READINGS

■ PROFESSIONAL ESSAYS

■ STUDENT ESSAYS

The Curious Writer

Custom Edition for University of New Orleans

Taken from:
The Curious Writer, Third Edition
by Bruce Ballenger

*The Curious Researcher: A Guide to Writing
Research Papers*, Sixth Edition
by Bruce Ballenger

Cover Art: Courtesy of Bobby de Vay, *Land Camera Series: Miss River*, 2010. Instant Print.

Taken from:

The Curious Writer, Third Edition
by Bruce Ballenger
Copyright © 2011, 2008, 2005 by Pearson Education, Inc.
Published by Longman
New York, New York 10036

The Curious Researcher: A Guide to Writing Research Papers, Sixth Edition
by Bruce Ballenger
Copyright © 2009 by Pearson Education, Inc.
Published by Longman

Pearson Learning Solutions, 501 Boylston Street, Suite 900, Boston, MA 02116
A Pearson Education Company
www.pearsoned.com

Printed in the United States of America

1 2 3 4 5 6 7 8 9 10 V354 16 15 14 13 12 11

0002000010270756849

ED

ISBN 10: 1-256-13057-5
ISBN 13: 978-1-256-13057-4

IMPORTANT!

To Our Students at UNO:

This customized text is designed specifically for ENGL 1157 and 1158.

In order to save you money, we have combined content from two textbooks and removed material that won't be covered in your Freshman Writing courses. You may notice that chapters and/or sections listed in the Table of Contents are missing from your custom-printed book. This is intentional, and the result is a significant savings.

Some instructors may not require this text, and others may require additional texts, so you should always check with your instructor before buying textbooks for your Freshman Writing courses.

This is the standard text for ENGL 1157/1158.

The Freshman Writing Program would like to thank Reggie Poché, Patricia Roger, David Rutledge, Katie Chosa, and Trisha Rezende. This custom text is a direct result of their efforts.

WRITING AS INQUIRY

WHAT IS A PROGRAM IDENTITY, & WHAT ARE ITS BENEFITS?

A program identity is the unifying concept that defines the first-year writing program. It provides a clear, succinct description of the focus we believe is best suited for providing our students with the knowledge and resources they need to produce successful writing, not only in our courses, but in the academy, their professions, and their public lives.

A program identity has the following benefits:

▸ Makes public a concise description of our approach to teaching writing

▸ Informs new faculty and teaching assistants of our focus

▸ Keeps us conscious and mindful of what informs our teaching and assessments

▸ Reveals what we value and what we believe is of value for our students

▸ Gives faculty a common purpose, which encourages a sense of community and facilitates the sharing of ideas, methods, and materials

▸ Encourages the development and use of a common, shared vocabulary of writing

▸ Provides direction for program and faculty development

▸ Underscores for students the relationship between the writing courses they are required to complete and their work in other courses

▸ Indicates what students can expect to gain from completing the First-Year Writing Program

▸ Serves as a reminder for students and the university that writing requires much more than standard grammar, usage, spelling, and punctuation

▸ Presents our program as we want it to be perceived

Writing as Inquiry defined

Inquiry-based freshman writing programs teach writing as part of the larger process of academic inquiry: asking questions, looking for answers, engaging with different viewpoints, and reflecting on what one has learned.

In an inquiry-based program, instructors lead students to recognize and practice the **habits of mind** essential to inquiry:
▸ Questioning
▸ Looking for answers
▸ Suspending judgment
▸ Seeking and valuing complexity
▸ Understanding that academic writing is a conversation
▸ Understanding that writing is a process (See Ballenger, *The Curious Writer* and Greene and Lidinsky, *From Inquiry to Academic Writing*)

Inquiry-based programs engage students as active participants in their own education, promote intellectual curiosity and open-mindedness, and encourage students to value writing as a way to learn, to communicate, and to reflect.

Our program

▸ Focuses on outcomes/strategies advocated by research into undergraduate education at research universities. *See http://naples.cc.sunysb.edu/Pres/boyer.nsf.*

▸ Fosters best practices as outlined in current composition scholarship. *See the bibliography at http://english.boisestate.edu/bballenger.*

▸ Coheres with the University s overall mission. *See http://www.dmar.uno.edu/strategicplans.htm.*

▸ Shares traits of writing programs at many of the University s peer institutions. *See the list of peer institutions at http://www.upcom.uno.edu/resources02.htm.*

▸ Emphasizes transferrable skills and strategies.

▸ Helps students see first-year writing courses as relevant to other areas of academic study, and to their lives.

The inquiry-based classroom

The inquiry-based course encourages students to be intellectually curious, to ask questions not only about themselves as writers but also about the nature of writing. To help foster this curiosity, students read and communicate in a variety of genres, learn and hone research methods, and apply a variety of rhetorical strategies. Student texts are developed through scaffolded assignments, consisting of interlinked low- and high-stakes assignments, as well as long and short compositions. These sequential assignments, including self-directed compositions and instructor-guided revisions, stimulate exploring, explaining, evaluating, and reflecting. They all work together to help students develop, test, and refine their own researchable questions and engage in self-discovery of the writing process.

OUTCOMES FOR THE FRESHMAN WRITING PROGRAM

Rhetorical Knowledge
Students should be able to

Determine purpose and audience in their own and others writing

Understand how purpose, audience, and context affect writing style, voice, and tone

Apply appropriate rhetorical strategies for diverse writing situations

Demonstrate familiarity with and/or compose in different genres (such as editorial writing, personal narratives, reviews, satires, dialogues, letters, or profile essays)

Demonstrate familiarity with and/or incorporate different media (such as power point presentations, web pages, pod casts, or visual essays)

Critical Thinking, Reading, and Writing
Students should be able to

Analyze and/or interpret texts and other forms of discourse in multiple genres

Use logical reasoning

Summarize, analyze, evaluate, and respond to the ideas of others

Understand writing as a process that involves invention, drafting, collaboration, and revision

Identify and incorporate persuasive techniques

Write informative, analytical, and persuasive essays

Incorporate the ideas and texts of others

Use library and non-library research methods

Evaluate sources

Knowledge of Conventions
Students should

Use standard grammar

Follow conventions for word choice, syntax, spelling, and punctuation

Follow conventions appropriate for the given genre and/or medium, such as style, diction, and format

Use a variety of sentence structures

Document sources in MLA style

Allow the goals of our program to drive your course design.

1156 and 1157 should introduce students to the concepts, strategies, and habits of mind that will lead to these outcomes.

Students who earn passing grades in 1158 should exhibit proficiency in each of the three areas that comprise our program s goals.

UNDERSTANDING 1156, 1157 & 1158

Freshman Composition students at all levels will read and communicate in a variety of genres, apply a variety of rhetorical strategies, and employ a variety of research methods. To help students to develop, test, and refine their own researchable questions and engage in self-discovery of the writing process, teachers create and employ **scaffolded assignments** that take students from low-stakes process exercises to high-stakes longer compositions.   These sequential assignments stimulate curiosity, exploration, and re-evaluation, and emphasize revision and reflection. The varieties of discourse in which students communicate comprise an entire **project**.

1156 & 1157	1158
students compose a minimum of 5000 words, 3000 of which should be formally assessed	
assignment sequences employ scaffolded assignments	
revision and reflection are an integral part of the writing process	
shorter, more frequent assignments	longer, more sustained assignments
suggested three projects minimum	suggested two projects minimum, one of which is an argument
more instructor-guided	more student-driven
students become familiar with different genres *(e.g., essays, summaries, analyses, reviews, narratives, arguments, letters to the editor, annotated bibliographies, proposals, blogs, public forum posts, photo essays, oral presentations)*	students compose in a variety of genres *(e.g., essays, summaries, analyses, reviews, narratives, arguments, letters to the editor, annotated bibliographies, proposals, blogs, public forum posts, photo essays, oral presentations)*
in 1156, students are introduced to research skills and methods; in 1157 students learn research skills and methods	students hone research skills, employing a variety of research methods

Understanding 1156, 1157 & 1158, continued

In 1156, students should be introduced to the conventions of college-level writing. To begin to master the process of writing effective college-level prose, students need intensive interaction with texts, their own and others'. Developing critical reading skills is crucial to their growth as writers. They need to read, react to, and analyze texts both in writing and class discussions. Students need to be taught to engage with the texts they read, especially non-fiction writing, which they are often unfamiliar with, and learn to find or construct the meaning within the texts. Instruction on how to read carefully and critically for content, then to go beyond the content to find the underlying attitudes and views prepares students for both the reading and writing required in this and future courses. Through intensive interaction, students learn the rhetorical principles of voice, audience, purpose, and appropriate usage and begin to master them in their own writing processes.

Writing should regularly occur in the classroom, but it should not be assessed as a high-stakes assignment. Revision and reflection are integral to the production of successful projects. Student-teacher conferencing should be emphasized as an essential part of the learning process in 1156. Moreover, all students in this course must spend one hour per week during the semester, excluding the first week of classes, in the Writing Center. Students should work one-on-one with a tutor when they have a draft or a paper in process; other weeks they may elect to attend group workshops, complete online exercises, or do other independent writing work under a tutor's supervision.

Ultimately, 1156 teachers need to ensure that students are introduced to the concepts, strategies, skills, and habits of mind that will lead to the programs outcomes. Having students write a formal reflection of their experience to accompany their best works or complete works portfolio during the final exam period will provide you with an effective assessment mechanism.

In 1157, students will produce a minimum of three projects, comprised of no less than 5000 words (total), 3000 of which are high-stakes (i.e., formally assessed). The scaffolded assignments that lead to the production of these three projects should introduce students to a variety of genres and their conventions, should teach students how to conduct research and to integrate their findings into their own writing, and should create opportunities for students to understand how audience and purpose govern the content, scope, organization, and expression of their own ideas.

Writing should occur in the classroom, but it should not be assessed as a high-stakes assignment. Revision and reflection are integral to the production of successful projects. Peer Collaboration (e.g., peer review, group work, and even group presentations) and student-teacher conferences may also be useful teaching tools. Ultimately, 1157 teachers need to ensure that students are introduced to the concepts, strategies, skills, and habits of mind that will lead to the program's outcomes. Having students write a formal reflection of their experience to accompany their best works or complete works portfolio during the final exam period will provide you with an effective assessment mechanism.

In 1158, students should continue to work toward the program's outcomes. To help students reach these goals, instructors should assign no less than two projects, comprised of at least 5000 words (total), 3000 of which are high-stakes (i.e., formally assessed). Some low-stakes writing must happen inside the classroom. At least one of these projects needs to create an opportunity for 1158 students to practice writing arguments. When ready, 1158 students may be given the freedom to craft their projects (by choosing, for example, its topic, scope, purpose, audience, kinds of writing, and/or presentation method). However, instructors need to guide students to make effective choices, ensuring that students employ a range of research methods, integrate others' ideas effectively, engage in discourse, and apply appropriate rhetorical strategies (e.g., considering opposing viewpoints or appealing to ethos). By the end of 1158, students should have met our program's outcomes. Only those students who exhibit proficiency in each of the three areas (Rhetorical Knowledge; Critical Thinking, Reading, and Writing; and Knowledge of Conventions) should earn a passing grade in 1158. Having students present their best project (or an arm of it) during the final exam period in addition to submitting their portfolios will allow you to easily assess their proficiency.

CONTENTS

All content from the first half of this book was taken from *The Curious Writer*, Third Edition, by Bruce Ballenger. All content from the second half of this book (after the colored divider page) was taken from *The Curious Researcher: A Guide to Writing Research Papers*, Sixth Edition, by Bruce Ballenger. Exceptions include the "To Our Students Letter" and "Writing as Inquiry" from the beginning of the book and Appendix A from the end of the book which were provided courtesy of the University of New Orleans.

1

THE SPIRIT OF INQUIRY

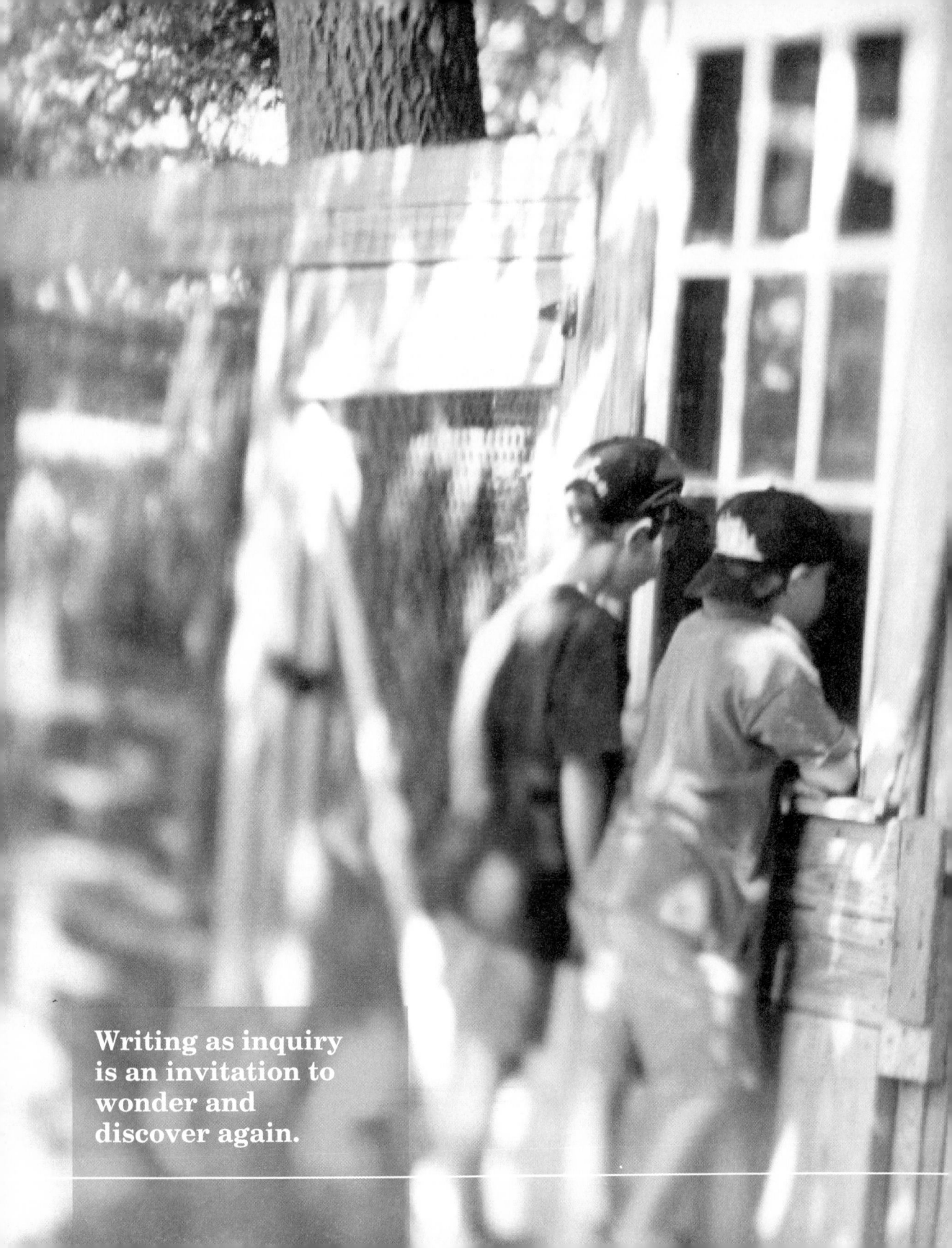

Writing as inquiry
is an invitation to
wonder and
discover again.

WRITING AS INQUIRY

Just the other night I was writing a card to my old friend Linda, some-one I went to college with and haven't seen in twenty-five years. As I wrote, my words scribbled in a heavy black pen, she began to appear before me again. I saw her in geology class, a few rows up, wearing a black raincoat and rubber boots, carefully putting her straight black hair behind an ear so she could see her notes. I hadn't seen her so clearly in years, and the writing brought her back. Most of us have had this experience—the power of words to summon images, memories, and feelings—which is why we sometimes indulge, often with pleasure, in writing letters, cards, and e-mails to friends and family.

Yet many of us admit that we really don't like to write, particularly when forced to do it, or we clearly prefer certain kinds of writing and dislike others: "I just like to write funny stories," or "I like writing for myself, and not for other people," or "I hate writing research papers." I can understand this, because for years I felt much the same way. I saw virtually no similarities between my note to Linda and the paper I wrote for my philosophy class in college. Words that had power in one context seemed flimsy and vacant in another. One kind of writing was fairly easy; the other was sweating blood. How could my experience as a writer be so fundamentally different? In other words,

> ## What You'll Learn in This Chapter
>
> - Why it pays to spend time thinking about your writing process.
> - Why learning to write well often involves *unlearning* things you already believe.
> - How understanding rhetoric will help you analyze writing situations.
> - What it means to be a writer who is motivated by a spirit of inquiry.
> - How to harness both creative and critical ways of thinking to come up with new ideas.

what's the secret of writing well in a range of contexts *and* enjoying it more? Here's what I had to learn:

1. All writing can offer the joy of discovery, the opportunity to speak and be heard, and the satisfaction of earned insight.
2. A key to writing well is understanding the *process* of doing it.

They're not particularly novel ideas, but both were a revelation to me when I finally figured them out late in my academic career, and they changed the way I wrote for good. These two insights—that the pleasures of writing can span genres and situations, and that thinking about *how* we write matters—are guiding principles of this book. After they read *The Curious Writer,* I won't guarantee that haters of writing will come to love it, or that lovers of writing won't find writing to be hard work. But I hope that by the end of the book you'll experience some of the same pleasures I found writing to my friend Linda in most writing situations, and that you'll be able to adapt your own writing process to meet the demands of whatever situation you encounter.

The process of becoming a more flexible and insightful writer must begin by exploring what you already believe it means to write well and learning a bit about how we can talk about writing as a process. In this chapter, I'll also introduce you to an idea that will be at the heart of every activity and assignment in *The Curious Writer:* the habits of mind and practices that will encourage you to adopt the "spirit of inquiry" as a motive for writing. This may sound a bit lofty and abstract. But by chapter's end I hope you'll recognize some practical implications of this approach that will help you with any writing assignment.

MOTIVES FOR WRITING

Why write? You could probably build a long list of reasons in a minute or two, perhaps beginning facetiously: "Because I *have* to!" But as you consider the many situations that call for writing and the purposes for doing it, I suspect that most will fall under a broad and obvious category: to say something to someone else. I'm less confident that you will see another broad motive for writing, partly because it gets less attention: we write to *discover* what we want to say.

These two motives for writing—to *share* ideas with others and to *discover* what the writer thinks and feels—are equally important.

But both these motives may arise from a still deeper spring: a sense of wonder and curiosity or even confusion and doubt, a desire to touch other people, or an urge to solve a problem. These feelings can inspire what I call the *spirit of inquiry,* a kind of perspective toward the world that invites questions, accepts uncertainty, and makes each of us feel some responsibility for what we say. This inquiring spirit should be familiar to you. It's the feeling you had when you discovered that the sun and a simple magnifying glass could be used to burn a hole in an oak leaf. It's wondering what a teacher meant when he said that World War II was a "good" war and Vietnam was a "bad" war. It's the questions that haunted you yesterday as you listened to a good friend describe her struggles with anorexia. The inquiring spirit even drives your quest to find the best DVD player, an effort that inspires you to read about the technology and visit consumerreports.org.

BELIEFS ABOUT WRITING

Most of us have been taught about writing since the first grade. We usually enter college with beliefs about how best to write a paper, which rules govern school writing, and even how to improve at composing. As I mentioned earlier, I've learned a lot about writing since my first years in college, and a big part of that learning involved unraveling some of my prior beliefs about writing. In fact, initially, I'd say that my development as a writer had more to do with *unlearning* some of what I already knew than it did with discovering new ways to write. What do you believe about how people get better at writing? You have theories that arise from all those years of school writing. Take a moment to find out what they are and whether they still make sense.

EXERCISE 1.1

What Do You Believe?

STEP ONE: From the following list, identify *the one belief* about writing that you agree with most strongly, and *one* that you're convinced isn't true.

1. Writing proficiency begins with learning the basics and then building on them, working from words to sentences to paragraphs to compositions.

2. The best way to develop as a writer is to imitate the writing of the people you want to write like.

3. People are born writers. Either you can do it or you can't.

4. The best way to develop as a writer is to develop good reading skills.

5. Practice is the key to a writer's development. The more a writer writes, the more he or she will improve.

6. Developing writers need to learn the modes of writing (argument, exposition, description, narration) and the genres (essays, research papers, position papers, and so on).

> ### RULES FOR FASTWRITING
>
> 1. There are no rules.
> 2. Don't try to write badly, but give yourself permission to do so.
> 3. To the extent you can, think through writing rather than before it.
> 4. Keep your pen moving.
> 5. If you run out of things to say, write about how weird it is to run out of things to say until new thoughts arrive.
> 6. Silence your internal critic to suspend judgment.
> 7. Don't censor yourself.

7. Developing writers should start with simple writing tasks, such as telling stories, and move to harder writing tasks, such as writing a research paper.

8. The most important thing that influences a writer's growth is believing that he or she can learn to write well.

9. The key to becoming a better writer is finding your voice.

STEP TWO: Spend five minutes writing in your notebook or journal about *why* you agree with the one belief and disagree with the other. This is an open-ended "fastwrite." You should write fast and without stopping, letting your thoughts flow in whatever direction they go.

Journal Prompts

- *When* did you first start agreeing or disagreeing with the belief? Can you remember a particular moment or experience as a student learning to write that drove this home?

- *What* do you mean, exactly, when you say you agree or disagree with the belief? Can you explain more fully why you think the belief is true or false?

- *Who* was most influential in convincing you of the truth or falsity of the belief?

ONE STUDENT'S RESPONSE

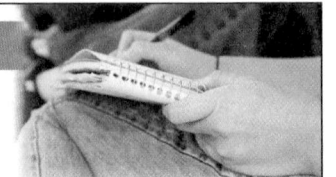

Bernice's Journal

EXERCISE 1.1
STEP TWO

I used to be a firm believer in the idea of born writers—it was a genetic thing. People were gifted with the gold pen genes, or they weren't. Writing as a process involved a muse, inspiration, and luck. Things uncontrollable by the writer. Then I started writing, mostly for my 101 class, and I started to feel powerful when I put words on paper. In control. The idea of my voice, my words just being on the page and other people reading it and maybe liking it was a rush. I was always the girl who specialized in the art of being unnoticed, unseen, blending in. My Comp 101 prof. liked my writing and pushed really hard to work on my basics, to think about my process, to prewrite and revise. I started to see a clear distinction between how to write and what to write. How is all mixed up with the process, with discipline, with practice and perseverance.... The how isn't something you are born with; its something you develop, something you practice, a skill you hone.... Becoming a good writer takes learning how to write, figuring out a process that works for you, and then letting your voice be heard on the page.

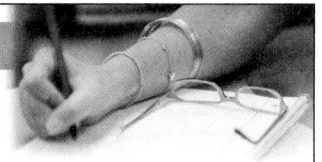

INQUIRING INTO THE DETAILS

Journals

Throughout *The Curious Writer*, I invite you to write in a journal. Some people hate journals. These are usually students who were forced to keep a journal in some class and found it a chore, or who tried to keep a journal at home and had little to show from the experience but blank pages. If you suffer from this condition, use a notebook instead of a journal. The two terms are synonymous. It's not what you call it that counts—it's what you do inside it!

Why do I want you to use a journal? One reason is that it is easier to write freely in this medium than it is when confronting the first page of a rough draft. Also, it's okay to write badly in journals and, as you will see later in this chapter, that's a good thing.

What kind of journal should you use? That's up to you. Some students just use the ubiquitous spiral notebook, which works just fine. Others find the digital journal best. They may be able to write faster and with more ease using a keyboard instead of a pen; keeping a journal on the computer might even be required if you're taking your class in a computer lab.

Unlearning Unhelpful Beliefs

You shouldn't be surprised when I say that I have a lot of theories about writing development; after all, I'm supposedly the expert. But we are *all* writing theorists, with beliefs that grow out of our successes and failures as students who write. Because you don't think much about them, these beliefs often shape your response to writing instruction without your even knowing it. For example, I've had a number of students who believe that people are born writers. This belief, of course, would make any kind of writing course a waste of time because writing ability would be a genetic problem.

A much more common belief is that learning to write is a process of building on basics, beginning with words, and then working up to sentences, paragraphs, and perhaps whole compositions. This belief was very common when I was taught writing. I remember slogging my way through Warriner's *English Grammar and Composition* in the seventh and eighth grade, dutifully working through chapter after chapter, beginning with parts of speech, parts of sentences, sentences, and then paragraphs.

Along with a lot of experts on writing instruction, I don't think that this foundational approach to writing development is very effective. I know it didn't help me become a better writer, and while I can still diagram a sentence, that's never a skill I call on when I'm composing. As a matter of fact, fifty years of research confirms that teaching formal grammar separately from writing essays is largely a waste of time. Despite this, formal grammar instruction persists, testimony to the subversive power of common sense. (Isn't it common sense that we should always learn the basics first?)

> Unlearning involves rejecting common sense if it conflicts with what actually works.

Unlearning involves rejecting common sense *if it conflicts with what actually works.* Throughout this book, I hope you'll constantly test your beliefs about writing against the experiences you're having with it. Pay attention to what seems to work for you and what doesn't; mostly, I'd like you at least initially to play what one writing instructor calls the believing game. Ask yourself, *What do I have to gain as a writer if I try believing this is true?*

The Beliefs of This Book

One of the metaphors I very much like about writing development is offered by writing theorist Ann E. Berthoff. She said learning to write is like learning to ride a bike. You don't start by practicing handlebar skills, move on to pedaling practice, and then finally learn balancing techniques. You get on the bike and fall off, get up, and try again, doing all of those separate things at once. At some point, you don't fall and you pedal off down the street. Berthoff said writing is a process that involves *allatonceness* (all-at-once-ness), and it's simply not helpful to try to practice the subskills separately. This is one belief about writing development shared by this book.

Any number of beliefs—the importance of critical thinking, the connection between reading and writing, the power of voice and fluency, and the need to listen to voices other than your own—all guide the structure of this book. One belief, though, undergirds them all: *The most important thing that influences a writer's growth is believing that he or she can learn to write well.* Faith in your ability to become a better writer is key. From it grows the motivation to learn how to write well.

Faith isn't easy to come by. I didn't have it as a writer through most of my school career because I assumed that being placed in the English class for underachievers meant that writing was simply another thing, like track, that I was mediocre at. For a long time, I was a captive to this attitude. But then, as a college freshman, I wrote a paper I cared about and the writing started to matter, not because I wanted to impress my instructor but because I discovered something I really wanted to say, and say well. I didn't settle for mediocrity after that.

As someone who wasn't too keen on writing for a very long time, I know how difficult it is to develop compelling reasons to write, particularly when the writing is required. I had to learn, among other things, that my teacher wasn't responsible for supplying the motivation (though I acknowledge that deadlines can help). I had to find a way to approach a writing assignment that made it seem like an opportunity to learn something.

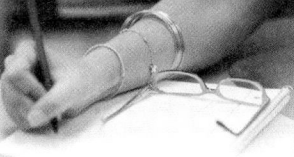

INQUIRING INTO THE DETAILS

Portfolios

One method for evaluating your development as a writer is to use a *portfolio,* which is a collection of work you assemble throughout a semester and submit to your instructor at the end of the course. If your instructor uses portfolios, he or she may grade some of your work as you go along, but will mainly assess your writing abilities by reviewing the total body of work in your portfolio. This means that until you hand in your final drafts, everything is pretty much a work in progress, and for much of the course you can focus on learning goals—say, finding new methods to begin and end your essays, or improving your editing skills. Performance goals, such as getting a decent grade, become a priority only at the end of the course. I'll have much more to say about portfolios later (see Appendix A).

WRITING SITUATIONS AND RHETORICAL CHOICES

Good writing is good writing, right? Well, it depends on the situation. For instance, here's what a friend of my daughter wrote as a comment on her blog the other day:

> im happy to be back w/ u guys it was a too long of a weekend- dancing friday then? u hailey and i runnin tomorrow- sounds fun 2 me

This isn't necessarily bad writing for Facebook and sites like it. The message uses online conventions that most of us are familiar with—text messaging abbreviations like "u" for *you* and "2" for *to*—and it possesses a level of informality and intimacy that seems appropriate for its context. Would it be good writing for a college essay? Obviously not.

Part of learning to write well, then, isn't simply learning how to craft transitions, organize information, and follow grammatical rules; it's learning to recognize that each writing situation asks you for something different. Actually, you know this already. You know, for example, that composing a letter to a landlord who refuses to return your security deposit will be fundamentally different from a letter to your sister describing your problem with the landlord. What you may not know is what to call this kind of knowledge: rhetoric.

One way of analyzing any writing situation is by using *the rhetorical triangle,* which reveals the dynamic relationships among the writer, the subject, and the reader (see Figure 1.1).

What the triangle implies is pretty straightforward—to write effectively, you must simultaneously address three main factors: your own perspective as the writer, the topic you are writing about, and the people you are writing for. The

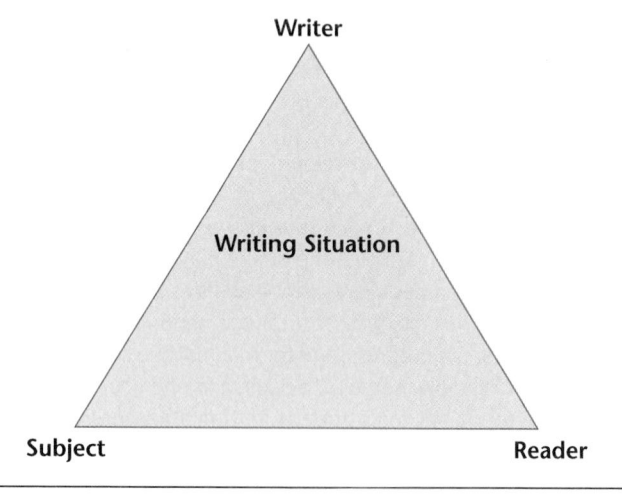

Figure 1.1   The rhetorical triangle

word *rhetorical,* of course, comes from *rhetoric*, the classical term for the study and practice of written and verbal communication. In fact, the rhetorical triangle has its origins in ancient Greece and the thinking of Aristotle, who first set down the principles of effective communication more than 2,000 years ago.

The three legs of the rhetorical triangle come together to shape the writing situation. The particularities of each leg—the writer, the subject, and the reader—determine the context of the writing situation. Consider again the security deposit problem. In that scenario, one thing is clear: Both of the proposed letters have a distinct—and different—*audience*. While the writer and the subject would seem to be the same for both letters, given the different audiences, the approach will be fundamentally different. In the letter to the landlord, the writer might adopt a formal, even legalistic, tone. The letter would be specific about what the writer is asking and when. The letter to the writer's sister would likely be informal, possibly more emotional. Its purpose would be to enlist a sibling's emotional support, not to persuade a landlord to return $500.

I'm pretty sure this is intuitively obvious to you. What may not be apparent is that you can use the same rhetorical knowledge to understand all kinds of writing situations, including academic ones. For example, consider next the opening two paragraphs from a writing assignment in Political Science 141: Contemporary Political Ideologies.

> This assignment aims to encourage students to connect the arguments being made by the thinkers in class to the issues and themes of our politics today. It aims to help students understand the relevance of political thinking for our political practice. Students are encouraged to share their judgments about the authors, only after they have shown that they understand the authors as the authors would understand themselves.

Use one of the following questions as the basis for a short essay. Your essay should be lucid and concise, and your argument should be thoroughly supported by relevant citations and allusions from the texts at hand. Grammar, spelling, punctuation, and syntax should be perfect.... Your paper is to be three to five pages in length, double-spaced, typed, and stapled in the upper left-hand corner. Please number your pages. A title page with an appropriate title must also be included, and all title pages should show what question the student is answering.

Using your own instincts about the rhetorical situation in this example, answer the following questions:

1. How would you characterize the instructor, and, based on that characterization, what kind of reader do you think he might be?

2. If you were in this class, how might your analysis of the rhetorical situation influence your approach to the writing assignment?

Writing well involves evaluating situations like these using your rhetorical knowledge.

HABITS OF MIND

When I first started teaching writing, I noticed a strange thing in my classes. What students learned about writing through the early assignments in the class didn't seem to transfer to later assignments, particularly research papers. What was I doing wrong, I wondered? Among other things, what I failed to make clear to my students was how certain "essential acts of mind" were present in every assignment, from the very first to the very last. What bound the writing course together was the idea of academic inquiry and the habits of mind—or *dispositions*, as one writer describes them—that lead students to see how writing can be a process of discovery.

Start with Questions, Not Answers

A lot of people think that writing is about recording what you already know, which accounts for those who choose familiar topics to write on when given the choice. "I think I'll write about _____," the thinking goes, "because I know that topic really well and already have an idea what I can say." Unfortunately, the result of writing about what you already know is too often an uninspired draft full of generalizations and clichés.

What do you do about this problem? *Make the familiar strange.* This means finding new ways to see what you've seen before. For years, I've asked some of my writing students to take photographs of any subject they want. Predictably, most students choose to take pictures of familiar things—their rooms or apartments, the trees outside the window, campus buildings, local landscapes—and they almost always take one picture of each subject. The result is that these photographs are rarely surprising. They see these familiar subjects in very familiar ways. But when I ask them to return to a single subject and take multiple pictures of it, there are almost always surprises and fresh ways of seeing the subject.

It's apparent that there are multiple ways of seeing the same thing, and of course this is one thing that we often admire about good writing—it offers a perspective on something familiar that we hadn't considered before. One of the ways writers accomplish this is by using questions. Questions shift a writer's perspective on a subject much as distance, angle, and light alter a photographer's ways of seeing. A shell is just a shell if you only look at it once and in one way. But if you want to see what you've seen before in a way you haven't seen it, you look again and again (see Figure 1.2). Questions are one way to keep shifting your gaze on any subject.

Therefore, in an inquiry-based approach to writing, you'll choose a writing topic that raises questions about how you think or feel over one that you have all figured out. Almost any topic can raise interesting questions. *There are no boring topics, only boring questions.* The key is to approach any topic with a sense of wonder and curiosity: *Why are houseflies so hard to kill? What distinguishes the cultures of skaters and snowboarders? When do most marriages fail and what can be done about it? Why do young people join gangs?*

Suspend Judgment

What's one of the most common problems I see in student writers? Poor grammar? Lack of organization? A missing thesis? Nope. *It's the tendency to judge too soon and too harshly.* A great majority of my students, including really smart, capable writers, have powerful internal critics, or as the novelist Gail Godwin once called them, "Watchers at the Gates." This is the voice you may hear when you're starting to write a paper, the one that has you crossing out that first sentence or that first paragraph over and over until you "get it perfect."

> It's okay to write badly. Resist the tendency to judge too soon and too harshly.

The only way to overcome this problem is to suspend judgment. In doing so, you essentially tell your Watchers this: *It's okay to write badly.*

I never try to write badly, of course, but whenever I'm stuck in the middle of something, or can't figure out what to say or where to begin, or even when I don't have a clue about my subject, I simply start writing. Sometimes it's absolutely horrible. But just as often, there's a glint of an idea, or direction, or topic, and away I go, trying to keep up with the vein of thought branching in all directions. The British novelist E. M. Forster once said, "How do I know what I think until I see what I say?" I've come to have a lot of faith in this idea. Rather than trying to use my journal the way I used to—to try to write beautiful, eloquent prose—I use the journal simply to think things through; that the prose sometimes stinks doesn't bother me anymore.

Figure 1.2   Good writing makes the familiar strange by offering multiple ways of seeing the same thing.

> ## CONDITIONS THAT MAKE "BAD" WRITING POSSIBLE
>
> 1. Willingness to suspend judgment
> 2. Ability to write fast enough to out-run your internal critic
> 3. Belief that confusion, uncertainty, and ambiguity help thought rather than hinder it
> 4. Interest in writing about "risky" subjects, or those that you don't know what you want to say about until you say it

We know how powerful our internal critics can be, insisting that every word be spelled right, and every thought sharp. Our Watchers can't abide bad writing. One of the conditions that makes bad writing possible for me is that my Watchers are not voices I honor in my journal, at least not when I want to use my journal to think something through.

Now I know it must seem odd that a book on writing would talk about the virtues of writing badly, but it can be a useful tool for solving all kinds of writing problems. I encourage you to use this approach throughout *The Curious Writer*. I've seen bad writing turn slow writers into faster ones, procrastinators into initiators. I've seen bad writing help students who always wrote short papers begin to generate longer, more thoughtful essays. Best of all, I've seen bad writing transform students who once hated writing into people who see writing as a useful tool for thinking, and even a source of pleasure.

Search for Surprise

One of the key benefits of writing badly is *surprise*. This was a revelation for me when I first discovered the virtues of bad writing in graduate school. I was convinced that you never pick up the pen unless you know what you want to say, which may account for my struggles with journal writing. Suddenly I stumbled on a new way to use writing—not to *record* what I already knew about a subject, but to *discover* what I actually thought. This way of writing promised a feast of surprises that made me hunger to put words on the page.

EXERCISE 1.2

A Roomful of Details

STEP ONE: Spend ten minutes brainstorming a list of details based on the following prompt. Write down whatever comes into your mind, no matter how silly. Be specific and don't censor yourself.

> Try to remember a room you spent a lot of time in as a child. It may be your bedroom in the back of the house at the edge of the field, or the kitchen where your grandmother kneaded bread or made thick red pasta sauce. Put yourself back in that room. Now look around you. What do you see? What do you hear? What do you smell?

STEP TWO: Examine your list. If things went well, you will have a fairly long list of details. As you review the list, identify one detail that surprises you the most, a detail that seems somehow to carry an unexpected charge. This might be a detail that seems connected to a feeling or story. You might be drawn to a detail that confuses you a little. Whatever its particular appeal, circle the detail.

STEP THREE: Use the circled detail as a prompt for a seven-minute fastwrite. Begin by focusing on the detail: What does it make you think of? And then what? And then? Alternatively, begin by simply describing the detail more fully: What does it look like? Where did it come from? What stories are attached to it? How does it make you feel? Avoid writing in generalities. Write about specifics—that is, particular times, places, moments, and people. Write fast, and chase after the words to see where they want to go. Give yourself permission to write badly.

> ## BRAINSTORMING
>
> - Anything goes.
> - Don't censor yourself.
> - Write everything down.
> - Be playful but stay focused.

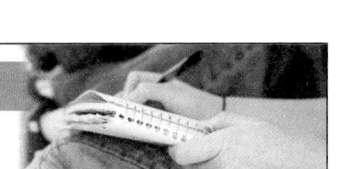

ONE STUDENT'S RESPONSE

Bernice's Journal

EXERCISE 1.2
STEP THREE

DETAIL: STAINLESS STEEL COUNTERS

When I was five or six my father and I made cookies for the first time. I don't remember what prompted him to bake cookies, he liked to cook but he didn't read very well so he didn't like to use cook books. I remember sitting on the cold stainless steel, the big red and white cook book splayed over my lap. I was reading it out loud to my dad. The kitchen was warm but everything gleamed; it was industrial and functional. It was the only room in our house that still looked like it belonged to the "Old Pioneer School." My dad and uncles had renovated every other room into bedrooms, playrooms, family rooms. The place was huge but cozy, it was home. I remember reading off ingredients until I got to the sugar. It called for $3/4$ cup and I didn't understand the fraction. I thought it meant three or four cups. We poured so much sugar into the bowl. The cookies were terrible. Hard and glassy, too sweet and brittle. It wasn't until years later that I understood that my dad didn't understand the measurement either. He was persistent though. We pulled down every cook book in the house until we found one that described the measuring cups and what they meant. We started all over and our second batch was perfect. My dad is one of the smartest people I know, inventive, imaginative

(continued)

One Student's Response (*continued*)

but he only has a rudimentary education. He can read and write enough to get by, he's gifted with numbers, but I can't help looking back and wondering what he could have been, what he could have done for the world if just one person had taken him by the hand and showed him what he showed me. If just one person had told him not to give up, to keep trying, that in the end it will be worth all the work, I wonder who he could have been if one person had seen his curiosity and imagination and fostered it instead of seeing his muscles and capable hands and putting him to work. If just one person had told him that his mind was the greatest tool he possessed. If just one person baked cookies with him.

You may experience at least three kinds of surprise after completing a fast-writing exercise like the preceding one:

1. Surprise about *how much* writing you did in such a short time
2. Surprise about discovering a topic you didn't expect to find
3. Surprise about discovering a *new way of understanding or seeing a familiar topic*

The kind of surprises you encounter doing this sort of writing may not always be profound. They may not even provide you with obvious essay topics. With any luck, though, by hunting for surprises in your own work you will begin to experience the pleasure of writing *to learn*. That's no small thing, particularly if you've always believed that writers should have it all figured out before they pick up the pen.

INQUIRING INTO THE DETAILS

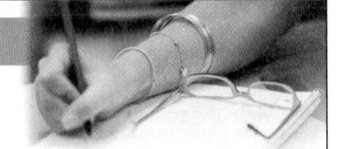

Invention Strategies

Perhaps without knowing it, you have already prac-ticed some writing techniques designed to help you generate material. These *invention strategies* include fastwriting, listing, brainstorming, questioning, and even conversation. You can use these techniques in any writing situa-tion when you need to gather more information, find a topic, or explore what you think. We call on these strategies often in the exercises and assignments that follow.

At first, spending time doing all this writing and thinking before you actually begin a draft may seem like a waste of time. After all, your goal is to finish the assign-ment. But if you want to find a focused topic that means something to you and write it with enough information, then invention strategies such as fastwriting will prove invaluable. They produce the raw material that can be shaped, like clay on a potter's wheel, into something with form and meaning. But really the best thing about inven-tion strategies is that they often generate material that is ripe with surprise.

INVENTION STRATEGIES

- *Fastwriting:* The emphasis is on speed, not correctness. Don't compose, don't think about what you want to say before you say it. Instead, let the writing lead, helping you discover what you think.

- *Listing:* Fast lists can help you generate lots of information quickly. They are often in code, with words and phrases that have meaning only for you. Let your lists grow in waves—think of two or three items and then pause until the next few items rush in.

- *Clustering:* This nonlinear method of generating information, also called *mapping,* relies on *webs* and often free association of ideas or information. Begin with a core word, phrase, or concept at the center of a page, and build branches off it. Follow each branch until it dies out, return to the core, and build another.

- *Questioning:* Questions are to ideas what knives are to onions. They help you cut through to the less obvious insights and perspectives, revealing layers of possible meanings, interpretations, and ways of understanding. Asking questions complicates things but rewards you with new discoveries.

- *Conversing:* Conversing is fastwriting with the mouth. When we talk, especially to someone we trust, we work out what we think and feel about things. We listen to what we say, but we also invite a response, which leads us to new insights.

- *Researching:* This is a kind of conversation, too. We listen and respond to other voices that have said something or will say something if asked about topics that interest us. Reading and interviewing are not simply things you do when you write a research paper but activities to use whenever you have questions you can't answer on your own.

- *Observing:* When we look closely at anything, we see what we didn't notice at first. Careful observation of people, objects, experiments, images, and so on generates specific information that leads to informed judgments.

WRITING AS A PROCESS

There is a process for doing almost anything—fixing a broken washing machine, learning how to play tennis, studying for the SAT, and, of course, writing. It might be hard to imagine, therefore, why some English teachers seem to make such a big deal out of the writing process. Here's why:

- The process of writing, like anything that we do frequently, is not something that we think about.

- When we focus, as we often do in writing, on *what* rather that *how,* on the product rather than the process, then when problems arise we don't see many options for solving them. We get stuck and we get frustrated.

- As we start to pay attention to how we write in a variety of situations, two things happen: We become aware of our old habits that don't always help, and that may actually hurt our success with writing. Second—and this is most important—we begin to understand that there are actually *choices* we can make when problems arise, and we become aware of what some of those are.

- The result of all of this is a simple yet powerful thing: The more we understand writing processes, the more control we get over them. Getting control of the process means the product gets better.[1]

Here's an example of what I mean. Chauntain summarized her process this way: "Do one and be done." She always wrote her essays at the last minute and only wrote a single draft. She approached nearly every writing assignment the same way: Start with a thesis and then develop five topic sentences that support the thesis with three supporting details under each. This structure was a container into which she poured all her prose. Chauntain deliberated over every sentence, trying to make each one perfect, and as a result she spent considerable time staring off into space searching for the right word or phrase. It was agony. The papers were almost always dull—she thought so, too—and just as often she struggled to reach the required page length. Chauntain had no idea of any other way to write a school essay. As a matter of fact, she thought it was really the *only* way. So when she got an assignment in her economics class to write an essay in which she was to use economic principles to analyze a question that arose from a personal observation, Chauntain was bewildered. How should she start? Could she rely on her old standby structure—thesis, topic sentences, supporting details? She felt stuck.

Not only did she fail to see that she had choices in this writing situation, she had no clue what those choices were.

That's why we study process. It helps us to solve problems like these. This must begin with a self-study of your own habits as a writer, identifying not just how you tend to do things but the patterns of problems that might arise when you do them.

EXERCISE 1.3

What Is Your Process?

Take a moment and analyze your own writing challenges. The following questions might help you develop a profile of your writing process in certain situations, and help you identify problems you might want to address by altering your process.

STEP ONE: Complete the Self-Evaluation Survey.

---

[1]There is considerable research in learning theory that confirms these conclusions; in particular, so-called "metacognitive thinking"—the awareness of how you do things—increases the transfer of relevant knowledge from one situation to another. In other words, what you learn about how to do something in one situation gets more easily activated in another.

Self-Evaluation Survey

1. When you're given a school writing assignment, do you wait until the last minute to get it done?

    Always——Often——Sometimes——Rarely——Never

2. How often have you had the experience of learning something you didn't expect through writing about it?

    Very often——Fairly often——Sometimes——Rarely——Never

3. Do you generally plan out what you're going to write before you write it?

    Always——Often——Sometimes——Rarely——Never

4. *Prewriting* describes activities that some writers engage in before they begin a first draft. Prewriting might include freewriting or fastwriting, making lists, brainstorming or mapping, collecting information, talking to someone about the essay topic, reading up on it, or jotting down ideas in a notebook or journal. How much prewriting do you tend to do for the following types of assignments? Circle the appropriate answer.

    ■ A personal essay:

    A great deal——Some——Very little——None——Haven't
    written one

    ■ A critical essay about a short story, novel, or poem:

    A great deal——Some——Very little——None——Haven't
    written one

    ■ A research paper:

    A great deal——Some——Very little——None——Haven't
    written one

    ■ An essay exam:

    A great deal——Some——Very little——None——Haven't
    written one

5. At what point in writing an academic paper do you usually get stuck? Check all that apply.

    ❑ Getting started

    ❑ In the middle

    ❑ Finishing

    ❑ I never get stuck (go on to Question 9)

    ❑ Other _____

6. If you usually have problems getting started on an academic paper or essay, which of the following do you often find hardest to do? Check

all that apply. (If you don't have trouble getting started, go on to Question 7.)

❑ Deciding on a topic

❑ Writing an introduction

❑ Finding a good place to write

❑ Figuring out exactly what I'm supposed to do for the assignment

❑ Finding a purpose or focus for the paper

❑ Finding the right tone

❑ Other_____

7. If you usually get stuck in the middle of a paper, which of the following causes the most problems? (If writing in the middle of a paper isn't a problem for you, go on to Question 8.)

❑ Keeping focused on the topic

❑ Finding enough information to meet page length requirements

❑ Following my plan for how I want to write the paper

❑ Bringing in other research or points of view

❑ Organizing all my information

❑ Trying to avoid plagiarism

❑ Worrying about whether the paper meets the requirements of the assignment

❑ Worrying that the paper just isn't any good

❑ Messing with citations

❑ Other_____

8. If you have difficulty finishing an essay or paper, which of the following difficulties are typical for you? Check all that apply.

❑ Composing a last paragraph or conclusion

❑ Worrying that the paper doesn't meet the requirements of the assignment

❑ Worrying that the paper just isn't any good

❑ Trying to keep focused on the main idea or thesis

❑ Trying to avoid repeating myself

❑ Realizing I don't have enough information

❑ Dealing with the bibliography or citations

❑ Other_____

9. Rank the following list of approaches to revision so that it reflects the strategies you use *most often to least often* when rewriting academic

papers. Rank the items 1–6, with the strategy you use most often as a 1 and least often as a 6.

_____ I usually just tidy things up—editing sentences, checking spelling, looking for grammatical errors, and performing other proofreading activities.

_____ I mostly look for ways to reorganize existing information in the draft to make it more effective.

_____ I generally try to fill holes by adding more information.

_____ I do more research.

_____ I often completely change the focus or even the main idea in the revision, rewriting sections, adding or removing information, and rearranging the order of things.

_____ I rarely do any rewriting at all.

10. Finally, do you tend to impose a lot of conditions on when, where, or how you think you write most effectively? For example, do you need a certain pen, do you always have to write on a computer, must it be quiet or noisy, or do you often write best under pressure? Do you need to be in certain kinds of places to write effectively? Or can you write under a range of circumstances, with few or no conditions? Circle one.

    Lots of conditions———Some———A few———No conditions

If you do impose conditions on when, where, or how you write, list some of those conditions here:

1.

2.

3.

4.

STEP TWO: In small groups, discuss the results of the survey. Begin by picking someone to tally the answers to each question. Post these on the board or a sheet of newsprint so they can be added to the class totals. Analyze the results for your group. In particular, discuss the following questions:

- Are there patterns in the responses? Do most group members seem to answer certain questions in similar or different ways? Are there interesting contradictions?

- Based on these results, what "typical" habits or challenges do writers in your class seem to share?

- What struck you most?

Thinking About Your Process

The survey you completed is the beginning of reflection on your own writing process. You will do this kind of reflection again and again throughout this book so that by the end you will have written a narrative of thought that tells the story of your reading and writing processes, and how you change those processes to produce better writing more efficiently. The reflective letter in your portfolio (see Appendix A) might be where you finally tell that story in full, perhaps beginning with what the survey revealed about your own habits, rituals, and challenges as you began this book.

However, now is a good time to begin telling yourself that story.

What do you remember about your own journey as a writer both inside and outside of school? One of my earliest, most pleasant memories of writing is listening to the sound of the clacking of my father's old Royal typewriter in the room down the hall as I was going to sleep. I imagine him there now, in the small study that we called the "blue room," enveloped in a cloud of pipe smoke. It is likely that he was writing advertising copy back then, or perhaps a script for a commercial in which my mother, an actress, would appear. I loved the idea of writing then. The steady hammering of typewriter keys down the hall sounded effortless, yet at the same time solid, significant. This all changed, I think, in the eighth grade when it seemed that writing was much more about following rules than tapping along to a lively dance of words.

Spend some time telling your own story about how your relationship to writing evolved.

EXERCISE 1.4

Literacy Narrative Collage

Generating Ideas

When you get a writing assignment, your habit is probably to sit down and simply write it, composing on the computer. This time, however, we'll begin by generating ideas (classical rhetoricians call this "invention").

To begin working toward a draft essay on your personal writing history, we'll start in your journal with a collage of moments, memories, or reflections. *For each prompt, write fast for about four minutes. Keep your pen moving and give yourself permission to write badly.* After you've responded to one prompt, skip a line and move on to the next one. Set aside about twenty minutes for this generating activity.

1. What is your earliest memory of writing? Tell the story.
2. We usually divide our experiences as writers into private writing and school writing, or writing we do by choice and writing we are required to do for a grade. Let's focus on school writing. Tell the story of a teacher, a

class, an essay, an exam, or other moment that you consider a *turning point* in your understanding of yourself as a writer or your understanding of writing.

3. Writing is part of the fabric of everyday life in the United States, and this is truer than ever with Internet communication. Describe a typical day for you in which writing plays a part, and think about how this has changed in your lifetime so far.

4. What is the most successful (or least successful) thing you've ever written in or out of school? Tell the story.

Congratulations. You've made a mess. But I hope this collage of your experiences as a writer is an interesting mess, one that brought some little surprises. As you look at these four fragments of fastwriting, you might sense a pattern between them. Is there a certain idea about yourself as a writer that seems to emerge in these various contexts for thinking about it? It's more likely that one or perhaps two of the prompts really took off for you, presenting trails you'd like to continue following. Or maybe nothing happened. For now, set your journal aside. We'll return to this material soon.

Writing Creatively, Writing Critically: A Process of Writing

Here was my writing process when I was in school:

1. Get the assignment. Find out when it was due and how long it was supposed to be.
2. Wait until the night before it was due and get started.
3. Stare off into space.
4. Eat ice cream.
5. Write a sketchy outline.
6. Write a sentence; then cross it out.
7. Stare off into space.
8. Write another sentence, and then squeeze out a few more.
9. Think about Lori Jo Flink, and then stare off into space.
10. Write a paragraph. Feel relief and disgust.

I would get the work done eventually, but the process was agonizing and the product mediocre. What did I conclude from this back then? That I wasn't good at writing, which was no big surprise because I pretty much hated it. Something happened to me to change that view, of course, because you hold my book in your hands. Among other things, I came to understand that the processes I was using for writing were really just habits I applied without thought no matter what the situation. I also was dedicated to the idea that I needed to know exactly what I was trying to say before I said it.

But more than anything, I thought writing was a process like this:

When it's really like this:

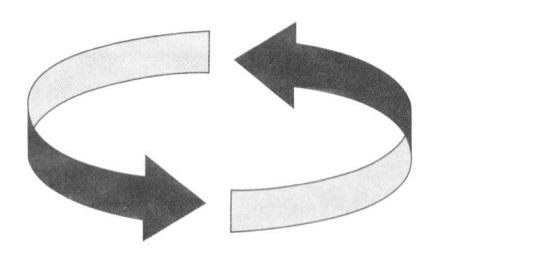

   In other words, I had always thought that writing was a straight march forward from beginning to end; I had to wait for something to come into my head and then tried to get it down. At all costs, I avoided things like new ideas or other ways of seeing a topic—anything that might get in the way of the drive to the conclusion. If I thought about anything, it was trying to find the "perfect" way of saying things or worrying about whether I was faithfully following a certain structure. I rarely learned anything from my writing. I certainly never expected I should.
   But this isn't the way experienced writers work at all. The writing process isn't a linear trajectory, but a looping, recursive process—one that encourages *thinking,* not simply recording the thoughts that you already have. Writing doesn't involve a series of steps that you must follow in every situation but is a much messier zigzag between collecting information and focusing on it, exploring things and thinking about them, writing and rewriting, reviewing and rearranging, and so on. The process is always influenced by the writing situation. For instance, experienced writers approach the process of writing an essay exam quite differently than they would a lab report. Some writers learn this flexibility slowly through experience. A faster way is to combine experience writing for all

kinds of situations *and* monitoring the processes you use for each one and applying your knowledge of what works.

   While there isn't a single writing process, I do think there are certain kinds of thinking that we can apply to most writing situations. Rather than read my explanation of it now, try the exercise that follows and maybe you'll see what I mean.

EXERCISE 1.5

Alternating Currents of Thought: Generating and Judging

Let's return to the subject you began writing about in Exercise 1.4—your experiences as a writer—but let's spend more time thinking about the third prompt in that exercise: your experience with writing technology.

Generating

STEP ONE: What are your earliest memories of using a computer for writing? Begin by telling the story and then let the writing lead from there. Keep your pen moving and allow yourself to write badly.

STEP TWO: Brainstorm a list of words or phrases that you associate with the word "literate" or "literacy."

Reread what you just wrote in your notebook or journal, underlining things that surprised you or that seem significant or interesting to you. Skip a line and respond in writing to the next set of prompts.

Judging

STEP THREE: Choose one of the following sentences as a starting point, and then write a paragraph about it. This time, compose each sentence thinking about what you want to say before you say it and trying to say it as well as you can.

> *What I understand now about my experiences with writing on computers that I didn't understand when I started out is _____.*
>
> *When they think about writing with computers, most people think _____, but my experience was _____.*
>
> *The most important thing I had to discover before I considered myself "computer literate" was _____.*

Reflecting

If you're like most people, then the parts of this exercise that involved generating felt different than the part where you judged what you had written. But *how* were they different? How would you distinguish between the experience of generating and judging? Talk about this or write about it in your journal.

Thinking and Writing Dialectically

At the heart of the strategy of inquiry, which is at the heart of *The Curious Writer*, is the following model:

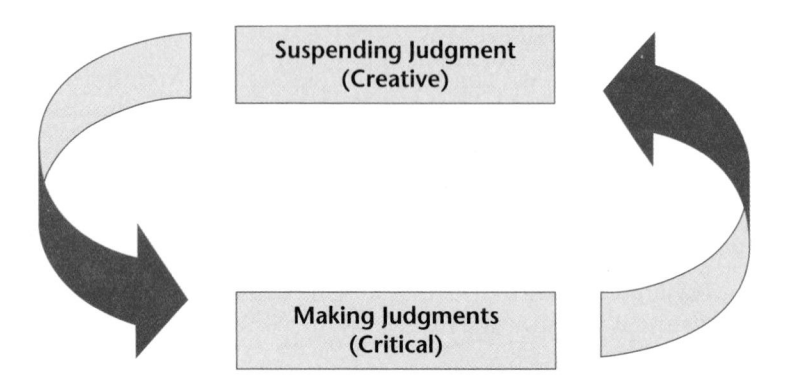

The two parts of Exercise 1.5, generating and judging, were designed to simulate this shift from suspending judgments and making judgments as you wrote about your early experiences using a computer for writing. In the first two steps, you spent some time fastwriting without much critical interference, trying to generate some information from your own experience. In the third step, which began with "seed" sentences that forced you into a more reflective, analytical mode, you were encouraged to look for patterns of meaning in what you generated.

> Suspending judgment feels freer, exploratory.... Making judgments shifts the writer into an analytical mode.

For many writers, these are two distinct ways of thinking. *Suspending judgment* feels freer, is exploratory, and may spark emotion. *Making judgments* shifts the writer into an analytical mode, one that might lower the temperature, allowing writers to see their initial explorations with less feeling and more understanding. Another way of distinguishing between these two modes of thought is to label the open-ended thinking we often associate with fastwriting as "creative" and the more closed-ended thinking we associate with judging or analyzing as "critical."

INQUIRING INTO THE DETAILS

Organizing Your Computer Files

In a writing class, you typically have lots of documents and frequently multiple versions of the same document. How do you make sure that you can find them? Take a little time to establish conventions for naming your files. Start by establishing a folder for your class, and then decide on what might be helpful naming categories to apply to each document. For example,

- Genre (e.g., essay, exercise, letter, response, and so on)
- Title of document
- Version number
- Date

Using the underscore key, separate each element when naming your document. For example, *essay_importanceofwritingbadly_v2_2008-December-12.* It takes a little more time to compose a more elaborate file name than *doc.1* but it ultimately saves time by helping you locate documents more easily.

Combining these two modes of thinking gives both thinking and writing more range and depth. Creative thinking creates the conditions for discovery—new insights or ways of seeing—while critical thinking helps writers refine their discoveries and focus on the most significant of them.

Figure 1.3 lists other ways you can visualize creative and critical thinking. In narrative writing, for instance (the kind of writing you likely did in the previous exercise), creative thinking helps you generate information about *what happened,* while critical thinking may lead you to insights about *what happens.* Likewise, in research writing, investigators often move back and forth between their *observations of* things and their *ideas about* them. More broadly speaking, when we think creatively we collect, and when we think critically we evaluate what we have collected.

Note that in Figure 1.3 double-ended arrows link the items in each pair. The process is *dialectical;* it consists of a back-and-forth movement between the two opposing modes of thought. Many writers do this instinctively. As they compose, they constantly shift between contrasting modes of thought, from collecting to focusing, from generating to criticizing, from showing to telling, from exploring to reflecting, from believing to doubting, from playing to judging.

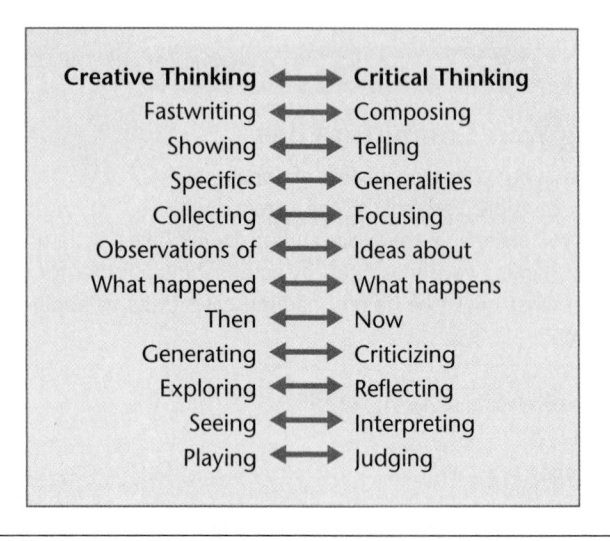

Figure 1.3 When writers use dialectical thinking, they move back and forth between two opposing modes of thought—the creative and the critical. One seems playful and the other judgmental; one feels open ended and the other more closed. Certain activities such as fastwriting or brainstorming promote one mode of thought, and careful composing or reflection promotes another.

Certain activities—such as fastwriting and composing—encourage one way of thinking or the other. Learning to balance these opposing forces is what dialectical thinking is all about. In practice, however, many beginning writers give too much emphasis to either one mode of thinking or the other, a tendency that accounts for many of the challenges these writers face within their own writing processes.

Spend too much time locked in the critical mode of thinking and your internal critic takes over. This voice pinches off the flow of material generated by creative thinking. The writing then comes slowly and painfully, and it rarely yields surprise. Topics are abandoned before the writer has fully explored their potential. Working from scarcity, the writer is compelled to use all the material he or she has at hand, often resulting in writing that feels forced, incomplete, or obvious.

On the other hand, give too much free rein to creative thinking and the artist runs wild. The problem here isn't scarcity but rather overabundance. It's a poverty of riches, for without a critical eye to provide shape and direction, the writer cannot present all of his or her material in a coherent and meaningful fashion.

Other challenges result when writers fail to move back and forth between creative and critical modes. One excursion into creative thinking followed by a second into critical thinking is rarely enough to produce good writing.

Writers need to move back and forth between the two modes until they come to see their topics in interesting ways that differ from what they might have creatively or critically thought about the topic when they started the writing process.

Put simply, the goal of this dialectical thinking is to address a question that ultimately all writing must answer:

So what?

So what? can be a pretty harsh question, and I find that some students tend to ask it too soon in the writing process, before they've fully explored their topic or collected enough information. That may have been your experience when you suddenly found yourself high and dry, forced to reflect on possible meanings of a moment you've written about for only eight minutes. When you can't come up with an answer to *So what?,* the solution is usually to generate more information.

There's another danger, too. In their enthusiasm to answer *So what?,* some writers seize on the first convenient idea or thesis that comes along. This abruptly ends the process of inquiry before they've had a chance to explore their subjects. These writers squander the opportunity to be surprised by what they discover.

Opening Questions

Using the dialectical thinking process is all well and good, but first you've got to have something to think about. The inquiry approach promoted by *The Curious Writer* is grounded in the idea that the writing process depends, more than anything else, on finding the right questions. What makes a question "right"? First and foremost, you must find it interesting enough to want to think and write about it for awhile.

I recently visited teachers in Laredo, Texas, and I told them that a good question can make even the most boring topic interesting. I would prove it, I said, and picked up a lemon that was sitting on a table and asked everyone, in turn, to ask a question about the lemon or about lemons. Twenty minutes later, we generated sixty questions, and in the process began to wonder how the scent of lemons came to be associated with cleanliness. We wondered why lemons appeared so often in wartime British literature. We wondered why the lime and not the lemon is celebrated in local Hispanic culture. We wondered a lot of interesting things that we never expected to wonder about because a lemon is ordinary. Questions can make the familiar world we inhabit yield to wonder.

The point is this: *There are no boring topics—just poor questions.*

Writing as inquiry, therefore, begins with questions and not answers. We pursue a subject because we want to find out what we think about it, and certain kinds of questions are much more likely to sustain our investigation than others. For example, I had a student once who really, really wanted to know whether Elvis was really dead. Yep, the King is gone. End of story. A better question for writing and thinking would have been to ask *why* we keep asking whether Elvis is dead. What is it about him that seems to sustain such a blind hope in his existence among certain people?

Learning to find the right question, one that will be worth spending time with, is an essential skill, and there are certain qualities that most good questions seem to share. Here are a few of them:

- The writer is genuinely interested in the question and the answers.
- People other than the writer have a stake in the answers to the question.
- It raises more questions; there isn't a simple answer.
- Something has been said already about the question. There's information out there.
- The question is a manageable size. It's isn't too broad ("What is the meaning of lemons?") or too specific ("What is the meaning of that lemon?").

QUESTIONS, CREATIVITY, AND CRITICAL THINKING: A STRATEGY FOR INQUIRY

If you combine the power of good questions with the back-and-forth process of writing creatively and critically discussed earlier in the chapter, you have a model for a strategy of inquiry that you can use for every assignment in this book (see Figure 1.4). Typically you begin exploring a subject, sometimes generating some initial thoughts through fastwriting, listing, or other invention methods. Subjects are like landscape shots in photography—they cover a huge amount of ground. You need to find a narrower topic, or some *part* of the landscape to look at more closely. Take popular music, for example. That's a huge subject. But as you write and read about it a little, you begin to see that the topic that interests you most is the blues, and maybe something about its influence on American popular music. Here's how it works:

- You start with a *subject* that makes you curious—music—and then work toward a *topic*—the influence of blues—that is beginning to focus your attention for a closer look.

Ultimately you are searching for a few questions about your topic that both interest you and will sustain your project. These are the questions that will help

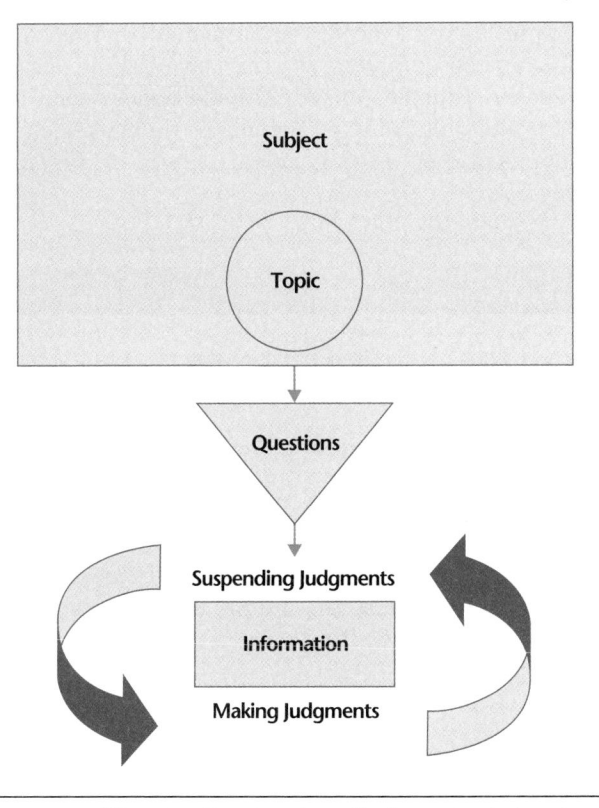

Figure 1.4   The process of inquiry first involves finding a topic in a larger subject that raises interesting questions, refining those questions, and then using them to collect information. Investigate the significance of what you've found by thinking creatively and critically—withholding judgments and then making judgments—working toward fresh understandings and new discoveries that lead you to what you want to say.

you focus your topic, that guide your research into yourself or other sources of information, and that may eventually become the heart of an essay draft on your topic. For example, you might arrive at a question like this one:

■   Beginning with a topic—the influence of the blues on pop music—you work toward questions that might power your writing project—questions, say, like this: *What was the influence of Mississippi delta blues on white performers like Elvis who were popular in the fifties and sixties?*

An inquiry question may be no more than a train station in a longer journey. As you continue to write, you may find another, better question around which to build your project. But a good opening question will keep you on the tracks. This is enormously helpful as you collect information, either from research or from your own experiences and observations, working toward some answers to the questions you pose. And some of the best insights you get about what those answers might be will come from the alternating currents of thought—generating and judging, suspending judgment and making judgments—that energize your writing and thinking processes.

EXERCISE 1.6

Writing with the Wrong Hand and Other Ways of Thinking About Yourself as a Writer

Though you may not have noticed it, you've already begun using this inquiry strategy in this chapter. In Exercise 1.4 (Literacy Narrative Collage) you started exploring your own background as a writer, first generating material about your past experiences and then stepping back and judging their significance. I provided most of the questions. So far, everything you've written about your literacy narrative is in your journal. Let's use the inquiry process to shape the material into a three- to five-page essay draft. But before we do that, we'll continue with a little more journal work.

Generating

STEP ONE: This four-minute fastwrite begins strangely. If you're right-handed, put your pen in your left hand. If you're left-handed, put it in your right. Write the following phrase in your journal with your "wrong" hand: *Writing with my wrong hand reminds me of...* Now switch the pen to your writing hand, and in a fastwrite explore the connections you can make, if any, with the experience of writing with the wrong hand. Let the writing lead, especially to stories, particular people, specific memories, or times in your life.

Judging

STEP TWO: Based on what you wrote in step one, compose a brief answer to one or more of the following questions:

- What's the thing that surprised you most when you wrote about writing wrong-handed?
- If you were going to explain the significance of this experience to someone else, what would you say?
- If you were going to do this experiment with a friend, what would you ask him or her about it afterward?

Generating

STEP THREE: The information we generate from our experiences and observations is only one kind of information we can generate for writing. Reading is another. The passage that follows is the opening of an essay by David Bartholomae, a writing theorist, which begins his look at how students in their first years of college must adjust to writing in academic discourses. Carefully read the passage, and in your journal *copy at least three passages* from the Bartholomae excerpt that struck you. Maybe you agreed or disagreed with them, or you found them interesting or confusing, or they spoke in some way to your own experiences so far in college.

From "Inventing the University"
David Bartholomae

Every time a student sits down to write for us, he has to invent the university for the occasion—invent the university, that is, or a branch of it, like history or anthropology or economics or English. The student has to learn to speak our language, to speak as we do, to try on the peculiar ways of knowing, selecting, evaluating, reporting, concluding, and arguing that define the discourse of our community. Or perhaps I should say the *various* discourses of our community, since it is in the nature of a liberal arts education that a student, after the first year or two, must learn to try on a variety of voices and interpretive schemes—to write, for example, as a literary critic one day and as an experimental psychologist the next; to work within fields where the rules governing the presentation of examples or the development of an argument are both distinct and, even to the professional, mysterious.

The student has to appropriate (or be appropriated by) a specialized discourse, and he has to do this as though he were easily and comfortably one with his audience, as though he were a member of the academy or an historian or an anthropologist or an economist; he has to invent the university by assembling and mimicking its language while finding some compromise between idiosyncrasy, a personal history, on the one hand, and the requirements of convention, the history of a discipline, on the other hand. He must learn to speak our language. Or he must dare to speak it or to carry off the bluff, since speaking and writing will most certainly be required long before the skill is "learned." And this, understandably, causes problems.

STEP FOUR: Now fastwrite for four or five minutes about the Bartholomae excerpt, and begin by exploring your reactions to the passages you selected. This time, tell the story of your thinking as it develops in your bad writing by beginning with your first thoughts: *The first thing I think when I consider what Bartholomae is saying is…And then I think…And then.* Follow the writing.

Judging

STEP FIVE: Reread your fastwriting from the preceding step, and spend a full minute generating a list of questions, either about the Bartholomae excerpt or about your response to it.

STEP SIX: Finally, craft one or two strong sentences that might begin an essay you write in response to "Inventing the University." A strong first sentence is one that would make a reader want to read the next sentence and the one after that.

Writers are almost always better off when they work from abundance rather than scarcity. That makes choosing what to put in and what to leave out of a draft much easier and makes it much more likely that the resulting piece will have a strong focus. That's also why we've spent so much time in this chapter beginning to generate and shape material about your own experiences as a writer. If you go over your journal work on this topic, you should see some or all of the following, depending on what your instructor assigned:

- Your earliest memory of writing
- The story of a turning point in your sense of yourself as a writer or your understanding of writing
- Writing you do on a typical day
- The story of the most or least successful thing you've ever written
- Your earliest memory of writing with a computer
- Your definitions of the word "literate"
- Your exploration of the experience of writing with the wrong hand
- A response to an excerpt on how college students must "learn to speak the language" of the university by "compromising" their "personal history" as writers

That's a fair amount of writing, and most of it probably isn't very good. But now you're ready to try and shape some of that material into a first draft, writing that might make sense to someone other than you.

THE WRITING PROCESS

INQUIRY PROJECT: THE WRITING LITERACY MEMOIR

Drawing on the writing you've done on the topic so far and the writing you will continue to generate, compose a three- to five-page essay that is a memoir of your history as a writer. Like all inquiry projects, this essay should investigate some question about your writing experiences, and this question should be behind the stories you tell. To start with, look for a question that explores a relationship between two things in your writing life. For example, "What is the relationship between my success with online writing and my struggles with school writing?" Or something like this: "What is the relationship between my memories of earning praise about my writing from teachers and the lack of confidence in writing I've always felt, and still feel?"

For additional reading, writing, and research resources, go to **www.mycomplab.com**

Obviously, you've already started this assignment, and you have pages of writing in your journal from which to work. Let the inquiry question you come up with help you decide what to put in and what to leave out. As you are drafting, also consider opportunities to generate new information that will help to develop your essay. For example, there might be a key moment in your narrative that deserves particular emphasis because of its relevance to your question or its importance in developing what it is you might be trying to say. Use the "Explode a Moment" revision strategy on page 341 of Chapter 9 to help with this. This is a chapter you'll use often for many of the assignments in *The Curious Writer*. It's a toolbox of techniques that will help you develop your drafts, no matter what the subject.

As you compose your writing history, consider the following:

- Don't just tell one story. Tell several from different parts of your life that might illuminate your question.

- Does it make sense to tell your story out of order, in a structure that doesn't strictly follow chronology?

- Incorporate other sources. Nonfiction writers, no matter what the genre, can turn to four sources of information: personal experience, observation, interview, and reading. While this assignment will mine your personal experience most heavily, would it be useful to talk to a parent about your writing? Can you use any of the Bartholomae excerpt we read in Exercise 1.6? Might you find a relevant fact online?

■ SAMPLE STUDENT ESSAY

For the last thirty or so pages of this chapter, you've watched a student, Bernice Olivas, work alongside you, doing the exercises, generating material and then judging what she came up with. Here is her writing memoir draft:

Writing a New Path

Bernice Olivas

1   It's getting cold. The leaves have turned from green to gold and orange. A few weeks ago an unexpected snowstorm turned the world white for a few hours. Winter is coming, and with it the holiday season. As a child I lived for this time of year because it brought out the kid in my father. He decorated a tree, hung stockings, and the house was filled with the people we loved. In last five years that celebration has crumbled around us. My sisters treat each other like spun glass, afraid to reignite old fires over old arguments, afraid of what they might say if they speak, afraid of what they can't say out loud. My little brothers swagger in and out of my mother's house as if they owned the place, their young wives and children underfoot. They play house while my mother works herself haggard and my father slips in and out of the house, never staying at home for long.

2   We talk to each other in a way we'd never speak to a stranger, our voice filled with scorn, anger, and indifference. We disrespect each other, we belittle each other, and it's as if we've forgotten how much we love each other. The little ones, my boys, my nieces and nephews run around taking it all in as if such pain was normal. To them it is. I've perfected excuse after excuse to avoid the drive to Jerome because it hurts too much to watch.

3   We've grown up, we've grown apart, or maybe I've just lost the rose colored glasses that let me see a warm, loving home in a household scarred by poverty, and haunted by all the harsh realities of life for a Mexican American family trying to make it up north. Most days I console myself with the fact that my brothers are young, they'll grow up. I tell myself my sisters will come around, after all we're family. Occasionally things slip back into what they used to be and I tell myself time will heal the wounds but come Christmas time I find myself hard pressed to believe myself. I miss them. I miss who we used to be. I let myself wallow in just how much I miss them. Last year three little nieces and nephews joined the family and I couldn't stand the idea that these babies would never know the family the way we used to be.

4   I needed to get it all out of my head so I started writing short stories, memories really, of my siblings, my childhood. As I lost myself in retelling these family stories I recaptured something, a feeling, a sense of self and family I haven't felt in a long time. I wrote for days and finally when I was done I felt closer to my family than I had in years. I decided to make copies of these stories, have them bound, and give them as gifts to my family. As each of my siblings read them, and my mother cried over them, we shared a moment of just being together. It was quick, almost invisible, but for a moment, we were laughing together, leaning into each other, our bodies relaxed. It was good.

5   There were no spoken words that could have given us that little moment because our spoken language is heavy with years of family baggage. Putting it on paper lets each of us experience the camping trips, the smell of baking cookies, the inside jokes all over again. Such is the power of the written word. And it's a power that I had no idea existed until I was twenty-four, married, and the mother of two and going back to college.

I planned to get my teaching degree, work at a high school, and earn a little stability   6
for my children. It simply never occurred to me to want more. Just being at college was
more than I'd ever expected to achieve because people like me don't go to college. People
like me, and my family, work with our hands, and there is a deep sense of pride, almost a
reverence, attached to the conceptualization of ourselves as a strong, working class family.

My classes were amazing. I was learning so much and I loved the buzz and energy of   7
campus, but it was so hard. I'd been out of school for a long time, and even when I was in
high school no one ever asked me to write the way they were asking me to write in my college classes. My spelling sucked, my grammar was worse, and I was sure I'd fail my Comp
101 class. My Composition 101 teacher was ruthless, going over and over my drafts, pushing me to think on the page, to ask questions, to push myself past simply reporting information. I hated him for the first semester but found myself signing up for his early morning
class in the spring. Somewhere along the way I'd fallen in love with writing.

I'd found my voice and it felt good to write. I loved being able to write out all the noise   8
in my head; it was messy but once it was on the page I could work through it slowly, carefully,
untangling it until it was something new and exciting and all my own. The written word is a
language unto itself, a form of expression that opens up the world to be explored and navi-
gated in a way that is entirely unique. It was a language I wasn't fluent in. Like the rest of my
family, I could write enough to get by, in the same sense a beginning Spanish speaker gets by
in Latin America, and I had no idea how much of the conversation I was missing.

My grades improved and that nasty little voice that snuck up on me in the middle of   9
the night and whispered that I didn't belong, that there was no place amid all these
intellectuals for someone like me, disappeared. Four years later I'm a writing major, and
I'm headed to graduate school where I'll earn my PhD. After that I plan to write books,
and teach writing at a university. Finding my voice did more than just help me through
a few classes. It gave me a sense of power over my own life, a way to communicate with
the world at large. These days I go online and discuss politics with people in Australia,
London, and Quebec. I write my opinions to the school editor and occasionally they
print them. I'm slowly writing my way through my childhood and seeing it, myself, my
family, my people, and history in a whole new way. I'm writing a new path for my own
children.

Whenever I go to a family gathering someone asks me why I want to be a writer, why I   10
want to teach writing. They ask me why I don't do something more productive, more useful.
Nothing I say seems to make them understand. Nothing I can say satisfies them, and they
go away, still confused, reassuring themselves that I was always a little weird, a little off.
They remind each other that I was born left handed and my mom had to train me to use my
right hand. They remind themselves that I didn't start talking till I was almost four, and
then there was that nasty bump on the head that landed me in the hospital when I was six.

After all nobody else in the family writes. In fact Grandpa Domingo was illiterate,   11
could barely sign his own name, until the day he died. He did all right, built a trucking
company right up out of the ground and left Grandma the house, the land, and a healthy
savings account, and he never wrote a word.

(continued)

(continued)

12   How can I tell them that I write because it makes me more me, in a way I wasn't before. How can I tell them that being voiceless in the written word is dehumanizing in a way I cannot articulate verbally. How can I tell them how much I hurt to think of my grandfather navigating in this world, voiceless? How I can tell them that as a family, as a community, we are powerless without a voice on the page.

13   How can I make them feel the elation I feel when I write, when I learn something new? How can I tell them that writing is a powerful tool, which gave me the courage to step up and take on the responsibility of changing my life, the courage to offer my sons a life of more than backbreaking labor, and the audacity to dream of contributing on a wider scale to the world around me?

14   I can't; I have no words to tell them any of those things. They wouldn't understand if I tried. I don't have the right words to speak, but I can write them, explore them until they're filled with a power of their own, until I find truth within them. Then maybe my family can read them and understand me just a little better. Such is the power of the written word.

EXERCISE 1.7

Taking a Reflective Turn

After you've finished drafting your writing memoir, back away from the experience and think about how it went. Sadly, reflecting like this about something we've written is rare. But as I said earlier, this focus on *how* instead of *what* will do for you as a writer what a tennis coach can do for a player: help her to see that she's making often unconscious choices that affect her play. As a writer, you can see that in any writing situation you have a range of choices, not just one—but you can see this only if you make time to reflect on the choices you've made.

Let's do that with your writing memoir. In your notebook, use one or more of the following prompts for a fastwrite:

- What was different about how you approached the process of writing this essay from the way you approach other writing for school?

- Where did you run into problems? How might you have solved them if you had the chance to repeat the process of writing this essay?

- What did your writing memoir reveal to you about your writing habits, beliefs, and hopes? What do you see more clearly now that you didn't see before you wrote it?

You'll also have the chance to try out dialectical thinking, a process that may seem a little dizzying. In a way, it should, because both the writing process and dialectical thinking involve a great deal of back-and-forth movement, the sort of mental gymnastics you perform with the pen in your hand or your fingers on the keyboard.

Does it feel natural? Probably not. At least not yet. But I hope you'll find that your understanding of the writing process becomes more intuitive as you read further in the book. You may modify your writing process, add a step here or skip one there, prolong the process, or cut it short, depending on the writing situation and your rhetorical concerns. Whatever you do, though, you need to make choices based on an understanding of how they will influence your process. This is the key to making you a productive, confident writer.

USING WHAT YOU HAVE LEARNED

When I was in college I used to say this to anyone who asked how I felt about writing: *I don't like writing but I love having written.* What I meant, of course, is that I often felt satisfaction with the product of writing—the paper or essay—but didn't like the work that it took to produce it. This belief didn't help me improve as a writer because it prevented me from finding things about the process that could actually be okay, and even pleasurable: things like discovery. I never imagined surprise was possible. I hope this chapter initiated a reexamination of your own beliefs about writing. I hardly expect a revolution in your thinking, but maybe one or two things you once thought were true of writing may at least be in doubt, particularly if you think those beliefs get in the way of your progress. Carry that openness to revise your thinking into every assignment in this book and you may be surprised at what you can do.

You now know more about your writing process. You've identified what seems to go well and when you get into trouble. The habit of reflecting on your process will be invaluable as you face each new writing situation because each one presents different problems and choices. Understanding the basic rhetorical principles—considering how to present yourself to particular audiences on particular subjects—will help. You already know more than you think about rhetoric.

Reading to inquire opens a conversation with a text in which the words on the page are only part of the dialogue between the author and the reader.

READING AS INQUIRY

Here's what you might be thinking as you read this sentence: *This is a chapter about reading (in a textbook about writing) and I'm really hungry and could eat some potato chips and I already know about reading; I've been reading for years; this guy has a strange way of opening a textbook chapter, how does he know what I'm thinking, he probably doesn't want to know....* Okay, so I don't know exactly what you're thinking. But I do know that you're not simply sitting there decoding the meaning of each word I've written. For one thing, you're reading faster than that, looking at chunks of language. However, a lot of what is going on in your head isn't directly related to the words here. You're thinking about what kind of book you're reading—the textbook genre—and making mental predictions about what is going to come next. You're thinking about the subject— "reading as inquiry"—and considering what you may already know about it. And you're thinking about your purpose in reading these sentences or this book, trying to use that purpose as a guide to help you navigate my meaning and its relevance to you. However, I'm probably wrong about the potato chips.

I hope the image you get from reading this account is that what *you* bring to the reading situation is much more powerful than the words on the page. Experienced readers are aware of this, and like experienced writers, they can bring this knowledge to a range of reading situations and make choices about *how* to read. This rhetorical knowledge of reading is especially important in

What You'll Learn in This Chapter

- How your existing beliefs about reading might be obstacles to reading rhetorically.
- What connections exist between the writing and reading processes.
- How to use the double-entry journal to encourage dialectical thinking.
- How to apply some of the same strategies to reading pictures that you do to reading texts.
- How to understand the unique grammar of images.
- How to design the "look" of your writing.

college. First, you'll be reading a lot, and you'll be introduced, in classes across campus, to new genres and specialized writing that are entirely new to you. Sometimes you might feel as if you're in a wrestling match with texts whose moves are so novel that they threaten to pin you every time you confront them. But you can learn the moves, and in many cases you already know them.

My students fret about writing. But they don't seem to get very worked up about the challenges of reading. As you've seen, however, reading is complex, and in this chapter I'll show you how the writing process involves some of the same mental activities and even similar rhetorical choices used in reading. I'll also show you how writing can help you read better.

When we think of reading we usually associate the act exclusively with written texts, but so many of the images we encounter are, like written texts, crafted to communicate and persuade and so, whether we recognize it or not, we read images, too. In this chapter we'll use images as a metaphor to talk about all kinds of reading strategies, but we'll also focus on the unique grammar of visual literacy and how images work to influence a "reader."

MOTIVES FOR READING

Why read? In the case of best-selling popular fiction such as *The Da Vinci Code* or the Harry Potter books, the answer seems pretty clear: These are entertaining books. But pleasure is not a motive that seems to apply to most academic reading—we usually regard such reading as something we have to do to study for the test or write the paper. However, reading to inquire, while not always a source of pleasure, can offer the satisfaction of surprise and discovery, just as writing to inquire can. This is because what's behind an encounter with a text can be a desire to answer a question that interests you. Reading to inquire is, like writing to inquire, an open-ended process in which you set out to discover what you think, and along the way welcome confusion and ambiguity as a natural condition of the search. In other words, you never read just to collect information; you read to have a conversation with the information. You go back and forth between what an author says and what you think about what he or she says. *Does this help answer a question I've posed? Does it inspire me to see things differently? Does it complicate what I already believe?*

> Reading with the spirit of inquiry turns books, essays, and articles into one side of a dialogue that you're having with yourself and an author.

Reading with the spirit of inquiry turns books, essays, and articles into one side of a dialogue that you're having with yourself and an author. The meaning of a text (or an image) isn't fixed forever—engraved in stone tablets like a message from above—but worked out between the two of you, the author and the reader. This turns reading into a much more complicated intellectual activity, but it also makes reading more interesting because you create the conditions for surprise, for learning, and for discovery.

BELIEFS ABOUT READING

Most of us aren't very aware of our reading strategies and habits. Why should we be? After all, isn't reading just reading? How many ways can you do it? The way we go about learning how to read, however, is similar to the way we learn how to write. We start at an early age, perhaps even before we go to school. Along with the learning, we acquire beliefs that inform our response to *how* we read. These beliefs, though, can help or hinder our progress as readers. Once again, then, we need to assess our beliefs. Only by understanding *how* we read in certain situations can we acquire more control over what we get out of the reading experience.

EXERCISE 2.1

What Do You Believe?

STEP ONE: In your journal, draft a brief definition of a "good" reader. What exactly is a good reader able to do?

STEP TWO: Answer the following questions in your journal.

- Do you think you're a good reader? Why or why not?
- How would you describe your own reading habits and methods?

STEP THREE: It's helpful to think about the characteristics of a "good" reader in certain contexts. For example, what should a good reader be able to do when

- taking computerized exams like the ACT and the SAT?
- researching a paper for school?
- reading a textbook for an exam?
- analyzing a poem or short story?
- reading a text message?
- reading a friend's Facebook page?
- reading instructions on how to set up a new computer?
- reading a novel for pleasure?

Choose two of these reading situations (or two others that you can imagine), and in your journal write a definition of what a good reader should be able to do in each situation.

ONE STUDENT'S RESPONSE

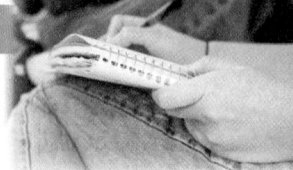

Briana's Journal

STEP ONE:

Good readers read with an open mind and an
open heart but cannot be too malleable. They have to be able to empathize and
still be able to judge with some sense. They have to immerse themselves in the
literature. I love when I read something and I feel something. Good readers
have to be able to pick up a variety of materials at any given time and be able
to have the skill to immerse themselves into that piece. They need to be able
to get the full scope of the writing and see the big picture through the small
details.

STEP THREE:

Reading a text message: Inflection is absent in this form of communication. And
because it is a casual type of communication, we tend to text like we talk. You
have to be able to recall the sender's personality and look at the words he or she
has chosen and the order in which he or she has placed them; this takes a high
level of analysis.

Most reading instruction seems to focus on comprehension—you know, the SAT- or ACT-inspired kind of situation in which you are asked to read something and then explain what it means. This often becomes an exercise in recall and vocabulary, an analytical challenge in only the most general way. Essentially, you train yourself to distinguish between specifics and generalities and to loosely follow the author's reasoning. In English classes, sometimes we are asked to perform a similar exercise with stories or poems—what is the theme or what does it mean?

> Only by understanding how we read in certain situations can we acquire more control over what we get out of the reading experience.

Questions such as these send students off on what is essentially an archaeological expedition where they must dig for hidden meaning. The "right" answers to the questions are in the text, like a buried bone; you just have to find them. Sometimes the expedition is successful, sometimes not. The trouble with this type of exercise has less to do with its success rate than with the belief that it tends to foster, which is that *all meaning resides in the text and the reader's job is merely to find it*. This belief limits the reader's interaction with the text. If meaning is fixed within the text, embedded like a bone in antediluvian mud, then all the reader has to do is dig to find that meaning. Digging isn't a bad thing, but reading can be so much more than laboring at the shovel and sifting through dirt.

READING SITUATIONS AND RHETORICAL CHOICES

You know those elaborate machines at the eye doctor's office that you look through while the optometrist tries various combinations of lenses, asking which make the fuzzy letters on the wall seem sharper? These devices are called phoropters (see Figure 2.1) and they immediately come to mind when I think about how we read. When we read anything—writing, images, graphics—we are looking through lenses. In a given situation, the right combination of lenses will help us to read better, and when we do we have found the right "prescription" for seeing a particular text for a particular purpose.

However, unlike the optometrist's phoropter, we can exercise more control over which lenses we use. Skillful readers are in command of the machine. This control comes from the same skill that gives writers more control: awareness of their own process and recognition of what each reading situation might demand. In Exercise 2.1 you began to think about both of these things, particularly

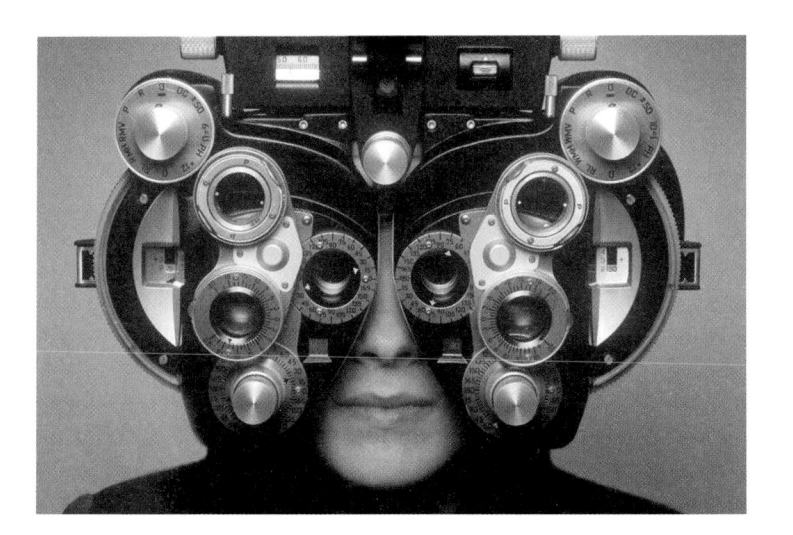

Figure 2.1 Reading is like looking through an optometrist's phoropter: The right combination of lenses will help us read better. Skillful readers are in command of the machine.

in Step 3, when you began to think about different contexts for reading, from SAT tests to text messages. Each situation demands different lenses that bring certain things—and not others—into sharper focus. The five most important types of lenses that influence how you see a text include the following:

- **Purpose:** Why are you reading?
- **Genre:** What do you know about this kind of text and what do you therefore expect?
- **Self-perception:** How good do you think you are at this kind of reading?
- **Knowledge:** What do you already know about the subject of the reading?
- **Rhetorical awareness:** What might be the purposes behind the text? What is it trying to do?

Imagine, for example, that you just purchased an iPhone and you're reading a page of instructions on how to use the video feature. Your purpose in reading in this case is entirely informational. You're motivated to learn how to use your new phone. You also probably have some experience with this genre—the instruction manual—because you've been buying electronics much of your life. Maybe you think you're a pretty good reader of the genre as a result. I know I'm not. I misread or misinterpret instructions, or ignore them altogether. I've also got a cell phone, but I've never used an iPhone, so I bring very little knowledge to my reading about how it works. If I were looking through the metaphorical phoropter, I'd start out with a pretty poor combination of lenses: difficulty with the genre, limited knowledge of the subject, and poor self-perception. If you were in my situation—or if you were advising me about how to be a better reader of this text—what would you do or say?

Let's look at an example of another kind of text. Last night I was reading a challenging piece on curiosity by two philosophers. It was published in the journal *Educational Theory*. The piece exemplifies a type of academic discourse that would be fairly typical in the discipline of philosophy. Here's an excerpt from the concluding paragraph of the article:

> In this article, we have characterized curiosity about a topic as attention to the topic giving rise to, and in turn sustained by, a motivationally original desire to know. Curiosity is biased by our practical and epistemic[1] interests. It is tenacious, typically involving a disposition to inquire into topics related to the topic of curiosity. And its motivational originality allows it to be some degree independent of practical and epistemic interests. The value of curiosity depends on these features. Its interest bias and tenacity together lead to deep inquiry than is motivated by practical and epistemic interests.[2]

---

[1]Of or related to knowledge.
[2]Schmitt, Fredrick F. and Reza Lahroodi. "The Epistemic Value of Curiosity." *Educational Theory* 58.2 (2008): 125–148.

This is pretty rough going for most readers. One of the problems has to do with purpose. Why are you reading this excerpt in the first place? I really didn't give you a reason. Now reread the passage once more, but this time your purpose is *to understand it well enough to write a two- or three-sentence summary of what you think the authors are saying.* After you're done, talk in class or in your journal about one or more of the following questions:

1. How competent do you think you are at reading this kind of writing? How did you feel when reading it? How do you often feel when reading difficult material?

2. You're probably not familiar with this genre of academic writing. What do you notice about its conventions: the language, the tone, the manner in which information is presented, and so on?

3. Curiosity is a condition of childhood, so we all bring some knowledge of it to this reading. Does this passage change anything about the way you think about your own curiosity? Does that make you think of a story?

4. What do you infer from reading this passage about the authors' purpose and audience for their article on curiosity? What exactly did you notice that inspired those inferences?

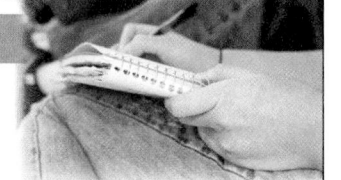

ONE STUDENT'S RESPONSE

Briana's Journal

READING ACADEMIC DISCOURSE

1. I feel like this piece is written for a certain kind of audience and that audience is not me. There are a lot of big words, some I am not sure what they mean and some I do but I have never heard or read them in that combination. As I read on I realize that it is not that difficult and they are really using a lot of words that people learn about that they are curious about. When I read difficult material I usually read the first sentence, then the second, realize that it is difficult and then sigh and then try and dig deeper and understand it and then I find that 4–5 sentences in I am not even paying attention and I usually altogether stop reading it.

2. It is not written plainly or for people that are not extremely knowledgeable in the subject; no one else would bother to read this. The info is presented in what I would consider a highly florid way; they are saying the same thing just in different ways and bringing in a minimum amount of new info.

(continued)

One Student's Response (*continued*)

3. It makes me think that when I find something interesting I will find all the books that I can on the subject and read them. Like I saw the movie *Marie Antoinette* and then I watched the special on the History channel and then I read her autobiography. Then my curiosity expanded to another queen, Queen Elizabeth. I watched the movies about her, and then I read her biography as well.

4. I am not sure what the authors' purpose is; I will presume it is to inform and I get the feeling that they also want to make others think that they are really smart. Like intellectual showoffs. I was under the assumption that that's what journals were for. But I am finding again that they are not saying a whole lot with all the words. This section is also a conclusion "we have characterized" part, maybe why it doesn't offer a lot of new information.

Figure 2.2 shows a genre that you might not be able to read very well.

Obviously, the electrical circuit diagram is a very specialized kind of text, and it presents tremendous challenges to novice readers. Even the most difficult academic discourse at least uses recognizable words, a symbol system that we've used most of our lives. But this is written in another language. Assume for a moment, though, that your assignment was to become a good

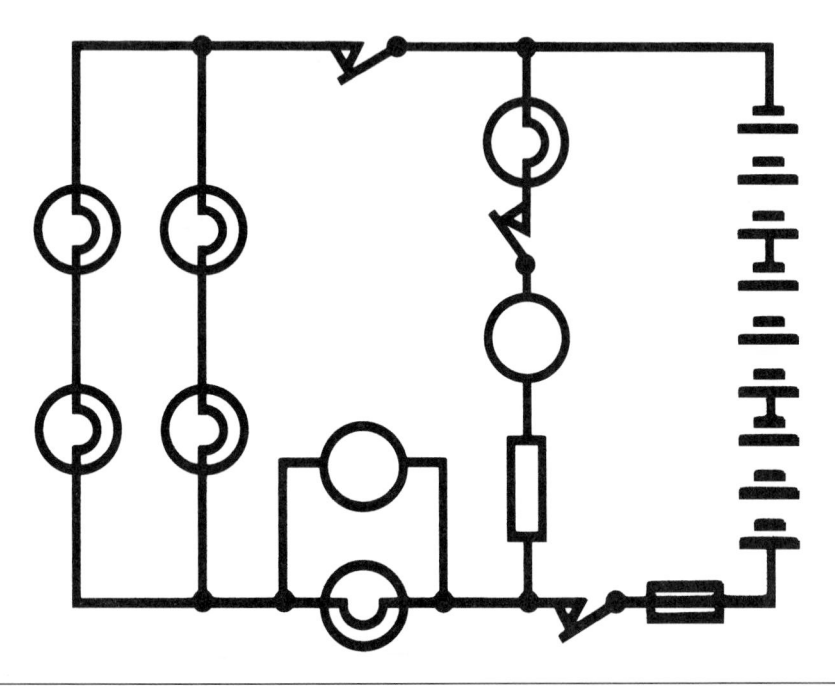

Figure 2.2 An electrical circuit diagram is a specialized kind of text that presents tremendous challenges to novice readers.

enough reader of this kind of text to be able to explain some of what this diagram is saying.

- How would you do that?
- What steps might you take?
- Might you generalize those steps or strategies to apply to any situation in which you're confronted with a difficult text?

Each of these three reading situations—an iPhone instruction manual, an excerpt from an academic journal, and an electrical circuit diagram—make different demands on you as a reader. One way of understanding these demands is to return to the rhetorical triangle we discussed in the last chapter (see Figure 2.3). Reading is a sometimes tricky negotiation between you, what you know, the subject and genre of the text, and the author's purpose behind it.

In the reader's rhetorical triangle, the reader moves to the apex of the triangle and the writer (or text's author, in this case) moves down to one of the lower legs (see Figure 2.3). The reader's portion of the triangle includes the reader's purpose for reading the text and knowledge of the subject and genre. Readers' self-perceptions—how competent they feel working with a particular text—strongly influence their motivation to wrestle with an unfamiliar work. The subject includes not only the main topic of the reading but the form or genre in which it is presented. The author's purpose shapes the third portion of the triangle. Combined, the three work to determine the context of each reading situation. The verbal SAT exam, for instance, in part involves reading short passages and answering multiple-choice comprehension questions. Speed is important. The significance of the test and the speed required to complete it influence the

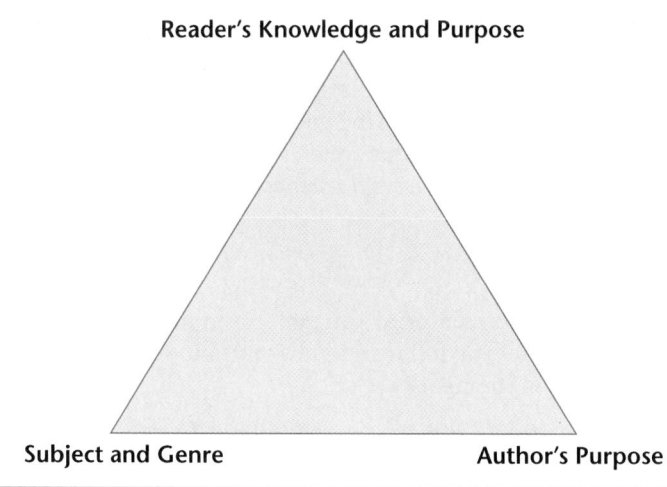

Reader's Knowledge and Purpose

Subject and Genre   **Author's Purpose**

Figure 2.3   **The reader's rhetorical triangle.** Reading is a negotiation between you, what you know, the subject and genre of the text, and the author's purpose.

reader's portion of the triangle. So too does the subject, which is presented in the form of multiple-choice questions. The author's intent in composing the questions—to test comprehension—also shapes the reading situation.

Each reading situation, like each writing situation, presents you with a range of choices. Becoming a good reader, like becoming a good writer, involves learning to recognize those situations and being flexible about how you respond to them. The path to becoming a more sophisticated reader, like being a stronger writer, begins with a look at your history and habits dealing with texts.

EXERCISE 2.2

Reading Autobiography

How do you think of yourself as a reader? Let's explore that self-perception in your journal. As in the last chapter, you'll be working toward a memoir essay, but this time on yourself as a reader.

Generating

STEP ONE: Think back to an experience with reading—or being read to—that stands out in your memory. I immediately think about my father reading *Lassie Come Home* aloud to me as a child. My head was on his chest and I could feel the words vibrate, and once I caught him weeping. For five or six full minutes, tell your own story with as much detail as you can. This is a fastwrite, so give yourself permission to write badly.

STEP TWO: Skip a line, and then write about another experience with reading. Write for five minutes.

STEP THREE: Imagine that you've been given a reading assignment in a class. You must read the first three chapters in the textbook. There are hints about the material being on an exam. Describe yourself, in the third person, doing this reading. Write this as a scene. For example, *He is sitting at a cluttered desk with his earphones on in an otherwise darkened room staring at the open book before him. His eyes wander…*

Judging

STEP FOUR: Look over the material you generated in the first three steps. In your journal, finish each of the following phrases, follow it until the writing dies out, and then move on to the next one.

1. *The thing that surprised me most about what I wrote is…*
2. *If someone else were to read what I wrote, they would probably see…*
3. *Overall, the one thing my writing seems to say about me as a reader is…*

READING AS A PROCESS

The difference between novice readers and more experienced readers comes down to this: Experienced readers always keep their purposes for reading in mind. Generally, these purposes arise from these three questions:

- Will this give me pleasure?
- What can I *learn* from this?
- What can I *do* with this?

Obviously, an act of reading can involve a combination of these motives, but reading for inquiry is ultimately concerned with the last: How can what I'm reading be used to explore the questions that interest me? Learning and the pleasure that arises from chasing after the answers to questions that interest you is a wonderful byproduct of the inquiry process, but as a writer your reading goal is much more utilitarian: You want to see if you can *use* what you're reading in your writing.

Reading to Write

The process of reading to write is going to be different than, say, reading for pleasure. For example, I'm currently stuck in an odd obsession with reading Lincoln biographies. I just can't get enough of them. My motives are both learning and pleasure, but I really don't plan on writing anything about Lincoln, so I don't bother with things like taking notes, marking passages, mining the bibliography, and other things like that. I certainly think about what I'm reading, and sometimes I even talk about what I've learned and bore everybody to death who isn't a Lincoln fan. I am, in short, a much less active reader when I'm not worrying about what I can do with what I'm reading.

Lately, I've been working on an essay in which I am exploring why certain landscapes—usually the ones we know best from our childhoods—often get under our skins even if we no longer live in those places. My reading for this project has led me to all kinds of sources—articles in anthropology, history, and literary works. This reading is enjoyable, but it's also work. In the back of my mind, I'm always asking, *Does this relate to the questions I'm interested in?* It's a reading process that is much more directed by my goals, my interests, and my desire to use what I'm reading in my own writing.

Reading for inquiry is a process that looks something like Figure 2.4.

Prereading. Before I read to write, I'm thinking:

- What are my inquiry questions? What do I want to find out?
- How might this text provide new answers, extending or changing what I think now?

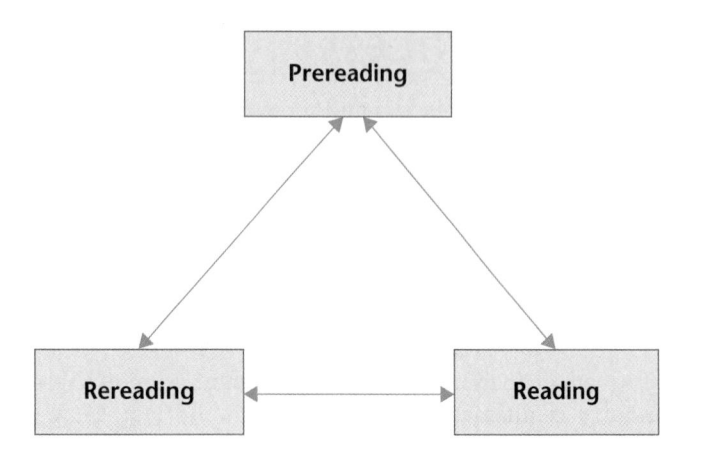

Figure 2.4   A process for reading to write. Reading, like writing, is a recursive process.

- What do I assume about the author's purposes?
- What do I know about how to read this kind of text?

Reading. When I read to write, I'm thinking:

- Is this relevant to what I want to know?
- Is this reliable?
- What does this say that I don't expect?
- What do I *think* about what it says?
- *How* might I use this in my writing?

Rereading. If the text seems relevant, I'll read it again, focused on not just the whole but also the parts, asking myself questions like these:

- What do I understand this to be saying?
- How does this connect with what I already know?
- Does it change the questions I'm asking?
- In my own words, what is the significance of this?
- How might the author's motives influence what this says?
- *Where* might I use this in my writing?

This process, like the writing process, is recursive. What I read may change the questions I'm asking, and every time I reread I'm also rereading my impressions from my first reading. But one thing doesn't change at any point in the process: My reading is always consciously goal-directed.

Goal-Directed Reading

Given a particular goal for reading, more experienced readers tend to agree on what's important. They learn to recognize certain patterns in a text that help them to use it more effectively. For example, I gave the following passage to sixty English majors. It's the concluding paragraphs of an essay by Christine Rosen[3] on the impact of social networking sites like Facebook on friendship. I then asked the students to assume that their purpose in reading the passage was to write a summary of what they understood Rosen to be saying about the effect of virtual relationships on human relationships, and I urged them to underline the words, phrases, or sentences in the excerpt that they thought would help them write it.

I've highlighted the sentences and phrases that my students consistently underlined the most. Keeping the goal of their reading in mind—to write a summary of this passage—what do you notice about the pattern of underlinings? What does this infer about where, in an article like this, readers can often find the most important information?

> We should also take note of the trend toward giving up face-to-face for virtual contact—and, in some cases, a preference for the latter. Today, many of our cultural, social, and political interactions take place through eminently convenient technological surrogates—Why go to the bank if you can use the ATM? Why browse in a bookstore when you can simply peruse the personalized selections Amazon.com has made for you? In the same vein, social networking sites are often convenient surrogates for offline friendship and community. In this context it is worth considering an observation that Stanley Milgram made in 1974, regarding his experiments with obedience: "The social psychology of this century reveals a major lesson," he wrote. "Often it is not so much the kind of person a man is as the kind of situation in which he finds himself that determines how he will act." To an increasing degree, we find and form our friendships and communities in the virtual world as well as the real world. These virtual networks greatly expand our opportunities to meet others, but they might also result in our valuing less the capacity for genuine connection.
>
> *(continued)*

---

[3]Rosen, Christine. "Virtual Friendship and the New Narcissism." *The New Atlantis* 2007 (Summer): 15–31.

(continued)

As the young woman writing in the *Times* admitted, "I consistently trade actual human contact for the more reliable high of smiles on MySpace, winks on Match.com, and pokes on Facebook." That she finds these online relationships more *reliable* is telling: it shows a desire to avoid the vulnerability and uncertainty that true friendship entails. Real intimacy requires risk—the risk of disapproval, of heartache, of being thought a fool. Social networking websites may make relationships more reliable, but whether those relationships can be humanly satisfying remains to be seen.

Sometimes we can learn the most about ourselves as readers by watching ourselves deal with a genre with which we're unfamiliar. Our knowledge about how the text works is limited so we're not quite sure where to direct our attention. We don't really trust ourselves to read the text "correctly." This may be exactly how you feel when you try to "read" a work of abstract art like the one by the artist Bridget Riley titled *Hesitate* (1964), shown in Figure 2.5. Riley was one of the most prominent artists in the short-lived Optical Art movement that began in the United States in the sixties.

Suppose you were asked by your art history professor to write a persuasive interpretation of *Hesitate*. Where would you begin? I would hope your instructor would have prepared your "reading" by helping you to understand how a painting like this one might be analyzed. What parts of this visual text should you pay attention to? How might you interpret the language of abstract art like this? One of the most important aspects of prereading is

Figure 2.5 Where would you begin if you were asked to write a persuasive interpretation of a piece of abstract art like *Hesitate* (1964), by Bridget Riley?

tapping the knowledge you have about the subject, genre, and conventions of the text you're working with. If you don't have that knowledge, you're likely to read it pretty poorly. If you've never really read a painting or know little about "optical art," then you'll probably be at a loss when pressed to say anything insightful about *Hesitate*.

EXERCISE 2.3

What Do You Know and When Did You Know It?

What *do* you know about how to read certain kinds of texts?

Generating

STEP ONE: Think for a moment about what you *believe you read pretty well* and perhaps what you've always liked to read: science fiction, auto repair manuals, blogs, short stories, song lyrics, poetry, newspapers, recipes, comic books? In your journal, begin by telling yourself the story of how you came to enjoy that genre. What moments or situations come to mind? What were particularly influential encounters with that type of text? Write fast for at least three minutes.

Judging

STEP TWO: Reflect on the genre you wrote about in step one and finish the following sentence in your journal at least four times:

*One of the things I learned about how to read_____ is that you should
_____.*

Our knowledge about reading comes to us accidentally, unexpectedly, and often unconsciously. We just do it, and eventually, if we're lucky, we get better at it. Eventually, we work tacitly from a series of assumptions about what it means to read something well, and we measure our success or failure against those assumptions. Perhaps several of those assumptions surfaced in this exercise. Examine them if they did. Do they still make sense? If you were going to teach someone else about how to read a recipe book, a comic book, or a poem, would these be the suggestions you might make?

Obviously, one way to become a more sophisticated reader is to expand this genre knowledge to other forms that you encounter with which you're less familiar, especially those you want to learn how to use in your writing.

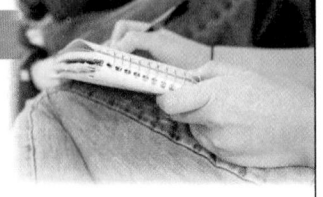

ONE STUDENT'S RESPONSE

Briana's Journal

EXERCISE 2.3
STEP ONE: Generating

I read novels really well, but who doesn't? Generally they are easy reads and they are on topics of my personal choice. But I really get into them. When I read a suspenseful part I can feel my muscles clench. I once read a thriller book and my jaw hurt after I read a chapter or two everyday and I couldn't figure out why. Apparently I had been clenching my jaw the whole time. When there is a sad part I will feel my heart hurt and I will get mad at the person or event that caused the sadness on the inflicted's behalf. I have always been empathetic, so it goes to reason that it also extends to fictional things as well. Call me a bleeding heart.

I also love to read textbooks and nonfiction books. In between college when I was taking my seven-year break, I would find textbooks somewhere and appropriate them or buy them online; and read them from cover to cover. I think that it is really important to keep learning and growing as a human; don't let your brain be idle. Of course all the books I chose were on subjects that I was interested in: physics, history, biographies on infamous queens, music theory, Che Guevara, or Eastern European culture. I will get "stuck" on a subject and then have to learn everything about it. I want to know, so I pay close attention and will have great retention of the information.

STEP TWO: Judging

- ■ ***One of the things that I learned about how to read*** textbooks ***is that you should*** really be interested in the subject that you are reading about.

- ■ ***One of the things that I learned about how to read*** a novel ***is that you can*** skip the boring parts that you don't like and fill in the blanks (I pretty much skipped all of the Elvish poetry in *The Two Towers*).

- ■ ***One of the things that I learned about how to read*** either novels or textbooks ***is that you should*** be interested in the subject, and if it is an area that you are not interested in and you have to read it, say for an assignment, then try and stay open-minded and try and find something that interests or intrigues you about it.

Inquiry Questions for Reading to Write

Writing to inquire, as you learned in the last chapter, begins with questions, not answers, and learning to craft a good question—one that will sustain your writing and thinking for some weeks—is an essential skill. Questions can also crack open a text and lead to new discoveries. To begin with, questions give you an initial reason for reading. I can imagine many kinds of questions that might

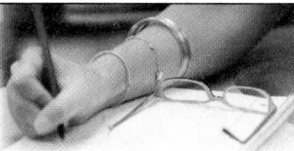

INQUIRING INTO THE DETAILS

Reading Perspectives

When we read, we always adopt certain perspectives toward a text, usually unconsciously. But one of the best ways to read strategically is to consciously *shift* our perspective while we read. Like changing lenses on a camera or changing the angle, distance, or time of day to photograph something, this shift in reading perspective illuminates different aspects of a text. Here are some of the perspectives you might take:

- **Believing:** What the author says is probably true. Which ideas can I relate to? What information should I use? What seems especially sound about the argument?

- **Doubting:** What are the text's weaknesses? What ideas don't jibe with my own experience? What are the gaps in the information or the argument? What isn't believable about this?

- **Updating:** What does this add to what I already know about the subject?

- **Hunting and gathering:** What can I collect from the text that I might be able to use?

- **Interpreting:** What might be the meaning of this?

- **Pleasure seeking:** I just want to enjoy the text and be entertained by it.

- **Connecting:** How does this information relate to my own experiences? What is its relationship to other things I've read? Does it verify, extend, or contradict what other authors have said?

- **Reflecting:** How was this written? What makes it particularly effective or ineffective?

- **Resisting:** This doesn't interest me. Why do I have to read it? Isn't *Survivor* on television right now?

guide your reading (also see "Inquiring into the Details: Reading Perspectives," above), but when you're reading to write, the following four categories of questions are the most common:

- Exploring questions
- Explaining questions
- Evaluating questions
- Reflecting questions

Questions in all four of these categories shift the way we see something. Years ago, I spent an afternoon taking photographs of an old wagon on a rolling New Hampshire hillside. I got up early on a September morning, hoping to take advantage of the slanting light and the shreds of mist that hung on the hayfield. I resolved to shoot an entire roll of film of the wagon, and I literally circled it, clicking away. By the fourth or fifth shot, I started to see the wagon in ways I'd never seen it, even though I had driven by it on my way to work for years. I saw how the beads of dew covered the bleached wood of the wagon's wheel. I saw how the ironwork of the driver's bench created a shadow on the grass that was a tangle of geometric shapes.

What I'm describing is the process of revision. But the anecdote also comes to mind now because it illustrates how different questions can shift your gaze on a topic. They help you to circle the wagon, changing your angle and revealing certain aspects of the subject. Behind each question is a different perspective on the subject. For example, take this finding from studies on computer literacy:

Boys generally outperform girls in knowledge and use of computers.

Suppose that you want to think about this. If you want to tap the power of questions, here are some that you might start with that fall into each of the four categories:

1. Do my own experiences and observations with computers tell me anything about what I think about this proposition? (Exploration)
2. How would I define "computer knowledge" in this context? (Explanation)
3. What have I seen, read, or experienced that provides support—or opposing evidence—for this idea? (Evaluation)
4. What do I notice about how each of the preceding questions shifts my way of seeing the claim about gender and computer use? (Reflection)

Can you see how each of these questions shifts your relationship to the topic and triggers different ways of thinking about it? Obviously, these aren't the only categories into which questions can be put, but they are very useful ones for reading to write.

You'll find exploring, explaining, evaluating, and reflecting questions (Figure 2.6) following readings throughout *The Curious Writer*. These form a launching point for your inquiry into the texts.

Exploration. To explore is to see a topic with wide-eyed wonder. *What might this mean to me? What do I feel or think about this?* Through questions like these, writers can openly investigate the things they read and there can be a big pay-off: You *discover* what you think. Obviously, exploratory questions about texts and the writing they inspire are most useful when you're writing about a topic that's relatively new to you. But you can also explore your existing beliefs, feelings, or ideas and you might also be surprised by what you find.

Here are some opening questions that might put you in an exploratory mode about any reading:

- What does this mean to me, or how do I think or feel about it?
- What are my first thoughts about this? And then what? And then?

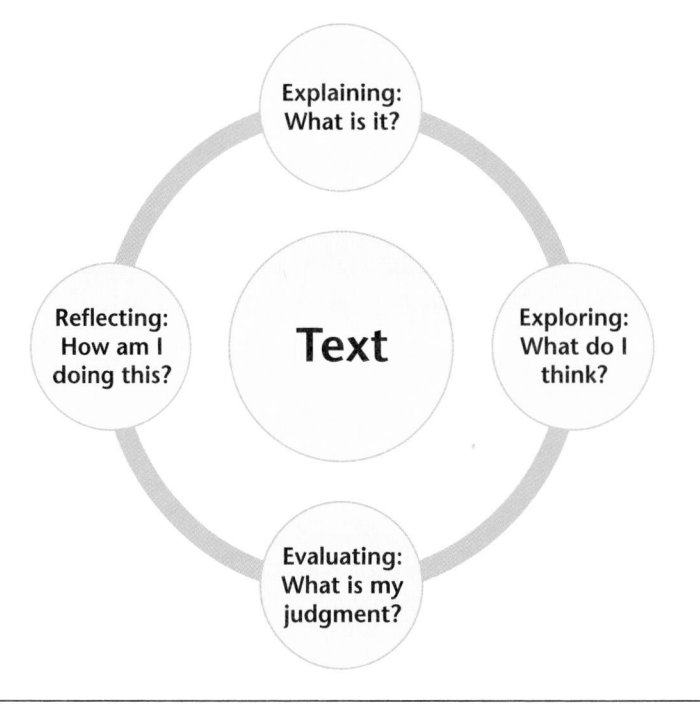

Figure 2.6   The four question categories—exploring, explaining, evaluating, and reflecting—will shift your gaze as a reader, encouraging you to see different things.

- What interests me most about this? What additional questions does it raise?
- What is the relationship between _____ and _____?
- How do my personal experiences and knowledge affect the way I feel and what I see?
- What surprises me about the way I see or think about this?

Explanation.   We explain things all the time. Just a minute ago, Jim, the plumber who is working on our bedroom remodel, explained to me how the boiling water tap works on our sink. We use it for making tea, and it was sputtering and coughing and generally looking like it had symptoms of influenza. When we explain things, we usually have a particular audience in mind. We want audience members to _understand_ something, but we are not merely reporting information. We're thinking about it too, trying to clarify in our own minds what we know or see and what we want to say about it.

    Some of the most common types of explanations involve defining, describing, categorizing, and comparing, often inspired by questions like these:

- What kind of text is this?
- What is its purpose?

- How is it put together?
- What is the text trying to do?
- How does it compare to something someone else has said?
- What do I understand this to be saying?

Evaluation. To evaluate something is to judge it or form an opinion about it. Evaluating things—restaurants, the quality of play in the NBA, the religious motives of Islamic extremists, the latest rap offering—is something we do all the time. These evaluations tend to lead us to do and say certain things and then to offer reasons and evidence that make them sound reasonable. If exploration is about *finding out* what we think about what we read, evaluation is often about using a reading to *prove our ideas*.

Don't misunderstand me, though. While we often have opinions about a topic, reading inquiry questions that move us to evaluate often inspire us to do more than simply find support for those opinions in what we read. We also evaluate the opinions themselves, and in the process we may begin to think differently.

Evaluation questions include the following:

- What's my opinion about what this reading seems to be saying, and what are my reasons?
- What is most convincing here? What is least convincing?
- What does the text assume to be true that might not be?
- What do I agree with? What do I disagree with?
- What does the author fail to see? How might it be seen differently?
- Who do I believe?

Reflection. If you did Exercise 2.3, you might have reflected on what you know about *how to read* the kinds of things you like to read. We often develop this kind of knowledge—knowledge about how to do things—slowly over time. But you can speed up the process by making time to ask yourself questions that encourage reflection.

You probably already have experience with this. We reflect on all kinds of processes that we want to get better at—things like playing golf, learning to act, and, of course, reading and writing. How am I executing that back swing? How might I do it differently? What new technique can I try that will deepen the emotional response of the character I'm playing? When we reflect like this on golf or acting, we discover other choices we can make that will help us perform better. The same is true when we reflect on how we think or write. The benefit of doing this is significant for everyone, but it's huge when you have problems with a process or you want to get better at it.

Inquiry questions that prompt reflection about how you read include:

- What do I notice about how I'm reading this?
- What assumptions do I bring to the reading that might influence what I think or how I feel about what it says?

- How do I compare how I approach this task with how I approach another one?
- When did I have the most problems with the text? What were they?
- How did this add to my knowledge about how to become a better reader?

READING DIALECTICALLY

Opening questions will give us goals for reading, as they do for writing, and we can also use the method of combining creative and critical thinking to help us get more out of what we read (see Figure 2.7). Remember the inquiry process described in Chapter 1 for combining creative and critical thinking?

You have already used this process extensively in the writing exercises so far, moving from suspending judgment when you generate ideas to making judgments when you analyze what you've generated. When we read to write, we can also use these alternate modes of thinking to ultimately answer the same question that all writing must answer: *So what*? What are you trying to say to others about what you've read that they might care to know? On the way to answering the "so what" question, we're trying to figure out what *we* think and, in particular, how a text helps us to think about the questions that moved us to look at it

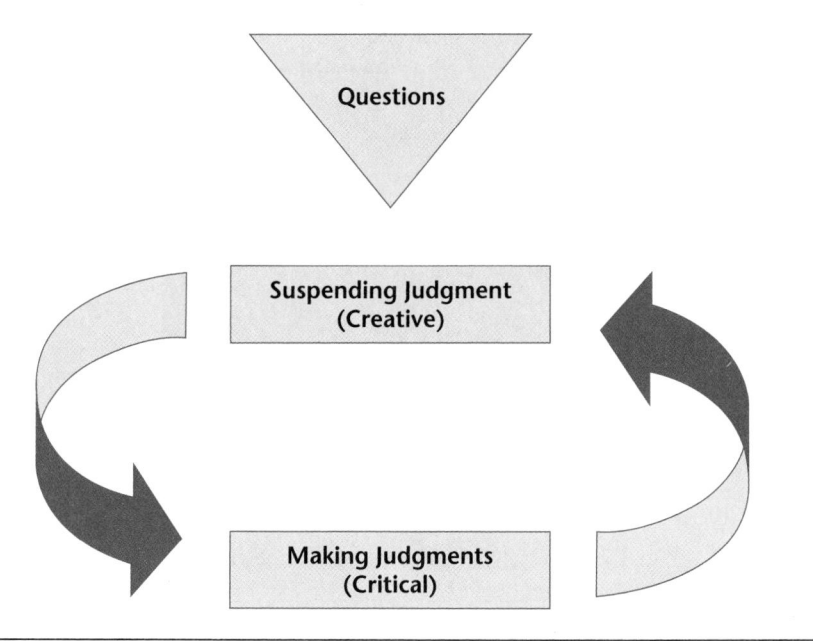

Figure 2.7   The inquiry process combines creative and critical thinking.

in the first place. Let's see how this might work with a visual text and then, later, a print text.

Suppose you were asked to *explain* the image in Figure 2.8, by famed American photographer Edward Weston, in a short response, offering your own idea about what it means based on particular things you see in the photograph.

You could approach this in two ways:

1. You could just make something up without thinking about it much and leave it at that. "Gee, this looks like, um, a bull's nostril."

2. You could withhold judgment and spend a little more time figuring out what you think.

The first option is a closed, cursory reading. It starts with answers rather than questions, and sidesteps any genuine inquiry into the text. The second option is more open-ended, and it requires that you look more closely at the text and *then* develop ideas about it. Reading dialectically is a method that can encourage that kind of inquiry.

When we read to write, we work from a question that gives our reading a goal. In the case of the photograph, we're asking an explaining question: "What is this image trying to do?" As you know, knowledge of *how* to read a kind of text with which we may not be familiar will really help us work toward a good reading

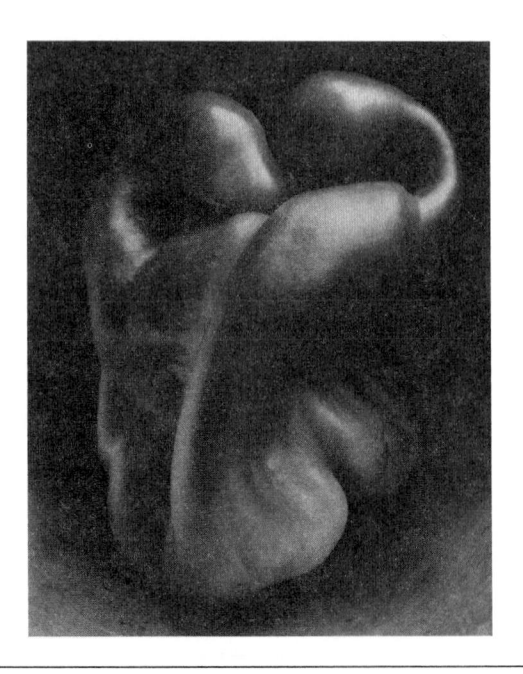

Figure 2.8   How would you explain this photograph?

(see "Inquiring into the Details: Visual Literacy: Reading Photographs, page 64). With this background knowledge, here's one way of finding an answer to our question:

- Start with two blank, opposing pages in a journal. Beginning on the left page, note your observations of the photograph. Writing fast, use your knowledge of how to read a photograph and explore what exactly you see in the image, describing this as specifically as you can.

- On the right page, compose your initial thoughts in response to the question, looking at the information you collected on the left page to help you think about what you are trying to say.

For example:

Observations of	Ideas about
What's interesting is that the setting of the image is stripped down and bare so that the green pepper is without question the most important visual subject here. The framing is so simple, really. All we need to know is before us. It's realistic and it's abstract at the same time. I can see the pepper, particularly the bruise in the bottom and the curving ribs of the thing, but the light seems to emphasize not the structure of the green pepper but the skin. The skin is amazing. The light has this amazing range reflecting on the skin—very dark at the top where the pepper turns into itself in contrast with the sheen on the edges. . . .	By stripping away any context and filling the frame with the image of a single green pepper, Weston's photograph emphasizes its abstract qualities. And yet, though we know it's a pepper, it's impossible to avoid seeing the play of the light on its skin as incredibly suggestive. It's sensuous and has some of the qualities of flesh, especially the curves and the muscular ridges.

Reading dialectically like this mimics the process you've already practiced in Chapter 1, moving back and forth from creative and critical, collecting and focusing, observations and ideas, specifics and generalizations. On the left page you are withholding judgment, trying to think through writing about what you see. On the right, you work toward making some kind of judgments about what you see. Obviously, this method—what writing theorist Ann Berthoff called the "dialogue journal" or double-entry journal—takes more time than just making a pronouncement like "It's a pepper!" or "It looks like two wrestling dinosaurs!" But by postponing the rush to a conclusion, you use the inquiry process to come up with better, more insightful, more informed ideas.

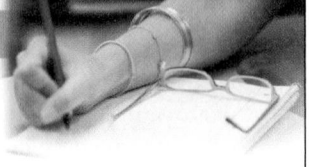

INQUIRING INTO THE DETAILS

Visual Literacy: Reading Photographs

As you know by now, it helps enormously when reading a new text to have some knowledge of *how* to read it. Here are some aspects to consider:

- *Framing:* As in writing, what the photographer chooses to leave in an image and what she chooses to leave out profoundly affect the story, idea, or feeling a photograph communicates.

- *Angle:* A front-on view of a subject creates a different effect than looking up— or down—at it.

- *Setting:* While good photographs emphasize certain visual elements and not others, some try, directly or indirectly, to communicate other information about where and when the photograph was taken. It's also significant when setting or context is missing.

- *Arrangement:* In writing, we give certain information emphasis by where we place it in a sentence, in a paragraph, or in the whole composition. Visual information also uses the physical arrangement of objects for emphasis, making some things larger or smaller, in the foreground or background, to one side or the other. Focus, or what is clear and what is fuzzy, is one way to manage visual arrangement.

- *Light:* What is most illuminated and what is in shadows—and everything in between—also influences what is emphasized and what is not. But since light is something we strongly associate with time and place, it also has an emotional impact.

EXERCISE 2.4

Reading Creatively, Reading Critically

Now that you've seen how the dialectical thinking approach can help analyze an image, let's try it with a more familiar kind of text. I published the essay "The Importance of Writing Badly" some years ago, but I think it still expresses several of the main ideas behind this book. I'd like you to read the piece critically, though, using the double-entry journal method we used when interpreting the pepper photograph.

As before, you'll use opposing pages of your journal. At the top of the left page write the word "Collecting," and at the top of the right page write the word "Focusing."

STEP ONE: Read the essay once through, and then once again. The second time through, carefully *copy* lines of passages from the essay on the left page of your notebook that:

- Connected with your own experience and observations
- Raised questions for you
- Puzzled you
- You thought seemed a key point
- You disagreed or agreed with or you think about differently
- You found surprising or unexpected

The Importance of Writing Badly
Bruce Ballenger

I was grading papers in the waiting room of my doctor's office the other day, and he said, "It must be pretty eye-opening reading that stuff. Can you believe those students had four years of high school and still can't write?"   1

I've heard that before. I hear it almost every time I tell a stranger that I teach writing at a university.   2

I also hear it from colleagues brandishing red pens who hover over their students' papers like Huey helicopters waiting to flush the enemy from the tall grass, waiting for a comma splice or a vague pronoun reference or a misspelled word to break cover.   3

And I heard it this morning from the commentator on my public radio station who publishes snickering books about how students abuse the sacred language.   4

I have another problem: getting my students to write badly.   5

Most of us have lurking in our past some high priest of good grammar whose angry scribbling occupied the margins of our papers. Mine was Mrs. O'Neill, an eighth-grade teacher with a good heart but no patience for the bad sentence. Her favorite comment on my writing was "awk," which now sounds to me like the grunt of a large bird, but back then meant "awkward." She didn't think much of my sentences.   6

I find some people who reminisce fondly about their own Mrs. O'Neill, usually an English teacher who terrorized them into worshipping the error-free sentence. In some cases that terror paid off when it was finally transformed into an appreciation for the music a well-made sentence can make.   7

But it didn't work that way with me. I was driven into silence, losing faith that I could ever pick up the pen without breaking the rules or drawing another "awk" from a doubting reader. For years I wrote only when forced to, and when I did it was never good enough.   8

(continued)

(continued)

9   Many of my students come to me similarly voiceless, dreading the first writing assignment because they mistakenly believe that how they say it matters more than discovering what they have to say.

10   The night before the essay is due they pace their rooms like expectant fathers, waiting to deliver the perfect beginning. They wait and they wait and they wait. It's no wonder the waiting often turns to hating what they have written when they finally get it down. Many pledge to steer clear of English classes, or any class that demands much writing.

11   My doctor would say my students' failure to make words march down the page with military precision is another example of a failed education system. The criticism sometimes takes on political overtones. On my campus, for example, the right-wing student newspaper demanded that an entire semester of Freshman English be devoted to teaching students the rules of punctuation.

12   There is, I think, a hint of elitism among those who are so quick to decry the sorry state of the sentence in the hands of student writers. A colleague of mine, an Ivy League graduate, is among the self-appointed grammar police, complaining often about the dumb mistakes his students make in their papers. I don't remember him ever talking about what his students are trying to say in those papers. I have a feeling he's really not that interested.

13   Concise, clear writing matters, of course, and I have a responsibility to demand it from students. But first I am far more interested in encouraging thinking than error-free sentences. That's where bad writing comes in.

14   When I give my students permission to write badly, to suspend their compulsive need to find the "perfect way of saying it," often something miraculous happens: Words that used to trickle forth come gushing to the page. The students quickly find their voices again, and even more important, they are surprised by what they have to say. They can worry later about fixing awkward sentences. First, they need to make a mess.

15   It's harder to write badly than you might think. Haunted by their Mrs. O'Neill, some students can't overlook the sloppiness of their sentences or their lack of eloquence, and quickly stall out and stop writing. When the writing stops, so does the thinking.

16   The greatest reward in allowing students to write badly is that they learn that language can lead them to meaning, that words can be a means for finding out what they didn't know they knew. It usually happens when the words rush to the page, however awkwardly.

17   I don't mean to excuse bad grammar. But I cringe at conservative educational reformers who believe writing instruction should return to primarily teaching how to punctuate a sentence and use *Roget's Thesaurus*. If policing student papers for mistakes means alienating young writers from the language we expect them to master, then the exercise is self-defeating.

18   It is more important to allow students to first experience how language can be a vehicle for discovering how they see the world. And what matters in this journey—at least initially—is not what kind of car you're driving, but where you end up.

STEP TWO: Now use the right page of your notebook to think further about what you wrote down on the left page. Remember these inquiry questions that can guide your thinking and writing:

- *Exploring:* What do I first notice about notes I took on "The Importance of Writing Badly?" And then what do I notice or think? And then?
- *Explaining:* What is it that I understand this to be saying?
- *Evaluating:* What is most convincing here? What is least convincing?

Write for five or six minutes without stopping.

STEP THREE: Reread what you've written. Again, on the right page of your notebook write your half of the dialogue below with someone who is asking you about the idea of "bad writing."

Q: I don't understand how bad writing can help anyone write better. Can you explain it to me?

A:

Q: Okay, but is it an idea that makes sense to you?

A:

Q: What exactly (i.e., quotation) does Ballenger say that makes you feel that way?

A:

STEP FOUR: Finish the exercise by reflecting in your journal for five minutes on what, if anything, you noticed about this method of reading. In particular:

- How did it change the way you usually read an article like this?
- How might you adapt it for other situations in which you have to read to write?
- What worked well? What didn't?
- Do you think the method encouraged you to think more deeply about what you read?

ONE STUDENT'S RESPONSE

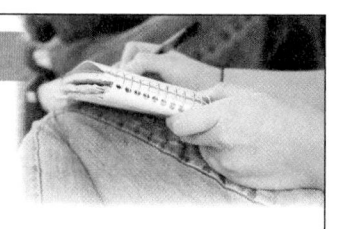

Briana's Journal

**EXERCISE 2.4 READING CREATIVELY,
READING CRITICALLY**
STEP TWO:

I took pieces of the sentences, not necessarily writing down the whole sentence but the parts that were the most poignant. I mostly chose sentences that I found to be clever, amusing, or just liked the way they sounded...I also created a dichotomy,

(continued)

One Student's Response (*continued***)**

focusing on two things: 1) the "proper" way of writing, which is English elitism, and is focusing on grammatical perfection and 2) the "artsy" way of writing, which focuses on writing as a thought process to help create understanding and growth. While I was writing down my notes and sentences, I was thinking that I have never had a Mrs. O'Neil. This has not been my experience. I write to write, and mostly to amuse myself or as a form of cheap therapy (also cheaper than cable). I also think that sometimes "grammatical imperfection" can add to the style and the voice of a piece. I also value voice and style over perfection…I see this piece as saying that writing is like a thinking process, like thinking out loud but you have an invaluable record of your thoughts. I also get that you need to write and write a lot. The more the better; it gives you more to work with. I also think that it helps you write better and enjoy it because you are getting a lot of experience. It's not so much about how you wrote it as it is about what you write about.

STEP THREE

Q: I don't understand how bad writing can help anyone write better. Can you explain it to me?

A: What you have to say is just as important as how you write it. Writing is a way of thinking, sort of like thinking out loud—a way of thinking through things and reflecting more deeply on things. It feels awesome to write with reckless abandon and show no concern for punctuation or grammar. It helps you think unhindered, to find out how you truly think and feel. Thoughts and feelings have little concern for these things. Looking back at your thoughts that you have written you can see your thoughts. Then you can look at how you have written. Being observant and introspective of your own writing will help you develop better writing skills.

Q: Okay, but is it an idea that makes sense to you?

A: Definitely, I prefer to write badly. I believe that it's a better expression of my actual thoughts, flaws and all. When I write on my computer my spellcheck goes crazy with "fragment sentences." But who cares? That's what I want to say and that is how it comes out and how it sounds in its natural state. I don't change it. Give me all your green squiggly underlinings, Windows Vista. It has been driven into so many students that we have to write perfectly—use correct punctuation, no vague pronouns, correct verb tense, good sentence syntax, and structure. I think that writing should be more than that. I think that it should be more of a form of expression.

Q: What exactly (i.e., quotation) does Ballenger say that makes you feel that way?

A: "Many of my students come to me similarly voiceless, because they mistakenly believe that how they say it matters more than discovering what they have to say."

I have never actually used the "double-entry" journal method before. I think it gave me a more articulate and clear idea of what I thought and how I came to think that. It became a map of my thought process. I usually have trouble pulling my thoughts in my writing together, but this gave me my thoughts more concisely. I also liked that

I had a record of my thoughts and that regardless of the quality of writing, it was an accurate record because we all know that memory is not all that reliable. I think that method would be good when you have to opine on a subject at length. I liked the explore, explain, evaluate, and reflect structure because when you are writing off the top of your head it is easy to lose focus. So this helps keep you on track.

Read to Write and Write to Read

In this chapter I'm making a case for an approach to reading that is probably unfamiliar to you. It includes the following:

1. **When you read to write, do it with certain goals in mind.** For many of us this isn't new—we often do read with purpose—but these goals are often limited to two things: comprehending and cherry-picking. The lesson of the SAT is that comprehension is what reading is all about since that is what you get tested on. Similarly, the five-paragraph theme and other formulaic forms of writing, which are so popular in school, teach us that reading to write is no more than plucking information from sources to plug into paragraphs to support topic sentences. But reading can also be a kind of conversation in which we talk with others with an open mind.

2. **Questions shift your perspective on what you read.** When we read to write we may have only one question in mind: What do I understand this to be saying? That's a good question, of course, but it's not the only one that can guide your thinking. Photographers consciously change lenses, angles, and distances on their subjects to see them in new ways. Questions have the same effect when you read—especially those that *explore, explain, evaluate,* and *reflect.*

3. **When you read to write you can write *and* read.** Some of us underline, highlight, and even make marginal notes when we read to write. But I'm encouraging you to do much more writing than that as you read, and after you read. If writing about your personal experiences can be a process of discovery, as I claimed in Chapter 1, then you can use the same method to explore anything else you want to think about. In other words, if you're trying to figure out what you think about what you're reading, then you can *write* your way to new understandings.

4. **Good readers develop *rhetorical knowledge*.** You already have more of this kind of knowledge than you think. You know, for example, to read a text message differently than a textbook. But the best readers pay a lot of attention to learning explicitly about this. They remember what different reading situations demand from them. For example, they learn to distinguish goals for reading to write about a short story from goals for reading to write about marketing. They also develop knowledge about genre. Good readers, for instance, know that Web pages are often designed to put the most important information across the top and down the left side.

THE WRITING PROCESS

INQUIRY PROJECT: THE READING LITERACY MEMOIR

In Chapter 1 you wrote a memoir on your writing life. This chapter will end the same way, but this time your three- to five-page essay will focus on your experiences as a reader. You've already started writing and thinking about this in Exercises 2.1 and 2.2. If you can, draw on some of that material and draft a personal essay that does two things:

- Tells stories about some of your reading experiences, in school and out
- Reflects on what you understand about those experiences now, as you look back on them

For your reflection, exploit, if you can, some of the information in this chapter, particularly ideas about what the differences might be between a "good" reader and a novice reader and where you see yourself as a reader now, what you think you need to learn, and why it matters.

For additional reading, writing, and research resources, go to **www.mycomplab.com**

Unfortunately, schooling can brand us and give us ideas about ourselves that are hard to change. I was told in subtle and unsubtle ways that I was not good at English. When it comes to reading—the major focus of language arts classes—one moment stands out that affected the way I thought about myself as a reader for a long time. My memoir, for example, might start like this:

In 1965, I moved from green to orange in the SRA reading packet but never moved again. In those days, orangeness was a sign of mediocrity. The shame of never busting through orange to blue, the color Jeff Brickman, Mark Levy, and Betsy Cochran seemed to achieve with such ease quite naturally made it easy to convince me that reading was just not my thing. From then on I hated English (a feeling I freely shared on the inside covers of my class yearbooks), except the time we studied the lyrics of Simon and Garfunkel's "The Sounds of Silence." I was a high school sophomore, and while I would sometimes, in my own way, think deeply on things, I was attached more to *the idea* of thinking deeply on things, usually expressed in the ponderous and self-consciously deep lyrics of early Simon and Garfunkel's. To *feel* deep, I thought, was to *be* deep.

■ STUDENT ESSAY

Reading Literacy Memoir
Briana Duquette-Shackley

I was born into a very blue-collar family, almost anti-intellectual. You read recipes, you read car repair manuals, you read the TV guide or on occasion you read those novels that they sell on the shelf at the checkout aisle. There was very little emphasis on learning or intellect. Instead you were told to be who you are and do what you like best. There was never anyone pushing me to be a doctor and when I said I wanted to be one, my parents said "OK." I said I wanted to be a racecar driver and they said "if that's what you want to do." I said that I wanted to be a fashion designer and they said "that's a fine idea."   1

Under this intellectual neutrality I just went with what interested me and I blossomed in the reading and language department. I could speak and read at an early age and was reading at a college freshman level in the fifth grade. If I wanted a book, my parents bought it; so when I asked for *The Scarlet Letter* at an early age, they didn't seem concerned about the content or the level of reading. I read it. There were some things that I had to reread, but I read it. I was a good student and consistently on the honor roll.   2

It was not that my parents didn't praise me for my academics, but they just didn't push me in any one direction. I found a love of reading, and once I started to read I didn't want to stop. I would read anything that I could get my hands on, and I continue to be like that to this day. I read *People*, *Us Weekly*, and *Good Housekeeping*, not because they are what I love to read but because it's the only thing to read at work. I could spend days in Barnes and Noble and not buy anything. And all the librarians at my local library know me by name.   3

In kindergarten I remember reading the books that they have that teach you how to read, the same "decodable" books I read to my own daughter, and I loved them. I would read aloud at the kitchen counter as my mom cooked dinner. I now find myself with a compulsion to read anything that is in front of me no matter how lame: cereal boxes, random pamphlets, those weird quips in the phonebook. I love the communication and the nuances between words, their meanings, and their usage. It's like how I look at fashion magazines for ideas on how to dress, I look to literature to show me examples of how to speak and write, and even to try out who I might want to be.   4

I have gone through phases where I want to explore an area of myself or life and I will turn to literature for information about it. During my punk rock phase in high school, I read books and periodicals about revolution and anarchy and became very politically savvy. I went through an artistic phase where I wanted to learn about the great artists and how to revolutionize the art world. I went to the library and checked out art book after art book. I went through an indie rock, intellectual phase and read exclusively books by the beat writers. Then I went through a Che Guevara phase and read *The Motorcycle Diaries* and his lengthy autobiography. I noticed toward the end of the bio that I didn't even want to read it; I really couldn't   5

(continued)

(continued)

care less about the flawed bureaucracy of the new Cuban government. I was mostly in love with the romantic ideal of the revolutionist, no matter how misguided. But I read it all, to have the sense of accomplishment and for fear that I might miss out on something.

6   Reading is something less that I do because I want to; it seems more like a compulsion. It's part pleasure and part practicality. I read for information, but I only read about things that I want to know about. I always have at least one book by my bed that I am reading. When I was a child, my parents read to me every night before bed. Even when I could read they would still read to me. But this wasn't about learning; it was about enjoyment. It was something that they shared with me; they liked doing it and I like being read to. So through the two—information and enjoyment—this compulsion arose.

7   Unfortunately, this passion for reading did not always help me in school. In elementary school, I struggled with reading comprehension. I guess I equated reading really fast with being a good reader. I didn't think about what the words were saying. When we would have a test I would read the piece and then not be able to answer any of the questions about what I had just read. When I would get my test back I would have A's in everything but reading comprehension. Working with my teacher after school, I learned to slow down to understand the words instead of merely repeating them.

8   Even now I will find myself "just trying to make it through" texts that I am not really all that into. And then I will look back and think that I have gotten absolutely nothing out of what I have just read and then have to reread it. I read extremely slowly when I am really trying to read and comprehend something that I don't really want to read. Yet when I am reading something that I really like, the same slow reading makes all else in my environment fade. When I read what I want and what I enjoy, comprehension is totally effortless. I have to give the piece value, and then I can enjoy it; I have to try to find one thing that I can derive pleasure from, and then I can get into it.

9   I think that my love of reading comes from the fact that I come from a blue-collar background. And herein lies the irony. Blue-collar people, from my observations, tend to be more rebellious. I guess reading and becoming more literate was my way of rebelling, too. And maybe that was what asking for *The Scarlet Letter* was all about. Reading a book that was considered a "great" or a "classic" was my equivalent to getting a facial piercing or a tattoo. Also, it is just in my nature to be curious and want to know about things. Since I always hated to ask anyone, for whatever reason, going and reading a book seemed like a much better and more direct route. I have a friend who told me that there is this Jewish philosophy that says that the only thing that you can take with you when you die is knowledge. Now I don't necessarily agree with this, but I think that knowledge can and will make the life that you are currently living much more rich and fulfilling. And the best place to get information is to read it. There are countless books and other sources of text, literature, prose, and everything in between. Thanks to the Internet you can read about anything at the touch of your fingertips, and you don't even have to get up. Reading to get information just makes good sense in my world.

10   At the moment, I am going through an, as of yet, unnamed phase, but I am reading Aleister Crowley. Someday, I hope to look back and see the story of myself in what I was reading and hope that what I was reading made my life better in some way.

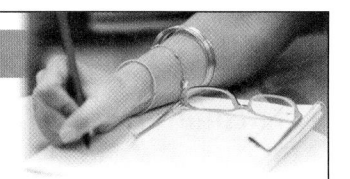

INQUIRING INTO THE DETAILS

The Double-Entry Journal

A double-entry journal is essentially a written dialogue between a reader and a text. As a reader you ask questions, make connections, and note memories and associations.

Here's how it works: You can either draw a line down the middle of a page to make two columns, or you can use the spine of your notebook for the line and use two opposing pages.

What the Text Says	What I Think
In the left column, write out the passages from the reading that confuse you, surprise you, make you think of other ideas, seem key to your understanding of what it says, and so on.	In the right column, write out your response to those passages. Sometimes you'll do a fastwrite; other times you may simply jot down quick thoughts.

- Jot down direct quotes, paraphrases, summaries, facts, claims.

- Note page numbers next to each passage or summary/paraphrase. Put them in the far right margin next to the borrowed material or ideas.

Play the doubting game, questioning the source; play the believing game, trying to find its virtues, even if you disagree.

- Shift to other reading perspectives.

- Tell the story of your thinking about what you're reading: *My initial reaction to this is... but now I think...and now I think...*

- List questions you have about the source's ideas, your emotional responses, other ideas or readings it connects to.

Continue this process for the entire reading, moving back and forth across the columns. Remember that you want to explore your response to a text, make connections to other works and your own writing, and analyze the writer's choices in terms of language, style, detail, and so forth. *Be sure to note all the bibliographic information from the source at the top of the page.*

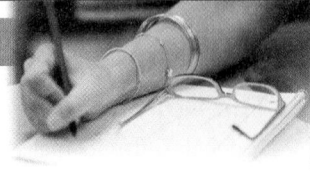

INQUIRING INTO THE DETAILS

Encountering Unfamiliar Genres

The only time most of us ever really pay attention to genre is when we encounter one that defies our expectations. When the low-budget film *Memento* was released several years ago, its puzzling narrative structure (beginning at the end of the story and proceeding to the beginning), its use of an unreliable narrator, and its alternation between black-and-white and color took audiences by surprise and generated lots of print by movie critics. Ultimately, the film became a phenomenal success, partly because its approach was so unexpected. *Memento* got people talking about a completely different way to think about filmmaking.

The response to the movie was so significant because we are a nation of moviegoers who are quite familiar with the genre, and *Memento* made us wonder how much we really know about film. These kinds of *Memento* movements happen to readers all the time, especially when we're in an academic setting and aren't familiar with the genres we're asked to read—a poem, a lab report, an academic argument, a minimalist painting. Our first response might be to question how well we can read, even though we've all been reading for a very long time.

An ad for the film *Memento*

One way of dealing with this is to simply apply reading strategies that we've used successfully in other genres. For example, because your verbal score on the reading comprehension portion of the SAT was so high, why not approach reading the essay on the need for a new immigration policy the same way, and try to decode exactly what the writer must have meant and leave it at that? Well, your instructor will likely say, "Fine, but I want to know what you think about his argument."

A better approach when you encounter types of readings that are new to you is to let the reading situation be your guide.

- Ask yourself, *Why am I reading this? How is it relevant to my inquiry question?* or *What exactly is my instructor asking me to do with this text?*

- Are there clues in the text about how it might be efficiently read? For instance, do subheadings provide guidance? Is there a preface that reviews the argument? Does the concluding section have the most weight?

- Who is the intended audience for this text and what clues does that provide about the writer's purpose? Might that explain not only how she composed the text—its language, organization, and so on—but also what she hoped to accomplish with it?

- Whenever possible, "frontload" before you read something challenging; that is, learn as much as you can about the subject and even the writer's relationship to the subject. This knowledge will make a big difference in how much you understand.

USING WHAT YOU HAVE LEARNED

Inquiry-based writing and reading begins with an open-eyed sense of wonder. Instead of initially asking, *What should I say?* you ask, *What do I think?* You begin by trying to find questions that interest you, knowing that there isn't necessarily a single right answer. At the same time, you know that just as you open up possible meanings, at some point you need to narrow them. You are both creative *and* critical, moving back and forth between collecting and focusing, exploring and evaluating, narrating and reflecting.

As you continue in *The Curious Writer*, I'll encourage you to apply this process to nearly every assignment. Before long, it will become second nature to you; you'll find yourself naturally shifting back and forth between the creative and the critical, whether you're exploring a topic for an assignment, reading an essay that you'll discuss in class, or analyzing an advertisement. Techniques that you've already practiced such as fastwriting and listing, the double-entry journal, and generating questions will help this along.

INQUIRY PROJECTS

Writing a personal essay is like seeing an old picture of yourself. This publicity photograph of my mother, my brother, and me in the 1950s returns me to that world—a time when fathers were often missing from the picture.

WRITING A PERSONAL ESSAY

WRITING ABOUT EXPERIENCE

Most us were taught and still believe that we need to know what we are going to write before we actually pick up the pen or sit in front of the computer. My student Lynn was typical.

"I think I'll write about my experience organizing the street fair," she told me the other day. "That would be a good topic for a personal essay, right?"

"Do you think so?" I said.

"Well, yes, because I already know a lot about it. I'll have a lot to write about."

"Okay, but is there anything about this experience that you want to understand better?" I said. "Anything about it that makes you curious?"

"Curious? It was just a street fair," she said.

"Sure, but is there something about what happened that makes you want to look at the experience again? Is there a chance that you might learn something about yourself, or about street fairs, or about the community, or about people, or...?"

Lynn was clearly sorry she asked. What I should have said was much more to the point: The best essay topics are those that are an itch you need to scratch. These tend not to be topics you have already figured out. While the topics can be familiar to you, the results of your inquiry are usually much better if you don't yet know what you think about your topics and you're interested to learn more about them.

> ### What You'll Learn in This Chapter
> - How personal essays can help you with academic writing.
> - What distinguishes a personal essay from other forms.
> - How to write a sketch.
> - Why a confusing topic may be better than one you have all figured out.
> - Questions for revising personal essays.

The best topics ask to be written about because they make you wonder *Why did I do that? What does that mean? Why did that happen? How did I really feel? What do I really think?*

Unlike most other forms of inquiry, the personal essay invites an initial display of confusion or uncertainty from writers regarding their subjects. In other words, writers do not have to have their subjects figured out when starting a personal essay. This form of inquiry is a vehicle for writers to work through their thinking and feeling on a subject directly in front of their readers.

> The personal essay is a vehicle for writers to work through their thinking and feeling on a subject directly in front of their readers.

As a form, the *personal* essay places the writer at center stage. This doesn't mean that once she's there, her responsibility is to pour out her secrets, share her pain, or confess her sins. Some essays do have these confessional qualities, but more often they do not. Yet a personal essayist, no matter the subject of the essay, is still *exposed*. There is no hiding behind the pronoun "one," as in "one might think" or "one often feels," no lurking in the shadows of the passive voice: "An argument will be made that...." The personal essay is first-person territory.

In this sense, the personal essay is much like a photographic self-portrait. Like a picture, a good personal essay tells the truth, or it tells *a* truth about the writer/subject, and it often captures the writer at a particular moment of time. Therefore, the experience of taking a self-portrait, or confronting an old picture of oneself taken by someone else, can create the feeling of exposure that writing a personal essay often does.

But it does more. When we gaze at ourselves in a photograph we often see it as yanked from a larger story about ourselves, a story that threads its way through our lives and gives us ideas about who we were and who we are. This is what the personal essay demands of us: We must somehow present ourselves truthfully and measure our past against the present. In other words, when we hold a photograph of ourselves we know more than the person we see there knew, and as writers of the personal essay, we must share that knowledge and understanding with readers.

MOTIVES FOR WRITING A PERSONAL ESSAY

Essai was a term first coined by the sixteenth-century French nobleman Michel de Montaigne, a man who had lived through occurrences of the plague, the bloody civil war between French Catholics and Protestants, and his own ill health. These were tumultuous and uncertain times when old social orders and intellectual traditions were under assault, and it proved to be ideal ferment for the essay. The French verb *essaier* means "to attempt" or "to try," and the essay became an opportunity for Montaigne to work out his thoughts about war, the education of children, the evils of doctors, and the importance of pleasure. The personal essay tradition inspired by Montaigne is probably unlike the essays you are familiar with in school. The school essay is often formulaic—a five-paragraph theme, or thesis-example paper—while the personal essay is an open-ended form that allows for uncertainty and inconclusiveness. It is more about the process of coming to know than presenting *what* you know. The personal essay attempts *to find out* rather than *to prove*.

It is an ideal form of inquiry if your purpose is exploratory rather than argumentative, and if you're particularly interested in working out the possible relationships between your subject and yourself. Because the personal essay is openly subjective, the writer can't hide. The intruding *I* confronts the writer with the same questions over and over again: *Why does this matter to me? What do I make of it? How does this change the way I think of myself and the way I see the world?* Because of this, one of the principal dangers of the personal essay is that it can become narcissistic; it can go on and on about what the writer thinks and feels, and the reader can be left with that nagging question—*So what?* The personal essayist must always find some way to hitch the particulars of his or her experience to something larger—an idea, a theme, or even a feeling that readers might share.

On the other hand, one of the prime rhetorical advantages of the personal essay is its subjectivity. Because it is written with openness and honesty, the essay is often a very intimate form, inviting the reader to share in the writer's often concealed world. In the personal essay, we often get to see the face sweating under the mask. Honesty is one of the essay's primary virtues, and because the form allows for uncertainty and confusion, the writer doesn't need to pretend that he has *the* answer, or that he knows more than he lets on about his subject.

THE PERSONAL ESSAY AND ACADEMIC WRITING

In some ways, the personal essay might seem like a dramatic departure from the kind of academic writing you've done in other classes. Openly subjective and sometimes tentative in its conclusions, the personal essay is a relatively open form that is not predictably structured, like much academic writing. Additionally, the tone of the personal essay is conversational, even intimate, rather than impersonal and removed. If your sociology or economics professor will never ask for a personal essay, why bother to write one in your composition class?

It's a fair question. While the pleasures of personal essay writing can be significant, and reason alone to write essays, there are other important reasons to practice the form. The most obvious is that the essay, more than any other form, gives you an opportunity to use exploration as a method of inquiry, and to practice those habits of mind that are so important to academic inquiry: suspending judgment, tolerating ambiguity, and using questions to challenge easy assumptions.

> The essay, more than any other form, gives you an opportunity to use exploration as a method of inquiry.

But the purpose of writing personal essays in your composition class goes beyond this. For one thing, the essay emphasizes the *process* of coming to know about yourself and your subject, exposing your reasoning and the ways you use knowledge to get at the truth of things. Reflecting on these things in a personal essay can tell you a lot about how you think. The *dialectical thinking* required by the personal essay—the movement back and forth between critical and creative thinking—is a useful mental exercise for a range of academic situations. Finally, much of what you are asked to write in college depends on your willingness to step forward and express a belief, make an assertion, or pose a relevant question. The personal essay is a form that puts the writer in the spotlight. You can't hide in the wings, concealed in the shadow of other people's opinions or someone else's findings. What *you* think is what the essay is all about.

FEATURES OF THE FORM

There are many different kinds of personal essays, of course, but certain conventions are present in most of them. Keep these in mind as you read the professional essays that follow. Which of the conventions listed here seem to be present? Can you detect any others?

- *Personal essays are usually written in the first person.* There is no pretense of scientific objectivity in personal essays.

- *The subject of the essay is often commonplace.* Although essayists sometimes write about dramatic things, they most often are interested in the drama of everyday life.

- *Narrative is often the primary method of development.* Personal essays often tell two kinds of stories—they relate narratives of the writer's experiences and observations, and they tell the story of the writer's thinking about what those experiences and observations might mean.

- *The thesis can be implicit, and it frequently emerges late, rather than at the beginning, of the essay.*

- *Of the four sources of information, the personal essay relies on memory and observation most of all.* Because of the subjectivity of the essay, the writer often reports *what has happened* to her as a means to account for *what happens*.

- *The essay often mimics the dialectical process that helped the writer compose it, shifting back and forth from the then and now, what happened to what happens, and showing and telling.*

READINGS

■ PERSONAL ESSAY 1

The essayist Scott Russell Sanders once observed that an essay "scatters a bunch of rabbits that go bounding in all directions.…If you refuse to chase any of them, and keep plodding along in a straight line, you and your reader will have a dull outing. If you chase too many, you will soon wind up lost in a thicket of confusion.…" In "Buckeye," Sanders flushes a few rabbits of his own, chasing down ideas about coping with grief, the life in a piece of wood, and learning to love land that doesn't yield easily to such affection. In this sense, it's a complicated essay; in another, it's as simple as an Ohio buckeye, rubbed shiny from handling. The essay that follows exemplifies one of the most appealing features of the personal essay: Its subject is often ordinary, familiar. In "Buckeye," Sanders is doing no more than telling stories about his father, a handmade wooden box, and a November afternoon. Yet the piece is anything but ordinary in its language, and especially in what it comes to say about how to "dwell in our place with a full heart."

BUCKEYE
Scott Russell Sanders

Years after my father's heart quit, I keep in a wooden box on my desk the two buck-eyes that were in his pocket when he died. Once the size of plums, the brown seeds are shriveled now, hollow, hard as pebbles, yet they still gleam from the polish of his hands. He used to reach for them in his overalls or suit pants and click them together, or he would draw them out, cupped in his palm, and twirl them with his blunt carpenter's fingers, all the while humming snatches of old tunes.   1

"Do you really believe buckeyes keep off arthritis?" I asked him more than once.   2

He would flex his hands and say, "I do so far."   3

My father never paid much heed to pain. Near the end, when his worn knee often slipped out of joint, he would pound it back in place with a rubber mallet. If a splinter worked into his flesh beyond the reach of tweezers, he would heat the blade of his knife over a cigarette lighter and slice through the skin. He sought to ward off arthritis not because he feared pain but because he lived through his hands, and he dreaded the swelling of knuckles, the stiffening of fingers. What use would he be if he could no longer hold a hammer or guide a plow? When he was a boy he had known farmers not yet forty years old whose hands had curled into claws, men so crippled up they could not tie their own shoes, could not sign their names.   4

"I mean to tickle my grandchildren when they come along," he told me, "and I mean to build doll houses and turn spindles for tiny chairs on my lathe."   5

(continued)

(continued)

6   So he fondled those buckeyes as if they were charms, carrying them with him when our family moved from Ohio at the end of my childhood, bearing them to new homes in Louisiana, then Oklahoma, Ontario, and Mississippi, carrying them still on his final day when pain a thousand times fiercer than arthritis gripped his heart.

7   The box where I keep the buckeyes also comes from Ohio, made by father from a walnut plank he bought at a farm auction. I remember the auction, remember the sagging face of the widow whose home was being sold, remember my father telling her he would prize that walnut as if he had watched the tree grow from a sapling on his own land. He did not care for pewter or silver or gold, but he cherished wood. On the rare occasions when my mother coaxed him into a museum, he ignored the paintings or porcelain and studied the exhibit cases, the banisters, the moldings, the parquet floors.

8   I remember him planing that walnut board, sawing it, sanding it, joining piece to piece to make foot stools, picture frames, jewelry boxes. My own box, a bit larger than a soap dish, lined with red corduroy, was meant to hold earrings and pins, not buckeyes. The top is inlaid with pieces fitted so as to bring out the grain, four diagonal joints converging from the corners toward the center. If I stare long enough at those converging lines, they float free of the box and point to a center deeper than wood.

9   I learned to recognize buckeyes and beeches, sugar maples and shagbark hickories, wild cherries, walnuts, and dozens of other trees while tramping through the Ohio woods with my father. To his eyes, their leaves, their bark, their winter buds were as distinctive as the set of a friend's shoulders. As with friends, he was partial to some, craving their company, so he would go out of his way to visit particular trees, walking in a circle around the splayed roots of a sycamore, laying his hand against the trunk of a white oak, ruffling the feathery green boughs of a cedar.

10   "Trees breathe," he told me. "Listen."

11   I listened, and heard the stir of breath.

12   He was no botanist; the names and uses he taught me were those he had learned from country folks, not from books. Latin never crossed his lips. Only much later would I discover that the tree he called ironwood, its branches like muscular arms, good for axe handles, is known in the books as hophornbeam; what he called tuliptree or canoewood, ideal for log cabins, is officially the yellow poplar; what he called hoop ash, good for barrels and fence posts, appears in books as hackberry.

13   When he introduced me to the buckeye, he broke off a chunk of the gray bark and held it to my nose. I gagged.

14   "That's why the old-timers called it stinking buckeye," he told me. "They used it for cradles and feed troughs and peg legs."

15   "Why for peg legs?" I asked.

16   "Because it's light and hard to split, so it won't shatter when you're clumping around."

He showed me this tree in late summer, when the fruits had fallen and the   17
ground was littered with prickly brown pods. He picked up one, as fat as a lemon,
and peeled away the husk to reveal the shiny seed. He laid it in my palm and closed
my fist around it so the seed peeped out from the circle formed by my index finger
and thumb. "You see where it got the name?" he asked.

I saw: what gleamed in my hand was the eye of a deer, bright with life, "It's   18
beautiful," I said.

"It's beautiful," my father agreed, "but also poisonous. Nobody eats buckeyes,   19
except maybe a fool squirrel."

I knew the gaze of deer from living in the Ravenna Arsenal, in Portage County,   20
up in the northeastern corner of Ohio. After supper we often drove the Arsenal's
gravel roads, past the munitions bunkers, past acres of rusting tanks and wrecked
bombers, into the far fields where we counted deer. One June evening, while mist
rose from the ponds, we counted three hundred and eleven, our family record. We
found the deer in herds, in bunches, in amorous pairs. We came upon lone bucks,
their antlers lifted against the sky like the bare branches of dogwood. If you were
quiet, if your hands were empty, if you moved slowly, you could leave the car and
steal to within a few paces of a grazing deer, close enough to see the delicate lips, the
twitching nostrils, the glossy fathomless eyes.

The wooden box on my desk holds these grazing deer, as it holds the buckeyes   21
and the walnut plank and the farm auction and the munitions bunkers and the
breathing forests and my father's hands. I could lose the box, I could lose the
polished seeds, but if I were to lose the memories I would become a bush
without roots, and every new breeze would toss me about. All those memories
lead back to the northeastern corner of Ohio, the place where I came to consciousness, where I learned to connect feelings with words, where I fell in love
with the earth.

It was a troubled love, for much of the land I knew as a child had been ravaged.   22
The ponds in the Arsenal teemed with bluegill and beaver, but they were also laced
with TNT from the making of bombs. Because the wolves and coyotes had long since
been killed, some of the deer, so plump in the June grass, collapsed on the January
snow, whittled by hunger to racks of bones. Outside the Arsenal's high barbed
fences, many of the farms had failed, their barns carving in, their topsoil gone.
Ravines were choked with swollen couches and junked washing machines and cars.
Crossing fields, you had to be careful not to slice your feet on tin cans or shards of
glass. Most of the rivers had been dammed, turning fertile valleys into scummy playgrounds for boats.

One free-flowing river, the Mahoning, ran past the small farm near the Arsenal   23
where our family lived during my later years in Ohio. We owned just enough land to
pasture three ponies and to grow vegetables for our table, but those few acres
opened onto miles of woods and creeks and secret meadows. I walked that land in

(continued)

(continued)

every season, every weather, following animal trails. But then the Mahoning, too, was doomed by a government decision; we were forced to sell our land, and a dam began to rise across the river.

24   If enough people had spoken for the river, we might have saved it. If enough people had believed that our scarred country was worth defending, we might have dug in our heels and fought. Our attachments to the land were all private. We had no shared lore, no literature, no art to root us there, to give us courage, to help us stand our ground. The only maps we had were those issued by the state, showing a maze of numbered lines stretched over emptiness. The Ohio landscape never showed up on postcards or posters, never unfurled like tapestry in films, rarely filled even a paragraph in books. There were no mountains in that place, no waterfalls, no rocky gorges, no vistas. It was a country of low hills, cut over woods, scoured fields, villages that had lost their purpose, roads that had lost their way.

25   "Let us love the country of here below," Simone Weil urged. "It is real; it offers resistance to love. It is this country that God has given us to love. He has willed that it should be difficult yet possible to love it." Which is the deeper truth about buckeyes, their poison or their beauty? I hold with the beauty; or rather, I am held by the beauty, without forgetting the poison. In my corner of Ohio the gullies were choked with trash, yet cedars flickered up like green flames from cracks in stone; in the evening bombs exploded at the ammunition dump, yet from the darkness came the mating cries of owls. I was saved from despair by knowing a few men and women who cared enough about the land to clean up trash, who planted walnuts and oaks that would long outlive them, who imagined a world that would have no call for bombs.

26   How could our hearts be large enough for heaven if they are not large enough for earth? The only country I am certain of is the one here below. The only paradise I know is the one lit by our everyday sun, this land of difficult love, shot through with shadow. The place where we learn this love, if we learn it at all, shimmers behind every new place we inhabit.

27   A family move carried me away from Ohio thirty years ago; my schooling and marriage and job have kept me away ever since, except for visits in memory and in flesh. I returned to the site of our farm one cold November day, when the trees were skeletons and the ground shone with the yellow of fallen leaves. From a previous trip I knew that our house had been bulldozed, our yard and pasture had grown up in thickets, and the reservoir had flooded the woods. On my earlier visit I had merely gazed from the car, too numb with loss to climb out. But on this November day, I parked the car, drew on my hat and gloves, opened the door, and walked.

28   I was looking for some sign that we had lived there, some token of our affection for the place. All that I recognized, aside from the contours of the land, were two weeping willows that my father and I had planted near the road. They had been slips the length of my forearm when we set them out, and now their crowns rose higher

than the telephone poles. When I touched them last, their trunks had been smooth and supple, as thin as my wrist, and now they were furrowed and stout. I took off my gloves and laid my hands against the rough bark. Immediately I felt the wince of tears. Without knowing why, I said hello to my father, quietly at first, then louder, as if only shouts could reach him through the bark miles and years.

Surprised by sobs, I turned from the willows and stumbled away toward the drowned woods, calling to my father. I sensed that he was nearby. Even as I called, I was wary of grief's deceptions. I had never seen his body after he died. By the time I reached the place of his death, a furnace had reduced him to ashes. The need to see him, to let go of this land and time, was powerful enough to summon mirages; I knew that. But I also knew, stumbling toward the woods, that my father was here.   29

At the bottom of a slope where the creek used to run, I came to an expanse of gray stumps and withered grass. It was a bay of the reservoir from which the water had retreated, the level drawn down by engineers or drought. I stood at the edge of this desolate ground, willing it back to life, trying to recall the woods where my father had taught me the names of trees. No green shoots rose. I walked out among the stumps. The grass crackled under my boots, breath rasped in my throat, but otherwise the world was silent.   30

Then a cry broke overhead and I looked up to see a red-tailed hawk launching out from the top of an oak. I recognized the bird from its band of dark feathers across the creamy breast and the tail splayed like rosy fingers against the sun. It was a red-tailed hawk for sure; and it was also my father. Not a symbol of my father, not a reminder, not a ghost, but the man himself, right there, circling in the air above me. I knew this as clearly as I knew the sun burned in the sky. A calm poured through me. My chest quit heaving. My eyes dried.   31

Hawk and father wheeled above me, circle upon circle, wings barely moving, head still. My own head was still, looking up, knowing and being known. Time scattered like fog. At length, father and hawk stroked the air with those powerful wings, three beats, then vanished over a ridge.   32

The voice of my education told me then and tells me now that I did not meet my father, that I merely projected my longing onto a bird. My education I've read, no lesson reached by logic has ever convinced me as utterly or stirred me as deeply as did that red-tailed hawk. Nothing in my education prepared me to love a piece of the earth, least of all a humble, battered country like northeastern Ohio; I learned from the land itself.   33

Before leaving the drowned woods, I looked around at the ashen stumps, the wilted grass, and for the first time since moving from this place I was able to let it go. This ground was lost; the flood would reclaim it. But other ground could be saved, must be saved, in every watershed, every neighborhood. For each home ground we need new maps, living maps, stories and poems, photographs and paintings, essays and songs. We need to know where we are, so that we may dwell in our place with a full heart.   34

Inquiring into the Essay

Throughout *The Curious Writer*, I'll invite you to respond to readings such as "Buckeye," using questions based on the four methods of inquiry discussed in Chapter 2. The following questions, therefore, encourage you to explore, explain, evaluate, and reflect to discover and shape what you think about the reading. If you're using a double-entry journal, use these questions to prompt writing on the right page of your notebook. Use the opposing left page to collect passages, details, and quotations from the reading that you think might be important.

1. Sanders handles a pair of buckeyes that once belonged to his father, and this triggers stories that allow him to look into ideas about grief and love of the land. It's a powerful thing, this recognition that the same ordinary objects hold a "deeper center," a meaning we don't often recognize unless we stop to look. In your journal, brainstorm a list of objects that hold significance for you. Choose one, and spend seven full minutes fastwriting in your journal about the stories it inspires. If the writing stalls, choose another. Keep your pen moving. Finally, skip a line and finish this sentence: *What surprised me most about what I just wrote is…*

2. Personal essays often tell two stories: the story of what happened, and the story of what the writer came to understand about the meaning of what happened. Explain your understanding of that second story in "Buckeye."

3. Though we rarely link the personal narrative and the argument, personal essays often make at least implicit arguments. "Buckeye" does. For example, Sanders writes that the steady destruction of the Ohio landscape has to do with the absence of a "shared lore" or art or literature that celebrates the land in the Midwest. "The Ohio landscape never showed up on postcards or posters," writes Sanders, "never unfurled like tapestry in films, rarely filled even a paragraph in books." What does Sanders assume to be true for this claim to be believable? Do you agree?

4. While "Buckeye" is not a confessional essay, it is quite personal. Reflect on how comfortable you are writing, as Sanders did, about the details of your life.

■ PERSONAL ESSAY 2

America is a nation of immigrants, and their stories often haunt their children. Judith Ortiz Cofer moved from Puerto Rico as a child with her family in the mid-1950s to a barrio in Paterson, New Jersey. There she became both part of and witness to a familiar narrative, that of the outsider who finds herself wedged between two worlds, two cultures, and two longings: the desire to return "home" and the desire to feel at home in the new place. While this is a story most immigrants know well, it is also a deeply personal one, shaded by particular places, prejudices, and patterns.

In "One More Lesson," Cofer describes both the places that competed for her sense of self—the Puerto Rico of her childhood, where she spent time as a child while her Navy father was away at sea, and an apartment in New Jersey where she would go when he returned.

One More Lesson
Judith Ortiz Cofer

I remember Christmas on the Island by the way it felt on my skin. The temperature dropped into the ideal seventies and even lower after midnight when some of the more devout Catholics—mostly older women—got up to go to church, *misa del gallo* they called it; mass at the hour when the rooster crowed for Christ. They would drape shawls over their heads and shoulders and move slowly toward town. The birth of Our Savior was a serious affair in our *pueblo*.   1

At Mamá's house, food was the focal point of *Navidad*. There were banana leaves brought in bunches by the boys, spread on the table, where the women would pour coconut candy steaming hot, and the leaves would wilt around the sticky lumps, adding an extra tang of flavor to the already irresistible treat. Someone had to watch the candy while it cooled, or it would begin to disappear as the children risked life and limb for a stolen piece of heaven. The banana leaves were also used to wrap the traditional food of holidays in Puerto Rico: *pasteles*, the meat pies made from grated yucca and plantain and stuffed with spiced meats.   2

Every afternoon during the week before Christmas Day, we would come home from school to find the women sitting around in the parlor with bowls on their laps, grating pieces of coconut, yuccas, plantains, cheeses—all the ingredients that would make up our Christmas Eve feast. The smells that filled Mamá's house at that time have come to mean anticipation and a sensual joy during a time in my life, the last days of my early childhood, when I could still absorb joy through my pores—*when I had not yet learned that light is followed by darkness, that all*   3

(continued)

(continued)

of creation is based on that simple concept, and maturity is a discovery of that natural law.

4   It was in those days that the Americans sent baskets of fruit to our barrio—apples, oranges, grapes flown in from the States. And at night, if you dared to walk up to the hill where the mango tree stood in the dark, you could see a wonderful sight: a Christmas tree, a real pine, decorated with lights of many colors. It was the blurry outline of this tree you saw, for it was inside a screened-in-porch, but we had heard a thorough description of it from the boy who delivered the fruit, a nephew of Mamá's, as it had turned out. Only, I was not impressed, since just the previous year we had put up a tree ourselves in our apartment in Paterson.

5   Packages arrived for us in the mail from our father. I got dolls dressed in the national costumes of Spain, Italy, and Greece (at first we could not decide which of the Greek dolls was the male, since they both wore skirts); my brother got picture books; and my mother, jewelry that she would not wear, because it was too much like showing off and might attract the Evil Eye.

6   Evil Eye or not, the three of us were the envy of the pueblo. Everything about us set us apart, and I put away my dolls quickly when I discovered that my playmates would not be getting any gifts until *Los Reyes*—the Day of the Three Kings, when Christ received His gifts—and that even then it was more likely that the gifts they found under their beds would be practical things like clothes. Still, it was fun to find fresh grass for the camels the night the Kings were expected, tie it in bundles with string, and put it under our beds along with a bowl of fresh water.

7   The year went by fast after Christmas, and in the spring we received a telegram from Father. His ship had arrived in Brooklyn Yard. He gave us a date for our trip back to the States. I remember Mother's frantic packing, and the trips to Mayagüez for new clothes; the inspections of my brother's and my bodies for cuts, scrapes, mosquito bites, and other "damage" she would have to explain to Father. And I remember begging Mamá to tell me stories in the afternoons, although it was not summer yet and the trips to the mango tree had not begun. In looking back I realize that Mamá's stories were what I packed—my winter store.

8   Father had succeeded in finding an apartment outside Paterson's "vertical barrio," the tenement Puerto Ricans called *El Building*. He had talked a Jewish candy store owner into renting us the apartment above his establishment, which he and his wife had just vacated after buying a house in West Paterson, an affluent suburb. Mr. Schultz was a nice man whose melancholy face I was familiar with from trips I had made often with my father to his store for cigarettes. Apparently, my father had convinced him and his brother, a look-alike of Mr. Schultz who helped in the store, that we were not the usual Puerto Rican family. My father's fair skin, his ultra-correct English, and his Navy uniform were a good argument. Later it occurred to me that my father had been displaying me as a model child when he took me to that store with him. I was always dressed as if for church and held firmly by the hand. I imagine he did the same with my brother. As for my mother,

her Latin beauty, her thick black hair that hung to her waist, her voluptuous body which even the winter clothes could not disguise, would have been nothing but a hindrance to my father's plans. But everyone knew that a Puerto Rican woman is her husband's satellite; she reflects both his light and his dark sides. If my father was respectable, then his family would be respectable. We got the apartment on Park Avenue.

Unlike El Building, where we had lived on our first trip to Paterson, our new home was truly in exile. There were Puerto Ricans by the hundreds only one block away, but we heard no Spanish, no loud music, no mothers yelling at children, nor the familiar *¡Ay Bendito!*, that catch-all phrase of our people. Mother lapsed into silence herself, suffering from *La Tristeza*, the sadness that only place induces and only place cures. But Father relished silence, and we were taught that silence was something to be cultivated and practiced.   9

Since our apartment was situated directly above where the Schultzes worked all day, our father instructed us to remove our shoes at the door and walk in our socks. We were going to prove how respectable we were by being the opposite of what our ethnic group was known to be—we would be quiet and inconspicuous.   10

I was escorted each day to school by my nervous mother. It was a long walk in the cooling air of fall in Paterson and we had to pass by El Building where the children poured out of the front door of the dilapidated tenement still answering their mothers in a mixture of Spanish and English: "Sí, Mami, I'll come straight home from school." At the corner we were halted by the crossing guard, a strict woman who only gestured her instructions, never spoke directly to the children, and only ordered us to "halt" or "cross" while holding her white-gloved hand up at face level or swinging her arm sharply across her chest if the light was green.   11

The school building was not a welcoming sight for someone used to the bright colors and airiness of tropical architecture. The building looked functional. It could have been a prison, an asylum, or just what it was: an urban school for the children of immigrants, built to withstand waves of change, generation by generation. Its red brick sides rose to four solid stories. The black steel fire escapes snaked up its back like an exposed vertebra. A chain-link fence surrounded its concrete playground. Members of the elite safety patrol, older kids, sixth graders mainly, stood at each of its entrances, wearing their fluorescent white belts that criss-crossed their chests and their metal badges. No one was allowed in the building until the bell rang, not even on rainy or bitter-cold days. Only the safety-patrol stayed warm.   12

My mother stood in front of the main entrance with me and a growing crowd of noisy children. She looked like one of us, being no taller than the sixth-grade girls. She held my hand so tightly that my fingers cramped. When the bell rang, she walked me into the building and kissed my cheek. Apparently my father had done all the paperwork for my enrollment, because the next thing I remember was being led to my third-grade classroom by a black girl who had emerged from the principal's office.   13

Though I had learned some English at home during my first years in Paterson, I had let it recede deep into my memory while learning Spanish in Puerto Rico. Once again I   14

(continued)

(continued)

was the child in the cloud of silence, the one who had to be spoken to in sign language as if she were a deaf-mute. Some of the children even raised their voices when they spoke to me, as if I had trouble hearing. Since it was a large troublesome class composed mainly of black and Puerto Rican children, with a few working-class Italian children interspersed, the teacher paid little attention to me. I re-learned the language quickly by the immersion method. I remember one day, soon after I joined the rowdy class when our regular teacher was absent and Mrs. D., the sixth-grade teacher from across the hall, attempted to monitor both classes. She scribbled something on the chalkboard and went to her own room. I felt a pressing need to use the bathroom and asked Julio, the Puerto Rican boy who sat behind me, what I had to do to be excused. He said that Mrs. D. had written on the board that we could be excused by simply writing our names under the sign. I got up from my desk and started for the front of the room when I was struck on the head hard with a book. Startled and hurt, I turned around expecting to find one of the bad boys in my class, but it was Mrs. D. I faced. I remember her angry face, her fingers on my arms pulling me back to my desk, and her voice saying incomprehensible things to me in a hissing tone. Someone finally explained to her that I was new, that I did not speak English. I also remember how suddenly her face changed from anger to anxiety. But I did not forgive her for hitting me with that hard-cover spelling book. Yes, I would recognize that book even now. It was not until years later that I stopped hating that teacher for not understanding that I had been betrayed by a classmate, and by my inability to read her warning on the board. *I instinctively understood then that language is the only weapon a child has against the absolute power of adults.*

15   I quickly built up my arsenal of words by becoming an insatiable reader of books.

Inquiring into the Essay

Explore, explain, evaluate, and reflect on Cofer's "One More Lesson."

1. In the 1950s and 1960s, many saw America as a "melting pot." The idea then was that although we may have many different immigrant backgrounds, we should strive toward some common "Americanism." For some, this is still a powerful idea, but for others the melting pot is a metaphor for cultural hegemony or even racial prejudice, a demand that differences be ignored and erased rather than celebrated. In your journal, write about your own feelings on this controversy. Tell the story of a friend, a relative, a neighbor who was an outsider. Tell about your own experience. What did it mean to assimilate, and at what cost?

2. Personal essays, like short fiction, rely heavily on narrative. But unlike fiction, essays both *show* and *tell*; that is, they use story to reveal meaning (*show*) and they also explain that meaning to the reader (*tell*). Identify

several places in the essay where Cofer "tells." What do you notice about the placement of these moments of reflection?

3. Does this essay make an evaluation, and, if so, what is it asserting about cultural assimilation in America during the 1950s and 1960s? Is Cofer's evaluation still relevant?

4. One of the most common reasons students cite for liking a story is that "they could relate to it." Does that criterion apply here? Reflect on whether it's a standard you often use as a reader to judge the value of something. What exactly does it mean to "relate to" a text?

SEEING THE FORM

Nautilus Shell

We think of most forms of writing as linear—beginning to end, thesis to supporting evidence, claims to reasons—in a steady march to a conclusion. And yes, much writing is like that. The essay is not. Or at least that's true of the essay inspired by the first essayist Montaigne, a sixteenth-century French nobleman who coined the term "essai," which in its verb form means to attempt, to try. A better analogy for the essay is the spiral rather than the line. It is the uncoiling of thought. The essay begins, much like a nautilus shell, when writers make tight spirals around a particular moment, object, observation, or fact that

(continued)

Seeing the Form (*continued*)

makes them wonder. The personal essay is an inductive form, working from the small things to larger ideas about them, with larger turns of thought. The work challenges writers to move outward from small, private chambers of experience to finally emerge into the more open spaces that others can share, meanings that others can understand even though they don't share exactly the same experience.

WRITING IN THE DISCIPLINES

The Personal Academic Essay

"You can't use 'I' in an academic essay," one of my students insisted. "It's just not done."

This is always the beginning of a great discussion about academic conventions, objectivity, and personal writing. Many of us accept, without question, the "rules" that we've learned about writing, especially school writing. Here are the things my fifteen-year-old daughter reports that she "can't do" in an essay:

1. Use first person.

2. Put a thesis anywhere but the first paragraph.

3. Write a paragraph without a topic sentence.

Anything that violates these rules is something called "creative" writing. Where do these ideas come from? The injunction against using "I" in academic writing, probably the most common assumption, isn't without support. After all, a great deal of academic writing avoids any reference to the author, or if it must, uses the more neutral pronoun "one." The question that is rarely asked is, Why is this so?

One reason is that scholars believe that "objectivity"—or at least the appearance of objectivity—gives their research more authority. In addition, in some disciplines, especially the sciences, the attention needs to be on the data and not the author. For these reasons, among others, avoiding first person in academic writing became a tacit tradition.

And yet, there are a surprising number of academic articles published in the first person, and not just in the humanities where you might expect authors to be more likely to acknowledge bias. While "autobiographical criticism" has been around for some time in literature, there is personal scholarship in many disciplines, including business, anthropology, education, nursing, and even geology. This first-person writing often tells a story, sometimes through a case study, a narrative of the writer's experiences, or an account of his or her intellectual journey.

Essaying "This I Believe"

The essay genre, which has been around for about 500 years, is a vibrant and increasingly common form of writing on the radio and online audio. Why? One reason might be that the intimacy of the essay—the sense of a writer speaking directly to a reader without the masks we often wear when we write—seems particularly powerful when we *hear* the voice of writing embodied in speech. Certainly, the ease with which we can "publish" essays as podcasts accounts for the explosion of online essayists.

"This I Believe," a program on National Public Radio, is typical of the radio programs (which are then subsequently published as podcasts) that actively seek student writing. The program began in the 1950s by famed journalist Edward R. Murrow, who invited radio listeners and public figures to submit very brief (350–500 word) essays that stated some core belief that guides the writers' "daily lives." The program, which was revived several years ago, is enormously popular on NPR and features work from people from all walks of life, including college students who may have written a "This I Believe" essay in their writing courses.

The program's Web site offers this advice to essayists:

1. Find a way to succinctly and clearly state your belief.

2. If possible, anchor it to stories.

3. Write in your own voice.

4. "Be positive," and avoid lecturing the listener.

THE WRITING PROCESS

> ## INQUIRY PROJECT: WRITING A PERSONAL ESSAY
>
> Write a 1,000-word personal essay that explores some aspect of your experience. Your instructor may provide additional details. Choose your topic carefully. Because of the essay's exploratory methods, the best topics are those that you want to write about *not* because you know what you think, but because you want to *discover* what you think. The essay should have the following qualities:
>
> - It must do more than tell a story; there must be a *purpose* behind telling the story that speaks in some way to someone else.
> - It should, ultimately, answer the *So what?* question.
> - Your essay should include some reflection to explain or speculate about what you understand *now* about something that you didn't understand *then*.
> - It should be richly detailed. Seize opportunities to *show* what you mean, rather than simply explain it.

PEARSON
mycomplab

For additional reading, writing, and research resources, go to www.mycomplab.com

Thinking About Subjects

When you are assigned a personal essay, it's essential to embrace uncertainty and be willing to suspend judgment. This is risky. Obviously, one of the risks when you start out with uncertainty is that you also might end up that way; your draft may just seem to go nowhere. The key to writing strong personal essays is accepting that first drafts might be real stinkers. But there's a payoff to this risk—the personal essay frequently yields surprise and discovery.

Generating Ideas

Begin exploring possible subjects by generating material in your notebook. This should be an open-ended process, a chance to use your creative side, not worrying too much about making sense or trying to prejudge the value of the writing or the subjects you generate. In a sense, this is an invitation to play around.

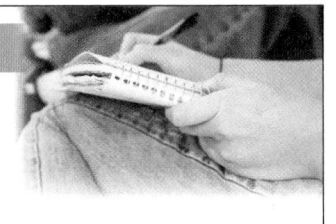

ONE STUDENT'S RESPONSE

Margaret's Journal: Listing Questions

Is my cat extremely unusual or can any cat be taught to walk and be as needy and attached as her?

Does testosterone really make one more confident? Is there a correlation between high T and aggressiveness?

How did I once find Dr. Laura so compelling?

Why are women seldom loyal to each other? How are female friendships different from male ones? Can women and men be friends without an underlying sexual tension?

Listing Prompts. Lists can be rich sources of triggering topics. Let them grow freely, and when you're ready, use an item as the focus of another list or an episode of fastwriting. The following prompts should get you started.

1. Make a fast list of experiences you've had that you can't forget. Reach into all parts and times of your life.

2. Make a list of questions that have always nagged you about some of the following: school, men or women, fast food, hair, television, public restrooms, shoes, and sports.

Fastwriting Prompts. In the early stages of generating possible topics for an essay, fastwriting can be invaluable, *if* you allow yourself to write "badly." Once you've tentatively settled on something, use a more focused fastwrite, trying to generate information and ideas within the loose boundaries of your chosen topic.

1. Choose an item from any one of the preceding lists as a prompt. Just start fastwriting about the item; perhaps start with a story, a scene, a situation, a description. Follow the writing to see where it leads.

2. Most of us quietly harbor dreams—we hope to be a professional dancer, a good father, an activist, an Olympic luger, or a novelist. Begin a fastwrite in which you explore your dreams. When the writing stalls, ask yourself questions: *Where did this dream come from? Do I still believe in it? In what moments did it seem within reach? In what moments did it fade?* Plunge into those moments.

3. What was the most confusing time in your life? Choose a moment or scene that stands out in your memory from that time, and, writing in the present tense, describe what you see, hear, and do. After five

minutes, skip a line and choose another moment. Then another. Make a collage.

4. What do you consider "turning points" in your life, times when you could see the end of one thing and the beginning of something else? Fastwrite about one of these for seven minutes.

Visual Prompts. Sometimes the best way to generate material is to see what we think in something other than sentences. Boxes, lines, arrows, charts, and even sketches can help us see more of the landscape of a subject, especially connections between fragments of information that aren't as obvious in prose. The clustering or mapping method is useful to many writers early in the writing process as they try to discover a topic. (See the "Inquiring into the Details" box on page 99 for more details on how to create a cluster.) Figure 3.1 shows my cluster from the first prompt listed here.

1. What objects would you most regret losing in a house fire? Choose a most-treasured object as the core for a cluster. Build a web of associations from it,

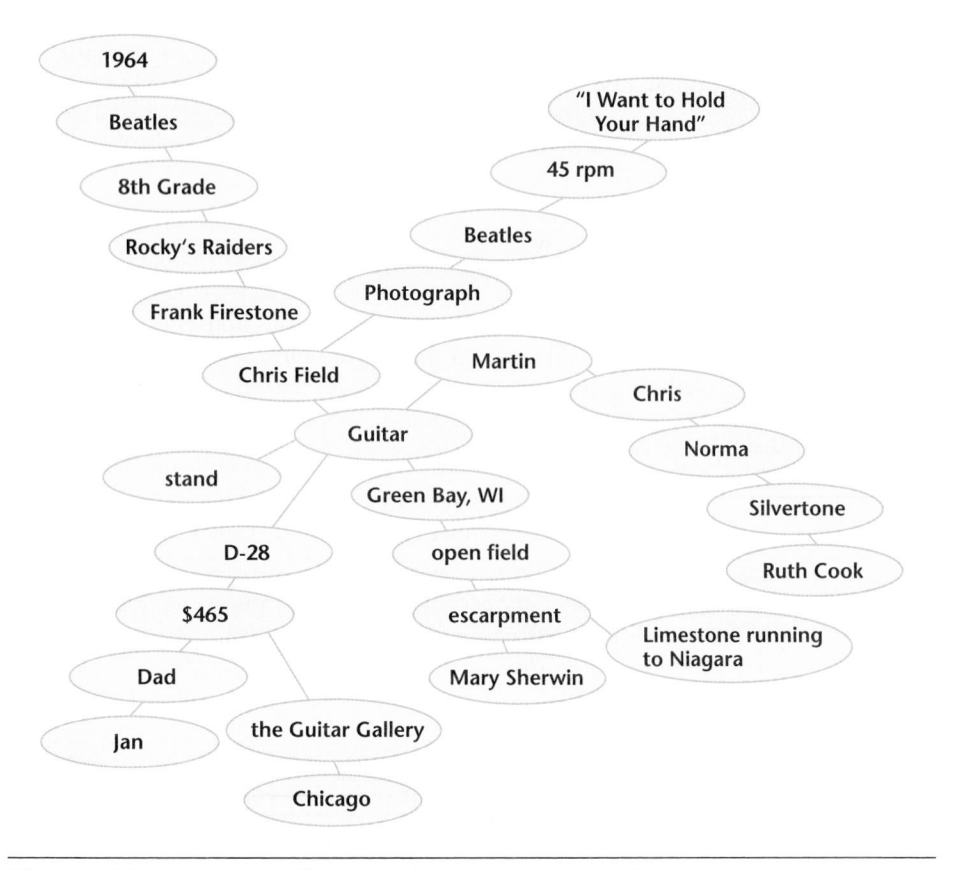

Figure 3.1 A cluster built around the one object I would most regret losing in a house fire: my Martin guitar

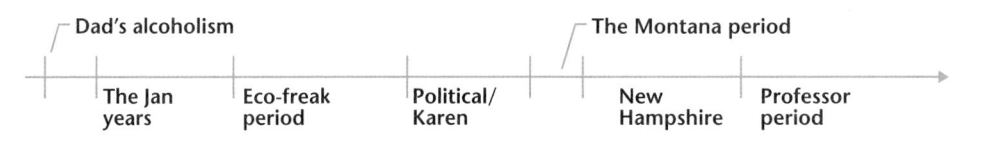

Dad's alcoholism   The Montana period

The Jan   Eco-freak   Political/   New   Professor
years   period   Karen   Hampshire   period

Figure 3.2   A sample timeline from my own life

returning to the detail in the core whenever a strand dies out. One of the wonderful complexities of being human is that we are sometimes deeply conflicted (I'm not suggesting this is always fun). Pair two opposed attributes that you consider typical of yourself. For example, *ambivalence/commitment, fear/risk taking, lonely/sociable, beautiful/ugly, composed/flaky,* and so on. Use these paired words as a core for a cluster.

2. Draw a long line on a piece of paper in your journal. This is your life. Divide the line into segments that seem to describe what feels like distinct times in your life. These may not necessarily correspond to familiar age categories like adolescence or childhood. More likely, the periods in your life will be associated with a place, a relationship, a dilemma, a job, a personal challenge, and so on, but because this is a timeline, these periods will be chronological. Examine your timeline and, as a fastwrite prompt, put two of these periods in your life together. Explore what they had in common, particularly how the earlier period might have shaped the later one. See Figure 3.2 for a sample timeline.

Research Prompts. Things we hear, see, or read can be powerful prompts for personal essays. It's tempting to believe that personal essays are always about the past, but just as often essayists are firmly rooted in the present, commenting and pondering on the confusions of contemporary life. In that sense, personal

INQUIRING INTO THE DETAILS

Clustering or Mapping

One of the virtues of clustering as a method of generating information is that it defies the more linear nature of writing, putting one sentence after another in a chain of thought. When you make a cluster, there are multiple chains, each growing from a core word, phrase, or idea. In Figure 3.1, I clustered the word *guitar*. I'm not just thinking of any guitar, of course, but my 1969 Martin D-28 with

(continued)

Inquiring into the Details (*continued*)

Brazilian rosewood and the ding on the front. This is the one object I'd rescue from a fire.

Clusters are in code; each item in the web says more than it says, at least to me, because I'm familiar with its meaning. You don't have that kind of knowledge, obviously, so my cluster wouldn't say much to you. Each strand suggests a story, an idea, or a feeling that I might explore.

Typically, clustering is most useful at the beginning of the writing process as you test a possible subject and want to see its landscape of possibilities. I can see, for example, possible essays about not only the significance of this guitar, but essays on the eighth grade, my old friend Chris Field, and the natural history of limestone. The best clusters are richly suggestive that way, but they're only starting places for more writing. How do you cluster?

1. Begin with a blank page in your journal. Choose a core word, phrase, name, idea, detail, or question; write it in the middle of the page and circle it.

2. Relax and focus on the core word or phrase, and when you feel moved to do so, build a strand of associations from the core, circling and connecting each item. Write other details, names, dates, place names, phrases, and so on—whatever comes to mind.

3. When a strand dies out, return to the core and begin another. Keep clustering until the page looks like a web of associations. Doodle, darkening lines and circles, if that helps you relax and focus.

4. When you feel the urge to write, stop clustering and use one of the strands as a prompt for journal work.

essayists are researchers, always on the lookout for material. Train your eye with one or more of the following prompts.

1. Return to the list of questions you made in the "Listing Prompts" section. Choose one nagging question about any of the subjects you were asked to consider and set aside time to explore it by carefully *observing* them. Write down exactly what you see…and what you think about it. (The double-entry notebook method is particularly useful for this.)

2. Newspaper "filler"—short stories, often about odd or unusual things—can be a wonderful source of inspiration for personal essays. Read your local paper for a few days, clipping these brief articles. Paste them in your journal and use them as prompts for fastwriting.

3. Although the Internet offers infinite opportunities for procrastination, with some focus it can also be a great source for jump-starting ideas. What happened to your best friend from kindergarten? Type her name into the Google search engine and find out. Think about your favorite vacation—a search for "Grand Canyon" might help jog your memory.

Judging What You Have

Generating may produce messy, incoherent writing that would earn you bad grades in most classes. If this material is going to go anywhere, it must be judged, shaped, and evaluated; the writer must emerge from particulars of his/her experience and find a vantage point to see what, if anything, those particulars add up to.

The initial challenge in producing a first draft is clarifying your topic: What are you really writing about? Suspend judgment for a bit and work through the following questions as you scrutinize the material you've collected so far in your journal.

What's Promising Material and What Isn't? A good topic for a personal essay need not be dramatic or profound; in fact, some of the most compelling essays are about quite ordinary things. But as you examine your journal writing so far, consider the following:

- **Abundance.** What subject generated the most writing? Do you sense that there is much more to write about?

- **Surprise.** What material did you find most confusing in interesting ways?

- **Confusion.** What subject raises questions you're not sure you can answer easily?

- **Honesty.** What subjects are you willing to write honestly about?

Questions About Purpose and Audience. Obviously, why you're writing and for whom will profoundly influence your approach. That's a fundamental principle of rhetoric, one that you applied when you jotted that note to your teacher explaining the late assignment or texted your friend about your new bicycle. With many types of writing, it's wise to consider your purpose and audience very early on—like, say, for an essay exam or an e-mail requesting information about a job. Sometimes, however, thinking too soon about purpose and audience will squeeze off your writing.

To begin with, then, embrace the open-ended process of "trying out" possible subjects. Initially, don't rule out anything because you think other people might find the topic boring. For now, you're the most important audience, and what you want to know from your writing is this:

- What topics raise questions about your experiences that you find puzzling or intriguing?

- What did you say that you didn't expect to say?

Choose a topic for your essay not because you know what you think but because you want to find out what you think.

Questions for Reflection. After you've generated enough material on your topic, seize opportunities to reflect. Remember that this move to reflect is an essential part of the dialectical thinking that helps writers make sense of things, going back and forth between *what happened* and *what happens*, between *showing* and *telling*, and *observations of* and *ideas about*. If you need help finding reflective distance, questions are the best way to do it. Use one or more of the following questions as prompts for thinking or writing in your journal.

- What do you understand now about this topic that you didn't fully understand when you began writing about it?
- What has surprised you most? Why?
- What seems to be the most important thing you're trying to say so far?
- Focus on how your thinking has changed about your topic. Finish this seed sentence as many times as you can in your notebook: once I thought _____, and now I think _____.
- Quickly write a narrative of thought about your topic: When I began writing about my father's alcoholism, I thought I felt relieved when he died. Then I decided that when he died some part of me died with him, and then I realized that the real truth is...
- Finish this sentence in your journal: As I look back on this, I realize that...Follow that sentence with another, and another, until you feel there's nothing more to say.

Writing the Sketch

It's hard to say when it's time to begin composing the draft, particularly with open-ended forms such as the personal essay. But bear in mind that working from abundance is particularly important when you're using writing to discover, the essayist's main motive.

Before you write a full draft, you'll compose a *sketch* or two of what seems to be the most promising material. A sketch is a brief treatment—probably no more than 300 words—that is composed with a sense of audience but not necessarily a clear sense of a thesis, theme, or controlling idea (see Chapter 1). Later, you'll revise a sketch into a draft personal essay.

Your instructor may ask you to write several sketches using the most promising material you've developed from the prompts. *The following guidelines apply to all sketches.*

- *The sketch should have a tentative title.* This is crucial because a title can hint at a possible focus for the revision.
- *The sketch should be approximately 300 to 500 words.* The sketch is a brief look at a topic that may later be developed into a longer essay.
- *The sketch should be a relatively fast draft.* Avoid the temptation to spend a lot of time crafting your sketch. Fast drafts are easier to revise.

- *The sketch may not have a clear purpose or theme.* That's what you hope to discover by writing the sketch.

- *The sketch should have a sense of audience.* You're writing your sketch to be read by someone other than you. That means you need to explain what may not be apparent to someone who doesn't know you or hasn't had your experiences.

- *The sketch should be richly detailed.* Personal essays, especially, rely on detail to help the writer and, later, the reader see the possible meanings of events or observations. Essayists are inductive, working from particulars to ideas. In early drafts especially, it's important to get down the details by drawing on all your senses: What exactly was the color of the wallpaper? How exactly did the beach smell at low tide? How exactly did the old man's hand feel in yours? What exactly did the immigration officer say?

■ STUDENT SKETCH

Amanda Stewart's sketch, "Earning a Sense of Place," faintly bears the outlines of what might be a great personal essay. When they succeed, sketches are suggestive; it is what they're not quite saying that yields promise. On the surface, "Earning a Sense of Place" is simply a piece about Amanda Stewart's passion for skiing. So what? And yet, there are lines here that point to larger ideas and unanswered questions. For example, Amanda writes that the "mental reel" of her swishing down a mountain on skis is "the image that sustains me when things are hard, and when I want to stop doing what is right and start doing what is easy." Why is it that such a mental image can be sustaining in hard times? How well does this work? The end of the sketch is even more suggestive. This really might be a piece about trying to find a "sense of place" that doesn't rely on such images; in a sense, the sketch seems to be trying to say that joy on the mountain isn't enough.

The pleasure of writing and reading a sketch is looking for what it might teach you, learning what you didn't know you knew.

Earning a Sense of Place
Amanda Stewart

The strings to my earflaps stream behind me, mixing with my hair as a rooster-tail   1
flowing behind my neck. Little ice crystals cling to the bottom of my braid and sparkle in
the sunlight. The pompom on top of my hat bobs up and down as I arc out, turning cleanly
across the snow. I suck in the air, biting with cold as it hits my hot lungs, and breathe deep
as I push down the run.

(continued)

(continued)

2   This is what I see when I picture who I want to be. It's the image that sustains me when things are hard, and when I want to stop doing what is right and start doing what is easy. I have made so many terrible decisions in the past that I know how far astray they lead me; I don't want that. I want the girl in the mental reel in her quilted magenta jacket and huge smile. She's what I grasp at when I need help getting through the day.

3   She's an amalgam of moments from the past mixed with my hopes for the future. I love to ski, and have since my parents strapped little plastic skis onto my galoshes when I was a year and a half old. From that day I flopped around our snow-covered yard, I've been in love with skiing. It's the only time I feel truly comfortable. Day to day I often feel so awkward. I wonder if my hair is right, or if my clothes fit. Last night, my roommate had a boy over, and as he sat on the couch talking to me, all I felt was discomfort and awkwardness. I didn't know what to say, felt judged, felt out of place. I never feel that way on skis. Even floundering in heavy, deep snow, or after a fall that has packed my goggles with snow and ripped the mittens off my hands I know exactly what to do. I'm a snow mermaid, only comfortable in my medium. I often wish I could trade in my walking legs for something like a tail that is more truly me.

4   My dad's coffee cup at home says, "I only work so I can ski," and for him, it's true. Sometimes I feel like I only push through my daily life so I can get to the next mountain and zip up my pants and go. I don't want to live like that though: it's too much time looking forward to something, and not enough looking at what I'm living in. I need to appreciate my life as it is, snowy cold or sunny warm. That sense of place I have on skis can probably be earned here on the flat expanses of campus just as easily as I got it pushing myself down the bunny slopes so long ago. I just have to earn it.

Moving from Sketch to Draft

A sketch is often sketchy. It's generally underdeveloped, sometimes giving the writer just the barest outline of his or her subject. But as an early draft, a sketch can be invaluable. A sketch might suggest a focus for the next draft, or simply a better lead. Learning to read your sketches for such clues takes practice.

Evaluating Your Own Sketch. Initially, you're the most important reader of your own sketches. It's likely that you're in the best position to sense the material's promise because you understand the context from which it sprang better than any reader can. What are the clues you should look for in a sketch?

1. What surprised you? Might this discovery be the focus of the draft? Chances are, if it surprised you, it will surprise your readers.

2. What is the most important line in the sketch? What makes it important? Might this line be a beginning for more fastwriting? Might it be the theme or controlling idea of the draft?

3. What scene, moment, or situation is key to the story you're telling? Could this be the lead in the draft?

4. What's your favorite part of the sketch? What would happen if you cut it?

Questions for Peer Review. If you'll be sharing your sketch with one or more of your classmates, you'll likely need the most help with clarifying your purpose and focus for a draft. Here are some useful questions that might guide peer responses to your personal essay sketches.

- What does the writer seem to want to say but doesn't quite say in the sketch?

- What line appears most important to the meaning of the sketch, as you understand it?

- What was most surprising about what the writer said or showed?

- What part of the story seems most important? What part might need to be told and isn't?

Reflecting on What You've Learned. Before you begin working on the draft of your personal essay, take a few minutes in your journal to think about your thinking. Finish the following sentence, and follow it in a fastwrite for at least five minutes. The thing that struck me most about writing and sharing my sketch on _____ was.... When you finish, quickly complete the following sentences:

1. The *real* story I seem to be trying to tell is _____.

2. So what? I'd answer that question by saying _____.

3. The main thing I'm planning to do in the draft is _____.

> **METHODS FOR PEER REVIEW OF SKETCHES**
>
> 1. Choose a partner, exchange sketches, read, and comment both in writing and through conversation.
>
> 2. Create a pile of sketches in the middle of the classroom. Everyone takes one (not his or her own, obviously), provides written comments, returns it to the pile, and takes another. Repeat this until everyone has read and commented on at least four sketches.
>
> 3. Share sketches online on the class Web site.

Research and Other Strategies: Gathering More Information

If everything has gone well so far, then your sketch has already given you a sense of direction and some ideas about how to develop your topic. But remember the importance of that dialectical movement between sea and mountain, or collecting and composing. Now that you have a topic and a tentative sense of purpose for your personal essay, journal work can be even more valuable because it can be *more focused*. Before you begin composing the draft—or during that process—consider using the following prompts to generate more information in your notebook:

- *Explode a moment.* Choose a scene or moment in the story or stories you're telling that seems particularly important to the meaning of the essay. Re-enter that moment and fastwrite for a full seven minutes, using all your senses and as much detail as you can muster.

- *Make lists.* Brainstorm a list of details, facts, or specifics about a moment, scene, or observation. List other experiences that seem connected to this one (see the *"Cluster"* point below).

- *Research.* Do some quick-and-dirty research that might bring in other voices or more information that will deepen your consideration of the topic.

- *Cluster.* In your journal, try to move beyond narrating a single experience and discover other experiences, moments, or scenes that might help you see important patterns. Use the preceding list of related experiences or observations and fastwrite about those, or develop a cluster that uses a key word, phrase, or theme as its core, and build a web of associations. For example, let's say your sketch is about your experience working with the poor in Chile. Have you had other encounters with extreme wealth or extreme poverty? Can you describe them? What do they reveal about your feelings or attitudes about poverty or your reactions to what happened in Chile? See Figure 3.3.

Composing the Draft

Some of my students get annoyed at all the "stuff" I encourage them to do before they begin a first draft of a personal essay. In some cases, all the journal work isn't necessary; the writer very quickly gets a strong sense of direction and feels

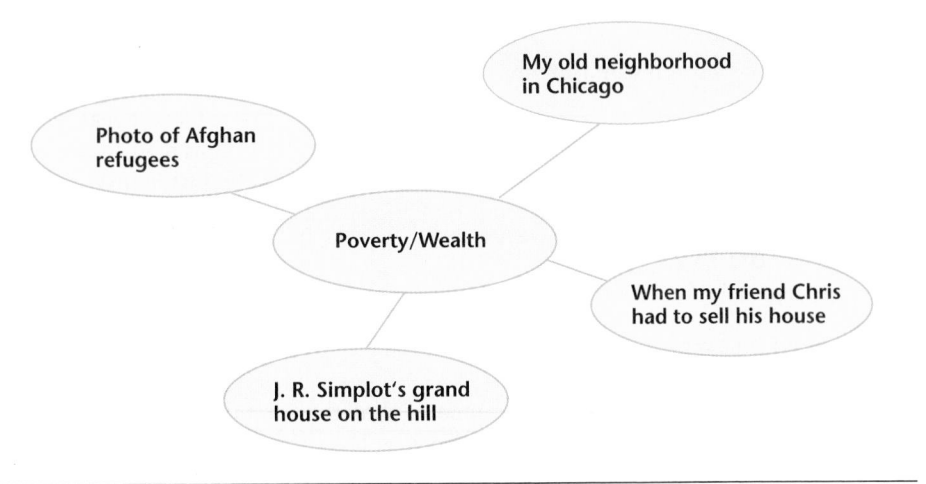

Figure 3.3   The start of a cluster built around poverty/wealth

ready to begin composing. But from the beginning I've encouraged you to gravitate toward topics that you find confusing, and with that kind of material exploratory writing is time well spent. Remember, too, that journal writing counts as writing. It not only offers the pleasures of surprise, but it can ultimately make the drafting process more efficient by generating material that you won't have to conjure up during those long, painful periods of staring at the computer screen wondering what to say next. This front-end work may also help abbreviate the end of the writing process—essentially, all this work in your journal and sketches is revision (see Chapter 9 for more on prewriting as a method of revision).

As you begin drafting, keep in mind what you've learned from your writing so far. For example:

- What is the question(s) behind your exploration of this topic?
- What do you understand now that you didn't understand fully when you started writing about it?
- How can you show *and* explain how you came to this understanding?
- Have you already written a strong first line for the draft? Can you find it somewhere in all your journal writing?

INQUIRING INTO THE DETAILS

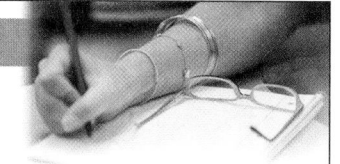

More Than One Way to Tell a Story

This is my daughter Julia telling a story:
"And she was like…"
"And then I was like…"
"And then she was like…"

Generally there are two structures for organizing information: reason and experience. Sometimes writing will combine both, but much academic writing is logically organized rather than experientially organized. Of course, when we think about organizing experiences—something that personal essays try to do—we immediately think of narrative, and then, naturally, we consider the most common narrative structure of all: chronology. This is Julia's method of oral storytelling, as it is for most of us.

Yet in essay writing, strict chronology—this happened and then this and then this—may not be the best way to tell a story. Once locked into a strictly chronological narrative, you may feel compelled to tell the *whole* story. It's a misconception that because it "happened that way" you have to tell the whole story in a personal essay. What you need to do is to tell those *parts* of the story (or stories) that are relevant to the question you're exploring or the thing you're trying to say.

(continued)

Inquiring into the Details (*continued*)

While chronological storytelling might be a good way to remember what happened as you explore your experiences in your journal or in early drafts, it isn't the only choice for structuring your essay. Structure in the personal essay, as in all writing, must be a servant to purpose. Simply put, purpose is how you might answer a potential reader who wants to know this: *So what?* Why should I read this?

Organize a narrative essay with the *So what?* question in mind. That means, first and foremost, that you start a narrative essay in that part of the story that illuminates the dilemma you're trying to solve, the question you're exploring, or the idea you're trying to understand. Typically, the beginning of the story ("The alarm clock went off at 6 AM, and I was groggy from sleep") isn't the best place to emphasize your dilemma, question, or idea. Sometimes, the middle or even the end is better for that.

Notice, for example, that Scott Sanders's essay "Buckeye" (see page 83) begins in the present, not the past, and in doing so he not only sidesteps the problem of telling his story from beginning to end, but he begins the essay reflectively. The most important part of organizing a personal narrative is not how you tell what happened. It is what you *now* think about the significance of what happened. It is this shift from past to present, from what you remember and what you understand about it now that you didn't then, that is the most important structure of all.

Methods of Development. How might you use some of the typical forms of development to develop your subject?

Narrative. The backbone of the personal essay is often, but not always, narrative. Remember, however, that narrative can work in an essay in at least three ways: (1) you tell an extended story of what happened, (2) you tell one or more anecdotes or brief stories, or (3) you tell the story of your thinking as you've come to understand something you didn't understand before. Often a single essay uses all three types of narrative.

Consider beginning your draft with an anecdote or the part of the story you want to tell that best establishes your purpose in the essay (see "Inquiring into the Details: More Than One Way to Tell a Story"). If you're writing about the needless destruction of a childhood haunt by developers, then consider opening with the way the place looked *after* the bulldozers were done with it.

A personal essay can stitch together not just one narrative but several stories, all of which are connected by the essay's theme or question. Time in writing is nothing like real time. You can write pages about something that happened in seven minutes or cover twenty years in a paragraph. You can ignore chronology, if it serves your purpose, too. The key is to tell your story or stories in ways that emphasize what's important. Ask yourself, *What does the reader most need to know to understand my thinking and feelings about this topic? What should I show about what happened that gives the reader a clear sense of what happened?*

Using Evidence. How do you make your essay convincing, and even moving, to an audience? It's in the details. This form thrives, like most literary genres, on particularity: What exactly did it look like? What exactly did she say? What exactly did it sound and smell like at that moment? Evidence that gives a personal essay authority are details that make a reader believe the writer can be trusted to observe keenly and to remember accurately. All of the professional essays in this chapter are rich in detail. There are the buckeyes, "as fat as a lemon," in Scott Russell Sanders' essay, and Laura Zazulak's neighbor with the "neon orange hunting cap" who rakes the same spot every day, and wilting banana leaves that curl around the coconut candy in Judith Ortiz Cofer's "One More Lesson." This focus on the particular—what it *exactly* looked like, smelled like, felt like, sounded like— makes an essay come alive for both writer and reader.

As you draft your essay, remember the subtle power of details. Tell, but always show, too.

Workshopping the Draft

If your draft is subject to peer review (see Chapter 10 for details on how to organize workshop groups), think carefully about the kind of responses you need from readers at this point in the process. In general, you should encourage comments that make you want to write again.

Reflecting on the Draft. To prepare for the workshop, make an entry in your journal that explores your feelings about the draft:

- What do you think worked?
- What do you think needs work?

Following the workshop session, do a follow-up entry in your notebook that summarizes what you heard, what made sense and what didn't, and how you plan to approach the next draft. Your instructor may ask you to share this information in a cover letter submitted with the revision.

Questions for Readers. A writer can structure responses to a draft in many ways. Some of them are discussed in detail in Chapter 10, "The Writer's Workshop." The key is to find a way to get what you need *at this stage in the writing process* that will be most helpful as you revise.

There are a few questions, however, that you might pose to your group that are particularly relevant to the personal essay:

1. Is there a story I'm telling that I need to develop more? Is there a story I'm not telling that I should?

2. What do you think is the *real* story? In other words, what idea or theme lurks beneath the accounts of my experiences and observations?

3. What seems the most important detail, the one that seems to say more than it says, that *reveals* some important feeling, attitude, or idea? What detail seems less important, less revealing?

4. Do my reflective observations seem obvious or overly abstract and general? If so, what questions do you have about what I say that might direct back into the essay's details, where I'm more likely to have better insights?

5. Do I explain things that are unnecessary to explain, that are better told through *showing* rather than *telling*?

Revising the Draft

Revision is a continual process—not a last step. You've been revising—literally "re-seeing" your subject—from the first messy fastwriting in your journal. But the things that get your attention during revision vary depending on where you are in the writing process. You've generated material, chosen a topic, done some research, and written both a sketch and a draft. Most students think that the only thing left to do is "fix things." Check for misspellings. Correct an awkward sentence or two. Come up with a better title. This is editing, not revision, and while editing is important, to focus solely on smaller "fixes" after writing a first draft squanders an opportunity to really *learn* from what the draft is telling you, or perhaps not quite telling you.

Chapter 9 can help guide these discoveries. The questions you can ask a draft fall into five categories: purpose, idea, information, development, and editing. Use the following chart to find the revision strategies in Chapter 9 that might help you re-see what you've written so far.

GUIDE TO REVISION STRATEGIES	
Problems in the Draft (Chapter 9)	**Page Number**
Unclear purpose ■ Not sure what the essay is about? Fails to answer the *So what?* question?	327
Unclear thesis, theme, or main idea ■ Not sure what you're trying to say?	333
Lack of information or development ■ Needs more details; more showing and less telling?	340
Disorganized ■ Doesn't move logically or smoothly from paragraph to paragraph?	344
Unclear or awkward at the level of sentences and paragraphs ■ Seems choppy or hard to follow at the level of sentences or paragraphs?	353

Personal essay drafts typically have some of the following problems:

- They don't answer the *So what?* question. Are you telling a story but don't help your readers understand *why* you're telling it?

- There is too much showing and not enough telling. In other words, do you *reflect* sufficiently in the draft, contributing your new understandings of what happened?

- There isn't enough detail. Because personal essays often rely heavily on narrative, they should show as well as tell. That is, help readers not only understand the significance of your experiences but in some small way experience those significant moments themselves.

Polishing the Draft

After you've dealt with the big issues in your draft—is it sufficiently focused, does it answer the *So what?* question, is it organized, and so on—you must deal with the smaller problems. You've carved the stone into an appealing figure but now you need to polish it. Are your paragraphs coherent? How do you manage transitions? Are your sentences fluent and concise? Are there any errors in spelling or syntax?

Before you finish your draft, work through the following checklist:

- ✓ Every paragraph is about one thing.
- ✓ The transitions between paragraphs aren't abrupt.
- ✓ The length of sentences varies in each paragraph.
- ✓ Each sentence is concise. There are no unnecessary words or phrases.
- ✓ You've checked grammar, particularly for verb agreement, run-on sentences, unclear pronouns, and misused words (*there/their, where/were,* and so on). (See the handbook at the end of the book for help with these grammar issues.)
- ✓ You've run your spellchecker and proofed your paper for misspelled words.

■ STUDENT ESSAY

In my part of the country, the seasonal migration of field workers occurs quietly; most of us rarely notice the cars parked on the country roads and the children sitting in the shade waiting near them. We don't notice the bent backs in the fields, moving methodically from row to row. We are dimly aware, of course, that seasonal workers are key to the beet and potato harvests, but these men and women are largely invisible to us.

Julia Arredondo's essay, "Beet Field Dreams," provides a glimpse of this life. She migrated from Texas to Idaho with her family for nearly fourteen years, where they worked the fields from May to October. For many years, when assigned the ubiquitous topic "What I Did on My Summer Vacation" in school, Julia made up stories about another Julia, one with a "normal" life of picnics, barbecues, and days spent at amusement parks. In this personal essay, the Julia who migrated "like a goose" comes to terms with the truth of those summers, and what they have come to mean.

Beet Field Dreams
Julia C. Arredondo

1   I was born in Welsaco, Texas, and for my entire childhood I considered myself Tejana—a Texan. It was true that I didn't live my entire life—or even my childhood—in the Rio Grande Valley of Southern Texas, but El Valle was my home, where my family and I lived on our own, where I went to school, where we celebrated the major holidays—Thanksgiving, Christmas, New Year's, and everyone's birthdays. Yet the Mini-Cassia, Magic Valley, area of Southern Idaho was also my home—and in a way, not my home—as a child. My father's parents—and their parents before them—were all migrant, seasonal farm workers. This was more than a kind of tradition; it was a way of life, a way of survival, and after a time, it began to feel that it was what my family was meant to do in this world.

2   Every year from late May to August my parents worked alongside my extended family hoeing sugar beets in the fields of Burley, Rupert, Heyburn, Paul, Oakley, and Twin Falls, Idaho. It was either thinning and chopping down beets to make room for more or searching for weeds to eliminate and protect the beets. From September to late October they worked in the spud harvest. Twelve to fourteen hour days picking clots out of the clusters of potatoes that flashed before their eyes, and they worked on combines, as if that's what God had put them here to do. And so we migrated. And migrated. And migrated.

* * *

3   School usually started in early September, but by the time we returned to Texas, Alamo public schools had been running for at least a couple of months. I hated being the new kid in school every year and I especially hated it when people started asking where I'd been, why I was coming into the semester late.

4   It was the infamous "How I spent my summer vacation" essay assignment that would always make me lie like Pinocchio. When the essay topic was assigned, I would panic and begin to feel my heart beat faster. I couldn't tell them what I had really been doing all five months of summer. I could not help it; I'd write about a stranger's summer: picnics, vacations, amusement parks, barbecues. A family trip to Fiesta Texas was the biggest, fictional vacation my elementary mind could conjure up and I think I believed the trip myself. I raved in my essay about how we'd spent an entire week in the

San Antonio amusement park, how the rides were awesome and how much fun I had had—all the while hoping, praying that no one would uncover the lies, and wishing that the teacher would never really read it. After all, they were only dreams that would never come true. I never told about the car. About the fields. Instead, I continued with the grand fabrications.

* * *

We slept in the car, of course. No hotels. Abandoned parking lots. Grocery store parking lots. My Dad liked to park the car somewhere where there was always a lot of light shining. One year in Moab, Utah, we had a really hard time finding a resting spot. First we stopped at a store on the main road that ran through the small town; but then a police officer came around and asked us to keep on moving. He said it was illegal for people driving through to just park anywhere to sleep and pointed us toward a rest area just on the edge of Moab. We went there. Dad parked the car under the only light post in the middle of the dirt parking lot. Then, he got off the car and walked to the pay phone just out of reach of the glowing light. Only a few minutes later, a large truck roared into the empty parking lot. Men's voices shouted and hollered from within as they circled our car, picking up speed, raising up dust clouds, tying a knot in my throat. And then just like that, they were gone. My dad came back to the car, got in, and we drove off.

After that, we mostly slept in truck stops. They were always lit, always alive. They were twenty-four-hour oases for travelers on the go. We had bathrooms available—no matter what time my bladder decided I needed to pee. We had hot food within reach. Hot coffee. So whenever Pa wanted to wake up and drive his family on, he could have a cup. It was almost as convenient as a hotel except that we slept amongst the trucks; their thunderous vibrations never really let me sleep. We'd put towels up as curtains, to block out some of the light—noise. But sometimes when I woke up in the middle of the night, and everyone in the car was asleep, I would look out and wonder where these monsters were going and whether they were as driven as we were to move.

* * *

As a kid I'd wake up on most summer mornings to the sound of doors slamming shut and cool breezes of fresh morning wind sweeping into the car, making me shiver. I could feel the weight of the car shift as the grown-ups pulled their hoes from the trunk. Their voices lingered outside the vehicle for minutes as they prepared for the day's work, waiting for the first light of day to guide their strokes. I'd lay still and listen as their voices became distant, then I would slowly drift back to my dreams.

Some mornings, when the sun wasn't quite strong enough to warm us up, my sister Debra and I would stay inside the car. I'd lounge around in the front seat—a place I hardly ever got to ride in—and impatiently wait for the adults to return to the *caheceras*. From the car they looked miniature as they moved at a hurried pace along the mile long rows. Debra and I would guess which one was Ma and which one was Pa. Sometimes we

(continued)

(continued)

were right. Sometimes I'd drift back to sleep and miss them reaching our end of the field. I'd awake to find they were already halfway back across the field and feel my heart weigh down.

9   I was always looking for a reason to join them in their hard labor; years later when I would have to really start working I knew exactly how hard it was. Still, I'd mention to my parents how I could work too, how we'd make more money that way. I'd ask them to break a hoe in half and let me have it. They only laughed and said when the time came for me to work I wasn't going to want to, so for me to just enjoy this time.

10   Sometimes near the field there would be a farmhouse from which laughter floated down towards us. Sometimes we could spot kids that looked our age jumping on their trampoline, swimming in their pool and I'd find myself longing to be them. Normal. Playing on a lawn, instead of a field. Waking in a bed, instead of a car's backseat. Eating lunch at a table, instead of from tin foil while I sat in the dirt on the shady side of the car to avoid the hot sun.

* * *

11   When I was fourteen we finally stopped moving. Field work continued being our main source of income, but we made Idaho our permanent home. And as the years passed, returning to Texas became preposterous; we were always too afraid to fall back into the old migrating lifestyle. Yet, even today I am a migrant. And it's not merely the fact that I've spent more than half my life migrating—like a goose—according to the seasons, but because it was a lifestyle that penetrates and becomes part of who I am for the rest of my life. As I grew older, I began to slowly acknowledge to others the kind of lifestyle my family lived during my childhood. Though no longer on the move, I will always be a migrant and sugar beet dreams will always haunt my sleep.

Evaluating the Essay

Discuss or write about your response to Julia Arredondo's essay using some or all of the following questions.

1. What is the essay's greatest strength? Is this something you've noticed in your own work, or the drafts of classmates?

2. Is the balance between exposition and narration, showing and telling, handled well in "Beet Field Dreams"? Does it read fairly quickly or does it drag at points?

3. The essay uses line breaks between sections. What do you think of this technique? What are its advantages and disadvantages?

4. What would you recommend to Arredondo if she were to revise "Beet Field Dreams"?

USING WHAT YOU HAVE LEARNED

My students often love writing personal essays. At its best, the genre is a rare opportunity to reexamine our lives and better understand our experiences. The insights we earn are often reward enough, but what have you learned in this assignment that you might apply in other writing situations?

1. The personal essay you wrote relies heavily on narrative and personal experience. How might an ability to tell a good story, using your experiences or the experiences of others, be a useful academic skill? How might you use it to write a paper for another class?

2. The personal essay is a deeply subjective form, seeming to put it at odds with formal academic writing, which strives for "objectivity." Are they at odds?

3. Based on your experience writing a personal essay, what do you think are its most important qualities? If you were to write more personal essays, what would you strive to do next time?

"If you want to write about mankind, write about a man," advises author E. B. White. The profile is a form that accomplishes this by giving an idea, a feeling, or an issue a human face.

WRITING A PROFILE

WRITING ABOUT PEOPLE

Some years ago, when I was writing a book on the culture of the New England lobster fishing industry, I wandered into the lighthouse keeper's house in Pemaquid Point, Maine. The lighthouse, built in 1827, was automated—like all but one lighthouse on the East Coast—but the empty keeper's house had been turned into a tiny fishing museum. I found my way there one late spring day, stepped inside, and was greeted by Abby Boynton, sitting on a folding chair working on needlepoint. I had come to look at historical objects related to lobster fishing, but instead I encountered Abby, an elderly widow whose husband, a local lobsterman, had died of cancer several years before.

We struck up a conversation, and within minutes she was leading me to the back of the museum to show me a picture book, now out of print, that documented a few days of her husband's work at the traps offshore from New Harbor, Maine. She told me the story of the New York photographer who asked her husband if he wouldn't mind company fishing that day. "He was always taking people out," she said, "so my husband said 'sure.'" That trip with the photographer led to other trips and the book that followed, *Fred Boynton, Lobsterman*. The museum copy was well thumbed and the binding was broken, but Mrs. Boynton assured me that there were still a few copies around. "I've got two copies at home," she said, "but I can't part with those. They'll be nice for the kids and the grandchildren."

What You'll Learn in This Chapter

- How the profile and the academic case study are related.
- What distinguishes the profile from other forms.
- The importance of close observation.
- Interview techniques.
- Ways to find a profile subject who is representative of a certain group of people.
- Questions for revising a profile.

Abby Boynton showed me a picture of the New Harbor house she had lived in with Fred all the years they were married. She moved three years ago because it was "too much house." As I was leaving she directed me to a model of her husband's boat, the *Dwayne B*, in a back room of the museum. It was named after their youngest son. A brass plaque on the boat model said, "In memory by his friends and fellow fishermen."

What was it like being a lobster man's wife? I asked, heading toward the sunshine. "Spent most of my time trying to keep his dinner warm," said Mrs. Boynton, resuming her post in the folding chair by the door. I glanced at the needlepoint in her lap, but couldn't read the stitched letters, which had not yet formed a word. After my fifteen minutes with Abby Boynton that seemed fitting; what didn't need a plaque or a label in this museum was the most powerful thing I found there. It occurred to me later that Abby Boynton was as bound to her husband's memory as she was to life. Only now she keeps more than his dinner warm as she waits.

This accidental interview with the lobsterman's wife reveals much more than I could explain about one aspect of community in Maine's fishing villages—the partnership between spouses who have chosen such a hard life. I can't imagine a better way to dramatize the level of devotion these marriages can demand than Abby Boynton's shrine to the memory of her husband—a worn book, a dusty model of his boat, and a picture of the New Harbor home they shared. You can hear it in her voice, too, and how quickly she directs a stranger to these relics. But all of this probably doesn't need explaining; you can sense it from the vignette.

> There may be no better way of dramatizing the impact of a problem or the significance of an idea than showing how it presents itself in the life of one person.

This piece could have easily continued, perhaps including information from the book *Fred Boynton, Lobsterman* or interviews about Abby and Fred from others in New Harbor who knew them. It might have included statistics about the divorce rate among Maine fishing families, or information about the economic pressures on families during a bad fishing season—all the factors that might easily make it hard for a marriage to survive. Most of all, I might have spent more time with Abby Boynton. The result would have been a profile, not a vignette, that would put a face on the idea that lobster fishing is difficult, but for many, a good life.

MOTIVES FOR WRITING A PROFILE

E. B. White, author of the children's classics *Charlotte's Web* and *Stuart Little* and many essays for the *The New Yorker* magazine, once offered this advice: "If you want to write about mankind, write about a man." The profile is a form that accomplishes this by giving a general idea or feeling a face. Through Abby Boynton we presumably can see something about other lobster-men's wives and families. In that sense, the profile is like the personal essay—the experiences and particulars about a living subject create, as Scott Russell Sanders once said, "a door through which [readers] might have passed." In a profile, however, the obvious subject is usually not the writer but the person he writes about.

The profile is a familiar form in the popular magazine. We can't seem to know enough about other peoples' lives. The celebrity profile is ubiquitous, but some of the best profiles are of ordinary people like Abby Boynton who are typical in some way of the people touched by the subject a writer is interested in. There may be no better way of dramatizing the impact of a problem, the importance of a question, or the significance of an idea than showing how it presents itself in the life of one person.

THE PROFILE AND ACADEMIC WRITING

While the profile may not be a common academic form, the case study is, and in a sense a profile is a form of extended case study. Almost any topic affects people's lives (if it doesn't, is it really that significant or interesting?). The profile or case study attempts to document these impacts. For example, suppose you're interested in examining the success of your university's commitment to ethnic and racial diversity—a principle the administration has publicly embraced. One way to approach the topic is to profile one international student. What has been her experience on campus? Which campus programs have proved useful? What programs are needed? The voice of your profile subject and the details of her experience would help dramatize an otherwise abstract policy debate, and the story she tells could offer a foundation from which to explore the issue.

> The profile relies on interviews and observation, particularly those revealing details that say something about the character or feelings of the person profiled.

You can write a profile in the service of an argument or as a way to explore the personal impact of an event. The profile may be part of a larger project that examines some aspect of a local culture, cultural trend, or place. It can, like good fiction, provide insight into the complexities of the human mind and soul.

More than any other form of inquiry, the profile relies on interviews for information—the voice of the writer's subject should come through—as well as observation, particularly those revealing details that say something about the character or feelings of the person profiled. In some cases, these details are merely descriptive—what the subject looks like, for instance. However, telling details can often be indirect evidence of a person's character, things like the way one man stands with his feet apart and arms folded on his chest to emphasize his biceps (arrogant), how a woman carefully knots the scarf around her neck (fastidious), and so on. Writers who want to practice interview skills—a key method of collecting information in communications and the social sciences—will find the profile a useful challenge.

FEATURES OF THE FORM

Some typical characteristics of the form include the following:

- *A profile usually provides a detailed look at one person.* The key is to decide who that person should be.

- *Alone, a profile may not provide enough substantiation for an argument.* While the writer may choose a profile to dramatize a problem or support a claim, it's always dangerous to generalize from a single case, particularly if the typicality of the subject is in doubt.

- *A profile uses narrative as a method of organization.* As in the personal essay, storytelling is frequently the backbone of the profile. This may take the form of a series of anecdotes about the writer's subject, or the subject's account of an experience.

- *The profile is usually written from one of two points of view—either the writer narrates in the first person or the subject is portrayed in the third person, and the writer stays out of the way.* A profile told in the first person can give an added dimension of the writer's own feelings and reactions, but risks distracting the reader from the real subject, the person being profiled. Portraying the subject in the third person loses the drama of the interaction between the writer and the person profiled, but keeps the focus on the subject.

- *Profiles go beyond mere description of subjects and reveal information about character much as a short story does, through telling details and the subject's own voice.* Letting the subject speak for herself is particularly important, but to do this well makes special demands on the writer. (See "Inquiring into the Details: Recording Interviews" later in the chapter.)

- *A strong beginning is essential, particularly when the subject of a profile isn't famous.* We read a celebrity profile because of the fame of its subject. But when writing about ordinary people, we need to quickly give readers a reason to be interested.

- *Scene and setting often provide useful information in a profile.* We know characters not just by what they say but what they do and where they do it.

- *The more time writers can spend with their subjects, the more revealing the profile.* The more information you have about your subject, the easier it is to focus the piece, and the more likely you are to get to the truth of things about your subject.

READINGS

■ PROFILE 1

One of the most memorable segments on the TV show *Seinfeld* was about the "Soup Nazi," a character inspired by the following profile. Published in *The New Yorker* by one of the staff writers, "Soup" profiles soup chef Albert Yeganeh, the tough-talking, impatient, demanding owner of a small restaurant on West Fifty-fifth Street. The force of Yeganeh's personality comes through brilliantly in this piece especially because the writer steps aside and lets the man speak for himself through extensive—and sometimes lengthy—quotations. It's hard to over-state how important it is to allow readers to hear the voices of profile subjects.

But this essay is also a great example of how important close and careful observation is to a profile. We can know people by the contexts in which they live and work, something that we could simply explain—"Yeganeh owns a soup restaurant on West Fifty-fifth Street in New York"—or describe—"The first thing you notice about it is the awning, which proclaims 'Homemade Hot, Cold, Diet Soups.'" These more specific observations bring the man's tiny world to life around him and contribute powerfully to our understanding of who he is.

Soup

Anonymous, The New Yorker

When Albert Yeganeh says "Soup is my lifeblood," he means it. And when he says "I am extremely hard to please," he means that, too. Working like a demon alchemist in a tiny storefront kitchen at 259-A West Fifty-fifth Street, Mr. Yeganeh creates any-where from eight to seventeen soups every weekday. His concoctions are so popular that a wait of half an hour at the lunchtime peak is not uncommon, although there are strict rules for conduct in line. But more on that later.

"I am psychologically kind of a health freak," Mr. Yeganeh said the other day, in a lisping staccato of Armenian origin. "And I know that soup is the greatest meal in the world. It's very good for your digestive system. And I use only the best, the freshest ingredients. I am a perfectionist. When I make a clam soup, I use three different kinds of clams. Every other place uses canned clams. I'm called crazy. I am not crazy. People don't realize why I get so upset. It's because if the soup is not perfect and I'm still selling it, it's a torture. It's *my* soup, and that's why I'm so upset. First you clean and then you cook. I don't believe that ninety-nine percent of the restaurants in New York know how to clean a tomato. I tell my crew to wash the parsley *eight* times. If they wash it five or six times, I scare them. I tell them they'll go to jail if there is sand in the parsley. One time, I found a mushroom on the floor, and I fired that guy who left it there." He spread his arms, and added, "This place is the only one like it in…in…the whole earth! One

(continued)

(continued)

day, I hope to learn something from the other places, but so far I haven't. For example, the other day I went to a very fancy restaurant and had borscht. I had to send it back. It was *junk*. I could see all the chemicals in it. I never use chemicals. Last weekend, I had lobster bisque in Brooklyn, a very well-known place. It was *junk*. When I make a lobster bisque, I use a whole lobster. You know, I never advertise. I don't have to. All the big-shot chefs and the kings of the hotels come here to see what *I'm* doing."

3   As you approach Mr. Yeganeh's Soup Kitchen International from a distance, the first thing you notice about it is the awning, which proclaims "Homemade Hot, Cold, Diet Soups." The second thing you notice is an aroma so delicious that it makes you want to take a bite out of the air. The third thing you notice, in front of the kitchen, is an electric signboard that flashes, saying, "Today's Soups...Chicken Vegetable... Mexican Beef Chili...Cream of Watercress...Italian Sausage...Clam Bisque...Beef Barley...Due to Cold Weather...For Most Efficient and Fastest Service the Line Must... Be Kept Moving...Please...Have Your Money...Ready...Pick the Soup of Your Choice...Move to Your Extreme...Left After Ordering."

4   "I am not prejudiced against color or religion," Mr. Yeganeh told us, and he jabbed an index finger at the flashing sign. "Whoever follows that I treat very well. My regular customers don't say anything. They are very intelligent and well educated. They know I'm just trying to move the line. The New York cop is very smart—he sees everything but says nothing. But the young girl who wants to stop and tell you how nice you look and hold everyone up—*yah!*" He made a guillotining motion with his hand. "I tell you, I hate to work with the public. They treat me like a slave. My philosophy is: The customer is always wrong and I'm always right. I raised my prices to try to get rid of some of these people, but it didn't work."

5   The other day, Mr. Yeganeh was dressed in chef's whites with orange smears across his chest, which may have been some of the carrot soup cooking in a huge pot on a little stove in one corner. A three-foot-long handheld mixer from France sat on the sink, looking like an overgrown gardening tool. Mr. Yeganeh spoke to two young helpers in a twisted Armenian-Spanish barrage, then said to us, "I have no overhead, no trained waitresses, and I have the cashier here." He pointed to himself theatrically. Beside the doorway, a glass case with fresh green celery, red and yellow peppers, and purple eggplant was topped by five big gray soup urns. According to a piece of cardboard taped to the door, you can buy Mr. Yeganeh's soups in three sizes, costing from four to fifteen dollars. The order of any well-behaved customer is accompanied by little waxpaper packets of bread, fresh vegetables (such as scallions and radishes), fresh fruit (such as cherries or an orange), a chocolate mint, and a plastic spoon. No coffee, tea, or other drinks are served.

6   "I get my recipes from books and theories and my own taste," Mr. Yeganeh said. "At home, I have several hundreds of books. When I do research, I find that I don't know anything. Like cabbage is a cancer fighter, and some fish is good for your heart but some is bad. Every day, I should have one sweet, one spicy, one cream, one vegetable soup—and they *must* change, they should always taste a little different." He added that he wasn't sure how extensive his repertoire was, but that it probably

includes at least eighty soups, among them African peanut butter, Greek moussaka, hamburger, Reuben, B.L.T., asparagus and caviar, Japanese shrimp miso, chicken chili, Irish corned beef and cabbage, Swiss chocolate, French calf's brain, Korean beef ball, Italian shrimp and eggplant Parmesan, buffalo, ham and egg, short rib, Russian beef Stroganoff, turkey cacciatore, and Indian mulligatawny. "The chicken and the seafood are an addiction, and when I have French garlic soup I let people have only one small container each," he said. "The doctors and nurses love that one."

A lunch line of thirty people stretched down the block from Mr. Yeganeh's doorway. Behind a construction worker was a man in expensive leather, who was in front of a woman in a fur hat. Few people spoke. Most had their money out and their orders ready.   7

At the front of the line, a woman in a brown coat couldn't decide which soup to get and started to complain about the prices.   8

"You talk too much, dear," Mr. Yeganeh said, and motioned her to move to the left. "Next!"   9

"Just don't talk. Do what he says," a man huddled in a blue parka warned.   10

"He's downright rude," said a blond woman in a blue coat. "Even abusive. But you can't deny it, his soup is the best."   11

Inquiring into the Essay

Use the four methods of inquiry—exploring, explaining, evaluating, and reflecting—to generate a response to "Soup."

1. Use a "narrative of thought" response to explore your initial reactions to "Soup." Immediately after reading the piece, open your notebook and begin a five-minute fastwrite, starting with the following phrase: The first thing that comes to mind after reading this essay is _____. And then...And then...Whenever the writing stalls, seize on the phrase *and then* to get you going. Feel free, however, to digress on some aspect of the profile you want to think about through writing. After five minutes, stop and finish the following sentence: Now that I look back on what I've said about "Soup," the thing that strikes me the most is...

2. If you're profiling someone famous, you really don't have to worry much about reader interest; fame alone gives you a rhetorical advantage. But when you write about someone, like Yeganeh, who is relatively unknown, you have to "hook" your readers within the first paragraph or two, giving them a reason to read on. Explain how the writer of "Soup" attempted to do this in the first paragraph of the essay.

3. Review the essay and any writing you've done on the essay. Make a quick list of words that best describe Yeganeh. Choose one of them and, using evidence from the essay, find specific information that supports the choice. What is the strongest evidence you found that best explains the

aptness of the word you chose to describe him? Evaluate the qualities of good evidence in a profile essay.

4. Go ahead and admit it. You like reading *People* occasionally (or maybe often). Now consider how you felt about reading "Soup." Were your motives and responses the same? How would you distinguish between a *People* piece on Nicole Kidman and the *New Yorker* profile of Albert Yeganeh?

■ PROFILE 2

It's possible to profile the dead. The growth of archives that include interview transcripts, photographs, audio recordings, and video clips—much of it online

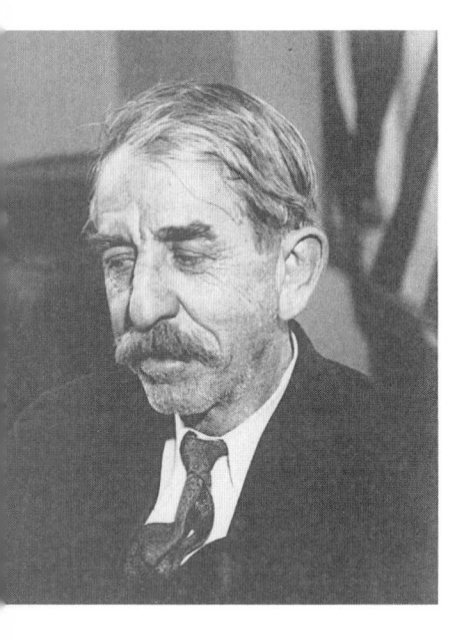

(see "Writing in the Disciplines," page 149)—makes it easier than ever before to create a portrait of both famous and ordinary people who died decades ago. This is the work of historians, of course, but novices like the rest of us, especially with the accessibility of archives, can do it too.

William Henry David Murray (nicknamed "Alfalfa Bill") was elected governor of Oklahoma in 1930. He was a man "who could talk for hours without interruption, fueled by caffeine and nicotine," writes Timothy Egan. "He drank two pots of black coffee a day and was never without a cigar." Murray was also a hopeless bigot who presided—ineffectively—over the Dust Bowl in Oklahoma, America's worst environmental tragedy. "Alfalfa Bill" is one of many compelling profiles in Egan's stunning history of the drought and destruction that overtook parts of Texas, Kansas, Colorado, and Oklahoma in the 1930s. The excerpt that follows, from Egan's book *The Worst Hard Time*, is a wonderful example of a different kind of profile that relies on archival information. It is possible, after all, to bring the dead to life.

Alfalfa Bill

Timothy Egan

1   The new governor of Oklahoma gave people hope, but he also tried to get them to hate. William Henry David Murray had been elected in 1930 after scandal drove the last two governors from office, both of them impeached. With a campaign slogan that railed against what he called "The Three C's—Corporations, Carpetbaggers, and Coons,"

Murray won by a huge margin, 301,921 votes to 208,575. He was known as "Alfalfa Bill" for his ceaseless advocacy of agriculture as the cornerstone of society. Alfalfa Bill said anything could grow in Oklahoma. His daddy, David, had made wine not long after grabbing a piece of dirt in the 1889 Sooner land rush; his Murray Mosel was so well-known that President Teddy Roosevelt had declared it "the bulliest wine of the land." Alfalfa Bill was himself a bully, but these times needed such a man, he said. Born in Toadsuck, Texas, in 1869, Murray ran away from home at the age of twelve, worked on a series of farms, and then got involved in populist politics. He bought a newspaper, educated himself so well he passed the bar, and made a name as president of the Oklahoma statehood convention in 1906. Oklahoma, he said at the time, could be a great state only if blacks were separated from whites and kept in the proper jobs—in the fields or factories. Next door, in Texas, lawmakers had institutionalized that sentiment forty years earlier with Reconstruction laws that said blacks could work only as field hands. Blacks were inferior to whites in all ways, Murray said, and must be fenced from society like quarantined hogs. At the start of the twentieth century, many people felt otherwise, but Alfalfa Bill tried to set his view into the proposed constitution. At the same time, he welcomed even black support, if done properly.

"I appreciate the old darkie who comes to me talking softly in that humble spirit which should characterize their actions and dealings with the white man," he said to wide applause at the constitutional convention. Murray hated Jews as well. Blacks had some virtues, but Jews had none, in his view. Nor did he like the handful of Italians who had come to the High Plains. The "low grade races" of southern Europe, he said, were a threat to civilization. Oklahoma became the forty-sixth state only after President Theodore Roosevelt forced Murray to remove the segregationist planks of the constitution. Murray was furious; he never let go of his grudge against the Roosevelt family.   2

At the start of the Depression, Alfalfa Bill was a mustachioed, haunt-eyed, big-eared man of sixty who could talk for hours without interruption, fueled by caffeine and nicotine. He drank two pots of black coffee a day and was never without a cigar—his method of ingesting "the great civilizer," as he called tobacco. Storming around Oklahoma in 1931, he said he could not make the sun less oppressive, but he promised to use muscle to fix the broken land. His muscle was the National Guard. As governor, Murray ruled by martial law, calling out the guard twenty-seven times in his first two years in office. When oil prices fell to a new low in 1931, the governor sent his troops to the oil fields to force a shutdown of three thousand wells as a way to drive up prices. When Texas backed a toll bridge across the Red River on the border with Oklahoma, Murray sent the guard to the bridge, nearly provoking a shooting war between the two states. In the midst of the standoff he showed up with an antique revolver, waving it in the faces of Texas Rangers. And when blacks tried to hold an Emancipation Day parade in a park in Oklahoma City, the governor imposed martial law on the city and ordered his guard troops to shut them down. Blacks were supposed to be invisible in his state, quietly working the   3

(continued)

(continued)

land or manning a factory station. All told, the governor issued thirty-four declarations of martial law during his four years in office.

4   The land dried up in the spring of 1932. Month after month, going into the height of the growing season, there was no rain. The sky was white and hot, and it took until well after midnight for the heat to dissipate. Alfalfa Bill urged people to fight nature with force. The unemployment rate in his state was 29 percent. To show them what could be done, he plowed up the grass on the grounds of the capitol and let people plant vegetable gardens. And to demonstrate how water could be taken from the ground, Murray went on a building binge, trying to create lakes and ponds in places that had neither. The ground could be mined at the deepest levels for water, using new and powerful centrifugal pumps, to create the garden state of Oklahoma. They could grab onto that underground lake, the Ogallala Aquifer, like the Sooners had grabbed the old Cherokee lands, and so what if the water was nearly seven hundred feet deep and had taken at least a hundred centuries to build up—it was there to be grubstaked.

5   In Boise City, Alfalfa Bill's plans sounded like a tonic. God knows they needed water. It wasn't trickling out of the distant Rockies. The Cimarron, once a roaring river, was now a tear trail. And it wasn't coming from overhead. It rained barely ten inches in all of 1932. The sun glared down at nesters in No Man's Land, every dawn a new punishment. It was time for man to stand up to the puckered face of the elements.

6   "Human progress has now reached the stage where it can master these mighty forces of nature," wrote the *Boise City News*, in support of a proposed dam in No Man's Land.

7   In the spring of 1932, Alfalfa Bill decided to run for president. He would follow the model that got him elected governor. In running for the statehouse, he had campaigned on the Three C's. Now he ran on a platform of promising people the "Four B's: Bread, Butter, Bacon, and Beans." That a governor could run for the highest office of the land with a campaign that offered people calories said something about 1932.

Inquiring into the Essay

1. According to Timothy Egan, "Alfalfa Bill" was a racist and an anti-Semite. Is it possible for you to get past these two serious character flaws and find anything redeeming in someone like Governor Murray? Does the historical context in which he lived matter at all? Explore these two questions in your journal in a four-minute fastwrite.

2. Choose a single word that you would use to describe your dominant impression of William Murray (other than "racist" and "anti-Semite"). Go back to the profile and find specific evidence that seems to support that dominant impression. Then, if you can, find some evidence that does not support it.

3. *The Worst Hard Times*, the book from which this character sketch of "Alfalfa Bill" was taken, is an environmental history. It makes the argument that there are aspects of the Dust Bowl that will help us understand all environmental disasters. Though you have to read the book to really appreciate that argument, speculate about how this profile might contribute to the idea that the Dust Bowl is a cautionary tale. What do you infer from the profile of William Murray about how his response to Oklahoma's environmental disaster is relevant, even today?

4. Reflect on what archival sources Timothy Egan could have used to write this piece.

▪ PROFILE 3

Joe Cool, aka Lonnie Beasley, worked in the produce department at Kroger, and he was the emcee of overstock. "Hey folks," he said on the store PA, "this is Joe Cool and my manager's jumpin' all over me 'cause I done stacked too many beans out there....So, please—come on over and buy some of these beans so I can get my manager off my back." The following profile of Beasley was originally published in the *Journal of Management Inquiry*. It is a work of academic scholarship, even if it doesn't read like one.

The discipline of business and economics, like many academic fields, is finding that this kind of alternative scholarship offers knowledge that traditional forms of research lack. For example, one business scholar who reviewed "Learning About Work from Joe Cool" wrote that "this story represents a more holistic view of work...than is usually the case in studies of organizational behavior." Another wrote that this profile is "powerful in reminding us that the analysis of work is ultimately etched in the life experiences of workers." The chance to look into the life of someone like Beasley, these scholars argue, provides knowledge that traditional quantitative research does not.

Learning About Work from Joe Cool
Gib Akin

The announcement over the supermarket PA system cut through the anonymous burble of shopping talk: "Hey folks, this is Joe Cool and my manager's jumpin' all over me 'cause I done stacked too many beans out here. Old Joe won't be COOOOL no more if he don't get these things movin'. So, please—come on over and buy some of these beans so I can get my manager off my back. And while you're here we've got a great buy on California navel oranges."   1

(continued)

(continued)

2   Here's Joe Cool himself: slim, angular, small turned-up nose on a face that is slightly dished, older than what you would expect from the name. But that's part of what makes him cool, acting so youthful, even at 55, and sporting an intensely white beard. The hair is striking in its contrasting black, and is parted in the middle, with a wing-like sweep back over each temple, plastered flat. It gives him an old fashioned look, like your jolly barkeep from the 1890s. A name tag on his denim apron makes it official that he really is Joe Cool. He's constant motion and constant talk, moving produce, keeping the customers, especially women customers, happy.

3   Lonnie Beasley became Joe Cool in the Kroger produce department, first only behind the scenes and then out front with the customers. He started produce work in 1971 and by 1975 his coworkers had begun to corroborate the Joe Cool persona. They gave him a pair of sunglasses to emulate the Peanuts cartoon showing Snoopy as Joe Cool. Stickers of the cartoon character began appearing on his locker, as well as near the water fountain and the time clock. The back room was becoming Joe Cool's domain. The work there was physically demanding, and all were amazed at Lonnie's youthful strength and endurance— lifting, unloading trucks, and stacking and moving large four-wheeled carts of produce.

4   But the idea that Lonnie was cool came mainly from his constant joking, talking, and relentlessly youthful attitude. "He would say anything." The mostly younger coworkers liked it that someone older could be like them, always fooling around, not serious, "a nut." But he also retained his seniority, and was paternal as well. He helped everybody. Susan Marsh remembers that "he always made me feel like a daughter he hadn't seen in quite a while." (She didn't know the circumstances that give her simile its keenness.)

5   And, he rode a motorcycle to work, the crash helmet worn for protection also creating his nineteenth-century hairdo. He didn't ride a mean machine as an aging outlaw biker, but a friendly, playful one as the fresh-air kid. That was really cool. He had a sly affection for the slightly wild image of a motorcyclist, even though he claimed he started riding motorcycles because of the good gas mileage.

6   When the store moved to a new location, a system of weighing and pricing produce in the section rather than at the register was started, and Lonnie was given the "out front" job as scale man. That's when grocery shoppers got to meet Joe Cool. Donald Linke, who also worked in produce and like Lonnie had come from the other store, now made an "official" name tag that read JOE COOL.

7   From his new job out front, Lonnie also became the idol of the airwaves. When he got on the PA system to announce some special promotion, people in the store would be quiet so they could hear what Joe Cool was going to say. On one Fourth of July holiday, the store manager, in response to running out the year before, had over-

stocked hamburger and hot dog rolls. As the day wore on and there were mountains of unsold buns remaining, Lonnie gave the play-by-play: "Folks, the manager has gone crazy, flipped his lid, gone bananas. He's giving away rolls, two for the price of one." And ten minutes later, "He's getting worse, now the poor fool has gone completely over the edge. He's giving four for the price of one. Y'all better get over here and stop this before we have to carry him off." As people arrived, Lonnie would load their baskets and whisk them off. What to do with all the buns? Nobody worried; it was Joe Cool.

Someone said to the manager, "Do you hear what that guy is saying about you?"   8

"Don't bother me none. Them rolls are moving aren't they?"   9

Lonnie was especially attentive to the ladies. He claimed that his beard had turned white as a result of all the smooching he had done (wink, touch your shoulder). Women shoppers always knew that both they and their vegetables were beautiful. Having been raised on a farm and always having his own garden even when living in town, Lonnie knew about produce and would help women pick the best vegetables and then advise on preparation.   10

Attention to women was also about kids. Kids loved Joe Cool and would have their mothers take them to see him.   11

The grocery store job was a second one, even though for most of the time it was a 40-hour-a-week commitment, a full-time job in its own right. Lonnie had always been a two-job man. "I guess working is just my thing." He had worked as a salesman at Sears and drove a Yellow cab as a second job. He sold life insurance as a first job and sold tires at the B. F. Goodrich store as a second. In 1971, he joined the University of Virginia police department working the graveyard shift and soon after began working days at the supermarket.   12

The police job had a lot of the same opportunities to help people. Lonnie claimed only 30 percent was crime fighting, and 70 percent was helping people and doing PR. And especially with University police, you got to deal with better people. Still, the people in produce were an antidote to some of the unfixable unhappiness he saw as a police officer.   13

Coworkers at the store would wonder how, and why, he would do it. "How much sleep you get?"   14

"Three or four hours."   15

"You call that living?"   16

"Depends on your aim."   17

Lonnie had two aims in work. One was simple, conventional, economic, and easy to talk about. Lonnie described himself as a depression baby, born in 1931. His parents separated when he was five, and his mother carried him back to the   18

(continued)

(continued)

country where her people were. They never had anything but always worked to pay their way. You didn't want to owe anything or anybody. And what you did was work.

19   He had always wanted to go back to the country, and the work earnings eventually allowed the purchase of a house and seven acres—not really a farm, but a place that could be lived on farm-like. In an open, ramshackle barn, is stored his second motorcycle, a blue 500cc Yamaha that replaced the Honda 350 he started with in 1976. They look faded and scrawny next to his current ride, a huge Honda Gold Wing with a sidecar. There's also a little-used RV. Three old cars live on the acreage, only three of many projects in various states of completion.

20   Depression babies, who never had anything, don't throw things away. Lonnie and Nancy's house was full of things collected deliberately or just impossible to part with. And they all had stories connected with them. Lonnie told the stories while Nancy listened. She sometimes interjected to show physical traces of the story, a photo, a card, a toy, a piece of clothing. (There was quite a collection of icons of the Snoopy Joe Cool character, modeled in banks, T-shirts, soap, a radio.) In retrieving one thing, something else always surfaced, and that kicked off another story. It wasn't having the things themselves, it was that they provided a kind of archaeology, the shards in which their life was encoded, an aid to the remembering and telling that make things real.

21   The accumulation has now attained some sort of critical mass so that there is not the same need to work so much. (Nancy, who Lonnie always calls "Mamma" or "doll," has never worked.) Part of the fullness has been achieved by inheriting some money, primarily from Nancy's side of the family. The farmers who were her kin may have lived poorly, but in the end their land had substantial cash value, which helped Lonnie and Nancy finally have something.

22   The other aim of Lonnie's work was less conventional and harder to tell.

23   Lonnie and Nancy referred to their son, James Irvin, as the achievement of their life. He was born in 1954, two years after they were married. At the age of two, James Irvin was taken sick with encephalitis and spent the rest of his life in need of special care. He died in a hospital in Lynchburg, 60 miles away from his family, in 1976. While he was alive, Lonnie, always devoted to helping people, couldn't really help as he would have liked.

24   During the time when James Irvin was alive and after his death, work was a form of therapy. "Cheaper than a psychiatrist," Lonnie claimed. It was a way to keep busy, a way to keep from worrying himself into the hospital.

25   Nancy quietly did most of the direct care giving, while Lonnie, feeling more and more distressed, took a second job and spent more time working. A friend admonished Nancy that Lonnie was running away and not helping. But Nancy, uncharacteristically, stood up strong, defending that Lonnie was doing his

part by working to pay the bills, doing what he could do in his own way for James Irvin.

When his son died, Lonnie cried, but he kept on working.   26

Lonnie also couldn't help his daughter as he would have liked. Born seven   27
years after James Irvin and named Nancy like her mother, she always knew her dad was cool. What was really cool was being delivered to school by taxi, a regular treat when Lonnie worked a second job as a driver for Yellow Cab. She recalled motorcycle trips to visit relatives in the Tidewater and that her dad would do anything to help someone in need, including her and her stricken brother.

The younger Nancy was married before finishing high school. Her dad didn't   28
exactly approve ("I may be Joe Cool, but I'm a square"). He remained supportive of her, nevertheless. Nancy and her husband had a daughter, but soon separated, and Nancy went to California—a place that for Lonnie was mysterious and dangerous, a place that changed people and made his daughter into someone he didn't know. He worried that she was drawn to men who were bad for her. But he was still there for her, even helping her move back to California after some time back at home. When she left with "her fellah" (Lonnie still can't say the name of the man he so disliked), Nancy's daughter Amber stayed with her grandparents.

Later, Lonnie and Nancy sued for custody of Amber, who was living with them. At   29
the time, the younger Nancy was angry that her parents were trying to take her daughter away. She now sees it differently, that Lonnie had to make this arrangement to be able to get Amber into school and to be able to provide medical care. Her reframing keeps alive the father she knows as helping people, as being supportive of her even if not approving.

When the younger Nancy's "fellah" was killed in an accident, Lonnie paid for the   30
funeral and helped Nancy get resettled. And Nancy, exactly as her father would have done, managed the pain and confusion by going to work. Employed as a receptionist at a psychiatric hospital, she was back at her job the next day. When a fellow employee, surprised that she was working so soon after the loss, asked what she was doing there, she replied, "To keep from going crazy. And if I do go crazy here you can just put me in one of the rooms down the hall." Work as therapy seemed to be an idea with genetic connections.

Lonnie doesn't like to talk about these times. It's as if he doesn't know how, that   31
there is no understandable face to put on it, no way to make anyone happy. It's not like what he could do at work.

There is less pain now, and there are fewer bills to pay. Lonnie wants to spend   32
time with Amber. And with the two Nancys. Be at home more. Lonnie is so social at work you might expect him in retirement to want to be around other people. He's a self-declared "people person," but that doesn't mean just being social: it means being

(continued)

(continued)

personal. Sociability covers much of the pain that comes from not being able to help, to make someone else happy. There's less of that now, so there isn't as much need for work as therapy.

33   When an early leave plan was offered by the grocery company in late 1986, Joe Cool could retire. He still worked the graveyard shift as a university police officer, but spent more time at home with Amber and Nancy, his wife of 41 years and a "right cute chick" he still likes to do things for.

34   On a recent Sunday, as Lonnie, Amber, and the two Nancys were strolling the local shopping mall, they were approached by a young mother. "Aren't you Joe Cool? I want you to say hello to my son."

Inquiring into the Essay

Once again, use the four methods of inquiry to investigate your thoughts and feelings about Akin's profile, "Learning About Work from Joe Cool."

1. Academic reviews of this essay suggest that this kind of scholarship offers us knowledge of subjects that traditional academic research does not. In your notebook, explore that idea. Take three minutes to make a fast list in response to this question: *What does knowing Joe Cool through this profile tell me about the nature of some workers and workplaces?*

2. Choose one or more of the segments in this essay—the sections separated by white space—and explain its purpose. What particular knowledge about workers or workplaces does the segment seem to offer? Why was it included?

3. Evaluate the effectiveness of "Joe Cool" as research. Do you agree that this kind of research—informal case studies that read like stories—make a valuable contribution to our knowledge of a subject? What are their strengths and weaknesses?

4. Reflect on what you would do if you were Gib Akin, the author of this story, charged with writing a profile of Joe Cool. What parts of the process would you enjoy? What parts would you find hard? As you consider writing your own profile of somebody, do you anticipate any personal challenges?

SEEING THE FORM

Roy Takeno Reading Paper in Front of Office by Ansel Adams

The photographer and the painter who are after a truthful portrait of someone confront the same problem as the writer: How can you possibly capture the complexity of a human being in a single image or on a few pages? The answer, of course, is that you can't. The best you can do is find, in the moment when you press the shutter release, a picture that says something more. A good photographic portrait, like a good written profile, reveals some aspect of who the subjects are, creates some particular impression, or, as in this photograph by Ansel Adams, uses the portrait to comment not just on the subject but a larger problem.

In 1943, Adams, best known for his landscape photographs, took more than 200 photographs at the Manzanar War Relocation Center in California, one of a number of internment camps created by the U.S. government to detain Japanese Americans during World War II. Look closely at Adams's picture of Roy Takeno. If this were a written profile about the man, what would be an idea around which the profile is organized?

Ansel Adams, *Roy Takeno Reading Paper in Front of Office*, 1943 (Library of Congress Prints and Photographs Division).

THE WRITING PROCESS

INQUIRY PROJECT: REPRESENTATIVE PROFILE

Write a 1,000- to 1,200-word profile of someone who strikes you as representative, in some ways, of a larger group. For example, write a profile of your neighbor, the Harley Davidson aficionado, because he seems typical, in some ways, of bikers. Profile a nurse because that's a profession you're interested in. Write about an African American student on your predominantly white campus to discover what of his or her experience might represent the experience of other minority students there. Your instructor may give you additional instructions.

Work toward a profile that has the following qualities:

- It is ultimately organized around ways your profile seems representative or typical of the larger group to which your subject belongs.
- The profile includes at least three anecdotes, or little stories, that help reveal this theme.
- You bring in the voice of your subject through selective quotations.
- The end of the essay circles back to the beginning.

PEARSON
mycomplab

For additional reading, writing, and research resources, go to www.mycomplab.com

---

Thinking About Subjects

Sometimes you don't choose the subject; he or she chooses you. That was frequently my experience when I researched my book on lobsters—as I traveled and talked to people about the subject I was researching, I found fascinating people whose experience, like Abby Boynton's, would powerfully reveal some aspect of lobstering that seemed important. One way to find suitable profile subjects, therefore, is simply to look for them in the course of doing your research. Who have you read or heard about or perhaps met who might provide a useful focus for a subject in which you're interested?

On the other hand, you might have an idea of who you'd like to profile now, someone you know or would like to know. But if you'd like to play around with some ideas, the following prompts should help. As always, keep generating ideas until you feel you have some potentially promising material.

Generating Ideas

Play with possible subjects, withholding judgment for the moment about what might be a good one. Again, as in the previous chapter, don't let your critical side stifle your creative side. At this point in the process, you can let yourself explore freely.

Listing Prompts. To select a topic within which you'd like to find someone to profile, try the following:

1. Make these lists in your journal, quickly generating each one in thirty seconds. Consider doing a profile of someone in one of the categories you generate.

    ■ List types of people—categories like "musicians" or "car mechanics"— that either interest you or with whom you have had contact.

    ■ Make a list of local issues, controversies, or problems that you feel something about.

    ■ Make a list of jobs that interest you.

2. Develop a "snapshot profile." Go to a public place—a café, the campus library, a fast-food restaurant—and observe people. Choose someone whom you can discreetly observe for at least ten minutes. Generate a list of observations of that person, double-entry style, in your notebook, using the left-facing page. Concentrate on particulars.

ONE STUDENT'S RESPONSE

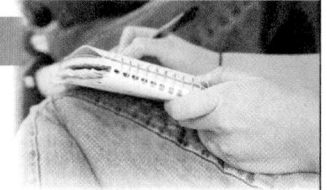

Jennifer's Journal

LIST OF OBSERVATIONS:
CELL PHONE SALESWOMAN

blonde and brown streaked hair	silver watch
straight to shoulders	"hey you" to girlfriend passing by
black cotton sweater	black nametag
low-cut green patterned blouse	Kimberly
long fingernails, painted white	eyebrows rise when smiles
pecks at computer keys carefully	"Get the only RAZR that's got it all"
cell phone to ear	looks into eyes of customer when talking
performs one-handed: writing form, pecking at computer, opening boxes	takes long strides when walking
	black pants
	black shoes, low heels

SNAPSHOT PROFILE
CELL PHONE SALESWOMAN

Kimberly does her job one-handed because the other hand is always holding a cell phone to her ear. Selling cell phones obviously means using cell phones while you sell them. She is young, perhaps 22, and has long nails that are carefully enameled in white. These present problems when she types on the computer, slowing down

(continued)

> **One Student's Response** (*continued*)
>
> her hunting and pecking considerably, a process that is performed, as always, with her right hand, since the left holds the cell phone to her ear. Kimberly works at a Verizon wireless counter that is a kind of island in the middle of the mall, and she moves effortlessly in the small square area behind the counter that she shares with two other salespeople. They share a private joke, and she smiles, and when she does one of her eyebrows lifts. This is not a freak accident. It happens again and again, and makes her seem skeptical. She unfolds a large brochure showing the company's national service area—accomplished once more single handedly—and points with a long white fingernail at something. The customer nods. Kimberly smiles, and the eyebrow lifts once again.

Fastwriting Prompts. Fastwriting is a great way to loosen up your creative side and at the same time generate raw material. Here are a few prompts to get you writing:

1. Choose the name of someone you know who you might want to profile. Use the "seed sentences" below to launch two separate fastwrites on your subject, each lasting at least three minutes (unless you can't stop writing).

   - When I first think of _____, I think of _____.
   - The one word I would use to describe _____ would be _____.
   - _____ had a strange habit.
   - Typically, _____ would _____.
   - _____ is best known for _____.
   - The one thing that most people fail to notice about _____ is _____.
   - When I first met _____, I noticed _____.
   - _____ said, "_____."

2. Review the data you collected for your "snapshot profile" under Listing Prompt 2, especially noting those that are suggestive in some way about your subject and how exactly you see her. On the right-facing page of your notebook, compose a fast paragraph that uses the best evidence you collected, all working toward some dominant impression or idea about your subject that you'd like to communicate to a reader. Use this material as the basis for a short vignette.

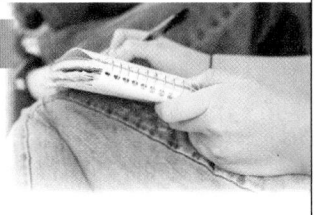

Javier's Fastwriting

When I think of my roommate, Ciaran Brenan, I think of his drums among other things. He's always playing the drums and I enjoy it because I really like music; although sometimes, it's annoying when I'm trying to study. The one word I would use to describe him is charismatic. When we go out, he always has this energy and he's always cracking jokes that make everybody laugh.

When I first met Ciaran, the first thing that came to my mind was "this guy is nuts" as I saw him with his mohawk and all the accessories he was wearing that day. When I moved into the apartment, I can tell you that I wasn't that wrong after getting to know him for a month. He's the type of guy that doesn't worry too much about things. He really takes it easy and goes with the flow.

Visual Prompts. Maps, clusters, lines and arrows, charts, and even sketches can help us piece together subjects in ways that writing sometimes cannot. Consider the following options:

1. Put the name of a possible profile subject in the center of a cluster. Build a web of associations for five minutes, and then begin fastwriting when you feel the urge.

2. Go through old photographs for ideas about profile subjects; this might be especially useful for reminding yourself of family and friends who might be good subjects.

Research Prompts. It is impossible to write a profile without conducting research of some sort, if not in the library or online, then in the field with one's subject. Doing some research up front, then, can be a useful way to find a subject to write about.

1. Return to the list you generated earlier in the "Listing Prompts" section. Choose a controversy in the community or on campus as the focus for your profile. Check the community and campus newspapers to discover who has been active as an advocate on the issue, or who has been impacted by it. Is any one person suitable for a profile?

2. Discuss your topic with your friends or people in your class. Who do they know who would be good as a profile subject?

3. On the Internet, search the archives of the local newspaper to find the names of potential profile subjects on an issue or controversy in which you're interested.

4. If you have a career interest, a profile of a working member of the profession can be compelling. Call the state professional association for suggestions about how to find an interview subject, or ask friends and family for suggestions.

Judging What You Have

You should have a considerable body of material to work with. It may not be coherent at this point, but again it's always better to work from abundance than from scarcity.

What's Promising Material and What Isn't? Let's look critically at the material you've generated. How will you choose the best profile subject? Consider the following criteria:

- *Accessibility.* The greatest subject in the world is no good to you if he or she is inaccessible.

- *Background.* Lacking time to spend with an interview subject, writers often look for information that may already exist: perhaps an article or two, a diary, a cigar box full of old pictures. Might you have access to such information on a possible subject?

- *Typicality.* Is the subject representative in some way of an aspect of a topic you'd like to investigate?

- *Extremity.* On the other hand, you may look for a subject who represents not the norm in a category of experience but an extreme.

- *Spontaneity.* Less experienced subjects, the kind you are most likely to profile, often have appeal because they *aren't* practiced at talking about themselves. There's freshness and even naiveté sometimes about what they say and how they say it that makes profiles particularly compelling.

- *Quotability.* Sometimes you simply can't know how quotable a subject might be until the interview. But if you do know beforehand that someone speaks in an interesting way, you may have a great profile subject.

- *Willingness.* I put this last for a reason. Most of us assume that people resist the kind of interviews a profile demands. A few profile subjects may, at first, resist the *idea* of being interviewed, but in reality people simply love to talk about themselves. An interview gives a subject a willing listener; how often do we enjoy the undivided attention of someone who is vitally interested in what we have to say about ourselves?

Questions About Audience and Purpose. As always, profile writing begins with a personal motivation. Is there something you think you can learn from your subject, perhaps something about an aspect of the world you are interested in, or something about the human spirit? By interviewing someone else is it possible to even learn something about yourself? You might also begin with a simpler, less grand, but no less important motive: Is there something this subject knows or feels that should be documented and preserved?

> The profile can, like good fiction, provide insight into the complexities of the human mind and soul.

As you evaluate the material you've generated, consider some of the following purposes that transcend your personal ones.

- *Which possible profile subject best fits the details of the assignment?* Your instructor may have provided guidance on how to approach the profile, including suggestions about choices of a profile subject or things to consider about audience. Which subject seems to best fit these guidelines?

- *Does this profile subject help illuminate an idea, issue, or controversy that might interest some of your readers?* The historical profile earlier in this chapter of "Alfalfa Bill," governor of Oklahoma during the Dust Bowl, is a small window through which readers can see the causes of environmental devastation. When given a face, a larger issue has a focus.

- *Does a profile subject represent a "type" of person that might interest readers?* Perhaps you're interested in the culture of sorority life on your campus and you have a willing subject who has belonged to Kappa Kappa Gamma for the last three years. Or perhaps you want to become a registered labor and delivery nurse. A profile of a working obstetric nurse will not only teach you something about your career choice but convince others that such a job is interesting, demanding, or not for them.

- *Is the profile subject an interesting character?* What often makes profile subjects interesting is that they shatter our assumptions about people and how they are in the world—a ninety-year-old man who still hikes fourteen-thousand-foot peaks, a fourteen-year-old college student, a therapist with marital problems, a lesbian activist in rural Mississippi, the president of an antifraternity fraternity. We are all composed of contradictions like these, but some are more surprising than others.

- *Who is your audience?* A key factor in any writing situation is audience. Who are you writing for in this assignment and which possible profile subjects would that audience find most compelling?

Interviewing

His interview subjects sometimes see John McPhee, one of the great profile writers, as "thick-witted." At times McPhee seems to ask the same questions over and over, and he frequently seems to possess only the most basic information about his subjects. According to William Howarth, when McPhee "conducts an interview he tries to be as blank as his notebook pages, totally devoid of preconceptions." His theory is that unless his interview subjects "feel superior or equal to their interviewer" they won't talk as freely or at length. McPhee never uses a tape recorder, but jots down spare notes in a notebook—these are the telling details and facts that reveal his subject's character.

McPhee is what some have called an *immersion journalist,* someone who spends substantial time with his subjects, getting to know them more intimately. This is the best basis for writing a profile because it generates enough information to get closer to the truth about the subject.

The following tips on researching techniques should help you start developing a plan for your interviews.

Making Contact. I'm a fairly shy guy. In fact, when I began writing nonfiction articles many years ago, the worst part of the work was calling people to ask for their time to do an interview. These conversations almost always ended well for a simple reason—people love to talk about themselves. That's hardly surprising.

Asking a family member or friend to be an interview subject is easy, but how do you ask a stranger? You start by introducing yourself and straightforwardly describing the profile assignment, including your feeling that the subject would be a great focus for your piece. You must be prepared to answer the almost inevitable follow-up question: "Well, gee, I'm flattered. But what is it about me that you find interesting?" Here's where McPhee's elementary knowledge is crucial: Although you need to know only a very little about your interview subject, you must know enough to say, for instance, that you're aware of his role in a bit of history or his involvement in a local issue, or recognize him as being knowledgeable about a topic you find of interest.

What you want from this initial contact is time. The conventional interview—when you sit across from your informant asking questions and writing down answers—can be very useful, but it may be more productive if you can spend time *doing* something with your profile subject that relates to the reason you've chosen him. For example, if you are profiling a conservative activist, spend an hour watching him work the telephone, lining up people for the meeting at city hall. Your interview with a homeless woman could take place during lunch at the local shelter. *Seeing* your subject in a meaningful situation can generate far more information than the conventional interview. Imagine what those situations might be.

What do you do if your subject doesn't want to be interviewed? In that unlikely event, you're permitted to ask why. If your reassurances aren't sufficient to change the person's mind, then you need to find another subject.

WRITING IN YOUR LIFE

Digital Profiles

Susan is a graduate student of mine who is working on a memoir about growing up on a farm in the desolate desert country of southern Idaho. Though her plan is to publish her book, Susan's project is typical of the kind of family history projects that have inspired millions to unravel genealogies, interview aging grandparents, and revisit the places where family roots run deep.

Interviews with living family members can become compelling profiles; they are characters in a longer story we can discover about ourselves. For example, Susan's Uncle Al, her father's brother, was not only an invaluable source of information; he became a memorable presence in her story and a richer portrait than any photograph or painting could be.

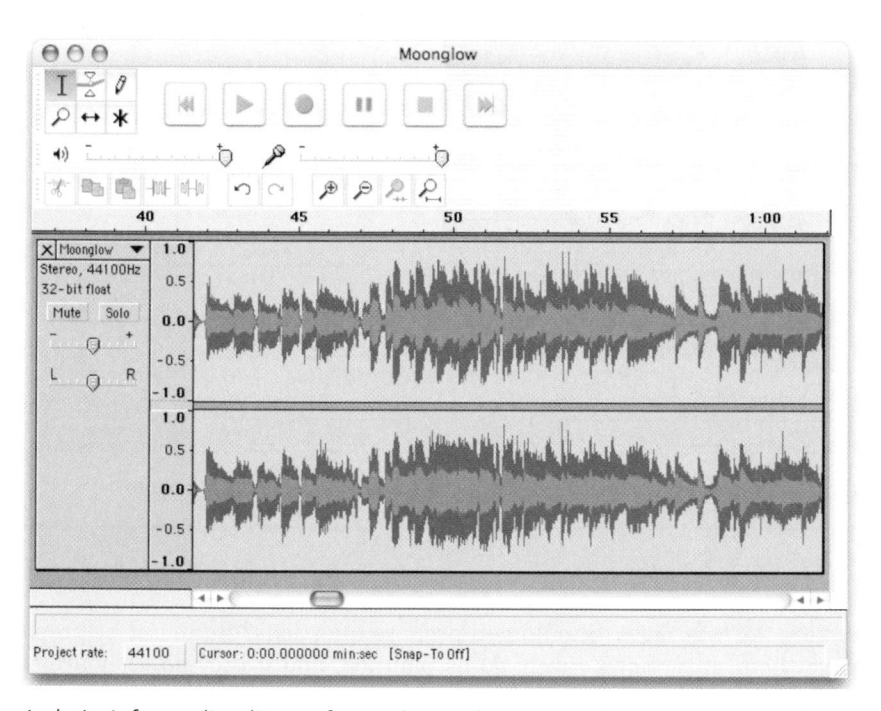

Audacity is free audio editing software that can be used to edit interviews for profiles.

There are many genealogical resources online (just try Googling "researching family history") but the audio recordings you make of your living family members create profiles that likely wouldn't exist unless you took the time to do them. It's

(continued)

Writing in Your Life (*continued*)

easier than ever. Digital recording, which has largely replaced tape, is easily edited on your computer using free audio editing software like Audacity. You can trim and move audio clips from your interview into a more coherent profile, and even add voice-overs or music. Your audio files can be easily converted to MP3 format, which can be played on MP3 players and computers and sent to your relatives in Kansas. These family profiles can also be combined with visuals using a program like Microsoft's Photo Story, another free download, and you can tell an even more powerful story about someone who matters in your family.

Microsoft Photo Story, a free download, can be used to tell a story with photos.

Conducting the Interview. Should you prepare questions? Sure, but be prepared to ignore them. Interviews rarely go as planned, and if they do, they are often disappointing. An interview is a *conversation,* and these are best when they head in unexpected directions.

Certain generic questions can reveal things about a subject's character. These are *open-ended questions* that often lead in surprising and interesting directions. Some of these open-ended questions include the following:

- In all your experience with _____, what has most surprised you?
- What has been the most difficult aspect of your work?

- If you had the chance to change something about how you approached _____, what would it be?

- Can you remember a significant moment in your work on _____? Is there an experience with _____ that stands out in your mind?

- What do you think is the most common misconception about _____? Why?

- What are significant trends in _____?

- Who or what has most influenced you? Who are your heroes?

- If you had to summarize the most important thing you've learned about _____, what would you say? What is the most important thing that people should know or understand?

Notetaking during an interview is a challenge. A popular method is to use a tape or digital recorder (see "Inquiring into the Details: Recording Interviews"), but even if you do it's essential to take handwritten notes as well. Jot down any facts, details, phrases, mannerisms, or even personal reactions you have during the interview.

INQUIRING INTO THE DETAILS

Recording Interviews

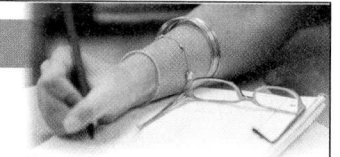

Digital recorders have made tape recorders obsolete. This is good. For one thing, it's much easier to manage and edit digital files, and "running out of tape" in the middle of an interview is not a problem. The hard drives on digital recorders hold a lot of interviews.

Here are some tips on recording your interviews digitally:

- ***You can use your MP3 player.*** If you have the music player—and don't have a digital recorder—then you can buy an adapter that turns your MP3 player into a digital recorder. It's cheap, too. One manufacturer sells the adapter for less than $20.

- ***You can record phone conversations.*** A $20 adapter will also allow you to record phone conversations, but legally you must ask your subject's permission to do so. Covert recordings are very uncool. You can also use Skype to record phone conversations.

- ***You can use software to transcribe recordings.*** Several free programs (e.g., www.transana.org and www.trans.sourceforge.net) available online, for example, will help you control the playback speed so you can more easily type what you're hearing and will allow you to label and reorganize interview clips.

- ***Take notes.*** A combination of old (well, really old) technology, like handwritten notes, with the new technology, like digital recording, makes it more likely that your interview will yield the best material. Your notes—even if sketchy—provide an outline of what you've recorded and help you to find that great quote or essential piece of information more easily.

While my students have used the double-entry journal effectively as a note-taking format for profiles, putting the observed information and quotations on the left page and personal responses on the right, I'm keen on those pocket-sized memo books. They're incredibly unobtrusive and easy to carry, and they force you to be spare. I especially like the ease with which I can take the memo book out and put it away, at times using it to signal to my subject that I'm more—or less—interested in something he's saying.

Listening and Watching. The art of interviewing relies, more than anything else, on the craft of listening. Few of us are good listeners, which is why profile writing can be so hard. First you must control your anxiety about getting things down, asking the next question, and making your subject relaxed.

What makes a good conversation? When it generates the kind of information that will help you write the profile, including the following:

- *Stories.* Interesting stories and anecdotes help you build a narrative backbone to your essay.

- *Memorable quotations.* A typical interview produces only a handful of these, so don't desperately write down everything a subject says. Wait until you hear something that is nicely put or distinctive, particularly quotes that reveal something about your subject's character.

- *Background information.* This can be in the form of stories, but might also be basic but essential information such as your subject's age, place of birth, and history of involvement in relevant jobs or issues.

- *Feeling.* A good conversation is an honest one in which the subject is willing to let the mask slip to reveal the face sweating underneath. Be alert to those moments of feeling when your subject seems to be revealing herself—what *really* matters to her, what might be hard, where she finds joy.

■ INTERVIEW NOTES

Below are interview notes that Javier Carvajal took in preparation for writing the profile "The Rhythm of a Musician" that appears at the end of this chapter.

Interview Notes:
"The Rhythm of a Musician:

Javier Carvajal

In all your experience with music, what has most surprised you?

Who's good and who's not. Sometimes you see someone and you don't think he's good, but then, he plays and you realize he's really good. You always learn something from somebody no matter how good you are.

What has been the most difficult aspect of your work as a musician?

Absolutely finding work. You really have to try hard to find places to work. It can be very frustrating as you have to negotiate with club owners and you have to make sure you are not being taken advantage of.

If you had the chance to change something about how you approached music, what would it be?

I wouldn't change anything. The only thing is that I'd like to not make it my living. I could just make it for fun if I had an unlimited supply of money because making it a job takes the fun out of it, and the reason I do music is because I love it.

Can you remember a significant moment while becoming a musician?

It was the first time I'd been to this place called Kaya's Kitchen, which is a vegetarian restaurant. Every night they have music, and on Saturdays, they have open mic nights. It was really crowded—maybe 50 or 60 people. When we started playing a song, literally every single person was on his/her feet dancing. It was awesome to know that I was the reason that people were having a good time.

Is there any artist that you admire that stands out in your mind?

I met Stanton Moore a month ago. He was stoned. I thought he was funny.

What do you think is the most common misconception about music and why?

When people think about musicians, they think of rock stars like Bon Jovi, but it's not like that at all. It's hard to be a musician. It's not just partying and rock and roll.

Who or what has most influenced you?

Every single piece of music has influenced me. Part of my music is taking all of what I've heard and making my own sound with it.

If you had to summarize the most important thing you've learned about music, what would you say?

Music isn't just about talent and it isn't about getting famous. When you pick a career, you should do something that you love and music is probably the best example of that. The reason I do music is because music is probably the thing that I care about most out of anything on Earth.

Writing the Sketch

When you think you've collected enough information about your profile subject from interviews, observations, and background research, compose a 500-word typewritten sketch. The sketch is a brief treatment of a promising subject that may lack a clear sense of purpose but does not lack specific information. For your profile sketch, your instructor will tell you which of the following elements you should incorporate:

- At least two potentially revealing anecdotes or brief stories about your profile subject.
- At least two strong quotations from your subject.
- A title.
- A paragraph of background information, including your informant's age, a physical description, and perhaps relevant job or personal history.
- A strong lead (perhaps one of the anecdotes) and an ending that somehow returns to the beginning.

Sketch:
"At the Sound of the Drumset"
Javier Carvajal

At eight forty-four in the morning, the alarm next door goes off. WWOZ is blasting some kind of music we don't have in Venezuela, and Ciaran Brennan rolls out of bed. He throws some clothes on, groggily stumbles past his drum set, grabs his skateboard, and heads off to music theory class. When he gets back from class, however, after the endless world of music has woken him, Ciaran is much more awake. He heads straight to his set, closes the door, and begins to practice. I can hear the ring-ping-tang of the cymbals and the rat-a-tat of the snare drum. I unconsciously find myself bobbing my head to the beat.

Ciaran Patrick Brennan is my roommate. And he is not like anyone else I've met before. He's got a loud, charismatic personality, and a very strange sense of humor. He has an instantly recognizable laugh that ranges in pitch from deep-belly to high-pitched-little-girl. His favorite saying is "Hell yeah, Homeboy!" which he yells at me all of the time. He is a hard partier and a heavy drinker, and I often come home to find him stupidly drunk. But behind his impulsive exterior is an intelligent, musical mind with a passion for what it knows best.

One casualty of being a foreign student is that I need to study much harder than other students, and unfortunately, I have to ask Ciaran to do something that is very hard for him to do: stop playing for a little while. When I walk in, I look at him. He doesn't notice me because his eyes are closed, and he is feeling the music in his own world. He briefly opens his eyes and is surprised to see me. "Oh. What's good, Javier?" he asks. I look at him for a second. He is eighteen years old, light-skinned, and average-sized, edging toward smallish. He has a drummer's forearms and a wide smile. He is clean-shaven with buzzed dark-brown hair, a nose that looks as if it has been broken one too many times, and grey-blue eyes with a ring of gold around the pupil. He already knows what I'm going to ask him to do, and I can see his face fall.

When I mentioned the typical rock star stereotype that most people have in their heads when they think about musicians, he shot me down: "When everyone thinks of musicians, they think about rock stars like Bon Jovi or the Beatles. It's not like that at all. It's hard to be a musician. The hardest thing is actually finding work. You really have to try hard to find places to play, and at every club, there's a manager or club owner trying to short your pay, and you have to negotiate." "Most places," he says, "just throw your CD out when you go in to get a job. You've got to work at it."

Moving from Sketch to Draft

A sketch is generally underdeveloped, sometimes giving the writer just the barest outline of his subject. But as an early draft, a sketch can be invaluable. It might hint at what the "real" subject is, or what questions seem to be behind your inquiry into the subject. A sketch might suggest a focus for the next draft, or simply a better lead. Here are some tips for finding clues in your sketch about directions you might go in the next draft.

Evaluating Your Own Sketch. You must begin evaluating your sketch with more reasonable ambitions. It *is* impossible to capture the whole person, but what you are working toward in your profile is to capture an *aspect* of that person, some particular quality that stands out. Read your sketch, paying attention to one or both of those purposes:

1. *Dominant impression.* What feeling or personality trait do I want to communicate about my profile subject? Can I name it? Is there evidence in the sketch that points to this?
2. *Role.* What exactly am I trying to show—or might I show in the next draft—about my subject's participation in an idea, an issue, or an event?

Questions for Peer Review. Peer review of sketches can help writers clarify purpose. You've already done some thinking about that; now ask readers for help. You might pose the following questions:

- If you were to use one word to describe your main impression of the person I profiled, what would it be?
- What evidence would you point to in the sketch that contributes to that impression?
- Did you find my portrait sympathetic or critical?
- In a sentence, what seems to be my subject's main point of view, attitude, or belief?
- What one detail—a fact, observation, description, or quotation—struck you as most revealing? What did it reveal?
- What would you like to know more about in the next draft?
- After reading the draft, what did you come to understand about the type of person profiled that you didn't know when you began the draft?

Reflecting on What You've Learned. Before you begin composing the next draft, make a journal entry that explores your thinking about the sketch and everything you heard. Begin an entry with the prompt, Based on what I've learned so far about my profile subject, the main thing I seem to be trying to show is _____.

Follow this prompt, continuing to reflect on what your intentions might be in the next draft. When the writing stalls, skip a line and make a quick list: The three things I heard during peer review that I want to remember are: (1) _____; (2) _____; and (3) _____.

Research and Other Strategies: Gathering More Information

If you emerged from the experience of writing and sharing your sketch with a stronger sense of purpose, then you're close to being ready to draft. If you didn't, return to your notes or share your sketch with a few more readers. In either case, you'll probably need to collect more information before you begin the draft. Most important, plan another interview with your subject. This one will likely be quite different; now that you have a clearer purpose for your profile, your questions will be directed at getting the information you need to more fully develop your piece.

You might consider other sources of information as well:

- Interview people who know your profile subject.
- If your subject is a public figure, do library or Web research for background.

- Do background research on your profile subject. Find out more about what she does or where she does it. Find out how she fits into a larger context. If you're writing about a nurse-midwife, find out how many are working in the state and what their licensing requirements might be.

The quotes and information you gather can be used in your profile, usually with attribution. Research the idea, issue, or event, if any, that provides the context for your profile.

Composing the Draft

If you haven't collected enough information, you'll run aground pretty quickly in the draft.

If you're confident that you're working from abundance, consider beginning the drafting process by writing multiple leads. For example, work toward three one-paragraph beginnings—perhaps each focused on a different anecdote—and decide which one seems to point the draft in the direction you want it to go and is most likely to capture your

WRITING IN THE DISCIPLINES

Giving History a Face and a Voice

Historians profile people all the time, from vignettes of individuals in larger narratives (see "Alfalfa Bill" on page 124) to book-length biographies. Much of this work relies on so-called "primary sources"—original materials from sources who were first-hand witnesses or that come from a profile subject's own mouth and hand. Examples include letters, newspaper accounts, journals, transcripts, and oral histories. Libraries often archive this material. The Library of Congress (loc.gov) may be one of the richest sources of primary documents on a wide range of topics, and increasingly these are available online. You can find digital copies of historic photographs, letters written by famous (and ordinary) people, recorded interviews, oral histories, and original documents. This is interesting stuff. For example, you can hear the voices of individuals who suffered through the depression, endured slavery, fought in World War I, witnessed the 9/11 attacks, or pioneered the blues. These materials can bring any historical research project to life by providing profiles of the people who were there when it happened.

readers. Once you've chosen a lead, follow it. You'll likely find that the leads you didn't use find a place for themselves somewhere else in the draft.

Methods of Development. You can pursue various strategies to develop your profile.

Narrative. The profile form often relies on narrative. It can do this in several ways; perhaps the most familiar is that the piece tells the story of the writer's encounter with her subject. For example, the profile of Albert Yeganeh (see p. 121), the "soup Nazi," is organized around the writer's visit one day to Yeganeh's Soup restaurant. The account includes the writer's reactions to what he was saying and doing. Profile writers are often drawn to the first-person account—my day with my subject—which is obviously a convenient structure if that matches the experience of the interviewer. However, consider whether a first-person point of view interrupts the narrative too much and interferes with the reader's view of the profile subject. After all, the writer isn't the subject of the profile.

Known to Unknown. If your profile subject is a public figure and your motive is to reveal a less well-known aspect of your subject's life or work, beginning the essay with information that first seems to confirm public perceptions but then promises to challenge them—in other words, moving from what's known to what's less known—can be an effective way to structure the profile. This method of development is quite common for celebrity profiles.

Using Evidence. The most authoritative information in a profile is the voice of your subject. It is also the information that will be most heavily scrutinized by the subject herself: "Did I really say that?" Readers of the profile often believe that the subject's voice is the most authentic information because it is less mediated by the writer, an assumption that isn't always accurate. After all, unless quotations come directly from the tape recorder, interviewers must rely on their notetaking skill. Even with a recorded transcription, writers commonly tidy up bad grammar and remove irrelevant utterances such as "uh" and "um."

A profile writer must also establish his authority by giving readers a sense that he is a keen and careful observer; he does so by carefully using not just quotation but detail, description, and research. Consider how the author of "Soup" did this when profiling restaurant owner Albert Yeganeh.

Workshopping the Draft

If your draft is subject to peer review (see Chapter 10 for details on how to organize workshop groups), think carefully about the kind of responses you need from readers at this point in the process. The following questions might help you prepare.

Reflecting on the Draft. As you prepare your draft for peer review, think about what you most need in a response. Are you reasonably confident that the purpose and focus of your profile is clear? Or are you feeling anxious about how well you managed to pull it all together? Your initial feelings about the draft will be a factor in the kind of response you request from your group.

- Make a journal entry in which you reflect in a five-minute fastwrite about how you feel about the draft. What worked? What needs work?
- If the writing stalls, consider this question: *If I could change the process of writing this draft, from initially generating a subject to write about to this first draft, what would I change?* Follow this with a fastwrite until you have nothing more to say.

Questions for Readers. As you prepare for peer review, certain questions are also particularly useful to consider when drafting profiles. Pose to your group any of these questions that seem relevant to your draft or possible plans for revision.

1.   What dominant impression did the draft create of its subject? What words would you use to describe that impression?

2.   In a sentence or two, what does the draft seem to be *saying* about its subject?

3.   Does the end strain to return to the beginning, or does it give the profile a sense of wholeness or unity?

4.   What is the strongest/weakest quote? What is the strongest/weakest anecdote?

5.   What do you want to know about the profile subject that the draft doesn't say?

6.   Did you find this person interesting? Why or why not?

7.   Did you learn anything about this type of person?

Revising the Draft

Revision is a continual process, not a last step. You've been revising—literally "re-seeing" your subject—from the first messy fastwriting in your journal. But the things that get your attention during revision vary depending on where you are in the writing process. You've generated material, chosen a topic, done some research, and written both a sketch and draft. Most students think that the only thing left to do is "fix things." Check for misspellings. Correct an awkward sentence or two. Come up with a better title. This is editing, not revision, and while editing is important, to focus solely on smaller "fixes" after writing a first draft squanders an opportunity to really *learn* from what the draft is telling you, or perhaps not quite telling you.

Chapter 9 can help guide these discoveries. The questions you can ask about a draft fall into five categories: purpose, idea, information, development, and editing. Use the following chart to find the revision strategies in Chapter 9 that might help you re-see what you've written so far.

Profiles typically have some of the following problems, most of which can be addressed by selecting appropriate revision strategies, or by repeating some of the earlier steps in this chapter.

- The draft lacks a single coherent theme, or dominant impression. Is your profile organized from beginning to end around one main thing you're trying to say about your subject?

- The theme or dominant impression is obvious but isn't developed with enough specific information. Do you need to do another interview?

- You find your subject interesting, but you haven't given your readers enough reason to agree. Does your lead make a strong enough case? Is there another story you should tell?

GUIDE TO REVISION STRATEGIES

Problems in the Draft (Chapter 9)	Page Number
Unclear purpose ■ Not sure what the essay is about? Fails to answer the *So what?* question?	327
Unclear thesis, theme, or main idea ■ Not sure what you're trying to say?	333
Lack of information or development ■ Needs more details; more showing and less telling?	340
Disorganized ■ Doesn't move logically or smoothly from paragraph to paragraph?	344
Unclear or awkward at the level of sentences and paragraphs ■ Seems choppy or hard to follow at the level of sentences or paragraphs?	353

Polishing the Draft. After you've dealt with the big issues in your draft—is it sufficiently focused, does it answer the *So what?* question, is it organized, and so on—you must deal with the smaller problems. You've carved the stone into an appealing figure, but now you need to polish it. Are your paragraphs coherent? How do you manage transitions? Are your sentences fluent and concise? Are there any errors in spelling or syntax?

Before you finish your draft, work through the following checklist:

✓ Every paragraph is about one thing.

✓ The transitions between paragraphs aren't abrupt.

✓ The length of sentences varies in each paragraph.

✓ Each sentence is concise. There are no unnecessary words or phrases.

✓ You've checked grammar, particularly verb agreement, run-on sentences, unclear pronouns, and misused words (*there / their, where / were,* and so on). (See the handbook at the end of the book for help with these grammar issues.)

✓ You've run your spellchecker and proofed your paper for misspelled words.

■ **STUDENT ESSAY**

The Rhythm of a Musician

Javier E. Carvajal

At eight forty-four in the morning, the alarm next door goes off. WWOZ is blasting some kind of music we don't have in Venezuela, and Ciaran Brennan rolls out of bed. He throws some clothes on, groggily stumbles past his drumset, grabs his skateboard, and heads off to music theory class. When he gets back from class, he submerges himself into the world of music. He heads straight to his set, closes the door, and begins to practice. I can hear the ring-ping-tang of the cymbals and the ratatat of the snare drum. I find myself unconsciously bobbing my head to the beat.

Ciaran Patrick Brennan is my roommate. He is not like anyone else I have met before. He has a loud, charismatic type of personality and a very strange sense of humor. He has an instantly recognizable laugh, which ranges in pitch from a deep-belly to the high-pitched laugh of a little girl. His favorite saying is "Hell yeah, homeboy!" which he yells at me all of the time. He is a hard partier and a heavy drinker, and I often come home to find him stupidly drunk. The first week he arrived here, he talked our other two roommates into donning Mohawk style haircuts. He has a collection of stolen traffic cones. He has broken the blinds on the window, put holes in the walls, and smashed numerous bottles. But behind his impulsive actions is an intelligent musical mind with a great passion for playing the drums.

Unfortunately, I have to ask this passionate musician to do something extremely difficult. Since one of the casualties of being a foreign student is that I have to study much harder than my peers, I have to ask Ciaran to stop playing for a while. When I walk in, I look at him. He doesn't notice me because his eyes are closed, and he is in his own world, feeling the music. He opens his eyes briefly and is surprised to see me. "Oh, what's good Javier?" he asks. I look at him for a second. He is eighteen years old, light-skinned and average-sized, edging towards smallish, with a drummer's forearms and a wide smile. He is clean shaven with buzzed dark-brown hair (he recently shaved off his Mohawk), a nose that looks like it has been broken one too many times, and grey-blue-ringed-with-gold eyes. He already knows what I'm going to ask him to do, and I can see his face fall as he puts down his drumsticks.

Later, when I am done studying, I put my books away. I go to Ciaran's room, and I ask him about his musical background. He started playing the drums when he was eleven, but was raised with music from a much younger age. His father is a music teacher in Belmar, New Jersey, his hometown, and his father's profession influenced Ciaran since birth. He banged on pots and pans and sang with his dad when he was a toddler, started taking piano lessons when he was an adolescent, and moved onto the drumset once he hit the double digits. He joined a band that, unlike most other bands their age, played blues, funk, and

(continued)

(continued)

jazz music. Since the age of fourteen, he has had the dream of coming to New Orleans to get involved in the rich jazz environment. He knows that is difficult; it is not easy to hit the big time. However, he is unique, talented, and equipped with the skills needed to succeed.

He does not want to fit the mold in anything that he does. In fact, he gets defensive when I mention the typical "rock-star" stereotype: "Everyone thinks . . . when they think of musicians . . . they think about rock-stars like Bon Jovi or the Beatles or something like that. It's not like that at all. It's hard to be a musician." I could tell, from the way his normally cheerful demeanor changes to a more serious one, that he has gained this knowledge from experience. "The hardest thing about it is actually finding work. You really have to try hard to find places to play, and at every club there's a manager or club owner trying to short you in pay, and you always have to negotiate. Most places," he says, "just throw your CD out when you go in and try and get a job. You've got to work at it." Despite all the barriers and difficulties Ciaran has to deal with, he is determined to go for it because the music runs through his veins.

Ciaran's love for music is clear, regardless of the difficulty involved in actually being a musician. His passion for funk and jazz musicians is remarkable. "I met Stanton Moore a month ago," he tells me. Stanton Moore is a local drummer, and one of Ciaran's drum idols. "Moore's got this awesome old-school funky style based in New Orleans rhythm and blues, but he throws in a bunch of modern jazz fills and stuff. He's also got great timing and an awesome feel. When you listen to Stanton Moore, you groove." Every single piece of music he listens to influences him—"Part of music is taking all of what you've heard and making what you will out of it."

All of a sudden, as if prompted by thinking of Stanton Moore, a big smile crosses Ciaran's face, and he asks me, "Do you want to hear a story?" and without waiting for me to answer, he starts telling me about the first time he performed with his band. "So, this one time, me and the band I was in back in New Jersey were playing an open mike night at this vegetarian restaurant called Kaya's Kitchen, which was run by hippies." He stops for a second, goes to the fridge and grabs an Abita beer. "I remember I was seventeen years old, yeah, and we went on at about midnight. We were jamming, and as we kept on playing, more and more people were showing up and getting into it, and all of a sudden this place was standing room only. And then we broke into this second-line kind of jam, and everyone in the entire place is up and dancing. Every face had a smile on it. Every pair of feet was moving. It was like nothing I've ever felt before. It was so surreal, I knew me and my music, us and our music, was the reason for these people's happiness. That's what music is about." As he is talking to me, I could picture myself in the place and feel the energy of the crowd as he describes it.

I begin to smile, and he continues, "Making people happy is what it's all about. It's never about making money. Yeah, you've got to turn it into a job, but if you don't love it, get a new profession. If you can't imagine yourself doing anything but music, then you know you're doing the right thing. I do it because I love it. The music moves me." From the look in his eyes, the smile on his face, and the passion I see when I watch him play his drumset, I can see how much Ciaran means what he is saying to me.

After hearing those words, I feel terrible every time I ask Ciaran to stop playing. Watching him pursuing his dreams so passionately inspires me to pursue mine. I've got to work hard if I want to be successful in America. And therefore, I need peace and quiet. So I ask him, "Sorry man, I need to study, could you stop playing?" He grins, and says, "Sure man. Asshole."

USING WHAT YOU HAVE LEARNED

You've read published profiles and one written by a student. You've also had the chance to write your own. What have you learned about the profile genre of writing and how might you use this in other writing situations?

1. What are the ethical obligations of writers to their profile subjects? For example, do you think it should be standard practice for subjects to approve profiles before they're published? What is reasonable for a profile subject to expect from a writer?

2. While a profile isn't an academic form, can you imagine how you might use some of the methods and approaches you tried here in papers for other classes?

3. A profile of one person who is representative of a larger social group is decidedly unscientific. It just isn't possible to make scientifically reliable generalizations about the group from a single case. Then what good is a profile?

Reviewer Mark Kermode describes Johnny Depp as a "brilliantly physical performer" capable of "finely honed movements," yet regards his work as Captain Jack Sparrow in *Pirates of the Caribbean: Dead Man's Chest* as some of his "very worst work to date."

WRITING A REVIEW

WRITING THAT EVALUATES

One of the occasions when I feel fairly stupid is after watching a movie with my wife, Karen. She always wants to know what I think. I don't have much of a problem arriving at a gut reaction—I loved the movie *Amelie,* for example, but I have a hard time saying why. Beyond statements such as, "It was pretty good," or "It was pure Hollywood," a comment I mean to be critical, the conversation scares me a little because Karen is wonderfully analytical and articulate when describing her feelings about a film. In comparison, I stutter and stammer and do my best to go beyond a simple judgment.

Essentially, Karen is asking me to evaluate a film, to make a judgment about its quality. This is something we do all the time. Buying a pair of jeans involves evaluating the reputation of the manufacturer, the quality of the denim and its particular design, and especially aesthetic judgments about how the jeans look on us when we wear them. I think most of us like to think these decisions are quite rational. On the contrary, many of our evaluations are more emotional than logical. We *really do* buy that pair of jeans because an ad suggests that we'll look sexy or attractive in them. Or consider this: How would you evaluate the quality of your mother's or father's parenting? Will this be a rational judgment? It's unlikely. Even though we're qualified to make such a judgment—after all, who is a better authority on the parenting skills of parents than their children—our views toward our parents are always awash in feelings.

You know, then, that part of the challenge of evaluating something is keeping an open mind, sometimes *despite* our initial feelings about it. Because all evaluation stems from what are essentially subjective value judgments, a tension

> ### What You'll Learn in This Chapter
> - The role of evaluation in a review.
> - How feelings and reason can form the basis of evaluation.
> - How to develop criteria for making judgments.
> - Questions that will help you revise a review.

always exists between our *desire* to prove our point and our *need* or *willingness* to learn more about the subject.

That emotion figures into our judgments of things isn't a bad thing. It's a human thing. But one of the reasons it's useful to consciously consider *how* we make such judgments is that we're more likely to introduce logical considerations in mostly emotional evaluations, or emotional considerations in mostly logical ones. This awareness also helps us suspend judgment long enough to get a more balanced look at something.

Evaluation involves three things:

1. *Judgment.* Something is good or bad, useful or not useful, relevant or not relevant, convincing or not convincing, worth doing or not worth doing, or perhaps shades in between.

2. *Criteria.* These form the basis by which we judge whether something is good or bad, useful or not useful, and so on. Often our criteria are implicit; that is, we aren't even consciously aware of the criteria that inform judgments. The more familiar we are with the thing—say, cars, movies, or mystery novels—the more elaborate and sophisticated the criteria become.

3. *Evidence.* Criteria provide the principles for making a judgment, but evidence—specific details, observations, or facts about the thing itself—is what makes an evaluation persuasive.

If this sounds a lot like making an argument, you're right, because evaluation is the basis of argument. But I suspect that emotion, at least initially, figures more in our judgments of things than our reasoned arguments about them. In fact, evaluation can be a way of seeding the field of argument because it helps you identify the things about which you have strong opinions.

MOTIVES FOR WRITING A REVIEW

Evaluative writing is one of the most common kinds of writing I do, from commenting on student papers, to writing reference letters for former students, to writing a memo to my colleagues about a proposed departmental policy. Evaluative writing is an enormously practical form, relevant in all sorts of situations in and out of school. Quite simply, we turn to it when we are asked to make a judgment of value, and then develop that judgment into something that goes beyond a gut reaction and unstated assumptions.

I once had a professor, Peter Sandman, who had a theory of behavior that was inspired, in part, by advertising research. Sandman argued that while we want to believe that our actions are based on reasoned judgments, frequently we decide to do something based on an "irrational motivator." We buy toothpaste, for example, not because of the evidence of its effectiveness but on the promise of sex appeal. It's only *after* we behave irrationally that we actively seek out information that makes our choice seem sensible. That's one reason why, after you purchase a car, you start noticing that make and model everywhere and feel pleased with yourself that others endorse your choice.

A motive for turning to evaluative writing like reviews is to work against emotion as a sole reason for doing or thinking something. When the worth of our judgments must be measured against particular criteria and evidence, sex appeal isn't enough to justify buying Crest toothpaste. We need to really know what we're talking about.

> Evaluative writing is an enormously practical form, relevant in all sorts of situations in and out of school.

Evaluative writing helps you work from that feeling outward into reason, which will make your judgment persuasive to others *and* help shape your future judgments about other similar things. That's why my conversations with Karen about movies, once I stop feeling stupid, can be so helpful: because she challenges me to find reasons for what I feel, reasons that I am slowly learning to apply to my judgments of other films.

If you feel strongly about something, turn to evaluative writing and thinking as a way to help yourself and others understand why.

THE REVIEW AND ACADEMIC WRITING

We don't usually think of the review as an academic form, although you may be asked to review a film you're shown in an English class or perhaps a performance in a theater class. But evaluative writing, a process you'll practice when writing a review, is among the most common types of writing in all kinds of college classrooms.

Once you start thinking about evaluative writing, you'll find it everywhere—the book reviews in the Sunday *Times,* the music reviews in *Spin,* the analysis of Web sites on WebSitesThatSuck.com. It's probably the most common form of

---

WRITING IN THE DISCIPLINES

Evaluation Across the Disciplines

Evaluation is an important part of academic writing in many disciplines. Here are a few examples of the different types of evaluative writing you may be asked to compose in your college courses.

- In a science class, you may need to evaluate the methodology of an experiment.
- Business writing may require evaluation of a marketing strategy, a product, or a business plan.
- Philosophy frequently involves the evaluation of arguments.
- In a literature class, you may be asked to evaluate the effectiveness of a story or a character.
- In a theater class, you may write a review of a dramatic performance.
- In a composition class, you're often asked to evaluate the writing of peers.

workplace writing, too, from assessing the performance of an employee to evaluating a plan to preserve historic buildings.

FEATURES OF THE FORM

Like all forms of writing, evaluation genres vary widely. Perhaps the least likely form is one in which the writer formally announces a judgment, lists criteria, and then offers evidence using the criteria. That is, at least, an approach that you'll have a hard time finding outside school. Much evaluative writing is more subtle than that—and much more interesting—because the writer blends judgments, criteria, and evidence seamlessly throughout. If you've ever read a review of a band, a computer, or a book, you probably never noticed its structure because if the review is well written the structure isn't noticeable. But most reviews share some features, and many of them are a part of all kinds of evaluative writing.

- *A review is usually clear about categories.* Of course, the effectiveness of all writing depends on responding to a certain situation, but evaluative writing is particularly sensitive to the *category* of thing you're writing about. For example, the inverted pyramid in Figure 5.1 shows the narrowing of categories of film, working toward a more limited category—say, feature films about space travel. It's easier to come up with convincing criteria to judge a narrower category than a broad, general one.

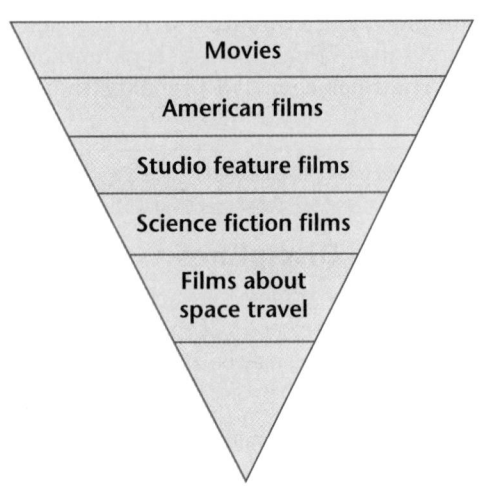

Figure 5.1   Narrowing the category of evaluation. One of the keys for developing useful and relevant criteria for judging something is making sure that you're focusing on the neighborhood, not the globe. In this example, it's much more helpful to talk about what makes a good Hollywood science fiction film about space travel than attempt to describe the qualities of the much broader category—all movies. After all, what makes a foreign art film effective is probably different from what makes a romantic comedy effective.

- *Reviews usually describe the thing they evaluate.* How much you describe depends on your readers' knowledge of what you're evaluating. If they haven't seen the performance, don't know the actor, haven't read the book, or don't know the type of product you're reviewing, then readers need the necessary background to understand what exactly you're talking about. Summaries can be vital.

- *Evaluation criteria are matched to purpose, category, and audience.* Obviously, a writer has reasons for making a judgment about something. Always in the back of the writer's mind is the purpose of the evaluation: what exactly he or she is writing about (and *not* writing about). If your aim is to help businesses understand which Web sites are likely to sell the most T-shirts, your criteria will be different from those used to evaluate the Web sites nonprofit groups might use to educate people about world hunger. Like all persuasive writing, the review is shaped by its audience.

- *In reviews, feelings often lead judgment but they are never enough.* Although evaluation is a form of argument, reason doesn't always lead judgment. Frequently, we first *feel* something—the Web site turns us off, or the new music video is captivating, or the reading assignment puts us to sleep. These feelings often lead us to an initial judgment—something we might acknowledge to readers—but they are never enough. The challenge of persuasive evaluation is to introduce reason into the process.

- *Judgments range from an overall assessment (it was good or bad, helpful or useless, and so on) to more specific commentary on particular evidence or aspects of the thing.* These judgments don't reside in one place in some kind of grand thesis, but are scattered throughout a review essay, working toward a more complicated assessment of the movie, book, or performance you're evaluating.

> The challenge of persuasive evaluation is to introduce reason into the process.

- *Reviews frequently attempt to offer a balanced assessment.* Hey, it can't be all bad. (Okay, sometimes it is.) The most persuasive negative evaluations tend to include some positive judgments, and positive evaluations frequently make some concessions about a thing's flaws.

- *Criteria may be stated or unstated.* You'll rarely find a piece of evaluative writing that neatly lists all the criteria used to judge the thing; in fact, some criteria may be implicit. Why? A common reason is that the writer and audience *share* certain assumptions about how to judge the value of a thing.

- *Relevant comparisons may form the backbone of a review.* Our fascination with winners and losers is reflected in one of the most ubiquitous evaluations in American culture: rankings. We rank cars, movies, music videos, celebrities' tastes in fashion, colleges, cameras, diets, and Web sites. The key, of course, is making sure that the things you're comparing do indeed belong in the same class, that you're comparing apples to apples and not apples to oranges.

READINGS

■ REVIEW 1

Mark Kermode is a British film critic who recently called the 2006 film *Little Man* "genuinely evil," and added "if you go and see it, shame on you." While I don't think I've heard him be that unequivocal about the faults of a film, Kermode's dislike of the *Pirates of the Caribbean* series, which stars the actor Johnny Depp, is well known to the fans who listen to his reviews on the BBC. In the review that follows, Kermode takes the second film in the trilogy, *Pirates of the Caribbean: Dead Man's Chest*, to task for its absence of narrative, its "pout performances," and most of all, its "interminable length."

Popular film criticism relies heavily on what Aristotle called *ethos,* or the character of the speaker. As readers, we want to appreciate the wit and intelligence of a reviewer, even when we disagree with him or her. A mindless rant or vacant praise simply won't engage readers. As you read Kermode's movie review, consider why you find him persuasive or why you don't.

Pirates of the Caribbean: Dead Man's Chest

Mark Kermode

1   Given my contempt for the first *Pirates of the Caribbean* movie, a triumph of turgid theme-park hackery over the art of cinema, it was assumed that I would have nothing positive to say about this sequel. On the contrary: the digitally enhanced squid-face of villain Davy Jones (he of the locker) is very well rendered, demonstrating the wonders of CGI and motion-capture technology. Reliable British actor Bill Nigh performs the human duties behind the high-tech make-up, lending an air of rancid fun to this slimy sea beast, who yo-ho-hos around the ocean accompanied by a crew of rum-sodden crustaceans.

2   There are a few moments of zany slapstick too, such as a fruit-throwing chase scene in which a skewered Captain Jack Sparrow becomes a human kebab, harking back to the days when the film's director, Gore Verbinski, made such innocuous fare as the slapstick farce *MouseHunt*. And I did laugh at one verbal gag about 'making the pleasure of your carbuncle'. So that's a thumbs up for the squid, the kebab and the carbuncle. Which is three more things than I liked about the last one.

Other than that, it's boring business as usual for this second instalment in   3
what is now a trilogy in the manner of all things post-*Lord of the Rings*. The plot
(and I use the word loosely) is episodic to the point of incoherence, constantly
reminding us that this is a film franchise based upon a fairground ride. Every five
minutes a new quest is announced, sending us rattling off on another tack, each
more fatuously inconsequential than the last. Go get Jack Sparrow's magic compass! Go seek out this magic key! Go track down the Flying Dutchman! Go dig up
Davy Jones's locker! Go and harvest 99 souls in three days! An early line about
'setting sail without knowing his own heading' seems to apply to the screenwrit-
ers as much as the pirates, and it's a full 40 minutes before any sense of direction
is established at all.

The romping tone may aspire to the nostalgic swashbuckle of Steven Spielberg's   4
Raiders of the Lost Ark series (replete with John Williams-lite 'ta-ran-ta raaa' score by
Hans Zimmer), but it is the rambling blather of Lucas's *Star Wars* prequels which is
most pungently evoked. So muddled is the narrative that the characters have to keep
stopping and explaining the story to each other ('You mean, if I find the chest, I will
find Will Turner...'). By the time the closing credits roll the story hasn't actually gone
anywhere, and there's still a whole other movie to come.

In the absence of narrative we are left with a string of 'spectacular' set pieces to   5
hold our attention. Verbinski may be a witless hack, but he understands the laws of
supply and demand and doesn't skimp on the money-shots. Thus we get giant-
tentacled Kraken attacks, ghost ships rising from the dead, and multiple storm-riven
battle scenes. When it comes to directing performances, however, Verbinski is completely at sea, leaving his rudderless cast to indulge themselves to their heart's
content.

The fact that Johnny Depp received an Oscar nomination for his boggle-eyed,   6
drawl-mouthed Keith Richards' impression doesn't change my opinion that the role
of Jack Sparrow has produced some of the actor's very worst work to date. Depp is
a brilliantly physical performer whose finely honed movements have breathed
eerie life into characters as diverse as Ed Wood and Edward Scissorhands, and
whose expressive voice lent an air of melancholy magic to the animated gem
Corpse Bride.

Yet Verbinski is no Tim Burton, and under his slack direction Depp defaults to an   7
untrammelled showiness not seen since the sub-Buster Keaton antics of Benny and
Joon. In *Dead Man's Chest,* every moment is a symphony of eye-rolling, hair-tossing,
lip-pouting, finger-fiddling narcissism. It's like being trapped in a room with a drunk
karaoke singer who's having much more fun than his audience.

As for poor old Orlando Bloom, where does one start to document the tidal   8
wave of wetness which he brings to these proceedings? No matter how much sea
water Verbinski throws at the set, nothing gets as damp as Mr. Bland, whose
expressions run the gamut from perky to peeved with occasional interludes of
petulance.

(continued)

(continued)

9   An early scene finds an imprisoned Keira Knightley saucily telling her fiancé: 'If it weren't for these bars, I'd have you already.' The idea of anyone 'having' this doe-eyed waif is hilarious, and a frightened looking Orlando promptly runs away to sea, leaving a trail of froth in his wake. Knightley, meanwhile, puts her best teeth forward and does her haughty Head Girl act, stopping only to lock lips with Depp in a red herring subplot which will presumably spark some dreary love triangle misunderstanding in Part Three. How on earth will Orlando react? I'm betting on 'prissy'.

10   Lumpen direction, lousy writing and pouting performances aside, the worst thing about *Dead Man's Chest* is its interminable length. The entire *Pirates of the Caribbean* franchise may be a horrible indicator of the decline of narrative cinema (and probably Western civilization), but the rank consumerist decrepitude of it all would be tolerable if the film wasn't quite so boring. At a bum-numbing two-and-a-half hours, this is what weak-bladdered studio boss Jack Warner used to refer to as 'a three-piss picture'—in every sense. Thank heavens for the squid.

Inquiring into the Essay

Explore, explain, evaluate, and reflect on "Pirates" by Mark Kermode.

1. Initiate a conversation in your journal with Kermode about his review. Imagine that you're engaged in an instant-message conversation with Kermode. He's just sent you a message that observes that "it's boring business as usual for this second installment" of *The Pirates of the Caribbean,* adding that in *Dead Man's Chest* "every moment [watching Depp] is a symphony of eye-rolling, hair tossing, lip-pouting, finger-fiddling narcissism." Write back. Try to play the believing and doubting games in your response. How do you agree? How do you disagree? What has Kermode failed to consider?

2. Analyze the ways that "Pirates" reflects the "Features of the Form" listed earlier in the chapter. Explain exactly where in Kermode's review he seems to incorporate those features.

3. All reviews make an argument, but it often can't be reduced easily to a single thesis or central claim. Reread Kermode's review, and try to list the claims he's making about the film. Which do you find most persuasive? Which are least persuasive? Why?

4. One way to get better as a writer who persuades readers is to pay attention to how *you* respond to written arguments. Tell the story of your thoughts and feelings as you read Kermode's review. Reread the review, pausing after the first paragraph to write for two minutes in

your journal about what you're feeling about Kermode, what he's saying, and how he's saying it. What story do these three episodes of writing tell about your experience of the review? What do they suggest about effective argument?

■ REVIEW 2

Criterion for a great car: You turn the key and it starts. Okay, so I don't have sophisticated taste in automobiles. For better or for worse, we are a car-loving culture, and, for some, every detail of an automobile like the Lotus Exige S 240, from the size of the intercooler to the automated launch-control system, is a source of fascination. It isn't the $70,000 price tag that inspires such devoted interest. Some people just love cars at any price. Though with diminishing oil reserves and global warming, many of us are now devoted to our bicycles, the vast majority of us still drive cars, and even if you're not a fan it makes sense to pay attention to judgments about quality.

We're not talking about Fords here, though. *New York Times* writer Ezra Dyer's review of the 2008 Lotus that follows is clearly written for automobile aficionados. It's interesting, however, even for readers who are not—particularly if they notice those moments when the piece seems to work for them and moments when it does not. These are moments that say a lot about how a piece of writing is crafted with a particular rhetorical situation in mind.

The 2008 Lotus Exige S 240.

A Ton (Just Barely) of Fun

Ezra Dyer

1   Colin Chapman, the racecar builder and founder of Lotus, followed a straightforward path to high performance: ignore the horsepower wars and focus on keeping weight low.

2   In 1990, a Lotus Esprit SE driven by Richard Gere made a memorable cameo in *Pretty Woman*. That car was powered by a small turbocharged 4-cylinder engine, yet with a weight of less than 3,000 pounds it was able to reach 60 miles an hour in less than five seconds.

3   Since then, the industry trend has been toward vehicles that are bigger, heavier and more powerful. Not at Lotus, the British sports car maker: the 2008 Exige S 240 is smaller, lighter and less powerful than that 1990 Esprit. It's also faster.

4   In another couple of decades, you might expect the Lotus flagship to be an electron with a steering wheel. Even then, they'll be trying to get it down to a quark.

5   Building a car with an emphasis on austerity and light weight starts a happy chain reaction of performance-enhancing consequences. For instance, because the Exige is light—just 2,077 pounds, Lotus says—it can generate ferocious road grip with relatively skinny tires. Each of the 195-width front tires on the Exige is actually a bit narrower than the rear tire of a 2009 Yamaha Vmax motorcycle.

6   As a result, the Exige gets by without power steering, trimming away a few more pounds. (Fearless assertion: the Exige has the most delicious steering feel of any current production car.) And you might even sweat off a few pounds wrestling that nonassisted steering at parking-lot speeds. Who needs Jenny Craig when you've got Colin Chapman?

7   The Exige is more comfortable than it looks. The seats are wafer-thin and barely adjustable. (The driver's seat moves fore and aft; the passenger seat is bolted to the floor.) But once you've limboed your way inside, it's not a bad place to be.

8   There is plenty of legroom and those severe-looking seats actually prove surprisingly accommodating. Need to adjust the passenger-side door mirror? It's not motorized, but you can reach it from the driver's seat. As for amenities, there's air-conditioning, power windows, power locks and even a strikingly minimalist cup holder consisting of little more than a small ring of aluminum that suspends a leather strap. Lotus should trademark this design and call it the Coffee Thong.

9   The S 240 is powered by a 1.8-liter Toyota 4-cylinder, supercharged to an output of 240 horsepower, that drives the rear wheels. The mid-mounted engine has a huge intercooler perched on top, so rearward visibility could charitably be described as compromised. You learn to back into parking-lot spaces, because reversing into traffic would be an invitation to catastrophe.

10   Lotus says the Exige S 240 is the quickest car it has ever made ever, with a zero-to-60 time of 4.1 seconds. (The S 240's "quickest Lotus" honors will probably cede next month to the Exige S 260, which has 17 more horsepower and, through generous use of carbon fiber, is 50 pounds lighter.)

The supercharger, besides cranking up the horsepower, smoothes out the power delivery. With the naturally aspirated version of the little engine—originally developed with Yamaha for the Toyota Celica GT-S—output was tepid until the variable valve timing shifted into its high-r.p.m. mode, unleashing an abrupt surge of power.

11

With the S 240, you don't have to work that hard. There's still a manic rush to the rev limiter (which, for brief moments, can allow up to 8,500 r.p.m.), but the Exige also feels tractable around town. You can shoot the gaps in traffic without crossing your fingers and hoping the power will arrive in time. Which is important when you're driving a car so small it has you looking up from the driver's seat to see the tailpipe of a Camry.

12

The Exige isn't shy about proclaiming its racecar intentions. Its Yokohama Advan Neova tires have a treadwear rating of 60, the lowest (and hence stickiest) number I have ever seen on a street tire. (A Porsche GT3 comes in at 80.) On a skid pad, this thing grips so hard that *you feel like an astronaut in a centrifuge.*

13

The Exige is so good at convincing you it's a racecar that you'll pull into gas stations and scream, "Gimme new tires on the right side and set the wing for more downforce at the rear!"

14

Speaking of gas stations, two fill-ups of the 10.6-gallon tank cost $18 and $19, respectively, even with the required premium fuel. The E.P.A. mileage rating is 20 m.p.g. in town and 26 on the highway, reasonable numbers for a vehicle with this level of performance.

15

Say what you will about the economy, but premium gas for less than $2 a gallon makes it really cheap to run your Lotus. Which is nice, because the rather heady base price of $65,815 ($70,650 as tested) puts the Exige S 240 in the territory of a Corvette Z06 or a Nissan GT-R.

16

Either of those cars is generally more agreeable on public roads. With the Lotus, you'll occasionally find yourself driving with a shoeless right foot: the pedals are so close you'll be mashing the brake when trying to accelerate.

17

The quirks don't end there. The headlights and instruments are always lighted, but at night you must remember to click the light switch to activate the taillights—an electrical idiosyncrasy (for a 2008 car, anyway) that I learned about thanks to a helpful local constable. And you'll inadvertently honk the horn at inopportune moments because the buttons are right where your thumbs tend to land on the steering wheel spokes.

18

In the era of ultra-refined, focus-grouped transport modules, the Exige still gives the impression that it was designed by an autocrat with a penchant for speed and a belief that ergonomics are an urban legend.

19

From that, you might conclude that the Exige is a throwback, a relic of simpler days. On the contrary, I see it as a harbinger of the future. *It's simple, light and fun. Its mileage is good. It shows how much performance can be wrung from modest engines.* If volatile oil prices and the faltering economy conspire to push sports cars toward a more spartan ideal, that might not be a bad thing.

20

The Exige has its warts, but once you've felt the tingle of electricity coming through that little Momo steering wheel, once you've clicked off a perfect motorcycle-quick upshift just as the motor reaches its snarling peak, even the most jaded proponent of V-8-powered excess will admit that Lotus is onto something.

21

Inquiring into the Essay

1. Explore your own experience with a car. Tell the story of a first car, a worst car, a car that got you through a particular time in your life, or one that helped you to define that time. Fastwrite about this for six minutes. It should be fun. Skip a line and write for two more minutes about how the review of the Lotus connects—or does not connect—in some way to the experience you wrote about.

2. Explain who you think was the audience for the Lotus review. Describe the demographics of that audience, and identify passages from the review that seem particularly geared toward those readers.

3. Evaluate the effectiveness of "A Ton (Just Barely) of Fun" for a reader like you. How could it be revised to be more interesting to another audience? Be specific.

4. Reading in college often involves an experience like the one you may have had reading this review. Did you feel like an insider or an outsider as a reader of the piece? When did you first feel that and how did it influence your response to the piece?

■ REVIEW 3

The video gaming industry hauls in something like $10 billion a year, so it's no surprise that more writers are penning reviews of the latest releases. These reviews, if they're any good, have to balance technical information about the game with attention to the experience of playing it. It is a well-described gaming experience, not arcane detail, that will appeal to most readers. That's why Seth Schiesel's review of "Grand Theft Auto IV," a hugely popular video game released in 2008, is such a great example of how to write a review that might make even non-video game players interested in giving it a try.

Like many reviews, the criteria Schiesel uses to determine the qualities of a good game are largely implicit. But it isn't hard to find them. One criterion he clearly uses is what we often look for in film and literature: "fully realized characters." When you think about it, this is a pretty extraordinary accomplishment in a video game. After all, characters in a game like "Grand Theft Auto IV" must consistently service the action, making things (usually violent things) happen, and this wouldn't seem to provide the time or the situations to develop character. But according to Schiesel, the protagonist of the fourth version of the game, Niko Bellic, is "one of the most fully realized characters that video games have yet produced."

Seth Schiesel sidesteps the ethics of producing games like "Grand Theft Auto IV," which makes efficient killing a key to advancement. But this is a review, not a public argument on the virtues of gaming, and his readers likely

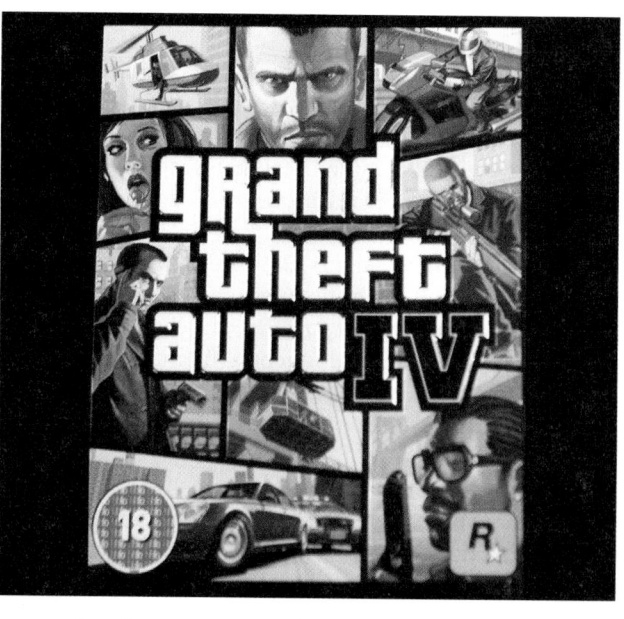

Niko Bellic (top center) is the main character of the video game "Grand Theft Auto IV," a game that Seth Schiesel calls "violent, intelligent, profane, endearing, obnoxious, sly, richly textured and throughly compelling."

aren't interested in such ethical and moral questions. They just want to know whether the game is any good. As you read "Grand Theft Auto Takes on New York," consider what exactly Schiesel means by that. On what other criteria does he base his judgment?

Grand Theft Auto Takes on New York

Seth Schiesel

I was rolling through the neon deluge of a place very like Times Square the other night in my Landstalker sport utility vehicle, listening to David Bowie's "Fascination" on the radio. The glittery urban landscape was almost enough to make me forget about the warehouse of cocaine dealers I was headed uptown to rip off.

Soon I would get bored, though, and carjack a luxury sedan. I'd meet my Rasta buddy Little Jacob, then check out a late show by Ricky Gervais at a comedy club around the corner. Afterward I'd head north to confront the dealers, at least if I

(continued)

1

2

(continued)

could elude the cops. I heard their sirens before I saw them and peeled out, tires squealing.

3   It was just another night on the streets of Liberty City, the exhilarating, lusciously dystopian rendition of New York City in 2008 that propels Grand Theft Auto IV, the ambitious new video game to be released on Tuesday for the Xbox 360 and PlayStation 3 systems.

4   Published by Rockstar Games, Grand Theft Auto IV is a violent, intelligent, profane, endearing, obnoxious, sly, richly textured and thoroughly compelling work of cultural satire disguised as fun. It calls to mind a rollicking R-rated version of Mad magazine featuring Dave Chappelle and Quentin Tarantino, and sets a new standard for what is possible in interactive arts. It is by far the best game of the series, which made its debut in 1997 and has since sold more than 70 million copies. Grand Theft Auto IV will retail for $60.

5   Niko Bellic is the player-controlled protagonist this time, and he is one of the most fully realized characters video games have yet produced. A veteran of the Balkan wars and a former human trafficker in the Adriatic, he arrives in Liberty City's rendition of Brighton Beach at the start of the game to move in with his affable if naïve cousin Roman. Niko expects to find fortune and, just maybe, track down someone who betrayed him long ago. Over the course of the story line he discovers that revenge is not always what one expects.

6   Besides the nuanced Niko the game is populated by a winsome procession of grifters, hustlers, drug peddlers and other gloriously unrepentant lowlifes, each a caricature less politically correct than the last.

7   Hardly a demographic escapes skewering. In addition to various Italian and Irish crime families, there are venal Russian gangsters, black crack slingers, argyle-sporting Jamaican potheads, Puerto Rican hoodlums, a corrupt police commissioner, a steroid-addled Brooklyn knucklehead named Brucie Kibbutz and a former Eastern European soldier who has become a twee Upper West Side metrosexual.

8   Breathing life into Niko and the other characters is a pungent script by Dan Houser and Rupert Humphries that reveals a mastery of street patois to rival Elmore Leonard's. The point of the main plot is to guide Niko through the city's criminal underworld. Gang leaders and thugs set missions for him to complete, and his success moves the story along toward a conclusion that seems as dark as its beginning. But the real star of the game is the city itself. It looks like New York. It sounds like New York. It feels like New York. Liberty City has been so meticulously created it almost even smells like New York. From Brooklyn (called Broker), through Queens (Dukes), the Bronx (Bohan), Manhattan (Algonquin) and an urban slice of New Jersey (Alderney), the game's streets and alleys ooze a stylized yet unmistakable authenticity. (Staten Island is left out however.)

9   The game does not try to represent anything close to every street in the city, but the overall proportions, textures, geography, sights and sounds are spot-on. The

major landmarks are present, often rendered in surprising detail, from the Cyclone at Coney Island to the Domino Sugar factory and Grand Army Plaza in Brooklyn and on up through the detritus of the 1964–65 World's Fair in Queens. Central Park, the Empire State Building, various museums, the Statue of Liberty and Times Square are all present and accounted for. There is no Yankee Stadium, but there is a professional baseball team known, with the deliciousness typical of the game's winks and nods, as the Swingers.

At least as impressive as the city's virtual topography is the range of the game's audio and music production, delivered through an entire dial's worth of radio stations available in almost any of the dozens of different cars, trucks and motorcycles a player can steal. From the jazz channel (billed as "music from when America was cool") through the salsa, alt-rock, jazz, metal and multiple reggae and hip-hop stations, Lazlow Jones, Ivan Pavlovich and the rest of Rockstar's audio team demonstrate a musical erudition beyond anything heard before in a video game. The biggest problem with the game's extensive subway system is that there's no music underground. (Too bad there are no iPods to nab.)   10

The game's roster of radio hosts runs from Karl Lagerfeld to Iggy Pop and DJ Green Lantern. It is not faint praise to point out that at times, simply driving around the city listening to the radio—seguing from "Moanin'" by Art Blakey and the Jazz Messengers to the Isley Brothers' "Footsteps in the Dark" to "The Crack House" by Fat Joe featuring Lil Wayne—can be as enjoyable as anything the game has to offer.   11

Grand Theft Auto IV is such a simultaneously adoring and insightful take on modern America that it almost had to come from somewhere else. The game's main production studio is in Edinburgh, and Rockstar's leaders, the brothers Dan and Sam Houser, are British expatriates who moved to New York to indulge their fascination with urban American culture. Their success places them firmly among the distinguished cast of Britons from Mick Jagger and Keith Richards through Tina Brown who have flourished by identifying key elements of American culture, repackaging them for mass consumption and selling them back at a markup.   12

It all adds up to a new level of depth for an interactive entertainment experience. I've spent almost 60 hours practically sequestered in a (real world) Manhattan hotel room in recent weeks playing through Grand Theft Auto IV's main story line and the game still says I have found only 64 percent of its content. I won't ever reach 100 percent, not least because I won't hunt down all 200 of the target pigeons (known as flying rats here) that the designers have hidden around the city.   13

But like millions of other players I will happily spend untold hours cruising Liberty City's bridges and byways, hitting the clubs, grooving to the radio and running from the cops. Even when the real New York City is right outside.   14

Inquiring into the Essay

Explore, explain, evaluate, and reflect on the review, "Grand Theft Auto Takes on New York" using the following questions:

1. This review doesn't address the moral and ethical questions raised by a game that celebrates "gloriously unrepentant lowlifes" including pot-heads, gangsters, and "crack slingers." "Grand Theft Auto IV" may be no worse than other violent video games, and unless you've played it, criticism or praise of this particular game is unfair. But in a four-minute fastwrite, explore your own feelings about violent video games. In his review, Schiesel argues that "Grand Theft Auto IV" is cultural satire. Can games like this serve a larger, even useful purpose?

2. Define, in your own words, what Seth Schiesel seems to believe are the qualities of a good video game.

3. Evaluate the rhetorical effectiveness of this review. Imagine what parts of the piece would work—or wouldn't—for the following categories of readers:

    a. People who have never played a video game in their lives but might consider it.

    b. People who are avid and experienced gamers.

    c. People who, when asked, usually consider playing video games a "waste of time."

4. Video game reviews are but one of a growing number of review genres, including movies, books, blogs, Web sites, best and worst dressed, and so on. Consider the reviews you read or might read. What exactly would you be looking for in a "good" review on that subject?

SEEING THE FORM

Choosing the Best Picture

When documentary photographer Dorothea Lange encountered Florence Thompson and her family camped by a frozen pea field, she came away with one of the most indelible images of the Depression, a picture that was later titled *Migrant Mother*. But Lange took multiple pictures that day, and only one of them became famous. Why? If you were charged with evaluating all six shots that Lange took of Thompson and her family that you see here, on what basis would you choose the best shot? What criteria would you use for making such a judgment?

Six photographs Dorothea Lange took of Florence Thompson.

THE WRITING PROCESS

INQUIRY PROJECT: WRITING A REVIEW

Write a 1,000- to 1,200-word review. You choose the subject—a performance, a book, a Web site, a consumer product, a film, whatever. Just make sure your review has the following qualities:

- You're able to put your subject in a manageable category for more useful comparisons; for example, rather than evaluating a Web site against all others, you're going to focus on Web sites for classroom use.
- The essay has all three elements of evaluation: judgment, criteria, and evidence.
- The criteria are reasonable and appropriate for what you're evaluating; they aren't overly idealistic or general.
- The evaluation seems balanced and fair.

Thinking About Subjects

Possible subjects for a review abound. What will you choose? Perhaps you're a sports fan who regularly seeks information on the Web. Which sites strike you as the most informative? Which would you recommend? Or maybe you are interested in photography, but really don't have any idea how to evaluate the landscape shots you took during a recent trip to Maine. Are they any good? The best inquiry projects begin with a question, not an answer, so try to choose a topic because you want to discover what you think instead of one about which you already have a strong opinion. You'll learn more and probably write a stronger, more balanced, more interesting essay.

> The best inquiry projects begin with a question, so choose a topic because you want to discover what you think instead of one about which you already have a strong opinion.

Generating Ideas

Play around with some ideas first by using some of the following triggers for thinking-through-writing in your journal. Suspend judgment. Don't reject anything. Explore.

Listing Prompts. Lists can be rich sources of triggering topics. Let them grow freely, and when you're ready, use an item as the focus of another list or an episode of fastwriting. The following prompts should get you started.

1. Fold a piece a paper into four equal columns. You'll be making four different brainstormed lists. In the first column, write "Things I Want." Spend two minutes making a quick list of everything you wish you had but don't—a new computer, a classical guitar, a decent boyfriend, and so on.

2. In the next column, write "The Jury Is Still Out." In this column, make a fast list of things in your life that so far are hard to judge—the quality of the school you attend, this textbook, your opinion about the films you saw last month, how well Susie cuts your hair, and so on.

3. In the third column, write "My Media." Devote a fast list to particular films, TV shows, books, Web sites, or musicians you like or dislike—jot down whatever you watch, listen to, or read regularly.

4. Finally, make a list of "Things of Questionable Quality." Try to be specific.

Fastwriting Prompts. Remember, fastwriting is a great way to stimulate creative thinking. Turn off your critical side and let yourself write "badly."

1. Choose an item from any of the four preceding lists as a prompt for a seven-minute fastwrite. Explore your experience with the subject, or how your opinions about it have evolved.

2. Begin with the following prompt, and follow it for five minutes in a fastwrite: *Among the things I have a hard time judging is* _____.... If the writing stalls, shift subjects by writing, *And another thing I can't judge is* _____....

Visual Prompts. Sometimes the best way to generate material is to see what we think represented in something other than sentences. Boxes, lines, webs, clusters, arrows, charts, and even sketches can help us see more of the landscape of a subject, especially connections between fragments of information that aren't as obvious in prose.

1. On a blank page in your journal, cluster the name of an artist, musician, film, book, author, performance, band, building, academic course or major, restaurant, university bookstore, PDA, computer, food store, or pizza joint. Cluster the name of anything about which you have some sort of feeling, positive or negative. Build a web of associations: feelings, details, observations, names, moments, facts, opinions, and so on. Look for a single strand in your essay that might be the beginning of a review.

2. Draw a sketch of what you think is an *ideal version* of something you need or use often: a computer, a classroom, a telephone, a wallet or handbag, and so on. If you could design such a thing, what would it look like? Use this as a way of evaluating what is currently available and how it might be improved.

Research Prompts. The depth of a review depends on the writer's knowledge of the criteria and evidence through which she judges her subject. Unless she is already an expert on her subject, research of some form will be a necessity. At this stage in the writing process, a little advance research can help you find a subject.

1. Do an Internet or library search for reviews on one of your favorite films, books, sports teams, artists, and so on. Do you agree with the evaluations? If not, consider writing a review of your own that challenges the critics.

2. Take a walk. Look for things to evaluate that you see as you wander on and off campus—downtown architecture, the quality of local parks, paintings in the art museum, neighborhoods, coffee shops. You'll be amazed at how much is begging for a thoughtful judgment.

3. Here's an entertaining generating activity: Plan a weekend of movie watching with a few friends. Ask each of them to contribute two or three titles of their favorite films, then rent a slew of them, and when you're thoroughly spent watching movies, discuss which might be most interesting to review.

Judging What You Have

Generating may produce the messy, incoherent writing that would earn you bad grades in most classes. Its virtue, however, should be obvious by now: "Bad" writing gives a writer material to work with. Remember that it's always better to work from abundance than scarcity. But if this material is going to go anywhere, it must be judged, shaped, and evaluated.

WRITING IN YOUR LIFE

Online Product Reviews

Amazon, the biggest bookseller in the world, publishes thousands of customer book reviews, and these have a big enough impact on sales that authors and publishers monitor them closely. One study suggests, in fact, that nearly a quarter of Americans who buy products online first consult customer reviews. British online consumers are apparently even more dedicated to reading reviews. Seventy percent report that they first read customer reviews of a product before they buy it. Few pieces of self-published writing wield that kind of influence.

It's possible to get paid for online reviews. Epinions.com is probably the best known site that pays contributors for product reviews, a sum that's calculated on how often your review is seen. But the best motive for writing product reviews is the satisfaction of influencing how people think about something you love (or don't). Like any persuasive writing, an online product review must be readable and convincing. It's a genre that requires honesty and directness. The relative brevity of these reviews makes it especially important that your point is clear. Since you aren't necessarily an authority on the thing you review, establishing a convincing ethos or persona is key. You want to come across as someone who is thoughtful and fair, and yet feels strongly.

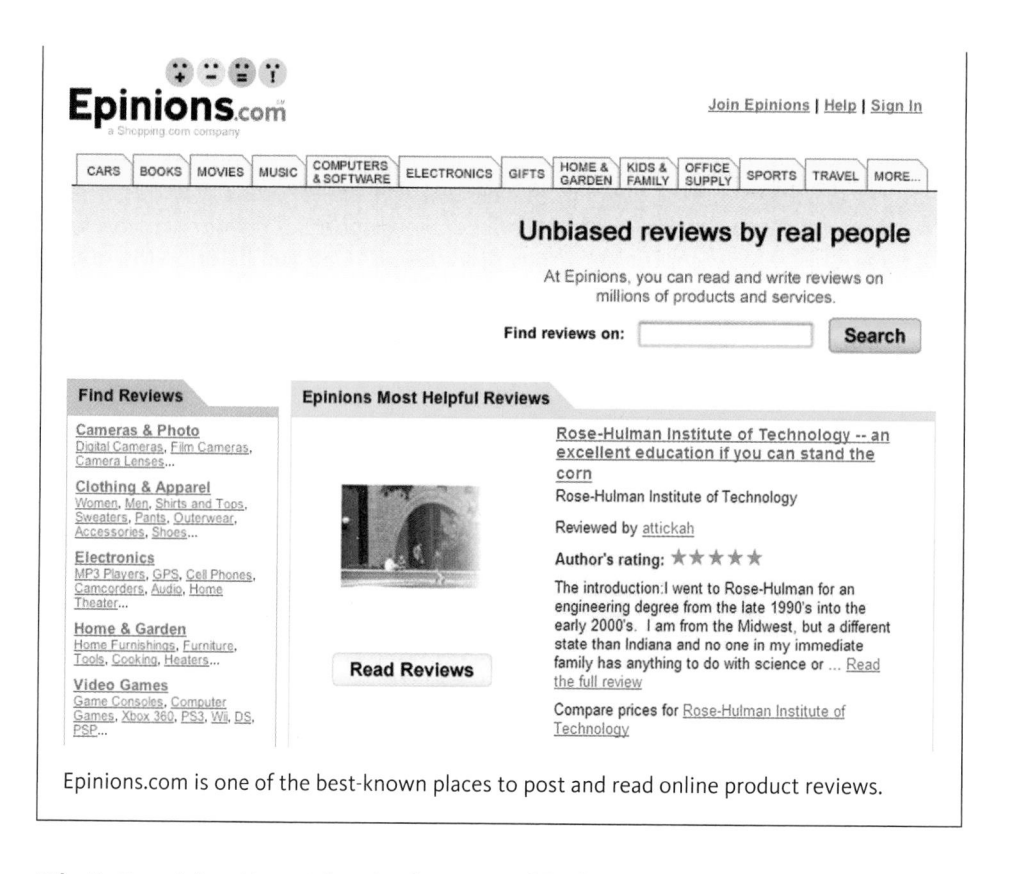

Epinions.com is one of the best-known places to post and read online product reviews.

What's Promising Material and What Isn't? My favorite coffee shop in my hometown of Boise, Idaho, is a place called the Flying M. It's a funky place with an odd assortment of furniture, overstuffed couches, worn armchairs, and wobbly tables. On the walls, there's work from local artists, mostly unknowns with talent and unusual taste. There are other coffee places in town, including the ubiquitous Starbucks and another more local chain called Moxie Java. I don't find much difference in the coffee at any of these places, and they're all rather pleasant. What makes me prefer the Flying M?

I've never really thought about it. That's one of the reasons I liked the idea of reviewing my favorite local coffeehouse when the Flying M appeared on one of my lists. The best inquiry-based projects begin when you're not quite sure what you think and want to explore a topic to find out.

- *Is there anything in your lists and fastwrites that you might have an initial judgment about but really haven't considered fully?* For example, you really dislike the sixties architecture that dominates your campus, but you're not quite sure what it is about it that leaves you cold.

- *As you consider possible subjects for your review, do some clearly offer the possibility of comparison with other similar things in that category?* Often judgment is based on such comparisons, although we may not really think about it much. Comparison isn't always essential, however, but it can be helpful. For instance, while I can't really distinguish the coffee served at Starbucks, Moxie Java, or the Flying M—it's all good—I'm pretty sure that my preferences have more to do with the atmosphere.

■ *Do any of your possible subjects offer the possibility of primary research, or research that might involve direct observation?* Can you listen to the music, attend the performance, read the novel, examine the building, visit the Web site, look at the painting? If I were doing this assignment, I'd choose a review of local cafés over other possible topics because it would give me an excuse to drink coffee and hang out in some of my favorite haunts. This is called research. Seriously.

Questions About Audience and Purpose. If I write a review of Boise's coffeehouse scene, I can immediately think of where I could publish it. *The Boise Weekly* is a local alternative magazine that frequently features food reviews and has an audience that certainly includes a high percentage of gourmet coffee drinkers. Many readers of the *Weekly* have direct experience with the coffeehouses I'd review and may even have judgments of their own about which are best. I'm reasonably confident that they might care about what I have to say on the topic.

The Internet is the easiest and fastest way to find an audience for a review. Sites like Epinions.com (see the feature "Writing in your Life" on page 176) invite, and sometimes pay for, reviews of a wide range of products. If you're devoted to a certain kind of product—books, movies, video games, or whatever—then consider blogging your review. It's easy to set up a blog (try www.blogger.com), and if your work is well-written and informative, you'll find an audience.

EXERCISE 5.1

From Jury to Judgment

Writing an evaluation of a thing requires that you become something of an expert about it. As you complete the following steps of the exercise, you'll generate material to work with that will make writing the draft much easier.

STEP ONE: Begin with a focused fastwrite that explores your initial feelings and experiences, if any, about your subject. In your notebook, use one of the following prompts to launch an exploration of your personal experiences with your topic. If the writing stalls, try another prompt to keep you going for five to seven minutes.

■ *Write about your first experience with your subject.* This might be, for example, the first time you remember visiting the restaurant, or hearing the performer, or seeing the photographs. Focus on scenes, moments, situations, and people.

- *Write about what you think might be important qualities of your subject.* Ideally, these would be what the thing should be able to do well or what effects it should have on people who use it or see it. Say you're evaluating laptop computers for college students. Under which conditions would a laptop be most useful? What have you noticed about the way you use one? In which common situations do student laptops prove vulnerable to damage? What have you heard other people say they like or dislike about their machines?

- *Write about how the thing makes you feel.* So much of our evaluation of a thing begins with our emotional responses to it. You love the photography of Edward Weston, or the music of Ani DiFranco, or you really dislike Hitchcock movies. Explore not just your initial good, bad, or mixed feelings about your subject but the place from where those feelings arise.

- *Compare the thing you're evaluating with something else that's similar.* I appreciate the Flying M café largely because it's so different from Starbucks. Focus your fastwrite on a relevant comparison, teasing out the differences and similarities and thinking about how you feel about them.

STEP TWO: Research your subject on the Web, gathering as much relevant background information as you can.

- *Search for information on product Web sites or Web pages devoted specifically to your subject.* If your review is on Ford's new electric car, visit the company's Web site to find out what you can about the vehicle. Find Green Day's home page or fan site for your review of the band's new CD.

- *Search for existing reviews or other evaluations on your subject.* One way to do this is to Google using the keyword "review" or "reviews" (or "how to evaluate") along with your subject. For example, "laptop reviews" will produce dozens of sites that rank and evaluate the machines. Similarly, there are countless reviews on the Web of specific performers, performances, CDs, consumer products, and so on.

STEP THREE: If possible, interview people about what they think. You may do this formally by developing a survey, or informally by simply asking people what they like or dislike about the thing you're evaluating. Also consider whether you might interview someone who's an expert on your subject. For example, if you're evaluating a Web site, ask people in the technical communications program what they think about it, or what criteria they might use if they were reviewing something similar.

STEP FOUR: This may be the most important step of all: *Experience* your subject. Visit the coffeehouses, examine the Web site, listen to the music, attend the performance, read the book, view the painting, visit the building, look at the architecture, watch the movie. As you do this, gather your impressions and collect information. The best way to do this methodically is to collect field notes, and the double-entry journal is a good note-taking system for this purpose. Put your observations on the left page and explore your impressions and ideas on the opposing right page of your notebook.

By now, you have some background information on your subject and have gathered observations and impressions that should shape your judgment about it. Maybe you've decided the film is a stinker, the CD is the best one you've heard, or the student union isn't meeting students' needs. After comparing Starbucks and the Flying M—and visiting both places—I'm even more convinced about which one I prefer. But why? This is a key stage in the process of evaluation: On what basis do you make the judgment? In other words, what *criteria* are you using?

Thinking About Criteria

Professional reviewers—say, consultants who evaluate marketing plans or people who write film reviews—may not sit down and make a list of their criteria. They're so familiar with their subjects that they've often internalized the criteria they're using, and their clients and readers may not insist on knowing on what they base their judgments. But it can be enormously helpful at this stage in the process to try to articulate your criteria, at least as a way of thinking more thoroughly about your subject.

Criteria might be quite personal. There are certain things that *you* think are important about a coffeehouse, student union, modern dance performance, fusion jazz CD, and so on. These opinions are what make the review yours, and not somebody else's. But they should be reasonable to others. Your criteria for judgment shouldn't set an unrealistic standard or seem nitpicky or irrelevant.

I asked my daughter Rebecca, a dancer, what criteria she would use to judge a modern performance (see the accompanying box). I don't completely understand all of the criteria she listed because I know little about dance, but her list seems sensible and I can imagine how it might guide her in evaluating the next performance of the Balance Dance Company. What I don't understand, she can explain to me.

As you write your sketch, keep your criteria in mind. You may not mention all of them, or even any of them in your draft, but they'll help direct you to the evidence you need to make your judgment seem persuasive to others.

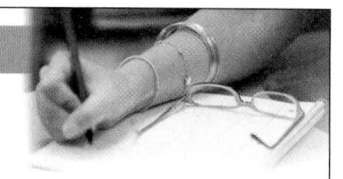

INQUIRING INTO THE DETAILS

Collaborating on Criteria

Need help determining the criteria for your evaluation? Asking others for their opinions can help. Consider the following strategy:

1. Write the category of the thing you're reviewing—a modern dance performance, coffeehouses, a hip-hop CD, a science fiction novel, and so on—on the top of a piece of newsprint.

2. Post your newsprint on the wall of your classroom.

3. For twenty minutes, everyone in class rotates around the room to each newsprint, trying to answer the following question about the category listed there: *In your judgment, what makes a particularly good* _____? (rap song, science fiction story, coffeehouse, and so on).

4. Briefly list your criteria for judging each category on the newsprint, or elaborate on a criteria that is already there. In other words, in your mind, what makes a good _____?

5. If you don't know that much about the category, make a reasonable guess about a basis for judging it.

BECCA'S CRITERIA

A good modern dance performance has...

1. Interesting features—props, comedy, or music?
2. Something improvised
3. Visible expressions of the dancers' enjoyment
4. Interesting variation
5. Good balance in choreography between repetition and randomness
6. Beginning, middle, and end, seamlessly joined

Writing the Sketch

As with the other inquiry projects, begin with a sketch of your review. This should be about 500 to 600 words (two to three double-spaced pages) and include the following:

- A tentative title.
- An effort to help readers understand why they might have a stake in the thing you're evaluating. What's significant about this particular CD, book, performance, place, or product?
- Specific evidence from the thing itself to help explain and support your judgment of it.

Moving from Sketch to Draft

A sketch usually gives the writer just the barest outline of his or her subject. But as an early draft, a sketch can be invaluable. It might hint at what the real subject is, or what questions seem to be behind your inquiry into the subject. A sketch might suggest a focus for the next draft, or simply a better lead. Learning to read your sketches for such clues takes practice. The following suggestions should help.

Evaluating Your Own Sketch. A sketch is an early draft; it should help expose gaps that you can fill in revision. Begin evaluating your sketch by looking for the following possible omissions:

1. Do you provide enough background about what you're reviewing so that readers unfamiliar with the subject know enough to believe and understand your claims?
2. Do you feel that your treatment of the topic was balanced? For example, did you include perspectives that differ from yours? Did you consider some positive qualities of your topic in an unflattering review or negatives in a positive review?
3. Do you use any helpful comparisons?
4. Are your judgments supported by specific evidence? Is there enough of it?
5. Having written the sketch, has your judgment changed at all? Should you strengthen, qualify, or elaborate on it? Do you feel as if it would be more honest to change it altogether?

Questions for Peer Review. Because a review is a form of persuasive writing, comments from other readers are crucial. In your workshop session, get your peers to comment on how persuasive they find your sketch by asking some of the following questions:

- After reading the sketch, what one thing do you remember most?
- Do you agree with my review of _____? If so, what did you find *least* convincing? If you disagreed, what did you find *most* convincing?

- What criterion seemed key to my judgment? Are there others that you thought I might mention but didn't?

- How do I come across in the sketch? Do I seem to know what I'm talking about? Or does it seem like a rant?

Reflecting on What You've Learned. Following your workshop session, write for five to seven minutes in your journal, beginning with a fastwrite in which you try to remember everything that you heard. Do this double-entry style, on the left page of your notebook. It will help you remember if you tell the story of your workshop session: The workshop began when...And then,...And then,.... When you're done trying to recall everything you can about what group members said to you, shift to the opposing right page and fastwrite about your reactions to what they said. What made sense? What didn't? How might you try one or more of the suggestions you like in the next draft?

Research and Other Strategies: Gathering More Information

If your workshop went well, you might feel ready to start the next draft. But remember this: It is always best to work from an abundance of information. It almost always pays off to resist the temptation to rush the draft and spend a little more time collecting information that will help you write it. Consider the following:

Re-Experience. Probably the single most useful thing you can do to prepare for the next draft is to collect more observations of your subject. Why? You're much more focused now on what you think, what criteria most influence that judgment, and what particular evidence you were lacking in the sketch that will make your review more convincing.

Interview. If you opted not to spend much time talking to people, you should strongly consider collecting the comments, opinions, and observations of others about the subject of your review. If you reviewed a concert or other event, find others who attended to interview. If you reviewed a film, get a small group of friends to watch the movie with you and jot down their reactions afterward. If it would be helpful to collect data on how people feel, consider designing a brief survey.

Also consider interviewing someone who is an expert on the thing you're reviewing.

Read. Go to the library and search for information about your subject. That will make you more of an expert. Look for books and articles in the following categories:

- *Information about how it's made or designed.* You love Martin's newest classical guitar but you really don't know much about the rosewood used in it. Search for books and articles on the qualities of wood that guitar makers value most.

- *Other reviews.* Search the Web and the library for other reviews of your subject. If you're reviewing a consumer product or some aspect of popular culture, check a database of general-interest periodicals such as *The General Reference Center* or *Reader's Guide Abstracts.* Also check newspaper databases. Has anyone else written about your topic?

- *Background information on relevant people, companies, traditions, local developments, and so on.* For example, if you're reviewing Bob Dylan's new CD, it would be helpful to know more about the evolution of his music. Check the electronic book index for a Dylan biography. Reviewing a modern dance performance? Find out more about the American tradition in the genre by checking the *Encyclopedia of Dance and Ballet* in the library's reference room.

Composing the Draft

Seth Schiesel's review of the fourth version of the video game "Grand Theft Auto" (see page 169) begins this way:

> I was rolling through the neon deluge of a place very like Times Square the other night in my Landstalker sport utility vehicle, listening to David Bowie's "Fascination" on the radio. The glittery urban landscape was almost enough to make me forget the warehouse of cocaine dealers I was headed uptown to rip off.

It isn't simply the punchy language that makes this lead paragraph compelling (e.g., "neon deluge" and "rip off"). It does three things that good beginnings should do:

1. Raises questions the reader might want to learn the answers to.
2. Creates a relationship between reader and writer.
3. Gets right to the subject without unnecessary scaffolding.

While we know from the title of the piece that this is about a video game, Schiesel's opening makes us wonder about what exactly is going on here, who this guy is, and what he is talking about. And the lead does what reviews of video games should do: get right to the *experience* of playing the game. He doesn't squander his beginning on providing background information, or talking about himself, or unnecessary pronouncements ("This paper will blah, blah, blah.").

Here are some other approaches to a strong lead for a review:

- Begin with a common misconception about your subject and promise to challenge it.
- Begin with an anecdote that reveals what you like or dislike.
- Help readers realize the relevance of your subject by showing how it's used, what it says, or why it's needed in a familiar situation.
- Provide interesting background that your readers may not know.

Methods of Development. What are some ways to organize your review?

Narrative. If you're reviewing a performance or any other kind of experience that has a discrete beginning and end, then telling a story about what you saw, felt, and thought is a natural move. Another way to use narrative is to tell the story of your thinking about your subject, an approach that lends itself to a delayed thesis essay where your judgment of final claim comes late rather than early.

Comparison/Contrast. You already know that comparison of other items in the same category you're evaluating—say, other science fiction films, or other electric cars, or laptops—can be a useful approach to writing an evaluation. If comparison is an important element, you might structure your essay around it, looking first at a comparable item and then contrasting it with another.

Question to Answer. One of the most straightforward methods of structuring a review is to simply begin by raising the question we explored earlier: *What makes _____ good?* This way, you make your criteria for evaluation explicit. From there, the next move is obvious—how well does the thing you're evaluating measure up?

Using Evidence. The most important evidence in an evaluation is your observations of the thing itself. These should be specific. Who was the best performer, or who was the worst? When did that become obvious during the show? What did he or she say or do? You will most likely obtain this evidence through *primary research*. You'll attend the concert, listen to the CD, or visit the coffeehouse. You may also use evidence from secondary sources; for example, what did another critic say or observe? But in general, the most authoritative evidence in an evaluation comes from direct observation.

Workshopping the Draft

If your draft is subject to peer review, see Chapter 10 for details on how to organize workshop groups and decide on how your group can help you, something that depends on how you feel about the work so far and the quality of your draft. The following journal activities and questions should help you make the most of your opportunity to get peer feedback on your work in progress.

Reflecting on the Draft. Prepare for peer review of your draft by spending three minutes fastwriting in your journal from the following prompt: The thing that I liked most about this draft was… Now fastwrite for three more minutes beginning with the following prompt: The thing that bothered me most about this draft was…

Finally, choose one part of your draft that you are *least* sure of; perhaps you think it's unconvincing or cheesy or unclear. Present this passage to your workshop group and ask what they think without initially voicing your concerns about it.

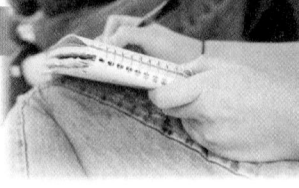

ONE STUDENT'S RESPONSE

Christy's Journal

REFLECTING ON THE DRAFT

The thing I liked most about this draft is the introduction. However, it does need some work structurally. But I feel I came in strong. The next paragraph gives the reader some clue as to what my criteria are, which gives me a foundation and a slant for the rest of the paper.

    The thing I liked least about the paper is the ending. The conclusion needs to be bulked up a bit, and I think I need to say a little more about Ilsa's character. I need to look at thoughts that might be a little too condensed, and try to elaborate on them.

Questions for Readers. Because evaluative writing is meant to be persuasive, pose some questions for your workshop group that help you gauge how convincing your draft is.

1. At what point in the draft did you think my argument was most effective?

2. When was it least effective?

3. Did you care about what I was evaluating? If not, how might I make you care more?

4. How do I come across as a speaker in this essay? What descriptive words would you use to describe me (*fair, critical, serious, nitpicky,* and so on)?

5. Is there a relevant comparison I might have made here but didn't?

OPTION FOR REVIEW ESSAY WORKSHOP

1. Divide each workshop group into two teams—believers and doubters.

2. Believers are responsible for presenting to doubters why the writer's review is convincing and fair.

3. Doubters challenge the writer's judgments and respond to the believers' claims.

4. The writer observes this conversation without participating.

5. After five minutes, believers and doubters drop their roles and discuss suggestions for revision with the writer.

Revising the Draft

Revision is a continual process, not a last step. You've been revising—literally "reseeing" your subject—from the first messy fastwriting in your journal. But the things that get your attention during revision vary depending on where you are in the writing process. You've generated material, chosen a topic, done some research, and written both a sketch and draft. Most students think that the only thing left to do is "fix things": Check for misspellings. Correct an awkward sentence or two. Come up with a better title. This is editing, not revision, and while editing is important, to focus solely on smaller "fixes" after writing a first draft squanders an opportunity to really *learn* from what the draft is telling you, or perhaps not quite telling you.

Chapter 9 can help guide these discoveries. The questions you can ask a draft fall into five categories: purpose, idea, information, development, and editing. Use the chart on the next page to find the revision strategies in Chapter 9 that might help you resee what you've written so far.

Review drafts also have some fairly typical problems, most of which can be addressed by repeating some of the steps in this chapter or selecting appropriate revision strategies in Chapter 9.

- Do you provide enough background on your subject for readers who aren't as familiar with it as you?

- Is the draft's *ethos* effective? In other words, do you come across as judgmental yet fair, authoritative yet cautious? Is the tone or voice of the draft persuasive to its audience?

- Is there enough evidence? Does the draft offer enough specific information about its subject so that the reader can understand exactly why you make a particular judgment about it?

- Do you go beyond a simple assessment of the subject—"it was good or bad because..." and offer a range of commentary on the subject's strengths and weaknesses?

Polishing the Draft

After you've dealt with the big issues in your draft—is it sufficiently focused, does it answer the *So what?* question, is it well organized, and so on—you must deal with the smaller problems. You've carved the stone into an appealing figure, but now you need to polish it. Are your paragraphs coherent? How do you manage transitions? Are your sentences fluent and concise? Are there any errors in spelling or syntax?

Before you finish your draft, work through the following checklist:

✓ Every paragraph is about one thing.
✓ The transitions between paragraphs aren't abrupt.
✓ The length of sentences varies in each paragraph.

GUIDE TO REVISION STRATEGIES

Problems in the Draft (Chapter 9)	Page Number
Unclear purpose ■ Not sure what the essay is about? Fails to answer the *So what?* question?	327
Unclear thesis, theme, or main idea ■ Not sure what you're trying to say? Judgment isn't clear?	333
Lack of information or development ■ Needs more details; more evidence from the review subject? ■ Criteria need work?	340
Disorganized ■ Doesn't move logically or smoothly from paragraph to paragraph?	344
Unclear or awkward at the level of sentences and paragraphs ■ Seems choppy or hard to follow at the level of sentences or paragraphs?	353

✓ Each sentence is concise. There are no unnecessary words or phrases.

✓ You've checked grammar, particularly verb agreement, run-on sentences, unclear pronouns, and misused words (*there/their, where/were*, and so on). (See the handbook at the end of the book for help with these grammar issues.)

✓ You've run your spellchecker and proofed your paper for misspelled words.

■ STUDENT ESSAY

Bayley Crow reviews Michael Pollan's book, *In Defense of Food: An Eater's Manifesto*, during a semester in which we focused on the topic of food. As we read and discussed the book, students kept a Reading Journal in which they summarized each section of the book and noted their reactions and questions. Bayley agreed with Pollan's declaration: "Eat Food. Mostly Plants. Not Too Much." In her Reading Journal, Bayley commented on Pollan's sense of humor, as well as his effective use of information and scientific studies. As she developed her review, she based her judgment that Pollan's book is both convincing and entertaining on these criteria: a clear argument, sufficient and relevant evidence, and an effective connection with readers. In her essay, she explains Pollan's argument and gives examples of studies he cites and jokes he makes.

Give Food a Chance
Bayley Alyson Crow

Michael Pollan's book *In Defense of Food* is at times hard to stomach. This is due to the fact that the information he is presenting is both, at times, hard to hear and a close hit to home. Though the information being presented is difficult, Pollan makes it easier to handle by interspersing his book with bits of sarcasm and humor that at times cause laugh-out-loud moments. His tone throughout the book helps to keep the reader sane even with all of the difficult information being presented. Pollan's main argument is that, although humans are able to live off of many different types of diets, the one that Americans choose and the one that is spreading to most industrialized countries is basically toxic to the human body. This diet has a name, the Western diet, and though people are already suffering the effects of this diet, Pollan does give hope for the future. By first explaining the origins of the Western diet and the circumstances during which it was popularized, he sets up the last section of his book in which he gives advice on how to change.

Pollan's purpose for writing *In Defense of Food* is clear: to inform readers about a potentially serious threat caused by the popular diets of Americans today. Readers are offered a background on nutritionism's birth and just how food scientists came to be. Pollan outlines some of the big confusion that people face about what to eat: "The history of modern nutritionism has been a history of macronutrients at war: protein against carbs; carbs against proteins, and then fats; fats against carbs" (30). The problem with all of these "wars" of macronutrients is the simple fact that they all deal with a nutrient and not an actual food source. One nutrient may not be responsible for the positive or negative effects that are heralded. Also, because the experiment is being done on a nutrient's effect on a person, the nutrient has to be replaced by a substitute, which cannot be accounted for in the experiment. The need to focus on nutrients was solidified in 1977 when the Senate Select Committee on Nutrition and Human Needs "issued a fairly straightforward set of dietary guidelines, calling on Americans to cut down on their consumption of red meat and dairy products" (23). This information was released with the support of "a growing body of scientific opinion," which "held that the consumption of fat and dietary cholesterol, much of which came from meat and dairy products, was responsible for rising rates of heart disease during the twentieth century" (23). The release of this information sparked a lot of backlash from both the meat and dairy industries, which resulted in a second set of guidelines to be released by the committee, which avoided telling people to cut down on a type of whole food, and advised, "Choose meats, poultry, and fish that will reduce saturated fat intake" (23). This wording made saturated fat the culprit behind disease, not the actual foods in which the saturated fat is contained. The problem with trying to pick out just one part of a food that is either good or bad is that there is really no way to test out the theory because every nutrient that is taken out must be replaced by something else, which makes the experiment unstable. Indeed, in 2001, a study was released called "Types of Dietary Fat and Risk of Coronary Heart Disease: A Critical Review," which gives a very interesting bit of

(continued)

(continued)

news early on in the review: "It is now increasingly recognized that the low-fat campaign has been based on little scientific evidence and may have caused unintended health consequences" (43). The experiments may not have gone as food scientists planned, but little had been known of these findings. Pollan warns about possible heart disease and other "unintended health consequences" and of how unreliable nutrition science seems to be. The information that he gives is attention-getting and tells about the origins of popular diets and the dangers they may hold.

3   In a study performed by Kerin O'Dea, Pollan is able to offer evidence that, though the problems with eating a Western diet are severe, they can be reversed, or at least made to be not so terrible. After seeking out ten Aborigines in Australia who had migrated from living in the bush to living near a city, O'Dea found that they had developed type two diabetes and some form of heart disease, O'Dea coaxed them to move back to the bush for seven weeks where they would have to hunt and gather their own food. O'Dea stayed with them and monitored their health conditions and kept a record of what they ate. By the end of the seven weeks, the results were phenomenal. Pollan reports O'Dea's findings:

4   All had lost weight (an average of 17.9 pounds) and seen their blood pressure drop. Their triglyceride levels had fallen into the normal range. The proportion of omega-3 fatty acids in their tissues had increased dramatically. "In summary," O'Dea concluded, "all of the metabolic abnormalities of type II diabetes were either greatly improved or completely normalized in a group of diabetic Aborigines by a relatively short reversion to traditional hunter-gatherer lifestyle." (87)

5   In another study that Pollan reports, before World War II, a dentist, Weston A. Price, who had born in the late 1800s and thus witnessed the decline of the condition of teeth firsthand, decided to seek out those peoples eating their original natural diets. His findings were shocking. This dentist discovered that most peoples who were eating diets unlike the Westernized one had little to no need for dentists. He studied and documented many different diets of many different peoples and found their amount of tooth decay to be little to none. What Pollan deciphered from Price's research is simple, sort of: "The human body is adapted to, and apparently can thrive on an extraordinary range of different diets, but the Western diet, however you define it, does not seem to be one of them" (100). Though this bit of information seems harsh, Pollan cushions it by informing the reader that there are ways to get away from the Western diet, and even to reverse the deleterious effects of it, by giving his readers some guidelines on how to shop and how to eat.

6   In his book, Pollan displays very serious information, but luckily, he intersperses it with his own humor to give a little sugar with the spoonful of medicine he is doling out. During his discussion of nutritionism, Pollan throws in, "It seems to be a rule of nutritionism that for every good nutrient, there must be a bad nutrient to serve as its foil, the latter a focus for our food fears and the former for our enthusiasm" (30). Though there is truth to this statement, Pollan is playing off of everyone's knowledge of the timeless battle of good versus evil, as seen in countless Disney movies. To me, this statement sparks the ideas of Simba versus Scar; Aladdin versus Jafar; Snow White versus her evil step-mother the Queen/Witch. While speaking of the "health claims" that many products are now able to

carry, Pollan warns about "the Cocoa Puffs and Lucky Charms" that "are screaming their newfound 'whole-grain goodness' to the rafters" while the "most healthful foods in the supermarket sit there quietly in the produce section, silent as stroke victims" (39). The imagery that Pollan uses is what makes this description deserve at least a little chuckle; even if that chuckle has a bit of nervousness at the heart of it. As he is musing over what would happen if the information got out that nutrition scientists have been wrong about the lipid hypothesis, he wonders what the government could be afraid of. He answers, "That we'll binge on bacon double cheeseburgers? More likely that we'll come to the unavoidable conclusion that the emperors of nutrition have no clothes and never listen to them again" (45). Pollan is able to play off of stories and ideas that are considered common knowledge to make a point. His way of writing is very clever because he makes the information that he is presenting easier to handle by giving it to the readers with an inside joke.

Pollan's book makes a clear point and gives the evidence necessary to back it up. He 7 makes himself personable to the reader by including details and humor. The fact that the Western diet is no good for humans is made less severe by Pollan telling us that there are many diets out there that are good for humans to eat. Pollan makes a point to outline the problems that nutritionism presents, whether it is the problem with focusing on just one nutrient from a nutritional point of view or from a scientific point of view. By including valid research and different studies, Pollan gives his argument a very clear basis, which makes his argument feasible to the average reader.

Work Cited

Pollan, Michael. *In Defense of Food: An Eater's Manifesto*. New York: Penguin, 2008.

USING WHAT YOU HAVE LEARNED

1. A review is a form of argument. Spend sixty seconds making a focused list of everything you learned about how to write persuasively from this assignment.

2. Judgments aren't always rational; in fact, we often have gut reactions that guide our evaluations of people and things. What have you learned in this chapter about how you might approach judgments in ways that combine both feelings and reason?

3. Suppose you had to evaluate the methodology of a biology experiment, or the effectiveness of a business plan. What are the first three things you would do?

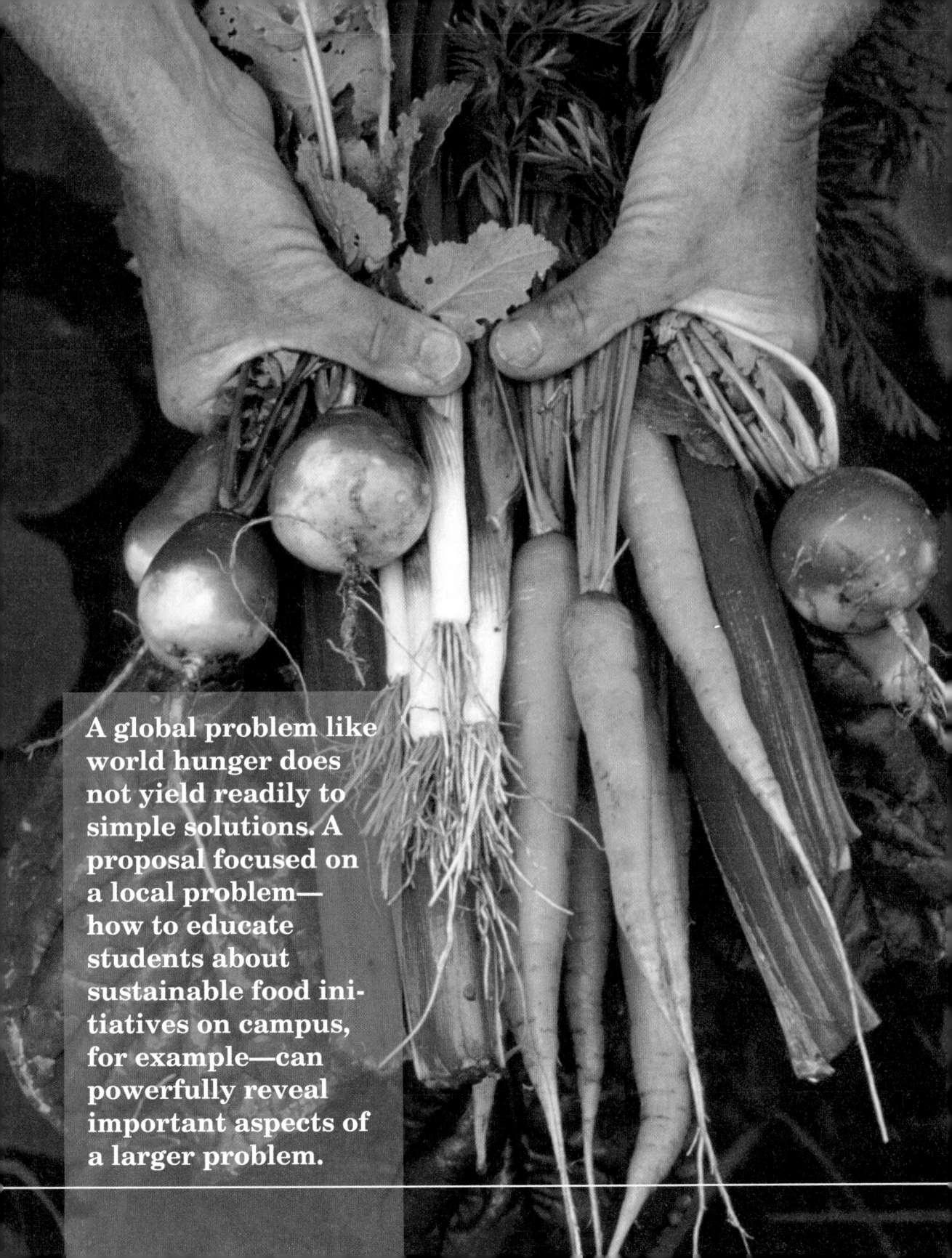

A global problem like world hunger does not yield readily to simple solutions. A proposal focused on a local problem—how to educate students about sustainable food initiatives on campus, for example—can powerfully reveal important aspects of a larger problem.

WRITING A PROPOSAL

WRITING ABOUT PROBLEMS AND SOLUTIONS

A small group of students sits around the round table in my office. Two are college sophomores, one is a junior, and the other is about to graduate. We're talking about problems each of us would love to solve. "I've got a short story due at three this afternoon and I've only written three pages," says Lana. Everyone nods sympathetically. "I'd really like to feel better about work," confides Amy, who works as a chef at a local restaurant. "Most days I just don't want to go." Margaret, who sits across the table from me, is a history major, familiar with the making and unmaking of nations and other grand narratives of colonialism, war, and social change. Her problem, however, is a bit more local. "I can't get my boyfriend to clean up the apartment," she says.

What about you, they ask me?

"The problem I most want to solve today is how to avoid getting scalded in the shower when someone in my house flushes the toilet," I say, getting into the spirit of things.

This conversation had not gone quite the way I expected. I know these students are socially engaged, politically aware, and academically gifted people. When I asked about problems that need solutions I expected that they might mention local issues such as housing developments that threaten the local foothills, or perhaps the difficulty of nontraditional students adjusting to the university, or possibly budget cuts that threaten the availability of courses next semester. If they had been thinking on a larger scale, say nationally or even internationally, perhaps the conversation would have turned to the spiraling federal deficit, the

What You'll Learn in This Chapter

- How to define a problem so that your readers have a stake in the solution.
- How to write a research proposal.
- What makes a proposal persuasive.
- Questions that will help you revise a proposal.

conflict in Darfur, or even some of the little-known problems associated with the use of cotton in the garment industry. Of course, I hadn't asked them to suggest social or economic problems. I had simply asked them what problems most vexed them at the moment.

I should not have been surprised that these would be boredom with work, too little time, and a messy boyfriend. These problems are quite real, and they demand attention, *now*. One was easy to solve. Lana would carve out extra time in the afternoon to finish her story—"I already know what I need to do," she said. But the other two problems—disenchantment with work and a boyfriend who's a slob—well, both Amy and Margaret saw these not so much as problems but realities they had to live with. In fact, all the students admitted that they rarely look at the world from the perspective of problem solving.

"What if you did?" I asked.

"Then I guess I'd ask myself if there was an opportunity to learn something," said Amy.

Problems of Consequence

While not all problems are equally solvable, the process of seeking and proposing solutions can be rewarding if you see, as Amy did, the opportunity to learn. There's another motivation, too: If the problem is shared by others, whatever you discover may interest them. Part of the challenge is recognizing problems *of consequence*. What makes a problem consequential?

1. It potentially affects a number of people.
2. The solution may not be simple.
3. There may be multiple solutions and people disagree about which is best.

My problem with getting scalded in the shower if somebody flushes a toilet is certainly a problem of consequence for me. It's painful. And I know that more than a few people have this problem. But the solution isn't complicated; all I need to do is go to Ace Hardware and buy a device for the shower head that senses dramatic temperature change. Problem solved. But what about Margaret's problem with her boyfriend? Is that a problem of consequence? Undoubtedly there are lots of people with messy mates, the solution is not at all obvious (just ask Margaret), and there are likely multiple ways of dealing with the problem. But has anyone else said anything about the topic? Like many other forms of inquiry, problem solving usually requires some research. After all, if we already knew the solution, we wouldn't have the problem. A final consideration, then, is whether anyone else has said something about the problem that might help you think about the best ways to solve it.

> While not all problems are equally solvable, the process of seeking and proposing solutions can be rewarding if you see the opportunity to learn.

A quick search of the Web and several of the university library's databases of articles produced an article on the psychological need of some women for tidiness, a Web page with advice on "Living with a Messy Man," and several scholarly articles on orderliness in the workplace and perceptions of messiness. That's not a bad beginning for background on an essay that looks at the problem and proposes some possible solutions. While Margaret may not succeed in her effort to get her boyfriend to pick up his socks, she will probably learn a few things about how to deal with the problem.

Problems of Scale

While our personal problems are very real, and they can be problems of consequence, the challenges of world hunger, war, environmental destruction, economic development, and human rights matter to far more people on the planet. These are also among the most complex problems to solve. I'm always delighted when writers in my classes are passionate about these issues, and they certainly can be great topics for writing. But as always, narrowing the topic to something manageable—with a limited focus that allows you to decide what *not* to consider—is a crucial first step. Obviously, you're not going to have anything meaningful to say about solving the world's hunger problems in a five-page essay (see Figure 6.1). But it might be possible to write a focused essay about the troubles

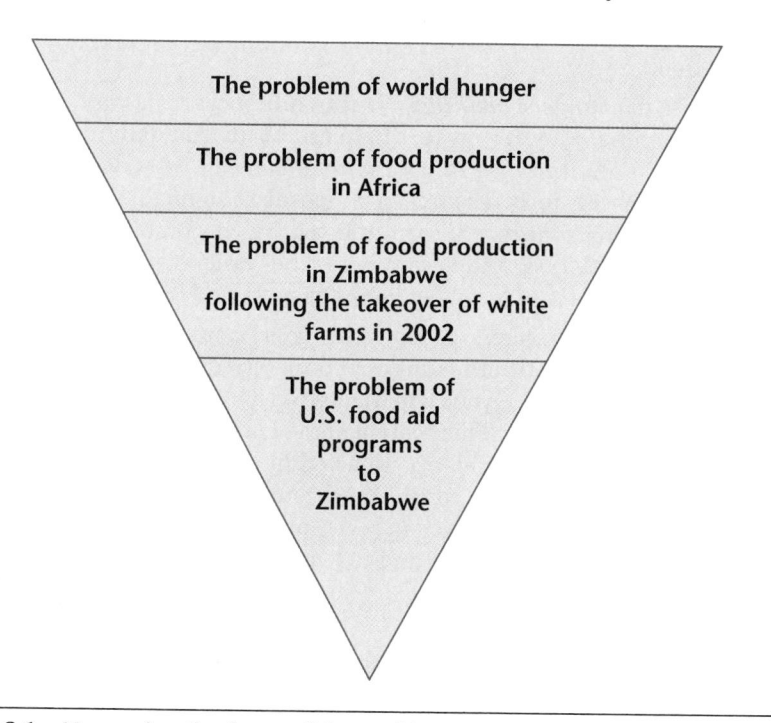

The problem of world hunger

The problem of food production in Africa

The problem of food production in Zimbabwe following the takeover of white farms in 2002

The problem of U.S. food aid programs to Zimbabwe

Figure 6.1   Narrowing the focus of the problem. Most of us want to find solutions to the big problems of the world, but big problems such as world hunger are complicated and do not readily yield to simple solutions. Unless you are writing a book-length proposal, it is better to narrow the focus of the problem to which you will propose solutions.

over food production in Zimbabwe, once one of Africa's most productive agricultural nations. Even better, narrow the topic further and investigate the particular U.S. aid policies that are failing to help feed hungry Zimbabwe children. Your interest in hunger can also easily lead to topics with a local angle—say, the reluctance of some hungry families in your community to use food stamps because of a local supermarket's policies. By focusing on the narrower problem, you can often reveal aspects of the larger problem much more powerfully.

The *scale* of the problems that you choose to explore, and their potential consequences, are two initial considerations when writing to solve problems. But why would you want to write about a problem in the first place?

MOTIVES FOR WRITING A PROPOSAL

Motives for writing a proposal include the following:

- *You* care *about the problem.* Whether it's something in your personal life—avoiding procrastination, having a more obedient dog, or finding a way to use less water in the garden—or a public issue—protecting bicyclists from traffic, increasing neighborhood police protection, or battling adolescent obesity—you should feel that the problem deserves your attention.

- *You hope to change something.* Writing a proposal is a way of overcoming powerlessness. Maybe you feel helpless about the daily deluge of scammers and junk messages in your e-mail. You can just complain about it. I do. But you can also research a proposal that might help you—and in turn the many others who are affected by the problem—better protect yourself from the Nigerian scammers who want to "give" you $8.5 million if you just send them a copy of your passport and $1,750.

- *You hope to learn something.* Does this go without saying? I don't think so. A proposal is like all other inquiry projects: You choose a topic because you're motivated to discover things you don't know. This motive alone isn't sufficient, of course. Others must be affected by the problem and have a stake in considering your solution. But if the problem is sufficiently complex and the solutions varied, then you stand to learn a lot.

> Writing a proposal is a way of overcoming powerlessness.

THE PROPOSAL AND ACADEMIC WRITING

Numerous academic situations involve writing to solve problems. The case-study approach, popular in business, medicine, and some social sciences, is essentially the presentation of a real-world problem for you to solve. Related to this is the growing popularity of problem-based learning, particularly in the sciences. Problem-based learning is an approach to inquiry that begins with a messy problem, rather than a question, and involves learners in coming up with tentative solutions. In these cases, writers' intentions may be less to persuade readers that certain solutions are best than to suggest a range of possibilities to consider.

In some classes, you'll be asked to write proposals. For example, political science courses may include an assignment to write a policy proposal, or an essay that looks at a specific public policy problem—say, the organization of the city government, or the state's role in wolf management (a big issue here in Idaho)—and suggest some possible solutions. In a marketing class, you might be asked to draft a proposal for dealing with a particular management problem. How do you motivate workers in a period when wages and benefits are flat? Research proposals are very common in the natural and physical sciences. These identify a particular problem—air pollution inversions in the valley, energy inefficiencies in buildings, declining populations of bull trout—and then propose a certain research program to study it. All of these forms of the proposal differ in the details but share many features and certainly an overall purpose: to get people to do something differently.

FEATURES OF THE FORM

The proposal is an academic form but it's even more common in everyday settings and situations. You can find writing that solves problems in the brochure at your doctor's office that suggests ways to deal with depression; you'll find it in your local newspaper in editorials that back a tax to create more parks; you'll find it in the case studies on marketing a new toy in your business textbook; you'll find it in the countless magazine articles and books that focus on "how to" and "self-help," on topics from anorexia to removing water marks on antique furniture.

The proposal is one of the most common forms of writing about problems and solutions. Here are some of its features:

- *Proposals usually deal with* both *problems and solutions*. What's interesting is seeing how the emphasis on each varies (see the next two points).

- *Proposals that emphasize solutions usually work from the premise that there is agreement on the problem*. That brochure in the doctor's office on depression may devote a single panel to describing the various ways the illness presents itself, and the rest of the brochure to what those who suffer from depression can do about it. Everybody agrees that depression is a problem, so it isn't necessary to persuade readers of the fact; therefore the emphasis is on solutions.

- *Proposals that emphasize the problem usually work from the premise that the problem isn't well known or well understood*. I recently read an article in the *New York Times* that described, at length, the problem that teen stars like Britney Spears have in holding their audience as they get older. Apparently, it's a problem shared by virtually all people who become celebrities as children, and "the majority don't get to the next level." Much of the article explored the nature of this problem because it isn't widely understood. The discussion of solutions was relatively brief, and of course featured an analysis of Madonna's many successful transformations.

■ *The writer usually includes outside perspectives on the problem or its solutions.* If you're writing about a problem of consequence, then other people have said something about it or will have something to say if you ask them. Occasionally, the writer might be an expert on the topic and won't think it's necessary to do much research. But more often, we learn about the problem as we seek to solve it and actively seek outside perspectives and ideas.

■ *Proposals that advocate certain solutions often use visual rhetoric.* If a main motive is to persuade people to buy something, support something, fund something, vote for something, or otherwise change their behavior, then writers may focus on the many visual ways they might get their point across. Some proposals use graphic devices such as bulleted lists or boldfaced headlines and other techniques for emphasis, drawing readers' attention to elements of the proposal that make it easier to read or more convincing, or give the impression that the writer is professional.

■ *Proposals justify their solutions.* You know, of course, that any claim is more convincing with supporting evidence, and solutions are a kind of argumentative claim. Typically proposals that offer certain solutions over others offer evidence—or justifications—for why. A proposal that calls for erecting a memorial statue that pays tribute to Vietnam veterans rather than creating a rose garden in their name might feature evidence from interviews with local vets or information about the success of similar monuments in other communities. Successful grant proposals depend on a convincing justification that would persuade a foundation or agency to fund one solution over competing ones.

READINGS

■ PROPOSAL 1

David Johnston has a problem and it's personal. But it's also a problem for others like him—military service members who find themselves stuck with homes they can't sell and debt they can't handle because they were called for duty in some other state or country. The economy these days is bad news for nearly everybody, but Johnston argues in "Housing and Our Military" that service people who often have no choice about when and where they'll be posted may be forced to sell their homes at a major loss. Worse, some banks may hold the sellers responsible for paying off the debt on the lost equity. Johnston finds himself paying a mortgage on a home he doesn't even own anymore. There's an appealing simplicity to Johnston's proposal. The problem-solution structure of the essay is obvious and it's concise and to-the-point. But like any argument (and proposals are a form of argument), "Housing and Our Military" works from premises or "warrants" that may or may not be obvious. In other words, what do you have to believe is true to find Johnston's solutions persuasive?

A few pages ago, I noted that an important motive for writing a proposal is that you hope to change something. Soon after David Johnston's essay was published in *USA Today,* several members of Congress read the piece and adopted most of Johnston's recommendations, in some cases word for word. Forty days later, the reforms he advocated became law as part of the American Recovery and Reinvestment Act of 2009. "I think forty days from argument essay to law of the land must be some kind of record," Johnston noted. "Words have power but timing is indispensible."

Housing and Our Military
David S. Johnston

The collapsing housing market has prompted many political and financial leaders to make urgent pleas to aid those owners who are facing the loss of their homes. But there is one group that gets little attention in that regard: the military family. 1

When change-in-duty-station orders arrive, these families do not have the option of waiting out the market for a return to pre-slump prices. Many military homeowners have lost equity in their houses and now owe more for their homes than they are worth. 2

I know this firsthand. Like many other servicemembers, I purchased a home near a military installation before the 2006 real estate decline. My family was too large to be given on-post housing in the Washington, D.C., market in 2004. But at the time, 3

(continued)

(continued)

we thought, "No problem," since we had just received a small inheritance that we could use for a down payment. If we got orders to move, we planned to rent or sell the house because we had equity and the market was climbing.

Change of Duty Station

4   I got orders sooner than I expected in the spring of 2006. So my wife and I put our house on the market for rent or sale and moved away. Then it happened: That same summer, the housing market began to crumble.

5   For the next two years, we were unable to sell the house. We lost our inheritance, all of our equity, and sold it for 40 percent less than its market high. Worse, the lenders levied the difference against us after the house was sold. We are now making payments on a house we no longer own.

6   If I declare bankruptcy, that jeopardizes my security clearances, so I am stuck. And I have heard similar stories from other soldiers. Although changes of duty stations are a part of military life, there should be a safety net in the travel regulations not unlike the rules for base closure/reduction-in-force regulations.

7   In response to the rise in home foreclosures, the Defense Department has heightened awareness of its family assistance programs that focus on financial counseling and education. But this does little to forestall the pressure of foreclosure or bankruptcy caused by the economic downturn.

Necessary Changes

8   Here's what I think should be done: First, the Pentagon should set up a program, perhaps in conjunction with the Veterans Benefits Administration (VBA), to refinance homes of struggling military members at 95 percent of the current market value while subsidizing the difference.

9   For those members who have lost their homes in foreclosure or by "short sell," and whose banks did not forgive any of the loss in the home's value, the government should provide incentives for the banks to forgive them or, potentially, assume the remainder of the unsecured loan.

10   Furthermore, the VBA should reconsider its loan program qualifications so that it would still allow good loans to families with poor credit if and only if that poor credit was a result of the housing market collapse and not of personal financial mismanagement.

11   Second, if the military relocates a servicemember who is a homeowner and the local housing market drops, a relocation assistance program ought to be available similar to Pentagon civilian programs that provide funds to cover a relocation.

12   When all options have been exhausted and the home will not sell, the servicemember should have the option to sell the property to the government at the amount owed. If the government acts soon, it can help many military families overcome these financial problems.

13   Nobody saw this coming, but military families really are hurting as never before.

Inquiring into the Essay

Use the four categories of inquiry questions—exploring, explaining, evaluating, and reflecting—to examine your ideas about David Johnston's "Housing and Our Military."

1. Explore your reaction to the premises behind Johnston's argument that the government should provide incentives and subsidies to service people who lose big on real estate because they were forced to sell when posted elsewhere. One premise, for example, is that while most enter the service knowing they may move around a lot, people who serve should be protected from big real estate losses when the market turns sour. Write fast for three minutes about what you think about this.

2. Explain other premises or (as logician Toulmin noted) "warrants" that you have to buy to find Johnston's solutions convincing.

3. Remember Aristotle's rhetorical triangle? (See page 10.) Evaluate how effectively this essay uses ethos, pathos, and logos. Which of these does it emphasize most? How might that reflect how Johnston imagines his audience?

4. Not every personal problem will be useful as a focus for a public proposal like this one. Here's a list of what's bugging me today: The dog won't stop barking, my income tax materials are all over the place, my daughter Julia keeps borrowing my favorite guitar, my Windows computer boots up sloooowly, and the gray February weather is depressing. Which of these might be problems that others share and have solutions in which others might have some stake? In other words, what makes a personal problem worthy of a proposal like the ones we're discussing in this chapter?

■ PROPOSAL 2

A lot of people can't imagine a proposal without PowerPoint (or Keynote for Mac users). It's a remarkably versatile program that exploits the potential of visual rhetoric. You can combine images with text, animation, and even audio. Presentation slides challenge the user to think about what ideas to emphasize and which visual arrangements might dramatize them to an audience. Depending on how you order the slides, you can tell a different story. Maybe because of all these possibilities, PowerPoint presentations can be boring. There may be too much text, the animation can be obnoxious, or the images might be distracting. Worse still, the presenter uses presentation slides like a script rather than a technique for focusing emphasis on key points. Watching someone's back while he or she reads a PowerPoint text is an invitation to nod off.

The following PowerPoint proposal, "Green Dining," describes how the dining services at University of California–Santa Cruz are trying to solve the problem of energy inefficiency in the kitchen. This proposal doesn't dramatize the problem. It doesn't really need to since most everyone agrees that wasting energy in dining halls (or any other campus building, for that matter) is a problem. This slide presentation focuses on some solutions, and it works well because the proposal has modest ambitions. It addresses one very specific aspect of the campus dining operation: dishwashing. Even better, there is concrete evidence that one solution is already making a difference in energy use. After documenting this success, "Green Dining" goes on to present other measures that should have a similar impact.

Notice how much can be accomplished with simple images, minimal text, and logical arrangement.

Green Dining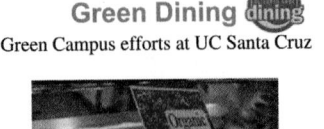
Green Campus efforts at UC Santa Cruz

Green Campus dining objectives

- Achieve Monterey Bay Green Business Certification
- Acquire new efficient technology
- Educate students about sustainable dining practices
- Adjust policies and procedures to conserve energy

Monterey Bay Green Business Certification

- An official recognition awarded by the *Monterey Bay Area Green Business Program*
- Businesses must take extensive measures to conserve resources prevent pollution, and minimize waste.

Savings Opportunities

- A typical dishwashing operation can use **over 2/3** of all water consumed at an establishment

- Often **1/2** of that water use is consumed by **pre-rinse spray nozzles**

- And that water is heated with energy

Smart Rinse Spray Nozzles

Low-flow "Smart-rinse" nozzles are one upgrade that can save hot water when rinsing and help businesses achieve Green Business Certification.

Spray Nozzle Specs

- Fisher "Ultra Spray"
- 1.15 GPM @ 60 PSI
- 1-hole clearance
- Easy-use, "knife spray" action that allows food to be easily removed
- Cost: roughly $50/unit

Benefits

- Saves water
- Saves energy
- Saves money
- Cleans faster
- Less splash back
- Covers larger surface area

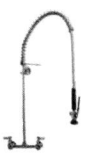

Success at UC Santa Cruz

5 "low-flow" nozzles were installed in various locations:	Nozzles were supplied and installed FOR FREE through the "Smart Rinse Program," a program of Ecology Action, a local Santa Cruz non-profit
• Crown/Merrill Dining • College 8/9 Dining • Owl's Nest Café • Terra Fresca Cafe	

Quantifiable Savings

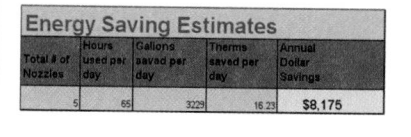

Energy Saving Estimates				
Total # of Nozzles	Hours used per day	Gallons saved per day	Therms saved per day	Annual Dollar Savings
5	65	3229	16.23	$8,175

Current Dining Projects

T8 Lighting retrofit

- 5 major dining halls
- Upgrade 32 watts → 28 Watts
- 1248 Lamps counted
- Roughly 5 KW saved

Future Dining Project

Variable control exhaust hoods

- Controls for commercial kitchen ventilation exhaust hoods
- Reduce energy costs by up to 70% during slow cooking periods

Project Benefits

- Massive energy savings
- Improved indoor air quality
- Optimum kitchen comfort
- Improved fire safety
- 1–4 year payback
- $1,500–$10,00 in annual savings

Questions?

Inquiring into the Essay

Explore, explain, evaluate, and reflect on "Green Dining."

1. Finish the following sentences in your journal, and follow them for a minute if you can. Write quickly.

   a. *As far as I'm concerned, PowerPoint is _____.*

   b. *The best slide presentations _____.*

   c. *The worst slide presentations _____.*

   d. *When I do PowerPoint (or Keynote), the main thing I think about is _____.*

   e. *A lot of times, people do PowerPoint when they should _____.*

2. Using some of the ideas you generated in the first question, craft a definition of an effective PowerPoint proposal, identifying specifically what qualities it should have.

3. Use your definition in the previous question to evaluate "Green Dining." Is it persuasive?

4. The preceding series of questions, if used consecutively, constitutes a method for thinking through writing about what you've read, working toward a more thoughtful evaluation. Reflect on how that process worked for you. Did you end up getting better ideas about what you think because you took time to do the prewriting?

■ PROPOSAL 3

Psychologists talk about people who have learned helplessness. Like Eeyore in *Winnie the Pooh,* they are people who feel like their world basically stinks and there is nothing they can do about it. "Why bother?" they say. "What difference will it make?" And yet, it's hard not to feel a little like Eeyore in the face of climate change. It's such a big problem, and what can the little guy do? Michael Pollan, quoting Wendell Berry, argues in the following essay that this is the "cheap-energy mind" talking, the one that encourages us to believe that we're hopelessly dependent on other people and their grand technologies to get what we need. The climate problem *is* huge, but in "Why Bother?" Pollan has a simple solution: Grow a vegetable garden, even a tiny one. What is so intriguing about his essay is not just the simplicity of the solution it offers but that Pollan manages to make it persuasive. See if you agree.

Why Bother?

Michael Pollan

Why bother? That really is the big question facing us as individuals hoping to do   1
something about climate change, and it's not an easy one to answer. I don't know
about you, but for me the most upsetting moment in *An Inconvenient Truth* came
long after Al Gore scared the hell out of me, constructing an utterly convincing case
that the very survival of life on earth as we know it is threatened by climate change.
No, the really dark moment came during the closing credits, when we are asked
to…change our light bulbs. That's when it got really depressing. The immense dis-
proportion between the magnitude of the problem Gore had described and the puni-
ness of what he was asking us to do about it was enough to sink your heart.

But the drop-in-the-bucket issue is not the only problem lurking behind the "why   2
bother" question. Let's say I do bother, big time. I turn my life upside-down, start bik-
ing to work, plant a big garden, turn down the thermostat so low I need the Jimmy
Carter signature cardigan, forsake the clothes dryer for a laundry line across the yard,
trade in the station wagon for a hybrid, get off the beef, go completely local. I could
theoretically do all that, but what would be the point when I know full well that
halfway around the world there lives my evil twin, some carbon-footprint *doppel-
gänger* in Shanghai or Chongqing who has just bought his first car (Chinese car ownership is where ours was back in 1918), is eager to swallow every bite of meat I for-
swear and who's positively itching to replace every last pound of CO_2 I'm struggling
no longer to emit. So what exactly would I have to show for all my trouble?

A sense of personal virtue, you might suggest, somewhat sheepishly. But what good   3
is that when virtue itself is quickly becoming a term of derision? And not just on the
editorial pages of the *Wall Street Journal* or on the lips of the (former) vice president,
who famously dismissed energy conservation as a "sign of personal virtue." No, even in
the pages of the *New York Times* and the *New Yorker,* it seems the epithet "virtuous,"
when applied to an act of personal environmental responsibility, may be used only
ironically. Tell me: How did it come to pass that virtue—a quality that for most of history
has generally been deemed, well, a virtue—became a mark of liberal softheadedness?
How peculiar, that doing the right thing by the environment—buying the hybrid, eating
like a locavore—should now set you up for the Ed Begley Jr. treatment.

And even if in the face of this derision I decide I am going to bother, there arises   4
the whole vexed question of getting it right. Is eating local or walking to work really
going to reduce my carbon footprint? According to one analysis, if walking to work
increases your appetite and you consume more meat or milk as a result, walking
might actually emit more carbon than driving. A handful of studies have recently suggested that in certain cases under certain conditions, produce from places as far away
as New Zealand might account for less carbon than comparable domestic products.

(continued)

(continued)

True, at least one of these studies was co-written by a representative of agribusiness interests in (surprise!) New Zealand, but even so, they make you wonder. If determining the carbon footprint of food is really this complicated, and I've got to consider not only "food miles" but also whether the food came by ship or truck and how lushly the grass grows in New Zealand, then maybe on second thought I'll just buy the imported chops at Costco, at least until the experts get their footprints sorted out.

5   There are so many stories we can tell ourselves to justify doing nothing, but perhaps the most insidious is that, whatever we do manage to do, it will be too little too late. Climate change is upon us, and it has arrived well ahead of schedule. Scientists' projections that seemed dire a decade ago turn out to have been unduly optimistic: the warming and the melting is occurring much faster than the models predicted. Now truly terrifying feedback loops threaten to boost the rate of change exponentially, as the shift from white ice to blue water in the Arctic absorbs more sunlight and warming soils everywhere become more biologically active, causing them to release their vast stores of carbon into the air. Have you looked into the eyes of a climate scientist recently? They look really scared.

6   So do you still want to talk about planting gardens?

7   I do....

8   For us to wait for legislation or technology to solve the problem of how we're living our lives suggests we're not really serious about changing—something our politicians cannot fail to notice. They will not move until we do. Indeed, to look to leaders and experts, to laws and money and grand schemes, to save us from our predicament represents precisely the sort of thinking—passive, delegated, dependent for solutions on specialists—that helped get us into this mess in the first place. It's hard to believe that the same sort of thinking could now get us out of it.

9   Thirty years ago, Wendell Berry, the Kentucky farmer and writer, put forward a blunt analysis of precisely this mentality. He argued that the environmental crisis of the 1970s—an era innocent of climate change; what we would give to have back *that* environmental crisis!—was at its heart a crisis of character and would have to be addressed first at that level: at home, as it were. He was impatient with people who wrote checks to environmental organizations while thoughtlessly squandering fossil fuel in their everyday lives—the 1970s equivalent of people buying carbon offsets to atone for their Tahoes and Durangos. Nothing was likely to change until we healed the "split between what we think and what we do." For Berry, the "why bother" question came down to a moral imperative: "Once our personal connection to what is wrong becomes clear, then we have to choose: we can go on as before, recognizing our dishonesty and living with it the best we can, or we can begin the effort to change the way we think and live."

10   For Berry, the deep problem standing behind all the other problems of industrial civilization is "specialization," which he regards as the "disease of the modern character." Our society assigns us a tiny number of roles: we're producers (of one thing) at work, consumers of a great many other things the rest of the time,

and then once a year or so we vote as citizens. Virtually all of our needs and desires we delegate to specialists of one kind or another—our meals to agribusiness, health to the doctor, education to the teacher, entertainment to the media, care for the environment to the environmentalist, political action to the politician....

Here's the point: Cheap energy, which gives us climate change, fosters precisely the mentality that makes dealing with climate change in our own lives seem impossibly difficult. Specialists ourselves, we can no longer imagine anyone but an expert, or anything but a new technology or law, solving our problems. Al Gore asks us to change the light bulbs because he probably can't imagine us doing anything much more challenging, like, say, growing some portion of our own food. We can't imagine it, either, which is probably why we prefer to cross our fingers and talk about the promise of ethanol and nuclear power—new liquids and electrons to power the same old cars and houses and lives.

11

The "cheap-energy mind," as Wendell Berry called it, is the mind that asks, "Why bother?" because it is helpless to imagine—much less attempt—a different sort of life, one less divided, less reliant. Since the cheap-energy mind translates everything into money, its proxy, it prefers to put its faith in market-based solutions—carbon taxes and pollution-trading schemes. If we could just get the incentives right, it believes, the economy will properly value everything that matters and nudge our self-interest down the proper channels. The best we can hope for is a greener version of the old invisible hand. Visible hands it has no use for.

12

But while some such grand scheme may well be necessary, it's doubtful that it will be sufficient or that it will be politically sustainable before we've demonstrated to ourselves that change is possible. Merely to give, to spend, even to vote, is not to do, and there is so much that needs to be done—without further delay. In the judgment of James Hansen, the NASA climate scientist who began sounding the alarm on global warming 20 years ago, we have only 10 years left to start cutting— not just slowing—the amount of carbon we're emitting or face a "different planet." Hansen said this more than two years ago, however; two years have gone by, and nothing of consequence has been done. So: eight years left to go and a great deal left to do.

13

Which brings us back to the "why bother" question and how we might better answer it. The reasons not to bother are many and compelling, at least to the cheap-energy mind. But let me offer a few admittedly tentative reasons that we might put on the other side of the scale:

14

If you do bother, you will set an example for other people. If enough other people bother, each one influencing yet another in a chain reaction of behavioral change, markets for all manner of green products and alternative technologies will prosper and expand. (Just look at the market for hybrid cars.) Consciousness will be raised, perhaps even changed: new moral imperatives and new taboos might take root in the culture. Driving an SUV or eating a 24-ounce steak or illuminating your McMansion like an airport runway at night might come to be regarded as

15

(continued)

(continued)

outrages to human conscience. Not having things might become cooler than having them. And those who did change the way they live would acquire the moral standing to demand changes in behavior from others—from other people, other corporations, even other countries.

16   All of this could, theoretically, happen. What I'm describing (imagining would probably be more accurate) is a process of viral social change, and change of this kind, which is nonlinear, is never something anyone can plan or predict or count on. Who knows, maybe the virus will reach all the way to Chongqing and infect my Chinese evil twin. Or not. Maybe going green will prove a passing fad and will lose steam after a few years, just as it did in the 1980s, when Ronald Reagan took down Jimmy Carter's solar panels from the roof of the White House.

17   Going personally green is a bet, nothing more or less, though it's one we probably all should make, even if the odds of it paying off aren't great. Sometimes you have to act as if acting will make a difference, even when you can't prove that it will. That, after all, was precisely what happened in Communist Czechoslovakia and Poland, when a handful of individuals like Vaclav Havel and Adam Michnik resolved that they would simply conduct their lives "as if" they lived in a free society. That improbable bet created a tiny space of liberty that, in time, expanded to take in, and then help take down, the whole of the Eastern bloc.

18   So what would be a comparable bet that the individual might make in the case of the environmental crisis? Havel himself has suggested that people begin to "conduct themselves as if they were to live on this earth forever and be answerable for its condition one day." Fair enough, but let me propose a slightly less abstract and daunting wager. The idea is to find one thing to do in your life that doesn't involve spending or voting, that may or may not virally rock the world but is real and particular (as well as symbolic) and that, come what may, will offer its own rewards. Maybe you decide to give up meat, an act that would reduce your carbon footprint by as much as a quarter. Or you could try this: determine to observe the Sabbath. For one day a week, abstain completely from economic activity: no shopping, no driving, no electronics.

19   But the act I want to talk about is growing some—even just a little—of your own food. Rip out your lawn, if you have one, and if you don't—if you live in a high-rise, or have a yard shrouded in shade—look into getting a plot in a community garden. Measured against the Problem We Face, planting a garden sounds pretty benign, I know, but in fact it's one of the most powerful things an individual can do—to reduce your carbon footprint, sure, but more important, to reduce your sense of dependence and dividedness: to change the cheap-energy mind.

20   A great many things happen when you plant a vegetable garden, some of them directly related to climate change, others indirect but related nevertheless.

Growing food, we forget, comprises the original solar technology: calories produced by means of photosynthesis. Years ago the cheap-energy mind discovered that more food could be produced with less effort by replacing sunlight with fossil-fuel fertilizers and pesticides, with a result that the typical calorie of food energy in your diet now requires about 10 calories of fossil-fuel energy to produce. It's estimated that the way we feed ourselves (or rather, allow ourselves to be fed) accounts for about a fifth of the greenhouse gas for which each of us is responsible.

21 Yet the sun still shines down on your yard, and photosynthesis still works so abundantly that in a thoughtfully organized vegetable garden (one planted from seed, nourished by compost from the kitchen and involving not too many drives to the garden center), you can grow the proverbial free lunch—CO_2-free and dollar-free. This is the most-local food you can possibly eat (not to mention the freshest, tastiest and most nutritious), with a carbon footprint so faint that even the New Zealand lamb council dares not challenge it. And while we're counting carbon, consider too your compost pile, which shrinks the heap of garbage your household needs trucked away even as it feeds your vegetables and sequesters carbon in your soil. What else? Well, you will probably notice that you're getting a pretty good workout there in your garden, burning calories without having to get into the car to drive to the gym. (It is one of the absurdities of the modern division of labor that, having replaced physical labor with fossil fuel, we now have to burn even more fossil fuel to keep our unemployed bodies in shape.) Also, by engaging both body and mind, time spent in the garden is time (and energy) subtracted from electronic forms of entertainment.

22 You begin to see that growing even a little of your own food is, as Wendell Berry pointed out 30 years ago, one of those solutions that, instead of begetting a new set of problems—the way "solutions" like ethanol or nuclear power inevitably do—actually beget other solutions, and not only of the kind that save carbon. Still more valuable are the habits of mind that growing a little of your own food can yield. You quickly learn that you need not be dependent on specialists to provide for yourself—that your body is still good for something and may actually be enlisted in its own support. If the experts are right, if both oil and time are running out, these are skills and habits of mind we're all very soon going to need. We may also need the food. Could gardens provide it? Well, during World War II, victory gardens supplied as much as 40 percent of the produce Americans ate.

23 But there are sweeter reasons to plant that garden, to bother. At least in this one corner of your yard and life, you will have begun to heal the split between what you think and what you do, to commingle your identities as consumer and producer and citizen. Chances are, your garden will re-engage you with your neighbors, for you will have produce to give away and the need to borrow their tools. You will have

(continued)

(continued)

reduced the power of the cheap-energy mind by personally overcoming its most debilitating weakness: its helplessness and the fact that it can't do much of anything that doesn't involve division or subtraction. The garden's season-long transit from seed to ripe fruit—*will you get a load of that zucchini?!*—suggests that the operations of addition and multiplication still obtain, that the abundance of nature is not exhausted. The single greatest lesson the garden teaches is that our relationship to the planet need not be zero-sum, and that as long as the sun still shines and people still can plan and plant, think and do, we can, if we bother to try, find ways to provide for ourselves without diminishing the world.

Inquiring into the Essay

Explore, explain, evaluate, and reflect on Michael Pollan's "Why Bother?"

1. Fastwrite in your journal for five minutes without stopping and explore how your life might operate from a "cheap-energy mind." You might tell yourself the story of what you did, say, yesterday that shows how that mindset operates. Be specific.

2. Test your understanding of Pollan's argument. After reading "Why Bother?" compose a fast paragraph that summarize how Pollan answers his own question: Why bother? Do this on the left page of your journal.

3. So are you convinced? On the right journal page, answer this question: Will you be digging up the lawn to plant zucchini?

4. Proposals like this, which advocate lifestyle change, seek to do something that is enormously difficult—to get people to change not just their behavior but their habits. Reflect on what you think are the best ways to accomplish this. What *kinds* of persuasion does changing behavior demand?

WRITING IN THE DISCIPLINES

Writing a Research Proposal

A research proposal is a kind of action plan that explains your research question, what you expect might be the answer, how your investigation contributes to what has already been said on the topic, and how you will proceed.

While the format varies, most research proposals aim to persuade readers that (1) the project is reasonable given the investigator's time and resources, (2) the research question or problem is significant, and (3) the researcher has a good plan for getting the job done.

The following elements are typically included in a research proposal:

- **Title:** Short and descriptive.

- **Abstract:** A brief statement of what you intend to do, including your research question and hypothesis, if you've got one.

- **Background or context:** Why is the project worth doing? What problem does it solve, or how does it advance our understanding of the subject? This key section establishes where your question fits into the ongoing conversation about your topic, in your class, in the academic literature, or both. You also want to demonstrate that you've done your homework—you've got a handle on the relevant literature on your topic and understand how you might build on it.

- **Methodology or research design:** How will you try to answer your research question? How will you limit your focus? What information will you need to gather, and how will you do it?

- **Results:** This isn't a common section for proposals in the humanities, but it certainly is in the sciences. How will you analyze the data you collect?

- **References or works cited:** Almost all research proposals, because they review relevant literature, include a bibliography. Sometimes you may be asked to annotate it (see Appendix C, "The Annotated Bibliography").

Because the research proposal is a persuasive document, craft it to keep your reader engaged; find a good balance between generalities and detail, avoid jargon, and demonstrate your curiosity and eagerness to pursue your question.

SEEING THE FORM

A Problem in Pictures

When members of the San Francisco Bicycle Coalition (SFBC) wanted to dramatize the problem of insufficient space for bikes on a city commuter train, they did it with pictures. It was a powerfully simple idea. They took shots of three morning trains, each overloaded with bicycles and nearly empty of passengers. The contrast is obvious. And so is the solution to the problem: Add more space for bicycles on trains. A few months later, transit authorities did just that.

(continued)

Seeing the Form (*continued*)

No Space for Bikes:
A photo study of trains bumping cyclists out of SF.

1: Train 134: Sept 22 9:07 AM

2: Train 134: Sept 22 9:07 AM

3: Train 230: Sept 24 8:53 AM

4: Train 230: Sept 24 8:53 AM

5: Train 332: Sept 30 8:56 AM

6: Train 332: Sept 30 8:56 AM

Submitted to JBP Oct 2
by Benjamin Damm

THE WRITING PROCESS

INQUIRY PROJECT: WRITING A PROPOSAL

A problem needs to be solved and you have an idea how to do it. Developing your idea and presenting it is the general purpose of this assignment. Ultimately, you'll write a 1,000- to 1,500-word draft that has the following features:

- It addresses a problem of consequence and is written to an audience that might be interested in solutions.
- It is a problem of local concern. In other words, the scale of the problem is limited to the details that in some way affect your community.
- You justify the solutions you propose.
- The form of your proposal is linked to your purpose and audience.

mycomplab

For additional reading, writing, and research resources, go to
www.mycomplab.com

Thinking About Subjects

Amy, Lana, and Margaret, the three students with whom I talked about problems at the start of this chapter, didn't have much trouble coming up with them: Amy hates her work, Lana procrastinates, and Margaret has a messy boyfriend. Initially, each problem seemed a relatively private matter, hardly a suitable topic for a proposal. But it became apparent later that at least one of them—Margaret's problem with her boyfriend—was actually something that was both shared by other women and a topic about which something had been said.

> The explosion of "how to" and "self help" books and articles is evidence of the popularity of writing that attempts to solve problems.

Perhaps you already have a topic in mind for your proposal. But if you don't, or you want to explore some other possibilities, begin by generating a list of problems you'd like to solve without worrying about whether they're problems of consequence. Also don't worry too much yet about whether you have solutions to the problems you're generating. You can come up with those later. Try some of the generating exercises that follow.

Generating Ideas

Play with some ideas about subjects for the proposal assignment. Remember not to judge the material at this stage.

Listing Prompts. Lists can be rich sources of triggering topics. Let them grow freely, and when you're ready, use an item as the focus of another list or an episode of fastwriting. The following prompts should get you started.

ONE STUDENT'S RESPONSE

Caesar's Journal

LISTING PROMPTS

Problems in my life

Procrastination
Can't stick to a budget
Credit card debt
Hate the winter
Failing calculus
Girlfriend prefers Hector
Balancing studying and social life
Can't afford to travel
Work too much

Problems on campus

No sense of community
Drying up of work-study funds
Not enough diversity
Lines at the registrar
Recent tuition hike

Legislature underfunds higher
  education
Lousy food at the SUB
Textbooks are too expensive
Waiting list for child-care center

Problems in community

Overdevelopment of foothills
Litter and degradation of Boise River
Too few child-care options
Hate crimes
Concert venues inadequate
Traffic
Air pollution in Valley
Smell from sugar beet factory
Range fires

1. In your journal, spend three minutes brainstorming a list of problems in your personal life that you'd like to solve. Let the ideas come in waves.

2. Spend three minutes brainstorming a list of problems *on your campus, at your workplace*, or *in the local community* that affect you in some way, or that you feel something about. Don't worry about repeating items from the list you made in Listing Prompt 1.

3. Explore some possible causes of the problem by finishing the following sentence as many times as you can: This is a problem because _____.

Fastwriting Prompts. In the early stages of generating possible topics for an essay, fastwriting can be invaluable, *if* you allow yourself to write badly. Initially, don't worry about staying focused; sometimes you find the best triggering topics by ranging freely. Once you've tentatively settled on something, use a more focused fastwrite to try to generate information and ideas within the loose boundaries of your chosen topic.

1. Pick any of the items from the preceding lists as a launching place for a five-minute fastwrite. Explore some of the following questions:

    ▪ When did I first notice this was a problem?

    ▪ What's the worst part about it?

- What might be some of its causes?
- What moment, situation, or scene is most typical of this problem? Describe it as if you're experiencing it by writing in the present tense.
- How does this problem make me feel?
- What people do I associate with it?

2. Depending on how familiar you are with a problem that interests you, do a five-minute focused fastwrite that explores solutions, beginning with the sentence I think one of the ways to deal with _____ is _____. Follow that sentence as long as you can. When the writing stalls, use the following prompt: Another possible solution to the problem of _____ might be _____. Repeat these prompts as often as you can for ten minutes.

ONE STUDENT'S RESPONSE

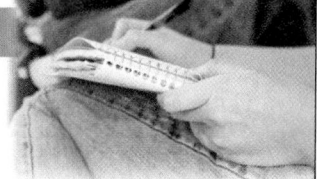

Gina's Journal: Fastwrite

I first became aware of how wasteful the modern lifestyle is about three years ago, when I first started dating Vinnie. What's bad is that most people aren't aware of the destruction they cause the environment, believe there is no other way, or are too lazy to think progressively. It's unfortunate when people choose to follow old habits instead of making daily active choices. This problem makes me feel dread, helplessness, and anger. I feel angry because I know that people can make a difference; I believe change is possible in the smallest and easiest of actions. I think the cause of this problem is the example the government leads, some of the media, and the influence parents have on their children. One specific example of this problem and how one small decision could greatly impact the Earth is with the restaurant chain, Subway. Right now, Subway wraps every sandwich it makes for customers in paper and then places it in a plastic bag. The plastic bags create an enormous amount of waste. If Subway merely made the decision to ask people if they wanted a bag, then less plastic would pollute the Earth. I believe many people wouldn't want a bag because they are immediately going to eat their sandwich and throw the bag away anyway.

   One solution to this problem is being open to change and new modes of thinking. People would need to question everything and think through the logistics completely. Some people may not know how to start, in which case I recommend reading literature and magazines that propose solutions such as *Ode*, *Back Home*, and *Mother Jones*. They could also attend renewable energy festivals and take workshops if they want to increase their awareness even further. I think one of the ways to deal with modern thinking and living styles is providing a good example for others. Make your choices wisely and don't give in to the "easy" decision.

Visual Prompts. Cluster a problem that concerns you. Build associations that help you think about people you associate with the problem, situations when it's most obvious, how it makes you feel, things that might cause the problem, and even possible solutions.

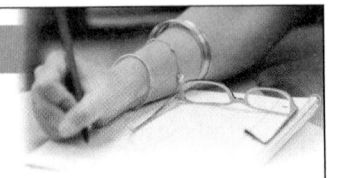

INQUIRING INTO THE DETAILS

Causation

One of my favorite clichés is, "This is a solution in search of a problem." Obviously, there's no point in proposing a solution if you can't win agreement that there's a problem in the first place. But once you do establish that there is a problem, the next thing is to examine what *causes* the problem. Controlling some of the causes may be the beginning of finding the solution. This exercise might help you discover those possibilities in the problem you've chosen to explore.

Begin with some journal work to flesh out your initial understandings and feelings about the problem.

1. At the top of a journal page, write *Causes*. Brainstorm a quick list of things that you believe contribute to or cause the problem. These might be composed as "because" statements. For example, if the problem is the lack of diversity on your campus, make a fast list of possible reasons by beginning with There is a lack of diversity on the Boise State campus because...

   - Idaho is sometimes perceived as a state with racial problems.
   - too few scholarships are targeted to minorities.
   - the history of African Americans and Latinos in Idaho isn't widely known among whites.
   - campus organizations don't do enough to promote diversity.
   - too few courses in the curriculum would appeal to minority students.
   - and so on.

   Remember that at this point you're brainstorming a fast list of *possible* causes. You may or may not know enough about the causes of the problem to be very certain about what you're saying here.

2. Choose *one* of the causes on your list that seems most plausible to you as contributing significantly to the problem, *or* that you find most interesting. Use this as a prompt for a five-minute fastwrite. Explore some of the following questions:

   - Do you have any personal experience with this particular cause?
   - In what ways, exactly, might it contribute to the problem?

> - Does this possible cause of the problem suggest anything about a possible solution?
> - When you compare it with other possible causes, what makes this one unique or significant?
>
> If the writing stalls, choose another cause from your list in Step 1, and explore it through writing using the preceding questions, if they're helpful.
>
> One of the things this exercise might do is help you to use cause/effect as a mode of inquiry that exposes relationships, and not just the connections between the problem and some of the reasons it exists, but also the problem and its possible solutions. Remember, your goal is to write a proposal; it's not enough to simply dramatize the problem.

Research Prompts. Research—reading, observing, and talking to people—can be enormously generative at any stage in the inquiry process, including the beginning. It's one of the best ways to discover a topic, and it almost always generates information you can use later in your essay once you've chosen a topic. Try some of the following research prompts to help you along.

1. Interview your classmates about what they think are the biggest problems facing them as students. Interview student or faculty leaders or administrators about what they think are the biggest problems facing the university community. Do the same with community leaders.

2. Design an informal survey targeted to a particular group that you're interested in—students, student-athletes, local businesspeople, sports fans, migrant workers, and so on. This group may or may not be one to which you belong. Discover what they believe are the most serious problems they face.

3. Become a student of a local newspaper. In particular, pay attention to the letters to the editor and the local community pages. What seems to be a recurrent problem that gets people's attention? Clip articles, letters, or editorials that address the problem.

Judging What You Have

Feeling a little overwhelmed? See problems everywhere? It can be wearing to focus on what's wrong with your life, your university, and your community. But remember that your ultimate goal is to write a proposal that suggests ways these problems might be resolved. You may have already explored some of these solutions, but if you haven't, don't worry; you'll get the chance later. Begin by scrutinizing the material you generated for possible topics.

What's Promising Material and What Isn't? We've talked about some initial judgments you can make. Now look at the material you generated in the fastwrites, lists, research, or clusters and ask yourself which of the problems listed *do you* *care about the most*, or which *are you most interested in*? Once you've selected some tentative topics for your proposal, narrow them down using the following questions:

- *Does someone aside from you have a stake in finding a solution?* Remember that you want to develop a proposal that addresses a problem that isn't merely a private matter but one that others care about, too.

- *Is there an identifiable audience for proposals about how to solve the problem?* A key part of the assignment is writing your proposal with a particular audience in mind. Can you readily identify who that audience might be?

- *Have other people said something somewhere about the problem or solutions?* Are you aware, through your initial research, whether there are experts, articles, reports, studies, Web pages, and other sources that explore your topic?

- *Which subject offers you the most opportunity for learning?* Amy saw problem solving as an opportunity to learn. This is most likely to occur if you choose to write about something that you may not fully understand. These are almost always the best topics for an inquiry-based project.

Questions About Audience and Purpose. This assignment asks you to identify an audience for your proposal. When you do, consider what exactly might be your purpose with respect to that audience. Do you want to:

- *Inform* them about the problem and explore possible solutions?

- *Advocate* certain solutions as the best ways to solve the problem?

- *Inform and advocate*, dramatizing the problem because your audience may not fully appreciate and understand it, and then persuade them to support the solutions you favor?

These purposes will shape your approach. But also consider how your audience might already think and feel about both the problem you're tackling and the solutions you offer. Use the chart in Figure 6.2.

Questions of Form. Although it might be premature to decide the *form* your proposal will take, sometimes an awareness of purpose and audience will suggest an approach. For example, if Cheryl's purpose is to advocate for a new nontraditional student center on campus, and her audience is school administrators, then she'll need to consider how best to get her message across. She might, for example, write her proposal in the form of a letter to the university's president. Gerald's proposal on how to deal with Internet plagiarism on campus might be written as a Web page that could be used as a link on the writing program or writing center's site.

Research Considerations. Research provides crucial support for most proposals and it is not too soon to do a little even at this early stage in the process. While

Awareness of the problem	If low, increase emphasis on dramatizing the problem.	If high, emphasize proposed solutions.
Initial disposition toward proposed solution	If favorably disposed, emphasize action that needs to be taken to implement solution. Emphasize pathos over logos.	If unfavorably disposed, offer balanced treatment of possible solutions before stating yours. Emphasize logos over pathos.
Attitude toward speaker	If positive, emphasize stronger action to solve the problem.	If negative, emphasize the views or experience speaker *does* share with audience.

Figure 6.2   Audience analysis chart

it's useful to do some quick and dirty research on your topic (for which the Web is ideal), avoid the temptation to while away the hours doing it. Collect just enough information to get you thinking and to give you relevant material you might incorporate into the sketch.

Writing the Sketch

Begin by drafting a sketch of your proposal. It should:

- be at least 500 to 600 words
- have a tentative title
- be written with the appropriate audience in mind
- not only dramatize the problem, but advocate or explore solution(s)

You might also develop this sketch in a form that you think might be particularly effective given your purpose and audience. Perhaps your sketch will be a letter, for example, or the text of a brochure, or an ad, or an essay.

■ STUDENT SKETCH

Gina's journal work kept pointing her to a potential problem—the wastefulness of American consumerism. Initially, we often circle subjects like birds lifted high on thermals, seeing an entire landscape below us. This is especially true when we focus on problems we think need to be solved. Gina had the good sense to know that consumerism was too large to work with, so she descended quickly and in her sketch landed on something far more focused: clothing. Later, in her draft, notice how she narrows this topic even further.

Clothing Optional
Gina Sinisi

1   Should you wear your green T-shirt and corduroys today or your leather jacket and combat pants? Perhaps you feel like wearing your good old trustworthy blue jeans instead. No matter what you choose, you must choose something because in American society getting dressed is not an option. While you are not allowed to roam freely in your birthday suit, whatever suit you do wear is your decision, as is where you get your clothes and what they are made of. It's easy to drive to the mall and consume to your heart's desire, but what about these traditional American clothing stores? Are they the best shopping option? What if I told you your blue jeans are deadly? Literally. Are they worth the life of another person? Would you trade them for your mom? It's important to know what you're wearing, who made it, and where it came from. It's also important to know you have choices.

2   Blue jeans are the favorite pants of Americans, but because of the toxic dyeing processes used to make them and the unfortunate chemical-laden cotton growing practices, they put their creators in dangerous situations. I believe in the good old "Do unto others as you would have done to yourself" mantra, and like I mentioned earlier, would you trade your mom for your jeans? No? Then why ask someone else to do the same?

3   If you are attached to wearing jeans, and your old ones are too worn out for your liking, then it is still possible to find some new ones. One great alternative to buying new clothes is buying secondhand, used, or vintage clothing. This option is the most environmentally friendly one because it's reusing what already exists and doesn't add to material waste. Secondhand shopping is also a great bargain and usually incredibly cheap. Garage sales are a great means for selling or buying new clothes and it's usually possible to bargain over the price. If you really get excited about clothes and know people who have enviable wardrobes, organizing a clothing swap is another option. This way, you can always borrow something back if you miss it too much, and you also know your clothes can be found on friendly bodies.

4   If you have a fair budget and you feel that secondhand shopping doesn't always suit your needs, then buying clothing made out of organic cotton or hemp is another agriculturally responsible decision. Typical cotton production is toxic and dangerous. "Because the cotton plant is susceptible to disease and pests, it's usually doused with a potent mix of agricultural chemicals. Some of these poisons are carcinogenic; others have been linked to headaches, dizziness, lung infections, asthma, depression and birth defects" (Visscher 22). While hemp is a much more sustainable plant than cotton and grows easily almost anywhere, the government unfortunately doesn't allow farmers to grow it in the States, so if you buy a product made of hemp, understand that you are not buying locally or nationally, but instead supporting a different country and contributing to major transportation costs.

5   While searching through the racks at secondhand stores and reading labels takes more time than bouncing from store to store at the mall, it is kind of like a treasure hunt and the harder you work at searching for the treasure the better the treasure is. You have to get

dressed. You don't have an option. You do, however, have the option of deciding what to wear and what role you want to play in the American clothing industry.

Works Cited

Visscher, Marco. "Imps & Elfs: Fashion Sense." *Ode* Apr. 2006: 22–24. Print.

Moving from Sketch to Draft

Prepare to revise your sketch by assessing it yourself and inviting comments from peers in workshop.

Evaluating Your Own Sketch. Before your proposal is subject to peer review, answer the following questions. Your instructor may ask you to hand in your responses with your sketch or simply make an entry in your notebook.

1. Assume that you're a reader who might be critical of your proposals. What do you say in the sketch that such a reader might disagree with? What might those objections be? Have you adequately responded to them or addressed them in the sketch?

2. Are there parts of the problem you're addressing here that you don't understand yet? Are there things about the solutions you propose that you need to know more about? What are they?

3. Have you changed your mind about anything on this topic after writing the sketch? If so, what?

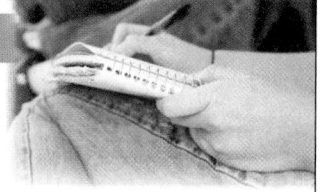

ONE STUDENT'S RESPONSE

Gina's Journal

1. A reader might disagree with my idea that the current American clothing industry is harmful to the environment and human health. I did not support my claims with enough factual evidence to be believable and get the reader's attention. It seems that I devoted more time to proposing solutions than exploring the problem.

2. There is one part of the problem that I don't quite understand which is the dyeing process of blue jeans. I'm not sure where current factories are located and what methods they use. I have only heard negative rumors regarding current practices. I have also heard opposing information regarding synthetic dyes versus natural indigo. I'm not sure which is worse or better. I would also like to know more about hemp, which is one of the solutions I propose.

(continued)

> **One Student's Response** (*continued*)
> 3. I have slightly changed my mind regarding this topic and that is because I'm not sure about natural and synthetic dyes. I used to think synthetic ones were more harmful, but now I'm not sure.

Questions for Peer Review. Because the assignment asks you to draft your proposal with a particular audience in mind, your workshop discussions may require a bit more imagination than usual. As when you evaluated your own sketch, you may have to ask your peer reviewers to imagine themselves as the readers you want them to be.

Begin your peer review session by clarifying your audience. Then the group might discuss the following questions about your sketch.

- After reading the sketch, repeat the problem you believe the sketch is addressing and why this solution is the best one?
- Is the solution offered sufficiently justified?
- Can you imagine other solutions the writer might consider?
- What part of the proposal did you find most interesting?
- Given the purpose and audience of the proposal, is there another form it might take?

Reflecting on What You Learned. While your proposal sketch is being peer reviewed, record the comments. Draw a line down the middle of a journal page, and on the left side jot down every suggestion or comment about the sketch that you hear—everything, even if you don't agree with it. Following the workshop, fastwrite on the right side about all of the comments you received. Explore how you might follow those suggestions and how they might change your approach to the next draft.

Research and Other Strategies: Gathering More Information

Unless you're an expert on the problem you're writing about, you're going to need to do more research. While the quick and dirty research you did earlier might have given you enough information to draft the sketch, at the very least you'll likely need to fill gaps in your explanation of the problem or more fully justify or explore alternatives to the solutions you propose. Where should you look?

- *Exploit local publications.* Because the assignment asks you to choose a topic of local interest, then sources such as the local daily newspaper, government reports, and university policies may be important sources for your proposal. Some of these, such as local newspapers and government documents, may be available in your campus library.

Grant Proposals and Group Ethos

If your career takes you into the sciences, engineering, or nonprofit work, then you'll be writing grant proposals. Expert grant writers say that finding a potential funder for your project isn't the hardest part. Proposals often fail because they aren't persuasive or don't follow the application guidelines. The effectiveness of a grant proposal depends on some of the same things that you're trying in this chapter, but they are also a specialized genre.

Imagine that you will often be competing with hundreds—and in some cases, thousands—of others who are chasing the same dollars from government and foundation grant programs. And unlike a proposal from an individual, grant proposals often come from institutions and organizations. Consequently, when you propose a solution that you think should be funded, you're selling two things: the proposed solution *and* your organization.

This is one of the ways that workplace writing is distinct from academic writing. Remember Aristotle's rhetorical triangle? One of the three elements of persuasion was ethos, or the credibility of the speaker. Usually we think of ethos as merely reflecting the writer's persona, but frequently writers are speaking for an institution and not for themselves. Suppose you are writing a foundation grant proposal for a local library to seek funds for a new reading program that will boost outreach into low-income neighborhoods. If you were the proposal writer, how would you want the library to come across, and how would you manage that presentation? When you're writing for a group and not for yourself, how does that change things like voice, tone, the information you might emphasize, or your methods of persuasion? How does the writing you do on behalf of a group differ from the writing you do for you?

Fortunately, if you want to write a grant, there is an industry waiting to help you: countless books, training seminars, and services to locate funders. Here are two helpful places to start online:

- *The Foundation Center* (http://foundationcenter.org/), a site that focuses on funding opportunities from private foundations.

- *Grants.gov*, a one-stop shop for all grant opportunities from the federal government.

- *Interview experts*. In Chapter 4, you practiced interview skills. Here's a chance to put them to use again. One of the most efficient ways to collect information for your revision is to talk to people who have knowledge about the problem. These may be experts who have researched the problem or people affected by it.

■ *Search for experience with similar solutions elsewhere.* If your proposal calls for an education program on binge drinking, what other universities might have tried it? What was their experience? Search for information using keywords that describe the problem you're writing about ("binge drinking"), and try adding a phrase that describes the solution ("binge drinking education programs"). Also check library databases that might lead you to articles in newspapers, magazines, and journals on the problem and its solutions.

Composing the Draft

Establishing the problem your proposal addresses and possibly even dramatizing the problem is a very common way to begin the form. As you begin your draft, consider how much you need to say in the beginning about the problem. If your readers aren't aware of the problem, should you dramatize it in some way, perhaps telling a story of someone who is a victim of the problem, or forcefully describing its effects?

Alternatively, you might want to begin the next draft by establishing your solution, a particularly strong beginning if your motive is advocacy and your audience already recognizes the problem. For example, everyone agrees that 9/11 is a national tragedy. There's no need to make that argument in a proposal for a memorial, so the architects' proposal began simply:

> *This memorial proposes a space that resonates with the feelings of loss and absence that were generated by the destruction of the World Trade Center and the taking of thousands of lives on September 11, 2001, and February 26, 1993.*

Here are some possible approaches to beginning your next draft:

1. Consider opening with an anecdote, image, description, or profile that dramatizes the problem you're writing about.
2. Lead with an explicit explanation of your proposal, simply stating the problem and advocating your solution.
3. Sometimes the form will influence your method of beginning. For example, if you're writing a brochure, the front panel—the first part readers will see—might include very little text and perhaps a graphic. A Web page might have similar constraints. A grant proposal might begin with an abstract. Choose a beginning that is appropriate to the form or genre of your proposal.
4. Frame the question or pose the problem. What is the question that you're trying to answer, or what part of the problem most needs a solution?

Methods of Development. What are some ways you might organize your proposal?

Problem to Solution. This is the most straightforward way to structure the draft, one that you'll commonly find in proposals of all kinds. In its simplest form, a proposal that works from problem to solution will devote varying emphasis to each, depending on how aware the intended audience is of the problem the proposal addresses. Obviously, more emphasis will be placed on establishing the problem or helping readers understand it if they lack awareness.

The problem–solution structure need not be a simple two-step perform-ance—first problem, then solution—but rather a two-part harmony in which the writer moves back and forth between discussion of an aspect of the problem and a solution that addresses it.

Cause and Effect. It's only natural when presented with a problem to ask, *What causes it?* This can be an essential part of explaining the problem, and also a way to introduce solutions; after all, most proposals address in some way the causes of the problem. If one of the causes of procrastination is perfectionism, then a solution will be to have more realistic expectations, perhaps by lowering your standards.

Conventions of the Form. Because this assignment encourages you to consider writing a proposal that might depart from the usual essay form, the method of development might be determined, in part, by the conventions that govern that genre. For example, a proposal for a new course, say, on Chicano litera-ture, written for the English department's curriculum committee, might have to follow a certain format, beginning with the course description followed by a justification. Sometimes these conventions might be more subtle or flexible. Web pages have no strict format, but Web designers do work from some gen-eral principles that you'd do well to learn before you design one. This can be one aspect of your research for this assignment. Sometimes merely looking closely at examples of a genre helps you infer some of the basic techniques of writing in that form.

Combining Approaches. As always, the methods of development often involve combining these and other approaches to structuring your draft. The sample proposals in this chapter are a mix of problem to solution, cause and effect, and genre-specific ways of organizing the material.

Using Evidence. What kind of evidence and how much of it you provide to justify the solutions you propose depends, as it often does, on your audience. *How much* evidence you need to provide depends on whether your intended audience is likely to be predisposed to agree or disagree with the solutions you propose. Obviously, if readers need convincing, you need to offer more justification. The "Inquiring into the Details: Evidence—A Case Study" box illustrates how the *type* of evidence you provide is a function of audience, too. As you compose your draft, consider who your readers will be and the kinds of evidence they will find most persuasive.

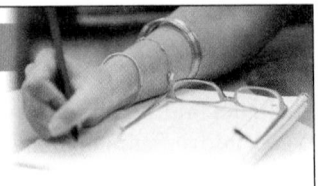

INQUIRING INTO THE DETAILS

Evidence—A Case Study

Suppose a proposal argues that the university needs an alternative or independent film series. The proposal, in the form of a memo, is written to the Student Activities Board, a group of students who decide how to spend student fee money collected at registration. Which of the following types of evidence used to justify such a film series would be *most* persuasive to that audience?

1. The writer's personal enjoyment of foreign films.

2. A petition signed by 100 people that supports the idea.

3. A quotation from Woody Allen about the educational and cultural virtues of independent films.

4. Information about the success of the independent film theater in town.

5. A quote from an English professor supporting the idea.

6. An estimate that shows that the cost of renting five independent films is half the cost of renting the same number of Hollywood films.

7. A survey of 200 students that indicates that 60 percent support the idea.

8. Data on good attendance at a similar series at another larger university.

Choosing the strongest evidence in a proposal is an exercise in audience analysis. Is your audience likely to favor your idea, oppose it, or have no opinion? If they're neutral or opposed, then you'd better be sure you not only have *appropriate* evidence but a lot of it. What makes evidence appropriate for a particular audience? *It is evidence the audience members are most likely to believe.*

Workshopping the Draft

If your draft is subject to peer review, see Chapter 10 for details on how to organize workshop groups and decide on how your group can help you. The following journal activities and questions should help you make the most of your opportunity to get peer feedback on your work in progress.

Reflecting on the Draft. After you've finished the draft, make an entry in your journal that follows these prompts:

- If I were going to write this over again, the one thing I think I'd do would be...

- The most important thing I learned about writing a proposal so far is...

- The most difficult part of the process for me was…
- The biggest question I have about the draft is…

Your instructor may ask you to hand in your responses to these prompts with your draft.

Following the workshop session, repeat the method of reflection you used following peer review of your sketch, drawing a line down the middle of a notebook page and recording your group's comments and suggestions on the left side and, later, your reactions on the right.

Questions for Readers. Again remind your workshop group about the particular audience you had in mind for your proposal. The group might then consider the following questions as they discuss the draft.

1. On a scale from 1 to 5, with 5 being "extremely serious" and 1 being "not serious at all," how would you describe your feelings about the severity of the problem addressed in this draft? Discuss the reasons for your ranking. Remember to imagine that you're the audience for whom the proposal was intended.

2. On the same scale, rank how convinced you were that the solutions proposed in the draft were the best ones. A 5 would indicate that you were totally convinced and a 1 would indicate that you weren't convinced at all. Discuss what was convincing and/or how the solutions offered could be more convincing. Be specific.

3. What questions did you have that weren't adequately answered in the draft?

Revising the Draft

Revision is a continual process—not a last step. You've been revising—literally "re-seeing" your subject—from the first messy fastwriting in your journal. But the things that get your attention during revision varies depending on where you are in the writing process. You've generated material, chosen a topic, done some research, and written both a sketch and draft. Most students think that the only thing left to do is "fix things." Check for misspellings. Correct an awkward sentence or two. Come up with a better title. This is editing, not revision, and while editing is important, to focus solely on smaller "fixes" after writing a first draft squanders an opportunity to really *learn* from what the draft is telling you, or perhaps not quite telling you.

Chapter 9 can help guide these discoveries. The questions you can ask a draft fall into five categories: purpose, idea, information, development, and editing. Use the following Guide to Revision Strategies chart to find the revision strategies in Chapter 9 that might help you re-see what you've written so far.

GUIDE TO REVISION STRATEGIES

Problems in the Draft (Chapter 9)	Page Number
Unclear purpose ■ Not sure what the essay is about? Fails to answer the *So what?* question?	327
Unclear thesis, theme, or main idea ■ Not sure what you're trying to say? Proposal isn't clear?	333
Lack of information or development ■ Needs more information to justify proposed solution? ■ Evidence offered isn't persuasive enough?	340
Disorganized ■ Doesn't move logically or smoothly from paragraph to paragraph?	344
Unclear or awkward at the level of sentences and paragraphs ■ Seems choppy or hard to follow at the level of sentences or paragraphs?	353

Proposals also have some fairly typical problems at this stage in the process, most of which can be addressed by repeating some of the steps in this chapter or selecting appropriate revision strategies in Chapter 9. Here are some questions to consider as you decide which of these strategies might be most helpful.

✓ Have you done enough to dramatize the problem if you're writing for an audience that may not recognize the problem? Should you do more to establish how your readers have a stake in solving the problem?

✓ How well have you justified your solution? Is there enough evidence? Is it appropriate evidence for your audience?

✓ Have you overemphasized one solution at the expense of others? Would your proposal be more balanced and persuasive if you considered alternatives, even if you ultimately reject them?

When you refer to Chapter 9, "Revision Strategies," for ideas on how to revise your draft following your workshop, use the preceding table as a guide. Remember that a draft may present problems in more than one category.

Polishing the Draft

After you've dealt with the big issues in your draft—is it sufficiently focused, does it answer the *So what?* question, is it well organized, and so on—you must deal with the smaller problems. You've carved the stone into an appealing figure, but now you need to polish it. Are your paragraphs coherent? How do you manage transitions? Are your sentences fluent and concise? Are there any errors in spelling or syntax?

Before you finish your draft, work through the following checklist:

- ✓ Every paragraph is about one thing.
- ✓ The transitions between paragraphs aren't abrupt.
- ✓ The length of sentences varies in each paragraph.
- ✓ Each sentence is concise. There are no unnecessary words or phrases.
- ✓ You've checked grammar, particularly verb agreement, run-on sentences, unclear pronouns, and misused words (*there/their, where/were*, and so on). (See the handbook at the end of the book for help with these grammar issues.)
- ✓ You've run your spellchecker and proofed your paper for misspelled words.

■ STUDENT ESSAY

It's August in Boise and cotton is king. I'm sitting here clothed from head to toe in 100 percent cotton, but until I read Gina Sinisi's essay on the problems of cotton production, I never imagined that these shorts, manufactured in Sri Lanka, might have contributed to obscenely low wages in foreign manufacturing plants and health problems among American workers who harvest the crop. But Gina's essay, like all good proposals, doesn't leave it at that. There are things we can do, beginning with being aware that our consumer choices echo into other people's lives, some of whom live on the other side of the world.

Clothing Optional
Gina Sinisi

Should you wear your green T-shirt and corduroys today or your leather jacket and combat pants? Perhaps you feel the urge to strut in your trustworthy blue jeans instead. While you are not allowed to roam freely in your birthday suit, whatever suit you do   1

(continued)

(continued)

choose is up to you, along with where you get it and what it is made of. It is easy to drive to the mall and consume to your wardrobe's content, but what about these traditional North American clothing stores? Are they the best shopping option? What if I told you your blue jeans are deadly? Literally. Are they worth the life of another person? Would you trade them for your mom? Your dad? It's important to know what you're wearing, who made it, and where it came from. It's also imperative to know you have choices. The impact of your political and social ideals on the clothing industry begins with your underwear.

2   The United States yields to the high demand of cotton by closely following China as the number two producer of cotton in the world, growing enough to manufacture about 9 billion T-shirts ("Clothes for a Change"). The good news is that North Americans can support local farmers by purchasing cotton grown in the United States; the downside is that North American citizens are also the ones directly affected by the chemicals sprayed on the cotton. According to the World Health Organization, pesticide poisoning annually afflicts three million people, killing between 20,000 and 40,000 of them ("Clothes for a Change"). While this statistic doesn't single out cotton as a cause of human health problems, the crop does require unusually high applications of pesticides. While as an agricultural product, cotton only takes up 3% of the world's farmland, it demands a quarter of the globe's pesticides and fertilizers ("Cotton and the Environment"). According to Visscher, "Because the cotton plant is susceptible to disease and pests, it's usually doused with a potent mix of agricultural chemicals. Some of these poisons are carcinogenic; others have been linked to headaches, dizziness, lung infections, asthma, depression and birth defects" (22).

3   I believe in the familiar credo, "Do unto others as you would have done to yourself," and to repeat my earlier question, would you trade your mom for your jeans? No? Then why ask someone else to do the same?

4   Cotton contributes not only to poor environmental and health standards, but also to poor working conditions. Because the majority of consumers are not willing to pay higher prices for well-made clothing, and instead prefer cheap clothing that changes with the seasons, most manufacturers have "outsourced" their production to countries like Viet Nam and China, where workers are paid extremely low wages, "as low as 13 cents an hour" ("Clothes for a Change"). If you buy these products you are condoning unacceptable work ethics. You can choose otherwise.

5   If you feel that common cotton growing and production practices are unnecessary and hazardous but can't detach yourself from cotton clothing and blue jeans, there is an agriculturally responsible decision you can make. Organic cotton is being grown in more than 18 countries worldwide, including the United States ("Clothes for a Change"), and worldwide sales are increasing by about 25% annually (Eshelby). If you can't find clothing made from organic cotton in your city, there are hundreds of clothing stores available online that support humane and environmentally conscious clothing practices.

6   A second alternative to traditional cotton clothing is buying hemp clothing products. Before the industrial revolution, hemp was a popular fiber in the United States because it

is strong and grows quickly and easily in a variety of soil types. The first paper was made from hemp, and, ironically some say, the Declaration of Independence was written on hemp paper.

Growing hemp in the United States is currently illegal because it is frequently confused with marijuana. While pot and hemp are the same plant species, hemp contains "virtually no" THC, the ingredient in marijuana that makes users "high." Most likely, hemp is illegal because it would dramatically drown the cotton industry and because of the ignorance that surrounds its false connection with marijuana.

7

While it is currently illegal to grow hemp in the United States, it is legal to sell hemp clothing products. A few clothing stores do exist throughout the country, but once again, it is always possible to easily find these products online. Unlike some rumors that declare hemp is itchy and rough on your skin, it is actually softer, more absorbent, extremely breathable and significantly longer lasting than clothing made from cotton.

8

One dilemma you must face when deciding to buy hemp products is whether or not you want to support a nonlocal product and all of the energy it takes to get the product from its point of origination to your body. Hemp has a high rate of "embodied energy," which is a term used to define all of the energy a product uses to be created and then transported to its final destination.

9

If you have a hard time choosing between the damage caused by cotton practices, the embodied energy included in hemp, and the petroleum base in many synthetic fabrics, and don't like ordering organic cotton clothing online without being able to try it on first, there is one final solution: A great alternative to buying new clothes is buying secondhand or vintage clothing. This option is the most environmentally friendly one because it's reusing what already exists and doesn't add to material waste. Secondhand shopping is usually incredibly cheap and a great means for selling or buying new clothes. It's usually possible to haggle for a lower price, too.

10

Vintage clothing is often more sturdy and durable than recently produced clothing; you also don't need to worry about anyone else showing up to a party wearing the same outfit as you. If you are a fashion fox and know people who have enviable wardrobes, organizing a clothing swap is another option. This way, you can always borrow something back if you miss it too much, and you also know your clothes can be found on friendly bodies. A final reason why it is better to buy used clothing is because old clothes no longer off-gas their chemicals into your skin and the air you breathe. They are safer, cheaper, and readily available.

11

While searching through the racks at secondhand stores and reading labels takes more time than bouncing from store to store at the mall, it is time well spent. When you know your clothes come from a righteous source, you can flaunt them with pride and revel in your own good health. You have to get dressed. You don't have an option. You do, however, have the option of deciding what to wear and what role you want to play in the clothing industry. Does the day call for an organic cotton T-shirt with hemp shorts, or a vintage tunic with Salvation Army jeans? You decide.

12

(continued)

(continued)

Works Cited

"Clothes for a Change." *Organic Consumers Association.* Web. 1 Aug. 2006.
"Cotton and the Environment." *Organic Trade Association.* Web. 1 Aug. 2006.
Eshelby, Kate. "Organic Cotton." *Ecologist* 36.1 (2006): 34–39. *Academic Search Premier.*
    Web. 7 Aug. 2006.
Visscher, Marco. "Imps & Elfs: Fashion Sense." *Ode* Apr. 2006: 22–24. Print.

Evaluating the Essay

1. The authority of a proposal depends on the evidence. Assess the evidence Gina provides to make her case that nonorganic cotton production is a serious problem. Do you find it convincing?

2. Is the solution she offers—use of organic cottons, hemp, or "vintage" clothing—a viable one? How could she strengthen the case for her proposal?

3. Can you imagine how this essay might have incorporated visuals—pictures, graphs, tables, and so on—that would have enhanced the argument?

USING WHAT YOU HAVE LEARNED

1. Think about the proposal draft you've written, and all those that you've read, both in this chapter and in your workshop group. Spend one minute answering, in writing, the following question: *What do you need to know to write an effective proposal?*

2. Draw a line down the middle of the page of your journal. Compare the proposal with another genre of writing you've tried in this book, looking specifically at the following:

   ■ degree of difficulty (which was harder, and why?)

   ■ audience awareness (when and how much did you consider who you were writing for?)

   ■ level of discovery (how much did you learn about your subject, or about yourself?)

■ application to other situations (how much and what might you use from this form of writing and apply in other writing situations?)

3. What approaches or ideas will you borrow from proposal writing that you can apply to other forms of writing and other writing situations? Can you imagine revising an essay you've already written in another genre using what you've learned here?

Arguing is a civic duty. It is an essential activity in any democratic culture and a major element of academic discourse. Academic argument is one of the key means of making new knowledge.

WRITING AN ARGUMENT

WRITING TO PERSUADE PEOPLE

Where I live, public arguments about wolf reintroduction, saving salmon, growing property taxes, and the need for a local community college are waged on the editorial pages of the local newspaper, *The Idaho Statesman*. The paper's editorials and so-called op-ed articles (short persuasive essays that are literally on the opposite page from editorials) present usually well-reasoned arguments of 250 to 600 words, but the real slugfest takes place in the letters to the editor. Reading letters to the editor is a form of recreation here. One correspondent complained a few years ago that the song "Rain, Rain, Go Away" was objectionable because it made her children dislike precipitation. Another letter writer, an angry animal rights activist, is a regular who always generates heated rebuttals here in cattle country. Last week, she railed about the evils of "Rocky Mountain oysters" (fried cattle testicles), which were served up at the Eagle Fire Department fundraiser. I can't wait to see the responses to that one.

Letters to the editor, while an important opinion forum, frequently feature great examples of flawed arguments, including logical fallacies, poor reasoning, and a pitiful lack of audience awareness. In the hands of a good writer, however, a short persuasive essay like the op-ed can move people to think and act. It is a genre that attracts some of the best nonfiction writers in the country—Ellen Goodman, George Will, Bob Greene, Anna Quindlen, and others—but op-ed essays are also written by anyone with an idea about a public problem. Across the

What You'll Learn in This Chapter

- New ways to understand the purpose of argument.
- Some differences between formal and informal arguments.
- The basic argument strategies most writers use.
- How to map an argument.
- How to avoid common logical fallacies.
- Revision strategies to fine-tune your argument.

United States, newspapers and magazines publish the opinion pieces of ordinary citizens, and these essays are among our liveliest forums for public debate.

While we often think of persuasive writing as stiff and formal, the op-ed essay is usually lively and engaging. Here's a sample of some opening lines from published op-ed pieces:

> Many of the hundreds of thousands of Hispanic demonstrators who poured out into the streets on Monday may not know much English, but they've learned the language of American politics: Flags. Tons of flags. And make them American.
>
> —"Immigrants Must Choose," Charles Krauthammer

> Maybe it was at the moment I found myself on my knees in my bathrobe, carefully prying tiny shards of paper out of the immobilized teeth of the shredder, that it finally hit me: The shredder had a paper jam. I had an info jam.
>
> —"C'mon, America, Fire Up Those Shredders," Lisa Johnston

> On the premise that spring is too beautiful for a depressing topic like Iraq, I thought I'd take up a fun subject—global warming.
>
> —"Global Warming: What, Me Worry?" Molly Ivins

> *Persuasive essays like the op-ed are a great way to participate in public debates that affect your campus and community, and even your nation.*

While these essays are often informal, they are still persuasive forms, and as you'll see later, they often employ the same methods of more formal arguments. However, unlike formal arguments—the kind you might write in a logic or philosophy course—persuasive essays of this kind have a much larger audience, and they are a great way to participate in public debates that affect your campus and community, and even your nation. In this chapter, you'll learn how to use some principles of argument to write persuasive essays like the op-ed that will give voice to things you care about, and that will increase the likelihood that voice will be heard.

What Is Argument?

Argument is not war.

When I was growing up, argument meant only one thing: indigestion. My father loved to argue at the dinner table, hotly pursuing any stray comment that would give him the chance to demonstrate his superior knowledge and logic. What I remember about these "arguments" was the hot-faced humiliation and anger I felt back then, and later, the feeling that I would prefer to avoid an argument at any cost. When I mention argumentative writing to my students, I think I recognize in the slumped shoulders and distant looks of some of them that they might have similar feelings.

Some of us think argument is impolite. It means uncomfortable conflict. It is the verbal equivalent of war.

And yet, we engage in argument every day when we attempt to persuade an instructor to extend the deadline on a paper, try to convince our spouse to help more around the apartment, or seek a loan from a bank.

Arguments *can* involve conflict, but they are rarely combat—despite the war metaphors like "finding ammunition" or "attacking a position." Far more often, the motives for arguing are more benign. We want others to consider seeing the world the way we see it. Or we want to encourage them to *do* something we believe is in their interests as well as ours. These are the motives behind the attempts at persuasion of several of the assignments you may have completed earlier in *The Curious Writer:* the review, the proposal, and the critical essay.

In a sense, all writing is persuasive. *See the world my way*, we ask of readers, *at least for a moment.*

> **There aren't just two sides.**

Two Sides to Every Argument?

TV talk shows stage "discussions" between proponents of diametrically opposed positions. Academic debating teams pit those for and those against. We are nurtured on language like *win* or *lose, right* and *wrong,* and *either/or*. It's tempting to see the world this way, as neatly divided into truth and falsehood, light and dark. Reducing issues to two sides simplifies the choices. But one of the things that literature—and all art—teaches us is the delightful and nagging complexity of things. By inclination and upbringing, Huck Finn is a racist, and there's plenty of evidence in *Huckleberry Finn* that his treatment of Jim confirms it. Yet there are moments in the novel when we see a transcendent humanity in Huck, and we can see that he may be a racist, *but.* ... It is this qualification—this modest word *but*—that trips us up in the steady march toward certainty. Rather than *either/or,* can it be *both/and?* Instead of two sides to every issue, might there be thirteen?

Here's an example:

One side: General education requirements are a waste of time because they are often irrelevant to students' major goal in getting a college education—getting a good job.

The other side: General education requirements are invaluable because they prepare students to be enlightened citizens, more fully prepared to participate in democratic culture.

It's easy to imagine a debate between people who hold these positions, and it wouldn't be uninteresting. But it *would* be misleading to think that these are the only two possible positions on general education requirements in American universities. One of the reasons why people are drawn to arguing is that it can be a method of discovery, and one of the most useful discoveries is some side to the story that doesn't fall neatly into the usual opposed positions. The route to these discoveries is twofold: *initially withholding judgment* and *asking questions.*

For instance, what might be goals of a university education other than helping students get a good job and making them enlightened citizens? Is it possible that a university can do both? Are general education courses the only route to enlightenment? Are there certain situations in which the vocational motives of students are inappropriate? Are there certain contexts—say, certain students at particular schools at a particular point in their education—when general education requirements might be waived or modified?

All of these questions, and more, tend to unravel the two sides of the argument and expose them for what they often are: *starting points* for an inquiry into the question, *What good are general education requirements?*

Premises are what hold up claims.

I actually asked my first-year students recently what they thought of general education or "core" classes at our university. It provoked a lively debate. Here's what one of them said:

> "I am all for the rant about higher education costing a fortune. The core classes are a joke, to be quite honest. Who hasn't had math, science, and history in high school?"

What interests me here is not the claim that "core classes are a joke" but a key assumption behind the claim that the writer assumes her readers agree with. Are high school math, science, and history classes equivalent to university core classes in the same subjects? It's a premise that isn't addressed, yet her argument fundamentally depends on our consent that it is true. In logical persuasion, not all premises need explanation because the audience may grant their truth without it—racism is bad, depression is a treatable condition, citizens in a democracy have a right to vote. But when writers ignore controversial premises, the argument is a house of cards, vulnerable to the slightest push back.

In argument, premises or assumptions are reasons that we believe something is true, and one way to find the path back from a claim to a reason is to use the word "because." *Core classes are a joke <u>because</u> their content is similar to what most students learn in high school.*

Arguments prove claims with appropriate evidence.

"I have a headache" is a statement, not a claim, because no one is likely to disagree with it. "Headaches can be caused by secondhand smoke" is a statement that is a claim because reasonable people might agree or disagree with it. Claims are at the heart of argument, and if you think about it, you already know this. Every time you make a judgment, interpretation, or evaluation, you make a claim. We do this daily: "Macs are better than PCs." "The food in this place sucks." "This town needs more buses."

However, unlike these often-offhand comments, argumentative writing is organized around convincing someone else that the claim is true. This means not only establishing the reasons behind why we think so, but providing evidence that seems convincing. For example, a comparison between the syllabi for my high school history course and my college core course in history shows that 60 percent of the time they cover the same material. Hmmm. Maybe core classes can be a "joke."

Not just any evidence will do, of course. It depends on the situation (see "Writing in the Disciplines," page 276). For example, statistical data are appropriate evidence in an environmental health paper on the effect of inversions and

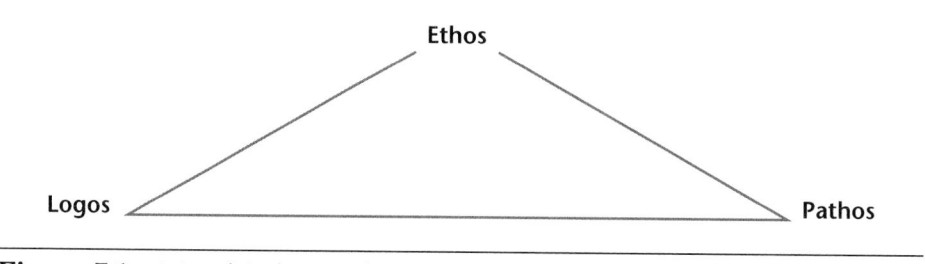

Figure 7.1   Aristotle's rhetorical triangle

not personal experience. An opinion essay on the need to act on air inversions might use statistics but is just as likely to use the writer's personal experience.

There is an artful balance between persona, emotion, and logic.

Persuasion, as Aristotle reminded us a few thousand years ago, depends not just on good reasoning (*logos*), but on moving an audience (*pathos*) and making it believe the speaker is someone worth listening to on the subject (*ethos*). Figure 7.1 shows Aristotle's famous rhetorical triangle, a visual presentation of this idea.

What may be a little misleading about Aristotle's graphic is the idea that the recipe for good argument is equal measures of ethos, pathos, and logos. Not at all. These are blended in varying amounts depending on the situation. One factor, for example, is the disposition of an audience toward your claim.

Figure 7.2 broadly describes the balance between Aristotle's three categories of appeals in the three most common rhetorical situations: when an audience is resistant to what you're trying to say, neutral about it, or receptive. For instance, direct-mail marketers, particularly those trying to raise money for nonprofit groups and political causes, make a living buying and cultivating lists of people who might be receptive to their messages. Direct-mail letters, therefore, are strong on emotional appeals (*pathos*): The humane society will include photographs of a sad-looking abandoned puppy, a conservative political action group will raise fears about threats to "family values," and so on. There's no need to spend a great deal reasoning (*logos*) with an audience that already agrees with your message. Move them with emotion!

In contrast, resistant audiences immediately suspect the credibility of speakers or writers (*ethos*), and so their challenge is to establish some common

Disposition of Audience	*Ethos*	*Pathos*	*Logos*
Resistant	Most important	Least important	Most important
Neutral	Important	Important	Important
Receptive	Least important	Most important	Least important

Figure 7.2   Audience and the balance of ethos, logos, and pathos

ground with their audiences. Emotional appeals will be unlikely to move this audience, at least initially.

Neutral audiences may be difficult to gauge. Sometimes an emotional appeal will spark its members' interest. Sometimes a well-reasoned argument (*logos*) will move them, and sometimes a neutral audience will be persuaded by the credibility of the speaker. Frequently, a careful combination of all three of Aristotle's appeals transforms a neutral audience into one that is receptive to what you have to say.

For many of us, then, argument in civic and private discourse is bound by our *feelings* about argument—how comfortable we are with conflict, how confident we are in our ability to say what we think, and how strongly we feel about our opinions. These feelings are complicated by our beliefs about the purpose of argument. Sorting through these beliefs can help us discover new, perhaps more productive ways of approaching argument. Does argument make you uncomfortable? What do you consider a "good" argument? What is a "bad" argument?

Argument and Inquiry

Like all inquiry projects, the process of writing an argument involves both suspending judgment and making judgments (see Figures 7.3 and 7.4). Directly or indirectly, arguments address some kind of problem that needs to be solved—global warming, lack of funding for local preschool education, online music piracy, or whatever issue is complex and interesting.

Suspending Judgment. When you suspend judgment you openly explore a problem, including your own initial assumptions about it, if you have any. This is your chance to discover what you think by looking at the evidence and arguments others have already put forward. One of the things this might inspire is clarifying what the problem really is that most needs a solution.

Making Judgments. Since all arguments are organized around a claim, clarifying the problem will help you determine what that might be. This is the most important judgment you'll make. From there, the process is a more familiar one of establishing the reasons behind your claim and then finding and organizing the relevant evidence that will make them convincing to someone else.

Inquiry arguments work best under the following conditions:

1. You choose a topic that you find confusing in interesting ways, which may not yield easily to obvious solutions.
2. You may have tentative ideas about what you think, but you're willing to change your mind.
3. You're willing to wrestle with viewpoints other than your own, even after you've decided on the claim you want to prove.

Suspending Judgment

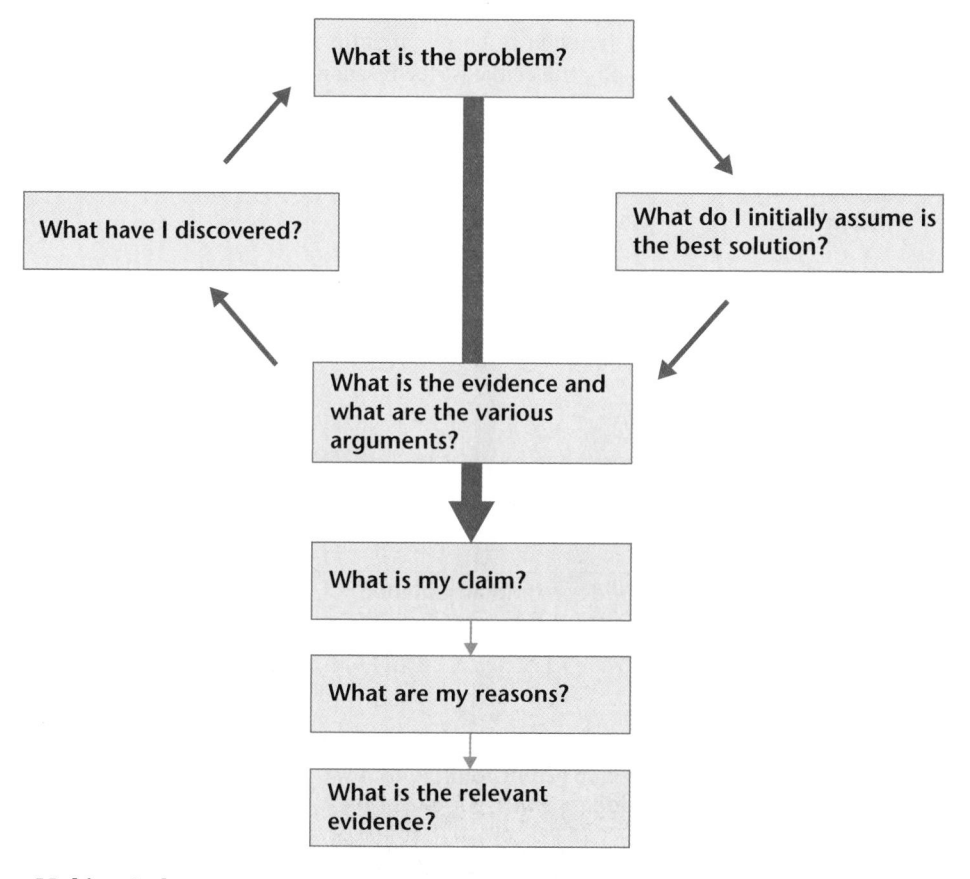

Making Judgments

Figure 7.3　An inquiry argument. Rather than rushing to judgment, inquiry-based arguments begin with an open exploration of the problem. The aim, as always, is discovery. These discoveries are the basis for clarifying the problem and then making a claim about what should be done about it. (See Figure 7.4 for an example of how this might work.)

Analyzing Argument

How might you analyze this letter writer's argument?

> Dear editor,
>
> As part of my required humanities class, I was forced to see the art exhibit "Home of the Brave" at the university gallery. As a combat veteran, what I saw there deeply offended me. I saw so-called "art" that showed great American military leaders like General Petraeus with skulls superimposed on their faces, and a photo of a man with an American flag wrapped around his head and lashed

with a plastic tie at his neck. It's popular to say these days that we should support the troops. Apparently, a group of artists who haven't defended our freedom feel free to use that freedom to be unpatriotic. I wonder if they would feel differently if they had to pay the real cost for freedom of speech.

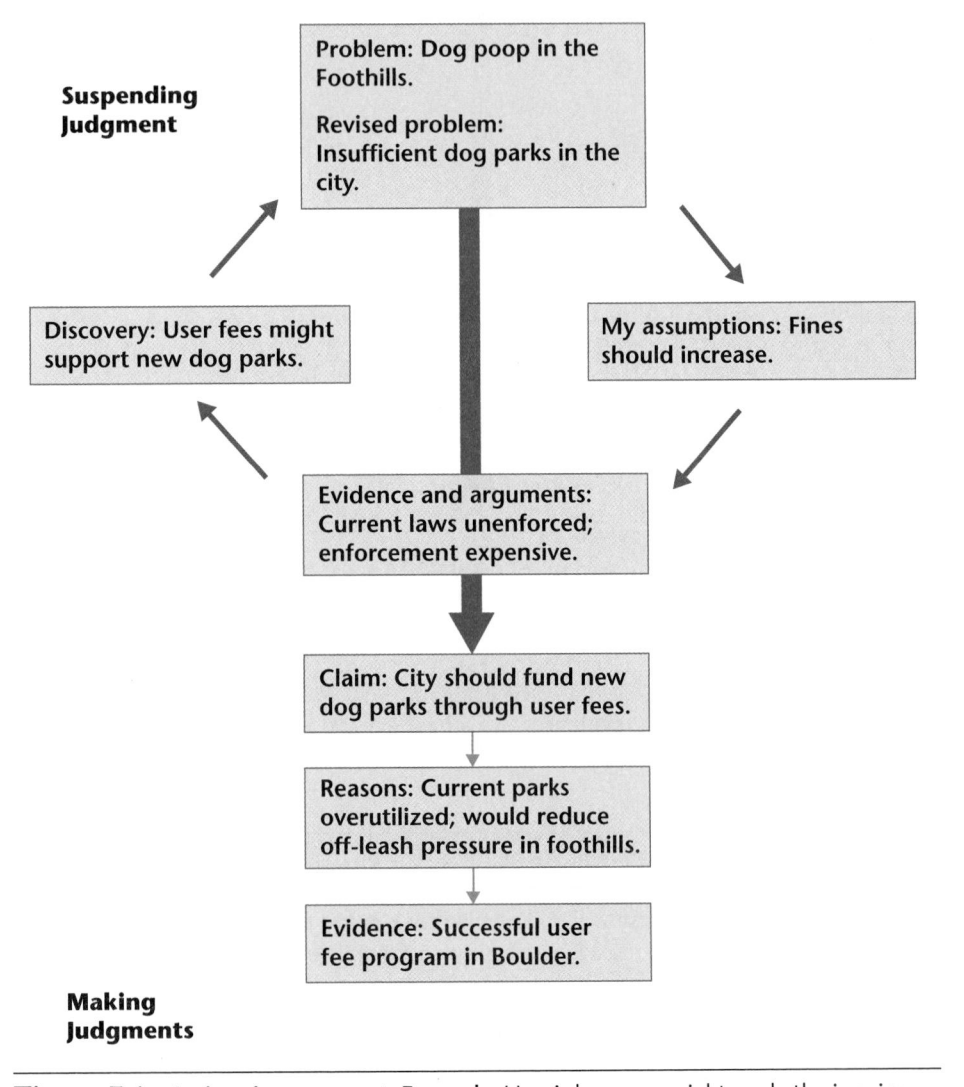

Figure 7.4   An inquiry argument: Example. Here's how you might apply the inquiry process to discovering an argument. In Boise, Idaho, where I live, there are more dogs per capita than nearly every other city in the U.S. That's a lot of dog poop, particularly on trails in the surrounding foothills. When you don't rush the claim and suspend judgment for a bit you're more likely to find a more insightful—and more focused—argument. For instance, instead of simply declaring, "There are too many dog piles on hiking paths!" you might discover a more interesting and useful claim: "Boise needs more off-leash dog parks."

Most arguments like this don't provoke an analytical response at first. We react emotionally: "This guy is so full of it!" or perhaps, "It's about time someone spoke up about the cost of freedom!" This letter, like many that raise controversial issues, triggers a whole set of deeply held beliefs about things like patriotism, freedom of speech, and the purpose of art. These are things that *should* provoke discussion—and inevitably trigger feelings. But without involving the head as well as the heart, it's impossible to have a civil discussion—one that will lead to new understanding. We need to understand not only what we ourselves believe but also what the other guy believes.

Using Toulmin. Fortunately, there are tools to help with this analysis. For example, Stephen Toulmin, an English philosopher, argued that arguments about any subject have features that include:

- claims
- evidence (grounds)
- warrants (reasons)
- backing

The most penetrating aspect of Toulmin's approach is the idea that *warrants*—or assumptions about the way things are—are key to the logical relationship between evidence and claims. For example, my colleague Dr. Michelle Payne does an exercise with her students in which she empties her purse and asks, "What claim might you make about what kind of person I am based on the evidence before you?" Michelle's students once inferred, for example, that the fact she carries three credit cards meant that she had a lot of money (she doesn't). Others claimed that the cards suggested she carried a lot of debt (actually, no). How might these opposing claims be evaluated? That's where warrants come in. "What do you need to believe is true," Michelle asked, "if your claims from the evidence are valid?" The backers of the high-debt claim agreed they would have to believe that there is a relationship between the number of credit cards one has and the amount of debt one carries. That's the warrant, and there actually is some factual backing for it. The success of any argument, Toulmin believed, depends on the validity of its warrants.

Earlier in the chapter, we talked about warrants as assumptions or premises, and they're pretty much the same things, except that Toulmin's model highlights a more formal relationship between evidence, claims, warrants, and backing. Figure 7.5 shows how we might use Toulmin to chart the claim Michelle's students made about the contents of her purse.

As you can see, arguing well isn't simply a matter of lining up ducks. The task isn't to make a claim and then hunt up evidence to support it. Toulmin reminds us that wedged between evidence and claims are warrants—things the writers assume must be true for their claims to be believable. These warrants may be implicit or explicit, and one of the best ways to analyze an argument is to figure out what the warrants are and to decide if they have enough backing to be believable.

Evidence		**Claim**
If Michelle has 3 credit cards in her purse...		...Michelle must carry too much debt.

Warrants

There is a relationship between the number of credit cards and personal debt.

Backing

Kim and Devaney (2001) cite a positive relationship between the number of credit cards and a consumer's debt.

Figure 7.5 Toulmin's model shows how to analyze the claim that carrying three credit cards means that one is also carrying too much debt.

Let's apply Toulmin's approach to the letter to the editor that began this section. What's the claim? What are its warrants? Here's one take:

Evidence and Claim: If artists subject "great American military figures" to ridicule in a time of war, they are being unpatriotic.

Warrant #1: During wartime, Americans should temper their criticism of the military.

Warrant #2: Those who haven't seen military service don't fully appreciate the costs associated with protecting freedom.

Warrant #3: Art can be unpatriotic.

These are not the only warrants implied by the letter writer's claim, and it's certainly debatable if I've actually got the claim right. But if someone asked me to go beyond an emotional reaction to the letter and offer a reasoned response, then these warrants might be the ideas I would start with. Do I agree with them? Why or why not? What backing might support or refute a particular warrant?

Using Logical Fallacies. Toulmin's method is just one of many ways to analyze the arguments that we encounter in our reading.

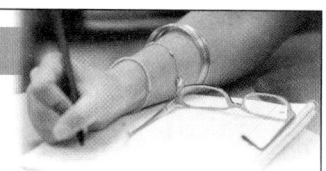

Common Logical Fallacies

An important way to evaluate the soundness of an argument is to examine its logic and, in particular, look for so-called logical fallacies that may lead writers' reasoning astray. Aristotle was one of the first to point out many of these, and a quick search on the Web using the term "logical fallacies" will reveal dozens and dozens of them that plague public argument. Many of them have indecipherable Latin names, testifying to their ancient origins.

Here are ten of the most common logical fallacies. I think they cover about 90 percent of the ways in which writers stumble when making an argument.

1. *Hasty generalization:* We're naturally judgmental creatures. For example, we frequently make a judgment about someone after just meeting him or her. Or we conclude that a class is useless after attending a single session. These are generalizations based on insufficient evidence. Hasty generalizations *might* be true—the class might turn out to be useless—but you should always be wary of them.

2. *Ad hominem:* When arguments turn into shouting matches, they almost inevitably get personal. Shifting away from the substance of an argument to attack the person making it, either subtly or explicitly, is another common logical fallacy. It's also, at times, hard to resist.

3. *Appeal to authority:* We all know that finding support for a claim from an expert is a smart move in many arguments. But sometimes it's a faulty move because the authority we cite isn't really an expert on the subject. A more common fallacy, however, is when we cite an expert to support a claim without acknowledging that many experts disagree on the point.

4. *Straw man:* One of the sneakiest ways to sidetrack reason in an argument is to misrepresent or ignore the actual position of an opponent. Unfortunately, the "straw-man" fallacy thrives in many political debates: "I can't support this proposal for universal health care," says politician A. "It's clear that politician A doesn't really take the problem in American health care seriously," says politician B. Huh?

5. *False analogy:* Analogies can be powerful comparisons in argument. But they can also lead us astray when the analogy simply doesn't hold. Are A and B *really* similar situations? For example, when a critic of higher education argues that a public university is like a business and should be run like one, are the two really analogous? Fundamentally, one is nonprofit and the other is designed to make money. Is this really a useful comparison? *(continued)*

Inquiring into the Details (*continued*)

6. ***Post hoc or false cause:*** Just because one thing follows another doesn't necessarily mean one *causes* the other. It might be coincidence, or the cause might be something else entirely. For example, if you're really keen on arguing that losing the football coach was the cause of the team's losing record, you might link the two. And it's possible that you're right, but it's also just as possible that the injury to the quarterback was one of the real reasons.

7. ***Appeal to popularity:*** In a country obsessed by polls and rankings, it's not hard to understand the appeal of reasoning that argues that because it's popular it must be good or true. Advertisers are particularly fond of this fallacy, arguing that because their brand is most popular it must be the best. In fact, this might not be the case at all. The majority can be wrong.

8. ***Slippery slope:*** I love the name of this one because it so aptly describes what can happen when reasoning loses its footing. You might start out reasonably enough, arguing, for example, that a gun control law restricts the rights of some citizens to have access to certain weapons, but pretty soon you start sliding toward conclusions that simply don't follow, such as that a gun control law is the beginning of the end of gun ownership in the country. Now you might really believe this, but logic isn't the route to get there.

9. ***Either/or fallacy:*** In a black-and-white world, something is right or wrong, true or false, good or bad. But ours is a colorful world with many shades. For instance, while it might be emotionally satisfying to say that opponents of the war in Iraq must not support the troops there, it is also possible that the war's opponents are against the war *because* they're concerned about the lives of American service people. Rather than *either/or* it might be *both/and*. We see this fallacy often in arguments that suggest that there are only two choices and each are opposites.

10. ***Begging the question:*** This one is also called circular reasoning because it assumes the truth of the arguer's conclusion without bothering to prove it. An obvious example of this would be to say that a law protecting people from Internet spam is good because it's a law, and laws should be obeyed. But *why* is it a good law?

MOTIVES FOR WRITING AN ARGUMENT

Argument, obviously, is a part of everyday life, though as I noted before, it doesn't always go well. I'm constantly trying to persuade my wife Karen that it would be a good thing if I added another guitar to my acoustic collection. I was thinking a new Martin with mahogany back and sides and onboard Fishman electronics would be good.

"You've already got seven guitars," she said. "How many more do you need?"

We argue to get something we want but these are often the least interesting arguments to make.

Classical rhetoricians like Plato, Aristotle, and Cicero had a great deal to say about how to argue well, and while their focus was largely on public speaking, their ideas are foundational for a modern understanding of argument. For

Aristotle, there were three arenas for persuasion—before the courts, before legislators and others who make public policy, and at social occasions.

Of course, there are plenty of other reasons to argue. In academic writing, the purpose of argument is usually to establish the truth of something. Modern advertising, the most common medium of modern persuasion, attempts to influence people's behaviors. Generally speaking, you can distinguish between these two purposes—to establish the validity of a certain way of seeing things and the desire to move people to action—but because the persuasive essay you will be writing in this chapter can do both, we won't make much of the distinction between these two purposes here.

Arguing is a civic duty. In fact, it is an essential activity in any democratic culture, and it's certainly a major element of academic discourse; academic argument is one of the key means of making new knowledge.

Knowing how to argue well has practical value, even if you don't become a lawyer. It might help you make the best case to a local legislator to support the bill providing tuition relief to students, or even bargaining with the used-car dealer for a better price on that black convertible Mazda Miata. Understanding argument helps you find the flaws in *other people's* arguments as well. Knowing how to analyze an argument gives me a language to talk about the flawed arguments in the letters to the editor in *The Idaho Statesman,* and it also helps me thoughtfully and critically read articles and essays that make claims.

Finally, the most important motive behind writing and studying argument is that you care about something. Throughout this book, I've argued that the personal motive for writing is the most powerful one of all; in this case, you're passionate about a question or an issue, and building a written argument channels that passion into prose that can make a difference.

THE ARGUMENT AND ACADEMIC WRITING

Argumentative writing is one of the most common of all academic forms. One reason for this is that the ability to argue well requires some command of subject matter. There is another motive for mastering argument in academic settings, however, and it has less to do with proving that you know your stuff. Argument is really about trying to get at the truth.

> Argument is one of the key means of making new knowledge.

In college, the audiences for your arguments are often your instructors. As experts in a particular discipline, professors argue all the time. They're not simply trying to be contrary but trying to get at the truth. Arguing is the main way that the academic community makes knowledge.

Notice I used the word *make*. While it often seems that the facts we take for granted are immutable truths—as enduring as the granite peaks I can see through my office window—things aren't often that way at all. Our knowledge of things—how the planet was formed, the best ways to save endangered species, the meaning of a classic novel, how to avoid athletic injuries—is entirely made up of ideas that are *contested*. They are less mountains than the glaciers that carved them, and in some cases the sudden earthquakes that bring them down. The primary tool for shaping and even changing what we know is argument.

FEATURES OF THE FORM

Generally speaking, persuasive writing can take many forms. Indeed, reviews and proposals, two essays addressed earlier in this book, both represent different types of persuasive writing. The argument essay we are covering in this chapter, however, more obviously embodies persuasive writing than either of these two other forms. This essay typically makes explicit claims and backs them up with hard evidence. It also employs the well-established rhetorical devices and the reasoning of formal argumentation in the effort to sway readers to its point of view. However, unlike more formal academic papers, the argument you'll be writing in this chapter is intended for a more general audience. It's what we might call a *public argument*. It's the kind of piece you might see in your local newspaper, or in a magazine. *Newsweek*'s "My Turn" column is an excellent example. (See Figure 7.6 for a comparison of argument essays.)

Here are some of the features of the public argument essay:

■ *Public arguments are often relatively brief treatments of a topic.* Readers of newspapers and many magazines read fast. They want to quickly get the gist

Rhetorical Context	Academic Argument Essay	Public Argument Essay
Audience	Academic discourse community	Publication's readers
Speaker	You as a member of above	You as an authority on subject
Purpose	To demonstrate your authority	To make something happen
Subject	Of academic interest	Of community interest
Voice	Conventional, academic	Personal, informed
Research	Always	Usually
Citations	Yes	No
Length	Varies, usually 8–25 pages	Varies, usually 500–1,000 words
How to read	Slowly, thoughtfully	Rapidly, mining for meaning

Figure 7.6 A comparison of academic and informal argument (Devan Cook, Boise State University)

of an essay or article and move on to the next story. In addition, space is often limited, particularly in newspapers. As a result, the op-ed or opinion piece rarely exceeds 1,000 words, or about four double-spaced manuscript pages.

■ *Subject matter often focuses on issues of public concern.* The magazines and newspapers that publish argument essays typically report on news, events, or issues that might affect a lot of people. Not surprisingly, then, writers of these essays are keen observers of public debates and controversies.

■ *A public argument has a central claim or proposition.* Sometimes we also call this a *thesis,* a term that's a holdover from the scientific terminology that dominated American scholarship from the end of the nineteenth century. Classical arguments, the kind many of us wrote in high school, usually state this central claim or thesis in the introduction. But many arguments, particularly essays that rely on narrative structure or explore the answer to a question or problem, may feature the thesis in the middle or at the end of the essay.

■ *The central claim is based on one or more premises or assumptions.* You already know something about this from the discussion earlier in the chapter. Basically, a premise suggests that something is true *because* of something else; it expresses the relationship between *what* you claim and *why* you believe that claim to be true. This is discussed at greater length later in the chapter.

■ *The public argument relies on evidence that a general audience will believe.* All arguments should use evidence appropriate for a particular audience. Academic writers in marine biology, for example, rely on data collected in the field and analyzed statistically because this kind of evidence is most persuasive to other marine biologists. Anecdotes or personal observation alone simply won't cut it in the *Journal of Marine Biology*. But the persuasive essay's more general audience finds a greater range of evidence convincing, including personal experience and observation. Writers of persuasive essays are likely to do the kind of research you use to write research papers—digging up statistics, facts, and quotations on a topic.

■ *They sometimes invite or encourage a response.* Earlier I noted a broad distinction between the purposes of argument: (1) to establish the validity of a writer's way of seeing what's true and (2) to move or persuade an audience to act a certain way. The second purpose is most obvious in the advertisement, which is a visual argument that asks viewers to *do* something—buy a Jeep or change toilet bowl cleaners. But public arguments sometimes ask for or imply a course of action readers should take. An op-ed piece might attempt to change the views and behaviors of political leaders, or influence how people vote for them. It might urge support for a school bond issue, or encourage fellow students to protest against the elimination of an academic program.

■ *Readers won't respond unless they know what's at stake.* An essential element of argument is establishing why a certain action, policy, or idea *matters*. How will opposition to the administration's strip-mining policies in West Virginia and Kentucky make a difference in the quality of life in those states, but even more important, why should someone in Boise, Idaho, care? The best arguments are built to carefully establish, sometimes in quite practical terms, how a certain action, belief, or idea might make a difference in the lives of those who are the argument's audience.

WRITING IN YOUR LIFE

Public Argument in a Digital Age

Winning an argument with Northwest Airlines over whether they owe you a lunch voucher after your flight was cancelled is typical of the way persuasion is an everyday concern. But in a larger sense—and probably more important one—arguing well and arguing ethically is a civic duty in a democratic society. A few thousand years ago, the Greeks and Romans created schools of rhetoric where people could learn the art of speaking persuasively in public settings.

These days, probably more than ever, argument is a vibrant part of civic life in the United States, particularly on the Internet. Here are a few of the many genres of public argument available to you for moving people to think or do something you consider important:

- *Op-ed essays:* These are possibly the most common brief argumentative essays for a general audience. The term "op-ed" refers to the editorial essays that are published opposite of the editorial page, a ubiquitous feature in most American newspapers.

- *Editorials:* Brief statements of opinion, often 500 words or less, represent the institutional judgment about a policy issue of a newspaper, radio or TV station, online publication, and so on.

- *Blogs:* One of the newest forms of public argument is the blog. Hosted by on-line sites like Google's "Blogger," the so-called blogosphere is sixty times larger than it was three years ago.

- *Photo essay:* Over 100 years ago, Jacob Riis used photographs of immigrants' squalid conditions in New York City tenements to incite a public outcry—and policy change—on how we treat the poor.

- *Letters to the editor:* These appear in print or online and, unlike editorials, people read them.

- *YouTube:* It's not just a forum for published videos on weird cat tricks.

- *PowerPoint:* Former Vice President Al Gore's slide presentation, "An Inconvenient Truth," made the point that there really is power in PowerPoint. Of course, more often these presentations are really awful.

READINGS

■ ARGUMENT 1

It's hard to imagine that one of the chief planners of the September 11, 2001, attacks on New York and Washington, D.C., might invoke George Washington as his hero. In the excerpt that follows, Kahlid Sheikh Mohammed, a commander for al Queda, who has been in custody since 2003, argues that Islamic extremists, like Washington, are just fighting for their independence. The language of war, says Mohammed, is universal, and that language is killing.

This partial transcript of Mohammed discussing his role in the 9/11 attacks, the murder of journalist Daniel Pearl, and the hotel bombings in Bali, was released by the U.S. Department of Defense and later appeared in *Harper's Magazine*.

The Language of War Is Killing

Khalid Sheikh Mohammed

I'm not making myself a hero when I said I was responsible for this or that. You   1
know very well there is a language for any war. If America wants to invade Iraq, they will not send Saddam roses or kisses. They send bombardment. I admit I'm America's enemy. For sure, I'm America's enemy. So when we make war against America, we are like jackals fighting in the night. We consider George Washington a hero. Muslims, many of them, believe Osama bin Laden is doing the same thing. He is just fighting. He needs his independence. Many Muslims think that, not only me. They have been oppressed by America. So when we say we are enemy combatants, that's right, we are. But I'm asking you to be fair with many detainees who are not enemy combatants. Because many of them have been unjustly arrested. You know very well, for any country waging war against their enemy, the language of the war is killing. If man and woman are together as a marriage, the others are kids, children. But if you and me, two nations, are together in war, the others are victims. This is the way of the language. You know forty million people were killed in World War I. Many people are oppressed. Because there is war, for sure, there will be victims. I'm not happy that three thousand have been killed in America. I feel sorry even. Islam never gives me the green light to kill people. Killing, in Christianity, Judaism, and Islam, is prohibited. But there are exceptions to the rule. When you are killing people in Iraq, you say, We have to do it. We don't like Saddam. But this is the way to deal with Saddam. Same language you use I use. When you are invading two thirds of Mexico, you call your war "manifest destiny."

(continued)

(continued)

It's up to you to call it what you want. But the other side is calling you oppressors. If now we were living in the Revolutionary War, George Washington would be arrested by Britain. For sure, they would consider him an enemy combatant. But in America they consider him a hero. In any revolutionary war one side will be either George Washington or Britain. So we considered American Army bases in Saudi Arabia, Kuwait, Qatar, and Bahrain. This is a kind of invasion, but I'm not here to convince you. I don't have to say that I'm not your enemy. This is why the language of any war in the world is killing. The language of war is victims. I don't like to kill people. I feel very sorry kids were killed in 9/11. What will I do? I want to make a great awakening in America to stop foreign policy in our land. I know Americans have been torturing us since the seventies. I know they are talking about human rights. And I know it is against the American Constitution, against American laws. But they said, Every law has exceptions. This is your bad luck—you've been part of the exception to our laws. So, for me, I have patience. The Americans have human rights, but enemy combatant is a flexible word. What is an enemy combatant in my language? The Ten Commandments are shared between all of us. We are all serving one God. But we also share the language of War. War started when Cain killed Abel. It's never gonna stop killing people. America starts the Revolutionary War, and then the Mexican, then the Spanish, then World War I, World War II. You read the history. This is life. You have to kill.

Inquiring into the Essay

Explore, explain, evaluate, and reflect on "The Language of War."

1. Does Mohammed have a point when he compares Islamic extremists who fight for "freedom" to American revolutionaries like George Washington who fought for independence? Fastwrite on this question in your journal for five minutes, exploring what you think. When you're done, skip a line and compose a one-sentence answer to this question: *What surprised you most about what you said in your fastwrite?*

2. Summarize in your own words what you think is Mohammed's main claim.

3. Make a list of reasons that he states in (or you infer from) the transcript that are meant to support Mohammed's main claim. Remember that reasons are ideas that can be attached to a claim using the word "because." For example, "Because most professors are liberals (reason), an open and balanced political discussion in the college classroom is unlikely (claim)." Choose one or more of these reasons, and evaluate whether they are convincing. If not, why not?

4. The September 11 attacks have, understandably, made many Americans very emotional about terrorism and terrorists. What did you notice about

your emotional reaction to Mohammed's argument in "The Language of War"? Did you find it difficult to read the transcript analytically, as the previous questions asked you to do? If so, is this a problem?

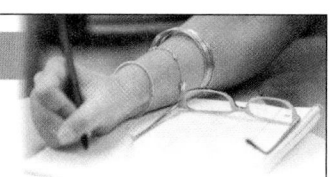

INQUIRING INTO THE DETAILS

Some Basic Argument Strategies

- ■ *Argument from generalization:* What I've seen or observed of a particular group is true of the group as a whole. *Risk: Are you sure that what you've observed is typical of the larger population?*

- ■ *Argument from analogy:* If it is true in one situation, it's likely true in another similar situation. *Risk: Are the situations* really *similar?*

- ■ *Argument from cause:* If one thing always seems present with something else, then one probably causes the other. *Risk: Is cause and effect* really *the relationship between the two things?*

- ■ *Argument from authority:* If an expert said it, it's true. *Risk: Is the expertise of the authority* really *relevant to the question at issue?*

- ■ *Argument from principle:* This general principle (which most of us agree with) applies in this case. *Risk: Is there* really *agreement on the rightness of the principle, and does it actually apply in this specific context?*

Adapted from Richard Fulkerson, *Teaching the Argument in Writing*. Urbana, IL: National Council of Teachers of English, 1996.

■ ARGUMENT 2

Faith and reason don't have to clash. In his encyclical on the subject, Pope John Paul II wrote that "faith and reason are like two wings on which the human spirit rises to the contemplation of truth." Before the modern era of science, any conflict between the two could be easily resolved by simply accepting that any proposition can, at the same time, be true by reason and false by faith. But these days, such a contradiction is hard to swallow. Take evolution. Darwin's scientific argument intensified the clash between faith and reason, and it still produces pitched battles between school boards and teachers, preachers and scientists, and believers and nonbelievers of all types.

One answer to the conflict is simple. Choose one or the other:

1. When science and scripture collide, scripture wins.
2. When science and scripture collide, science wins.

In the op-ed essay that follows, *Boston Globe* columnist Jeff Jacoby seems to offer another alternative. Using the intellectual success—and deep religious commitment—of one great figure, Jacoby argues that faith and reason aren't necessarily incompatible.

A Teacher with Faith and Reason
Jeff Jacoby

1   Did you hear about the religious fundamentalist who wanted to teach physics at Cambridge University? This would-be instructor wasn't simply a Christian; he was so preoccupied with biblical prophecy that he wrote a book titled *Observations on the Prophecies of Daniel and the Apocalypse of St. John.* Based on his reading of Daniel, in fact, he forecast the date of the Apocalypse: no earlier than 2060. He also calculated the year the world was created. When Genesis 1:1 says "In the beginning," he determined, it means 3988 BC.

2   Not many modern universities are prepared to employ a science professor who espouses not merely "intelligent design" but out-and-out divine creation. This applicant's writings on astronomy, for example, include these thoughts on the solar system: "This most beautiful system of sun, planets, and comets could only proceed from the counsel and domination of an intelligent and powerful Being…He governs all things, and knows all things that are or can be done."

3   Hire somebody with such views to teach physics? At a Baptist junior college deep in the Bible Belt, maybe, but the faculty would erupt if you tried it just about anywhere else. Many of them would echo Oxford's Richard Dawkins, the prominent evolutionary biologist, who writes in "The God Delusion" that he is "hostile to fundamentalist religion because it actively debauches the scientific enterprise….It subverts science and saps the intellect."

4   Equally blunt is Sam Harris, a PhD candidate in neuroscience and another unsparing foe of religion. "The conflict between religion and science is inherent and (very nearly) zero-sum," he has written. "The success of science often comes at the expense of religious dogma; the maintenance of religious dogma always comes at the expense of science." Less elegant but more influential, the National Science Education Standards issued by the National Academy of Sciences in 1995 classified religion with "myths," "mystical inspiration," and "superstition"—all of them quite incompatible with scientific study. Michael Dini, a biologist at Texas Tech University in Lubbock, made headlines in 2003 over his policy of denying letters of recommendation for any graduate student who could not "truthfully and forthrightly affirm a scientific answer" to the question of mankind's origin. Science and religion, he said in an interview at the time, "shouldn't overlap."

5   But such considerations didn't keep Cambridge from hiring the theology- and Bible-drenched individual described above. Indeed, it named him to the prestigious

Lucasian Chair of Mathematics—in 1668. A good thing too, since Isaac Newton—notwithstanding his religious fervor and intense interest in Biblical interpretation—went on to become the most renowned scientist of his age, and arguably the most influential in history.

Newton's consuming interest in theology, eschatology, and the secrets of the Bible is the subject of a new exhibit at Hebrew University in Jerusalem (online at jnul.huji.ac.il/dl/mss/Newton). His vast religious output—an estimated 3 million words—ranged from the dimensions of Solomon's Temple to a method of reckoning the date of Easter to the elucidation of Biblical symbols. "Newton was one of the last great Renaissance men," the curators observe, "a thinker who worked in mathematics, physics, optics, alchemy, history, theology, and the interpretation of prophecy and saw connections between them all." The 21st-century prejudice that religion invariably "subverts science" is refuted by the extraordinary figure who managed to discover the composition of light, deduce the laws of motion, invent calculus, compute the speed of sound, and define universal gravitation, all while believing deeply in the "domination of an intelligent and powerful Being." Far from subverting his scientific integrity, the exhibition notes, "Newton's piety served as one of his inspirations to study nature and what we today call science."

For Newton, it was axiomatic that religious inquiry and scientific investigation complemented each other. There were truths to be found in both of the "books" authored by God, the Book of Scripture and the Book of Nature—or as Francis Bacon called them, the "book of God's word" and the "book of God's works." To study the world empirically did not mean abandoning religious faith. On the contrary: The more deeply the workings of Creation were understood, the closer one might come to the Creator. In the language of the 19th Psalm, "The heavens declare the glory of God, and the sky above proclaims his handiwork."

To be sure, religious dogma can be a blindfold, blocking truths from those who refuse to see them. Scientific dogma can have the same effect. Neither faith nor reason can answer every question. As Newton knew, the surer path to wisdom is the one that has room for both.

Inquiring into the Essay

Explore, explain, evaluate, and reflect on "A Teacher with Faith and Reason."

1. Perhaps the central claim of this essay appears, as it often does in an op-ed essay, two thirds of the way into the piece, when Jacoby writes,

    > The 21st-century prejudice that religion invariably "subverts science" is refuted by the extraordinary figure who managed to discover the composition of light, deduce the laws of motion, invent calculus, compute the speed of

sound, and define universal gravitation, all while believing deeply in the "domination of an intelligent and powerful Being."

When you analyze an argument, it's often helpful to first explore—in a relatively open-ended way—what you think about the central claim. Do that now in a four-minute fastwrite in your journal. Do you agree or disagree that Isaac Newton's legacy "refutes" the current "prejudice" that religion undercuts scientific inquiry? Try writing a narrative of thought, beginning with "The first thing I think about this is…And then I think…And then…" Allow yourself to digress if that's where your writing takes you.

2. Define the two key terms in this debate—reason and faith—in your own words.

3. An argument about potential conflicts between faith and reason can easily become too abstract to evaluate well. So consider the case Jacoby mentions in his essay: A Texas Tech biology professor routinely refused to write recommendations for any graduate student who didn't provide a "scientific answer" to explain the beginnings of humankind. Do you find Jacoby's argument helpful in developing your own response to that particular situation?

4. This is one of those social issues that trigger strong feeling which, at times, can cloud reasoning. Reflect on your own response to issues like this one. When you have an emotional response to a public argument, how do you get past it?

■ ARGUMENT 3

During the fall semester, 2008, Laredo businessman Loye Young agreed to teach a business management class at nearby Texas A&M International University (TAMIU). Like many instructors, he toiled over his syllabus, trying to make sure his course policies were clear, especially a section on the consequences of plagiarism in his class. Young warned that plagiarists would not only flunk the course, they would be reported to university officials. That's fairly standard punishment at most universities. What got critics' attention was Young's warning that he would publicly humiliate any student caught cheating.

True to his word, when he caught six students plagiarizing a paper, Young published their names on his blog, and soon after, TAMIU officials fired him, arguing that he violated the Family Educational and Privacy Act, a policy designed to protect the confidentiality of certain student information. Young, a former attorney, strongly disagreed.

The firing ignited a national controversy and a wild debate in the blogosphere over whether Loye Young's decision to out students he suspected of academic dishonesty was effective, ethical, and fair. In response to one of his critics, Loye posted the following defense of his approach on his blog.

Is Humiliation an Ethically Appropriate Response to Plagiarism?

Loye Young

I'm a business owner in Laredo, Texas. I had never taught a college course before, and I never asked to teach. The department asked me to teach this course. I accepted because of my commitment to Laredo's future.   1

I worked hard on the syllabus, and everything in the syllabus was deliberate. Specifically, the language about dishonesty was based on moral and pedagogical principles. The department chairman, Dr. Balaji Janamanchi, reviewed the syllabus with me line-by-line, and I made a few changes in response to his comments.   2

I was surprised by how common and blatant plagiarism turned out to be. Six students in one class is an extraordinarily high number. I thought and prayed about what to do for about a week before following through on my promise. I decided I had only one moral choice. I am certain it was right.   3

My decision was guided by two factors: What is good for the students themselves? and What is good for other students?   4

What is good for the students themselves?   5

I am cognizant of the extraordinary moral difficulty involved when deciding what is in another's best interests. Nonetheless, I am convinced that public disclosure, including the concomitant humiliation, is in the interests of the student because it is the best way to teach the student about the consequences of dishonesty and discourage the student from plagiarizing again. Humiliation is inextricably part of a well-formed conscience.   6

The Vice President-elect, Senator Joseph Biden, is perhaps the most well-known plagiarizer in recent history. Biden was caught plagiarizing while at Syracuse Law School. The school gave him an F, required him to retake the course, and subsequently treated the incident as confidential.   7

Unfortunately, Biden didn't learn his lesson at law school. He continued to plagiarize for another 20 years. During the 1988 presidential campaign, Senator Biden's career of plagiarizing came to light, and he was forced to end his presidential bid.   8

It is my belief that the Syracuse incident left a subtle and subliminal message in Biden's mind: plagiarism is not a deal breaker. Consequently, he continued to plagiarize. Unfortunately for the Senator, the facts came to public light at the worst possible time: when he was running for President.   9

I believe that had the Syracuse incident been available publicly, Mr. Biden would have actually learned his lesson and would not have plagiarized later. Twenty years later, if the incident had come up at all, the Senator would have plausibly and convincingly maintained that the incident was a youthful mistake.   10

There is yet another reason for publicity in such cases: unjustly accused students are protected, for two reasons. One, a professor will be more careful before blowing   11

(continued)

(continued)

the whistle. I myself knew that posting the students' names would be appropriately subject to intense public scrutiny. Therefore, I construed every ambiguity in the students' favor. Two, public disclosure ensures that subsequent determinations by the university are founded on evidence and dispensed fairly.

12 What is good for other students?

13 On the second question, four reasons convince me: deterrents, fairness, predictability, and preparedness for life.

14 Deterrents—Only if everyone knows that violations of plagiarism will be exposed and punished will the penalties for plagiarism be an effective deterrent. (As a lawyer once told me after hearing of another lawyer's disbarment, "I'm damn sure not going to do THAT again!") In fact, one of the six students had not plagiarized (to my knowledge) until the week before I announced my findings. Had I announced the plagiarism earlier, it is possible that student would not have plagiarized at all.

15 Fairness—Honest students should have, in fairness, the knowledge that their legitimate work is valued more than a plagiarizer's illegitimate work. In my course, the students were required to post their essays on a public website for all to see. Thus, anyone in the world could have detected the plagiarism. Had another student noticed the plagiarism but saw no action, the honest student would reasonably believe that the process is unfair.

16 Predictability—By failing publicly to follow through on ubiquitous warnings about plagiarism, universities have convinced students that the purported indignation against deceit is itself deceitful and that the entire process is capricious. TAMIU's actions in this case have confirmed my suspicions that such a perception is entirely justified.

17 Preparedness for life—In the real world, deceitful actions have consequences, and those consequences are often public. Borrowers lose credit ratings, employees get fired, spouses divorce, businesses fail, political careers end, and professionals go to jail. Acts of moral turpitude rightly carry public and humiliating consequences in real life, and students need to be prepared.

18 In closing, I submit that education died when educators came to believe that greater self-esteem leads to greater learning. In fact, the causality is backwards: self-esteem is the result of learning, not the cause.

Inquiring into the Essay

Explore, explain, evaluate, and reflect on "Is Humiliation an Ethically Appropriate Response to Plagiarism?"

1. If you accept that plagiarism is a problem, then what should an instructor do about it? What would you consider not just an ethical policy but one that you think might be an effective deterrent? Fastwrite about this question in your journal for four minutes, exploring what you think.

2. How would *you* define plagiarism? Is it possible that some students might be understandably confused about what it means?

3. Loye Young writes, "Humiliation is inextricably part of a well-formed conscience." How would you evaluate that claim? Can you imagine the *reasons* that Young believes it's true? (Try filling in the blank in this sentence: *Because _____, humiliation is inextricably part of a well-formed conscience.*) Do you agree with them?

4. Reflect on the blog as a genre of public argument. How would you distinguish it from, say, an op-ed essay or a letter to the editor?

SEEING THE FORM

The "Imagetext" as Argument

While model Kate Moss is likely disturbed by the appropriation of her image by advocates in the pro-anorexia ("pro-ana") movement, Moss's picture along with those of other celebrities such as Calista Flockhart, Mary-Kate Olsen, and Keira Knightley appear as "thinspiration" on Web sites that argue that eating disorders are a "lifestyle choice," not a disease. Some of these images (though not this one) are digitally altered to make the models seem even thinner than they really are. In a recent article on the "imagetexts" used by these controversial Web sites, Robin Jensen observes that images rarely argue in isolation, a phenomenon that is particularly relevant to the Web, which often combines pictures and verbal texts. Jensen notes that when pictures like this one of Kate Moss are given a new "visual frame," quite different from the one originally intended, the meaning of the picture can be manipulated. Imagine, for instance, that the Kate Moss photograph appeared in a "thinspiration" gallery of celebrity photographs on a "pro-ana" Web site, and included the following caption: "Maintaining a weight that is 15 percent below your expected body weight fits the criteria for anorexia, so most models, according to medical standards, fit into the category of being anorexic." Analyze this "imagetext" rhetorically. How does this picture of Moss combined with the caption serve the purpose of the "pro-ana" movement? What message is it meant to convey and is it persuasive to its intended audience?

Kate Moss in ultra-thin pose.

THE WRITING PROCESS

For additional reading, writing, and research resources, go to www.mycomplab.com

Thinking About Subjects

Gun control, abortion rights, and other hot-button public controversies often make the list of banned topics for student essays. This is not because they aren't important public debates. Instead, the problem is much more that the writer has likely already made up his mind and sees the chance to ascend a soapbox.

> The best argument essays make a clear claim, but they do it by bowing respectfully to the complexity of the subject, examining it from a variety of perspectives, not just two opposing poles.

Now, I have my own favorite soapboxes; people with strong convictions do. But as you think about subjects for your essay, consider that the soapbox may not be the best vantage point for practicing inquiry. If you've already made up your mind, will you be open to discovery? If you just want to line up ducks—assembling evidence to support an unwavering belief—will you be encouraged to think deeply or differently? Will you be inclined to filter the voices you hear rather than consider a range of points of view?

The best persuasive essays often emerge from the kind of open-ended inquiry that you might have used writing the personal essay. What do you want to understand better? What issue or question makes you wonder? What controversies are you and your friends talking about? Be alert to possible subjects that you might write about *not* because you already know what you think, but because you want to find out. Or consider a subject that you might have feelings about but feel uninformed, lacking the knowledge to know exactly what you think.

Generating Ideas

Play around with some ideas first by using some of the following triggers for thinking-through-writing in your journal. Suspend judgment. Don't reject anything. Explore.

Listing Prompts. Lists can be rich sources of triggering topics. Let them grow freely, and when you're ready, use an item as the focus of another list or an episode of fastwriting. The following prompts should get you started.

1. In your journal, make a quick list of issues that have provoked disagreements between groups of people in your hometown or local community.

2. Make a quick list of issues that have provoked disagreements on your college's campus.

3. Make another list of issues that have created controversy between groups of people in your state.

4. Think about issues—local, statewide, regional, national, or even international—that have touched your life, or could affect you in some way in the following areas: environmental, health care, civil rights, business, education, crime, or sports. Make a quick list of questions within these areas you wonder about. For example, *Will there be enough drinking water in my well if the valley continues to develop at this rate?* Or *Will I be able to afford to send my children to the state college in twelve years?* Or *Do new domestic antiterrorism rules threaten my privacy when I'm online?* Or *Will I benefit from affirmative action laws when I apply to law school?*

5. Jot down a list of the classes you're taking this semester. Then make a quick list of topics that prompt disagreements among people in the field that you're studying. For example, in your political science class, did you learn that there are debates about the usefulness of the electoral college? In your biology class, have you discussed global warming? In your women's studies class, did you read about Title 9 and how it affects female athletes?

Fastwriting Prompts. Remember, fastwriting is a great way to stimulate creative thinking. Turn off your critical side and let yourself write "badly." Don't worry too much about what you're going to say before you say it. Write fast, letting language lead for a change.

1. Write for five minutes beginning with one of the questions you raised in Question 4 in the "Listing Prompts" section. Think through writing about when you first began to be concerned about the question, how you think it might affect you, and what you currently understand are the key questions this issue raises. Do you have tentative feelings or beliefs about it?

2. In a seven-minute fastwrite, explore the differences between your beliefs and the beliefs of your parents. Tell yourself the story of how your own beliefs about some question evolved, perhaps moving away from your parents' positions. Can you imagine the argument you might make to help them understand your point of view?

3. Choose an item from any of the lists you generated in the "Listing Prompts" section as a starting place for a fastwrite. Explore what you understand about the issue, what the key questions are, and how you feel about the issue at the moment.

Visual Prompts. In your journal, cluster one or more of the following phrases:

"Things that seem unfair"

"Things that bug me the most"

"There oughta be a law about..."

"Problems that must be solved"

"The worst thing about living here"

Let your cluster grow as many branches as possible; when one dies out start another. Focus on ideas, people, places, facts, observations, questions, experiences,

---

ONE STUDENT'S RESPONSE

Ben's Journal

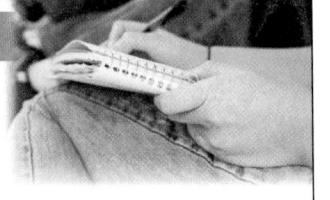

FASTWRITE
WHY DO STUDENTS SEEM SO APATHETIC ABOUT POLITICS?

We're in the midst of presidential elections and I can't seem to get anyone interested in talking about it. I wonder why that is? Are college students more cynical about politics and politicians than other groups? It seems like it to me. I can think of a few reasons right off the bat. First, college students are mostly young (though certainly not all at this school) so they don't have the habit of going to the polls. Whenever a generation loses the habit of voting, I'll bet the next generation is even more likely to be apathetic. I also think my generation has seen so few effective politicians. My dad talks about being inspired by the likes of JFK but I can't think of too many national politicians who have inspired me as much as JFK inspired him. I also wonder if there is that basic sense of powerlessness. We just don't feel like much of anything makes a difference. I wonder if that is also reflected in volunteerism. Do students volunteer less than they used to? Have to check on that. I guess I just find politics kind of interesting. I wonder why? Hmmm...I think it had something to do with my Dad. But I guess I also have this basic belief in voting as an important part of being a citizen. Seems like one of the best ways to be patriotic...

and details that pop into your mind when you focus on the pair of words at the center of your cluster. Look for interesting argument topics when you're done. See Figure 7.7 for an example.

Research Prompts. By definition, argument essays deal with subjects in which people beyond the writer have a stake. And one of the best ways to collect ideas about such issues is to do a little quick and dirty research. Try some of the following research prompts:

1. Spend a few days reading the letters to the editor in your local paper. What issue has people riled up locally? Is there one that you find particularly interesting?

2. Do a Web search to find op-ed essays written by one or more of the following national columnists: Ellen Goodman, Cal Thomas, George Will, David Broder, Nat Hentoff, Mary McGrory, Molly Ivins, Bob Herbert, or Clarence Page. Read their work with an eye toward topics that interest you.

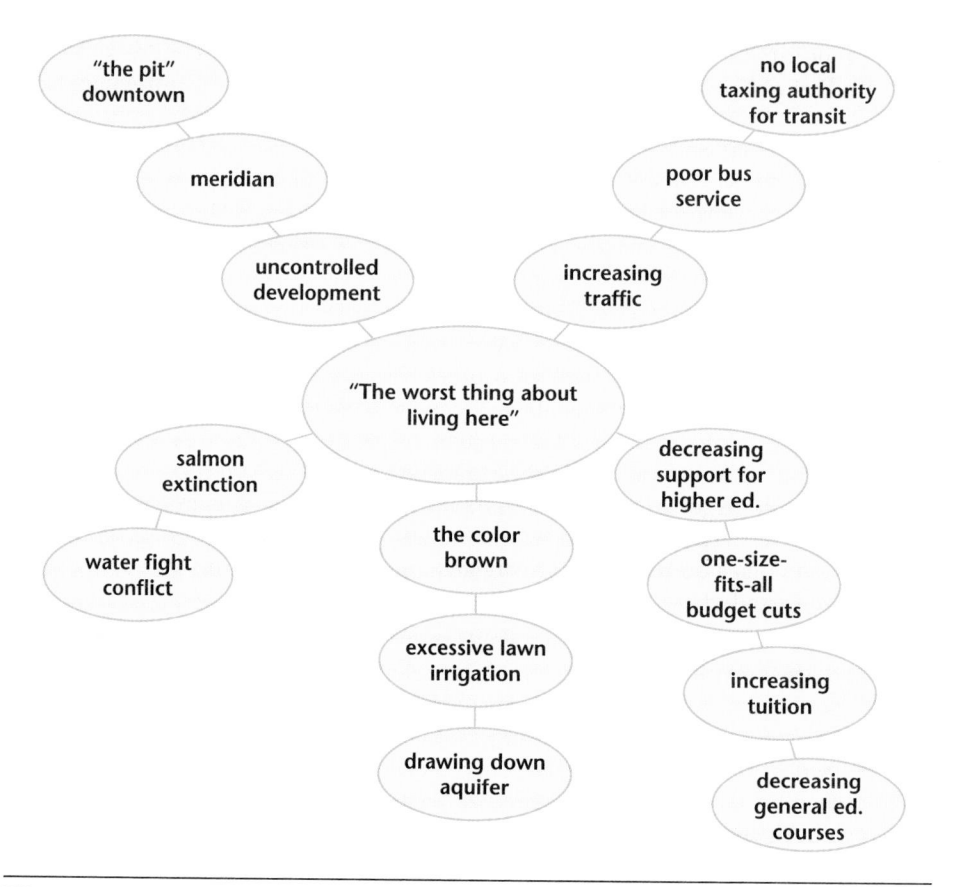

Figure 7.7   Sample cluster

3. Do a Google search for terms or phrases on an issue that interests you, such as "global warming Greenland glaciers" or "pro-anorexia Web sites." Did you produce any results that make you curious or make you feel something about the issue, one way or another?

4. Interview people you know—on or off campus—about the public issues that they care about most.

Judging What You Have

Shift back to your more critical mind and sift through the material you generated. Did you discover a topic that might be interesting for your argument essay? Did you stumble over some interesting questions you'd like to explore further? Did anything you wrote or read make you *feel* something? Evaluate the raw material in your journal and keep the following things in mind as you zero in on a topic for your argument essay.

What's Promising Material and What Isn't? Let's take a critical look at the subjects you've generated so far. What promising topics might be lurking there for an argumentative essay? Consider some of the following as you make your choice.

- *Interest.* This almost goes without saying. But you were warned earlier about seizing on a topic if you already have strong convictions about it. Do you already know what you think? If so, why not choose a topic that initially invites more open-ended inquiry? On the other hand, it matters a lot whether you *care*. What topic might touch your life in some way? Do you have some kind of stake in how the questions are answered?

- *Focus.* One of the most common flaws of student drafts in all genres is that they attempt to cover too much territory. A more *limited* look at a larger landscape is always best. Because these argument essays are brief, consider topics that you can do justice to in less than a thousand words. As you review potential topics for your essay, can you see how some aspect of a larger question can be addressed by asking a smaller question? You can't write a short piece about the negative impact of affirmative action policies on the nation's colleges and universities, but you can write a brief op-ed about the specific impacts on your school.

- *Disagreement.* A topic lends itself to argumentative writing if it leads to disagreement among reasonable people. *Is smoking bad for your health?* was once a question that was debatable, but now pretty much everyone concedes that this question has been answered. *Did the Holocaust really happen?* is a question that only blockheads debate. But the question, *What are the motives of people who deny the Holocaust?* is a question that would generate a range of views.

- *Information.* Is sufficient information available on the topic for you to make a reasonable judgment about what is true? Is it accessible? One great advantage of choosing a local question as the focus for an argumentative essay is that often the people are close by and the relevant information can easily be had. It's also essential that you can obtain information from more than just a single viewpoint on the question.

- *Question.* What makes a topic arguable is that it raises questions to which there are multiple answers. Which of them makes the most sense is at issue. But some questions are merely informational. For example, *How do greenhouse gases contribute to global warming?* is a question that will likely lead to explanations rather than argument. On the other hand, *Is the U.S. rejection of the Kyoto accords on global warming a responsible policy?* is an arguable, rather than informational, question.

Questions About Audience and Purpose. Persuasive writing is a very audience-oriented form. *To whom* you make your case in an argument matters a lot in *how* you make it, but audience also matters in *whether* one topic is a better choice for an essay than another topic. The public argument is written for a more general audience. Your readers are unlikely to be experts on your topic, and they are likely to read your essay quickly rather than slowly and thoughtfully. What does this imply about the best subjects?

- *Do your readers have a stake in the question you're answering?* The word *stake* can be broadly considered. For example, a topic may directly affect the readers of your essay; say you're writing for fellow college students on your campus, all of whom pay tuition, and your topic addresses whether a 12 percent hike in fees is justified. Sometimes, however, you choose a topic because readers need to know that they *do* have a stake in how a question is answered. For instance, the argument that new antiterrorist rules threaten online privacy is something you believe your readers, most of whom surf the Web, should consider.

- *Can you identify what your readers might already believe?* One of the key strategies of persuasion is to find ways to link the values and attitudes of your audience with the position you're encouraging them to believe. Does your potential topic lend itself to this kind of analysis?

- *Is your purpose not only to inform readers but also to encourage them to believe or do something?* As you know by now, one of the things that distinguishes argument essays such as the op-ed piece from other forms of writing is the writer's intention to change his or her audience.

Research Considerations. While writing this argument essay does involve some research, it isn't exactly a research paper. A research paper is a much more extended treatment of a topic that relies on more detailed and scholarly information than is usually needed for an argument essay. Internet research, library research, and evaluating sources are all skills that will help you with this project.

To develop a working knowledge of the topic for your public argument essay, focus your research on the following:

1. *The back-story:* What is the history of the controversy? When did it begin, who was involved, how was the issue addressed, what were the problems?

2. *Popular assumptions:* What do most people currently believe is true about the issue?

3. *The evidence:* Who has said what that seems to support your claim or provide backing for your assumptions?

4. *Opposing arguments:* Who offers a counterargument that you might need to consider?

Consider working through some of the following research strategies to find this information.

Researching on the Web

- Google (for relevant Web sites, online periodicals, and some newspapers)
- Google Scholar (if your topic is discussed by scholars)
- Google Blog Search (to get the gist of the public discussion of your topic)
- GPO Access (go to http://www.gpoaccess.gov/ to search for relevant federal documents)
- Online version of local newspaper (if your topic has a local angle)
- State and Local Government on the Net (go to http://www.statelocalgov.net/ if your topic is an issue of policy)

Researching in the Library

- General subject databases (these cover a wide range of subjects, and many include nonacademic publications as well)
- Newspaper databases (for example National Newspaper Index or Newspaper Source)
- Newspapers on microfilm (your university library might archive copies of the local paper on microfilm, going back for many years)

While both the Web and the university library are great sources of information on your topic, often the best way to learn about it—and get some good quotes for your essay—is to find someone to talk to. Your reading will probably give you the best clues about who to contact. Who is often quoted in news stories? Who has been writing or blogging about the issue? You might also be able to find someone on your own campus. If you're writing, say, about measures that attempt to protect students from date rape on your campus, someone in the Criminal Justice department or in Student Affairs can tell you more about the issue in a few minutes than you might learn in a couple hours online.

Narrowing the Question. I've been vaguely aware of the crisis in Medicaid funding—federal health care support for the poor—but the issue really came home when officials told Dorothy Misner, a ninety-two-year-old woman in nearby Nampa, that she would have to gum her food because the state refused to pay for dentures. Probably the best way to make a larger controversy a manageable writing topic is to find a local angle. In this case, for example, the larger question—*Should the national Medicaid program do more to support the poor without health insurance?*—becomes a much narrower question: *Is the state's Medicaid program failing people like Dorothy Misner?* Whenever possible, make big issues smaller by finding some connection to the local.

That isn't always possible, however. Unless you live in Alaska, for instance, the debate over development of the Arctic National Wildlife Refuge is hard to cut as a local issue. Then it becomes important to find a narrower question, something that may not be possible until after you've done a little research. For example, the question, *Should the Arctic National Wildlife Refuge be open to oil development?* could be narrowed by asking, *Are oil company claims about the potential of recoverable oil in the refuge reasonable?*

Another way to narrow the focus of an argument is to find a useful case study, anecdote, or example that somehow typifies some aspect of the issue you want to examine. Finally, do what journalists do: Peg your essay to a recent event related to the issue you're writing about. George Will's approach to many of his op-ed essays is to use a newly released study, report, academic article, or interview with an expert as the anchor for his piece. He then takes off on his own from there. Other events might include a relevant hearing, a protest, a court decision, a crime, an accident, and so on.

Writing the Sketch

Now draft a sketch of roughly 500 to 600 words with the following elements:

- It has a tentative title.
- It makes at least one claim and offers several reasons that support the claim.
- It presents and analyzes at least one contrasting point of view.
- The sketch includes specific evidence to support (or possibly complicate) the reasons offered in support of the claim, including *at least* several of the following: an anecdote or story, a personal observation, data, an analogy, a case study, expert testimony, other relevant quotations from people involved, or a precedent.

■ STUDENT SKETCH

Inspiring young voters isn't easy. In my own classes, I almost never hear younger students talk casually about elections. On the rare occasions that I actually see a button on a backpack for one candidate or another, I'm always a little surprised. Are young voters apathetic? And if they are, what should be done about it? Those were Ben Bloom's questions, both of which arose from a fastwrite. Here is his sketch on the topic. Where should he go from here? What should he research before the next draft? What should he consider that he doesn't consider here?

How to Really Rock the Vote

Ben Bloom

1   MTV sponsors "Rock the Vote." Presidential candidates swing through college campuses wearing blue jeans and going tieless. There's even an organization called "Kid's Vote" that tries to get high school students involved in the political process. It's pretty clear that student vote matters but are these efforts paying off?

2   It doesn't seem so. On my own campus, fewer than a few hundred students vote in the annual elections for the Student Senate. I can't even get my roommate to talk about the Presidential election, much less who's running for student body president.

3   What seems typical is the following comment from a college-age columnist: "On the issue of voter apathy, I look at myself first. I'm not even registered to vote, which is as apathetic as it gets. I do, however, educate myself about presidential candidates and their proposed policies—I just never have thought my one, lonesome vote could matter. I've neglected registering because it has never seemed logical to inconvenience myself, through the registration process, only to give another drop of water to an ocean (to add one vote to millions)."

4   "Never seemed logical to inconvenience" yourself to participate in the most basic part of the democratic process? Has it gotten this bad?

5   The student journalist above was responding to a survey that came out two years ago from a group called Project Vote Smart. It found what I suspected from my own experiences: young voters are staying away from the polls.

6   According to the study, there has been a decline in the numbers of 18- to 25-year-olds voting by 13% over the last twenty-five years. Actually, I think the situation is worse than that. The main reason they cite is that young people don't think their votes make a difference.

7   What should be done about this? How can we convince young voters to believe in the power of their vote? Are organizations like "Rock the Vote" or "Project Vote Smart" going to convince students like the guy who finds voting "inconvenient" that it's worth the effort?

8   In my opinion, celebrities and rock stars won't make a difference. The key is for political candidates to find a way to talk about issues so that young voters overcome their apathy and actually *feel* something. In the sixties, it was the draft. I'm not sure what the issues with emotional impact are these days. But the people who want students to vote have got to find them.

Moving from Sketch to Draft

A sketch is often sketchy. It's generally underdeveloped, sometimes giving the writer just the barest outline of his subject. But as an early draft, a sketch can be invaluable. It might hint at what the real subject is, or what questions seem to be behind your inquiry into the subject. A sketch might suggest a focus for the next draft, or simply a better lead. Here are some tips for finding clues in your sketch about directions you might go in the next draft.

Evaluating Your Own Sketch. You've read and written about an issue you care about. Now for the really hard part: getting out of your own head and into the heads of your potential readers, who may not care as much as you do. At least not yet. Successful persuasion fundamentally depends on giving an audience the right reasons to agree with you, and these are likely both logical and emotional, involving both *logos* and *pathos,* as you learned earlier in this chapter.

Another element of argument is the way the writer comes across to readers—his or her *ethos.* What's the ethos of your sketch? How might you be perceived by a stranger reading the sketch? Is your tone appealing, or might it be slightly off-putting? Do you successfully establish your authority to speak on this issue, or do you sense that the persona you project in the sketch is unconvincing, perhaps too emotional or not appearing fair?

As we develop convictions about an issue, one of the hardest things to manage in early argument drafts is creating a persuasive persona (*ethos*). Another is finding ways to establish connections with our audience; this does not merely involve connecting writers and readers but includes creating some common ground between readers and *the topic.* There are many ways to do this, including the following:

1. Connecting your readers' prior beliefs or values with your position on the topic.

2. Establishing that readers have a *stake,* perhaps even a personal one, in how the question you've raised is answered; this may be self-interest, but it may also be emotional (remember the advertiser's strategy).

3. Highlighting the common experiences readers may have had with the topic and offering your claim as a useful way of understanding that experience.

As you look over your sketch, evaluate how well you create this common ground between your topic and your intended audience. Might you revise it by exploiting one or more of the strategies listed here?

Finally, is there enough evidence to support the reasons you've provided to support your claims? Initial drafts commonly lack enough specifics. Do you see places in the sketch that could be developed with specific information in the next draft?

Questions for Peer Review. Because the argument essay is such an audience-oriented form, these initial peer reviews of your sketch are invaluable in helping you get your bearings. Much of what you might have felt about how you managed the ethos and connections with readers can be confirmed or challenged by this first public reading. Ask your workshop group some of the following questions:

- How is the *ethos* of the sketch? Do I come across in the sketch as an advocate for my position? For example, am I *passionate, preachy, reasonable, one-sided, sympathetic, overbearing, intimate, detached, objective, subjective, uncaring, empathetic, humorous, serious, angry, mellow, contemptuous, approachable, patronizing, respectful, thoughtful, presumptuous, fair,* or *judgmental?*
- In your own words, what do you think was my central claim?
- Which reasons did you find most convincing? Which were least convincing?
- What do you think was the best evidence I offered in support of my reasons? Where exactly did you feel that you needed more evidence?
- What were the stated or unstated "warrants" or assumptions behind the claims? What do you need to assume is true to believe in their validity?

Reflecting on What You've Learned. Spend a few minutes following your peer review workshop to generate a list of everything you heard, and then begin a five-minute fastwrite that explores your reaction to these suggestions and your tentative plan for revision. In particular, what will you change? What will you add, and what will you cut in the next draft? What problems were raised that you don't yet know how to solve? What problems *weren't* raised that you expected might be? Do you still need to worry about them? End your fastwrite by writing about what you understand now about your topic, and your initial beliefs about it, that you didn't fully understand when you began writing about it.

Research and Other Strategies: Gathering More Information

Here's a mortifying thought: You've completely changed your mind about what you think about your topic and what you want to say in your argument. That's unsettling, but it's also a sign that you're willing to allow things to get a bit messy before they get sorted out. This is good because it's much more likely to result in an essay that gets at the truth of what you feel than if you doggedly stick to a particular point of view, come what may. If you *have* changed your mind, you have a lot of collecting to do. Return to the Web sites of current publications and search for information that might be relevant to your emerging idea.

Another research strategy can be helpful whether you change your mind or not: the interview. People who are somehow involved in your topic are among the best sources of new information and lively material. An interview can provide ideas about what else you should read or who else you might talk to, and it can be a source of quotations, anecdotes, and even case studies that will make the next draft of your argument essay much more interesting. After all, what makes an issue matter is how it affects people. Have you sufficiently dramatized those effects?

When appropriate, you can also add images to dramatize your claims or your evidence. They're easier than ever to find on nearly any subject using on-line services like Google Image Search. But they must be relevant. Figure 7.8, for example, is an ad by the National Eating Disorders Association that focuses on the relationship between our genetic disposition to be a certain body size.

Figure 7.8   Sometimes your research for a public argument will include visual sources. This poster for National Eating Disorders Awareness Week reads, "Be comfortable in your genes. Your genes play a role in determining your body size and shape. So be kind to your body. Stop trying to turn it into something it's not. Wear jeans that fit the REAL you."
Source: http://www.gurze.com/productdetails.cfm?PC=1588 National Eating Disorders Association, http://www.nationaleatingdisorders.org/index.php

Imagine if the image was dropped into an argument essay—or a PowerPoint presentation—that argued for the strong influence of an "obesity gene."

For more information on face-to-face interviewing, see Chapter 4, "Writing a Profile." The Internet can also be a source for interview material. Look for e-mail links to the authors of useful documents you find on the Web and write to them with a few questions. Interest groups, newsgroups, or electronic mailing lists on the Web can also provide the voices and perspectives of people with something to say on your topic. Remember to ask permission to quote them if you decide to use something in your draft. For leads on finding Web discussion groups on your topic, visit the following sites:

- **Google Groups,** http://groups.google.com, allows you to search for online discussion groups on virtually any topic.
- **Yahoo Groups** offers a similar service, allowing you to search for groups by keyword. Find it at http://groups.yahoo.com.
- **Catalist,** the official catalog of electronic mailing lists, http://www.lsoft. com/lists/listref.html, has a database of about 15,000 discussion groups.

One of the most useful things you can do to prepare for the draft is to spend forty-five minutes at the campus library searching for new information on your topic. Consider expanding your search from current newspapers and periodicals to books or government publications. In addition, you can refer to almanacs such as *Infoplease* (http://www.infoplease.com) and the *CIA World Factbook* (http://www.odci.gov/cia/publications/factbook/) as well as statistical information available from sources such as the U.S. Census Bureau's *American Fact Finder* (http://factfinder.census.gov/home/saff/main.html?_lang=en), which is a wonderful resource that draws on the agency's massive database of information on U.S. trends.

Composing the Draft

As always, it's best to work from abundance rather than scarcity. If you don't have enough evidence to support your argument, find more. But if you're feeling reasonably well prepared to develop your argument essay from a sketch (or proposal) to a longer draft, then begin by crafting a strong lead. There are so many ways to begin an essay like this one; which is best? As always, think of a beginning that might not only interest your readers in your topic but also hints at or states your purpose in writing about it. Through tone, your beginning also establishes your relationship with your readers. Here's instructor Andrew Merton's lead in "The Guys Are Dumbing Down," a piece that argues that students' baseball caps in class indicate something other than studiousness.

Here is the big social note from the campus of the University of New Hampshire, where I teach: Dumbing down is in. For guys.

Merton's tone is a strong element of this lead. He begins casually—"Here is the big social note..."—suggesting some friendly, almost chatty relationship with his readers. This lead also does what many argument essay beginnings do: It states the writer's main claim. You may assume it is always required to state your thesis in your introduction, but this isn't true at all. Some argument essays, especially op-ed pieces, have a delayed thesis, in which the writer works methodically toward his or her point. Which approach should you use in your draft? In part, that depends on your method of development.

Methods of Development. What are some of the ways you might organize the next draft?

Narrative. Telling a story is an underrated way of developing an argument. Can you imagine a way to turn your topic into an extended story, perhaps by focusing on the experience of a particular person or group of people, in a particular place, at a particular time? Somehow the story must be logically linked to your claim; obviously, just any old story won't do.

There are other ways to use narrative, too. Anecdotes, or brief stories used to illustrate an idea or a problem, are frequently used in argument essays. One effective way to begin your essay might be to tell a story that highlights the problem you're writing about or the question you're posing.

Question to Answer. Almost all writing is an attempt to answer a question. In the personal essay and other open forms of inquiry, the writer may never arrive at a definite answer, but an argument essay usually offers an answer. An obvious method of development, therefore, is to begin your essay by raising the question and end it by offering your answer.

Are there several key questions around which you might organize your draft, leading to your central claim at the end?

Problem to Solution. This is a variation on the question-to-answer structure. But it might be a particularly useful organization strategy if you're writing about a topic readers may know very little about. In that case, you might need to spend as much time establishing what exactly the problem is—explaining what makes it a problem and why the reader should care about it—as you do offering your particular solution.

Effect to Cause or Cause to Effect. At the heart of some arguments is the *relationship* between two things, and often what is at issue is pinpointing the real causes for certain undesirable effects. Once these causes are identified, then the best solutions can be offered. Sadly, we know the effects of terrorism, but what are its causes? If you argue, as some do, that Islamic radicalism arose in response to U.S. policies toward Israel and the Palestinians, then the solution offered might be a shift in foreign policy. The international debate over global warming, for some participants, is really an argument about causes and effects. If you don't believe, for example, that U.S. contributions to atmospheric carbon dioxide in the next ten years will match contributions from the developing world, then the U.S. refusal to sign the Kyoto treaty—one proposed solution—may not matter that much. Some arguments like these can be organized simply around an examination of causes and effects.

Combining Approaches. As you think about how you might organize your first draft, you don't necessarily have to choose between narrative, problem-to-solution, or cause-to-effect structures. In fact, most often they work well together.

Using Evidence. All writing relies on evidence, usually some specific information in relationships with general ideas (see the "Inquiring into the Details: What Evidence Can Do" box). Evidence in an argumentative essay often has a *particular* relationship to ideas; most often it is offered to support ideas the writer wants the reader to believe. What *kind* of evidence to include is a rhetorical question. To whom are you writing, and what kind of evidence will they be more likely to believe? Generally speaking, the narrower and more specialized the audience, the more particular they will be about the types of evidence they'll find convincing.

For example, as you write more academic papers in your chosen major, the types of evidence that will help you make a persuasive argument will be more and more prescribed by the field. In the natural sciences, the results of quantitative studies count more than case studies; in the humanities, primary texts count more than secondary ones. The important thing for this argument essay, which you're writing for a more general audience, is that you attempt to *vary* your evidence. Rather than relying exclusively on anecdotes, include some quotes from an expert as well.

INQUIRING INTO THE DETAILS

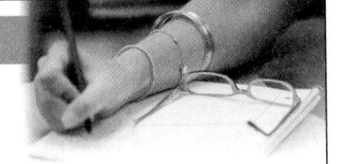

What Evidence Can Do

Usually we think of using evidence only to support an idea or claim we're making. But evidence can be used in other ways, too. For example, it can do the following:

- *support* an idea, observation, or assertion
- *refute* or challenge a claim with which you disagree
- *show* that a seemingly simple assertion, problem, or idea is really more complex
- *complicate* or even contradict an earlier point you've made
- *contrast* two or more ways of seeing the same thing
- *test* an idea, hypothesis, or theory

Workshopping the Draft

If your draft is subject to peer review, see Chapter 10 for details on how to organize workshop groups and decide on how your group can help you. The following
journal activities and questions should help you make the most of your opportunity to get peer feedback on your work in progress.

Reflecting on the Draft. After you've finished the draft, prepare for peer review
by making a journal entry that explores your experience writing the essay.

- What proved hardest?
- What most surprised you about the process?
- What did you find particularly gratifying? What was especially frustrating?
- How did your process for writing this type of essay differ from writing the
  personal essay or some other form?
- If you were going to start all over again, what would you do differently?

Discuss the insights that might have emerged from this open-ended writing
in class or in your workshop group. After your draft has been discussed, make
some notes in your journal in response to the following questions:

- What most surprised you about your group's response to your essay?
- What did you hear that most made you want to write again?
- What specifically do you think you need to do in the next draft?

Questions for Readers. Here are some questions that might prompt members of
your workshop group to offer helpful advice on your argument draft.

1. What was the most interesting part of the draft? What was the least
   interesting?
2. What did you believe about my topic before you read the draft? What did
   you believe after you read it?
3. What reason most strongly supported my main point? What reason
   seemed the weakest?
4. What was the most convincing evidence I offered? What was the least
   convincing?

Revising the Draft

Revision is a continual process—not a last step. You've been revising—literally
"re-seeing" your subject—from the first messy fastwriting in your journal. But
the things that get your attention during revision vary depending on where you
are in the writing process. You've generated material, chosen a topic, done some
research, and written both a sketch and draft. Most students think that the only
thing left to do is "fix things." Check for misspellings. Correct an awkward

WRITING IN THE DISCIPLINES

Argument in Academic Disciplines

Arguing is the main way that academic communities make knowledge. While the process for developing and making an argument can be applied in any discipline, the types of evidence and the forms of arguments can vary widely from one discipline to another. Knowing what kind of knowledge is valued in a particular discipline can help you to shape effective academic arguments as you move from subject to subject throughout your college career.

Discipline	Common Types of Argument	Valued Evidence
humanities	interpretive essays textual analyses reviews formal arguments	textual details personal observations and experience historical background personal insights biographical evidence about authors and creators ethnographic (small-scale) studies
social sciences	causal analyses historical trends projections about effects of policies	demographics and statistics research data large-scale studies interviews
natural sciences	lab reports experimental studies	experimental data quantitative data visual information
applied sciences	feasibility reports recommendations and proposals	quantitative data research data field research findings firsthand observations
business	proposals	case studies survey data

sentence or two. Come up with a better title. This is editing, not revision, and while editing is important, to focus solely on smaller "fixes" after writing a first draft squanders an opportunity to really *learn* from what the draft is telling you, or perhaps not quite telling you.

GUIDE TO REVISION STRATEGIES

Problems in the Draft (Chapter 9)	Page Number
Unclear purpose ■ Not sure what the paper is about?	327
Unclear thesis, theme, or main idea ■ Not sure what you're trying to say?	333
Lack of information or development ■ Need more convincing evidence? Need to check for logical fallacies?	340
Disorganized ■ Doesn't move logically or smoothly from paragraph to paragraph?	344
Unclear or awkward at the level of sentences and paragraphs ■ Seems choppy or hard to follow at the level of sentences or paragraphs?	353

Chapter 9 can help guide these discoveries. The questions you can ask about a draft fall into five categories: purpose, idea, information, development, and editing. Use the Guide to Revision Strategies chart above to find the revision strategies in Chapter 9 that might help you re-see what you've written so far.

Draft argument essays have some typical problems at this stage in the process. Do any of these apply to yours?

- Is your central claim or thesis stated clearly?

- Do you employ any logical fallacies? See "Inquiring into the Details: Common Logical Fallacies."

- Do you have sufficient evidence or information to make your assertions convincing? Do you need to gather more facts?

- Have you considered any counterarguments in your essay? This is especially important if you think the audience for your essay might not be inclined to initially agree with your position.

- Have you clearly established what stake your readers have in the issue you're writing about?

- Does the draft use *pathos, logos*, and *ethos* effectively? (See Figure 7.1.)

Polishing the Draft

After you've dealt with the big issues in your draft—is it sufficiently focused, does it answer the *So what?* question, is it well organized, and so on—you must deal with the smaller problems. You've carved the stone into an appealing figure, but now you need to polish it. Are your paragraphs coherent? How do you manage transitions? Are your sentences fluent and concise? Are there any errors in spelling or syntax? Part 5 of Chapter 9 can help you focus on these issues.

Before you finish your draft, work through the following checklist:

- ✓ Every paragraph is about one thing.
- ✓ The transitions between paragraphs aren't abrupt.
- ✓ The length of sentences varies in each paragraph.
- ✓ Each sentence is concise. There are no unnecessary words or phrases.
- ✓ You've checked grammar, particularly verb agreement, run-on sentences, unclear pronouns, and misused words (*there/their, where/were*, and so on). (See the handbook at the back of the book for help with these grammar issues.)
- ✓ You've run your spellchecker and proofed your paper for misspelled words.

■ STUDENT ESSAY

Many Americans are fond of talking about our country's native people in the past tense. We admire the tribal cultures as they existed a century or two ago, and borrow freely from them, engaging in "vision quests" and drumming circles. We feel the tug of nostalgia for these lost tribes, and yes, guilt for the sad history of relations between the mostly white immigrants who dispossessed the tribes and the Indian people who were confined to reservations. It's convenient to assume that the problems were in the past because contemporary Native Americans are largely invisible to us—except if you happen to drive through a reservation as Kelly Sundberg would on her way to visit friends at a nearby university.

Confronting Native Americans in the present tense forced Kelly to examine her own prejudices, and in the essay that follows she argues that the route to understanding begins at school.

I Am Not a Savage
Kelly Sundberg

1   Salmon, Idaho, is named after the river that runs through it, a river that is filled with turbulent whitewater punctuated by deep and calm pools and shallow riffles. In the spring, I have looked into these riffles and seen waves of silver and red moving gently just underneath the surface of the water.

2   We call them "reds"—spawning salmon. Nowadays, they are diminished in numbers, but at one time the river was full of them, and full of abundance as well for the

Lemhi Indians who once lived on the banks. For the Lemhi, the salmon was not solely for sustenance, but also an integral part of their culture and spirituality.

Today there are few "reds" and almost no Lemhi left in the valley.   3

The initial influx of Mormon settlers followed by migrations of Californians and   4
Midwesterners forced Native Americans out of the valley. Still, upon entering the Salmon city limits from Highway 28, a large sign proclaims, "Welcome to Salmon, Idaho. Birthplace of Sacagawea!" In a time when anything related to Lewis and Clark means profit, the city of Salmon, my hometown, has now chosen to capitalize on this marketable heritage, even though they once ignored it or treated it derisively.

My high school mascot is the "Salmon Savage." The marquee in front of the school has   5
a picture with an Indian warrior on it, and when the football team scores a touchdown a white girl wearing war paint and a "made in China" headdress will ride a horse around the track in celebration.

I never questioned the integrity or intent of these symbols until I was a sophomore at   6
the school. For Civil Rights Day, the school invited Rosa Abrahamson, a Lemhi Indian, to speak to the students. She cried as she spoke about the injustice of the name "savage." "My people are not savages," she said. "We are peaceful and do not take pride in that name." When she finished speaking the applause was polite but subdued.

The next speaker was a rancher named Bud, who lit into a tirade about the govern-   7
ment subsidizing "lazy Indians." As he finished with fists raised into the air, he was greeted by a standing ovation. For the first time in my life, I felt ashamed to be a part of the community.

It wasn't that those of us in the gym had consciously made the decision to be racist. It   8
was simply ignorance. Despite the history of the Lemhi in the valley, our ideas of their cul-ture are shaped from drives through the reservation on the way to campus visits at the University of Idaho. Our perceptions were safely gleaned from inside of an automobile and never involved real interaction with Native Americans.

Once, when asked to write our opinions about reservations in a U.S. government class,   9
I wrote that I thought the government was making it "too easy on the Native Americans and they had become apathetic and unmotivated because of subsidies."

I got a better glimpse at my Lemhi neighbors recently reading Sherman Alexie's   10
novel *The Lone Ranger and Tonto Fistfight in Heaven*. Alexie, a member of the Spokane/ Coeur d'Alene tribes, conveys the opposition between contemporary and traditional Native American culture. His characters are torn and struggle to reconcile the two: "At the halfway point of any drunken night, there is a moment when an Indian realizes he cannot turn back toward tradition and that he has no map to guide him toward the future."

My own community struggles to reconcile two conflicting ideas as well—we embrace   11
the symbols of savagery to inspire the football team, yet in order to make a profit we proudly claim Sacagawea as one of our own. Still, when the Lemhi wanted to build a school near Sacagawea's birthplace, the county refused to sell them the land, claiming it would become a "mini-reservation."

(continued)

(continued)

12   Ironically, Salmon shares more than it cares to admit with its neighbors on the reservation. Poverty, alcoholism, and depression are a way of life for many Salmon residents. Yet the perception in the community is that an alcoholic white man is somehow superior to a "drunk Indian."

13   In Salmon, all students are required to take an Idaho history class, yet this class makes almost no mention of Native American history in the valley. None of the readings in Advanced Placement English classes are by Native American authors, and government classes don't address Native American issues at all.

14   Is it any wonder that racism persists?

15   The local school system needs to lead. English teachers should require readings by authors like Alexie, they should provide field trips to local and national archeological sites, and they should bring in Native American interpreters to speak about local history. By letting go of negative and outdated ideas, the city of Salmon and the Lemhi can take the first step toward healing.

Evaluating the Essay

Discuss or write about your response to Kelly Sundberg's essay using some or all of the following questions:

1. What is the thesis of the essay? Where in the piece is it most clearly stated?

2. Refer to the box that lists ten common logical fallacies and reread Sundberg's essay. Do you suspect there are any logical fallacies in "I Am Not a Savage"?

3. Consider the *ethos* of this essay. How does the writer come across? Is her persona effective?

4. What do you think is the most effective paragraph in the essay? Why? What is the least effective?

USING WHAT YOU HAVE LEARNED

You've read published op-ed essays and a student draft. You've also worked on your own argument essay, a genre that may be new to you. Take a moment to consider how you might use what you've learned.

1. Reflect on how your thinking about argument and argumentative writing may have changed because of the reading and writing in this chapter by finishing the following sentence in your journal at least four times: Before I began this chapter I thought _____, but now I think _____.

2. The personal essay (discussed in Chapter 3) and the argument essay might seem at first to be fundamentally different kinds of writing. Do you see any connections between the two genres now?

3. Examine the letters to the editor or the editorials in your local newspaper. How do you read these pages differently after studying and writing an argument? Clip a letter or editorial that might best demonstrate what you've learned.

Writing an ethnographic essay will test your research skills by bringing them out of academia and into the field. That might be to a park where skateboarders gather, a hall where World War II veterans meet, a mall where fifteen-year-olds congregate, or the fields where migrant workers toil.

WRITING AN ETHNOGRAPHIC ESSAY

WRITING ABOUT CULTURE

My daughter hates spiders. In fact, she's so repulsed by spiders she refuses to utter the word, calling them "s-words" whenever she spots one of the bugs. In sadistic moments, I want to explain to her that there are invisible webs everywhere and that we walk into them all the time. In fact, we may spin a few threads ourselves occasionally. Like the spiders in our basement, subcultures abound right under our very noses. We just have to learn to see the webs they weave.

The "web of culture" is a good metaphor because, like spider webs, the many cultures and subcultures we encounter in our everyday lives are often difficult to detect. These webs are also something in which we are all enmeshed, whether we know it or not. To some extent they limit our movements, shape our beliefs, and determine our traditions.

Ethnography is a method of inquiry into culture that exposes the web in which members of a group are enmeshed, much the way the morning dew exposes the intricacies of a spider web in your backyard. In this chapter, you'll practice this approach to research and learn some ways that you can apply ethnographic techniques to all kinds of research projects. The real value of trying ethnography isn't that you'll be writing lots of ethnographies in other classes—you probably won't. Instead, writing an ethnographic essay will test your research skills by bringing them out of academia and into the field. That might be to the park where skateboarders gather, a hall where World War II veterans meet, a mall where fifteen-year-olds congregate, or

> ### What You'll Learn in This Chapter
> - How to sharpen your observation skills.
> - The many ways that culture disciplines our behavior.
> - Techniques for field research.
> - Awareness of more subjective methods of research.

the fields where migrant workers toil. You might even wander online, where electronic subcultures abound. You'll learn to be a more careful observer. And ethnography will also raise interesting questions about whether all research can be objective.

> Ethnography is a method of inquiry into culture that exposes the web in which members of a group are enmeshed.

MOTIVES FOR WRITING ETHNOGRAPHY

Ethnography may be new to you, but you've almost certainly enjoyed its nonacademic versions. Magazine articles on other cultures in *National Geographic* and *Discover* have some elements of ethnography, and arguably so do some of the reality TV shows. These popular versions of ethnography invite readers and viewers to briefly enter unfamiliar worlds and learn a little about other people's ways of seeing and knowing. Essentially, the goal of such articles and programs is to show how things work in particular social contexts—a Los Angeles police department, a poor village in South Africa, or the neighborhood bowling alley. While the study of a culture can take the researcher overseas, it can just as easily take him or her down the street or across town.

Why might fieldwork like this make sense? If the inquiry questions that interest you involve how certain people behave in social settings, then you can learn more by actually *watching* them operate in their own worlds. Sure, you can read published accounts, relying on the observations of others. And you should. But actually observing for yourself how labor and delivery nurses on the night shift interact with patients at your local hospital is a much richer source of data. Seeing for yourself is almost always better.

Of course, the world is not a laboratory. You can't control the many variables that influence what people say and what they do. But that's the point. From the outset, ethnography concedes that social communities are complicated. Fieldwork will never be able to completely untangle them. But it can unknot a few strands. Ethnographers try to do this while acknowledging their own bias. Like much "qualitative" research, ethnography is subjective, but in many ways this adds to the richness of the results. We get a truer look at the chemistry between the observer and the observed, something that is always present in research with human subjects but frequently hidden behind the veil of "objectivity."

ETHNOGRAPHY AND ACADEMIC WRITING

Interest in academic ethnography has boomed in recent years, something you'll probably discover if you take an anthropology course. But you may also encounter ethnographic ways of seeing—or interest in the ways social groups behave and believe—in sociology, English, and even the visual arts, where something called "visual ethnography" might be practiced in formal or informal ways. Some researchers are using both film and still photography to capture a subculture in action, something you might consider as you work on your own ethnographic project.

But even if you never are asked to write a formal ethnography for a college class, the skills and habits of mind you practice while writing one here will help you in several ways. Writing ethnographically requires that you expand your repertoire of research to include interview and fieldwork, two methods of collecting that can help you with all kinds of research projects. In addition, the ethnographic essay is closely related to the case study, a method of research frequently used in the social sciences and especially in business. Finally, the project you're about to tackle calls on something you've practiced already—the willingness to suspend judgment while you collect information and then interpret the possible significance of what you've found. Once again, you enact the dialectical thinking that's been a part of every inquiry project in *The Curious Writer:* your observations of and your ideas about something, your record of what happened, and your sense of what *happens.*

FEATURES OF THE FORM

Like other inquiry projects in this book, ethnography is a form with many variations. However, most ethnographic essays share some features:

- *They focus on groups of people who identify themselves as group members.* We all belong to subcultures that we don't recognize we belong to—or perhaps refuse to acknowledge. But ethnography tends to focus on people who, at least when pressed, freely identify with a specific group.

- *Ethnography depends on close observation over time.* More than in other forms of inquiry, ethnographers must spend time in the field simply watching and taking notes. Particularly if you're an outsider to the culture you're studying, you can't possibly discover its artifacts, rituals, and insider language unless you hang out long enough with group members.

- *The bulk of the research takes place in the natural settings where group members gather.* You want to research interstate truck drivers? Go to a truck stop on I-84. You're interested in the culture of college women's basketball? Go to the locker room and spend time at practice. The goal of ethnography is to observe a culture as it behaves normally in typical situations. The hard part, sometimes, is inserting yourself into these situations without disrupting the way things usually are, which is another reason why spending enough time in the field is important; it helps your study subjects get used to you.

- *Ethnography looks closely at the few to get hints about the many.* By carefully describing a very small subset of the larger group—a group of five teenage skateboarders, or one women's basketball team—they hope to be able to infer something about the big picture.

> More than in other forms of inquiry, ethnographers must spend time in the field simply watching and taking notes.

- *Ethnography is often openly subjective.* Since the writer/researcher is the instrument for collecting data as well as interpreting its significance, the subjectivity of the method is inescapable. Consequently, ethnographers frequently have a strong presence in their studies, acknowledging their particular angles of vision. But the aim of the ethnographer, ultimately, is to overcome the potential screen of subjectivity and *see the world the way their study subjects see it.*

READINGS

■ ETHNOGRAPHIC ESSAY 1

Identity, as any fifteen-year-old knows, is a transaction. You give a little and you get a little from the social groups you like, and you don't do business with those you don't, except maybe to make sure you don't look or act like "one of them." This is not, however, free enterprise. Certain identities carry more social power. In my high school, those were not just the varsity football and basketball players but the well-to-do kids whose homes had huge "rec rooms" in the basement where they held parties for a select few.

You don't have a choice, however, about belonging to some groups. For example, you may be African American, Latina, or Native American. Perhaps you are disabled. While there's more tolerance of difference these days, Judith Ortiz Cofer observes in "The Myth of the Latin Woman" that it is nearly impossible, as someone who is different, to escape the assumptions others have about who you are. Sometimes these perceptions have serious consequences—you aren't hired or you can't rent the house. What can you do about this? Understandably, you might get angry. In her essay, Cofer suggests another response: Sometimes it is "custom,…not chromosomes," that helps explain difference. Cofer's essay, like the others in this chapter, is not a formal ethnography, but it is a great introduction to ethnography as a form of inquiry. "The Myth of the Latin Woman" helps us to see how the people we observe look back at us. Since we are visitors in their world, doing ethnography means working hard to understand that world in *their* terms, not ours.

The Myth of the Latin Woman: I Just Met a Girl Named Maria

Judith Ortiz Cofer

1   On a bus trip to London from Oxford University where I was earning some graduate credits one summer, a young man, obviously fresh from a pub, spotted me and as if struck by inspiration went down on his knees in the aisle. With both hands over his heart he broke into an Irish tenor's rendition of "Maria" from *West Side Story*. My politely amused fellow passengers gave his lovely voice the round of gentle applause it deserved. Though I was not quite as amused, I managed my version of an English smile: no show of teeth, no extreme contortions of the facial muscles—I was at this time of my life practicing reserve and cool. Oh, that British control, how I coveted it. But María had followed me to London, reminding me of a prime fact of my life: you can leave the Island, master the English language, and travel as far as you can, but if you are a Latina, especially one like me who so obviously belongs to Rita Moreno's gene pool, the Island travels with you.

2   This is sometimes a very good thing—it may win you that extra minute of someone's attention. But with some people, the same things can make *you* an island—not so much a tropical paradise as an Alcatraz, a place nobody wants to visit. As a Puerto Rican girl growing up in the United States and wanting like most children to "belong," I resented the stereotype that my Hispanic appearance called forth from many people I met.

3   Our family lived in a large urban center in New Jersey during the sixties, where life was designed as a microcosm of my parents' casas on the island. We spoke in Spanish, we ate Puerto Rican food bought at the bodega, and we practiced strict Catholicism complete with Saturday confession and Sunday mass at a church where our parents were accommodated into a one-hour Spanish mass slot, performed by a Chinese priest trained as a missionary for Latin America.

4   As a girl I was kept under strict surveillance, since virtue and modesty were, by cultural equation, the same as family honor. As a teenager I was instructed on how to behave as a proper señorita. But it was a conflicting message girls got, since the Puerto Rican mothers also encouraged their daughters to look and act like women and to dress in clothes our Anglo friends and their mothers found too "mature" for our age. It was, and is, cultural, yet I often felt humiliated when I appeared at an American friend's party wearing a dress more suitable to a semiformal than to a

playroom birthday celebration. At Puerto Rican festivities, neither the music nor the colors we wore could be too loud. I still experience a vague sense of letdown when I'm invited to a "party" and it turns out to be a marathon conversation in hushed tones rather than a fiesta with salsa, laughter, and dancing—the kind of celebration I remember from my childhood.

I remember Career Day in our high school, when teachers told us to come dressed as if for a job interview. It quickly became obvious that to the barrio girls, "dressing up" sometimes meant wearing ornate jewelry and clothing that would be more appropriate (by mainstream standards) for the company Christmas party than as daily office attire. That morning I had agonized in front of my closet, trying to figure out what a "career girl" would wear because, essentially, except for Marlo Thomas on TV, I had no models on which to base my decision. I knew how to dress for school: at the Catholic school I attended we all wore uniforms; I knew how to dress for Sunday mass, and I knew what dresses to wear for parties at my relatives' homes. Though I do not recall the precise details of my Career Day outfit, it must have been a composite of the above choices. But I remember a comment my friend (an Italian-American) made in later years that coalesced my impressions of that day. She said that at the business school she was attending the Puerto Rican girls always stood out for wearing "everything at once." She meant, of course, too much jewelry, too many accessories. On that day at school, we were simply made the negative models by the nuns who were themselves not credible fashion experts to any of us. But it was painfully obvious to me that to the others, in their tailored skirts and silk blouses, we must have seemed "hopeless" and "vulgar." Though I now know that most adolescents feel out of step much of the time, I also know that for the Puerto Rican girls of my generation that sense was intensified. The way our teachers and classmates looked at us that day in school was just a taste of the culture clash that awaited us in the real world, where prospective employers and men on the street would often misinterpret our tight skirts and jingling bracelets as a come-on.

Mixed cultural signals have perpetuated certain stereotypes—for example, that of the Hispanic woman as the "Hot Tamale" or sexual firebrand. It is a one-dimensional view that the media have found easy to promote. In their special vocabulary, advertisers have designated "sizzling" and "smoldering" as the adjectives of choice for describing not only the foods but also the women of Latin America. From conversations in my house I recall hearing about the harassment that Puerto Rican women endured in factories where the "boss men" talked to them as if sexual innuendo was all they understood and, worse, often gave them the choice of submitting to advances or being fired.

It is custom, however, not chromosomes, that leads us to choose scarlet over pale pink. As young girls, we were influenced in our decisions about clothes and colors by the women—older sisters and mothers who had grown up on a tropical island where the natural environment was a riot of primary colors, where showing your skin was one way to keep cool as well as to look sexy. Most important of all, on the island,

(continued)

(continued)

women perhaps felt freer to dress and move more provocatively, since, in most cases, they were protected by the traditions, mores, and laws of a Spanish/Catholic system of morality and machismo whose main rule was: *You may look at my sister, but if you touch her I will kill you.* The extended family and church structure could provide a young woman with a circle of safety in her small pueblo on the island; if a man "wronged" a girl, everyone would close in to save her family honor.

8   This is what I have gleaned from my discussions as an adult with older Puerto Rican women. They have told me about dressing in their best party clothes on Saturday nights and going to the town's plaza to promenade with their girlfriends in front of the boys they liked. The males were thus given an opportunity to admire the women and to express their admiration in the form of *piropos:* erotically charged street poems they composed on the spot. I have been subjected to a few piropos while visiting the Island, and they can be outrageous, although custom dictates that they must never cross into obscenity. This ritual, as I understand it, also entails a show of studied indifference on the woman's part; if she is "decent," she must not acknowledge the man's impassioned words. So I do understand how things can be lost in translation. When a Puerto Rican girl dressed in her idea of what is attractive meets a man from the mainstream culture who has been trained to react to certain types of clothing as a sexual signal, a clash is likely to take place. The line I first heard based on this aspect of the myth happened when the boy who took me to my first formal dance leaned over to plant a sloppy overeager kiss painfully on my mouth, and when I didn't respond with sufficient passion said in a resentful tone: "I thought you Latin girls were supposed to mature early"—my first instance of being thought of as a fruit or vegetable—I was supposed to *ripen,* not just grow into womanhood like other girls.

9   It is surprising to some of my professional friends that some people, including those who should know better, still put others "in their place." Though rarer, these incidents are still commonplace in my life. It happened to me most recently during a stay at a very classy metropolitan hotel favored by young professional couples for their weddings. Late one evening after the theater, as I walked toward my room with my new colleague (a woman with whom I was coordinating an arts program), a middle-aged man in a tuxedo, a young girl in satin and lace on his arm, stepped directly into our path. With his champagne glass extended toward me, he exclaimed, "Evita!"

10   Our way blocked, my companion and I listened as the man half-recited, half-bellowed "Don't Cry for Me, Argentina." When he finished, the young girl said: "How about a round of applause for my daddy?" We complied, hoping this would bring the silly spectacle to a close. I was becoming aware that our little group was attracting the attention of the other guests. "Daddy" must have perceived this too, and he once more barred the way as we tried to walk past him. He began to shout-sing a ditty to the tune of "La Bamba"—except the lyrics were about a girl named María whose exploits all rhymed with her name and gonorrhea. The girl kept saying "Oh, Daddy" and looking at me with pleading eyes. She wanted me to laugh along with the others.

My companion and I stood silently waiting for the man to end his offensive song. When he finished, I looked not at him but at his daughter. I advised her calmly never to ask her father what he had done in the army. Then I walked between them and to my room. My friend complimented me on my cool handling of the situation. I confessed to her that I really had wanted to push the jerk into the swimming pool. I knew that this same man—probably a corporate executive, well educated, even worldly by most standards—would not have been likely to regale a white woman with a dirty song in public. He would perhaps have checked his impulse by assuming that she could be somebody's wife or mother, or at least *somebody* who might take offense. But to him, I was just an Evita or a María: merely a character in his cartoon-populated universe.

Because of my education and my proficiency with the English language, I have   11
acquired many mechanisms for dealing with the anger I experience. This was not true for my parents, nor is it true for the many Latin women working at menial jobs who must put up with stereotypes about our ethnic group such as: "They make good domestics." This is another facet of the myth of the Latin woman in the United States. Its origin is simple to deduce. Work as domestics, waitressing, and factory jobs are all that's available to women with little English and few skills. The myth of the Hispanic menial has been sustained by the same media phenomenon that made "Mammy" from *Gone with the Wind* America's idea of the black woman for generations; María, the housemaid or counter girl, is now indelibly etched into the national psyche. The big and the little screens have presented us with the picture of the funny Hispanic maid, mispronouncing words and cooking up a spicy storm in a shiny California kitchen.

This media-engendered image of the Latina in the United States has been docu-   12
mented by feminist Hispanic scholars, who claim that such portrayals are partially responsible for the denial of opportunities for upward mobility among Latinas in the professions. I have a Chicana friend working on a Ph.D. in philosophy at a major university. She says her doctor still shakes his head in puzzled amazement at all the "big words" she uses. Since I do not wear my diplomas around my neck for all to see, I too have on occasion been sent to that "kitchen," where some think I obviously belong.

One such incident that has stayed with me, though I recognize it as a minor of-   13
fense, happened on the day of my first public poetry reading. It took place in Miami in a boat-restaurant where we were having lunch before the event. I was nervous and excited as I walked in with my notebook in my hand. An older woman motioned me to her table. Thinking (foolish me) that she wanted me to autograph a copy of my brand new slender volume of verse, I went over. She ordered a cup of coffee from me, assuming that I was the waitress. Easy enough to mistake my poems for menus, I suppose. I know that it wasn't an intentional act of cruelty, yet of all the good things that happened that day, I remember that scene most clearly, because it reminded me of what I had to overcome before anyone would take me seriously. In retrospect I understand that my anger gave my reading fire, that I have almost always taken

(continued)

(continued)

doubts in my abilities as a challenge—and that the result is, most times, a feeling of satisfaction at having won a convert when I see the cold, appraising eyes warm to my words, the body language change, the smile that indicates that I have opened some avenue for communication. That day I read to that woman and her lowered eyes told me that she was embarrassed at her little faux pas, and when I willed her to look up at me, it was my victory, and she graciously allowed me to punish her with my full attention. We shook hands at the end of the reading, and I never saw her again. She has probably forgotten the whole thing but maybe not.

14   Yet I am one of the lucky ones. My parents made it possible for me to acquire a stronger footing in the mainstream culture by giving me the chance at an education. And books and art have saved me from the harsher forms of ethnic and racial prejudice that many of my Hispanic *compañeras* have had to endure. I travel a lot around the United States, reading from my books of poetry and my novel, and the reception I most often receive is one of positive interest by people who want to know more about my culture. There are, however, thousands of Latinas without the privilege of an education or the entrée into society that I have. For them life is a struggle against the misconceptions perpetuated by the myth of the Latina as whore, domestic or criminal. We cannot change this by legislating the way people look at us. The transformation, as I see it, has to occur at a much more individual level. My personal goal in my public life is to try to replace the old pervasive stereotypes and myths about Latinas with a much more interesting set of realities. Every time I give a reading, I hope the stories I tell, the dreams and fears I examine in my work, can achieve some universal truth which will get my audience past the particulars of my skin color, my accent, or my clothes.

15   I once wrote a poem in which I called us Latinas "God's brown daughters." This poem is really a prayer of sorts, offered upward, but also, through the human-to-human channel of art, outward. It is a prayer for communication, and for respect. In it, Latin women pray "in Spanish to an Anglo God / with a Jewish heritage," and they are "fervently hoping / that if not omnipotent, / at least He be bilingual."

Inquiring into the Essay

Explore, explain, and evaluate Cofer's "The Myth of the Latin Woman."

1. Being different and being born different are two quite different things. But different from what? Who gets to decide what is "normal" or "conventional"? And is there anything we can do about it? Fastwrite about these questions for four minutes without stopping.

2. Imagine that Cofer's essay is "data" for an ethnographic project on Latina culture, specifically first-generation Puerto Rican girls who attend an urban high school. In your own words, summarize what this "subject" (Cofer) contributes to your effort to understand those girls' world.

3. One thing that makes this essay interesting to read is Cofer's reliance on anecdote, and especially scenes, as a way of making her argument. This essay both shows and tells. Choose one of these moments (e.g., the London bus trip, high school Career Day, the hotel encounter, the poetry reading) and explain why you found it particularly persuasive.

4. Reflect on this problem: Ethnography doesn't pretend to be "objective." The writer/observer is intimately involved in collecting and interpreting the data. And yet, like all "qualitative" research, ethnographers hope to produce accurate insights. How can the ethnographer attempt to minimize bias?

ETHNOGRAPHIC ESSAY 2

In a multicultural nation like the United States, ethnic differences are among the most obvious webs in which we are enmeshed. I grew up in an Italian American family, and as a boy that meant that meals were social events and the quantity of food consumed was a measure of gratitude to the cook. Still, I was two generations away from the Italian immigrants in my family, and these rituals were fairly self-conscious expressions of my heritage. Most of the time, I didn't really feel that Italian.

Many among us, however, are recent immigrants, and ethnic ties bind these Americans more tightly to another place and culture. Among the challenges this group faces is how much to retain the rituals and traditions of the place from which they came, and how much to adopt and adapt to traditionally American ways. This dilemma is particularly hard for the children of immigrants. For those of us several generations away from this, it's hard to imagine how profound this dilemma can be.

For California teenage girls who are Muslim, one way these cultural tensions can be explored is by looking at a rite of passage that for many Americans symbolizes adolescence—the prom. How do the Muslim daughters of Pakistani-American parents celebrate the prom—one of high school's most important coming-of-age rituals—when their faith does not permit them to dress in a manner perceived as immodest around boys or allow boys to touch girls? The article that follows, "For the Muslim Prom Queen, There Are No Kings Allowed," is a fascinating look at the cultural adaptation of a new generation of sons and daughters of immigrants. Their solution to the dilemma of negotiating old and new cultures is to reshape the new culture to fit the old, rather than the other way around. Muslim teenagers can have a prom, but it won't look much like the one I attended.

Like most of the essays in this chapter, the piece that follows isn't a formal ethnography. But notice how much you can learn about culture by focusing on how people participate in a single ritual. In this case, it's the high school prom, but it could just as easily be an initiation rite of a fraternity, a funeral, or a birthday. Consider such an approach when you write your own ethnographic essay. Is there a ritual event that could be the focus of your essay?

For the Muslim Prom Queen, There Are No Kings Allowed

Patricia Leigh Brown

1   The trappings of a typical high school prom were all there: the strobe lights, the garlands, the crepe pineapple centerpieces and even a tiara for the queen. In fact, Fatima Haque's prom tonight had practically everything one might expect on one of a teenage girl's most important nights. Except boys.

2   Ms. Haque and her friends may have helped initiate a new American ritual: the all-girl Muslim prom. It is a spirited response to religious and cultural beliefs that forbid dating, dancing with or touching boys or appearing without a hijab, the Islamic head scarf. While Ms. Haque and her Muslim friends do most things other teenagers do—shopping for shoes at Macy's, watching "The Matrix Reloaded" at the mall or ordering Jumbo Jack burgers and curly fries at Jack in the Box—an essential ingredient of the American prom, boys, is off limits. So they decided to do something about it.

3   "A lot of Muslim girls don't go to prom," said Ms. Haque, 18, who removed her hijab and shawl at the prom to reveal an ethereal silvery gown. "So while the other girls are getting ready for their prom, the Muslim girls are getting ready for our prom, so we won't feel left out."

4   The rented room at a community center here was filled with the sounds of the rapper 50 Cent, Arabic pop music, Britney Spears and about two dozen girls, including some non-Muslim friends. But when the sun went down, the music stopped temporarily, the silken gowns disappeared beneath full-length robes, and the Muslims in the room faced toward Mecca to pray. Then it was time for spaghetti and lasagna.

5   It is perhaps a new version of having it all: embracing the American prom culture of high heels, mascara and adrenaline while being true to a Muslim identity.

6   "These young women are being very creative, finding a way to continue being Muslim in the American context," said Jane I. Smith, a professor of Islamic studies at the Hartford Seminary in Connecticut. "Before, young Muslims may have stuck with the traditions of their parents or rejected them totally to become completely Americanized. Now, they're blending them."

7   Non-Muslim students at San Jose High Academy, where Ms. Haque is president of the student body, went to the school's coed prom last month—renting cars or limousines, dining at the Sheraton, going to breakfast at Denny's and, for some, drinking. Ms. Haque, meanwhile, was on her turquoise cellphone with the smiley faces organizing the prom. She posted an announcement on Bay Area Muslim Youth, a Yahoo news group scanned by young people throughout the San Francisco Bay area, home to one of the country's largest and most active Muslim communities.

8   "We got so close, we wanted to hang," said Fatin Alhadi, 17, a friend, explaining the farewell-to-high-school celebration, which involved cooking, shopping and

decorating the room, rented with a loan from Ms. Haque's parents. "It's an excuse to dress and put makeup on. Everyone has so much fun at the prom."

The sense of anticipation was palpable at Ms. Haque's house this afternoon, including an occasional "Relax, mom!" For Ms. Haque and her friends, the Muslim prom—like any prom—meant getting your eyebrows shaped at the last minute and ransacking mother's jewelry box. It was a time to forget about the clock, to look in the mirror and see a glamorous woman instead of a teenager. To be radiant.

9

Ms. Haque and her Muslim girlfriends dwell in a world of exquisite subtlety in which modesty is the underlying principle. Though she wears a hijab, Ms. Alhadi recently dyed her black hair auburn. "Everyone asks me why, because nobody sees it," she said. "But I like to look at myself."

10

Ms. Haque, who will attend the University of California at Berkeley in the fall, is one of a growing number of young Muslim women who have adopted the covering their mothers rejected. Islamic dress, worn after puberty, often accompanies a commitment not to date or to engage in activities where genders intermingle.

11

Her parents immigrated from Pakistan, and her mother, Shazia, who has a master's degree in economics, does not wear the hijab.

12

Ms. Haque's decision to cover herself, which she made in her freshman year, was nuanced and thoughtful.

13

"I noticed a big difference in the way guys talked," she said. "They were afraid. I guess they had more respect. You walked down the street and you didn't feel guys staring at you. You felt a lot more confident." Her parents were surprised but said it was her decision.

14

Ms. Haque faced some taunting after the terror attacks on Sept. 11, 2001. "They call you terrorist, or raghead because high school students are immature," she said.

15

But she and her friends say Muslim boys, who are not distinguished by their dress, may have a tougher time in American society.

16

"The scarf draws the line," said Ms. Alhadi, the daughter of a Singaporean mother and Indonesian father. "It's already a shield. Without it everything comes to you and you have to fight it yourself."

17

Ms. Haque is enrolled in the academically elite International Baccalaureate program at San Jose High Academy, a public school where, as her friend Morgan Parker, 17, put it, "the jocks are the nerds."

18

But the social pressures on Muslims, especially in less-cloistered settings, can be intense.

19

"I felt left out, big time," said Saira Lara, 17, a senior at Gunn High School in Palo Alto, of her school's prom. But she gets a vicarious taste of dating by talking with her non-Muslim friends.

20

"The drama that goes on!" Ms. Lara said, looking dazzling at the Muslim prom in a flowing maroon gown. "The Valentine's Day without a phone call or a box of chocolates!"

21

Imran Khan, 17, a senior at Los Altos High School, admitted that his school's prom was not easy.

22

(continued)

(continued)

23   "When I told my friends I wasn't going, they all said, 'Are you crazy?'" he said in a telephone interview. "Prom is a you-have-to-go kind of thing. Obviously if all your friends are going and you're not, you're going to feel something. That day I was, 'Oh man, my friends are having fun and I'm not.' But I don't regret not going."

24   Most of Mr. Khan's school friends are not Muslim, and his Muslim friends are scattered across the Bay area.

25   "A lot of times it's difficult," he said. "We guys blend in so you can't tell we're Muslim. We're not supposed to touch the opposite gender. My friends who are girls understand, but when other girls want to hug you or shake your hand, it's hard. I don't want them to think I'm a jerk or something."

26   Adeel Iqbal, 18, a senior at Bellarmine College Preparatory, a boys' Catholic school in San Jose, went stag to his coed senior prom. Mr. Iqbal decided to go in his official capacity as student body president as well as a representative of his Muslim beliefs.

27   "Every day we're bombarded with images of sex and partying and getting drunk, in music and on TV, so of course there's a curiosity," he said. "When you see your own peers engaging in these activities, it's kind of weird. It takes a lot of strength to not participate. But that's how I've been raised. When your peers see you're different in a positive way, they respect it."

28   Nearly all parents of adolescents worry about the pressures of sex, drugs and alcohol, but the anxiety is especially acute in Muslim families who strictly adhere to traditional Islamic dress and gender separation. Many Muslim parents disapprove of what they see as an excessively secularized and liberalized American culture, and are deeply concerned that young Muslims, especially girls, not be put in compromising situations.

29   Ms. Haque's father, Faisal, a design engineer at Cisco Systems, said that the pressure to conform was "very significant." It is the subject of frequent family discussions.

30   "It's difficult at best," Mr. Haque said. "It takes a lot of self-control. I have a lot of respect for these kids."

31   The Haques supported their daughter's decision to organize the Muslim prom. "You have to live in this country," Mr. Haque said. "In order to function, the children have to adapt. Prom is a rite of passage. You don't want them to feel like they don't belong."

32   Ms. Haque would like the Muslim prom to become an annual event. "My goal is an elegant ballroom with a three-course dinner—no paper plates—women waiters and a hundred girls," she said.

33   Tonight, the prom room was filled with promise as the young women whirled around the dance floor, strobe lights blinking. "Show off whatever you've got!" Ms. Lara exhorted the throng, sounding like a D.J. "Come on, guys. This is the most magical night of your life!"

Inquiring into the Essay

Use the four ways of inquiring to think about your response to Patricia Leigh Brown's article.

1. If you went to an American high school, then you had to decide whether to attend the prom. Was this much of a decision for you? Fastwrite for five minutes in your journal about your social status then. Were you an insider or outsider? How was the prom at your school symbolic of the ways in which social status was expressed at your high school? In what ways was this reflected in how people dressed, what they did, who they hung out with, and how they behaved? Write about your own observations of this and your feelings about it back then.

2. Based on what you may have written in your journal in response to the first question, explain the markers of social status in your high school. How could you tell an insider from an outsider, the popular from the less popular, the socially mainstream from the less so? Be as specific as you can.

3. How would the students of your school respond to Fatima Haque, the girl who organized the Muslim prom described in the article, if she came to the prom in her hijab (head covering) and shawl? What does this suggest about the culture of your high school?

4. Critics of multiculturalism might read this article and argue that recent immigrants should work harder to assimilate and adopt conventional American traditions and rituals. In other words, perhaps what these girls needed to do was to find a way to bend their own beliefs to accommodate the typical prom, rather than appropriate the prom to conform to their own beliefs. How would you evaluate that claim?

5. Empathy is essential if we're going to understand the lives of people with different cultural, racial, or social backgrounds. When you read and write about people who are fundamentally different from you, how do you attempt to get outside of your own biases and the limitations of your own experience?

SEEING THE FORM

Mrs. Smith's Kitchen Table and Vanity the Day After She Died

My brother Buzz's neighbor, Mrs. Smith, lived in her small bungalow in Santa Cruz, California, for nearly all of her life. The day after she died, Buzz, a professional photographer, was in Mrs. Smith's house and took the pictures below. One of the many reasons I love these shots is how much can be revealed about a life by the things we choose to surround ourselves with. In these two pictures, I get a sense of a life

 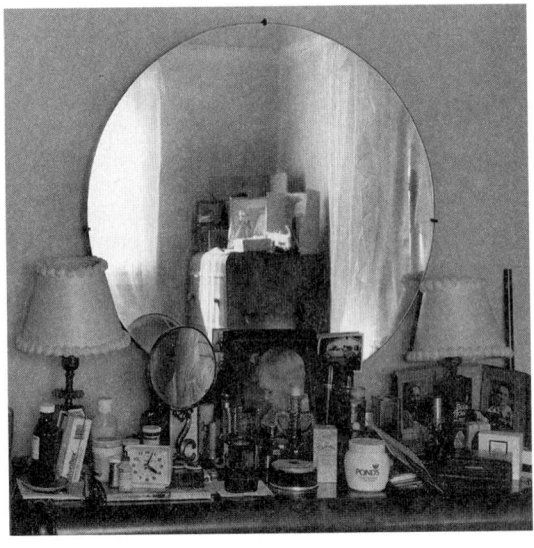

that was suddenly interrupted; we are confronted with the frozen image of a coffee cup and saucer, an open phone book, a crumpled tissue, bottles of medicine, and a picture of a fair-haired boy. An ethnographic "reading" of these pictures would place particular emphasis on what these things imply about Mrs. Smith's social status or as markers and artifacts of a culture to which she belonged.

Reading pictures like these, simply to speculate about the kind of person Mrs. Smith was, is a great exercise in ethnographic seeing. Spend a few minutes looking very closely at the pictures. Inventory as many details in the images as you can, perhaps cataloging them in your journal. As you consider these particulars, speculate about Mrs. Smith. What kind of person do you imagine she was? What kinds of things did she seem to care about? What does this brief moment in time suggest about the kind of life she was leading the day she died?

THE WRITING PROCESS

INQUIRY PROJECT: WRITING AN ETHNOGRAPHIC ESSAY

This assignment will take you into the field to observe a subculture in the community. You'll write a 2,500- to 3,000-word essay that uses field research and reading as the basis for an interpretation of how the subculture sees things. This necessarily will be a limited picture, so it should focus on some aspect of the culture that emerges from your observations.

The essay should also have the following qualities:

- Have a limited focus.

- Be organized around some thesis or interpretation of how this culture sees things. For example, how does the culture view authority figures, or what constitutes a leader in the group? (See the "Inquiring into the Details: Questions Ethnographers Ask" box, page 305.)

- Offer a rationale for why this group constitutes a distinct culture.

- Provide enough evidence from your field observations to make your interpretations and commentary convincing.

For additional reading, writing, and research resources, go to www.mycomplab.com

---

Thinking About Subjects

Like any of the inquiry projects described in *The Curious Writer,* success depends on what motivates you. What might make you curious about studying a certain local culture? Do you have a family member you've always wanted to know better who just happens to be a truck driver, a farmer, an emergency room nurse, a migrant worker? Maybe your best friend is a member of a social group you'd like to study—a Baptist youth group, rock climbers, or Deadheads—and can offer access. If you're an older student, perhaps you have a niece or a nephew or possibly one of your own children who is a member of the local girls' tennis team, the youth ballet company, or the bowhunters club.

Might your professional interests be relevant to this project? Say you want to be a police officer; might it be enlightening to hang out with a few officers to find out what the life is like? If you have an interest in writing, then the ethnography assignment promises to be a great learning experience, no matter what culture you choose to study. You'll get practice in observation, note taking, interviewing, and profiling—skills that are invaluable for writers of any kind.

Possible subjects for your ethnography are all around you. We are all enmeshed within intricate webs of cultures. But what should you choose to write about? If you're a student at an urban campus, then the possibilities are nearly

Commercial Ethnography

Ethnography isn't just for academics. Increasingly, businesses are using the method to analyze consumer behavior, and they are finding that ethnography is often better than the usual surveys, questionnaires, and focus groups. Why? Because the information researchers get from observing people where they work and live is a more accurate measure of what they think. Even more important, since ethnographers are interested in watching how people behave, not just in surveying their attitudes, researchers get a much more realistic picture about what people are willing to actually *do*. Using video, photographs, audio, interviews, and observation, commercial application of ethnography gives designers and marketers a glimpse into cultural norms or can reveal some of the ways a product may—or may not—fit into our ordinary lives.

limitless, but even if you attend a rural university you can still find a culture to study on your own campus.

Generating Ideas

Begin exploring possible subjects for a review by generating material in your notebook. This should be an open-ended process, a chance to use your creative side without worrying too much about making sense or trying to prejudge the value of the writing or the subjects you generate. In a sense, this is an invitation to play around.

Listing Prompts. Lists can be rich sources of triggering topics. Let them grow freely, and when you're ready, use an item as the focus of another list or an episode of fastwriting. The following prompts should get you started.

1. In class or in your journal, create a four-column table, labeling the first column Trends, the second Hobbies, the third Community Groups, and the fourth Campus Groups (see the following example). Brainstorm a list of *cultural trends* that are a visible part of American culture in the new millennium. For example, snowboarding is a sport that has boomed in recent years, nearly eclipsing skiing. Write the name of each trend under the first column in the table. Create a similar list for popular hobbies (note that trends and hobbies often overlap—snowboarding can also be a hobby) and write the name of each hobby in the second column. Finally, brainstorm a list of identifiable social groups in the community and on campus— fraternities, truck drivers, goths, and so on. Write these, respectively, in the third and fourth columns of your table.

Trends	Hobbies	Community Groups	Campus Groups
Snowboarding	Fly fishing	Kiwanis	Fraternities
Blogging (participating in Web logs)	Ballroom dancing	Pentecostal church	Black student alliance
	Computer games	Gospel singers	Graduate students
Atkins/South Beach/low-carb diet craze	Autograph collecting	Truck drivers	
Reality TV programming			

2. Create a new three-column table, labeling the first column Artifacts, the second Language, and the third Rituals. Now choose one of the trends, hobbies, community groups, or campus groups from your first table and under the first column of the new table list all of the artifacts—tools, equipment, devices, clothing—that you can think of that people typically use when they participate in the activity/group you have selected. In the second column, list the language—special terms, jargon, and other words or phrases—that group members regularly use. In the third column, list the rituals—habits, patterns of behavior, or traditions—that are typical of the activity/group. Creating the new table will help you expose some of the threads of a particular activity's or group's culture. Objects that group members typically use, their ways of speaking, and the traditions and rituals that govern their behavior are three key elements you need to consider when writing an ethnographic essay. The accompanying table identifies some of the artifacts, language, and rituals of fly fishing.

FLY FISHING

Artifacts	Language	Rituals
Fly rod (not "pole")	"Working water"	Keeping physical distance from other fly fishers
Artificial fly	"Skunked"	
Vest	"Meat fisherman"	Catch and release of fish
		Winter fly tying

Fastwriting Prompts. Choose an item from one of your lists as a fastwrite prompt. Write quickly, exploring each of the following questions:

1. What are your own experiences and observations with this trend, hobby, or group?

2. What are your presuppositions, biases, or assumptions about this trend, hobby, or group? What do you assume about the kind of people who participate in it, for example, and what might their motives be for belonging?

3. Based on what you know now, what things—or artifacts—seem particularly important to participants?

4. What questions do you have about why this trend exists, or why people participate in the group or hobby?

Visual Prompts. Sometimes the best way to generate material is to see what we think is represented in something other than sentences. Boxes, lines, webs, clusters, arrows, charts, and even sketches can help us see more of the landscape of a subject, especially connections between fragments of information that aren't as obvious in prose.

1. If you like to take photographs, go through your collection looking for suggestive pictures of subcultures you've captured. Perhaps you took pictures of an on-campus or community event, or you have some shots of people back home that represent certain social groups.

2. Take a word or phrase from the table you created from the first question in the "Listing Prompts" section and use it as a nucleus word for a cluster on a blank page of your journal. When you cluster a hobby, cultural trend, or community or campus group, build associations using the five W's: *what, when, where, who,* and *why. Where* do participants of this hobby, group, or trend gather, and *when? Who* are the kind of people who belong? *What* are their activities and rituals? *Why* do people belong?

Research Prompts. Research can be helpful even this early in the process. New or more detailed information might trigger ideas about possible topics for your paper that you otherwise would never have considered. At this stage, your research will be open-ended and not particularly methodical. Just enjoy poking around.

1. In the United States, there's a magazine for nearly every subculture. Go to a bookstore and survey the hobby and special-interest magazines. The Web also has useful sites with links to resources on American subcultures or information on cultural trends (see "Inquiring into the Details: Researching Trends and Subcultures on the Web"). Do any of these interest you?

2. One quick way to gain entry to a culture you don't belong to is to find someone in your class who is a member. Stay alert to what others in the class say about their own identification with certain social groups and interview any who belong to a culture that interests you.

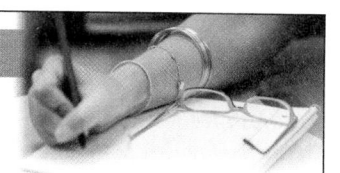

INQUIRING INTO THE DETAILS

Researching Trends and Subcultures on the Web

If you're browsing for ideas about a topic, or researching the cultural group you've chosen to investigate, a number of sites on the Internet can help.

- *The Pew Internet and American Life Project* features up-to-date information on trends in Internet use. http://www.pewinternet.org

- *The Statistical Abstract of the United States* is an annual Census Bureau publication that is a gold mine of data on all kinds of trends. http://www.census.gov/compendia/statab

- *The Gallup Poll* Web site features recent survey results on social trends. http://poll.gallup.com

- *The Open Directory Project,* a subject catalog of Web information, includes a useful directory on subcultures as varied as geeks and polygamists. http://dmoz.org/Society/Subcultures/

- *The Google Directory* also lists subcultures with links to resources on the Web. http://www.google.com/Top/Society/Subcultures/

- *Wikipedia,* the "free encyclopedia," isn't necessarily a good source for academic writing, but it is the "largest reference site on the Web." The list of subcultures is impressive. http://en.wikipedia.org/wiki/Category:Subcultures

Judging What You Have

Generating may produce the messy, incoherent writing that would earn you bad grades in most classes. Its virtue, however, should be obvious by now: "bad" writing gives a writer material to work with. And while it's always better to work from abundance rather than scarcity, this material still must be judged, shaped, and evaluated.

What's Promising Material and What Isn't? In deciding what to write about, keep in mind that you should choose a local culture that meets the following qualifications:

1. The culture is accessible to you.
2. The culture's members gather at places that you can visit.
3. The culture interests you in some way.
4. The culture might lend itself to library or online research.
5. You are not a member of this culture.

The last criterion—that you shouldn't be a member of the group you're studying—isn't a hard and fast rule, especially if you have just a few weeks to complete the assignment, but it is preferred. As an outsider, it takes a bit more time to gain access to the group and earn the members' trust, but this is a particularly useful vantage point for observing the culture because first impressions are enormously valuable. Also, as an outsider you'll be more open to what you see and more likely to see more.

How can you know whether a study subject will meet the definition of a culture? If the answer to the following questions is *yes,* then your subject probably will qualify:

- Does the group you want to study feel, at least implicitly, a sense of identification with each other as members? (This doesn't necessarily mean that they all like each other or always get along.)

- Do group members share certain behaviors, outlooks, beliefs, or motivations for belonging?

- Do they share a common language? Do they tend to describe things in similar ways, or use words or phrases that have special significance to the group?

- Do they share an interest in certain objects or artifacts? Do they invest these things with similar significance?

This list of questions might seem limiting, but because we are all immersed in social groups that have these kinds of cultural affinities you should find it easy to discover a culture to study from the ideas you generated. Cultures are everywhere, including your campus.

Questions About Audience and Purpose. No matter how fascinated you are by the people who do medieval battle reenactments at the park, you still have to have something *to say* about the subculture to readers who may not share your fascination. Most academic ethnographies are written to fellow experts. Researchers, to some extent, assume prior knowledge and interest in their subjects. However, you're writing an ethnographic *essay,* a much shorter, less extensively researched, and more general reader-friendly work. Imagine an audience that may know something about your subject—after all, most of us are aware of many social groups—but your essay should help readers to see what perhaps they've seen before in a way they haven't seen it. Good essays make the familiar strange.

How do you do this?

1. *Look hard and look closely.* If you're going to see anything new, you have to have as much data as you can. That means doing as much fieldwork as you can.

2. *Focus on what is less obvious.* If you're going to surprise your audience you need to surprise yourself. What are you noticing about those battle reenactors that you never noticed before?

3. *Find the question.* What aspect of your culture are you most interested in exploring?

4. *Discover one main thing you're trying to say.* You can't know what this is until you've done a lot of fieldwork and some reading. But in the final draft the main idea you're trying to get across about the group you observed should be clear.

5. *Tell stories, provide profiles, use dialogue, incorporate heavy description.* To bring the culture you studied to life for readers, try to employ some of the literary techniques you know from good storytelling.

Research Considerations. Prepare to do fieldwork by confirming the best places to conduct observations of the culture in which you're interested. Sometimes that's easy to figure out: Snowboarders hang out at the lodge, surfers at the beach, fraternity brothers at the fraternity house, homeless men at the shelter. But there will also be less obvious gathering places, locations you may only learn of through interviews with group members. Are there other locations where group members gather to socialize, plan activities, celebrate successes, or learn from each other?

> Writing ethnographically requires that you expand your repertoire of research to include interviews and fieldwork.

INQUIRING INTO THE DETAILS

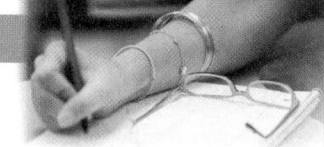

Questions Ethnographers Ask

When you study a social group, whether it's skateboarders or opera singers, there are certain basic things you want to find out about how that group operates. For example,

- How do group members view outsiders?
- What motivates members to belong?
- What artifacts are present, how are they typically used, and what significance is attached to them?
- What is the nature of gender relations in the group?
- Where does the group gather and why?
- What is the group's social hierarchy, and how is it organized and maintained?
- What's the relationship between this local culture and the larger culture with which it identifies?
- Does this group seem to define itself *in opposition to* other groups, and if so, why?
- What are the culture's most symbolic or significant rituals? Why is meaning assigned to them?
- Is there an initiation of some kind?

If the sites you want to visit aren't public, you may need permission to conduct your observation. In addition, make sure you plan for your own safety. While it's unlikely that you'll study a city gang or a gun-toting right-wing militia or some similar group that can be dangerous to outsiders, make sure that you will be safe wherever you go. Bring a friend with you; tell others where you'll be and for how long.

Taking Notes. The most important source of information for your essay will be the observation notes you take in the field. You've practiced notetaking during the profile assignment, but the notes for the ethnography project will involve more observation. In the initial stages, focus on your first impressions of the group you're studying. Jot down everything.

Photographs. Visual ethnography uses photographs, film, or video to document local culture. These can be enormously rich records because pictures extend our perception and preserve information for later study and analysis. In addition, sharing the photographs we take with our study subjects can yield valuable insight about the meanings of the things in the images. A twelve-year-old skateboarder, for example, might look at the picture of someone attempting a trick and offer a commentary about the rider's motives and techniques, and the meanings of his moves. Digital photography has made it possible to instantaneously share this material.

INQUIRING INTO THE DETAILS

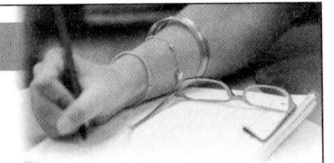

Ethnography and Ethics

Unlike most other undergraduate research projects, an ethnography involves work with human subjects. As you might imagine, this raises some ethical issues. How open should you be with your research subjects about your project? Do you need their permission? What responsibility do you have to protect your subjects' identities?

For faculty who do research with people, a university review board charged with protecting human subjects must approve the project. That probably won't be necessary for your ethnographic essay, but there are still ethical guidelines you should follow:

1. Let your research subjects know what you're doing and why you're doing it.

2. Obtain their permission to be included in your research. While a written "informed consent" may not be necessary, there should at least be a clear verbal understanding between you and the people you're studying.

3. Protect their anonymity. You have an obligation to make certain that your subjects' identities are protected. It's often a wise practice to use pseudonyms in your research.

For the American Anthropological Association's ethical guidelines, visit http://www.aaanet.org/committees/ethics/ethcode.htm.

Bring your camera along on your site visits and record what you see. When you print the pictures, attempt to place them in a meaningful order. Try to establish relationships among the pictures. Do they fall into certain categories of activity or significance? In addition, study the photographs for information that you might have missed in your field notes. What do you notice about artifacts, clothing, or the context in which the action is taking place?

Interviews. There is only so much we can see. Simply observing people won't tell us what they think or feel; we have to ask. Your earlier practice with interviews will have prepared you for this method of collecting information; see Chapter 4 for more information on interview methods and techniques.

Artifacts. If you can, collect or describe things from the site or that people in this culture routinely make, talk about, or use. For example, if you're studying a truck stop, collect menus, placemats, and so on. If you're studying people in a bowling league, describe the differences among bowling balls or collect score sheets. Photographs can also be helpful in identifying artifacts that you can't haul away. Collecting such things can help you to determine what meaning, if any, is assigned to them by group members. For example, do members of a male bowling league see the weight of a bowling ball as a measure of not only a bowler's strength but also his manhood?

Maps. One way to analyze a group's social relationships and the context in which activities take place is to observe where and how members occupy space. Imagine, for example, your own family dinner table as you were growing up. Did everyone sit in the same chair every night? Was there any logic to that arrangement? Does it say anything about the social roles of each family member? If you were to draw a map of your family's seating arrangement, and then add arrows that follow the movement of each member of your family during a typical meal, what would that suggest about social roles and relationships? In my family, my mother's chair was always nearest the kitchen, and she moved far more than the rest of us, mostly back and forth, to and from the oven, table, and sink. Consider making similar maps of your study site, noting the arrangement of things and people, as well as their movements.

Reading Research. Because you have weeks rather than months to write your ethnographic essay, you will probably need to rely somewhat on the work of others who have formally or informally studied the culture in which you're interested. This may include reading the hobby or specialty magazines that group members read; visiting Web sites, newsgroups, chat rooms, and electronic mailing lists that group members frequent online; and searching the library databases for any academic research that scholars may have published on the culture you're studying (see the "Inquiring into the Details: Useful Library Databases for Ethnography," page 312). You'd be surprised at how much work has been done on local culture in the United States.

■ FIELD NOTES

Rita Guerra hasn't bowled often in the past twenty years, but she has fond memories of holding birthday parties at the local bowling alley when she was a girl, and now her own children clamor from time to time to do some ten-pin bowling. Guerra remembers her hometown bowling alley as a social and cultural center for her small town. Wouldn't such a place be a great site to do some fieldwork for her ethnographic essay?

What follows are Guerra's field notes following her first visit to Emerald Lanes—"The Best Alley in the Valley." At this stage, she is focused on collecting data—transcribing conversations she hears, carefully describing what she sees, jotting down text from signs and notices, mapping the space, and simply watching to see what happens when. She uses double-entry field notes. On the left are her observations, and on the right are her impressions or ideas about what she sees, hears, smells, or feels. Notice that she gets a dialogue going between the two columns—speculating, interpreting, and raising questions on the right in response to specific information she collected on the left.

The success of your ethnographic essay depends on the success of your field notes. Always collect more information than you can use—which probably means multiple visits to your field sites—and push yourself to reflect on what you've found as you collect the information. Rita Guerra's field notes are a good model.

Field Notes on Friday Afternoon at Emerald Lanes

Rita Guerra

OBSERVATIONS OF

4/9/04
4:32 Sounds of balls hitting maple lanes, thundering toward pins. There is a constant hum of noise—rolling balls, lane chatter, country music, clanking of pins. Smells like cigarettes and beer. Smoking is allowed throughout the alley.

IDEAS ABOUT

A Friday afternoon at Emerald Lanes appear to be more family oriented, no league play. But I was impressed by how many strong bowlers, mostly young couples played. Emerald Lanes seems a family-friendly place though I was surprised that the entire place allowed smoking. This might be indicative of the bowling culture—smoking is still okay.

"That will be a triple," says a woman in shorts and green tank top. She is bowling with two other young couples and they all bowl well, alternating between strikes and spares. Successful frame usually produces a kind of dance, clenched fists, "yessss!" Poor frame—silence, stone faced.

Scores are tallied electronically on monitors above each lane. Large number of families on Friday afternoon, including birthday party in far lanes.

"Got it right where I wanted to," says young player with girlfriend. He cups the ball underneath before his swing and when releasing it give it a spin. Ball breaks from left to right. Wears own bowling shoes, no rentals, and black wrist band. Spends very little time preparing but picks up his ball, sights the pins, and goes into motion within 15 seconds.

"The Best Alley in the Valley"
"The Bowling Guy's Pro Shop" Ball polisher
Tropical theme—three plastic palm trees between lanes.
Budweiser sign: Welcome to Emerald Lanes. Good Family Fun?
Movement

Need to check for "bowling lingo" on the Internet. What is a "triple"? Three strikes in a row? I was really interested in watching the preparation and releases of bowlers. Seems like you could tell the experienced bowlers from inexperienced ones by the smoothness of their release and especially the velocity of the ball. But maybe more than anything, I began to interpret their reactions to a good frame and bad frame. Strike produces a "yesss!" and clenched fist but not extended celebration. Bad frame a stony face. No anger, no laughter. Seemed to be no difference in this between men and women. Less experienced bowlers would react with more exaggeration.

I need to learn more about the theories behind introducing spin in releasing the ball. The ability to do this seems to distinguish the more skilled from the less skilled bowlers. This player consistently produced a left-to-right break by cupping the ball and obviously spinning it right before he releases it.

Might be interesting to actually time how long it takes for bowlers to prepare to bowl when it is their turn. My impression is that more experienced bowlers waste very little time; novices diddle and dawdle.

Like a lot of bowling alleys I've seen this one seems a bit tacky from the outside, and inside seems friendly but with an atmosphere of Budweiser beer and smoke. On a Friday afternoon, though, it seemed family friendly. Need to plan next visit for a Saturday night during league play. I have a sense that it's an entirely different culture.

Writing the Sketch

Write a sketch that provides a verbal snapshot of the culture you're studying. Using the ethnographer's questions (posed earlier) as guides for your field observation, go to a place where you can observe your culture in action. Collect observations and interviews that will allow you to create a snapshot of your group in action. For example, if you're interested in gender relations among young skateboarders, go to the skateboard park and carefully observe how the boys and girls interact. If possible, talk to some of them. Take lots of notes, and consider taking photographs as visual records, too.

Try working through the following three steps in your journal in preparation for drafting your sketch.

1. **Narrative of thought.** In your notebook, tell the story of how your thinking has evolved. When you first chose your subject, what did you think about that culture? What assumptions did you make and what did you expect to find? And then? And then? And then? And how about now?

2. **Look at strands in the web.** Which of the following features of a culture apply to the one you're studying?

    ■ *Shared language* (for instance, are there insider phrases and words that have significance to group members?)

    ■ *Shared artifacts* (for instance, are there objects that have particular significance to group members?)

    ■ *Common rituals and traditions* (for instance, are there patterns of behavior that surround certain activities, or are there historical understandings of how something must be done?)

    ■ *Shared beliefs and attitudes* (for instance, are there common attitudes toward other insiders, toward outsiders, toward new initiates; do group members share beliefs in the significance of the group and its activities?)

    ■ *Common motivations* (for instance, do members participate for some of the same reasons?)

3. **Examine one strand.** Choose *one* of the preceding features. In your notebook/journal, generate specific evidence from your research or fieldwork that supports your finding.

After you complete the above steps, write a 500- to 600-word sketch that describes what you saw and heard during one or more of your field experiences. The key is not to simply *explain* what you noticed but to *show* it, too. In addition:

■ Choose a title for your sketch.

■ Whenever possible, *show* what you observed or heard using description, scene, dialogue, and similar literary devices.

■ Offer a tentative theory about a belief or attitude that group members seem to share based on your initial field observations and interviews.

Moving from Sketch to Draft

If it was successful, your sketch provided an initial snapshot of the group you're studying. The draft, of course, will provide a fuller picture. But what should that picture focus on? What kind of information should you try to gather now? Your sketch can provide some useful clues.

Evaluating Your Own Sketch. You have a significant advantage over the people in your workshop group who will read and discuss your sketch: you witnessed what you're writing about. You spent time in the field gathering impressions and information, but quite a bit of that probably didn't end up in your sketch. Use that extra knowledge to guide your revision. But before you workshop your sketch, reread it, and in your notebook fastwrite responses to the following questions:

1. *What is my strongest impression of the group so far? What kinds of things did I see, hear, or read that gave me that impression?*
2. *What is another impression I have?*
3. *Which one of these two impressions might be a focus for the next draft?*
4. *What do I most want to know now about the culture I'm observing? What questions do I have?*

Questions for Peer Review. Everyone in your workshop group is working on a similar ethnography project, so you can help each other out by identifying the typical problems that these early drafts present: too little information, lack of focus, and insufficient interpretation of the information. Questions for the group to consider about each ethnography sketch include the following:

- What information or observations in the sketch seemed most striking?
- Which of the questions listed in the "Inquiring into the Details: Questions Ethnographers Ask" box seem to be addressed in the sketch? If the next draft focused on one or two of these, what might they be?
- Based on what you've read so far about this group, what theory would you propose about how its members see things?

Reflecting on What You've Learned. Follow up your workshop by making a schedule that describes your plan for additional research and field observations over the next few weeks. For example:

Sunday	Monday	Tuesday	Wednesday	Thursday	Friday	Saturday
2–4 Field observations at the park		3 PM Pick up photos		7 PM Library research		10–12 Field observations, interview w/Karen

Research and Other Strategies: Gathering More Information

The most important thing you can do to improve the next draft of your ethnography is return to the field for more observations and interviews. This project doesn't permit the kind of immersion in a culture that most ethnographic researchers enjoy, so it's essential that you focus on gathering as much data as you can in the time you have. This will take careful planning and scheduling and your schedule will help. (In fact, your instructor may ask you to hand in your schedule.)

If photography is part of your data gathering, spend some time analyzing the pictures you've taken. Begin by arranging them in some kind of logical order, and note that chronology isn't the only arrangement that makes sense. Do you see the pictures grouping around certain typical activities? Do they seem relevant to any of your particular research questions? Does a sequence suggest something about how group members interact with each other or occupy space? Do certain arrangements of photographs tell a story that seems significant?

Study individual photographs as well. Because the camera's eye misses little, a single picture can be a rich source of detailed information about the context or setting in which important group activities take place. A picture can also capture data about artifacts and even the relationships among group members. All of this information can help you write a more informative, interesting draft and make your interpretations of what you've seen more convincing.

Finally, don't forget to continue library and Internet research. Consult specialized indexes and databases you might have skipped earlier (see "Inquiring into the Details: Useful Library Databases for Ethnography" below). What can you learn from what others have observed and said about the culture you're studying?

INQUIRING INTO THE DETAILS

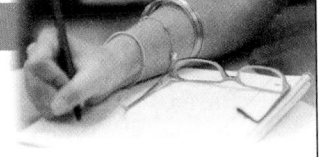

Useful Library Databases for Ethnography

Don't forget to research existing ethnographies that may be published on the culture you're studying. If your library has them, the following specialized databases are worth checking:

- Anthropological Index Online
- EHRAF Collection of Ethnography
- Sociological Abstracts
- Ethnographic Bibliography of North America
- Abstracts in Anthropology
- Abstracts of Folklore Studies
- International Bibliography of the Social Sciences

Composing the Draft

Here's a checklist to consider before you start drafting:

✓ *Do you have enough information?* Have you gathered sufficient field notes and done enough research?

✓ *Do you have a focus?* If you want your ethnographic essay to be interesting and informative, you must focus on an aspect of the culture you're studying.

✓ *Do you have a theory?* By now, you've hopefully got an idea or two about some significant patterns you've observed in the relationships, artifacts, rituals, and behaviors of the culture you're studying. What are they?

Methods of Development. As an extended form of inquiry, the ethnographic essay will probably combine some of the methods of development described here.

Narrative Structures. Because ethnography often involves scene or setting, character, dialogue, and action, it's a form that naturally accommodates storytelling. Try one or more of these narrative techniques.

1. *A typical day.* One way to capture your culture is to describe, in some detail, what happened on a single day that seems representative. This focus on a particular time, place, and people gives your ethnographic essay a dramatic and limited focus.

WRITING IN THE DISCIPLINES

Digital Ethnography

In 2007, Kansas State anthropology professor Michael Wesch, pondering the potential of digital texts compared with print, posted a video on YouTube, "The Machine is Us/ing Us." Within days the spot got millions of viewings. Along with his students, Wesch is now working on an ethnography of YouTube. Wesch's work dramatizes how easily and quickly information can be distributed on what is now called "Web 2.0." But he also argues that this new media isn't just an exciting new form of communication; it is fundamentally changing "human relationships," something that ethnographers should study. "We know the value of participant observation in understanding social worlds," he wrote recently. "Now we need to understand the new forms of sociality emerging in this quickly changing mediated world." The field is responding. Increasingly, ethnographies are published digitally, incorporating text with videos, photographs, and audio. Consider those possibilities with your own ethnographic essay. Can you imagine ways to present your findings using some combination of digital media?

2. *Collage.* Sometimes it's effective to generate a series of significant snap-shots of your subjects in their natural setting. For example, an ethnography of eighth-grade cheerleaders might feature a collage of scenes with titles like "Making the Team" or "The Squad's Social Hierarchy."

3. *Narrative of thought.* Tell the story of your initial presumptions about the culture and how your observations and research influenced those. Or state an initial theory and then tell the story of whether the evidence supported it.

Question to Answer. Inquiry projects are motivated by questions and you can use them to structure your draft.

Begin by establishing your focusing question (e.g., "What is the social hierarchy of dog handlers and how is it maintained?"). Then consider including some or all of the following:

- Provide some background from research about other studies (if any) that have directly or indirectly addressed the question.

- Explain the writer's interest in the question. What observations, inter-views, or readings suggest that the social hierarchy of dog handlers might be interesting or significant to look at?

- Explain the methods the writer used to focus on the question.

- Offer a theory, a possible answer to the question. For example, Based on my initial impressions, handlers and trainers who have established reputations as successful breeders tend to get the most respect.

Compare and Contrast. When I teach graduate workshops in creative nonfiction, I often wonder how gender shapes my students' responses to each other and the work being discussed. If I conducted a study that focused on such a question, I probably would find a range of ways in which men and women interact with each other. One useful way of exploring these would be to look for similarities and differences, to compare and contrast. In fact, it's hard to imagine any ethnography not exploiting this method of development in at least a small way, and it's easy to imagine that comparisons might form the backbone of some essays.

Using Evidence. Ethnographic research is distinctive because it studies social groups in their own environments. It follows, then, that the most important evidence in this kind of essay will be the investigator's detailed field observations. In addition, because the purpose of an ethnography is to attempt to see the world the way your study subjects see it, interviews that bring the voices of group members into the essay provide valuable evidence. After all, who can better articulate a group's beliefs and perspectives than its members? Ethnography mostly relies on *primary* research like this, but secondary sources—articles and essays about the group you're studying—can be useful, too, particularly if they come from academic sources. But it's time in the field that is the most important element in the success or failure of this kind of writing.

Workshopping the Draft

If your draft is subject to peer review, see Chapter 10 for details on how to organize workshop groups and decide on how your group can help you. The following journal activities and questions should help you make the most of your opportunity to get peer feedback on your work in progress. But first, are you happy with the way the first draft turned out? Here is a check to determine the strengths and weaknesses of your draft:

- Is your purpose clear? Do you think readers will understand the question that interests you or what your particular motives were when writing about this culture?

- Have you taken a landscape picture when you needed a close-up? Does the draft try to cover too much territory, include too much information, or say too much?

- Is there enough specific information—observations, scenes, facts, dialogue, and so on? Do you show as well as tell in the draft?

- Is it clear what you're trying to say about this group? Do you propose a certain theory about how it operates or sees things? Do you make a central claim or have a main point? Are you working toward a dominant impression or interpretation of the group?

Reflecting on the Draft. Review the preceding list, and fastwrite for seven minutes in your journal exploring your answers to some of the questions. End the fastwrite by generating a quick list of ideas in response to this question: *What things might I do to improve this draft when I revise it?*

Questions for Readers. Make the most of your peer review session by asking readers of your draft to answer one or more of the following questions:

1. If you had to summarize in a sentence or two your main impression of the group I studied, what would it be?

2. If you were to imagine the draft as a kind of documentary film that allows you to get a good look at a culture, where in the draft were the camera shots most vivid? Where in the draft did you wish there were close-ups, or long shots?

3. What questions did the draft seem to try to answer about the culture? Which of these seem most important or interesting?

Revising the Draft

Revision is a continual process—not a last step. You've been revising—literally "re-seeing" your subject—from the first messy fastwriting in your journal. But the things that get your attention during revision vary depending on where you are in the writing process. You've generated material, chosen a topic, done some research, and written both a sketch and draft. Most students think that the only thing left to do is "fix things." Check for misspellings. Correct an awkward sentence or two. Come up with a better title. This is editing, not revision, and while editing is important, to focus solely on smaller "fixes" after writing a first draft squanders an opportunity to really *learn* from what the draft is telling you, or perhaps not quite telling you.

Chapter 9 can help guide these discoveries. The questions you can ask of a draft fall into five categories: purpose, idea, information, development, and editing. Use the following chart to find the revision strategies in Chapter 9 that might help you re-see what you've written so far. Ethnographic essays typically have some of the following problems that should be addressed in revision:

- Does your draft fail to give clear enough pictures to readers about the group you studied? The problem is usually that there simply isn't enough information from field observations of the group. The solution? Get back out into the field.

- Do your self-references in the draft—how you felt at a particular moment, what you were thinking, and so on—serve a purpose? Do they contribute in some way to an effort to clarify your biases or methodology, or do they help readers understand how your study subjects see things? If not, cut those self-referential passages to keep the focus on your subjects.

- Does the draft try to say things about the group rather than focus on a single main thesis, interpretation, or question?

- If your time for fieldwork was limited, did you make up for it by finding some useful research about the culture you studied in the library or on the Web?

GUIDE TO REVISION STRATEGIES

Problems in the Draft (Chapter 9)	Page Number
Unclear purpose ■ Not sure what the paper is about?	327
Unclear thesis, theme, or main idea ■ Not sure what you're trying to say?	333
Lack of information or development ■ Need more convincing evidence?	340
Disorganized ■ Doesn't move logically or smoothly from paragraph to paragraph?	344
Unclear or awkward at the level of sentences and paragraphs ■ Seems choppy or hard to follow at the level of sentences or paragraphs?	353

Refer to Chapter 9, "Revision Strategies," for ideas about how to address these and many other problems. Use the following table to find other appropriate revision strategies. Remember that a draft may present problems in more than one category.

Polishing the Draft

After you've dealt with the big issues in your draft—is it sufficiently focused, does it answer the *So what?* question, is it well organized, and so on—you must deal with the smaller problems. You've carved the stone into an appealing figure but now you need to polish it. Are your paragraphs coherent? How do you manage transitions? Are your sentences fluent and concise? Are there any errors in spelling or syntax?

Before you finish your draft, work through the following checklist:

✓ Every paragraph is about one thing.

✓ The transitions between paragraphs aren't abrupt.

✓ The length of sentences varies in each paragraph.

✓ Each sentence is concise. There are no unnecessary words or phrases.

✓ You've checked grammar, particularly verb agreement, run-on sentences, unclear pronouns, and misused words (*there/their, where/were,* and so on). (See the handbook at the back of the book for help with these grammar issues.)

✓ You've run your spellchecker and proofed your paper for misspelled words.

USING WHAT YOU HAVE LEARNED

Will you be asked to write an ethnographic essay in another class? Probably not. But the experience of writing an essay like this one will help you be a better researcher and writer in a range of situations. It also raises some interesting questions about the very nature of research.

1. We often think that research requires "objectivity." In the sciences, the experimental method attempts to reduce the influence of the experimenter on the results. That's not possible, of course, with an ethnography. Does that make the information and the conclusions less reliable? Less useful? Can any researcher, even a scientific one, be purely objective?

2. Recall the inquiry model used throughout *The Curious Writer,* the process of moving back and forth from creative thinking to critical thinking. Is that a process that you used to write this essay? Can you imagine how you could apply it to nearly *any* essay?

3. In one minute, write a response to the following question: *Based on your experience with this assignment, how would you define culture?*

3

RE-INQUIRING

Revision is work. But it's also an opportunity for surprise. The trick is to see what you have written in ways you haven't seen it before.

REVISION STRATEGIES

RE-SEEING YOUR TOPIC

"I don't really revise," Amy told me the other day. "I'm usually pretty happy with my first draft."

Always? I wondered.

"Well, certainly not always," she said. "But I know I work better under pressure, so I usually write my papers right before they're due. There usually isn't much time for revision, even if I wanted to do it, which I don't, really."

Amy is pretty typical. Her first-draft efforts usually aren't too bad, but I often sense tentativeness in her prose, endings that seem much stronger than beginnings, and promises that aren't really kept. Her essay promises to focus on the dangers of genetically engineered foods to teenagers who live on Cheeze-Its and Cheetos, but she never quite gets to saying much about that. The writing is competent—pretty clear and without too many awkward passages—but ultimately it's disappointing to read.

You can guess what I'm getting at here—Amy's work could be much stronger if it were rewritten—but the logic of last-minute writing is pretty powerful: "I really think I need to bump up against a deadline."

The writing process has three phases: prewriting, drafting, and rewriting. Prewriting refers to a range of activities writers might engage in before they attempt to compose a first draft, including fastwriting, listing, clustering, rehearsing lines or passages, preliminary research, conversations, or even the kind of

> ## What You'll Learn in This Chapter
>
> - How genuine revision involves exactly that: revision, or *re-seeing* your topic.
> - Basic revision strategies for "divorcing the draft."
> - How to become a reader of your own work.
> - The five categories of revision.
> - Advanced revision strategies.

deep thought about a topic that for some of us seems to occur best in the shower. The drafting stage is hardly mysterious. It often involves the much slower, much more focused process of putting words to paper, crafting a draft that presumably grows from some of the prewriting activities. Rewriting is a rethinking of that draft. Although this typically involves tweaking sentences, it's much more than that. Revision, as the name implies, is a *re-seeing* of the paper's topic and the writer's initial approach to it in the draft.

DIVORCING THE DRAFT

Sometimes I ask my students to generalize about how they approach the writing process for most papers by asking them to divide a continuum into three parts corresponding to how much time, roughly, they devote to prewriting, drafting, and rewriting. Then I play "writing doctor" and diagnose their problems, particularly resistance to revision. Figure 9.1 depicts a typical example for most of my first-year writing students.

> Revision, as the name implies, is a *re-seeing* of the paper's topic and the writer's initial approach to it in the draft.

The writing process shown in Figure 9.1 obviously invests lots of time in the drafting stage and very little time in prewriting or rewriting. For most of my students, this means toiling over the first draft, starting and then starting over, carefully hammering every word into place. For students who use this process, strong resistance to revision is a typical symptom. It's easy to imagine why. If you invest all that time in the first draft, trying to make it as good as you can, you'll be either too exhausted to consider a revision, delusional about the paper's quality, or, most likely, so invested in the draft's approach to the topic that revision seems impossible or a waste of time.

There also is another pattern among resistant revisers. Students who tend to spend a relatively long time on the prewriting stage also struggle with revision. My theory is that some of these writers resist revision as a final stage in

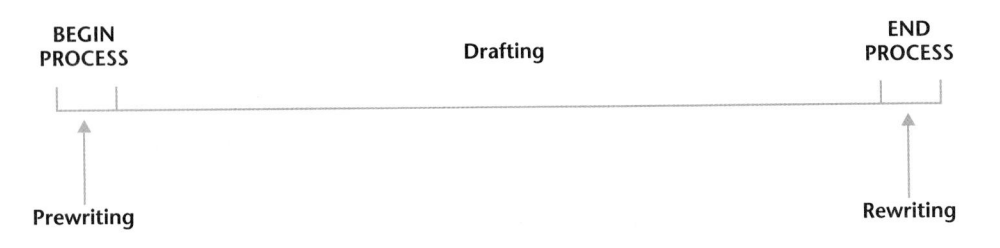

Figure 9.1   How some writers who resist revision typically divide their time between the three elements of the writing process: prewriting, drafting, and rewriting. The most time is devoted to writing the first draft, but not much time is given to prewriting and rewriting.

the process because *they have already practiced some revision at the beginning of the process.* We often talk about revision as occurring only after you've written a draft, which of course is a quite sensible idea. But the process of revision is an effort to *re-see* a subject, to circle it with questions, to view it from fresh angles; and many of the open-ended writing methods we've discussed in *The Curious Writer* certainly involve revision. Fastwriting, clustering, listing, and similar invention techniques all invite the writer to re-see. Armed with these discoveries, some writers may be able to write fairly strong first drafts.

What is essential, however, whether you revise at the beginning of the writing process or, as most writers do, after you craft the draft, is achieving some separation from what you initially thought, what you initially said, and how you said it. To revise well, writers must divorce the draft.

STRATEGIES FOR DIVORCING THE DRAFT

You can do some things to make separation from your work easier, and spending less time on the first draft and more time on the revision process is one of them. But aside from writing fast drafts, what are other strategies for re-seeing a draft that already has a hold on you?

1. **Take some time.** Absolutely the best remedy for revision resistance is setting the draft aside for a week or more. Professional writers, in fact, may set a piece aside for several years and then return to it with a fresh, more critical perspective. Students simply don't have that luxury. But if you can take a week or a month—or even a day—the wait is almost always worth it.

2. **Attack the draft physically.** A cut-and-paste revision that reduces a draft to pieces is often enormously helpful because you're no longer confronted with the familiar full draft, a version that may have cast a spell on you. By dismembering the draft, you can examine the smaller fragments more critically. How does each piece relate to the whole? Might there be alternative structures? What about gaps in information? (See Revision Strategy 9.18 later in this chapter for a useful cut-and-paste exercise.)

3. **Put it away.** Years ago I wrote a magazine article about alcoholism. It was about twenty-five pages long and it wasn't very good. I read and reread that draft, completely puzzled about how to rewrite it. One morning, I woke up and vowed I would read the draft just once more, then put it away in a drawer and start all over again, trusting that I would remember what was important. The result was much shorter and much better. In fact, I think it's the best essay I've ever written. Getting a troublesome draft out of sight—literally—may be the best way to find new ways to see it.

4. **Ask readers to respond.** Bringing other people's eyes and minds to your work allows you to see your drafts through perspectives other than your own. Other people have a completely different relationship with your writing

than you do. They will see what you don't. They easily achieve the critical distance that you are trying to cultivate when you revise.

5. **Write different leads.** The nonfiction writer John McPhee once talked about beginnings as the hardest thing to write. He described a lead as a "flashlight that shines down into the story," illuminating where the draft is headed. Imagine, then, the value of writing a new beginning, or even several alternative beginnings; each may point the next draft in a slightly different direction, perhaps one that you didn't consider in your first draft.

6. **Conduct research.** One of the central themes of *The Curious Writer* is that research isn't a separate activity but a source of information that can enrich almost any kind of writing. Particularly in genres such as the personal essay, in which the writer's voice, perspective, and experience dominate the draft, listening to the voices and knowledge of others about a topic can deepen and shift the writer's thinking and perspectives.

7. **Read aloud.** I always ask students in workshop groups to read their drafts aloud to each other. I do this for several reasons, but the most important is the effect that *hearing* a draft has on a writer's relationship to it. In a sense, we often hear a draft in our heads as we compose it or reread it, but when we read the words aloud the draft comes alive as something separate from the writer. As the writer listens to herself—or listens to someone else read her prose—she may cringe at an awkward sentence, suddenly notice a leap in logic, or recognize the need for an example. Try reading the work aloud to yourself and the same thing may happen.

8. **Write in your journal.** One of the strategies you can use to divorce the draft is to return to your notebook and fastwrite to yourself about what you might do to improve the piece. You can do this by asking yourself questions about the draft and then—through writing—attempt to answer them. The method can help you see a new idea that may become key to the structure of your next draft. Too often we see the journal exclusively as a prewriting tool, but it can be useful throughout the writing process, particularly when you need to think to yourself about ways to solve a problem in revision.

Later in this chapter, we'll build on some of these basic strategies with specific revision methods that may work with particular kinds of writing and with drafts that have particular problems. All of these methods encourage a separation between the writer and his or her draft or rely on that critical distance to be effective.

PHOTOGRAPHY AS A METAPHOR FOR REVISION

For several years, I taught composition by asking students to bring along a camera. The idea grew out of an experience I had in a graduate seminar with my friend and mentor Donald Murray, in which we were asked to apprentice to a creative activity and then write about how the process seemed to compare to the ways we write. I chose photography. It became clear almost immediately that there were dramatic parallels between the composing processes in each; the most striking was how much taking pictures taught me about revision.

What does it really mean to revise, or put another way, to *re-see*? What might be rewarding about such an effort? For many, revision may involve little more than proofreading a first draft. But when most experienced writers imagine revision, they mean something much less superficial (not that proofreading is unimportant!). Rewriting may involve adding or cutting information, reorganizing the draft, or even rebuilding around a new angle or purpose. This kind of revision grows from the conviction that when we first look at a topic there is much we don't notice, and this is a lesson photography teaches as well.

When I first ask my students to go out and take pictures, the only instruction I provide is that they must shoot an entire roll of film. I don't suggest photographic subjects, and I don't offer tips on technique. "Just go out and take a roll of pictures," I say, "and bring back the slides next week." The results are almost always the same: Every student in the class takes one photograph of every subject, a shot that usually captures it in the most familiar angle and light conditions—the school building from across the street, the roommate or friend squinting into the sun, the long shot down the beach at midday. Rarely were these particularly interesting pictures.

The same might be said of first drafts, especially those written in a rush the night before the paper is due. The writer pretty much goes with the first picture of his topic that he sees, and revision is pretty limited to "fixing" things here and there at the last minute. One common characteristic of these one-draft papers is that they often seize on the most obvious point or idea about their topics. A paper on the accuracy of "smart bombs" argues that they aren't always smart. Or a personal essay on fading friendships concludes that "true friends are hard to find." There isn't anything wrong with stating the obvious in a first draft *if* in a revision you plan to dig more deeply, working toward a fresher argument, a better insight, a less familiar way of seeing.

My students' first roll of film makes this point really well. When you take only one picture of a subject, you're not likely to see beyond what you've already seen. Our first look at almost anything is likely to reveal only what's most obvious about it. If we *really* want to see, if we really want to learn something we don't already know, we have to look and then look again. Speaking photographically, deep revision requires that we take more than one picture.

The value of taking more than one picture becomes apparent to my students when I ask them to complete a second assignment with their cameras. This time, I say, choose only two subjects from the first roll and take twelve shots of each one. Make every shot different by varying distance, angle, and light conditions. By composing multiple "drafts" of their subjects, even novice photographers discover new ways of seeing things they've seen before. They see the pattern of three kinds of stone that come together on the corner of Thompson Hall—something they never really noticed before although they walk by the building every day. They see the way the fire escapes cling like black iron insects to the west side of the building, its bricks bloodied by the setting sun. They see the delicate structure of a tulip or their best friend's hand, roughened by a summer of carpentry. Once my students get past the first few pictures of a subject, they really begin to see it freshly. More often than not, the twelfth picture is much more interesting than the fifth or sixth. The principle is simple: *The more you look, the more you see.*

Although the Greek meaning of the word is "light writing," photography, of course, is *not* writing. It really isn't hard to look through a camera, take a bunch of pictures, and re-see a subject. Doing this in writing is more difficult, because we must "see" through language. Words often get in the way. Yet the motive for revision in writing isn't much different from a photographer's inclination to take more than one shot—both writer and photographer know not to trust their first look at something. They know they won't see it well enough, so both writers and photographers use a process that helps them to see their subjects in new ways. The rewards for doing this are similar, too: the pleasure of surprise and discovery, of learning something new about their subjects and about themselves.

> The motive for revision is like a photographer's inclination to take more than one shot—both writer and photographer know not to trust their first look at something.

FIVE CATEGORIES OF REVISION

The following kinds of writers are typically ones who most need to revise:

1. Writers of fast drafts
2. Writers who compose short drafts
3. Writers who indulge in creative, but not critical, thinking
4. Writers who rarely go past their initial way of seeing things
5. Writers who have a hard time imagining a reader other than themselves
6. Writers who rely on limited sources of information
7. Writers who still aren't sure what they're trying to say
8. Writers who haven't found their own way of saying what they want to say
9. Writers who haven't delivered on their promises
10. Writers who think their draft is "perfect"

These are the usual suspects for revision, but there are many more. In general, if you think there's more to think about, more to learn, more to say, and better ways to say it, then revision is the route to surprise and discovery. Most writers agree that rewriting is a good idea, but where should they start?

Problems in drafts vary enormously. But the diagnosis tends to involve concerns in five general areas: purpose, meaning, information, structure, and clarity and style. Here are some typical reader responses to drafts with each kind of problem:

1. **Problems with Purpose**
   - "I don't know why the writer is writing this paper."
   - "The beginning of the essay seems to be about one thing, and the rest of it is about several others."
   - "I think there are about three different topics in the draft. Which one do you want to write about?"
   - "So what?"

2. **Problems with Meaning**
   - "I can't tell what the writer is trying to say in the draft."
   - "There doesn't seem to be a point behind all of this."
   - "I think there's a main idea, but there isn't much information on it."
   - "I thought the thesis was saying something pretty obvious."

3. **Problems with Information**
   - "Parts of the draft seemed really pretty vague or general."
   - "I couldn't really *see* what you were talking about."
   - "It seemed like you needed some more facts to back up your point."
   - "It needs more detail."

4. **Problems with Structure**
   - "I couldn't quite follow your thinking in the last few pages."
   - "I was confused about when this happened."
   - "I understood your point but I couldn't figure out what this part had to do with it."
   - "The draft doesn't really flow very well."

5. **Problems with Clarity and Style**
   - "This seems a little choppy."
   - "You need to explain this better. I couldn't quite follow what you were saying in this paragraph."
   - "This sentence seems really awkward to me."
   - "This doesn't have a strong voice."

PROBLEMS WITH PURPOSE

A draft that answers the *So what?* question is a draft with a purpose. Often enough, however, writers' intentions aren't all that clear to readers and they don't have a strong reason to keep reading.

It's a little like riding a tandem bike. The writer sits up front and steers while the reader occupies the seat behind, obligated to pedal but with no control over where the bike goes. As soon as the reader senses that the writer isn't steering anywhere in particular, then the reader will get off the bike. Why do all that pedaling if the bike seems to be going nowhere?

Frequently, when you begin writing about something, you don't have any idea where you're headed; that's exactly *why* you're writing about the subject in the first place. When we write such discovery drafts, revision often begins by looking for clues about your purpose. What you learn then becomes a key organizing principle for the next draft, trying to clarify this purpose to your readers. The first question, therefore, is one writers must answer for themselves: "Why am I writing this?" Of course, if it's an assignment it's hard to get past the easy answer—"Because I have to"—but if the work is going to be any good, there must be a better answer than that. Whether your topic is open or assigned, you have to find your own reason to write about it, and what you discover becomes an answer to your bike partner's nagging question, yelled into the wind from the seat behind you: "If I'm going to pedal this hard, you better let me know where we're going."

In general, writers' motives behind writing often involve more than one of these following four purposes.

1. **To explore.** One way to handle complicated questions is to approach the answers in an open-ended way; the writer writes to discover what he thinks or how he feels and reports to the reader on these discoveries.

2. **To explain.** Much of the writing we encounter in daily life is meant simply to provide us with information: This is how the coffeemaker works, or this is the best way to prepare for a trip to New Zealand. Expository writing frequently explains and describes.

3. **To evaluate.** In a sense, all writing is evaluative because it involves making judgments. For instance, when you explain how to plan a New Zealand vacation, you're making judgments about where to go. But when the explicit purpose is to present a judgment about something, the writer encourages readers to see the world the way the writer does. He or she may want the reader to think or behave a certain way: It makes sense to abolish pennies because they're more trouble than they're worth, or you should vote for the bond issue because it's the best way to save the foothills.

4. **To reflect.** Less frequently, we write to stand back from what we're writing about and consider *how* we're thinking about the subject, the methods we're using to write about it, and what we might learn from this writing situation that might apply to others.

Revision Strategy 9.1: The Motive Statement

It may help to begin a revision by attempting to determine your *primary motive* for the next draft. Do you want to explore your topic, explain something to your readers, offer a persuasive judgment, or step back and reflect on what you're saying or how you're saying it? The genre of writing has a great deal to do with this (see the following table). If you're writing a personal essay, your purpose is likely to be exploratory. If you're writing a review, a proposal, a critical essay, or an argument essay, it's likely your primary motive is to evaluate. One way, then, to get some basic guidance for the next draft is to carefully craft the second half of the following sentence: My primary motive in writing this paper is to explore/evaluate/explain/reflect about _____.

Genre	Primary Motive
Personal essay	Explore
Profile	Explore or explain
Review	Evaluate
Proposal	Evaluate
Argument	Evaluate
Critical essay	Evaluate
Ethnographic essay	Explore or evaluate
Research essay	Explore or evaluate
Reflective essay	Reflect

Of course, any one essay may involve all four motives, but for the purpose of this exercise, choose your *main* purpose in writing the essay. Composing the second half of the sentence may not be so easy because it challenges you to limit your subject. For instance, the following is far too ambitious for, say, a five-page essay: My main motive in writing this paper is to evaluate the steps taken to deal with terrorism and judge whether they're adequate. That's simply too big a subject for a brief persuasive paper. This is more reasonable: My main motive in writing this paper is to evaluate passenger screening procedures in Europe and decide whether they're better than those in the United States.

Since largely exploratory pieces often are motivated by questions, a writer of a personal essay might compose the following sentence: My main motive in writing this essay is to explore why I felt relieved when my father died.

After you craft your motive sentence, put it on a piece of paper or index card and post it where you can see it as you revise the draft. Periodically ask yourself, *What does this paragraph or this section of the draft have to do with my main motive?* The answer will help you decide what to cut and what needs more development in the next draft. Remember, the essay should be organized around this motive from beginning to end.

Revision Strategy 9.2: What Do You Want to Know About What You Learned?

Because inquiry-based writing is usually driven by questions rather than answers, one way to discover your purpose in a sketch or draft is to generate a list of questions it raises for you. Of course, you hope that one of them might be

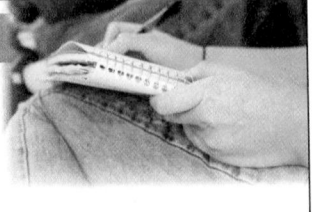

ONE STUDENT'S RESPONSE

Julia's Draft

What do I understand about this topic now that I didn't understand before I started writing about it?

After writing this essay, I understand more clearly that there's a relationship between a girl's eating disorders and how her father treats her as a child.

LIST OF QUESTIONS

- Why the father and not the mother?
- What is it about father/daughter relationships that make them so vulnerable to feminine body images?
- Is the father's influence on a girl's body image greater at certain ages or stages in her life?
- How can a father be more informed about his impact on a daughter's body image?

behind your purpose in the next draft. Try the following steps with a draft that needs a stronger sense of purpose.

1. Choose a draft or sketch you'd like to revise, and reread it.

2. On the back of the manuscript, craft an answer to the following question: *What do I understand about this topic now that I didn't understand before I started writing about it?*

3. Next, if you can, build a list of questions—perhaps new ones—that this topic still raises for you. Make this list as long as you can, and don't censor yourself (see "One Student's Response" above).

4. Choose one or more of the questions as a prompt for a fastwrite. Follow your writing to see where it leads and what it might suggest about new directions for the revision.

5. If you can't think of any questions, or find you didn't learn much from writing about the topic (step 2), you may have several options. One is to abandon the draft altogether. Is it possible that this topic simply doesn't interest you anymore? If abandoning the draft isn't possible, then you need to find a new angle. Try Revision Strategy 9.3.

Revision Strategy 9.3: Finding the Focusing Question

The best topics, and the most difficult to write about, are those that raise questions for you. In a sketch or first draft, you may not know what these questions are. But if your subsequent drafts are going to be purposeful and focused, then discovering the main question behind your essay is essential. This is particularly important in essays that are research based because the drafts are longer and you're often trying to manage a lot of information. This revision strategy works best when it's a class activity.

1. Begin by simply putting your essay topic on the top of a large piece of paper such as newsprint or butcher paper. If yours is a research topic—say, Alzheimer's disease—jot that down. Post your paper on the classroom wall.

2. Spend a few minutes writing a few sentences explaining why you chose to write about this topic in the first place.

3. Make a quick list of everything you *already know* (if anything) about your topic—for instance, surprising facts or statistics, the extent of the problem, important people or institutions involved, key schools of thought, common misconceptions, familiar clichés that apply to the topic, observations you've made, important trends, and typical perspectives. Spend about five minutes on this.

4. Now spend fifteen or twenty minutes brainstorming a list of questions about your topic that you'd love to learn the answers to. Make this list as long as possible.

5. As you look around the room, you'll see a gallery of topics and questions on the walls. You can help each other. Circulate around the room and do two things: add a question that you're interested in about a particular topic, and check the question (yours or someone else's) that seems most interesting.

When you return to your newsprint or butcher paper, it should be covered with questions. How will you decide which of them might provide the best focus for the next draft? Consider the following criteria as you try to make this decision:

- **What question do you find most intriguing?** After all, it's your essay, and it should be driven by your own interests in the subject.

- **Which question seems most manageable?** This mostly has to do with the level of generality or specificity of the question. You want a focusing question that isn't too general or too specific. For example, a question such as *What causes international terrorism?* is a landscape question—it contains so much possible territory that you'll never get a close look at anything. But a question such as *How effective has the Saudi royal family been in limiting terrorist activities?* is a much more focused, and therefore manageable, question.

- **What question seems most appropriate for the assignment?** For example, if you're assigned a research essay, certain questions are more likely than others to send you to the library. If you're writing a persuasive essay, gravitate toward a question that might point you toward a claim or thesis.

- **What seems most relevant to the information you've already collected?** It would be convenient if information from your research or first draft is relevant to the question that's behind the next draft. While this might make the revision go more quickly, always be open to the possibility that a question that takes you in new directions might simply be more interesting to you.

- **What question is likely to yield answers that interest your readers?** You already have a sense of this from the questions that students in your class added to your newsprint about your topic. The challenge in any piece of writing, of course, is to answer the *So what?* question. Does your focusing question promise to lead you somewhere that readers would care to go?

Revision Strategy 9.4: What's the Relationship?

One of the more common purposes for all kinds of essays is to explore a relationship between two or more things. We see this in research all the time. What's the relationship between AIDS and IV drug use in China? What's the relationship between gender and styles of collaboration in the workplace? What's the social class relationship between Huck and Tom in *The Adventures of Huckleberry Finn*?

One way, then, to clarify your purpose in revision is to try to identify the relationship that may be at the heart of your inquiry. Relationships between things can be described in a couple different ways.

- **Cause and effect.** What is the relationship between my father's comments about my looks and my eating disorder when I was a teenager? What is the relationship between the second Iraqi war and destabilization in Saudi Arabia? What is the relationship between the decline of the Brazilian rain forest and the extinction of the native eagles? What is the relationship between my moving to Idaho and the failure of my relationship with Kevin?

- **Compare and contrast.** How is jealousy distinguished from envy? How might writing instruction in high school be distinguished from writing instruction in college? What are the differences and similarities between my experiences at the Rolling Stones concert last month and my experiences at the Stones concert fifteen years ago?

Review your sketch or draft to determine whether what you're really trying to write about is the relationship between two (or more) things. In your journal, try to state this relationship in sentences similar to those listed here. With this knowledge, return to the draft and revise from beginning to end with this purpose in mind. What do you need to add to the next draft to both clarify and develop the relationship you're focusing on? What should you cut that is irrelevant to that focus?

PROBLEMS WITH MEANING

Fundamentally, most of us write something in an attempt to say something to someone else. The note my wife Karen left for me yesterday said it in a sentence: "Bruce—could you pick up some virgin olive oil and a loaf of bread?" I had no trouble deciphering the meaning of this note. But it isn't always that easy. Certain poems, for example, may be incredibly ambiguous texts, and readers may puzzle over them for hours, coming up with a range of plausible interpretations of meaning. (See Figure 9.2.)

Where Does Meaning Come From?

Depending on the writing situation, you may know what you want to say from the start or you may *discover* what you think as you write and research. Inquiry-based projects usually emphasize discovery, while more conventional argument papers may rely on arriving at a thesis earlier in the process. It's something like the difference between sledding with a saucer or a flexible flyer. The saucer is likely to veer off course and you might find yourself somewhere unexpected, yet interesting.

TERMS TO DESCRIBE DOMINANT MEANING

- Thesis
- Main point
- Theme
- Controlling idea
- Central claim or assertion

No matter what you think about a topic when you start writing—even when you begin with a thesis to which you're committed—you can still change your

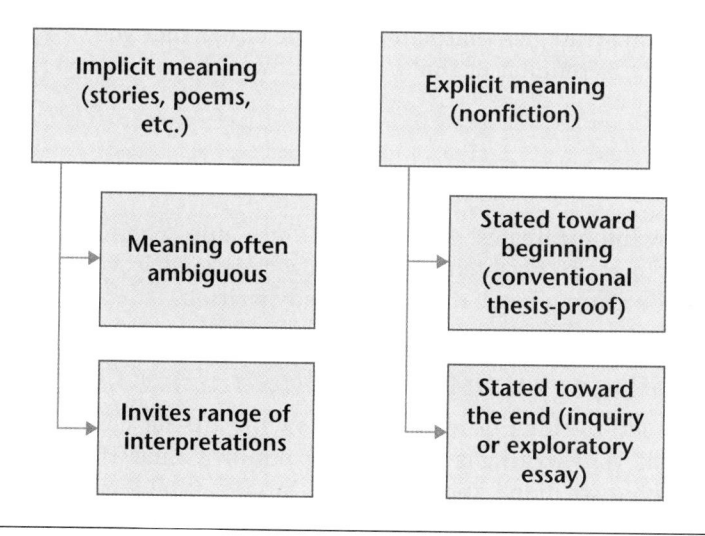

Figure 9.2   Depending on the genre, writers say it straight or tell it slant. In short stories, for example, the writers' ideas may be ambiguous, inviting interpretation. Nonfiction genres—the kind you will most often write in college and beyond—usually avoid ambiguity. Writers say what they mean as clearly and as persuasively as they can.

mind. You *should* change your mind if the evidence you've gathered leads you away from your original idea. Unfortunately, writers of thesis-driven papers and other deductive forms are far more resistant to any change in their thinking. In some writing situations—say, essay exams—this isn't a problem. But it's often important in academic writing, including arguments, to always be open to new insight.

Ideas about what we want to say on a writing topic grow from the following:

1. **Thesis.** This is a term most of us know from school writing, and it's most often associated with types of writing that work deductively from a main idea. Here's a sample thesis:

   The U.S. Securities and Exchange Commission is incapable of regulating an increasingly complex banking system.

2. **Theory.** We have strong hunches about how things work all the time, but we're not certain we're right. We test our theories and report on the accuracy of our hunches. Here's an example of a theory:

   Certain people just don't have a "head" for math.

3. **Question.** In a question-driven process, the emphasis is on discovery and you might work more inductively. You see or experience something that makes you wonder. Here's a question that led a writer to ideas about girls, advertising, and sexuality.

   Why does my ten-year-old want to dress like a hooker?

The revision strategies that follow assume either that you've got a tentative thesis and want to refine it or that you're still working on discovering what you want to say.

Methods for Discovering Your Thesis

Use the following strategies if you're not quite sure whether you know what you're trying to say in a sketch or draft. How can you discover clues about your main point or meaning in what you've already written?

Revision Strategy 9.5: Find the "Instructive Line"

It may seem odd to think of reading your own drafts for clues about what you mean. After all, your writing is a product of your own mind. But often a draft can reveal to us what we didn't know we knew—an idea that surfaces unexpectedly, a question that we keep asking, or a moment in a narrative that seems surprisingly significant. Part of the challenge is to recognize these clues to your own meanings, and understand what they suggest about the revision.

This isn't always easy, which is one reason it's often so helpful to share your writing with other readers; they may see the clues that we miss. However, this revision strategy depends on reading your own drafts more systematically for clues about what your point might be. What do you say in this draft that might suggest what you really want to say in the next one?

1. **Find the "instructive line."** Every draft is made up of many sentences. But which of these is *the most important sentence or passage*? What do I mean by *important*? Which line or passage points to a larger idea, theme, or feeling that seems to rise above much of the draft and illuminates the significance or relevance of many other lines and passages? The writer Donald Murray calls this the "instructive line," the sentence that seems to point upward toward the meaning of what you've set down. Underline the instructive line or passage in your draft. It may be subtle, only hinting at larger ideas or feelings, or quite explicitly stated. In a narrative essay, the instructive line might be a moment of stepping back to reflect—"As I look back on this now, I understand that..." In a review or persuasive essay, it might be an assertion of some kind—"American moviegoers are seduced by the 'twist' at the end of a film, and learn to expect it."

2. **Follow the thread of meaning.** If the instructive line is a ball of string, tightly packed with coils of meaning that aren't readily apparent, then to get any guidance for revision you need to try to unravel it. At the top of a journal page, write the line or passage you selected in your draft as most important. Use it as a prompt for five minutes of exploratory writing, perhaps beginning with the following seed sentence: I think/feel this is true because...and also because...and also...and also...

3. **Compose a thesis.** Reread your fastwriting in the preceding step and, keeping your original passage in mind, craft a single sentence that best captures the most important idea or feeling you'd like to bring into the next draft. For example, *Because of the expectation, encouraged by Hollywood, that every good movie has a surprise ending, American moviegoers often find even superior foreign films a disappointment.*

4. **Post it.** Put this thesis on the wall above your computer, or use a Post-it note and place the thesis on your computer screen. Revise with the thesis in mind, from beginning to end. Add information that will *illustrate, extend, exemplify, complicate, clarify, support, show, provide background,* or *prove* the thesis. Cut information from the draft that does none of these things.

Revision Strategy 9.6: Looping Toward a Thesis

I've argued throughout *The Curious Writer* for a dialectical approach to writing, moving back and forth between creative and critical modes of thinking, from your observations of and your ideas about, from generating and judging, from specifics and generalities. This is how writers can make meaning. The approach can also be used as a revision strategy, this time in a technique called *loop writing*. When you loop write, you move back and forth dialectically between both modes of thought—opening things up and then trying to pin them down. I imagine that this looks like an hourglass.

1. Reread the draft quickly, and then turn it upside down on your desk. You won't look at it again but trust that you'll remember what's important.

2. Begin a three-minute fastwrite on the draft in which you tell yourself the story of your thinking about the essay. When you first started writing it, what did you think you were writing about, and then what, and then...Try to focus on your ideas about what you were trying to say and how it evolved.

3. Sum up what you said in your fastwrite by answering the following question in a sentence: *What seems to be the most important thing I've finally come to understand about my topic?*

4. Begin another three-minute fastwrite. Focus on scenes, situations, case studies, moments, people, conversations, observations, and so on that stand out for you as you think about the draft. Think especially of specifics that come to mind that led to the understanding of your topic that you stated in the preceding step. Some of this information may be in the draft, but some may *not* yet be in the draft.

5. Finish by restating the main point you want to make in the next draft. Begin the revision by thinking about a lead or introduction that dramatizes this point. Consider a suggestive scene, case study, finding, profile, description, comparison, anecdote, conversation, situation, or observation that points the essay toward your main idea (see the "Inquiring into the Details: Types of Leads" box on page 350). For example, if your point is that your university's program to help second-language learners is inadequate, you could begin the next draft by telling the story of Maria, an immigrant from Guatemala who was a victim of poor placement in a composition course that she was virtually guaranteed to fail. Follow this lead into the draft, always keeping your main point or thesis in mind.

Revision Strategy 9.7: Reclaiming Your Topic

When you do a lot of research on your topic, you may reach a point when you feel awash in information. It's easy at such moments to feel as if you're losing control of your topic, besieged by the voices of experts, a torrent of statistics and facts, and competing perspectives. Your success in writing the paper depends on making it your own again, gaining control over the information for your own purposes, in the service of your own questions or arguments. This revision strategy, a variation of Revision Strategy 9.6, should help you gain control of the material you collected for a research-based inquiry project.

1. Spend ten or fifteen minutes reviewing all of the notes you've taken and skimming key articles or passages from books. Glance at your most important sources. If you have a rough draft, reread it. Let your head swim with information.

2. Now clear your desk of everything but your journal. Remove all your notes and materials. If you have a rough draft, put it in the drawer.

3. Now fastwrite about your topic for seven full minutes. Tell the story of how your thinking about the topic has evolved. When you began, what did you think? What were your initial assumptions or preconceptions? Then what happened, and what happened after that? Keep your pen moving.

4. Skip a few lines in your notebook, and write Moments, Stories, People, and Scenes. Now fastwrite for another seven minutes, this time focusing more on specific case studies, situations, people, experiences, observations, facts, and so on that stand out in your mind from the research you've done so far, or perhaps from your own experience with the topic.

5. Skip a few more lines. For another seven minutes, write a dialogue between you and someone else about your topic. Choose someone who you think is typical of the audience you're writing for. If it helps, think of someone specific—an instructor, a fellow student, a friend. Don't plan the dialogue. Just begin with the question most commonly asked about your topic, and take the conversation from there, writing both parts of the dialogue.

6. Finally, skip a few more lines and write these two words in your notebook: So what? Now spend a few minutes trying to summarize the most important thing you think your readers should understand about your topic, based on what you've learned so far. Distill this into a sentence or two.

As you work your way to the last step, you're reviewing what you've learned about your topic without being tyrannized by the many voices, perspectives, and facts in the research you've collected. The final step, Step 6, leads you toward a thesis statement. In the revision, keep this in mind as you reopen your notes, reread your sources, and check on facts. Remember in the rewrite to put all of this information in the service of this main idea, as examples or illustrations, necessary background, evidence or support, counterexamples, and ways of qualifying or extending your main point.

Revision Strategy 9.8: Believing and Doubting

In persuasive writing such as the argument, review, proposal, or research paper, we often feel that a thesis involves picking sides—"the play was good" or "the play was bad," "the novel was boring" or "the novel was fun to read." Instead of *either/or*, consider *both/and*. This might bring you to a more truthful, more sophisticated understanding of your subject, which rarely is either all bad or all good. One way to do this is to play Peter Elbow's doubting game and believing game.

1. Set aside ten to twelve minutes for two episodes of fastwriting in your journal or on the computer. First, spend a full five minutes playing the "believing game" (see the following prompts), exploring the merits of your subject even

if (and especially if) you don't think it has any. Then switch to the "doubting game." Write fast for another five minutes using a skeptical mind.

THE BELIEVING GAME	**THE DOUBTING GAME**
Give the author, performer, text, or performance the benefit of the doubt. Suspend criticism.	Adopt a critical stance. Look for holes, weaknesses, omissions, problems.
1. What seems true or truthful about what is said, shown, or argued?	1. What seems unbelievable or untrue?
2. How does it confirm your own experiences or observations of the same things?	2. What does it fail to consider or consider inadequately?
3. What did you like or agree with?	3. Where is the evidence missing or insufficient, or where do the elements not work together effectively?
4. Where is it strongest, most compelling, most persuasive?	4. How does it fail to meet your criteria for good in this category of thing?
5. How does it satisfy your criteria for being good, useful, convincing, or moving?	5. Where is it the least compelling or persuasive? Why?

2. From this work in your notebook, try to construct a sentence—a thesis—that is more than a simple statement of the worth or worthlessness of the thing you're evaluating, but an expression of *both* its strengths and weaknesses: Although _____ succeeds (or fails) in _____, it mostly _____. For example: Although reality television presents viewers with an often interesting glimpse into how ordinary people handle their fifteen minutes of celebrity, it mostly exaggerates life by creating drama where there often is none.

Methods for Refining Your Thesis

You may emerge from writing a draft with a pretty clear sense of what you want to say in the next one. But does this idea seem a little obvious or perhaps too general? Does it fail to adequately express what you really feel and think? Use one or more of the following revision strategies to refine a thesis, theme, or controlling idea.

Revision Strategy 9.9: Questions as Knives

Imagine that your initial feeling, thesis, or main point is like an onion. Ideas, like onions, have layers, and to get closer to their hearts you need to cut through the most obvious outer layers to reveal what is less obvious, probably more specific, and almost certainly more interesting. Questions are to ideas as knives are to onions: They help you slice past your initial impressions. The most important question—the sharpest knife in the drawer—is simply *Why? Why* was the Orwell essay interesting? *Why* do you hate foreign films? *Why* should the university do more for second-language speakers? *Why* did you feel a sense of loss when the old cornfield was paved over for the mall?

Why may be the sharpest knife in the drawer, but there are other *W* questions with keen blades, too, including *What?, Where?, When?,* and *Who?* In Figure 9.3 you can see how these questions can cut a broad thesis down to size. The result is a much more specific, more interesting controlling idea for the next draft.

1. Subject your tentative thesis to the same kind of narrowing. Write your theme, thesis, or main point as a single sentence in your notebook.
2. Slice it with questions and restate it each time.
3. Continue this until your point is appropriately sliced; that is, when you feel that you've gone beyond the obvious and stated what you think or feel in a more specific and interesting way.

As before, rewrite the next draft with this new thesis in mind, reorganizing the essay around it from beginning to end. Add new information that supports the idea, provides the necessary background, offers opposing views, or extends it. Cut information that no longer seems relevant to the thesis.

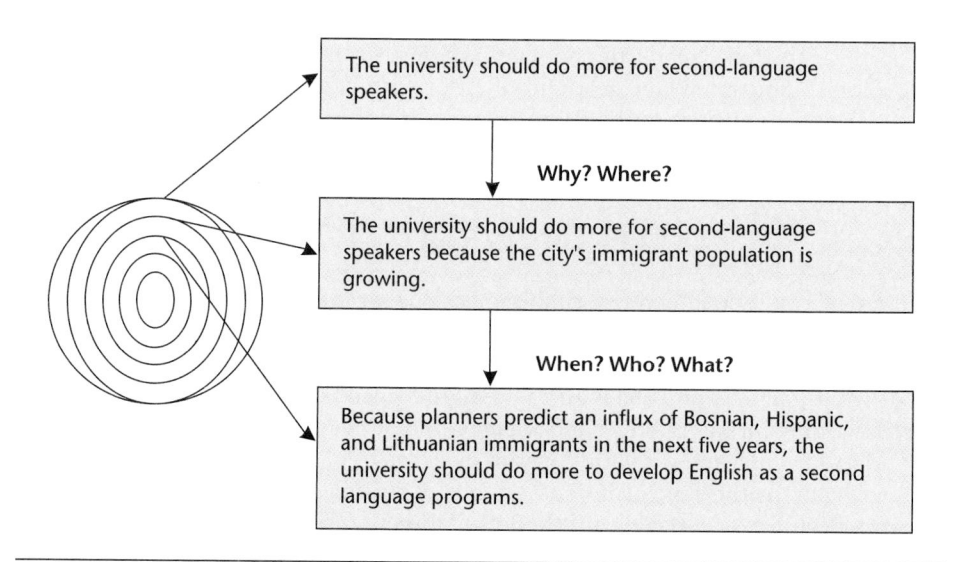

Figure 9.3   Why? Where? When? Who? and What? Using questions to narrow the focus of a thesis is like using a knife to cut into the heart of an onion.

Revision Strategy 9.10: Qualifying Your Claim

In your research you discovered that, while 90 percent of Americans think that their fellow citizens are too "fat," only 39 percent would describe themselves that way. This evidence leads you to make the following claim: *Although Americans agree that obesity is a national problem, their response is typical: it's somebody else's problem, an attitude that will cripple efforts to promote healthier lifestyles.* This seems like a logical assertion if the evidence is reliable. But if you're going to try to build an argument around it, a claim should be rigorously examined. Toulmin's approach to analyzing arguments provides a method for doing this.

1. Toulmin observes that sometimes a claim should be *qualified* to be more accurate and persuasive. The initial question is simple: *Is what you're asserting always or universally true?* Essentially, you're being challenged to examine your certainty about what you're saying. This might lead you to add words or phrases to it that acknowledge your sense of certainty: *sometimes, always, mostly, in this case, based on available evidence,* and so on. In this case, the claim is already qualified by specifying that it is limited to Americans, but it is also based on evidence from a single source. The claim, therefore, might be qualified to say this: *Although one survey suggests that Americans agree that obesity is a national problem, their response is typical: it's somebody else's problem, an attitude that will cripple efforts to promote healthier lifestyles.*

2. Imagining how your claim might be rebutted is another way to strengthen it. How might someone take issue with your thesis? What might be the exceptions to what you're saying is true? For example, might someone object to the assertion that Americans "typically" respond by putting their heads in the sand when personally confronted with problems? You must decide then whether this clever aside in your claim is something you're prepared to support. If not, cut it.

PROBLEMS WITH INFORMATION

Writers who've spent enough time generating or collecting information about their topics can work from abundance rather than scarcity. This is an enormous advantage because the ability to throw stuff away means you can be selective about what you use, and the result is a more focused draft. But as we revise, our purpose and point might shift, and we may find ourselves in the unhappy position of working from scarcity again. Most of our research, observation, or fastwriting was relevant to the triggering subject in the initial sketch or draft, not to the generated subject we decide is the better direction for the next draft. In some cases, this might require that you research the new topic or return to the generating activities of listing, fastwriting, clustering, and so on that will help provide information for the next draft.

More often, however, writers don't have to begin from scratch in revision. Frequently, a shift in the focus or refining a thesis in a first draft just means emphasizing different information or perhaps filling in gaps in later drafts. The strategies that follow will help you solve this problem.

Revision Strategy 9.11: Explode a Moment

The success of personal essays that rely on narratives frequently depends on how well the writer renders an important scene, situation, moment, or description. When you're telling a story from experience, not all parts of the story are equally important. As always, emphasis in a narrative depends on the writer's purpose in the essay. For example, Matt's essay on the irony of the slow poisoning of Butte, Montana, his home town, by a copper mine that once gave the city life would emphasize those parts of the story that best highlight that irony. Or a description of the agonizing death of the snow geese that unwittingly landed on the acid pond—their white beauty set against the deadly dark water—might be an important scene in Matt's next draft; it nicely portrays life and death, beauty and ugliness in much the same way the town and the mine might be contrasted. Matt should "explode that moment" because it's an important part of the story he's trying to tell about his Montana home town.

If you're trying to revise a draft that relies on narratives, this revision strategy will help you first identify moments, scenes, or descriptions that might be important in the next draft, and then develop these as more important parts of your story.

1. Choose a draft that involves a story or stories.

2. Make a list in your journal of the moments (for example, scenes, situations, and turning points) that stand out in the narrative.

3. Circle one that you think is most important to your purpose in the essay. It could be the situation that is most telling, a dramatic turning point, the moment of a key discovery that is central to what you're trying to say, or a scene that illustrates the dilemma or raises the question you're exploring in the draft.

4. Name that moment at the top of a blank journal page (for example, the snow geese on the acid pond, when the ice broke, or when I saw my grandfather in his coffin).

5. Now put yourself back into that moment and fastwrite about it for seven full minutes. Make sure that you write with as much detail as possible, *drawing on all your senses*. Write in the present tense if it helps.

6. Use this same method with other moments in the narrative that might deserve more emphasis in the next draft. Remember that real time means little in writing. An experience that took seven seconds can easily take up three pages of writing if it's detailed enough. Rewrite and incorporate the best of the new information in the next draft.

Revision Strategy 9.12: Beyond Examples

When we add information to a draft we normally think of adding examples. If you're writing a research essay on living with a sibling who suffers from Down syndrome, you might mention that your brother typically tries to avoid certain cognitive challenges. Members of your workshop group wonder, "Well, what kind of challenges?" In revision, you add an example or two from your own experience to clarify what you mean. This is, of course, a helpful strategy; examples of what you mean by an assertion are a kind of evidence that helps readers more fully understand your work. But also consider other types of information it might be helpful to add to the next draft. Use the following list to review your draft for additions you might not have thought of for revision.

- **Presenting counterarguments.** Typically, persuasive essays include information that represents an opposing view. Say you're arguing that beyond "avoidance" behaviors, there really aren't personality traits that can be attributed to most people with Down syndrome. You include a summary of a study that says otherwise. Why? Because it provides readers with a better understanding of the debate, and enhances the writer's ethos because you appear fair.

- **Providing background.** When you drop in on a conversation between two friends, you initially may be clueless about the subject. Naturally, you ask questions: "Who are you guys talking about? When did this happen? What did she say?" Answers to these questions provide a context that allows you to understand what is being said and to participate in the conversation. Background information like this is often essential in written communication, too. In a personal essay, readers may want to know when and where the event occurred or the relationship between the narrator and a character. In a critical essay, it might be necessary to provide background on the short story because readers may not have read it. In a research essay, it's often useful to provide background information about what has already been said on the topic and the research question.

- **Establishing significance.** Let's say you're writing about the problem of obesity in America, something that most of us are generally aware of these days. But the significance of the problem really strikes home when you add information from research suggesting that 30 percent of American adults are overweight, up from 23 percent just six years ago. It is even more important to establish the significance of a problem about which there is little awareness or consensus. For example, most people don't know that America's national park system is crumbling and in disrepair. Your essay on the problem needs to provide readers with information that establishes the significance of the problem. In a profile, readers need to have a reason to be interested in someone—perhaps your profile subject represents a particular group of people of interest or concern.

- **Giving it a face.** One of the best ways to make an otherwise abstract issue or problem come to life is to show what it means to an individual person. We can't fully appreciate the social impact of deforestation in Brazil without being introduced to someone such as Chico Mendes, a forest defender who was murdered for his activism. Obesity might be an abstract problem until we meet Carl, a 500-pound 22-year-old who is "suffocating in his own fat." Add case studies, anecdotes, profiles, and descriptions that put people on the page to make your essay more interesting and persuasive.

- **Defining it.** If you're writing about a subject your readers know little about, you'll likely use concepts or terms that readers will want you to define. What exactly do you mean, for example, when you say that the Internet is vulnerable to cyberterror? What exactly is cyberterror anyway? In your personal essay on your troubled relationship with your mother, what do you mean when you call her a narcissist? Frequently your workshop group will alert you to things in the draft that need defining, but also go through your own draft and ask yourself, *Will my readers know what I mean?*

Revision Strategy 9.13: Research

Too often, research is ignored as a revision strategy. We may do research for the first draft of a paper or essay, but never return to the library or search the Web to fill in gaps, answer new questions, or refine the focus of a rewrite. That's crazy, particularly because well-researched information can strengthen a draft of any kind. That has been one of the themes of *The Curious Writer* since the beginning of the book: Research is not a separate activity reserved only for the research paper, but a rich source of information for any type of writing. Try some of these strategies:

1. For quick facts, visit http://www.refdesk.com. This enormously useful Web site is the fastest way to find out the exact height of the Great Wall of China or the number of young women suffering from eating disorders in America today.

2. The *Library of Congress Subject Headings* will help you pinpoint the language you should use to search library databases on your topic. Particularly if the focus of your next draft is shifting, you'll need some fresh information to fill in the gaps. The *LCSH* will help you find more of it, more quickly.

3. To maximize Web coverage, launch a search on at least three different search engines (for example, Google, MSN Search, and Yahoo!), but this time search using terms or phrases from your draft that will lead you to more specific information that will fill gaps in the draft.

4. Interview someone relevant to your topic.

5. To ferret out some new sources on your topic, search library databases under author rather than keyword. Focus on authors that you know have something to say on your topic.

6. Develop as much knowledge as possible about your topic.

Revision Strategy 9.14: Backing Up Your Assumptions

Targeted research is particularly important when you're making an argument. In addition to providing evidence that is relevant to your thesis, frequently an argument rests on the assumptions behind that assertion. Stephen Toulmin calls these assumptions *warrants*. For example, suppose your claim is the following: *Although most Americans agree that obesity is a national problem, most don't describe themselves as fat, an attitude that will cripple efforts to promote healthier lifestyles.* Every claim rests on assumptions, or warrants. In other words, what do you have to believe is true to have faith in the accuracy of the claim?

1. Write your claim on the top of a journal page, and then list the assumptions or warrants on which it seems to rest. For example, the claim about obesity includes an assumption that most Americans equate the words *obesity* and *fat*. Also there's an assumption that public attitudes—particularly the view that there is a problem but it isn't my problem—hinder progress on public policy.

2. Which of the warrants behind your claim would be stronger if there were "backing" or evidence to support them? This will give you new direction for research. It might strengthen the argument on the obesity problem, for example, to draw on evidence from the civil rights struggle. Is there any evidence that attitudes toward personal responsibility for racism lagged behind acknowledgment of racial inequality as a national problem? Was progress finally made when this gap narrowed?

PROBLEMS WITH STRUCTURE

When it's working, the structure of a piece of writing is nearly invisible. Readers don't notice how the writer is guiding them from one piece of information to the next. When structure is a problem, the writer asks readers to walk out on a shaky bridge and trust that it will help them get to the other side, but the walkers can think of little else but the shakiness of the bridge. Some professional writers, such as John McPhee, obsess about structure, and for good reason—when you're working with a tremendous amount of information, as McPhee often does in his research-based essays, it helps to have a clear idea about how you'll use it.

It's helpful to distinguish two basic structures for writing. One typically organizes the information of experience, and one organizes our thinking so that it's clear and convincing. Typically, we use narrative, and especially chronology, to organize our experiences, though how we handle time can vary considerably. Writing that presents information based on the writer's reasoning—perhaps making an argument or reporting on an experiment—is logically structured. The most common example is the thesis-example, or thesis-proof, paper. Much formal academic writing relies on logical structures that use deduction or induction.

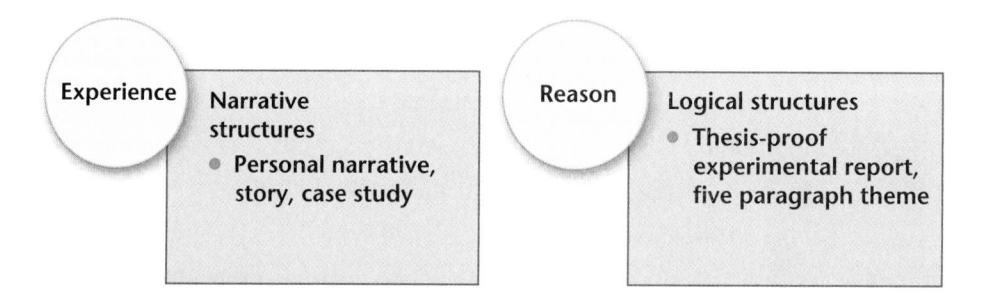

And yet some kinds of writing, like the researched essay or ethnography, may *combine* both patterns, showing how the writer reasoned through to the meaning of an experience, observation, reading, and so on. These essays tell a "narrative of thought."

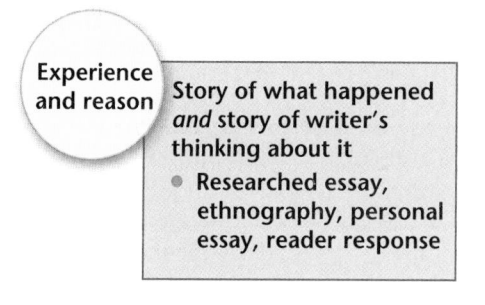

Formal Academic Structures

In some academic writing, the structure is prescribed. Scientific papers often have sections—Introduction, Methodology, Results, Discussion—but within those sections writers must organize their material. Certain writing assignments may also require you to organize your information in a certain way. The most common of these is the thesis/support structure. In such essays you typically establish your thesis in the first paragraph, spend the body of the paper assembling evidence that supports the thesis, and conclude the essay with a summary that restates the thesis in light of what's been said.

Thesis/support is a persuasive form, so it lends itself to arguments, critical essays, reviews, proposals, and similar pieces. In fact, you may have already structured your draft using this approach. If so, the following revision strategy may help you tighten and clarify the draft.

Beginning

- Establishes purpose (answers *So what?* question)
- Introduces question, dilemma, problem, theory, thesis, claim (sometimes dramatically)
- Helps readers understand—and feel—what's at stake for them

Middle

- Tests theory, claim, thesis against the evidence
- Develops reasons, with evidence, for writer's thesis or claim
- Tells story of writer's inquiry into question, problem, or dilemma

End

- Proposes answer, even if tentative, for writer's key question
- Revisits thesis or claim, extending, qualifying, contradicting, or reconfirming initial idea
- Raises new questions, poses new problems, or offers new understanding of what is at stake for readers

Revision Strategy 9.15: Beginnings, Middles, Ends, and the Work They Do

Stories, we are often told, always have a beginning, middle, and end. This may be the most fundamental structure of all, and it doesn't just apply to narratives. The figure above explains what a beginning, middle, and end might contribute to making nearly any piece of writing coherent and convincing. Apply some of these ideas to your draft.

1. Divide a draft you'd like to revise into three parts—beginning, middle, and end—by drawing lines in the paper to distinguish each section. Where you decide to divide the draft is entirely up to you; there's no formula to this. But you may change your mind as you go along.

2. Now use the figure above to analyze your beginning, middle, and end. Does each section do at least *one* of the listed tasks? If not, revise that section

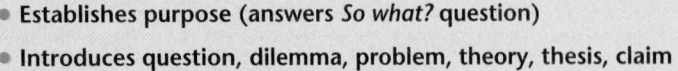

so that it does. This may involve adding one sentence or possibly paragraphs of new information, perhaps moving some from elsewhere in the draft.

3. Generally speaking, the middle of an essay does the most work, and so proportionally it should have the most information. For example, many essays look like this:

If you find, for example, that your beginning takes three pages of a five-page essay, then you might want to cut away at the first few pages and concentrate on developing the body of your essay.

Revision Strategy 9.16: Reorganizing Around Thesis and Support

Because the thesis/support structure is fairly common, it's useful to master. Most drafts, even if they weren't initially organized in that form, can be revised into a thesis/support essay. (Personal essays would be an exception.) The order of information in such an essay generally follows this design:

■ **Lead paragraph:** This paragraph introduces the topic and explicitly states the thesis, usually as the last sentence in the paragraph. For example, a thesis/support paper on the deterioration of America's national parks system might begin this way:

> Yellowstone National Park, which shares territory with Idaho, Montana, and Wyoming, is the nation's oldest park and, to some, its most revered. Established on March 1, 1872, the park features the Old Faithful geyser, which spouts reliably every 76 minutes on average. What isn't nearly as reliable these days is whether school groups will get to see it. Last year 60% of them were turned away because the park simply didn't have the staff. <u>This essay will argue that poor funding of our national parks system is a disgrace that threatens to undermine the Park Service's mission to preserve the areas "as cumulative expressions of a single national heritage" ("Famous Quotes").</u>

The thesis (underlined) is the final sentence in the paragraph, for emphasis.

- **Body:** Each succeeding paragraph until the final one attempts to prove or develop the thesis. Often each paragraph is devoted to a single *reason* why the thesis is true, frequently stated as the topic sentence of the paragraph. Specific information then explains, clarifies, and supports the reason. For example, here's a typical paragraph from the body of the national parks essay:

> <u>One aspect of the important national heritage at risk because of poor funding for national parks is the pride many Americans feel about these national treasures.</u> *Newsweek* writer Arthur Frommer calls the national park system among the "crowning glories of our democracy." He adds, "Not to have seen them is to have missed something unique and precious in American life" (12). To see the crumbling roads in Glacier National Park, or the incursion of development in Great Smoky Mountains National Park, or the slow strangulation of the Everglades is not just an ecological issue; it's a sorry statement about a democratic nation's commitment to some of the places that define its identity.

The underlined sentence is the topic sentence of the paragraph and is an assertion that supports and develops the thesis in the lead of the essay. The rest of the paragraph offers supporting evidence of the assertion, in this case a quotation from a *Newsweek* writer who recently visited several parks.

- **Concluding paragraph:** This paragraph reminds the reader of the central argument, not simply by restating the original thesis from the first paragraph but by reemphasizing some of the most important points. This may lead to an elaboration or restatement of the thesis. One common technique is to find a way in the end of the essay to return to the beginning. Here's the concluding paragraph from the essay on national park funding:

> We would never risk our national heritage by allowing the White House to deteriorate or the Liberty Bell to rust away. <u>As the National Park Service's own mission states, the parks are also "expressions" of our "single national heritage," one this paper contends is about preserving not only trees, animals, and habitats, but our national identity.</u> The Old Faithful geyser reminds Americans of their constancy and their enduring spirit. What will it say about us if vandals finally end the regular eruptions of the geyser because Americans didn't support a park ranger to guard it? What will we call Old Faithful then? Old Faithless?

Note that the underlined sentence returns to the original thesis but doesn't simply repeat it word for word. Instead, it amplifies the original thesis, adding a definition of "national heritage" to include national identity. It returns to the opening paragraph by finding a new way to discuss Old Faithful. Revise your draft to conform to this structure, beginning with a strong opening paragraph that explicitly states your thesis and with an ending that somehow returns to the beginning without simply repeating what you've already said.

Revision Strategy 9.17: Multiple Leads

A single element that may affect a draft more than any other is the beginning. There are many ways into the material, and of course you want to choose a beginning or lead that a reader might find interesting. You also want to choose a beginning that makes some kind of promise, providing readers with a sense of where you intend to take them. But a lead has less obvious effects on both readers and writers. How you begin often establishes the voice of the essay; signals the writer's emotional relationship to the material, the writer's ethos; and might suggest the form the essay will take.

This is, of course, why beginnings are so hard to write. But the critical importance of where and how we begin also suggests that examining alternative leads can give writers more choices and more control over their essays. To borrow John McPhee's metaphor, if a lead is a "flashlight that shines down into the story," then pointing that flashlight in four different directions might reveal four different ways of following the same subject. This can be a powerful revision strategy.

1. Choose a draft that has a weak opening, doesn't have a strong sense of purpose, or needs to be reorganized.

2. Compose four *different* openings to the *same* draft. One way to generate ideas for this is to cluster your topic, and write leads from four different branches. Also consider varying the type of lead you write (see the "Inquiring into the Details: Types of Leads" box on the following page).

3. Bring a typed copy of these four leads (or five if you want to include the original lead from the first draft) to class and share them with a small group. First simply ask your classmates to choose the beginning they like best.

4. Choose the lead *you* prefer. It may or may not be the one your classmates chose. Find a partner who was not in your small group and ask him or her the following questions after sharing the lead you chose:

   - Based on this lead, what do you predict this paper is about?
   - Can you guess the question, problem, or idea I'm writing about in the rest of the essay?
   - Do you have a sense of what my thesis might be?
   - What is the ethos of this beginning? In other words, how do I come across to you as a narrator or author of the essay?

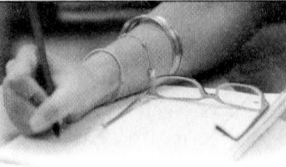

INQUIRING INTO THE DETAILS

Types of Leads

Writer John McPhee says beginnings—or leads—are "like flashlights that shine down into the story." If you imagine that information about your topic is collected in a darkened room, then where and how you choose to begin an essay will, like a flashlight, illuminate some aspect of that room. Different beginnings point the flashlight in different directions and imply the different directions the essay might develop. Consider a few types of leads:

1. *Announcement.* Typical of a thesis/support essay, among others. Explicitly states the purpose and thesis of the essay.

2. *Anecdote.* A brief story that nicely frames the question, dilemma, problem, or idea behind the essay.

3. *Scene.* Describe a situation, place, or image that highlights the question, problem, or idea behind the essay.

4. *Profile.* Begin with a case study or description of a person who is involved in the question, problem, or idea.

5. *Background.* Provide a context through information that establishes the significance of the question, problem, or idea.

6. *Quotation or Dialogue.* Begin with a voice of someone (or several people) involved or whose words are relevant.

7. *Comparison.* Are there two or more things that, when compared or contrasted, point to the question, problem, or idea?

8. *Question.* Frame the question the essay addresses.

If the predictions were fairly accurate using the lead you preferred, this might be a good alternative opening to the next draft. Follow it in a fastwrite in your notebook to see where it leads you. Go ahead and use the other leads elsewhere in the revision, if you like.

If your reader's predictions were off, the lead may not be the best choice for the revision. However, should you consider this new direction an appealing alternative for the next draft? Or should you choose another lead that better reflects your current intentions rather than strike off in new directions? Either way, follow a new lead to see where it goes.

Revision Strategy 9.18: The Frankenstein Draft

One way to divorce a draft that has you in its clutches is to dismember it; that is, cut it into pieces and play with the parts, looking for new arrangements of information or new gaps to fill. Writing teacher Peter Elbow's cut-and-paste revision can be a useful method, particularly for drafts that don't rely on narrative structures (although sometimes playing with alternatives, particularly if the draft is strictly chronological, can be helpful). Research essays and other pieces that attempt to corral lots of information seem to benefit the most from this strategy.

1. Choose a draft that needs help with organization. Make a one-sided copy.

2. Cut apart the copy, paragraph by paragraph. (You may cut it into smaller pieces later.) Once you have completely disassembled the draft, shuffle the paragraphs to get them wildly out of order so the original draft is just a memory.

3. Now go through the shuffled stack and find the *core paragraph*. This is the paragraph the essay really couldn't do without because it helps answer the *So what?* question. It might be the paragraph that contains your thesis or establishes your focusing question. It should be the paragraph that explains, implicitly or explicitly, what you're trying to say in the draft. Set this aside.

4. With the core paragraph directly in front of you, work your way through the remaining stack of paragraphs and make two new stacks: one of paragraphs that don't seem relevant to your core (such as unnecessary digressions or information) and those that do (they support the main idea, explain or define a key concept, illustrate or exemplify something important, or provide necessary background).

5. Put your reject pile aside for the moment. You may decide to salvage some of those paragraphs later. But for now focus on your relevant pile, including the core paragraph. Now play with order. Try new leads, ends, and middles. Consider trying some new methods of development as a way to organize your next draft (see the "Methods of Development" box). As you spread the paragraphs out before you and consider new arrangements, don't worry about the lack of transitions; you can add those later. Also look for gaps, places where more information might be needed. Consider some of the information in the reject pile as well. Should you splice in *parts* of paragraphs that you initially discarded?

6. As a structure begins to emerge, begin taping together the fragments of paper. Also splice in scraps in appropriate places and note what you might add in the next draft that is currently missing.

> ## METHODS OF DEVELOPMENT
>
> - Narrative
> - Problem to solution
> - Cause to effect, or effect to cause
> - Question to answer
> - Known to unknown, or unknown to known
> - Simple to complex
> - General to specific, or specific to general
> - Comparison and contrast
> - Combinations of any of these

Now you've created a Frankenstein draft. But hopefully this ugly mess of paper and tape and scribbled notes holds much more promise than the monster. On the other hand, if you end up with pretty much the original organization, perhaps your first approach wasn't so bad after all. You may at least find places where more information is needed.

Revision Strategy 9.19: Make a PowerPoint Outline

While outlines can be a useful tool for planning a formal essay, they can also help writers revise a draft. One of the best tools for doing this is a program such as PowerPoint that challenges you to develop brief slides in sequence. The ease of moving the slides around, the imperative to be brief and to the point, and the visual display of your logic all combine to make the program an ideal medium for playing with the order of information. This is often helpful even if you don't ever make a presentation.

Your goal in creating a PowerPoint outline isn't to transfer all your text to slides and then move it around, though you could do that if you thought it helpful. Your aim is to exploit the software to help you develop a logical outline. You have several options for doing this. One is to title separate slides using some of the conventional structures of academic essays, and then make bulleted lists of the information you might include in each (see the sample slide). For example, these could be slide titles:

- Abstract, Introduction, Literature Review, Thesis/Purpose, Methods, Results, Discussion, Conclusion
- The Problem/Question, Purpose of the Essay, Claim, Reasons and Evidence (separate slide for each reason), Conclusion

Sample PowerPoint slide outlining a plan for an essay.

- Introduction, Thesis, Example 1, Example 2, Example 3, etc., Conclusion
- Lead/Introduction, Background, Research Question, Significance of the Problem or Question, Other Voices on the Question, Thesis, Conclusion

Alternatively, you might use less formal methods of parsing the information in the draft onto slides. For example, can you label categories of information? In a narrative essay, it might be a particular scene, description, or reflection. In an argument it might be claims, warrants or assumptions, evidence, and counterarguments. A literary essay might be grouped on slides using key passages, the main idea, textual background, information on the author, and so on.

Whichever method you use, once you are able to disassemble your draft onto PowerPoint slides using some logic, don't just play with the order. Consider moving some of the information from slide to slide, too.

PROBLEMS WITH CLARITY AND STYLE

One thing should be made clear immediately: Problems of clarity and style need not have anything to do with grammatical correctness. You can have a sentence that follows all the rules and still lumbers, sputters, and dies like a Volkswagen bug towing a heavy trailer up a steep hill. Take this sentence, for instance:

> Once upon a point in time, a small person named Little Red Riding Hood initiated plans for the preparation, delivery, and transportation of foodstuffs to her grandmother, a senior citizen residing at a place of residence in a wooded area of indeterminate dimension.

Strong writing at the sentence and paragraph levels always begins with clarity.

This beastly sentence opens Russell Baker's essay "Little Red Riding Hood Revisited," a satire about the gassiness of contemporary writing. It's grammatically correct, of course, but it's also pretentious, unnecessarily wordy, and would be annoying to read if it wasn't pretty amusing. This section of the chapter focuses on revision strategies that improve the clarity of your writing and will help you consider the effects you want to create through word choice and arrangement. Your questions about grammar and mechanics can be answered in the handbook at the back of the book.

Maybe because we often think that work with paragraphs, sentences, and words always involves problems of correctness, it may be hard to believe at first that writers can actually manage readers' responses and feelings by using different words or rearranging the parts of a sentence or paragraph. Once you begin to play around with style, however, you will discover that it's much more than cosmetic. In fact, style in writing is a lot like music in movies. Chris Douridas, a Hollywood music supervisor who picked music for *Shrek* and *American Beauty*, said recently that he sees "music as an integral ingredient to the pie. I see it as helping to flavor the pie and not as whipped cream on top." Certainly people don't pick a movie for its music, but we know that the music is central to our experience of a film. Similarly, *how* you say things in a piece of writing powerfully shapes the reader's experience of *what* you say.

But style is a secondary concern. Strong writing at the sentence and paragraph levels always begins with clarity. Do you say what you mean as directly and economically as you can? This can be a real problem, particularly with academic writing, in which it's easy to get the impression that a longer word is always better than a shorter word, and the absence of anything interesting to say can be remedied by sounding smart. Nothing could be further from the truth.

Solving Problems of Clarity

Begin by revising your draft with one or more revision strategies that will make your writing more direct and clear.

Revision Strategy 9.20: The Three Most Important Sentences

Writers, like car dealers, organize their lots to take advantage of where readers are most likely to look and what they're most likely to remember. In many essays and papers, there are three places to park important information and to craft your very best sentences. These are,

- the very first sentence
- the last line of the first paragraph
- the very last line of the essay

The First Sentence. Obviously, there are many other important places in a piece of writing—and longer essays, especially, have more and different locations for your strongest sentences. But in an informal piece of modest length, the first sentence not only should engage the reader, it should, through strong language and voice, introduce the writer as well. For example, here's the first line of Richard Conniff's researched essay, "Why God Created Flies": "Though I've been killing them for years now, I have never tested the folklore that, with a little cream and sugar, flies taste very much like black raspberries." In more formal writing, the first line is much less about introducing a persona than introducing the subject. Here's the first line of an academic piece I'm reading at the moment: "Much of the international debate about the relationship between research and teaching is characterized by difference." This raises an obvious question—"What is this difference?"—and this is exactly what the author proposes to explore.

The Last Line of the First Paragraph. The so-called "lead" (or "lede" in journalism speak) of an essay or article does three things: It establishes the purpose of the work, raises interesting questions, and creates a register or tone. A lead paragraph in a shorter essay is just that—the first paragraph—while a lead in a longer work may run for paragraphs, even pages. Whatever the length, the last sentence of the lead launches the work and gets it going in a particular direction. In conventional thesis-proof essays, then, this might be the sentence where you state your main claim. In inquiry-based forms like the essay, this might be where you post the key question you're exploring or illuminate the aspect of the problem you want to look at.

The Last Line of the Essay. If it's good, this is the sentence readers are most likely to remember.

Try this revision strategy:

1. Highlight or underline each of these three sentences in your draft.
2. Ask yourself these questions about the first line and, depending on your answers, revise the sentence:
   - Is the language lively?
   - Does it immediately raise questions the reader might want to learn the answers to?
   - Will they want to read the second sentence, and why?
3. Analyze the last sentence of your "lead" paragraph for ideas about revision. Ask yourself this:
   - Is the sentence well-crafted?
   - Does it hint at or explicitly state your motive for asking readers to follow along with you in the paragraphs and pages that follow?
4. Finally, scrutinize your last sentence:
   - Is this one of the best-written sentences in the piece?
   - Does it add something?

Revision Strategy 9.21: Untangling Paragraphs

One of the things I admire most in my friends David and Margaret is that they both have individual integrity—a deep understanding of who they are and who they want to be—and yet they remain just as profoundly connected to the people close to them. They manage to exude both individuality and connection. I hope my friends will forgive the comparison, but good paragraphs have the same qualities: Alone they have their own identities, yet they are also strongly hitched to the paragraphs that precede and that follow them. This connection happens quite naturally when you're telling a story, but in expository writing the relationship between paragraphs is more related to content than time.

The following passage is the first three paragraphs from Paul de Palma's essay on computers, with the clever title "www.when_is_enough_enough?.com." Notice the integrity of each paragraph—each is a kind of mini-essay—as well as the way each one is linked to the paragraph that precedes it.

A paragraph should be unified, focusing on a single topic, idea, or thing. It's like a mini-essay in that sense.

In the misty past, before Bill Gates joined the company of the world's richest men, before the mass-marketed personal computer, before the metaphor of an information superhighway had been worn down to a cliché, I heard Roger Schank interviewed on National Public Radio. Then a computer science professor at Yale, Schank was already well known in artificial intelligence circles. Because those circles did not include me, a new programmer at Sperry Univac, I hadn't heard of him. Though I've forgotten details of the conversation, I have never forgotten Schank's insistence that most people do not need to own computers.

Note how the first sentence in the new paragraph links with the last sentence in the preceding one.

That view, of course, has not prevailed. Either we own a personal computer and fret about upgrades, or we are scheming to own one and fret about the technical marvel yet to come that will render our purchase obsolete. Well, there are worse ways to spend money, I suppose. For all I know, even Schank owns a personal computer. They're fiendishly clever machines, after all, and they've helped keep the wolf from my door for a long time.

As before, the first sentence links with the last sentence in the previous paragraph.

It is not the personal computer itself that I object to. What reasonable person would voluntarily go back to a typewriter? The mischief is not in the computer itself, but in the ideology that surrounds it. If we hope to employ computers for tasks more interesting than word processing, we must devote some attention to how they are actually being used, and beyond that, to the remarkable grip that the idol of computing continues to exert.

The final sentence is the most important one in a paragraph. Craft it carefully.

Well-crafted paragraphs like these create a fluent progression, all linked together like train cars; they make readers feel confident that this train is going somewhere. This might be information that clarifies, extends, proves, explains, or even contradicts. Do the paragraphs in your draft work well on their own and together?

1. Check the length of every paragraph in your draft. Are any too long, going on and on for a full page or more? Can you create smaller paragraphs by breaking out separate ideas, topics, discussions, or claims?

2. Now examine each paragraph in your draft for integrity. Is it relatively focused and unified? Should it be broken down further into two or more paragraphs because it covers too much territory?

3. In Figure 9.4, note the order of the most important information in a typical paragraph. Is each of your paragraphs arranged with that order in mind? In particular, how strong is the final sentence in each paragraph? Does it prepare readers to move into the next paragraph? In general, each paragraph adds some kind of new information to the old information in the paragraphs preceding it. This new material may clarify, explain, prove, elaborate on,

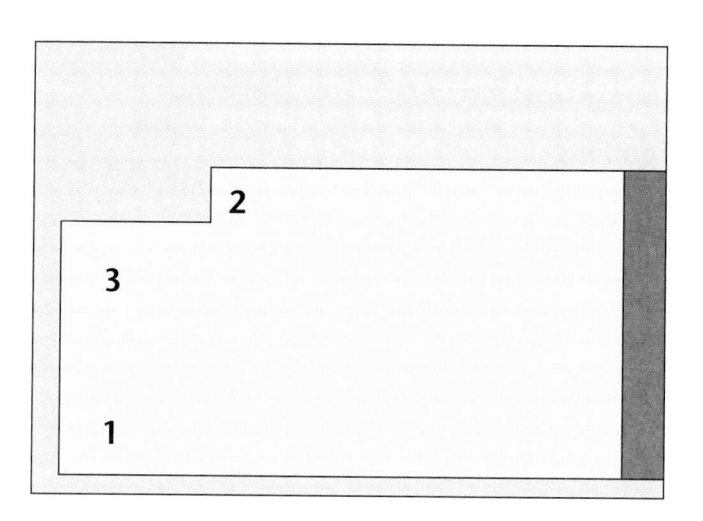

Figure 9.4   Order of important sentences in a paragraph. Often the first sentence is the second most important sentence in a paragraph. The third most important sentence follows immediately thereafter. The most important sentence usually comes at the end of the paragraph.

> contrast, summarize, contradict, or alter time. Sometimes you should signal the nature of this addition using transition words and phrases (see the "Inquiring into the Details: Transition Flags" box). Are there any awkward transitions? Should you smooth them using transition flags?

Revision Strategy 9.22: Cutting Clutter

Russell Baker's overinflated version of "Little Red Riding Hood" suffered from what writer and professor William Zinsser called "clutter." This disease afflicts much writing, particularly in academic settings. Clutter, simply put, is saying in three or four words what you might say in two, or choosing a longer word when a shorter one will do just as well. It grows from the assumption that simplicity means simplemindedness. This is misguided. Simplicity is a great virtue in writing. It's respectful of the readers, for one thing, who are mostly interested in understanding what you mean without unnecessary detours or obstacles.

In case Russell Baker's tongue-and-cheek example of cluttered writing isn't convincing because it's an invention, here's a brief passage from a memo I received from a fellow faculty member some years ago. I won't make you endure more than a sentence.

> While those of us in the administration are supporting general excellence and consideration of the long-range future of the University, and while the Faculty Senate and Caucus are dealing with more immediate problems, the Executive Committee feels that an ongoing dialogue concerning the particular concerns of faculty is needed to maintain the quality of personal and educational life necessary for continued educational improvement.

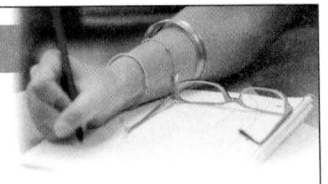

INQUIRING INTO THE DETAILS

Transition Flags

One way to connect paragraphs is to signal to a reader with words what the relationship is between them.

- **Clarifying:** *for example, furthermore, specifically, also, to illustrate, similarly*
- **Proving:** *in fact, for example, indeed*
- **Time:** *first…second…finally, subsequently, following, now, recently*
- **Cause or effect:** *therefore, consequently, so, accordingly*
- **Contrast or contradiction:** *on the other hand, in contrast, however, on the contrary, despite, in comparison*
- **Summarizing:** *finally, in the end, in conclusion, summing up, to conclude*

That's a 63-word sentence, and while there is nothing inherently wrong with long sentences, I'm pretty sure that at least half of the words are unnecessary. For the fun of it, see if you can cut at least thirty words from the sentence without compromising the writer's intent. Look for ways to say the same things in fewer words, and look for shorter words that might replace longer ones. What kinds of choices did you make to improve the clarity of the sentence?

Now shift your attention to one of your own drafts and see if you can be as ruthless with your own clutter as you were with the memo writer's.

1. One of the most common kinds of clutter is stock phrases, things we mindlessly say because we've simply gotten in the habit of saying them. *Due to the fact that…* is the one that drives me most crazy. Why not the simpler word *Because*? The following table lists some of the most common stock phrases used in student writing. Read your draft from beginning to end and when you see one of these, cut it down to size.

STOCK PHRASE	SIMPLER VERSION
Due to the fact that…	Because
At the present time…	Now
Until such time as…	Until
I am of the opinion that…	I think
In the event of…	When
This is an appropriate occasion to…	It's time
Proceed with the implementation of…	Begin
Referred to as…	Called
Totally lacked the ability to…	Couldn't
A number of…	Many
In the event of…	If
There is a need for…	Must

2. Another thing to consider is choosing a shorter, simpler word rather than a longer, more complicated word. For example, why not say *many* rather than *numerous*, or *ease* rather than *facilitate*, or *do* rather than *implement*, or *found* rather than *identified*. Go through your draft and look for opportunities such as these to use simpler, more direct words.

3. In his book *Style: Ten Lessons in Clarity and Grace*, Joseph Williams cleverly calls the habit of using meaningless words "verbal tics." These are words, he writes, that "we use unconsciously as we clear our throats." My favorite verbal tic is the phrase *in fact*, which I park at the front of a sentence when I feel like I'm about to clarify something. Mostly I can do without it. In fact, most of us have verbal tics, and we should learn to recognize them. Williams mentions a few common ones, including *kind of, actually, basically, generally, given, various,* and *certain*. For example, *It's generally assumed that certain students have various reasons for being apolitical these days.* A better version would be, *Students have reasons for being apolitical these days.*

Go through your draft and search for words and phrases that you use out of habit, and cut them if they don't add meaning.

Revision Strategy 9.23: The Actor and the Action Next Door

I live in a relatively urban neighborhood, and so I can hear Kate play her music across the street and Gray powering up his chainsaw to cut wooden pallets next door. I have mixed feelings about this. Kate and I have different taste in music and Gray runs the saw at dusk. But I am never confused about who is doing what. That's less obvious in the following passage:

> A conflict that was greeted at first with much ambivalence by the American public, the war in Iraq, which caused a tentativeness that some experts call the "Vietnam syndrome," sparked protests among Vietnam veterans.

The subject or actor of the sentence (*the war in Iraq*) and the action (*sparked protests*) are separated by a few city blocks. In addition, the subject is buried behind a long introductory clause. As a result, it's a bit hard to remember who is doing what. Putting actor and action next door to each other makes the writing livelier, and bringing the subject up front helps clarify who is doing what.

> The war in Iraq sparked protests among Vietnam veterans even though the conflict was initially greeted with public ambivalence. Some experts call this tentativeness the "Vietnam syndrome."

Review your draft to determine whether the subjects in your sentences are buried or in the same neighborhood as the verbs that modify them. If not, rewrite to bring the actors up front in your sentences and to close the distance between actors and actions.

Improving Style

These revision strategies will improve the style of your writing. In the same way that a John Williams score can make movies such as *Indiana Jones and the Temple of Doom* and *Star Wars* more memorable and moving, style in writing can add to readers' experiences of a text. These are often calculated moves. Writers adopt a style because it serves a purpose, perhaps encouraging a certain feeling that makes a story more powerful, enhancing the writer's ethos to make an essay more convincing, or simply giving certain information particular emphasis. For example, here's the beginning of an article about Douglas Berry, a Marine drill sergeant.

> He is seething, he is rabid, he is wound up tight as a golf ball, with more adrenalin surging through his hypothalamus than a cornered slum rat, he is everything these Marine recruits with their heads shaved to dirty nubs have ever feared or ever hoped a drill sergeant might be.

The style of this opening is calculated to have an obvious effect—the reader is pelted with words, one after another, in a breathless sentence that almost simulates the experience of having Sgt. Douglas Berry in your face. There's no magic to this. It is all about using words that evoke action and feeling, usually verbs or words based on or derived from verbs.

Revision Strategy 9.24: Actors and Actions

My favorite verb yesterday was *shattered*. I often ask my writing students to come to class and share their favorite verb of the day; last spring, my senior seminar consistently selected *graduate* as their favorite.

As you know, verbs make things happen in writing, and how much energy prose possesses depends on verb power. Academic writing sometimes lacks strong verbs, relying instead on old passive standbys such as *it was concluded by the study* or *it is believed*. Not only are the verbs weak, but the actors, the people or things engaged in the action, are often missing completely from the sentences. *Who* or *what* did the study? *Who* believes?

This is called *passive voice*, and while it's not grammatically incorrect, passive voice can suck the air out of a room. While reasons exist for using passive voice (sometimes, for instance, the writer wants the reader to focus on the action, not the actor), you should avoid it in your own writing. One of the easiest ways to locate passive voice in your drafts is to conduct a *to be* search. Most forms of the verb *to be* (see the Forms of *To Be* box on the next page) usually signal passive voice. For example,

> It is well known that medieval eating habits were unsavory by contemporary health standards. Cups were shared, forks were never used, and the same knives used to clean under fingernails or to gut a chicken were used to cut and eat meat.

What is missing, of course, are the actors. To revise into active voice you simply need to add the actors, whenever possible:

> Medieval diners had unsavory eating habits by contemporary health standards. They shared cups with friends, they never used forks, and they used their knives, the same ones they used to clean under their fingernails or gut a chicken, to cut and eat their meat.

1. Conduct a *to be* search of your own draft. Whenever you find passive construction, try to put the actor into the sentence.

2. Eliminating passive voice is only one strategy for giving your writing more energy. Try to use lively verbs as well. Can you replace weak verbs with stronger ones? How about *discovered* instead of *found*, or *seized* instead of *took*, *shattered* instead of *broke*. Review every sentence in the draft and, when appropriate, revise with a stronger verb.

> **FORMS OF *TO BE***
>
> - Is
> - Are
> - Was
> - Were
> - Has been
> - Have been
> - Will be

Revision Strategy 9.25: Smoothing the Choppiness

Good writing reads like a Mercedes drives—smoothly, suspended by the rhythms of language. One of the most important factors influencing this rhythm is sentence length, or, more precisely, pauses in the prose that vary as the reader travels from sentence to sentence and paragraph to paragraph. We rarely notice either the cause or the effect, but we certainly notice the bumps and lurches. Consider the following sentences, each labeled with the number of syllables:

> When the sun finally rose the next day I felt young again.(15) It was a strange feeling because I wasn't young anymore.(15) I was fifty years old and felt like it.(10) It was the smell of the lake at dawn that thrust me back into adolescence.(19) I remembered the hiss of the waves.(9) They erased my footprints in the sand.(9)

This really isn't awful; it could pass as a bad Hemingway imitation. But do you notice the monotony of the writing, the steady, almost unvarying beat that threatens to dull your mind if it goes on much longer? The cause of the plodding rhythm is the unvarying length of the pauses. The last two sentences in the passage each have 9 syllables, and the first two sentences are nearly identical in length as well (15 and 15 syllables, respectively).

Now notice how this choppiness disappears by varying the lengths of the pauses through combining sentences, inserting other punctuation, and dropping a few unnecessary words.

When the sun finally rose the next day I felt young again,(15) and it was a strange feeling because I wasn't young.(13) I was fifty years old.(6) It was the smell of the lake at dawn that thrust me back into adolescence and remembering the hiss of the waves as they erased my footprints in the sand.(39)

The revision is much more fluent and the reason is simple: The writer varies the pauses and the number of syllables within each of them—15, 13, 6, 39.

1. Choose a draft of your own that doesn't seem to flow or seems choppy in places.

2. Mark the pauses in the problem areas. Put slash marks next to periods, commas, semicolons, dashes, and so on—any punctuation that prompts a reader to pause briefly.

3. If the pauses seem similar in length, revise to vary them, combining sentences, adding punctuation, dropping unnecessary words, or varying long and short words.

Revision Strategy 9.26: Fresh Ways to Say Things

It goes without saying that a tried-and-true method of getting to the heart of revision problems is to just do or die. Do you know what I mean? Of course you don't, because the opening sentence is laden with clichés and figures of speech that manage to obscure meaning. One of the great challenges of writing well is to find fresh ways to say things rather than relying on hand-me-down phrases that worm their way into our speech and writing. Clichés are familiar examples: *home is where the heart is, hit the nail on the head, the grass is greener*, and all that. But even more common are less figurative expressions: *more than meets the eye, rude awakenings, you only go around once, sigh of relief*, and so on.

Removing clichés and shopworn expressions from your writing will make it sound more as if you are writing from your own voice rather than someone else's. It gives the work a freshness that helps readers believe that you have something interesting to say. In addition, clichés especially tend to close off a writer's thoughts rather than open them to new ideas and different ways of seeing. A cliché often leaves the writer with nothing more to say because someone else has already said it.

1. Reread your draft and circle clichés and hand-me-down expressions. If you're not sure whether a phrase qualifies for either category, share your circled items with a partner and discuss them. Have you heard these things before?

2. Cut clichés and overused expressions and rewrite your sentences, finding your own way to say things. In your own words, what do you really mean by "do or die" or "striking while the iron is hot" or becoming a "true believer"?

USING WHAT YOU HAVE LEARNED

Take a few moments to reflect on what you learned in this chapter and how you can apply it.

1. Which revision strategy has proved most helpful to you so far? Does it address one of your most common problems in your drafts?

2. Here's a common situation: You're assigned a paper for another class and the professor doesn't require you to hand in a draft. She's just interested in your final version. What incentive do you have to work through a draft or two?

3. If revision is rhetorical, then the kinds of revision strategies you need to use depend on the particular situation: to whom you're writing and why, and in what form. The kind of writer you are—and the kinds of problems you have in your drafts—also matters. Consider the following forms: the essay exam, the review, the annotated bibliography, the letter, the formal research paper, and the reading response. Which of the five revision strategies would probably be most important for each form?

Writers rarely experience the impact their writing has on readers. When they do experience this in a writing workshop, the idea of writing for an audience ceases to be an abstraction.

THE WRITER'S WORKSHOP

10

MAKING THE MOST OF PEER REVIEW

Sharing your writing with strangers can be among the most frightening and gratifying social experiences. It can be a key to the success of the next draft or a complete waste of time. One thing sharing your writing can't be, however, is avoided, at least in most composition courses, which these days frequently rely on small and large group workshops to help students revise. This is a good thing, I think, for three reasons:

1. It's useful to experience *being read* by others.
2. Workshops can be among the most effective ways for writers to divorce the draft.
3. The talk about writing in workshops can be enormously instructive.

Being Read

Being read is not the same thing as being read to. As we share our writing, sometimes reading our own work aloud to a group, we are sharing ourselves in a very real way. This is most evident with a personal essay, but virtually any piece of writing bears our authorship—our particular ways of seeing and saying things—and included in this are our feelings about ourselves as writers.

Last semester, Matthew told me that he felt he was the worst writer in the class, and that seemed obvious when I watched him share his writing in his workshop group. Matthew was quiet and compliant, readily accepting suggestions with little comment, and he seemed to rush

> ### What You'll Learn in This Chapter
> - The purpose of peer review.
> - The most common approaches for organizing writing workshops.
> - How to plan to make the most of the chance to share your draft.
> - What can go wrong and how to deal with it.
> - Response formats for guiding how readers evaluate your drafts.

the conversation about his draft as if to make the ordeal end sooner. When Matthew's drafts were discussed, his group always ended in record time, and yet he always claimed that they were "helpful."

Tracy always began presenting her drafts by announcing, "This really sucks. It's the worst thing I've ever written." Of course it wasn't. But this announcement seemed intended to lower the stakes for her, to take some of the pressure off of her performance in front of others, or, quite possibly, it was a hopeful invitation for Tracy's group members to say, "You're too hard on yourself. This is really good."

To *be read* in a workshop group can mean more than a critique of your ideas or sentences; for students like Matthew and Tracy it is an evaluation of *themselves,* particularly their self-worth as writers. Of course, this isn't the purpose of peer review at all, but for those of us with sometimes nagging internal critics, it's pretty hard to avoid feeling that both your writing and your writing self are on trial. This is why it's so helpful to articulate these fears before being read. It's also helpful to imagine the many positive outcomes that might come from the experience of sharing your writing.

While taking workshop comments about your writing personally is always a risk, consider the really rare and unusual opportunity to *see* readers respond to your work. I often compare my published writing to dropping a very heavy stone down a deep well and waiting to hear the splash. And waiting. And waiting. But in a workshop, you can actually hear the murmurs, the sighs, and the laughter of your readers as you read to them; you can also see the smiles, puzzled expressions, nodding heads, and even tears. You can experience your readers' experiences of your writing in ways that most published authors never can.

> In a workshop, you can actually hear the murmurs, the sighs, and the laughter of your readers as you read to them.

What is so valuable about this, I think, is that audience is no longer an abstraction. After your first workshop, it's no stretch to imagine the transaction that most writing involves—a writer's words being received by a reader who thinks and feels something in response. And when you take this back to the many solitary hours of writing, you may feel you have company; that members of your workshop group are interested in what you have to say.

This is a powerful thing. In some ways, it's the most important thing about the workshop experience.

Divorcing the Draft

Our writing relationships include our emotional connection to drafts, and this often has to do with the time we spent writing them. In Chapter 9, I described the ways we can get entangled in first drafts that blind us to other ways of seeing a topic. Sometimes we need to divorce a draft, and the best remedy for this is time away from it. But students rarely have that luxury.

Workshops provide an alternative to time away from a draft and are effective for the same reason some people see therapists—group members offer an "outsider's" perspective on your work that may give it new meanings and raise new possibilities. If nothing else, readers offer a preview of whether your current meanings are clear and whether what you assume is apparent *is* apparent to someone other than yourself. It's rare when a workshop doesn't jerk writers away from at least a few of their assumptions about a draft, and the best of these experiences inspire writers to want to write again. This is the outcome we should always hope to attain.

Instructive Talk

Consider a few comments I overheard during workshops recently:

- "I don't think the focus is clear in this essay. In fact, I think there are at least two separate essays here, and it's the one on the futility of antiwar protests I'm most interested in."
- "Do you think that there's a better lead buried on the third page, in the paragraph about your sister's decision to go to the hospital? That was a powerful scene, and it seemed to be important to the overall theme."
- "I was wondering about something. What is it about the idea that we sometimes keep silent not only to protect other people but to protect ourselves that surprised you? I mean, does knowing that change anything about how you feel about yourself as a parent?"
- "I loved this line. Simply loved it."

The talk in workshops is not always about writing. The "underlife" of the classroom often surfaces in workshops, a term one educator uses to describe the idle talk about the class itself. Most writing classes ask students to step out of their usual student roles. Rather than quietly listen to lectures or study a textbook, in a writing course you are asked to make your own meanings and find your own ways of making meaning. Whenever we are asked to assume new roles, some resistance can set in, and workshops can become an occasion for talk about the class, often out of earshot of the instructor. This talk isn't always complaining. Often workshops are opportunities to share understandings or approaches to assignments and especially experiences with them. They can also be a chance for students to try out new identities—"I really liked writing this. Maybe I'm an okay writer after all."

While this kind of talk may not be directly about a draft, it can help you negotiate the new roles you're being asked to assume in your writing class. This is part of becoming better writers who are confident that they can manage the writing process in all kinds of situations. However, the main purpose of workshop groups is to help students revise their drafts. But why seek advice from writers who are clearly less experienced than the instructor?

1. By talking with other students about writing, you get practice using the language you're learning in the writing classroom, language that helps you describe important features of your own work.

2. Because writing is about making choices among a range of solutions to problems in a draft, workshop groups are likely to surface possibilities that never occurred to you (and perhaps wouldn't occur to the instructor, either).

3. Your peers are also student writers and because they come from similar circumstances—demands of other classes, part-time jobs, and perhaps minimal experience with college writing—they are in a position to offer practical and realistic revision suggestions.

4. Finally, in most writing courses, the students in the class are an important audience for your work. Getting firsthand responses makes the rhetorical situation real rather than imagined.

Will you get bad advice in a peer workshop? Of course. Your group members will vary in their experience and ability to read the problems and possibilities in a draft. But in the best writing workshops, you learn together, and as time goes by the feedback gets better and better. Paradoxically, it pays off in your own writing to be generous in your responses to the work of others.

MODELS FOR WRITING WORKSHOPS

The whole idea of peer review workshops in writing classes has been around for years. Collaboration is hardly a novelty in the professional world, but small-group work in academia is a relatively recent alternative to lecture and other teaching methods in which the student listens to a professor, takes notes on what is said, and later takes a test of some kind. You won't learn to write well through lecture, although it may be a perfectly appropriate approach for some subjects. Because collaboration in the writing classroom fits in perfectly with the class's aim of generating knowledge about the many ways to solve writing problems, peer review of drafts in small groups is now fairly common. You'll find workshops in writing classes ranging from first-year composition to advanced nonfiction writing.

What will workshops be like in your course? Your instructor will answer that question, but the workshop groups will likely reflect one or more of the following models.

Full-Class Workshops

Sometimes you may not work in small groups at all. Depending on the size of your class and your instructor's particular purposes for using peer review, you may share your work with everyone in a full-class session. This approach is popular in creative writing classes, and it's typically used in composition classes to introduce students to the process of providing responses to other students' work. It also can work nicely in small classes with ten students or fewer.

In a full-class workshop, you'll choose a draft to share, and you (or your instructor) will provide copies for everyone either a few days before the workshop or at the beginning of the workshop session. On drafts you receive days ahead of the session, you're often expected to read and bring written comments to class with you. If you receive the draft at the beginning of the workshop session, you might make notes while the draft's author reads the piece aloud, or take some time to write some comments either immediately after the draft is read or following the group discussion.

Reading your draft aloud to your workshop group is a common convention in all kinds of workshop groups, large or small. This might be something you resist at first. It will quickly become apparent, however, how useful it is to read your own work aloud. It's an entirely different reading to literally give voice to your words. You'll stumble over passages in your draft that seemed fine when you read them silently, and you may notice gaps you glossed over. You'll hear what your writing voice sounds like in this particular essay, and whether it works for you and your readers.

Your instructor may lead the discussion in a full-class workshop, or she may sit back and wait while students share their responses. There may be guidelines and ground rules for responses as well (for some examples of these, see "The Reader's Responsibilities" section later in the chapter). If your draft is being discussed, your instructor may ask you to simply listen. Sometimes it's best to avoid defending certain choices you made in a draft and simply take in the range of responses you receive to what you have done. In other cases, you may be asked to present the large group with questions to consider. It certainly can be scary sharing your work with twenty or twenty-five people, but imagine the range of perspectives you'll get!

Small-Group Workshops

Far more typical is the workshop group of between three and seven members, either chosen randomly by your instructor or self-selected. These groups may stay together all semester or part of the semester, or you may find yourself working with fresh faces every workshop session. Each of these alternatives has advantages and disadvantages, all of which your instructor has considered in making a choice.

Ideally, your workshop group will meet in a circle, because when everyone, including the writer presenting a draft, is facing each other you'll have more of a conversation and be able to engage each other directly (see Figure 10.1). Like so many writing group methods, this is a basic principle of teamwork borrowed from the business world.

Some of the methods of distributing drafts apply to the small group as well as to the full-class workshop discussed earlier: Writers will distribute copies of their drafts either a few days before their workshops or at the beginning of the sessions. You will provide written comments to each writer either before or after the workshop.

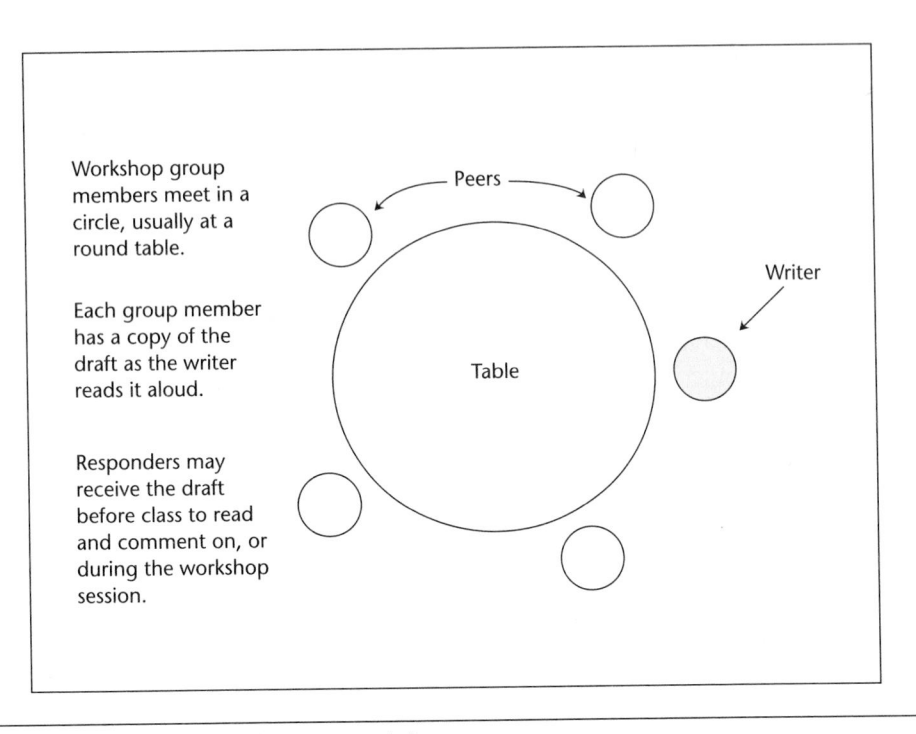

Workshop group members meet in a circle, usually at a round table.

Each group member has a copy of the draft as the writer reads it aloud.

Responders may receive the draft before class to read and comment on, or during the workshop session.

Peers

Writer

Table

Figure 10.1   The small-group workshop

One-on-One Peer Review

Your instructor also may ask you to work with a partner, exchanging drafts and discussing them with each other. While you lose some of the range and quantity of feedback by working with a single reader, this conversation is often richer because each of you is reading the other's work with particular care and attention. You'll probably also have more time to talk because you'll be discussing only two rather than four or five drafts.

One variation of this kind of one-on-one peer review is the draft exchange. Your instructor will ask you to make a pile of drafts at the front of the room and ask you to take a draft from the pile, comment on it, return it, and then take another. You may return multiple times to collect, comment on, and return a draft, and the result is that each draft may have three or four readers during the class session.

THE WRITER'S RESPONSIBILITIES

No matter what model your instructor chooses, the success of the workshop depends largely on the writers themselves. Sure, it can be harder to get what you need from some groups, but in the end, you can always get *some* help with a draft if you ask the right questions and seek certain kinds of responses.

How should you prepare for a workshop to make the most of it, and what are your responsibilities during the workshop? Here's a list you might find helpful:

- Make sure everyone in the group gets a copy of the draft in a timely way.

- Reread and reflect on the draft before the workshop session. What kinds of responses would be most helpful from your group? What questions do you have about the draft's possible problems?

- Time the discussion so that your draft gets the allotted time and no more, particularly if there are other drafts to discuss.

- Avoid getting defensive. Listen to comments on your work in an open-minded way. Your obligation is simply to listen, not to take all the advice you're offered.

- Take notes. There are two reasons for this. First, it will help you remember other students' comments and, second, it will signal that you take those comments seriously. This increases everyone's engagement with your work.

THE READER'S RESPONSIBILITIES

Tina poured her heart and soul into her personal essay draft, and she was eager to get some response to it. When it was her turn to workshop the piece, however, one of the group's members was absent, and two others failed to write her the required response. "It was so lame," she told me. "It was as if no one cared about my essay. It sure makes me feel less inclined to read their stuff carefully." If this workshop group were at Hewlett-Packard or any of the thousands of businesses that encourage teamwork, the slackers would be in trouble. But teamwork in the writing class depends more on internal motivation—a sense of responsibility to others—than any external reward or punishment. There is some external motivation: It pays to be generous with your responses to others' work because you'll learn more about your own.

You can increase your own learning in a workshop and contribute to a writer's positive experience by taking the following responsibilities seriously:

- Always read and respond to a writer's draft in a timely way. The writer may suggest the type of response that would be most helpful; if so, always keep that in mind.

- Whenever possible, focus your responses on particular parts or passages of the draft but, except in an editorial workshop, avoid a focus on grammar or mechanics.

- Offer suggestions, not directives. The word *could* is usually better than *should*. Remember that the purpose of the workshop is to help identify the range of choices a writer might make to improve a draft. There is almost always more than one.

- Identify strengths in the draft. This is often a good place to begin because it sets writers at ease, but, more important, writers often build on strengths in revision.

■   Consider varying the roles you play in conversation with your group (see the "Inquiring into the Details: Finding a Role" box). It's easy to fall into a rut in group work, pretty much sticking to saying the same kinds of things or developing certain patterns of response. Stay vigilant about this and try deliberately shifting the role you play in the workshop group.

WHAT CAN GO WRONG AND WHAT TO DO ABOUT IT

Lana is not a fan of workshops. In an argument essay, she complained that they "lack quality feedback," and sometimes workshop groups encourage "fault finding" that can hurt the writer and the writing. Things can go wrong in workshops, of course, and when they do students like Lana feel burned. Typically, unsuccessful

---

INQUIRING INTO THE DETAILS

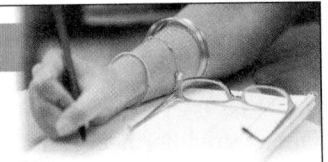

Finding a Role

"Slacker" is a role that's easy to slide into in small-group work. It's completely passive, and it's really pretty selfish. Active roles ask more of you, but they pay off big because you learn more about your own writing. You might assume any of several active roles in a workshop group. Try them out.

ROLES THAT HELP GROUPS GET THINGS DONE

Initiators: "Here's how we might proceed with this."
Information seekers: "What do we need to know to help the writer?"
Information givers: "This seems to be an important example."
Opinion seekers: "What do you think, Al?"
Opinion givers: "I think this works."
Clarifiers: "We all seem to be saying that the lead doesn't deliver, right?"
Elaborators: "I agree with Tom, and would add…"
Summarizers: "I think we've discussed the thesis problem enough. Should we move on to the evidence?"

ROLES THAT HELP MAINTAIN GROUP HARMONY

Encouragers: "I love that idea, Jen."
Expressivists: "My silence isn't because I'm not moved by the essay, but I'm still trying to figure out why. Is that why you're quiet, Leah?"
Harmonizers: "I think we disagree about this, but that's okay. Let's move on to discussing this next page."
Compromisers: "Maybe both Richard and Joseph are right, particularly if we look at it this way…"
Gatekeepers: "Jon, we haven't heard anything from you yet."

workshop groups suffer from two major problems: lack of commitment by group members and lack of clarity about the process of giving feedback. It's like a cold and a runny nose—when a group is afflicted with one problem it usually suffers from the other.

Lack of commitment is easy to see. The writer whose draft is to be discussed forgets to make copies for the rest of her group. Members who were supposed to provide written responses to a writer's draft before class hastily make notes on his manuscript as it's being discussed. The group is supposed to allot fifteen minutes to discuss each draft but finishes in five. Members are frequently absent and make no effort to provide responses to drafts they missed. Discussion is limited to general, not particularly thoughtful, compliments: "This is really good. I wouldn't change a thing," or "Just add a few details."

This lack of commitment is contagious and soon infects nearly every group meeting. Things rarely improve; they frequently get worse. Part of the problem may be that workshop participants are not clear on what is expected of them, a problem that should be minimized if you reviewed the checklists about the writer's and reader's responsibilities in workshop, discussed in the preceding sections. A solution that is beyond your control is that the instructor evaluates or even grades workshop participation, but a group can evaluate itself, too. Questions members should ask when evaluating their group can include: How effectively does your group work together? How would you evaluate the participation of group members? How do you feel about your own performance? How satisfied were you with the responses to your draft?

Groups that work together over a period of time should always monitor how things are going, and the group evaluations can be particularly helpful for this. If problems persist, the instructor may intervene or the group might consider intervention of its own (consider Exercise 10.1 as one option). Remember, the best workshops have a simple but powerful effect on writers who share their work: *It makes them want to write again.*

EXERCISE 10.1

Group Problem Solving

If group evaluations reveal persistent problems, devote ten minutes to exploring possible solutions.

STEP ONE: Choose a facilitator and a recorder. The facilitator times each step, directs questions to each participant, and makes sure everyone participates. The recorder takes notes on newsprint.

1. Discuss the patterns of problems identified by group members. Do writers seem dissatisfied? Do readers feel like they're performing poorly?
2. What is behind these problems? Brainstorm a list.

3. What might be done to change the way the group operates? You must come up with *at least* one concrete idea that you agree to try.

STEP TWO: After the next workshop session, set aside five minutes at the end to discuss whether the change improved the group's performance. Is there something else you should try?

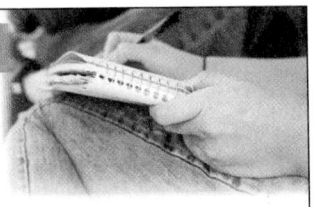

ONE STUDENT'S RESPONSE

Amy's Perspective On Workshops

WHEN THINGS GO RIGHT

In both small and large workshops things are most productive when the conversation delves deep into a couple of issues instead of skimming the surface on a broad range of topics. My best experiences have been in small workshops because the groups were willing to get more deeply involved in a piece. It probably helps that there aren't too many ideas in a small group and the ones that get thrown out for debate are well considered. I always appreciate it when the group writes notes on my paper for future reference and my absolute best workshops have been multiple sessions with the same small group. Assessing each other's progress really helps in the revision stages.

WHEN THINGS GO WRONG

Especially in a small workshop people can take things too personally and ruin the objective atmosphere, letting their own agenda take precedence over progression. In one of the worst workshops I've been a part of, we were assessing an essay by a writer who chose to write about her relationship with God. The essay had many problems, she used very vague metaphorical language, and the attempted symbolism didn't really work. It was a bit hard to read because of the overly sentimental tone of the piece. Instead of discussing these points, though, the workshop turned into an argument about outside topics and became pretty vicious. The writer was very open to most of the comments I made about some major changes that needed to happen in the piece, but very defensive (understandably) to the personal attacks. The communication simply broke down due to varying personal beliefs when they could have been a strength of the group.

In a large group a fine balance must be achieved. It is important that the conversation runs deep, but also that it covers more than one topic. Because of the multitude of opinions in a large group, the entire workshop can get stuck on one topic or section of the piece. Not only is it unproductive when the debate gets stuck, but it's also really hard to sit through.

METHODS OF RESPONDING

One thing I don't need with an early draft is someone telling me that I misspelled the word *rhythm*. It is a word I'll never be able to spell, and that fact makes me eternally grateful for spellcheckers. I do like to know whether an early draft delivers on its implied promises to the reader, and especially whether there is another angle or another topic lurking there that I might not have noticed. But I don't want my wife, Karen, to read my stuff until I have a late draft to show her because I sometimes find her comments on early drafts discouraging.

> The kinds of responses we seek to our writing in workshops depend on at least two things: where we are in the writing process and how we feel about the work in progress.

The *kinds* of responses we seek to our writing in workshops depend on at least two things: where we are in the writing process and how we feel about the work in progress. This is not particularly surprising. After all, certain kinds of problems arise during different stages of the writing process, and sometimes what we really need from readers of our work is more emotional than practical. We want to be motivated, encouraged, or validated, or feel any number of things that will help us work well.

Experiential and Directive Responses

It makes sense, then, to invite certain kinds of readings of your work that you'll find timely. In general, these responses range from experiential ("this is how I experienced your draft") to more directive ("this is what you could do to make it better"). Which of these two forms would make reader comments on your work most helpful? For example, depending on who you are and how you work, it may be most helpful to get less directive responses to your work early on. Some people feel that very specific suggestions undermine their sense of ownership of rough drafts. They don't want to know what readers think they should do in the revision but how readers experienced their draft. What parts were interesting? What parts were confusing? On the other hand, other writers feel particularly lost in the early stages of the writing process; they could use all the direction they can get. You decide (or your instructor will make suggestions), choosing from the following menu of workshop response methods. These begin with the most experiential methods of response to those that invite your readers to offer quite specific suggestions about the revision.

Response Formats

The following formats for responding to workshop drafts begin with the least directive, most experiential methods and move to the more directive approaches.

THE ETHICS OF RESPONDING

- Respect the writer.
- Everyone contributes.
- Say "could" rather than "should."
- Say "I" rather than "you," as in "I couldn't follow this" rather than "You weren't very clear."

While many of these formats feature some particular ways of responding to drafts, remember that the writer's and reader's responsibilities described earlier apply to all of them. Participate thoughtfully and ethically (see the box "The Ethics of Responding") and you'll be amazed at what you learn about your own writing from talking with other writers about theirs.

The No-Response Workshop. Sometimes the most useful response to your work comes from simply reading it aloud to your group and asking them to just listen—nothing more. Why? You may not be ready for comments because the work is unformed and you're confident that'll you discover the direction you want to go in the next draft. Comments may confuse or distract you. It's always helpful to read your work aloud to yourself, but it's also valuable to read to an audience even if you don't invite a response. You will read with more attention and awareness. Finally, you may simply feel unprepared for a response because your confidence is low.

The method couldn't be simpler. You read your draft with little or no introduction while your group quietly listens. They will not comment unless they want you to repeat something because it was inaudible. Remember to read slowly and clearly.

The Initial-Response Workshop. Robert Brooke, Ruth Mirtz, and Rick Evans[1] suggest a method that is useful for "maintaining your motivation to write while indirectly learning what to improve in your text." It might also be appropriate for an early draft.

They suggest that you invite three kinds of responses to your work: a "relating" response, a "listening" response, and a "positive" response. These three types of response to a draft could be made in writing, in workshop discussion, or both.

- **Relating response.** As the name implies, group members share what personal associations the writer's topic inspires. Perhaps they've had a similar or a contradictory experience. Maybe they've read something or seen something that is relevant to what the writer is trying to do in the draft.

---

[1]Robert Brooke, Ruth Mirtz, and Rick Evans, *Small Groups in Writing Workshops* (Urbana, IL: NCTE, 1994).

- **Listening response.** This is much like the "say back" method some therapists use with patients. Can you summarize what it is that you hear the writing saying in the draft? Is this something that is helpful to know?

- **Positive response.** What parts of the draft really work well and why? Might these be things the writer could build on in the next draft?

The Narrative-of-Thought Workshop. A writer who hears the story of readers' thinking *as they experienced the draft* can get great insight about how the piece shapes readers' expectations and how well it delivers on its promises. This method borrows a term from Peter Elbow— "movie of the mind"—to describe the creation of such a narrative response to a piece of writing.

The easiest way to create stories of your readers' experiences is to prepare your draft ahead of time to accommodate them. Before you make copies for your workshop group, create 2- to 3-inch white spaces in the manuscript immediately after the lead or beginning paragraph, and then again in the middle of the essay. Also leave at least that much white space after the end of the piece.

You will read your draft episodically, beginning by just reading the lead or introductory paragraph, then allowing three or four minutes for your group's members to respond in writing in the space you provided for some of the following questions. The writer should time this and ask everyone to stop writing when it's time to read the next section of the draft. Repeat the process, stopping at the second patch of white space after you've read roughly half of the essay. Give your group the same amount of time to respond in writing and then finish the essay to prompt the final episode of writing.

- **After hearing the lead:** What are your feelings about the topic or the writer so far? Can you predict what the essay might be about? What questions does the lead raise for you that you expect might be answered later? What has struck you?

- **After hearing half:** Tell the story of what you've been thinking or feeling about what you've heard so far. Has the draft fulfilled your expectations from the lead? What do you expect will happen next?

- **After hearing it all:** Summarize your understanding of what the draft is about, including what it *seems* to be saying (or not quite saying). How well did it deliver on its promises in the beginning? What part of your experience of the draft was most memorable? What part seemed least clear?

Discuss with your group each of the responses—after the lead, after the middle, and at the end of the draft. This conversation, and the written comments you receive when you collect their copies of your draft, should give you strong clues about how well you've established a clear purpose in your essay and sustained it from beginning to end. The responses also might give you ideas about directions to take the next draft that you hadn't considered.

The Instructive-Lines Workshop. Most essays balance on a thesis, theme, question, or idea. Like the point of a spinning top, these claims, ideas, or questions are the things around which everything else revolves. Essay drafts, however, may easily topple over because they lack such balance—there is no clear point, or there are too many, or some of the information is irrelevant. In discovery drafts especially, a writer may be seeking the piece's center of gravity—or *centers* of gravity—and a useful response from a workshop group is to help the writer look for the clues about where that center might be.

This format for a workshop invites the members to try to identify the draft's *most important lines and passages,* by clearly marking them with underlining or highlighting. What makes a line or passage important? *These are places where writers explicitly or implicitly seem to suggest what they're trying to say in a draft,* and they may include the following:

- A line or passage where the writer seems to state his or her thesis.

- A part of a narrative essay when the writer adopts a critical stance and seems to be trying to pose a question or speculate about the meaning of an experience or some information.

- A part of the draft in which the writer seems to make an important claim.

- A scene or comparison or observation that hints at the question the writer is exploring (or could explore).

- A comment in a digression that the writer didn't seem to think was important, but you think might be.

These portions of the text become the subject of discussion in the workshop session. Questions to consider include the following: Why did this particular line seem important? What does it imply about what you think is the meaning of the essay? Do the different underlined passages speak to each other—can they be combined or revised into a controlling idea or question for the next draft—or do they imply separate essays or treatments? Would the writer underline something else? How might the different interpretations of the draft be reconciled?

The Purpose Workshop. Sometimes writers know their purpose in a draft: "I'm trying to argue that the Enron collapse represented the failure of current methods of compensating CEOs," or "I'm proposing that having vegetarian fast-food restaurants would reduce American obesity," or "This essay explores the question of why I was so relieved when my father died." What these writers may need most from their workshop groups is feedback on how well the draft accomplishes particular purposes.

Before the workshop session, the writer crafts a statement of purpose similar to those in the preceding paragraph—a sentence that clearly states what the writer is trying to do in the draft. This statement of purpose should include a verb that implies what action the writer is trying to take—for example, *explore, argue, persuade, propose, review, explain,* or *analyze.* As you probably guessed, these verbs are usually associated with a particular form of inquiry or genre.

The writer should include this sentence *at the end* of the draft. It's important that you make group members aware of your purpose only after they've read the entire piece and not before. Discussion and written responses should then focus on some of the following questions:

- Were you surprised by the stated purpose, or did the essay prepare you for it?

- If the stated purpose did surprise you, what did you think the writer was trying to do in the draft instead?

- Does the lead explicitly state or hint at the stated purpose?

- What parts or paragraphs of the draft seemed clearly relevant to the stated purpose, and which seemed to point in another direction?

- Did the draft seem to succeed in accomplishing the writer's purpose?

If more directive responses would be helpful to you, consider also asking some questions such as whether there might not be a stronger beginning or lead buried elsewhere in the draft, or soliciting suggestions about which parts or paragraphs should be cut or what additional information might be needed. Which parts of the draft seemed to work best in the context of the writer's stated purpose, and which didn't work so well?

The Graphing-Reader-Interest Workshop. What commands readers' attention in a draft and what doesn't? This is useful to know, obviously, because our overall aim is to engage readers from beginning to end—which is difficult to do, particularly in longer drafts, and reader attention often varies from paragraph to paragraph in shorter drafts. But if three or four paragraphs or a couple of pages of your draft drone on, then the piece isn't working well and you need to do something about it in revision.

One way to know this is to ask your workshop group members to graph their response to your essay, paragraph by paragraph, and then discuss what is going on in those sections that drag.

For this workshop, consecutively number all the paragraphs in your draft. You or your instructor will provide each member of your group with a "reader interest chart" (see Figure 10.2), on which the corresponding paragraph numbers are listed. On the vertical axis is a scale that represents reader interest, with 5 being high interest and 1 being low interest in that particular paragraph. As you slowly read your draft aloud to your group's members, they mark the graph after each paragraph to roughly indicate their interest in what the paragraph says and how it says it.

When you're finished, you'll have a visual representation of how the essay worked, paragraph by paragraph, but the important work is ahead. Next, you

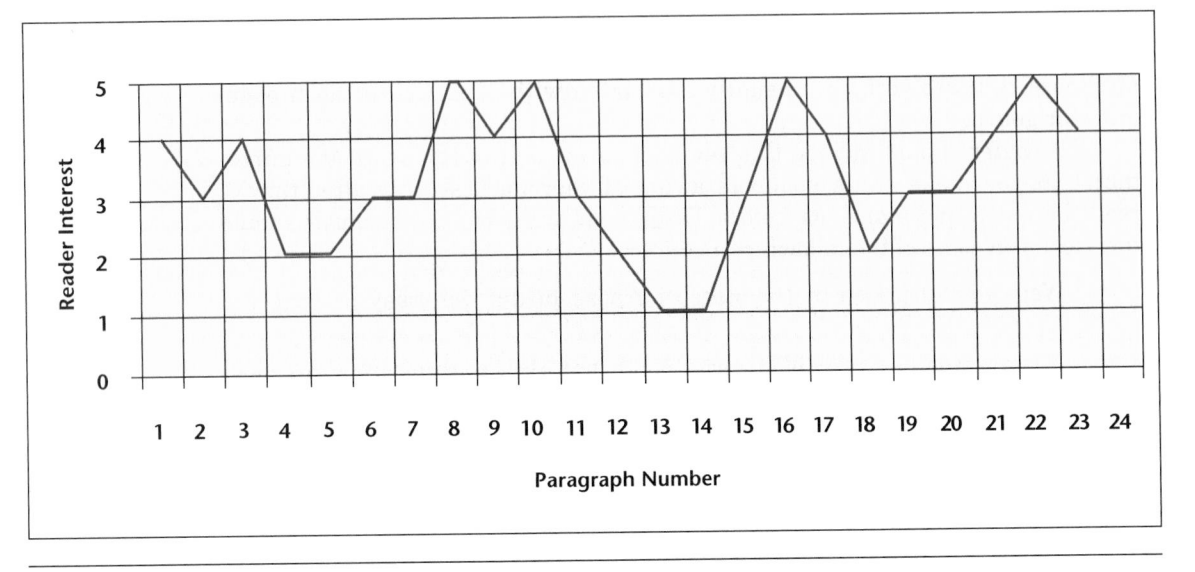

Figure 10.2 Reader interest chart

need to discuss with your group *why* a paragraph or section of the draft failed to hold some readers' attention. What is going on in those parts of the draft?

- Are they confusing?
- Do they needlessly digress?
- Is the prose awkward?
- Is there too much or too little explanation?
- Are they too loaded with facts and not enough analysis?
- Does the writer seem to lose his voice?

One way to find out what's going on with the weaker parts of your essay is to look at the stronger ones. What do you notice about those paragraphs that were rated 4 or 5 by your group members? What are the particular strengths of these sections? Can you do more of that in other, less lively sections of the draft?

The Sum-of-the-Parts Workshop. Like a watch, a well-written essay moves fluently forward because all of its parts work together. In workshops you can never talk about all those parts; there is too little time, and often it's hard to tease apart all the gears and the springs that make an essay go. But you can try to be as thorough as you can during a workshop, essentially running through a checklist of some of the most important elements, including purpose, theme, structure, information, and style. In this workshop, you attempt to cover as much territory as possible, so the responses you get will have breadth but not depth. You also invite some directive responses from your readers—suggestions for the revision and specific areas of confusion—as well as their interpretation of your purpose and theme.

One of the best ways to solicit this information is to use a worksheet like the one that follows. Typically, this worksheet would be filled out by your group's members outside class and before you workshop the draft. It would then be attached to the copies of your draft and returned to you after the group discusses the work. If your peers respond thoughtfully to the worksheet, it can generate a wealth of information for you about your draft.

The Thesis Workshop. An alternative to the sum-of-all-parts format is to focus on a single element of the draft that you are particularly concerned about, and no part is more important than the thesis. An essay without an implicit theme or an explicit thesis is an essay without meaning. No one is particularly interested in reading a pointless story or research essay, nor are most readers interested in points that seem unrelated to the information in the draft or that are painfully obvious. For example, the idea that the death of your Aunt Trudy was sad for you is a much less compelling theme to build an essay around than the idea that her death—and the deaths of family members generally—upset the family system in ways that helped you to take on new roles, new identities.

A thesis workshop will help you make sure there is a controlling idea or question behind the draft, and help you think more deeply about what you're trying to say. Your workshop members can help with this because they bring a range of perspectives and experiences to a conversation about your theme that might make it richer and more informative for you.

WORKSHOP WORKSHEET

Purpose: In your own words, what is the writer's motive in the draft? Use one of the following verbs to describe this in a sentence: *explore, explain, argue, analyze, review, report, propose, persuade, reflect.*

Theme: State in your own words what you think the thesis, main point, or central question is in this draft. What question does this idea or question raise for you?

Information: Name at least two specific places in the draft where you wanted more information to fully appreciate what the writer was trying to say. What kind of information do you suggest (anecdote, story, fact, detail, background, example, interview, dialogue, opposing perspective, description, case study, etc.)?

Design: Identify *at least* one paragraph or passage that seemed out of place. Any suggestions about where it belongs?

Style: Place brackets [ ] around several sentences or passages in the draft that seemed awkward or confusing to read.

In this workshop, group members receive the drafts ahead of time. Before the workshop session they should underline the thesis, main idea, theme, or question that seems to be behind the draft. This will be the *main thing* the writer seems to be saying or exploring. This isn't particularly difficult in essays with explicit thesis statements, such as arguments or proposals, but in personal essays and other more literary pieces, the theme may not be so explicit. In that type of essay, they should underline the passage that seems central to the meaning of the essay. This may be a reflective passage or it might be a scene or moment.

Second, at the top of a piece of paper, they should write down in a sentence or two—at most—the thesis or theme as they understand it. This may involve simply copying it down from the draft. However, if the thesis or theme is not that clear or explicit, each reader should write it down in his or her own words, trying to capture the main point of the draft.

Then members should fastwrite for five minutes about their own thoughts and experiences about the writer's thesis or theme, constantly hunting for questions it raises for them. Say the draft's thesis is that the university athletic programs have become too powerful and have undermined the university's more important academic mission. In the fastwrite, explore what you've noticed about the football team's impact on the school. Where does the football program get funds? Does it compete with academic programs? Then fastwrite about what you've heard—for instance, that athletics have strong alumni support. Keep the fastwrite focused on the thesis; if it helps, stop and reread it for another prompt.

The workshop session that follows will be a conversation largely focused on what people thought was the point of the draft, and their own thoughts and feelings about it. The writer should facilitate the conversation without comment and make sure the following two things are discussed in this order:

1. What seems to be the thesis, theme, or question behind the essay? Is it clear? Are there alternative ideas about what it might be?

2. What does each group member think or feel about what the writer seems to be saying? How do the reader's experiences and observations relate to the writer's main point or question? And especially, what questions should the writer consider in the next draft?

Although it may be hard to keep quiet if your draft is being discussed, the conversation will probably surprise you. You may discover that several of your group members either failed to understand what you were trying to say in the draft or give you a completely new idea about what you were up to. At its best, the thesis workshop inspires you to think more deeply about your theme or main idea as you consider the range of experiences and questions that other people have about it. Take lots of notes.

The Editing Workshop. In a late draft, the larger issues—for example, having a clear purpose, focus, and point, as well as appropriate information to support it—may be resolved to your satisfaction, or you may feel that you already have some pretty good ideas about how to deal with them. If so, what you may need most from your workshop group is editorial advice: responses to your work at the sentence and paragraph levels.

In the editing workshop, you invite your group members to focus on style and clarity (and perhaps grammar and mechanics). The questions that direct the reading of the draft might include some or all of the following:

- Did you stumble over any awkward passages that seemed to interrupt the fluency of the writing?

- Were there any sentences or passages that you had to read a few times to understand?

- Could any long paragraphs be broken down into smaller ones? Did any paragraphs seem to be about more than one thing?

- Are the first and last lines of the essay well crafted? Are the last lines of paragraphs strong enough?

- Were there any abrupt transitions between paragraphs?

- Was the voice or tone of the draft consistent?

- (Optional) Did you notice any patterns of grammatical problems, including run-on sentences, unclear pronoun references, or lack of subject–verb agreement?

Group members who see any of these problems should bracket [ ] the sentence or passage and refer to it when discussing the editorial issue with the group. The workshop discussion has the following ground rules:

- Be respectful of the writer's feelings. Some of us feel that style is a very personal issue, and that grammar problems are related somehow to our self-worth.

- Don't have arguments about editorial judgments. Group members don't have to agree. In fact, you probably won't agree about a lot of things. Offer your comments on style as suggestions and then move on, although don't hesitate to offer a differing opinion.

- Make sure to identify places in the draft where the writing is working just fine. Editorial workshops need not focus exclusively on problems. Sentences, paragraphs, or passages that work well stylistically can often help the writer see how to revise the less effective parts.

- If readers have some comments about larger issues in the draft, things such as purpose or theme, ask the writer first if he or she welcomes that kind of feedback. Otherwise, keep the workshop focused on editorial matters.

An editing workshop may sound a little harrowing. It really isn't, particularly if the group knows the ground rules. My students often tell me that these conversations about style are some of the best workshops they have had.

Everybody learns something—not just the writer—a principle that applies to many workshop formats and another reason that peer review is such a useful practice in the writing classroom.

Reflecting on the Workshop

The real work follows the workshop. Then you have the task of mulling over the things you've heard about your draft and deciding how you're going to rewrite it. This calls for a way of inquiring—reflection—that you've already practiced. As soon as possible after your workshop session, reread your notes and your readers' comments, then go to your journal and fastwrite for five minutes. Choose one of the following prompts to get—and keep—you going.

- What did I hear that seemed most useful? What did I hear that I'm not sure about?
- What responses to my draft do I remember most? Why?
- What did I think I needed to do to revise the draft before the workshop? Did my peer review experience change my mind? Did it reinforce my initial plans?
- What do I plan to do to revise this draft to make it stronger?

USING WHAT YOU HAVE LEARNED

The writing workshop is just one of many forms of collaboration that you'll likely experience both during and after college. Even unsuccessful workshops are instructive because they help you understand how groups work and what roles you can play to make them function better. Consider your experience so far.

1. What is the best workshop group experience you've had in this class? What made it so good? What was the worst experience? What made it so bad?

2. As you reflect on your own performance in groups, what have you learned about yourself as a collaborator? How would you describe yourself as a group member? How would you *like* to describe yourself?

3. If you're currently involved in a group project in another class, how would you compare your writing workshop with that other group project? Can what you've learned in one provide useful guidance for the other?

APPENDIX A

THE WRITING PORTFOLIO*

What Is a Portfolio?

You've probably heard about stock portfolios and artist portfolios, but the term *writing portfolio* may be something new. *Portfolio* in these three examples means a collection of stocks, photographs or paintings, or writings that represent something about the compiler: for example, if you have a stock portfolio in which 75 percent of your money is invested in high-risk growth funds and the other 25 percent is in safe bond funds, then you might be showing that you're a risk taker. If you are an artist and you select a range of photographs taken over a long period of time, you might be showing how you've developed and changed as a photographer.

Writing portfolios can reflect similar things about their authors. As a collection of the work you've done for a writing class, a portfolio can demonstrate how you've developed as a writer, it can show specific writing principles you've learned, or it can illustrate the range of genres you have worked with (to name a few). Often it will be a large percentage of your course grade, so the work you submit will have been revised several times and you might be asked to reflect on your assembled work, exploring what you want the portfolio to illustrate. In fact, the whole idea of using a portfolio to evaluate your work emphasizes the principles of inquiry and reflection at the heart of this book.

Instructors use portfolios in different ways: Some require certain essays and assignments to be included, some allow *you* to choose what to include, others ask that you choose according to particular guidelines (for example, pieces that demonstrate your ability to conduct research, to put a lesson plan together if it's a teaching portfolio, or to revise). It's important that you understand what kind of portfolio your instructor is requiring and why. We'll talk about why later—let's look first at the different kinds of portfolios you might be asked to assemble.

---

*Appendixes A, B, C, and D were written by Dr. Michelle Payne, English Department Chair at Boise State University.

Types of Portfolios

It's important here to distinguish between *unevaluated* and *evaluated* portfolios. An unevaluated portfolio would be one in which you are collecting all your work for the course, like a journal or working folder, but your instructor will not be evaluating the material. You keep class notes, doodles, drafts of essays, exercises, and anything else that relates to the course. From that folder, you then might be asked to *choose specific assignments*, continue working on them, and turn them in for your final portfolio. A final portfolio is one type of evaluated portfolio. Your instructor either gives you the evaluation criteria for it or helps the class develop those criteria with him or her. You turn in selected pieces from the course, either freely chosen by you or required by your instructor. The work is "final" in that you have stopped revising, done your best to make it as effective an essay as possible, and are ready to have it graded. Unevaluated portfolios, then, are places in which you experiment with, collect, and play around with your ideas and your writing, not worrying about evaluation as much as you would when you assemble an evaluated portfolio. All the activities in this book, for example, would be part of a writing journal or working folder that your instructor might not evaluate. Then, as you develop essays from those exercises, you revise them into final products that your instructor can grade.

Unevaluated Portfolios

The unevaluated portfolios you are most likely to encounter in your college writing are as follows:

- *A journal or working folder.* In this type of unevaluated portfolio, keep all your work for your writing course—everything that you do in and out of class, all your assignments and drafts. It's a place where you can track your progress as a writer because you have everything there. Some instructors ask you to turn this type of portfolio in for a holistic grade (that is, the entire body of work is evaluated, not individual pieces), based on criteria that are different from the criteria used for evaluating a portfolio of final drafts (for example, in evaluating a writing journal, your instructor might consider whether you've completed all the assignments, taken risks in your writing, and experimented).

- *A learning portfolio.* For this type of unevaluated portfolio, you collect materials from your course and possibly other places that reflect something about your learning process. Let's say your writing instructor wants you to keep a record of your learning in another course, such as sociology. You might include class notes that changed the way you understood a concept, restaurant napkins scribbled with conversations you've overheard, a paper you are assigned to write, and some reflections on how the theories you've been learning affect how you perceive your world. You can include both print and nonprint materials, such as photos or music. Learning portfolios often allow for free choice, so you have to carefully select what you will include and why. This type of portfolio may be helpful as you apply the concepts you learn in this course—about inquiry, essay writing, and reflection—to another course.

Evaluated Portfolios

Evaluated portfolios include the following types:

- *A midterm portfolio.* As the name suggests, this portfolio is assembled at midterm. Your instructor might ask you to include particular assignments—such as your two best reading responses and a revised essay—and write a cover letter that explains, for example, what you've learned about writing that is reflected in these pieces. You might also be asked to evaluate the portfolio yourself and discuss your goals for the rest of the course. A midterm portfolio might be evaluated, but it might also be used as a practice run for the final portfolio at the end of the course and not be evaluated.

- *A final portfolio—limited choice.* Your instructor may require you to include specific assignments and essays in the portfolio you turn in at the end of the course. Let's say your university's writing program requires all students to write a research essay in their first-year writing course and to demonstrate that they can use documentation effectively, support their claims with evidence, and do more than simply string information together. Your instructor, then, would ask you to include one or more research essays in the final portfolio so he or she can assess whether you have learned what is required. That might be the only required essay and you would have some choice about what else to include. Or you might be required to include a profile, an argument, and an ethnographic essay, as well. In addition, instructors might ask you to include a reflective essay with your final portfolio (explained in more detail next). In general, a final portfolio emphasizes the final products of the course, the revised and polished work that shows what you've learned for the entire term.

- *A final portfolio—open choice.* While all your work will be revised and polished, your instructor may ask you to choose your best writing for the course and not require particular essays. She might ask that you choose only from the essays you've written or that you choose from the informal writing you've done, as well (such as the writing exercises in this book). She may require a certain number of pages (say, twenty to twenty-five pages) or a certain number of assignments (three out of the five essays required in the course) or leave the length and number of assignments open. Here are a couple of examples: If you feel your research essay is better than your ethnographic essay, then you might include it and not work any further on your ethnographic essay. You might also include your personal essay, an argument, and your response to a particular writing exercises. You would include these pieces because you believe they are your best work, but you want to be sure you can talk specifically about *why* they are the best and *what* they show your instructor about what you've learned. For instance, do you want to show your growth, your success in using writing as inquiry, or what you've learned about crafting paragraphs?

Why Require a Portfolio?

Before we talk more about how to choose the materials to include in your portfolio, we should talk about why you will be expected to assemble one. If you are keeping an unevaluated portfolio, your instructor wants to emphasize your learning process at least as much as your final product. We rarely take the time to reflect on how we learn, but doing so can help you learn better in your other courses. Are you a visual learner? Do you learn best when you have a relationship with your teacher or when the teacher is more removed? If you learn more outside school, why? Learning portfolios enable you to develop even better learning strategies and understand why you might struggle with certain learning situations. The same is true for a writing journal or working folder. As you collect everything you do in a writing course, you can pause periodically and reflect on which writing strategies seem to sabotage your efforts, which seem to work well, how you might work through writer's block, or what principles about writing you've been learning. Many of the exercises in this book prompt you to reflect on your writing process, your reading strategies, and your learning and thinking, so if you've been doing them, you have already seen the benefits of reflecting on your process.

In both kinds of unevaluated portfolios, the *process* of whatever you're doing is being emphasized and valued. You don't have to worry about writing beautifully styled sentences the first time around or having a complicated reading all figured out the first time through. An unevaluated portfolio allows for—in fact encourages—the messiness of writing and thinking instead of focusing only on polished work. These kinds of portfolios emphasize risk, experimentation, and reflection on the process of writing and learning, all of which are central to the ideas in this book. These types of portfolios, then, reflect and reinforce what you've been learning about writing so far.

Evaluated portfolios are important for very similar reasons. In order to get your drafts to the point that they are ready to be evaluated, you are encouraged all term to experiment, rewrite, and critique them. In fact, most of the term you are working in your writing journal, exploring ideas, commenting on peers' drafts in workshop, revising your own drafts, and taking them apart again, all in an effort to learn more about writing and make your essays more effective.

Portfolios allow you to do all that over a long period of time and in a relatively "evaluation-free" zone, so you are graded based on your final product at the end, not in the middle, of the process.

Your final product, though, is the result and reflection of all that work you did throughout the semester. In addition, the reflection exercises in this book have had you thinking about your learning all term. You will be more conscious of the writing and reading strategies that work best for you, and so will be better prepared to write the reflective essay that your instructor may require in the portfolio.

Of course, the final product is what is evaluated in a final portfolio, so while this kind of portfolio reinforces the process of inquiry and reflection, it also emphasizes the way a sentence is crafted, the way an essay is organized, and the way a writer explores an idea. A portfolio, then, allows an instructor to evaluate *both* the process of writing and the quality of the final product.

Organizing Portfolios

Because a writing portfolio emphasizes the *process* of writing and learning as much as the final product, you'll want to keep your course materials organized— that is, the materials that reflect your process. Whether or not your instructor assigns a journal or working folder, it's a good idea to keep one yourself. You can do this on the computer or in a notebook. You can organize your writing journal or working folder in several ways, including these options:

1. **Organize by chronological order.** Keep everything that you do in the course in the order you complete it.

2. **Organize by assignments.** Within each category, include all the writing you've done (fastwriting, drafts, exercises), peer and teacher responses, notes, research materials, and so on. As an example, your portfolio might be broken out into the following categories:

   - Profile
   - Ethnographic essay
   - Review
   - Argument
   - Reflective exercises
   - Reading responses
   - Essay exam

3. **Organize by subjects.** Here you place your writing into categories defined by the subject or theme of the writing. For example:

   - Racism (profile, research essay)
   - Italy trip (personal essay, review, argument)

With this approach, you have a better sense of how you've explored a topic through different genres, comparing what you've learned about the subject as well as about the form.

4. **Organize by stage of process.** Here you place your writing into categories based on what place in the writing process it falls, starting with your fastwriting and journal writing and ending with your final drafts and reflective writing. For example:

- Fastwriting/journal writing
- Exercises
- Sketches
- Early drafts
- Peer responses
- Instructor responses
- Revisions
- Final drafts
- Reflective writing

You can also create your own categories to organize your class work. However you choose to organize your writing, be sure to keep everything you write for the course; don't throw anything away. If you are using a computer, *save all of your writing files and keep a separate backup copy.*

If you are expected to include a reflective letter or essay as a preface to your portfolio, it's a good idea to create a separate section in your journal or folder for all the reflective writing you've done in the class. You can do all the reflective exercises in that separate section, or you can include them for each separate assignment. However you do it, keeping your reflective writing in one place will make it easier to compose your reflective letter or essay.

Writing a Reflective Letter or Essay

You may have to preface your final portfolio with a letter or essay that introduces the pieces you've included and reflect on what you've learned about writing, reading, and inquiry. For some instructors, this letter or essay becomes crucial in evaluating the whole portfolio because it gives coherence and purpose to the material and articulates what you've learned. In my own classes, the reflective essay can make the difference of half a letter grade in the overall evaluation of the portfolio. As always, clarify with your instructor what is expected in the reflective letter or essay and how it will be weighed in the portfolio grade. While some instructors require a five- to seven-page essay or letter that begins the portfolio, others may require a prefatory letter for *each piece* you include in the portfolio. Some want only a reflection on the writing process for each essay; others may want only a narrative of how your thinking changed about each subject you wrote about. Regardless, you'll want to spend some time going through your writing journal or folder and reflecting on what you notice. Here are some questions that might help:

- **Patterns.** As you flip through the pages of your writing journal or folder, what patterns do you notice? What seems to happen frequently or stand out to you? For example, you might notice that you always begin your essays the same way, or you ended up writing about the same subject the whole semester without realizing it, or you got better at organizing your essays and using significant detail.

- **Reflective writing.** As you look only at the reflective writing you've done throughout the course (and the reflective exercises in this book), what do you notice? What five things have you learned about writing, reading, and inquiry based on that early reflective writing?

- **Change over time.** How did you describe your writing process (and/or reading process) at the beginning of the course? How would you describe it now? If it has changed, why and how?

- **Writing principles.** List five to seven principles about writing that you have learned in this course, the five to seven most important things you've learned about writing, reading, and inquiry. Or, list five to seven strategies for writing and reading that you will take with you into other writing situations.

- **Revision.** For each of the essays you are including in your portfolio, what would you do differently if you had more time?

- **Writing processes.** For each of the essays in your portfolio, describe the writing and thinking process that led to the final product. Emphasize the most important changes you made and why you made them.

- **Most and least effective writing.** Which essay in the portfolio is your strongest? Your weakest? Why?

- **Effect of peer response.** How have your peers and other readers of your work affected the revisions you've made?

- **Showing what you've learned.** What does your portfolio demonstrate about you as a writer, a student, a reader, a researcher? How? Be as specific as possible.

- **What's missing.** What is *not* reflected in your portfolio that you believe is important for your instructor to know?

- **Expectations.** How does your portfolio meet the expectations for effective writing defined in your class?

- **Applying the textbook.** How have you applied the principles about each essay form that are outlined in this textbook?

- **Personal challenge.** In what ways did you challenge yourself in this course?

TYPICAL PROBLEMS IN REFLECTIVE ESSAYS/LETTERS

- Use of overly general and vague comments.
- Not enough specific details.
- Giving the teacher only what you think he or she wants whether it's true or not.
- Critiquing the course (usually this is reserved for end-of-term evaluations that are confidential and anonymous); it's not wise to risk criticizing the person who is evaluating you.
- Comments that suggest you don't take the assignment seriously.

Your instructor might ask you to address only three or four of these questions in the letter or essay itself, but it's a good idea to do some fastwriting on all of them. Doing so will help your essay or letter be more specific, thoughtful, and persuasive.

As with any essay, you'll want to take this one through several revisions and get feedback from readers before you include it in the portfolio. Your instructor might even ask you to workshop a draft of this with your group. If you've done some fastwriting on the preceding questions, you are in good shape to compose a first draft of your reflective letter or essay. Keep in mind who your audience is—your teacher, teachers unknown to you, and/or your peers—and address what that audience expects. Be as specific as possible, citing examples from your work and drawing on the terms and principles you've discussed in class and read about in this book.

If you've been doing reflective writing all term, you will have plenty of material to draw from to make your reflective essay or letter concrete, substantive, and as honest as it can be (given the circumstances). You'll probably surprise yourself with all that you've learned.

Final Preparations

Before you turn your portfolio in, take time to proofread it carefully, possibly asking one of your peers for help. Check again to be sure you've met all the criteria for the portfolio, including what is required, assembling it appropriately, and formatting it as required. This is work that you are proud of, so the way you present it should reflect that pride. It should meet high standards for presentation and quality.

APPENDIX B
THE LITERATURE REVIEW

What Is a Literature Review?

Have you ever wondered why those academic articles you read for your research projects seem to begin with a list of the other people who've talked about the same ideas? Somewhere in the first few pages you find a section that seems to list everyone who's ever had anything to say about the subject of, say, Charlotte Brontë or quantum physics. This "who's who" list, though, is actually a common academic convention called the *literature review*. In it a writer reviews or summarizes what has already been said about his or her research question and then analyzes it.

An explicit example of giving this kind of background is the opening to "Is the Medium the Message?" by Ellen M. Bennet, et al. As you read it, notice the way the writers acknowledge the specific people who are a part of this conversation and try to accurately summarize their contributions (I've italicized some of the phrases these writers use to signal this summary). Imagine this as the writers' way of introducing us to the conversation that we've just walked into. The article begins:

> When Pennsylvania official Budd Dwyer committed suicide during a press conference in January 1987, television coverage of the incident was criticized sharply, although most stations cut the tape before the shot was fired. Somehow, coverage of this event by print reporters and photojournalists did not stir the same scorn from the critics or the public that TV news accounts evoked.
>
> The "bad news" bias of journalism professionals has been of increasing concern generally, and much of the criticism has been leveled specifically at television news. Both *practitioners of the profession and news consumers* have complained that TV news exploits graphic and grotesque news events for the purpose of increasing ratings in the competitive race for profits. *Two common responses* to these criticisms are that, first, the morbid event is newsworthy and, second, that this is what the audience wants.
>
> *A common criticism* leveled at television is that it is excessively morbid in its presentation of news. Even *those who have pioneered the field of television news* identify the medium as uniquely able to portray tragedy because it is so visual.

Researchers have also noted the near universal appeal of stories about disturbing, unpleasant, tragic events. *Haskins* has observed that "throughout history humans have been drawn to public spectacles involving bloody death and disfigurement, to helpless victims, to public hangings and crucifixions and decapitation." The purpose of the present study...

Although this introduction doesn't cover a wide range of specific experts in the field, it does summarize what most people in the field have said—or what people *outside* have said. It gives us an overview, a brief summary with background on the issue so we all know why it is important and what has been said about it already. After all, how can we determine how significant someone's research is unless they tell us how it compares with the work of other people in the same field?

So in a literature review, a writer gives readers an overview of the conversation that other scholars, writers, or researchers have been having over the years so they will understand why his question is important and where it comes from. But he also gives us this critical overview to signal that he's done his research, he knows who has said what and why it's important, and therefore he has credibility to write about the subject, too. A literature review, then, does at least three things:

1. **Summarizes the established knowledge** on a particular subject and **analyzes it** within the context of the writer's overall thesis or research question.

2. **Establishes why the writer's question is significant,** given what has already been said, and how it emerged as an important subject for further study.

3. **Establishes the writer's ethos or credibility,** signaling membership in a particular community (such as the field of biology or engineering) and demonstrating thoroughness in researching.

As you might guess, writing a literature review means you will focus on the two ways of inquiring we've discussed in this book: *explanation* and *evaluation*. The thinking and reading you do *before* you write the review, however, will demand that you use all four ways of inquiring, including reflection and exploration.

How to Write the Literature Review

The easiest and most efficient way to write a literature review is to approach its composition systematically. This will include gathering materials, reading strategies, organizing, and drafting processes.

Gathering Materials

First, you have to conduct some research: Do a thorough search for materials related to your research question and sort out which are most relevant and most important in the field. Often you can discover who the important researchers and scholars are in an area by looking at the bibliographies of the articles and books you have found. Whose name seems to occur frequently? Who seems to be cited quite often? Whose work seems to be central to the ideas you're talking about?

Sorting out what is relevant to your question all depends on your question and the scope of your research.

- If your research question hasn't been explored by others yet, then you need to look at material that helps you discuss *why* it hasn't been researched before.

- If you are using a particular theory or approach to your research—such as feminist literary theory to interpret *Jane Eyre* or an ethnographic approach to understand reading skills in third graders—you will need to discuss that particular theory or approach. What has been argued about this theory or approach? What are the key principles and arguments that will be relevant to your own work?

- If your research question touches on an area that has been written about a great deal—let's say Shakespeare or World War II—then you need to narrow your overview to the particular issue about that subject you are focusing on—say, gender in Shakespeare's tragedies or military strategies during the invasion of Normandy. Then you have to choose the sources that are most relevant and significant in the conversation that has been going on about the particular subject you're researching.

You cannot cover everything that has been said in the last seventy-five years—nor should you. You have to have criteria for deciding what you will include in your literature review. How many sources you discuss is often dependent on how long your project is (for a thesis or dissertation, a literature review is a chapter of about thirty pages; for a ten- to fifteen-page research paper, the review might be several paragraphs).

Reading Strategies

Like any other assignment, the reading strategies you use for this assignment will have a particular purpose. Your main task will be to understand well the argument each source is making, and then to judge its conclusions, methods of research, evidence, and relevance to your overall question or purpose. Most important, when you get ready to write your literature review, you need to have made connections among all the materials you've read, not only evaluating them against each other, but showing how each is related to the other. The following are some questions you should keep in mind as you read individual texts:

- What is the author's overall question and her conclusions? What argument is she making?

- What research methods does she use (for example, empirical, ethnographic, theoretical, case study)? What are the strengths and limitations of this method? Has she addressed them? How reliable are her conclusions?

- How well does she review the literature relevant to her subject?

- How effectively does she argue her case? Are her conclusions logical? Is her evidence relevant, specific, and substantial? Are her emotional appeals effective? Does she include counterarguments?

- What seem to be the gaps or unanswered questions in her research and/or conclusions? In other words, what does she not address or seem to dismiss or ignore that you think is relevant?

- What other approach might she have taken to this issue?

- How does this particular article/review/book/study fit into what has already been said? What is its relationship to other studies? For example, does it build on the work of another scholar, does it refute a long-standing theory, does it critique the research methods used, does it answer a question raised at the end of an earlier study?

After you finish reading individual texts, you will want to ask some broader questions:

- As you read all the material you've gathered, what overall patterns seem to emerge? For example, what seems to be common knowledge among the people in this area?

- Do the studies share similar research methods?

- Do they address different perspectives on the same question?

- Do they come to similar conclusions?

- Do they all seem to ignore similar assumptions or limitations?

- In other words, what kind of picture can you get about this conversation?

Finally, before you begin writing your literature review, use this seed sentence to help you summarize the material and articulate how your question is related to what you've read: *When most people think about/study/write about_____, they say/assert/argue _____. However, what they don't address is _____.*

Organizing

Once you have a sense of the conversation going on about your subject and you've carefully read and evaluated your sources, you need to figure out how you will organize your review. What you don't want to do is simply list all the relevant sources like a grocery list or a list of summaries, beginning each paragraph with "According to..." Although you'll want to introduce the authors using this kind of signal phrase, you don't want to organize your literature review by author. Instead, you need to organize the material around each source's *relationship* to the others and its significance to your project. That's what you've begun to do by answering the preceding questions about the patterns you see among all the sources you've read.

When you focus on the relationship among sources, you will be comparing, contrasting, and evaluating them based on particular criteria. You might, for example, want to focus on the trends in the research or compare the various conclusions of researchers. You need an organizing strategy. The following strategies are only a few of the possibilities:

- Trends in current research.
- Types of research methods used (quantitative, qualitative).
- Theoretical approaches.
- Specific purposes for the research/arguments.
- Conclusions reached.
- Gaps in the literature, questions not answered, and/or conflicts among theories, conclusions, evidence, or research methods.
- Chronology, or a history of how one idea led to the next.

The organizational strategy you choose will also be related to the question you're pursuing in your own research, especially if your literature review is part of a longer essay. If you are writing an essay about the medical uses of leeches, for example, you probably won't focus on the types of research methods used or the theoretical approaches. You might write a narrative of how leeches have been used in history, you might focus on what is known and what is not, or you might look at conflicting studies on the effectiveness of using leeches in medicine. The literature review should offer the reader context for your own question, reasons why it's important, and your own approach to the subject compared to that of others in the field.

You can use these organizational strategies to create sections in your literature review or to organize by paragraph. It all depends on the number of sources you plan to study and the length of your essay.

APPENDIX C

THE ANNOTATED BIBLIOGRAPHY

What Is an Annotated Bibliography?

You've had experience putting together a Works Cited or References page for your research essays, but you may not have had experience writing an annotated bibliography, which includes descriptions and comments about each of your sources. It is a list in which each citation is followed by a short descriptive and sometimes evaluative paragraph or annotation. Many scholars use published annotated bibliographies during their research to help them narrow down the material that seems most relevant to their work, but you might be asked to write one as part of a larger project for a class, sometimes in preparation for a literature review or a research proposal. Annotated bibliographies, then, can serve a lot of different purposes, so if you are assigned one, you want to be sure you understand your role as a researcher and writer.

We will examine four types of annotated bibliographies in this appendix.[1] Their purposes include indicating content and coverage, describing thesis and argument, evaluating the work, and a combination of these three. If you have looked at published annotated bibliographies, you have probably seen one of these types. When you are assigned to write an annotated bibliography, you'll need to decide which of the following four forms is the most appropriate, but you can also consider using these at various stages of your own research process.

Indicative Bibliography. Are you being asked to *indicate* what the source contains or simply identify the topic of the source, but *not evaluate or discuss the argument and evidence*? If so, explain what the source is about ("This article explores gender in Shakespeare's tragedies."). List the main ideas it discusses—this may include chapter titles, a list of authors included if the source is an anthology, or the main ideas included in the subsections if it's an article ("Topics covered include male homosocial desire, women as witches, and conceptions of romantic love."). Usually, in a descriptive annotation, you don't evaluate the source's argument or relevance, nor do you describe its overall thesis.

---

[1]The four forms discussed are found on the Writing Center Web site for the University of Wisconsin–Madison (http://www.wisc.edu/writing/Handbook/AnnBib_content.html).

WHY WRITE AN ANNOTATED BIBLIOGRAPHY?

- It can help you compile a list of sources on your subject that will need to be sorted through later. It can also help you decide if you want to return to a source later in your process.

- If you have been keeping a dialogue journal for your research project, you can refer to it in composing these annotations. This type of bibliography can help you further think through your own developing thesis or conclusions.

- This type of bibliography will also help you develop your own thesis, and it will help you write a literature review, as well.

Informative Bibliography. Are you being asked *to summarize the argument* for each source? If so, briefly state each work's thesis, the primary assertions and evidence that support the main argument, and any conclusions the author makes. You are not evaluating the effectiveness of the argument, nor are you delineating the content of the source (as you would in an indicative form); instead, you are informing your audience about the works' arguments and conclusions.

Evaluative Bibliography. Are you being asked *to evaluate the sources* you find? If so, your annotations will include a brief summary of the argument and conclusions and then move on to critically evaluate it: How useful is the source to your particular project? What are the limitations of the study or argument? What are the strengths? How reliable are the conclusions? How effective are the research methods? The criteria you use for evaluating each source depend on the purpose of the bibliography, whether you are compiling one to help focus your research project and sort out the most important articles or you are writing one to help others decide what is most relevant in the subject area. Be sure you are clear about the evaluation criteria.

Combination of Types. Are you being asked to be *both informative and evaluative*? Many annotated bibliographies have multiple purposes, so you will be combining the preceding forms. Because most annotations can be up to 150 words, you need to devote only a sentence or two for each purpose—in other words, a few lines to summarize and describe, a few to evaluate and comment. However, you may be told exactly what to include in the annotations and how many words or sentences to use. Your instructor might, for example, ask that you write one sentence summarizing each work's argument and then another sentence describing how the work relates to your own developing thesis.

How to Write an Annotated Bibliography

Before you can begin writing an annotated bibliography you must choose a subject on which to focus. From there you will move to gathering materials, applying reading strategies, and finally writing the annotated bibliography.

Gathering Materials

Find material relevant to your subject. Are you supposed to find a wide range of materials, such as reviews, scholarly articles, and books? Are you to focus only on materials from the last five years? What are the parameters for your researching? Be sure to clarify these issues with your instructor.

Reading Strategies

You'll again use the critical reading strategies you've learned as you read the sources you've decided to include in your bibliography. If the materials you've gathered will later become part of a research essay, then you will be taking notes and writing about them. But to create your annotated bibliography, you'll have an additional purpose for reading your sources. If you simply need to describe the content of the sources (indicative form), you will do little critical evaluation; instead, you'll focus on explanation. Once you determine the focus for your annotations, use the following questions (which apply primarily to evaluative forms of annotation, but also can help with informative and indicative forms) to guide your reading.

- Who is the intended audience for this article, review, or book?
- What central research question or claim does the material address? Write it out in one or two sentences.
- What kind of evidence is used to support the conclusions, argument, and thesis? How valid is it, given what the intended audience values? For example, literary examples wouldn't be taken seriously as evidence in a biology paper, nor would anecdotal evidence about an experiment.
- How effectively has the author addressed the central question or claim?
- Sketch out the main argument in a brief outline. Note the main subjects covered, the authors listed (if it's a collection of articles), and the general organization of the work.
- What is known about the credibility of this author(s)? Have you seen her name appear in other works on this subject? Is she publishing in her area of expertise?
- Note the dates of publication, usually on the copyright page. Is the material current? Does it need to be? Is this a revised edition?
- Compare the source to others on the same subject. Are the ideas similar enough to suggest that this author is working with accepted knowledge?
- If they aren't, do you find them valid, significant, or well researched? Is one source on this subject better than another, and why or why not? Does the source build on the ideas of others, critique them, and add new knowledge?

- How effectively is the source written?
- If you can, try to find reviews of the material or commentaries from other scholars in the area. This will give you a sense of how the work was received, what (if any) controversy it has generated, and what about it has been lauded and/or criticized.

Writing the Annotated Bibliography

Because annotations are so brief, it's tempting to think that they are easy to write. But as in any writing project, you need to have a lot of material to draw from—in this case, substantive notes and reflective writing about each work. It is better to work from abundance than from scarcity—remember, you need material to work with if you are going to identify what's worth keeping and what should be dropped.

Length. Depending on the requirements for and purposes of the annotations, they could be one paragraph or only a few sentences, so you have to choose your words carefully and use specific details judiciously. Clarify with your instructor the kind of writing style he expects; that is, does he want brief phrases, almost like a bulleted list of main points, or full sentences and paragraphs?

Content. Begin with the proper citation form for the source, following the guidelines for the specific documentation style your instructor requires (APA or MLA). Organize this list alphabetically. After each source, compose a paragraph or two that addresses your purpose for the bibliography. That purpose, again, will depend on the requirements your instructor has given you. If you are describing the content of the source, for example, begin with an overview of the work and its thesis, then select the specific points you want to highlight about it (such as chapter titles, subjects covered, authors included). If you are explaining the main argument of the work, begin with the central thesis and then include the main claims, evidence, research methods, and conclusions. Finally, if you are evaluating the source, add comments that summarize your critique.

Sample Student Annotated Bibliography

In the example that follows, Lauren Tussing wanted to apply what she's learned about feminist theory to the film *Lost in Translation*, and her annotated bibliography helped her focus her research question and decide which of the sources would be most useful in composing her essay. Notice that she has written an annotated bibliography that combines the informative and evaluative forms—she primarily summarizes the main argument of each source and then discusses its relevance to her research project.

Lauren Tussing

Instructor Michelle Payne

Engl 497

18 April 2004

Annotated Bibliography

Doane, Mary Ann. "Film and the Masquerade: Theorising the Female Spectator."

Feminism and Film. Ed. E. Ann Kaplan. Oxford: Oxford, 2000. 418–36. Print.

This is an article in a collection of articles on feminist film theory. In the essay, Doane works to create a theory for the female spectator, moving away from prior focus on the male spectator. Doane does, however, reintroduce the idea of Laura Mulvey's binary opposition of passive/female and active/male that she introduced in her essay "Visual Pleasure and Narrative Cinema." Doane applies the notion of distance to Mulvey's binary opposition.

This essay, written for an academic audience, is esoteric and sometimes difficult to understand, but it might be helpful for my paper if I decide to talk about the female spectator. Despite my difficulty with this essay, Doane did give me some ideas about how to think about *Lost in Translation,* the film that I discuss in my essay. A woman directs this film, so I wonder how her direction affects the gaze. Is there a uniquely female gaze for this film? Or does the film conform to the male gaze? How might viewers, both male and female, gaze upon this film?

Gaines, Jane. "White Privilege and Looking Relations: Race and Gender." *Feminism*

and Film. Ed. E. Ann Kaplan. Oxford: Oxford, 2000. 336–55. Print.

This essay, also included in the same collection as the above essay, argues that psychoanalysis isn't a good way to critique films, particularly because it overlooks racial and sexuality issues. Even when theorists use psychoanalysis to describe black family interaction, they impose "an erroneous universalisation and inadvertently reaffirm white middle-class norms" (337). When feminist theory uses gender first and foremost in discussing oppressions, it "helps to reinforce white middle-class values" (337). Also, Gaines argues, because feminist theory universalizes white middle-class values, it ideologically hides other forms of oppression from women.

This essay has given me new ideas about how to read *Lost in Translation*. Although I wasn't initially going to talk about issues of race, I might want to. Race actually plays a big role in the movie because it is about white people in an Asian country. Also, I think this essay is helpful in its critique of psychoanalysis. In my research of feminist film theory, I have found that you can't escape psychoanalysis. I don't particularly like psychoanalysis, but I realize that it is an important theory to understand. It is at the basis of many articles on feminist film theory. However, I don't think I will be discussing psychoanalysis in my essay.

Jayamanne, Laleen, ed. *Kiss Me Deadly: Feminism and Cinema for the Moment*. Sydney: Power Institute of Fine Arts, 1995. Print.

This is a collection of articles about feminism and film. The articles in this book focus mostly on directors, such as Kathryn Bigelow, Rainer Werner Fassbinder, Alexander Kluge, and Nicolas Roeg. Before looking at this book, I had never heard of any of these directors. I didn't find this book particularly helpful, especially because, as Jayamanne notes in the introduction, some of the directors and films discussed are "foreign to the semi-official canons of feminist film theory" (14).

Johnston, Claire. "Dorothy Arzner: Critical Strategies." *Feminism and Film*. Ed. E. Ann Kaplan. Oxford: Oxford, 2000. 139–50. Print.

In this essay, Johnston discusses Dorothy Arzner, a director from the 1920s to the 1940s who was nearly the only woman during her time to create a lucid bulk of work in Hollywood. Because not many studies have been written about Arzner—especially in male-dominated film studies—Johnston's purpose is to explore various approaches to Arzner's work and to discuss how her films are important for contemporary feminists.

   This essay also gave me a new idea about how to look at the film I will be discussing in my paper. I'd like to discuss the director of *Lost in Translation.* Are her films, particularly *Lost in Translation,* important for contemporary feminists?

Kaplan, E. Ann, ed. *Women in Film Noir.* London: British Film Institute, 1978. Print.

   This book is a collection of articles about film noir. Because the book is aimed at scholars who are educated in feminist film theory, it does not actually give a definition of film noir, and I didn't know what film noir was, so I looked it up in the Oxford English Dictionary. According to the Oxford English Dictionary, film noir is "a cinematographic film of a gloomy or fatalistic character." I don't think the film I will be discussing falls into this category, so I don't think I will be using this source for my essay.

———. *Feminism and Film.* Oxford: Oxford University Press, 2000. Print.

   This is a collection of articles on feminist film theory. Many of the essays in this book are esoteric and difficult to understand, but I think this is an invaluable resource to my research essay because of the range of essays it includes. The book is split into four phases: (1) Pioneers and Classics, (2) Critiques of Phase 1 Theories: New Methods, (3) Race, Sexuality, and Postmodernism in Feminist Film Theory, and (4) Spectatorship, Ethnicity, and Melodrama. By employing these different "phases" of feminist film theory, the book allows the reader to see the conversations within feminist film theory and its subsequent evolutions. I have summarized a few of the articles contained in this collection above.

Kuhn, Annette. *Women's Pictures: Feminism and Cinema.* London: Verso, 1994. Print.

   In this book, Kuhn argues that "feminism and film, taken together, could provide the basis for new forms of expression, providing the opportunity for a truly feminist alternative cinema in terms of film language, of reading that language and of representing the world." The book provides a systematic view of film. First, Kuhn discusses the dominant cinema. Then, she explores "rereading dominant cinema" from a feminist stance. Finally, she discusses "replacing dominant cinema" with feminist film.

I think this book will be helpful when I attempt to understand where *Lost in Translation* fits into film culture. Is the film part of dominant cinema? How can it be read from a feminist viewpoint? How is it a feminist film? How isn't it a feminist film?

APPENDIX D

THE ESSAY EXAM

The following table explains the differences between essay exams and the essays you write for class assignments. From this we can figure out which writing and reading strategies will be most useful when you're sitting in a classroom with only fifty minutes to craft an argument on one of Shakespeare's plays or apply an economic theory to a specific scenario.

	Essay Exam	Essay for Class Assignment
Time	Usually limited to a class period (60–75 minutes), within which time you have to generate ideas, focus, plan, draft, and revise.	Usually several days to several weeks to generate ideas, explore and focus them, draft, workshop, and revise.
Purpose	To show your instructor how well you know class material and how well you can *analyze and apply it*.	Depending on subject, genre, and focus of the class, this can vary from demonstrating competency at certain writing strategies to mastering a particular genre to making a persuasive argument.
Choice	While you may have a choice of which essay questions you'll respond to, often your choice of subject is limited by the question. Within the question you might have some choice over texts or materials to which you will refer.	Often students have a wider range of choices for subjects when writing for a class assignment.

(continued)

(continued)	Essay Exam	Essay for Class Assignment
Process	Your writing process is truncated into a shorter period, so you might go right to drafting an outline, drafting the response to the question, and then revising; you won't have time to experiment or explore ideas; your goals are to demonstrate your knowledge, not explore it.	More time to explore ideas, experiment, revise, and get feedback from other writers.
Methods of Inquiry	You will have little if any time for reflecting or even exploring ideas; instead, you will have to focus on explaining and evaluating, stating a claim, and providing explanation and evidence.	At various times you will use all the methods of inquiry: exploring, reflecting, explaining, and evaluating. The methods used in a particular paper depend on the assignment, the audience, the form, and the subject.
Form	Depending on the nature of the exam question, the form expected is something similar to a five-paragraph thesis essay: an introduction that states your thesis; supporting paragraphs that "prove" it using details from class materials; and a conclusion that wraps everything up (this is not true for short-answer essay questions). Essay exams are often expected to be close-ended forms.	Depending on the subject and audience: from narrative to thesis-example structure, open-ended to closed-ended form. Much more flexibility in choosing a form that fits the material than in an essay exam.
Thesis	Many instructors expect a thesis statement in the first paragraph.	Some instructors expect a thesis to be implied (as in the personal essay and the profile); others expect it to be explicit (as in the critical essay). How explicit it is depends on the genre, purpose, audience, and subject.

How to Write Essay Exams

Given the difference between essay exams and the essays you write for class assignments, you should employ very specific strategies when writing in this form.

Gathering Materials

Because the purpose of an essay exam is different from that of a regular essay, the sources of information are going to be different. This may seem obvious, but it's crucial to understanding how to prepare for the exam. For a research essay, textbooks are rarely considered good reference sources, and while class lectures can be used in a course paper, they cannot form the basis of the paper. Yet these sources are often the sole basis for essay exams, and you usually can't have these sources open at your side as you write. So how do you figure out what is important to focus on in this rhetorical context?

Let's talk first about the purposes of essay exams. For many instructors, the essay exam offers a forum for students to demonstrate one or more of the following achievements.

- Students *understand* the main course concepts.
- Students can *apply* those concepts to other kinds of information, situations, or problems.
- Students can *evaluate and support* that evaluation with relevant evidence and criteria.
- Students can *analyze* a subject: this includes *synthesizing and summarizing* a range of information, as well as *making connections* among that information by considering cause/effect and using comparison and contrast.

Anticipating the Exam

If you've been paying attention to the main ideas of the course and the methods of inquiry your instructor seems to value, then you are in good shape to anticipate the questions that might be on the exam. One of the best ways to prepare for an exam is to play the role of your instructor.

- What does she want you to learn and why?
- What kinds of questions has she asked on previous exams?
- What kinds of questions would best show how you've met the course goals?

After you've thought about these questions, generate a good list of possible exam questions and then answer them, either alone or in a small study group. You'll quickly learn what you need to go back and learn in more depth because you will be in a group reflecting on your learning process. And you may just find some version of those questions on the exam.

Because your instructor is your only audience and will be forming the questions, you might ask about the kinds of questions you can anticipate: How long will they be? What kinds of questions will there be? What criteria will be used for evaluating the answers? And, if they are available, look over previous exams from the same course and instructor.

If you've been engaging in inquiry throughout the course, then you will most likely have a good grasp of the main ideas in the course and your judgments about them. Inquiry can reduce the amount of time you spend memorizing the course material. You will have already been doing more than simply collecting facts and theories while your instructor lectures; you will have been posing questions, making connections, evaluating, and exploring, then reflecting on what you know and what more you need to know. You will, in short, understand the material. By the time you sit down to commit some key concepts and details to memory, you'll remember them better because you understand their purpose and their relationship to each other.

Analyzing Essay Questions

When you get the exam, read through all of it before you do anything else, and consider the following factors before you start writing your answers:

Time. Make some choices about how much time you will spend on each question based on:

- *Point value.* How many points is each question assigned? Prioritize them based on how much they are worth so you spend more time on those questions that are worth more. If you run out of time, then the questions you haven't responded to won't hurt you quite as much.
- *Priorities.* Based on your priorities, divide the time up for each question. Spend more time on questions worth more points. Try to stick to the time limits you've given yourself.
- *Ability to answer the question.* If you have a choice of questions, consider carefully which one you will answer. To decide, quickly brainstorm in the margins your ideas for each question. That will tell you how much you know about each and whether you can do what the question asks. For example, you might be able to explain a concept, but not compare it to something else, which is what the exam question actually demands that you do.

Key Phrases/Verbs. Once you've tentatively decided which questions you'll answer and how much time you'll devote to each, analyze the questions as quickly as you can. Your first step is to figure out what a question is asking you to *do*. Circle the key verbs that indicate your purpose when writing your answer. One way to understand what an essay question is asking you to do is to think of it in terms you already know: the ways of inquiring. In general, essay exams ask you to evaluate or explain. The accompanying table lists some of the verbs that imply one or the other way of inquiring.

Verbs of Evaluation	Required Action
Prove/justify/support	Offer reasons and evidence in support of a position.
Argue	Like *prove* and *justify*, this verb demands that you present an argument with reasons and evidence, but often the essay question gives you a position to take or asks you to choose a particular position.
Evaluate/assess	Make a judgment about the value or importance of a particular idea or subject, being clear about the criteria you're using for evaluation and supporting your claim with reasons and evidence.
Analyze	Usually this means you examine the parts of something—such as an argument—breaking it into sections and discussing the relationships among them; sometimes it may mean assessing those parts, or explaining your response. The rest of the question should indicate how much you should describe the parts and how much you should judge them.
Critique	To analyze and evaluate the subject in the essay question (an idea, argument, or theory).
Respond	Often this verb means that you must evaluate or justify your response to whatever the question asks of you.
Synthesize	Bring together two or more ideas/subjects/concepts that haven't been considered together and do more than simply summarize and compare them; explain why you have brought them together and what new understanding emerges from that.

Verbs of Explanation (Information)	Required Action
Define	Describe and give the meaning of the idea presented, using authoritative sources, comparing and contrasting it to other ideas that are related.
Enumerate	Present the steps, sequence, or events involved in a particular process in some detail.
Trace	Like *enumerate*, trace asks you to describe a series of events, but in chronological order.

(continued)

(continued) Verbs of Explanation (Information)	Required Action
List	Like *enumerate,* this verb asks you to name several things that are connected to a main idea presented in the question.
Review	Quickly summarize something.
Summarize	Present the main ideas of an argument or concept in an organized way.
Explain why/how	Offer reasons and examples of why and/or how something happened or relates to a larger idea.
Illustrate	Describe specific examples of something and their relationship to each other and the larger subject given in the question.
Identify	Like *illustrate,* this verb asks you to describe something and show its relationship to a larger idea, but often it implies looking at just one or two things.
Discuss	At length and from different perspectives, describe and analyze the idea presented in the question, using specific examples and evaluating the strengths and weaknesses.
Research	Just as it implies, gather sources and analyze what you've found.

Verbs of Explanation (Relationships and Connections)	Required Action
Compare	Illustrate the similarities of two or more things.
Contrast	Illustrate the differences of two or more things.
Relate	Show the relationships among various things.
Cause	Illustrate how various events relate to each other and resulted in a particular effect.
Apply	Illustrate how a theory or concept works in another situation.
Construct	Sometimes asks you to create a model or diagram through which to present your ideas.

Noun Phrases. Now that you know you need to contrast two different ideas, you need to be sure you know what to contrast. Some essay questions are rather long and it may be hard to decipher what, exactly, the subject of your answer should be. Usually the clues are in the noun phrases ("parts of the cell," "factors that led to the Civil War," "three influences on Sylvia Plath's poetry"). If the question begins with a quotation, read the question carefully to see whether it's background information for the question, or something you need to address in your answer. Underline all the key noun phrases that indicate the ideas/concepts you are expected to discuss.

Organizational Clues. Based on the subject and purpose of your answer, how might you best organize it? You may need to use a cause-effect, step-by-step, or thesis/support structure. Sometimes the question itself implies a structure. For example, if you are asked to analyze the cause and effect of the Great Depression, you'll use a cause-effect structure. If you are asked to identify three influences on Sylvia Plath's poetry and argue which is most significant, you'll name those three, then devote a separate paragraph for each one to discuss in more detail, ending with the one you believe is most significant. Before you begin writing, sketch an outline that seems appropriate for the question.

Planning and Drafting

Once you have analyzed the exam question and you have a good sense of what you are being asked to do, you need to draft an answer in a very short period of time. Before you begin writing your response, jot down a rough outline of what you'll say and the supporting details and examples you'll use. Put your points in the order of most to least important in case you run out of time. That way you know you've touched on the most important ideas before time is up. Then draft an introductory paragraph that summarizes your argument and gets right to your thesis statement at the end. Your lead doesn't need an attention grabber as much as it needs a clear direction for the essay and a clear statement of your answer in one or two sentences.

Focus your writing on the body of the essay, developing your points as fully as you can. Keep in mind what your instructor will value the most, and use the key terms that are used in the exam question to show how you are directly addressing it. Essay exams necessarily demand clear, simple, and direct writing. Leave some time at the end to reread your answer, editing it carefully and considering which sections need more information. Sometimes it helps to write on every other line of notebook or blue-book paper so you have space to write in when you revise. If you don't finish your answer in time, briefly describe for your instructor what you would do if you had more time. Write as legibly as you can, minimizing scratch-outs and keeping in mind how many exams your instructor will have to read.

When you analyzed the essay question, you paid some attention to the kind of structure the question was probably demanding. You may need to use a cause-effect pattern, a step-by-step pattern, or a thesis/support structure. Within the body of that structure, though, keep each paragraph to one main idea, using specific details to illustrate or support your main assertions. Then try to connect the idea in the paragraph back to your main thesis, explaining why it's important to what you are trying to say ("Another example of this phenomenon is _____ or "An additional factor that complicates this process is _____"). Your conclusion, then, will tie the essay together with a sentence or two restating your main claim and telling your instructor what all this information means.

HANDBOOK

This guide assumes that you, like other writers, sometimes have problems getting your sentences to come out right. These are problems in *usage*: how to use verbs, modifiers, and pronouns, for example. This discussion focuses on those problems, explaining the *how* more than the *what*, treating those problems as matters of writing, not of grammar. It avoids grammatical jargon as much as possible but defines terms where necessary for understanding the problem. This guide also gives you a quick review of punctuation, mechanics, spelling, style, and basic grammar. It also offers tips for ESL writers. Refer to this guide while writing and when your instructor suggests sections for you to study.

Here's how the sections are arranged:

1 Sentence Boundaries

Sentence boundaries are marked by end punctuation (7A): periods, question marks, or occasionally exclamation points. Because they mark the ends of sentences, each mark of end punctuation must be preceded by at least one independent clause (a complete statement containing a subject and a verb and not beginning with a subordinating word). Errors in sentence boundaries involve inappropriate punctuation: periods where commas or no punctuation should go, and commas or no punctuation where periods or semicolons should go. To develop your own sense of which marks to use, think of periods, semicolons, and commas as *strongest* to *weakest*. The weakest mark, the comma, is not interchangeable with the strongest mark, the period, and usually not with the semicolon. But periods and semicolons, depending on the writer's choice, *are* often interchangeable. The following discussions regarding sentence boundary errors are based on this reasoning.

1A Fragments

Sentence fragments are errors in which partial sentences are treated as sentences—begun with a capital letter and ended with a period. The fragment may be a subordinate clause, a phrase, or a combination of subordinate elements. What makes each a fragment is that it lacks a subject or a verb, or that it begins with a subordinating word. Only independent clauses can make independent statements.

Subordinate Clause Fragment

Recognition. A subordinate clause has a subject and a verb but cannot make an independent statement because of the connector that implies it is only part of a sentence. Here are two lists of the most common subordinating connectors.

Subordinating conjunctions, arranged by function

Time	Place
after	where
before	wherever
once	
since	Cause
until	as
when	because
whenever	since
while	
	Condition
Contrast	even if
although	if
even though	

though
while   in order that
                        so
so that
than   that
whether

who (whom, whose)   whoever (whomever, whosever)
which   whichever
that
what   whatever
where   wherever
when   whenever
why
unless
whereas

Any clause beginning with one of these words is *subordinate* and should not be written as a sentence. Here are examples of clause fragments (italicized):

The Vikings revolutionized shipbuilding with the keel. *Which allowed their ships to go faster and farther without stopping for supplies.*

Norway's Lapps are believed to be a nomadic people of Asian heritage. *Who follow reindeer herds through Norway's cold, rugged land.*

Because the northern part of Norway is so far north. It has long periods during the summer when the sun shines 24 hours a day.

Correction. There are mainly two ways of correcting clause fragments: (1) attaching them to the preceding or following sentence and (2) removing or changing the subordinating connector. These sentences illustrate both types of correction:

The Vikings revolutionized shipbuilding with the keel. *This innovation* allowed their ships to go faster and farther without stopping for supplies. The subordinating word of the fragment is changed.

Norway's Lapps are believed to be of Asian heritage—nomadic people who follow reindeer herds through Norway's cold, rugged land. The fragment is connected to the preceding sentence with a dash.

Because the northern part of Norway is so far north, it has long periods during the summer when the sun shines 24 hours a day. The fragment is connected to the following sentence with a comma.

Phrase Fragment
Phrase fragments lack a subject, a verb, or both. The most common phrases written as fragments are *verbal phrases* and *prepositional phrases*.

Recognition. A *verbal phrase* is a word group made up of a verb form and related modifiers and other words. As opposed to *verb phrases,* which are made up of verb parts (such as *has been gone*), a verbal phrase is constituted with a *verbal,* a word formed from a verb but not functioning as a verb. *Going,* for example, is a verbal, as is *gone.* You probably wouldn't write "Charles going to St. Louis" or "Charles gone to St. Louis." Instead, you would add helping verbs: "Charles *is going* to St. Louis" and "Charles *has gone* to St. Louis."

There are three kinds of verbals: gerunds, participles, and infinitives. Gerunds end in *-ing*; participles end in either *-ing* (present) or *-ed* (regular past); infinitives have no ending but are usually introduced by *to.* Here are a few examples of how verbals are formed from verbs:

Verb	Present participle and gerund	Past participle	Infinitive
snap	snapping	snapped	to snap
look	looking	looked	to look
want	wanting	wanted	to want
go	going	gone	to go
has	having	had	to have

Verbals function primarily as adjectives and nouns, most often in verbal phrases.

In the following examples, the italicized verbal phrases are fragments because they are written as sentences:

Eero Saarinen designed the 630-foot Gateway Arch for the St. Louis riverfront. *Imagining a giant stainless steel arch.* Participial phrase modifying *Eero Saarinen.*

Critics said that cranes could not reach high enough. *To lift the steel sections into place.* Infinitive phrase modifying *high.*

Under Saarinen's plan, a derrick would creep up the side of each leg of the arch. *Lifting each plate into position.* Participial phrase modifying *derrick.*

Saarinen knew that precision was of utmost importance. In *building the arch.* Gerund phrase as object of preposition *In.*

Correction. Verbal phrase fragments can be corrected in one of two ways: (1) by connecting them to a related sentence or (2) by expanding them to a sentence. Both ways are illustrated next.

Eero Saarinen designed the 630-foot Gateway Arch for the St. Louis riverfront. *He imagined a giant stainless steel arch.* The verbal fragment is expanded to a sentence.

Critics said that cranes could not reach high enough *to lift the steel sections into place.* The verbal fragment is connected to a related sentence.

Under Saarinen's plan, a derrick would creep up the side of each leg of the arch, *lifting each plate into position.* The verbal fragment is connected to a related sentence.

Saarinen knew that precision was of utmost importance in *building the arch.* The gerund phrase, object of the preposition *In,* is connected to a related sentence.

Recognition. A *prepositional phrase* is a word group made up of a preposition and its object. Together they contribute meaning to a sentence, usually modifying a noun or a verb. Like subordinating conjunctions, prepositions show relationships, such as time, place, condition, cause, and so on. Here are some of the most common prepositions:

about	concerning	onto
above	despite	out
according to	down	out of
across	during	outside
after	except	over
against	except for	past
along	excepting	regarding
along with	for	since
among	from	through
around	in	throughout
as	in addition to	till
at	in back of	to
because of	in place of	toward
before	in spite of	under
behind	inside	underneath
below	instead of	unlike
beneath	into	until
beside	like	up
between	near	up to
beyond	next	upon
but	of	with
by	off	within
by means of	on	without

In the following examples, prepositional phrases have been written as sentences and are therefore fragments:

The Vikings were descendents of Teutonic settlers. *Like most of today's Norwegians.*

Norway is a land of natural beauty. *From its fjord-lined coast to frigid Lapland.*

Correction. Preposition phrase fragments also can be corrected (1) by connecting them to a related sentence or (2) by expanding them to a sentence.

The Vikings were descendents of Teutonic settlers, *like most of today's Norwegians.* **or** *Like most of today's Norwegians,* the Vikings were descendents of Teutonic settlers. The prepositional phrase is connected to a related sentence.

Norway is a land of natural beauty. *Its charm extends from its fjord-lined coast to frigid Lapland.* The prepositional phrase is expanded to a sentence.

Incomplete Thoughts

Sometimes fragments are simply errors in punctuation: The writer uses a period when a comma or no punctuation would be correct. A more difficult type of fragment to correct is the incomplete thought, such as this one:

> A large concrete dock 50 feet short of a wooden platform anchored in the middle of the bay.

In this fragment, something is missing, and, as a result, a reader doesn't know what to make of the words "large concrete dock." With fragments of this sort, the writer needs to insert the missing information. The fragment might be revised like this:

> A large concrete dock juts out, stopping 50 feet short of a wooden platform anchored in the middle of the bay.

Acceptable Fragments

You probably encounter fragments every day. Titles are often fragments, as are answers to questions and expressions of strong emotion.

Titles: *The Curious Writer,* "A Fire in the Woods"

Answer to question: "How many more chairs do we need?" "Fifteen."

Expression of strong emotion: "What a great concert!"

And much advertising utilizes fragments:

> Intricate, delicate, exquisite. Extravagant in every way.

> Another successful client meeting. Par for the course.

Common as they are in everyday life, fragments are usually unacceptable in academic or business writing. Even though professional writers and advertising writers sometimes use them for emphasis, there are rarely cases when you will need intentional fragments for effective expression of your thoughts in school or business.

1B Comma Splices

Comma splices consist of two independent clauses (clauses that can stand alone as sentences) improperly joined together by a comma in the same sentence. Here are two examples:

> The economy of Algeria is in trouble, many citizens blame the government.

> The death of any soldier is tragic, however, death by friendly fire is particularly disturbing.

Recognition. The first step in avoiding comma splices is to identify them. Because they happen only in sentences with at least two independent clauses, you can test your sentences by substituting periods for your commas. If you end up with complete sentences, you probably have a comma splice.

In testing the first of the two preceding examples we come up with the following result:

The economy of Algeria is in trouble.

Many citizens blame the government.

Both of these clauses obviously qualify as complete sentences, so they must be independent clauses. They therefore cannot be connected with a comma. Remember this simple rule of punctuation: *Periods and commas are not interchangeable.* If a period is correct, a comma is not.

Correction. You can revise comma splices using five different strategies.

1. Separate the independent clauses using a comma and a *coordinating conjunction*. The list of coordinating conjunctions is short:

   and   or   for   yet
   but   nor   so

   To correct a comma splice, begin the second independent clause with one of these conjunctions preceded by a comma. For example:

   The economy of Algeria is in trouble, *and* many citizens blame the government.

2. Separate the independent clauses using a semicolon (with or without a transitional adverb). Semicolons are often interchangeable with periods and therefore can be used to separate independent clauses. For example:

   The economy of Algeria is in trouble; many citizens blame the government.

   The death of any soldier is tragic; *however,* death by friendly fire is particularly disturbing.

In the second example, *however* is a transitional adverb. Unlike coordinating conjunctions, *transitional adverbs* are not conjunctions and so do not join sentence elements. They do, however, connect ideas by showing how they relate to one another. Like conjunctions, they can show addition, contrast, result, and other relationships. Here are some of the common transitional adverbs, arranged by function:

Addition	Examples
in addition	for example
also	for instance
moreover	in fact
next	specifically
then	
finally	
	Contrast
	however
Comparison	nevertheless
likewise	on the contrary
similarly	on the other hand
in comparison	otherwise

Result	Time
therefore	meanwhile
consequently	subsequently
then	finally
as a result	then

A semicolon should always precede the transitional adverb that begins the second independent clause. A comma usually follows the transitional adverb, although in some instances, as in the following example, the comma is omitted:

> Air bags deflate within one second after inflation; *therefore* they do not interfere with control of the car.

Some comma splices result when writers use transitional adverbs as if they were coordinating conjunctions. If you have trouble distinguishing transitional adverbs from coordinating conjunctions, remember that none of the coordinating conjunctions is longer than three letters, and all of the transitional adverbs are four letters or longer. Also, keep in mind that transitional adverbs are movable within the sentence while coordinating conjunctions are not; for example, the preceding example could be rewritten as:

> Air bags deflate within one second after inflation; they do not *therefore* interfere with control of the car.

3. Make one of the independent clauses subordinate to the other by inserting a subordinating conjunction. When one of the clauses explains or elaborates on the other, use an appropriate subordinating conjunction to make the relationship between the two clauses more explicit (see 1A Fragments for a list of subordinating conjunctions). Consider the following comma splice and its revision:

> Henry forgot to fill in his time card on Friday, he is going to have a hard time getting paid for the overtime he put in last week.

> *Because* Henry forgot to fill in his time card on Friday, he is going to have a hard time getting paid for the overtime he put in last week.

4. Rewrite one of the independent clauses as a modifying phrase. A *modifying phrase* serves as an adjective or adverb within a sentence. By rewriting one of the independent clauses as a phrase you can eliminate unneeded words. For example, consider the following comma splice and its revision:

> The celebrity couple smiled for the cameras, they were glowing of wealth and fame.

> The celebrity couple smiled for the cameras, glowing of wealth and fame. Here *glowing of wealth and fame* acts as an adjective modifying the noun *couple*.

5. Punctuate each independent clause as a separate sentence. No law of grammar, punctuation, or style says you must present the two independent clauses together within one sentence, so you won't be cheating if you write

them as two separate sentences. The example from before is perfectly acceptable written as follows:

> The economy of Algeria is in trouble. Many citizens blame the government.

It may be to your advantage to divide long and/or complex independent clauses into separate sentences—doing so may help convey your meaning to readers more clearly.

1C Fused Sentences

Fused sentences, sometimes called *run-on sentences,* are similar to comma splices. However, instead of a comma between the two independent clauses, there is no punctuation; the two independent clauses simply run together. For example:

> The United States has 281 lawyers per 100,000 people Japan has only 11 attorneys per 100,000.

> The World Cup is the most popular sporting event in the world you would never know it based on the indifferent response of the average American.

Recognition. Unlike the comma splice, there is no punctuation in the fused sentence to guide you to the end of the first independent clause and the beginning of the second. As a result, it can be more challenging to identify independent clauses within fused sentences, particularly if the sentence also contains modifying phrases or dependent clauses set off by commas. The best way to do this is to read from the beginning of the sentence (reading aloud may help) until you have found the end of the first independent clause. Consider the following example:

> Even though I was still sick with the flu, I attended the awards banquet as my family watched, the coach presented me with the trophy for most valuable player.

This fused sentence contains two subordinate clauses (*Even though I was still sick with the flu* and *as my family watched*), each one attached to one of the two independent clauses (*I attended the awards banquet* and *the coach presented me with the trophy*).

Correction. Revise fused sentences using any one of the same five strategies employed for correcting comma splices (see 1B Comma Splices for more information on each strategy).

1. Separate the independent clauses using a comma and a coordinating conjunction. For example:

   > The United States has 281 lawyers per 100,000 people, *but* Japan has only 11 attorneys per 100,000.

2. Separate the independent clauses using a semicolon (with or without a transitional adverb). For example:

   > The United States has 281 lawyers per 100,000 people; Japan has only 11 attorneys per 100,000.

The World Cup is the most popular sporting event in the world; *however,* you would never know it based on the indifferent response of the average American.

3. Make one of the independent clauses subordinate to the other by inserting a subordinating conjunction. The newly formed dependent clause should explain the remaining independent clause. For example, consider the following fused sentence and its revision:

I run a marathon my feet get sore.

Whenever I run a marathon, my feet get sore.

4. Rewrite one of the independent clauses as a modifying phrase. Remember, modifying phrases act as adjectives or adverbs. Consider the following fused sentence and its revision:

Last night the tomcats fought outside my window they were crying and hissing for what seemed like hours.

Last night the tomcats fought outside my window, crying and hissing for what seemed like hours. Here *crying and hissing* acts as an adjective modifying the noun *tomcats.*

5. Punctuate each independent clause as a separate sentence. As with comma splices, you can write the independent clauses (and their related phrases and dependent clauses) as separate sentences. Indeed, this is often the easiest way to handle fused sentences. For example:

I attended the awards banquet even though I was still sick with the flu. As my family watched, the coach presented me with the trophy for most valuable player. Here the subordinate clause attached to the first independent clause *even though I was still sick with the flu* was also moved to the back of the first sentence for the sake of greater readability.

2 Sentence Inconsistencies

Sentences pose difficulties for readers when the grammar is confused or inconsistent. Such problems happen when writers pay attention to what they are saying and not to how they are saying it. Such attention is a natural condition of writing, and careful revision usually takes care of any problems.

2A Parallelism

Parallelism results when two or more grammatically equivalent sentence elements are joined. The sentence elements can be nouns, verbs, phrases, or clauses. (See 2B Coordination and Subordination.) Here is a sentence with parallel elements:

In a country where college education becomes increasingly everybody's chance, where executives and refrigerator salesmen and farmers play golf together, where a college professor may drive a cab in the summertime to keep his family alive, it becomes harder and harder to guess a person's education, income, and social status by the way he talks. —Paul Roberts

Here is the same sentence with the parallel elements arranged to be more visually accessible:

In a country

{where college education becomes increasingly everybody's chance,

{where {executives

and {refrigerator salesmen

and {farmers play golf together,

{where a college professor may drive a cab in the summertime to keep

his family alive,

it becomes {harder

and {harder to guess a person's {education

{income,

and {social status

by the way he talks.

This sentence has parallel clauses (each beginning *where*), parallel subjects (*executives, refrigerator salesmen,* and *farmers*), parallel adverbs (*harder* and *harder*), and parallel direct objects (*education, income,* and *social status*). As this sentence illustrates, the principle of parallelism does not require that elements be alike in every way. Some of these nouns have modifiers, for example, and the clauses have different structural patterns.

Parallelism becomes a problem when dissimilar elements are joined in pairs, in series, in comparisons using *than* or *as,* or in comparisons linked by correlative conjunctions. Consider the following examples of faulty parallelism:

She did not like rude customers or taking orders from her boss. The two elements in the pair are not parallel.

We were having a hard time deciding what to do in the afternoon: go snorkeling, go fishing, or swim out to the sand bar. The last of the three elements in the series is not parallel.

Michael decided to complete his degree next semester rather than studying abroad for another year. The two elements compared using *than* are not parallel.

My sister not only lost the race but also her leg got hurt. The two elements compared by the correlative conjunction *not only…but also* are not parallel. Other correlative conjunctions include *both…and, either…or, neither…nor, whether…or,* and *just as…so.*

Faulty parallelism can be corrected in various ways:

> She did not like *dealing with* rude customers or taking orders from her boss. Words were added to the first element to make it parallel to the second.

> We were having a hard time deciding what to do in the afternoon: go snorkeling, go fishing, or *go swimming*. The last element was rewritten to make it parallel with the others in the series.

> Michael decided to complete his degree next semester rather than *to study* abroad for another year. The verb form of the second element is changed from a participle to an infinitive to make it parallel with the verb form in the first element.

> My sister not only lost the race but also *hurt her leg*. The second element was rewritten to make it parallel with the first element.

Revision of faulty parallelism is usually fairly easy to achieve. What is difficult is recognizing it, and unfortunately there are no tricks to easy recognition. Even experienced writers find that in their own writing they need to make an editing trip through their drafts looking just at their parallel structures. The absence of faulty parallels is a sign of careful writing.

2B Coordination and Subordination

Most sentence relationships embody either coordination or subordination. That is, sentence elements are either grammatically equal to other elements (coordination) or grammatically dependent on other parts (subordination). For example, two independent clauses in a sentence are coordinate; but in a sentence containing an independent clause and a dependent clause, the dependent clause is subordinate (indeed, dependent clauses are also called subordinate clauses).

Coordination

When two or more equivalent sentence elements appear in one sentence they are coordinate. These elements can be words, phrases, or clauses. Only parallel elements can be coordinated: verbs linked with verbs, nouns with nouns, phrases with phrases, and clauses with clauses. (See 2A Parallelism.) For example:

> *Broccoli* and *related vegetables* contain beta-carotene, a substance that may reduce the risk of heart attack. Two nouns are joined by a coordinating conjunction.

> We *ran, swam,* and *cycled* every day while we were at the fitness camp. Three parallel verbs are joined in a series with commas and a coordinating conjunction.

> American medical devices are equally remarkable, *giving life to those with terminally diseased organs, giving mobility to those crippled with arthritic joints and deadened nerves,* and even, miraculously, *restoring the sense of hearing to those deprived of it.—Atlantic.* The participial (verbal) phrases are joined by commas and a final coordinating conjunction. Also, embedded in the second participial phrase, two coordinate noun phrases are joined by a coordinating conjunction: *arthritic joints and deadened nerves.*

The term "Big Bang" is common usage now with scientists, but it originated as a sarcastic rejection of the theory. Two independent clauses are joined by a comma and a coordinating conjunction.

Subordination

Subordination is an essential aspect of sentence relations. If all sentence elements were grammatically equivalent, the sameness would be tedious. Subordinate elements show where the emphasis lies in sentences and modify elements with independent clauses. A subordinate element—be it a phrase or clause—is dependent on the element it modifies for its meaning. At the same time, it often provides a fuller meaning than could be achieved exclusively through the use of independent elements.

For example:

For walking and jogging, the calorie expenditure is greater for people of greater body weight. The subordinate element is a prepositional phrase, modifying *is greater.*

Increasing both speed and effort in aerobic activities, the exerciser burns more calories. The subordinate element is a verbal phrase, modifying *exerciser.*

Because sedentary people are more likely to burn sugar than fat, they tend to become hungry sooner and to overeat. The subordinate clause modifies the verb *tend.*

People *who exercise on a regular basis* change certain enzyme systems *so that they are more likely to burn fat than sugar.* There are two subordinate clauses, one beginning with *who* and modifying *People,* and one beginning with *so that* and modifying the verb *change.*

Effective writing has both coordination and subordination—coordination that sets equivalent elements side by side, and subordination that makes some elements dependent on others. Both are useful writing tools.

2C Mixed Sentences

In mixed sentences, called faulty predications when they involve the mismatching of subject and predicate, two or more parts of a sentence do not make sense together. Like other inconsistencies, this kind of problem usually occurs when writers concentrate harder on meaning than on grammar.

The following mixed sentences are common in everyday speech and may not seem inconsistent to you. Indeed, in casual speech they are usually accepted. In standard written English, however, they qualify as grammatical errors.

By driving to the movie was how we saw the accident happen. The prepositional phrase *By driving to the movie* is treated as the subject for the verb *was.* Prepositional phrases cannot serve as subjects.

Just because the candidate once had a drinking problem doesn't mean he won't be a good mayor now. The adverb clause *because the candidate once had a drinking problem* is treated as the subject of the verb *doesn't mean*. Adverbs modify verbs and adjectives and cannot function as subjects.

A CAT scan is when medical technicians take a cross-sectional X-ray of the body. The adverb clause *when medical technicians take a cross-sectional X-ray of the body* is treated as a complement of the subject *CAT scan*—another function adverbs cannot serve.

The reason I was late today is because my alarm clock broke. The subject, *reason*, is illogically linked with the predicate, *is because*. *Reason* suggests an explanation, so the predicate, *is because*, is redundant.

Revise mixed sentences by ensuring that grammatical patterns are used consistently throughout each sentence. For cases of faulty predication either revise the subject so it can perform the action expressed in the predicate or revise the predicate so it accurately depicts an action performed by the subject. Also avoid using *is when* and *is where* to explain an idea and *The reason . . . is because* constructions in your writing.

There are often many ways to revise mixed sentences. In each of the following revisions the grammatical patterns are consistent and the subjects and predicates fit together logically:

While driving to the movie, we saw the accident happen.

Just because the candidate once had a drinking problem, we can't conclude that he won't be a good mayor.

A CAT scan is a cross-sectional X-ray of the body.

The reason I was late today is that my alarm clock broke.

2D Shifts

Shifts occur when writers lose track of their sentence elements. Shifts occur in a variety of ways:

In person

In music, where left-handed people seem to be talented, the right-handed world puts *you* at a disadvantage. Shift from *people*, third person, to *you*, second person.

In tense

Even though many musicians *are* left handed, instruments *had been designed for right handers*. Shift from present tense to past perfect.

In number

A left-handed *violinist* has to pay extra to buy *their* left-handed violin. Shift from singular to plural.

In mood

Every time the *violinist played, she could always know* when her instrument was out of tune. Shift from the indicative mood, *violinist played*, to the subjunctive mood, *she could always know*.

In voice

The sonata *was being practiced* by the violinists in one room while the cellists *played* the concerto in the other room. Shift from the passive voice, *was being practiced*, to active voice, *played*.

In discourse type

She said, "*Your violin is out of tune*," and that *I was playing the wrong note*. Shift from the direct quotation, *Your violin is out of tune*, to indirect quotation, that *I was playing the wrong note*.

Once you recognize shifts, revise them by ensuring that the same grammatical structures are used consistently throughout the sentence:

In music, where left-handed *people* seem talented, the right-handed world puts *them* at a disadvantage.

Even though many musicians *are* left handed, instruments *have been designed* for right handers.

Left-handed *violinists* have to pay extra to buy *their* left-handed violins.

Every time the violinist *played,* she *knew* when her instrument was out of tune.

The violinists *practiced* the sonata in one room while the cellists *played* the concerto in the other room.

She said, "*Your violin is out of tune and you are playing the wrong note.*"

3 Problems with Modification

One part of a sentence can be *modified* by another part. A part that is modified is changed in some way: limited or broadened, perhaps, or described, defined, identified, or explained. Adjectives and adverbs always serve modifying functions, but phrases and subordinate clauses also can be modifiers. This section deals with problems in modification. (See 2B Coordination and Subordination.)

3A Dangling and Misplaced Modifiers

Dangling and misplaced modifiers are words and word groups that, because of their position or the way they are phrased, make the meaning of a sentence unclear and sometimes even ludicrous. These troublesome modifiers are most commonly verbal phrases, prepositional phrases, and adverbs. Here are examples:

Reaching to pick up the saddle, the obnoxious horse may shake off the blanket. The dangling verbal phrase appears to relate to *horse*.

To extend lead out of the eversharp pencil, the eraser cap is depressed. The dangling verbal phrase implies that *the eraser cap* does something.

The eversharp pencil is designed to be used permanently, *only periodically replacing the lead*. The dangling verbal phrase implies that the pencil replaces the lead.

Dick *only* had to pay ten dollars for his parking ticket. The misplaced adverb should immediately precede *ten*.

Theodore caught a giant fish in the very same spot where he had lost the ring *two years later*. The misplaced adverb phrase confusingly appears to modify the last part of the sentence instead of, correctly, the first part.

Errors of this type are difficult for writers to recognize because to the writers they are not ambiguous.

Recognition. Verbal phrases always have implied subjects; in other words, somebody is performing the action. For clarity, that implied subject should be the same as the subject of the sentence or clause. To recognize your own dangling verbal modifiers, make sure that the implied subject of the verbal phrase is the same as the subject of the sentence. In the first example above, the implied subject of *Reaching* is not *the horse*. In the second example, the implied subject of *To extend* is not *the eraser cap*. And in the third example, the implied subject of *replacing* is not *the pencil*. Also check passive voice, because in a passive sentence the subject is not the doer of the action. In the second example, the dangler can be corrected when the verb, changed from passive to active voice, tells who should depress the eraser (see correction that follows).

Correction. Correcting dangling and misplaced modifiers depends on the type of error. Misplaced modifiers can often be moved to a more appropriate position:

Dick had to pay *only* ten dollars for his parking ticket.

Two years later, Theodore caught a giant fish in the very same spot where he had lost the ring.

Dangling modifiers usually require some rewording:

As you reach to pick up the saddle, the obnoxious horse may shake off the blanket. The dangling verbal phrase is converted to a clause.

To extend lead out of the eversharp pencil, *depress the eraser cap*. The main clause is revised so that *you* is the implied subject of *depress* (as it is for *To extend*).

The eversharp pencil is designed to be used permanently, *only periodically needing the lead replaced*. The dangling verbal phrase is revised so that the implied subject of *needing* is *pencil*.

3B Restrictive and Nonrestrictive Modifiers

Some modifiers are essential to a sentence because they *restrict,* or limit, the meaning of the words they modify; others, while adding important information, are not essential to the meaning of a sentence. The first type is called restrictive and the second nonrestrictive. The terms usually refer to subordinate clauses and phrases. Here are examples of restrictive and nonrestrictive modifiers:

Restrictive

People *who plan to visit Europe* should take time to see Belgium. Relative clause modifying and identifying *People*.

The industrialized country *between the Netherlands and France on the North Sea* is constitutionally a kingdom. Prepositional phrases modifying and identifying *country*.

The Kempenland was thinly populated *before coal was discovered there*. Subordinate clause modifying *was populated* and giving meaning to the sentence.

Language and cultural differences have created friction *that has existed for centuries*. Relative clause modifying and identifying *friction*.

Nonrestrictive

Belgium has two major populations: the Flemings, *who live in the north and speak Flemish,* and the Walloons, *who live in the south and speak French.* Two relative clauses, the first modifying *Flemings* and the second modifying *Walloons*.

With Brussels in the middle of the country, both groups inhabit the city. Prepositional phrases, together modifying *inhabit*.

NATO's headquarters is in Brussels, *where it has been since its beginning in 1950.* Subordinate clause modifying *Brussels*.

Covering southeastern Belgium, the sandstone Ardennes mountains follow the Sambre and Meuse rivers. Participial (verbal) phrase modifying *mountains*.

These examples illustrate several aspects of restrictive and nonrestrictive modifiers:

1. They *modify* a word in the clause or sentence; they therefore function as adjectives or adverbs.
2. They can appear at the beginning, somewhere in the middle, or at the end of a sentence or clause.
3. Most types of subordinate elements can be restrictive and nonrestrictive.
4. Whether a clause or phrase is restrictive or nonrestrictive depends on its function in the sentence.
5. Restrictive elements are not set off with punctuation; nonrestrictive elements are set off with commas (and sometimes dashes).

If you think the distinction between restriction and nonrestriction is not worth making, consider the following sentences, the first restrictive and the second nonrestrictive:

People who wear braces on their teeth should not eat caramel apples.

People, who wear braces on their teeth, should not eat caramel apples.

Set off with commas, the nonrestrictive *who* clause implies that all people wear braces on their teeth and should not eat caramel apples, which is clearly not the case. It does not *restrict,* or limit, the meaning of *people.* In the first sentence, however, the *who* clause does restrict, or limit, the meaning of *people* to only those who wear braces on their teeth. Often only the writer knows the intended meaning and therefore needs to make the distinction by setting off, or not setting off, the modifier.

Here are a few guidelines that might help you in making this fine distinction:

1. A modifier that modifies a proper noun (one that names a person or thing) is usually nonrestrictive, because the name is sufficient identification. Notice *Flemings* and *Walloons* in the previous example.

2. A *that* clause is almost always restrictive.

3. Adverbial subordinate clauses (those beginning with subordinating conjunctions such as *because* and *when*; see list on page 421) are almost always restrictive and usually not set off with commas when they appear at the end of their sentences. If they appear at the beginning of sentences, they are almost always set off with commas.

4. A nonrestrictive modifier at the beginning of a sentence is followed by a comma, one at the end is preceded by a comma, and one in the middle is enclosed with two commas.

3C Adjectives and Adverbs

Adjectives and adverbs, often called *modifiers,* describe nouns and verbs (see 9A Parts of Speech). Adjectives modify nouns; that is, they describe, limit, explain, or alter them in some way. By modifying, they *limit* the meaning of the nouns: *red car* is narrower in meaning than *car,* and *fast red car* is narrower than *red car.* Adverbs modify verbs, adjectives, and other adverbs, telling more than the words by themselves would tell: drive *carefully* (adverb modifying a verb), *unexpectedly* early (adverb modifying an adjective), drive *very* carefully (adverb modifying an adverb). Adverbs usually tell how, where, when, and how much.

Adjectives and adverbs occasionally present some problems for writers. Be careful not to use adjectives when adverbs are needed, as in this sentence:

The governor suspected that the legislators were not taking him *serious*. The sentence element receiving modification is the verb *were not taking* yet the modifier *serious* is an adjective, which can only modify nouns. The correct modifier for this sentence is the adverb *seriously*. (If you are not sure whether a word is an adjective or an adverb, check your dictionary, which should identify parts of speech.)

Another problem in form concerns the *comparative* and *superlative* degrees. The comparative form of adjectives and adverbs shows a greater degree between two things:

Your luggage is *stronger* than mine. Adjective comparing *your luggage* and *mine*.

Your luggage survives airport baggage handling *better* than mine does. Adverb comparing how the two *survive* handling.

The comparative degree is formed by adding *-er* to shorter adjectives and adverbs (*strong, stronger, hard, harder*); longer words are preceded by *more* (*beautiful, more beautiful; seriously, more seriously*). Do not use *-er* with *more* (not *more harder*).

The superlative form shows a greater degree among three or more things:

This is the *strongest* luggage I have ever seen. Adjective comparing the present luggage to all other luggage the writer has seen.

Your luggage survives airport baggage handling *best* of all luggage I've seen. Adverb comparing how all luggage the writer has seen survives handling.

The superlative degree is formed by adding *-est* to shorter adjectives and adverbs (*strong, strongest; hard, hardest*); longer words are preceded by *most* (*beautiful, most beautiful; seriously, most seriously*). Do not use *-est* with *most* (not *most strongest*).

Do not use adjectives and adverbs gratuitously, just to fill space or because you think you ought to. They are effective only when they add meaning to a sentence.

4 Verbs

Verbs are the central core of a sentence; together with subjects, they make statements. Verbs often tell what the subject is doing:

The company *agreed* to plead guilty to criminal charges.

Nearly every miner *can name* a casualty of black lung disease.

Another common function of verbs is to link subjects to complements:

Logan *is* an isolated county in the corner of the state.

Sometimes the verb tells something about the subject, as the following passive verb does:

Casualties of mining *cannot be measured* only by injuries.

Through changes in form, verbs can tell the time of the action (past, present, future), the number of the subject (singular or plural), and the person of the subject (first person, *I, we*; second person, *you*; third person, *he, she, it, they*).

4A Tense

The problems that writers sometimes encounter when using verbs in writing result from the fact that verbs, unlike most other words in English, have many forms, and a slight shift in form can alter meaning. Notice how the meanings of the following pairs of sentences change as the verbs change:

The fish *has jumped* into the boat.

The fish *have jumped* into the boat.

The concert *starts* at 8:15 p.m.

The concert *started* at 8:15 p.m.

In the first pair, the meaning changes from one fish to more than one fish jumping into the boat. In the second pair, the first verb implies that the concert has not yet begun; the second, that it had already begun. It is important, therefore, to use the verb form that conveys the intended meaning. Observe how the verb *vanish* changes in the following sentences to indicate differences in time, or *tense*:

Present:	Many agricultural jobs *vanish*.
Past:	Many agricultural jobs *vanished*.
Future:	Many agricultural jobs *will vanish*.
Perfect:	Many agricultural jobs *have vanished*.
Past Perfect:	Many agricultural jobs *had vanished*.
Future Perfect:	Many agricultural jobs *will have vanished*.

To omit an *-ed* ending or use the wrong helping verb gives readers a false message.

Helping (Auxiliary) Verbs. It is also important to use a form that is a *finite,* or an actual, verb. In the following example, the word that appears to be a verb (italicized) is not a finite verb:

The fish *jumping* into the boat.

The word *jumping* does not have one of the primary functions of verbs—telling time of the action, called *tense*. The time of the occurrence could have been the past (*the fish were jumping*), present (*the fish are jumping*), or the future (*the fish will be jumping*). We also don't know whether the writer meant one fish or many. The *-ing* form is a *verbal* and requires a helping, or auxiliary, verb to make it finite, or able to tell time: words such as *am, is, are, was, were* (forms of *be*). Other helping verbs are *do* (*Do* you *want* the paper? She *doesn't want* the paper) and *have* (I *haven't seen* the paper; *has* she *seen* it?).

Irregular Verbs. Most verbs change forms in a regular way: *want* in the present becomes *wanted* in the past, *wanting* with the auxiliary *be* (i.e., *is wanting*), and *wanted* with the auxiliary *have* (i.e., *have wanted*). Many verbs change irregularly, however—internally rather than at the ending. Here are a few of the most common irregular verbs:

Base form	Past tense	Present participle	Past participle
be (is, am, are)	was, were	being	been
come	came	coming	come
do	did	doing	done
drink	drank	drinking	drunk
give	gave	giving	given
go	went	going	gone
grow	grew	growing	grown
lie	laid	lying	lain
see	saw	seeing	seen
take	took	taking	taken
teach	taught	teaching	taught
throw	threw	throwing	thrown
wear	wore	wearing	worn
write	wrote	writing	written

Check your dictionary for the forms of other verbs you suspect may be irregular.

The verb form that is perhaps the most troublesome is the *-s* form in the present tense. This form is used for all singular nouns and the pronouns *he, she,* and *it*. (See 4D Subject–Verb Agreement.)

4B Voice

English sentences are usually written in the active voice, in which the subject of the sentence is the doer of the action of the verb:

> Scott misplaced the file folder. *Scott,* the subject of the sentence, performed the action, *misplaced.*

With the passive voice, the doer of the action is the object of a preposition or is omitted entirely:

> The file folder was misplaced by Scott. *File folder* is now the subject of the sentence.

> The file folder was misplaced. The person doing the action is not named.

At best, the passive voice is wordier than the active voice; at worst, it fails to acknowledge who performs the action of the verb. Use the passive voice when you do not know or want to name the doer or when you want to keep the subjects consistent within a paragraph.

To avoid the passive voice, look for *by* phrases near the ends of your sentences; if you find any, see if the subject of your sentence performs the action of your verb. If not, revise the sentence so that it does. Another way to find occurrences of the passive voice is to look for forms of *be*: *am, is, are, was, were, been, being.* Not all these verbs will be passive, but if they function as part of an action verb, see if the subject performs the action. If it does not, and if your sentence would be clearer with the subject performing the action, revise to the active voice.

4C Mood

Mood refers to the writer's attitude toward the action of the verb. There are three forms: indicative, imperative, and subjunctive. Verbs in the *indicative mood* are used to make statements, to ask questions, and to declare opinions. For example:

> Not many people today *think* the world *is* flat. Makes a statement.

> *Does* anybody today *think* the world is flat? Asks a question.

> Members of the Flat Earth Society *should reevaluate* their thinking. Declares an opinion.

Verbs in the *imperative mood* issue commands, requests, or directions. Imperative verbs never change form. When the subject of an imperative verb is not explicitly identified it is understood to be *you.*

Julia, *stop* teasing your baby brother. Issues command.

Please *complete* this report by tomorrow morning. Issues request.

Turn right at the light and *drive* for another two blocks. Issues directions.

Verbs in the *subjunctive mood* communicate wishes, make statements contrary to fact, list requirements and demands, and imply skepticism or doubt. They usually appear in clauses introduced by *if, that, as if,* and *as though.* Use the base form of the verb for the present tense subjunctive. For the past tense subjunctive of the verb *be,* use *were* for all subjects.

She wishes that her son's best friend *were* more responsible. Communicates wish.

If the world *were* to end tomorrow, we would not have to pay taxes anymore. Makes statement contrary to fact.

The jury summons requires that your cousin *arrive* punctually at 8:00 a.m. and *sign* in with the court clerk. Lists requirements.

His girlfriend talks as if she *were* a pop music diva. Implies skepticism.

Be sure to select the correct verb forms to express indicative, imperative, and subjunctive moods.

4D Subject–Verb Agreement

Clauses are made of subjects and verbs plus their modifiers and other related words. A fundamental principle of usage is that verbs agree with their subjects. In most cases, this principle presents no problem: You say "Birds *have* feathers," not "Birds *has* feathers." But not all sentences are this simple. Before getting into the problem areas, consider first that errors in subject–verb agreement occur only with present-tense verbs and the verb tenses that use present tense forms of helping verbs (such as *have* and *be*). And, except for the irregular verb *be* (with its forms *am, is, are, was, were*), the problem centers on third-person singular verbs with their *-s* ending. Here is the problem illustrated. Notice that only the verbs in the third-person singular are different. The unfortunate thing is that all nouns are third person and, when singular, require this form in the present tense.

	Present		Present Perfect	
	singular	plural	singular	plural
first person	I work	we work	I have worked	we have worked
second person	you work	you work	you have worked	you have worked
third person	he works (she, it)	they work	he has worked (she, it)	they have worked

It is the *-s* form, then, that you need to watch for to avoid errors in subject–verb agreement. Here are some situations that may cause problems.

Intervening Subordinate Element

When a subject and a verb are side by side, they usually do not present a problem. Often, however, writers separate them with subordinate elements, such as clauses, prepositional or verbal phrases, and other elements. The result may be a verb error. The following sentence illustrates this problem:

> The realization that life is a series of compromises never occur to some people. The subject is *realization*, a singular noun, and should be followed by the singular verb *occurs*. The corrected sentence would read "The realization that life is a series of compromises never occurs to some people."

Subject Complement

Subject complements follow some verbs and rename the subject, although they are not always in the same number as the subject. Because a singular subject may have a plural complement, and vice versa, confused writers might make the verb agree with the complement instead of the subject. Here's an example:

> The result of this mistake are guilt, low self-esteem, and depression. The subject is *result*, not *guilt, low self-esteem*, and *depression*; the singular subject should be followed by the singular verb *is*. The corrected sentence would read "The result of this mistake is guilt, low self-esteem, and depression."

Compound Subject

Two or more words may be compounded to make a subject. Whether they are singular or plural depends on their connector. Subjects connected by *and* and *but* are plural, but those connected by *or* and *nor* are singular or plural depending on whether the item closer to the verb is singular or plural. Here are examples:

> The young mother and the superior student *are* both candidates for compulsive perfectionism. Two subjects, *mother* and *student*, are joined by *and* and take a plural verb.

> Promotions or an employee award *tells* the perfectionist he or she is achieving personal goals. When two subjects, *promotions* and *award*, are joined by *or*, the verb agrees with the nearer one; in this sentence a singular verb is required.

> An employee award or promotions *tell* the perfectionist he or she is achieving personal goals. Here the plural verb, *tell*, agrees with *promotions*, the closer of the two subjects.

Indefinite Pronoun as Subject

Indefinite pronouns are defined and listed under 5C Pronoun Agreement. Although these words often seem plural in meaning, most of them are singular grammatically. When indefinite pronouns are the subjects of sentences or clauses, their verbs are usually singular. Here are examples:

> Everyone *has* at some time worried about achieving goals. The singular indefinite pronoun *everyone* takes a singular verb, *has*.

> Each car and truck on the highway *was* creeping along on the icy pavement. The singular indefinite pronoun *each* requires a singular verb, *was*.

> Neither of us *is* going to worry about being late. The singular indefinite pronoun *neither* takes a singular verb, *is*.

Nevertheless, some of us *are* going to be very late. The indefinite pronoun *some* (like *all*, *any*, and *none*) is singular or plural depending on context; compare "Some of the book *is* boring."

Inverted Sentence Order

Inverted sentence order can confuse your natural inclination to subject–verb agreement. Examples of inverted order are questions, plus sentences beginning with *there*. Sentences like these demand closer attention to agreement.

Have the results of the test come back yet? The plural subject, *results*, takes a plural verb, *have*.

There *are* many special services provided just for kids at hotels, ski lodges, and restaurants. The plural subject, *services*, takes a plural verb, *are*. *There* is never a subject; it only holds the place for the subject in an inverted sentence.

Intervening Relative Clause

Subordinate clauses that begin with the relative pronouns *who*, *which*, or *that* present special problems in subject–verb agreement. Their verbs must agree with their own subjects, not with a word in another clause. These subordinate clauses demand special attention because whether the pronouns are singular or plural depends on their antecedents. These sentences illustrate agreement within relative clauses:

Every person who *attends* the baseball game will receive a free cap. *Who*, the subject of *attends*, means "person," a singular noun.

John is one of the few people I know who *care* about frogs. *Who*, the subject of *care*, means "people," a plural noun.

John is the only one of all the people I know who *cares* about frogs. *Who* in this sentence means "one."

5 Pronouns

Pronouns can have all the same sentence functions as nouns; the difference is that pronouns do not have the meaning that nouns have. Nouns name things; a noun stands for the thing itself. Pronouns, however, refer only to nouns. Whenever that reference is ambiguous or inconsistent, there is a problem in clarity.

5A Pronoun Case

Case is a grammatical term for the way nouns and pronouns show their relationships to other parts of a sentence. In English, nouns have only two case forms: the regular form (the one listed in a dictionary, such as *year*) and the possessive form (used to show ownership or connection, such as *year's*; possessive nouns are discussed in 8C Apostrophe).

Pronouns, however, have retained their case forms. Here are the forms for personal and relative pronouns:

	Subjective	Objective	Possessive
Personal	I	me	my, mine
	you	you	your, yours
	he	him	his
	she	her	her, hers
	it	it	its
	we	us	our, ours
	they	them	their, theirs
Relative	who	whom	whose
	whoever	whomever	whosever

Notice, first, that possessive pronouns, unlike possessive nouns, do not take apostrophes—none of them. Sometimes writers confuse possessive pronouns with contractions, which do have apostrophes (such as *it's,* meaning *it is* or *it has*; and *who's,* meaning *who is*; for a further discussion, see 8C Apostrophe).

Another problem writers sometimes have with pronoun case is using a subjective form when they need the objective or using an objective form when they need the subjective.

Subjective Case. Use the subjective forms for subjects and for words referring to subjects, as in these examples:

Among the patients a nutritionist sees are the grossly overweight people *who* have tried all kinds of diets. *Who* is subject of the verb *have tried* in its own clause.

They have a life history of obesity and diets. *They* is the subject of *have.*

He and *the patient* work out a plan for permanent weight control. *He* and *the patient* are the compound subjects of *work.*

The patient understands that the ones who work out the diet plan are *he* and *the nutritionist. He* and *the nutritionist* refer to *ones*, the subject of the clause.

Notice that pronoun case is determined by the function of the pronoun in its own clause and that compounding (*he and the patient*) has no effect on case.

Objective Case. Use the *objective* forms for objects of all kinds:

"Between *you* and *me*," said the patient to his nutritionist, "I'm ready for something that works." *You* and *me* are objects of the preposition *between.*

An exercise program is usually assigned the patient for *whom* diet is prescribed. *Whom* is the object of the preposition *for.*

The nutritionist gives *her* a suitable alternative to couch sitting. *Her* is the indirect object of *gives.*

Modest exercise combined with modest dieting can affect *him or her* dramatically. *Him or her* is the direct object of *can affect.*

Having advised *them* about diet and exercise, the nutritionist instructs dieters about behavioral change. *Them* is the object of the participle *having advised*.

Notice again that the case of a pronoun is determined by its function in its own clause and is not affected by compounding (*you and me*).

Possessive Case. Use the possessive forms to indicate ownership. Possessive pronouns have two forms: adjective forms (*my, your, his, her, its, our, their*) and possessive forms (*mine, yours, his, hers, its, ours, theirs*). The adjective forms appear before nouns or gerunds; the possessive forms replace possessive nouns.

The patient purchased *his* supplements from the drug store *his* nutritionist recommended. Adjective form before nouns.

His swimming every day produced results faster than he anticipated. Adjective form before gerund.

His was a difficult task to accomplish, but the rewards of weight loss were great. Possessive form replacing possessive noun.

5B Pronoun Reference

Personal and relative pronouns (see the list in section 5A Pronoun Case) must refer to specific nouns or antecedents. By themselves they have no meaning. As a result, they can cause problems in clarity for writers. If you were to read "She teaches technical writing at her local technical college," you would know only that *someone,* a woman, teaches technical writing at the college. But if the sentence were preceded by one like this, "After getting her master's degree, my mother has achieved one of her life goals," the pronoun *she* would have meaning. In this case, *mother* is the antecedent of *she*. The antecedent gives meaning to the pronoun. For this reason, it is essential that pronouns refer unambiguously to their antecedents and that pronouns and antecedents agree.

Ambiguous pronoun reference may occur in various ways:

- More than one possible antecedent.
- Adjective used as intended antecedent.
- Implied antecedent.
- Too great of a separation between antecedent and pronoun.

Here are sentences in which the pronouns do not clearly refer to their antecedents:

The immunologist refused to admit fraudulence of the data reported by a former colleague in a paper *he* had cosigned. More than one possible antecedent. *He* could refer to *immunologist* or to *colleague*.

In Carolyn Chute's book *The Beans of Egypt, Maine*, **she** treats poverty with concern and understanding. Adjective used as intended antecedent (possessive nouns function as adjectives). In this case, *Carolyn Chute's* modifies *book* and cannot serve as an antecedent of the pronoun *she*.

It says in the newspaper that the economy will not improve soon. Implied antecedent. There is no antecedent for it.

At Ajax *they* have tires on sale till the end of the month. Implied antecedent. There is no antecedent for *they*.

This only reinforces the public skepticism about the credibility of scientists. Implied antecedent. There is no antecedent for *This*.

One of the primary rules for using humor in advertising is often broken, *which* is that the ad doesn't make fun of the product. Too great a separation between antecedent and pronoun. The antecedent of *which* is *rules*, but its distance from the pronoun makes reference difficult.

Faulty pronoun reference is corrected by clarifying the relationship between the pronoun and its intended antecedent. Observe how the example sentences have been revised:

The immunologist refused to admit fraudulence of the data reported by a former colleague in a paper *the immunologist* had cosigned. *The immunologist* replaces the unclear pronoun *he*.

In **her** book *The Beans of Egypt, Maine*, **Carolyn Chute** treats poverty with concern and understanding. The possessive pronoun *her* replaces the possessive noun and refers to the noun subject, *Carolyn Chute*.

The newspaper reports that the economy will not improve soon. The unclear pronoun *it* is replaced by its implied antecedent, *the newspaper*.

Ajax has tires on sale till the end of the month. The unclear pronoun *they* is replaced by *Ajax*.

This *kind of waffling* only reinforces public skepticism about the credibility of scientists. The unclear pronoun *this* is replaced by the adjective *this* modifying the intended antecedent *kind of waffling*.

That the ad doesn't make fun of the product is an often-broken primary rule for using humor in advertising. Parts of the sentence are moved around until they are clear.

Revising unclear pronoun reference is sometimes like working a jigsaw puzzle: finding and adding a missing piece or moving parts around to achieve the best fit. Often only the writer can make the right connections.

5C Pronoun Agreement

Some pronoun errors result because the pronoun and its antecedent do not agree. In the sentence, "When a student is late for this class, they find the door locked," the plural pronoun *they* refers to a singular antecedent, *a student*. There is no agreement in *number*. In this sentence, "When a student is late for this class, you find the door locked," again the pronoun, this time *you,* does not agree with the antecedent. This time the problem is *person.* Pronouns must agree with their antecedents in number, person, and gender. (See the list of pronouns in 5A Pronoun Case.)

Compound Antecedents

Problems sometimes occur with compound antecedents. If the antecedents are joined by *and;* the pronoun is plural; if joined by *or,* the pronoun agrees with the nearer antecedent. Here are examples of correct usage:

> In the pediatric trauma center, the head doctor and head nurse direct *their* medical team. The pronoun *their* refers to both *doctor* and *nurse.*

> The head doctor or the head nurse directs *his or her* team. The pronouns *his or her* refer to the closer antecedent, *nurse* (because the gender of the nurse is not known, the neutral alternatives are used).

> The head doctor or the other doctors give *their* help when it is needed. The pronoun *their* agrees with the closer antecedent, *doctors.*

Indefinite Pronouns as Antecedents

A particularly troublesome kind of agreement is that between personal or relative pronouns and *indefinite pronouns.* As their name implies, indefinites do not refer to particular people or things; grammatically they are usually singular but are often intended as plural. Here are the common indefinite pronouns:

all	every	none
any	everybody	nothing
anybody	everyone	one
anyone	everything	some
anything	neither	somebody
each	no one	someone
either	nobody	something

Like nouns, these pronouns can serve as antecedents of personal and relative pronouns. But because most of them are grammatically singular, they can be troublesome in sentences. Here are examples of correct usage:

> Everyone in the trauma center has *his or her* specific job to do. **or** *All* the personnel in the trauma center have *their* specific jobs to do. The neutral, though wordy, alternative *his or her* agrees with the singular indefinite *everyone.* The second sentence illustrates the use of plural when gender is unknown.

> *Each* of them does *his or her* job efficiently and competently. **or** *All* of them do *their* jobs efficiently and competently. *Each* is singular, but *all* is either singular or plural, depending on context (compare "*All* literature has *its* place").

Shifts in Person

Agreement errors in *person* are shifts between *I* or *we* (first person), *you* (second person), and *he, she, it,* and *they* (third person). These errors are probably more often a result of carelessness than of imperfect knowledge. Being more familiar with casual speech than formal writing, writers sometimes shift from *I* to *you,* for example, when only one of them is meant, as in these sentences:

> Last summer *I* went on a canoeing trip to northern Manitoba. It was *my* first trip that far north, and it was so peaceful *you* could forget all the problems back home. The person represented by *you* was not present. The writer means *I.*

See also 2D Shifts.

5D Relative Pronouns

Use relative pronouns to introduce clauses that modify nouns or pronouns. Personal relative pronouns refer to people. They include *who, whom, whoever, whomever,* and *whose.* Nonpersonal relative pronouns refer to things. They include *which, whichever, whatever,* and *whose.*

Most college writers know to use *who* when referring to people and *which* or *that* when referring to things, but sometimes carelessness or confusion can lead to errors. Many writers assume that *which* and *that* are interchangeable when they are not. Use *which* to introduce nonrestrictive clauses and *that* to introduce restrictive clauses (see 3B Restrictive and Nonrestrictive Modifiers). Another problem area concerns the correct use of *who* and *whom*. Use *who* to refer to the subject of the sentence and *whom* to refer to an object of the verb or preposition. Following are examples of common errors:

> The lawyer *that* lost the case today went to law school with my sister. Uses impersonal relative pronoun *that.*

> Conflict between the two parties led to the lawsuit *that* was finally settled today. The relative pronoun *that* introduces a nonrestrictive clause that modifies *lawsuit.* Nonrestrictive clauses supply extra information to the sentence, not defining information.

> The case resulted in a ruling, *which* favored the plaintiff. The relative pronoun *which* introduces a restrictive clause that modifies *ruling.* Restrictive clauses supply defining information.

> Later, the lawyer *whom* lost the case spoke with the jurors *who* we had interviewed. The first relative pronoun *whom* refers to the subject *lawyer* while the second relative pronoun *who* refers to the object of the verb *had interviewed.*

Once you recognize relative pronoun errors it is usually easy to fix them:

> The lawyer *who* lost the case today went to law school with my sister.

> Conflict between the two parties led to the lawsuit, *which* was finally settled today.

> The case resulted in a ruling *that* favored the plaintiff.

> Later, the lawyer *who* lost the case spoke with the jurors *whom* we had interviewed.

6 Style

Style in writing, like style in clothes, art, or anything else, is individual and develops with use and awareness. But even individual writers vary their style, depending on the situation. At school and work, the preferred style tends to be more formal and objective. The readings in this book provide abundant examples of this style. It is not stuffy, patronizing, or coldly analytical. It is simply clean, direct, and clear. This handbook section treats a few of the obstacles to a good writing style.

6A Conciseness

Nobody wants to read more words than necessary. When you write concisely, therefore, you are considerate of your readers. To achieve conciseness you do not need to eliminate details and other content; rather, you cut empty words, repetition, and unnecessary details.

In the following passage, all the italicized words could be omitted without altering the meaning.

> *In the final analysis, I feel that* the United States should have converted to the *use of the* metric system *of measurement* a long time ago. *In the present day and age,* the United States, except for Borneo and Liberia, is the *one and* only country in the *entire* world that has not yet adopted this measurement system.

Repetition of key words is an effective technique for achieving emphasis and coherence, but pointless repetition serves only to bore the reader.

Follow these guidelines to achieve conciseness in your writing:

1. **Avoid redundancy**. Redundant words and expressions needlessly repeat what has already been said. Delete them when they appear in your writing.

2. **Avoid wordy expressions**. Phrases such as *In the final analysis* and *In the present day and age* in the preceding example add no important information to sentences and should be removed and/or replaced with less wordy constructions.

3. **Avoid unnecessary intensifiers**. Intensifiers such as *really, very, clearly, quite,* and *of course* usually fail to add meaning to the words they modify and therefore are often unnecessary. Deleting them does not change the meaning of the sentence.

4. **Avoid excess use of prepositional phrases**. The use of too many prepositional phrases within a sentence makes for wordy writing. Always use constructions that require the fewest words.

5. **Avoid negating constructions**. Negating constructions using words such as *no* and *not* often add unneeded words to sentences. Use shorter alternatives when they are available.

6. **Avoid the passive voice**. Passive constructions require more words than active constructions (see 4B Voice). They can also obscure meaning by concealing the sentence's subject. Write in the active voice whenever possible.

Following are more examples of wordy sentences that violate these guidelines:

If the two groups *cooperate together,* there will be *positive benefits* for both. Uses redundancy.

There are some people *who* think the metric system is un-American. Uses wordy expression.

The climb up the mountain was *very* hard on my legs and *really* taxed my lungs and heart. Uses unnecessary modifiers.

On the day of his birth, we walked *to the park down the block from the house of his mother.* Uses too many prepositional phrases.

She *did not like* hospitals. Uses negating construction when a shorter alternative is available.

The door *was closed* by that man over there. Uses passive voice when active voice is preferable.

Corrections to the previous wordy sentences result in concise sentences:

If the two groups cooperate, both will benefit. This correction also replaces the wordy construction *there will be…for both* with a shorter, more forceful alternative.

Some people think the metric system is un-American.

The climb up the mountain was hard on my legs and taxed my lungs and heart.

On his birthday, we walked to the park near his mother's house.

She hated hospitals.

That man over there closed the door.

6B Appropriate Language

Effective writers communicate using appropriate language; that is, language that:

1. Suits its subject and audience.
2. Avoids sexist usage.
3. Avoids bias and stereotype.

Suitability

The style and tone of your writing should be suitable to your subject and audience. Most academic and business contexts require the use of *formal language*. Formal language communicates clearly and directly with a minimum of stylistic flourish. Its tone is serious, objective, and detached. Formal language avoids slang, pretentious words, and unnecessary jargon. *Informal language,* on the other hand, is particular to the writer's personality and also assumes a closer and more familiar relationship between the writer and the reader. Its tone is casual, subjective, and intimate. Informal language can also employ slang and other words that would be inappropriate in formal language.

As informal language is rarely used within an academic setting, the following examples show errors in the use of formal language:

The director told the board members to *push off*. Uses informal language.

Professor Oyo *dissed* Marta when she arrived late to his class for the third time in a row. Uses slang.

The *aromatic essence* of the gardenia was intoxicating. Uses pretentious words.

The doctor told him to take *salicylate* to ease the symptoms of *viral rhinorrhea*. Uses unnecessary jargon.

Employing formal language correctly, these examples could be revised as follows:

The director told the board members to leave.

Professor Oyo spoke disrespectfully to Marta when she arrived late to his class for the third time in a row.

The scent of the gardenia was intoxicating.

The doctor told him to take aspirin to ease his cold symptoms.

Sexist Usage

Gender-exclusive terms such as *policeman* and *chairman* are offensive to many readers today. Writers who are sensitive to their audience, therefore, avoid such terms, replacing them with expressions such as *police officer* and *chairperson* or *chair*. Most sexist usage in language involves masculine nouns, masculine pronouns, and patronizing terms.

Masculine Nouns. Do not use *man* and its compounds generically. For many people, these words are specific to men and do not account for women as separate and equal people. Here are some examples of masculine nouns and appropriate gender-neutral substitutions:

Masculine Noun	Gender-Neutral Substitution
mailman	mail carrier
businessman	businessperson, executive, manager
fireman	firefighter
man-hours	work hours
mankind	humanity, people
manmade	manufactured, synthetic
salesman	salesperson, sales representative, sales agent
congressman	member of Congress, representative

Using gender-neutral substitutions often entails using a more specific word for a generalized term, which adds more precision to writing.

Masculine Pronouns. Avoid using the masculine pronouns *he, him,* and *his* in a generic sense, meaning both male and female. This can pose some challenges, however, because English does not have a generic singular pronoun that can be used instead. Consider the following options:

1. Eliminate the pronoun.

   Every writer has an individual style. Instead of Every writer has his own style.

2. Use plural forms.

   Writers have their own styles. Instead of A writer has his own style.

3. Use *he or she, one,* or *you* as alternates only sparingly.

   Each writer has his or her own style. Instead of Each writer has his own style.

   One has an individual writing style. Instead of He has his own individual writing style.

   You have your own writing style. Instead of A writer has his own style.

Patronizing Terms. Avoid terms that cast men or women in gender-exclusive roles or that imply that women are subordinate to men. Here are some examples of biased or stereotypical terms and their gender-neutral substitutions:

Biased/Stereotypical Term	Gender-Neutral Substitution
lady lawyer	lawyer
male nurse	nurse
career girl	professional, attorney, manager
coed	student
housewife	homemaker
stewardess	flight attendant
cleaning lady	housecleaner

Biases and Stereotypes

Biased and stereotypical language can be hurtful and can perpetuate discrimination. Most writers are sensitive to racial and ethnic biases or stereotypes, but writers should also avoid language that shows insensitivity to age, class, religion, and sexual orientation. The accepted terms for identifying groups and group members have changed over the years and continue to change today. Avoid using terms that have fallen into disuse such as *Indian* or *Oriental*; instead, use accepted terms such as *Native American* or *Asian.*

7 Punctuation

Punctuation is a system of signals telling readers how the parts of written discourse relate to one another. They are similar to road signs that tell the driver what to expect: A sign with an arrow curving left means that the road makes a left curve, a "stop ahead" sign that a stop sign is imminent, a speed limit sign what the legal speed is. Drivers trust that the signs mean what they say. Readers, too, expect punctuation marks to mean what they say: A period means the end of a sentence, a colon that an explanation will follow, a comma that the sentence is not finished. Punctuation is a way for writers to help readers understand their words in the intended way.

Punctuation corresponds roughly to intonations and other physical signals in speech. When you speak, you use pitch levels, pauses, hand signals, head movements, and facial expressions to make sure your audience understands you. At the end of a sentence, you unconsciously let your voice drop—not just pause but decidedly drop in pitch. With some questions, your voice rises at the end, as in "Do you want to go?" With other questions, the pitch drops, as in "Do you want to go or not?" You can have brief pauses, or you can lengthen them to increase the drama of what you are saying. You can increase or decrease the sound volume of your words. None of these signals are available to writers. To make their situation even more difficult, writers do not have their audience right in front of them to look puzzled or to question them when meaning is unclear. So writers use punctuation.

Ends of sentences are punctuated with periods, question marks, or exclamation points. Semicolons function as "soft" periods, usually marking the end of independent clauses (as periods do) but not of complete thoughts. Commas show relationships within sentences, as do colons, dashes, quotation marks, parentheses, brackets, and ellipsis dots. These marks are explained in the sections that follow. Other marks, those used within words (apostrophes, hyphens, italics, and slashes), are explained in Section 8, Mechanics and Spelling.

Figure H-1 serves as a quick guide to sentence punctuation. For explanations, refer to the relevant entry.

7A End Punctuation

A period is the normal mark for ending sentences. A question mark ends a sentence that asks a direct question, and an exclamation point ends forceful assertions.

Period

Sentences normally end with a period.

> Studies suggest that eating fish two or three times a week may reduce the risk of heart attack. Statement.

> Eat two or three servings of fish a week. Mild command.

> The patient asked whether eating fish would reduce risk of heart attack. Indirect question.

Avoid inserting a period before the end of a sentence; the result will be a fragment (see 1A Fragments). Sentences can be long or short; their length does not determine their completion. Both of the following examples are complete sentences.

> Eat fish. Mild command; the subject, *you*, is understood.

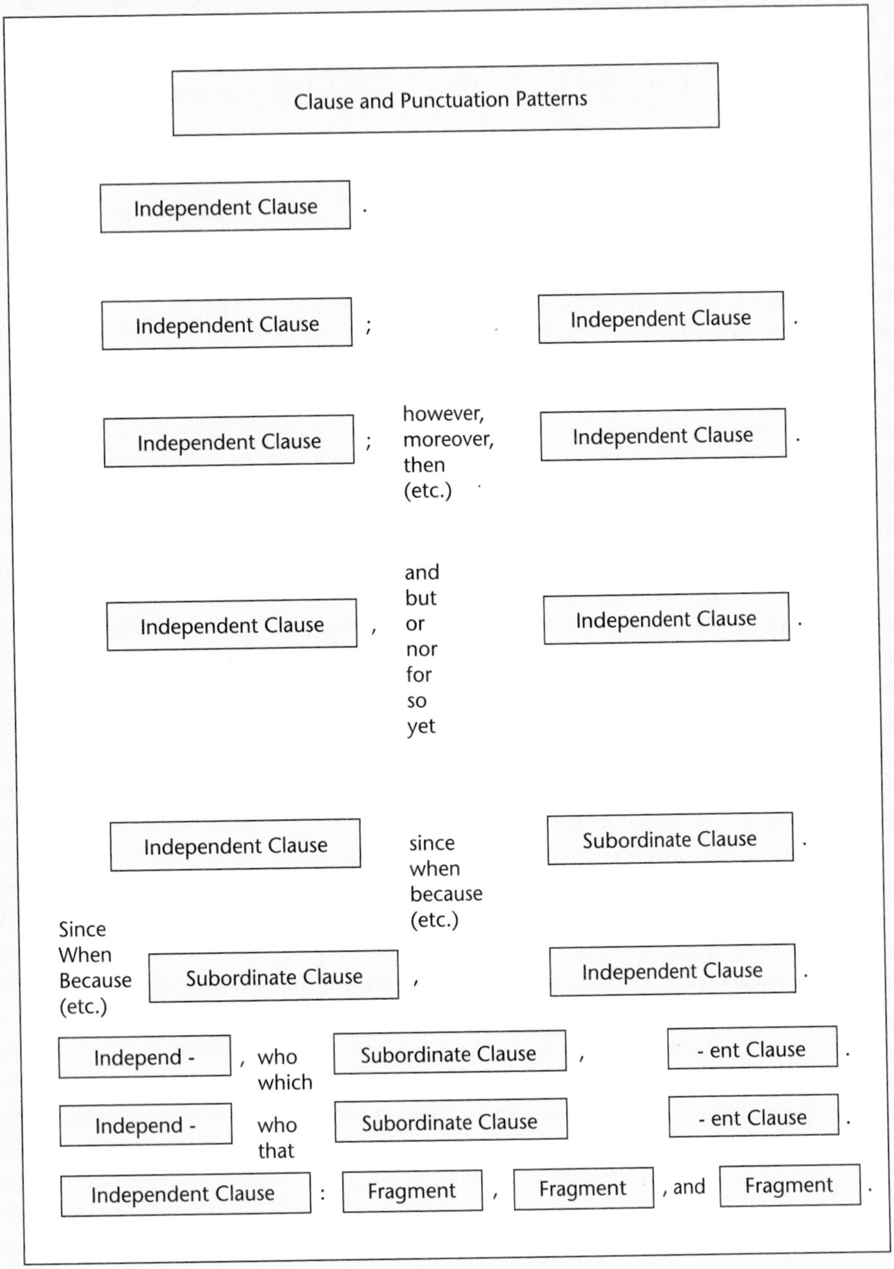

Clause and Punctuation Patterns

| Independent Clause | . |

| Independent Clause | ; | | Independent Clause | . |

| Independent Clause | ; | however,
moreover,
then
(etc.) | Independent Clause | . |

| Independent Clause | , | and
but
or
nor
for
so
yet | Independent Clause | . |

| Independent Clause | since
when
because
(etc.) | Subordinate Clause | . |

Since
When
Because
(etc.) | Subordinate Clause | , | Independent Clause | . |

| Independ - | , who
which | Subordinate Clause | , | - ent Clause | . |

| Independ - | who
that | Subordinate Clause | | - ent Clause | . |

| Independent Clause | : | Fragment | , | Fragment | , and | Fragment | . |

Figure H-1

In a two-year study of 1,000 survivors of heart attack, researchers found a 29 percent reduction in mortality among those who regularly ate fish or took a fish oil supplement. Statement; one sentence.

Question Mark

A sentence that asks a direct question ends in a question mark:

How does decaffeinated coffee differ from regular coffee?

Do not use a question mark to end an indirect question:

The customer asked how decaffeinated coffee differs from regular coffee.

With quoted questions, place the question mark inside the final quotation marks:

The customer asked, "How does decaffeinated coffee differ from regular coffee?"

Exclamation Point

The exclamation point ends forceful assertions:

Fire!

Shut that door immediately!

Because they give the impression of shouting, exclamation points are rarely needed in formal business and academic writing.

7B Semicolon

The main use for a semicolon is to connect two closely related independent clauses:

Dengue hemorrhagic fever is a viral infection common to Southeast Asia; it kills about 5,000 children a year.

Sometimes the second clause contains a transitional adverb (see 1B Comma Splices):

Dengue has existed in Asia for centuries; *however,* it grew more virulent in the 1950s.

Do not use a comma where a semicolon or period is required; the result is a comma splice (see 1B Comma Splices). In contrast, a semicolon used in place of a comma may result in a type of fragment (see 1A Fragments):

In populations where people have been stricken by an infectious virus, survivors have antibodies in their bloodstreams; *which prevent or reduce the severity of subsequent infections.* The semicolon makes a fragment of the *which* clause.

Do not confuse the semicolon with the colon (see 7D Colon). While the semicolon connects independent clauses, a colon ordinarily does not. The semicolon is also used to separate items in a series when the items contain internal commas:

Scientists are researching the effects of staphylococcus bacteria, which cause infections in deep wounds; influenza A virus, which causes respiratory flu; and conjunctivitis bacteria, which have at times caused fatal purpuric fever.

7C Comma

The comma is probably the most troublesome mark of punctuation because it has so many uses. It is a real workhorse for punctuation within a sentence. Its main uses are explained here.

Compound Sentences. A comma joins two independent clauses connected with a coordinating conjunction (see 1B Comma Splices):

> Martinique is a tropical island in the West Indies, *and* it attracts flocks of tourists annually.

Do not use the comma between independent clauses without the conjunction, even if the second clause begins with a transitional adverb:

> Faulty: Martinique is a tropical island in the West Indies, it attracts flocks of tourists annually. Two independent clauses with no conjunction; it is a comma splice.

> Faulty: Martinique is a tropical island in the West Indies, consequently it attracts flocks of tourists annually. Two independent clauses with transitional adverb; it is a comma splice.

Introductory Sentence Elements. Commas set off a variety of introductory sentence elements, as illustrated here:

> *When the French colonized Martinique in 1635,* they eliminated the native Caribs. Introductory subordinate clause.

> *Choosing death over subservience,* the Caribs leaped into the sea. Introductory participial (verbal) phrase.

> *Before their death,* they warned of a "mountain of fire" on the island. Introductory prepositional phrase.

> *Subsequently,* the island's volcano erupted. Introductory transitional adverb.

Short prepositional phrases sometimes are not set off:

> *In 1658* the Caribs leaped to their death.

Sometimes, however, a comma must be used after a short prepositional phrase to prevent misreading:

> *Before,* they had predicted retribution. Comma is required to prevent misreading.

Nonrestrictive and Parenthetical Elements. Words that interrupt the flow of a sentence are set off with commas before and after. If they come at the end of a sentence, they are set off with one comma.

In this class are nonrestrictive modifiers (see 3B Restrictive and Nonrestrictive Modifiers), transitional adverbs (see 1B Comma Splices), and a few other types of interrupters. Here are examples:

> This rugged island, *which Columbus discovered in 1502,* exports sugar and rum. Nonrestrictive *which* clause; commas before and after.

A major part of the economy, *however,* is tourism. Interrupting transitional adverb; commas before and after.

Tourists, *attracted to the island by its climate,* enjoy discovering its culture. Interrupting participial (verbal) phrase (see 1A Fragments); commas before and after.

A popular tradition in Martinique is the Carnival, *which occurs just before Lent each year.* Nonrestrictive *which* clause; one comma.

Martinique is an overseas department of France, *a status conferred in 1946.* An absolute, ending the sentence (participial phrase plus the noun it modifies).

Series

Commas separate items in a series:

Martiniquans dance to *steel drums, clarinets, empty bottles, and banjos.* Four nouns.

Dressing in colorful costumes, dancing through the streets, and thoroughly enjoying the celebration, Martiniquans celebrate Carnival with enthusiasm. Three participial (verbal) phrases.

Martinique has a population of over 300,000, its main religion is Roman Catholicism, and its languages are French and Creole dialect. Three independent clauses.

Various sentence elements can make up a series, but the elements joined should be equivalent grammatically (see 2A Parallelism, which discusses faulty parallelism). Common practice calls for a comma before the conjunction joining the last item in the series.

Quotations

Commas set off quoted sentences from the words that introduce them:

"A wise man," says David Hume, "proportions his belief to the evidence."

According to Plato, "Writing will produce forgetfulness" in writers because "they will not need to exercise their memories." The second clause is not set off with a comma.

"*X* on beer casks indicates beer which paid ten shillings duty, and hence it came to mean beer of a given quality," reports *The Dictionary of Phrase and Fable.*

Quotations introduced with *that* and other connectors (such as *because* in the second sentence here) are not set off with commas. Commas at the end of quotations go inside the quotation marks.

Coordinate Adjectives

Commas separate adjectives that equally modify a noun:

The "food pyramid" was designed as a *meaningful, memorable* way to represent the ideal daily diet. Two adjectives modify the noun *way* equally.

When you're not sure about using a comma, try inserting the coordinating conjunction *and* between the two adjectives to see if they are truly coordinate (*meaningful and memorable*). Another test is to reverse the order of the adjectives (*memorable, meaningful*). Do not use a comma between adjectives that are not coordinate or between the last adjective and the noun being modified. (See also 3C Adjectives and Adverbs.)

Addresses and Dates

Use a comma to separate city and state in an address, but do not set off the zip code:

Glen Ridge, New Jersey 07028 *or* Glen Ridge, NJ 07028

In a sentence, a state name is enclosed in commas:

The letter from Glen Ridge, New Jersey, arrived by express mail.

Dates are treated similarly:

January 5, 1886 *but* 5 January 1886

The events of January 5, 1886, are no longer remembered. When other punctuation is not required, the year is followed by a comma.

Commas to Avoid

Some people mistakenly believe that commas should be used wherever they might pause in speech. A comma does mean pause, but not all pauses are marked by commas. Use a comma only when you know you need one. Avoid the following comma uses:

1. To set off restrictive sentence elements:

   People, *who want a balanced diet,* can use the food pyramid as a guide. The restrictive *who* clause is necessary to identify *people* and should not be set off with commas.

2. To separate a subject from its verb and a preposition from its object:

   People who want a balanced diet, can use the food pyramid as a guide. The comma following the *who* clause separates the subject, *people*, from its verb, *can use*.

   The bottom level of the food pyramid contains food from grains, *such as,* bread, cereals, rice, and pasta. The preposition *such as* should not be followed by a comma.

3. To follow a coordinating conjunction (see 1B Comma Splices):

   The food pyramid describes a new approach to a balanced diet. But, the meat and dairy industries opposed it. The coordinating conjunction *but* should not be set off with a comma.

4. To separate two independent clauses (see 1B Comma Splices) not joined with a coordinating conjunction:

   The pyramid shows fewer servings of dairy and meat products, therefore consumers would buy less of these higher-priced foods. The comma should be replaced with a semicolon (7B).

5. To set off coordinate elements joined with a coordinating conjunction:

   Vegetables and fruits are near the bottom of the pyramid, *and should be eaten several times a day.* The coordinating conjunction *and* joins a second verb, *should be eaten,* not a second independent clause; therefore no comma is needed.

7D Colon

The colon is used most often to introduce an explanatory element, often in the form of a list:

> The space shuttle *Challenger* lifted off on January 28, 1986, with a seven-member crew: Francis R. Scobee, Michael J. Smith, Ronald E. McNair, Ellison S. Onizuka, Judith A. Resnik, Gregory B. Jarvis, and Christa McAuliffe. The list explains *crew.*

> A twelve-member investigating team discovered the cause of the disaster: a leak in one of the shuttle's two solid-fuel booster rockets. The phrase explains the *cause of the disaster.*

Do not use colons interchangeably with semicolons (see 7B Semicolon). Semicolons separate two independent clauses (see 1B Comma Splices); colons ordinarily are followed by a phrase or phrases. Also avoid using colons after verbs and prepositions (see 1A Fragments):

> The two causes of the O-ring failure were cold temperatures and design deficiencies. No colon after *were.*

> The commission investigating the disaster noted a number of failures in communication, such as one within the National Aeronautics and Space Administration. No colon after *such as.*

Colons have a few other set uses:

Time:	10:15 a.m.
Salutation in a business letter:	Dear Patricia Morton:
Biblical reference:	Genesis 2:3

7E Dash

The dash separates sentence elements with greater emphasis than a comma:

> In *The War of the Worlds* (1898), science fiction writer H. G. Wells described an intense beam of light that destroyed objects on contact—the laser.

It is also used to set off a nonrestrictive sentence element (see 3B Restrictive and Nonrestrictive Modifiers) that might be confusing if set off with commas:

> A number of medical uses—performing eye surgery, removing tumors, and unclogging coronary arteries—make the laser more than a destructive weapon. The three explanatory items separated by commas are set off from the rest of the sentence with dashes.

Like commas that set off nonrestrictive elements within a sentence, dashes often are used in pairs—at the beginning of the interruption and at the end.

A dash is sometimes used in place of a colon when a colon might seem too formal:

> Besides its medical uses, the laser serves many other functions—reading price codes, playing compact audio disks, and sending telephone messages.

Use the dash with caution; overuse gives the impression that you aren't familiar with alternative means of punctuation.

7F Quotation Marks

The main use for quotation marks is to set off direct quotations:

> Professor Charlotte Johnson announced, "Interdisciplinary science is combining fields of scientific knowledge to make up new disciplines."

> "Biochemistry," she went on to say, "combines biology and chemistry."

Quotations within quotations are marked with single quotation marks:

> "The term 'interdisciplinary science' thus describes a change in how processes are investigated," she concluded.

Use quotation marks correctly with other punctuation marks. Periods and commas (see 7C Comma) always go inside the end quotation marks; colons and semicolons almost always go outside the quotation. Dashes, question marks, and exclamation points go inside or outside depending on meaning—inside if the mark applies to the quotation and outside if it applies to the surrounding sentence:

> "Do you know the various branches of the physical sciences?" asked Professor Johnson. Question mark goes inside quotation marks because it applies to the quotation.

> Did the professor say, "Histology deals with tissues and cytology with the fine structures of individual cells"? Question mark goes outside quotation marks because it applies to the surrounding sentence, not the quotation.

Do not use quotation marks to set off indirect quotations:

> The professor said that histology and cytology are different branches of study.

Another use for quotation marks is to enclose titles of works that are not published separately, including short stories, poems, and essays:

> "You Are a Man," by Richard Rodriguez

> "The Incident," by Countee Cullen

Do not enclose titles of your own essays in quotation marks when they are in title position. (See 8D Italics for treatment of titles of works that are published separately.)

Quotation marks are sometimes used to enclose words used in a special sense, but be careful not to abuse this function:

> The "right" way to do a thing is not always the best way.

7G Other Marks

Parentheses

Parentheses enclose interrupting elements, setting them off from the rest of the sentence or discourse with a greater separation than other enclosing marks such as commas and dashes. They usually add explanatory information that might seem digressive to the topic.

> The Particle Beam Fusion Accelerator *(PBFA II)* is a device designed to produce energy by fusion. Parentheses set off an abbreviation that will henceforth be used in place of the full term.

> The PBFA II stores up to 3.5 million joules of energy. *(One joule is the amount of energy expended by a one-watt device in one second.)* Parentheses set off an explanation framed as a complete sentence.

Parentheses are always used in pairs. They might have internal punctuation (as in the second example), but marks related to the sentence as a whole go outside the parentheses. Parentheses are almost never preceded by a comma. Note the following example:

> During fusion *(joining of two atomic nuclei to form a larger nucleus),* mass is converted to energy. Parenthetical element is followed by a comma, showing that it relates to *fusion*. If it had been preceded by a comma, it would appear, illogically, to relate to *mass*.

Brackets

Square brackets have limited uses and are not interchangeable with parentheses. Their most common use is to mark insertions in quoted material:

> Describing the Great Depression, Frederick Lewis Allen says, "The total amount of money paid out in wages *[in 1932]* was 60 percent less than in 1929." The words *in 1932* were not part of the original text.

Some writers use brackets to enclose brief parenthetical material within parentheses:

> Jules Verne (*Journey to the Center of the Earth* [1864]) described giant apes and a vast subterranean sea at the core of the earth. The date of publication is parenthetical to the title of the book.

Ellipsis Dots

Ellipsis dots (spaced periods) are used in quotations to indicate where words have been omitted. Three spaced dots mark omissions within a sentence. If the omission comes at the end of your sentence but not at the end of the original sentence, use four spaced periods.

> One of the legacies of the Great Depression, says Frederick Lewis Allen, is that "if individual Americans are in deep trouble,...their government [should] come to their aid." Words following a comma in the original sentence are omitted within the sentence. The brackets enclose an inserted word.

This idea, adds Allen, "was fiercely contested for years...." Allen's sentence did not end at *years,* where the quoted sentence ends.

When using ellipsis dots, be careful not to distort the meaning of the original by your selection of what to include and what to omit.

8 Mechanics and Spelling

Some "rules" of writing are flexible, allowing choices, but this is not the case with spelling. With the invention of the printing press in the fifteenth century and the publication of dictionaries in the eighteenth century, flexibility in spelling all but vanished. Dictionaries spell almost all their words in exactly the same way as other dictionaries, and readers expect writers to do likewise. We have expectations about the way hyphens are used in compound words, the way apostrophes show possession or contraction, the way suffixes are added to root words, and so on. This section treats the formation of words—capitalizing, abbreviating, punctuating (apostrophes, italics, and hyphens), and spelling.

8A Capitalization

The rules for capitalization are relatively fixed. Following are examples of situations calling for capitalization.

Beginning of a sentence

In 1929, the whole credit structure of the American economy was shaken.

Proper names or nouns

With the onset of the *Great Depression, President Hoover* at first tried to organize national optimism. Historical period or event; person.

Bankers on *Wall Street,* manufacturers in *Detroit,* and legislators in *Washington* all had an effect on the economy. Place.

The Great Depression was part of a worldwide collapse, ending only with *World War II.* Historical period or event.

President Hoover set up the *Reconstruction Finance Corporation* to aid banks and businesses. Person; institution.

In 1900, most of the *African Americans* in this country lived in the *South.* Race and nationality; geographical region.

Jell-O, Pepsi, Rice Krispies Trade names.

Aunt Beatrice, Grandmother Dietz, Dad Relationships when they are part of the name; but not *my dad* and *my aunt and uncle.*

Titles

Death at an Early Age, by Jonathan Kozol; *The Dancing Wu Li Masters: An Overview of the New Physics,* by Gary Zukav. Capitalize first and last words, words following colons, and all other words except articles (*a, an,* and *the*) and conjunctions and prepositions of fewer than five letters (*and, but, in, by,* etc.).

Avoid capitalizing common nouns; for example:

For many people, the *winter* of 1902 was bleak. Seasons.

Many people moved *south* to a warmer climate. Compass directions.

My *great-grandparents* were among those who moved. Relationships.

Simon Waterson was a *professor of history* at the time. Titles that are not part of proper names.

8B Abbreviation

While abbreviations are part of the language, not all are acceptable in all circumstances. A general guideline is that they are less common in formal prose than in less formal circumstances.

Titles with proper names

Dr. Paul Gordon   Paul Gordon, Ph.D.
George Grossman, Jr.

Times and dates

11:15 A.M. *or* 11:15 a.m.   53 B.C.   A.D. 371

Names of organizations and countries

NATO   CIA   NBC

Use *U.S.* as an adjective (*in a U.S. city*) and *United States* as a noun (*a city in the United States*).

Latin abbreviations (write out except in source citations and parenthetical comments)

etc.   and so forth (*et cetera*—applies to things)
i.e.   that is (*id est*)
e.g.   for example (*exempli gratia*)
cf.   compare (*confer*)
et al.   and others (*et alii*—applies to people)
N.B.   note well (*nota bene*)

Abbreviations to be avoided in most prose

The school board not bd. met on Tuesday not Tues. February 3 not Feb.

William not Wm. Townsend was a guest lecturer in the economics not econ. class.

Townsend arrived from Pittsburgh, Pennsylvania not *PA* or *Penn.* late last night. For letters and envelopes, use the U.S. Postal zip codes, such as PA for *Pennsylvania* and IL for *Illinois*. Note that both letters are capitalized and are not followed by periods.

Consult your dictionary when you have questions about specific abbreviations.

8C Apostrophe

The apostrophe has two main uses in English—to mark possessive nouns and to show contractions—plus a few specialized uses. Avoid all other uses.

Possessive Nouns

Ownership or connection is marked on nouns with apostrophes:

> Norton's resume is short and concise. The resume belongs to Norton.
>
> This week's newsletter will be a little late. The newsletter of this week.
>
> The article's title is confusing. The title of the article.

To make nouns possessive, follow one of these steps:

1. For singular nouns, add *'s* (*nature + 's = nature's*; *Tess + 's = Tess's*).
2. For plural nouns ending in *s*, add *'* (*strangers + ' = strangers'*).
3. For plural nouns not ending in *s*, add *'s* (*men + 's = men's*).

Do not use apostrophes to make nouns plural. (See 8G Spelling.) And do not use apostrophes with possessive and relative pronouns. (See 5A Pronoun Case and the Contractions section that follows.)

For example:

> The *Harris's* are in Florida. Incorrectly uses apostrophe to make the noun *Harris* plural.
>
> The family lost *it's* home in the fire. Incorrectly uses apostrophe with the pronoun *it* to make it possessive.

Contractions

Apostrophes stand in place of omitted letters in contractions:

doesn't	does not
isn't	is not
I'd	I would
you've	you have
it's	it is *or* it has
who's	who is *or* who has
let's	let us
we'll	we will

Because contractions reflect a casual style, they are usually not acceptable in formal writing. Do not confuse the contracted *it is* (*it's*) and *who is* (*who's*) with the possessive pronouns *its* and *whose*. (See 5A Pronoun Case.)

Special Uses

Plurals of letters, numbers, and words used as terms

> I am hoping to get all *A*'s this year.
>
> The memo had four misspelled *there*'s. See 8D Italics, which discusses underlining words used as terms.
>
> All the *7*'s are upside down in the 1990s catalog. The plural for years is usually formed without apostrophes.

Omitted letters or numbers

We'll never forget the summer of '78. Restrict to informal writing.

"Be *seein'* ya," Charlie said. Dialect in quoted speech.

8D Italics (Underlining)

Italic type slants to the right and is used in printed material in the same way that underlining is used in handwritten or typed copy. It has specialized uses.

Titles of works published independently

The Atlantic Monthly (magazine)

A Farewell to Arms (book)

The Wall Street Journal (newspaper)

Desperate Housewives (television program)

Cats (play)

Ships, aircraft, spacecraft, and trains

Challenger (spacecraft)

Leasat 3 (communications satellite)

San Francisco *Zephyr* (train)

Words, letters, and numbers used as themselves

The process of heat transfer is called *conduction*.

The Latin words *et cetera* mean "and other things."

The letter *e* is the most commonly used vowel.

Many people consider *13* to be an unlucky number.

Emphasis

"I said, '*Did* you buy the tickets?' not '*Would* you buy the tickets?' "

Many people writing with computers use italics instead of underlining. If you are writing a documented paper for class, find out if your teacher approves of italics for titles.

8E Hyphens

Hyphens have three main uses: to divide words at the ends of lines, to form compound words, and to connect spelled-out numbers.

Dividing Words

There are three general rules to remember when using hyphens to divide words at the ends of lines: (1) always divide between syllables, (2) don't divide one-syllable words, and (3) don't divide words so that only two letters carry over to the second line. Consider the following examples:

After the results came back, the doctor sat me down and explained my *condi-tion*.

While they could not cure the condition, at least they could alleviate its *symp-toms*.

In the end, after months of waiting and mountains of legal fees, the court *ru-led* against him. Incorrectly divides the one-syllable word *ruled*.

Needless to say, when the court ruled against him, he was not *particular-ly* pleased. Incorrectly divides the word *particularly* so that only the last two letters carry over to the second line.

Forming Compound Words

Knowing when to hyphenate compound words can be tricky. This is because some compound words can be written as single words (for example, *graveyard* or *postmaster*) while others can be written as two separate words (for example, *place kick* or *executive secretary*). Complicating matters further, compound adjectives take hyphens when they precede nouns but not when they follow nouns. Here are some examples of the correct and incorrect use of hyphens:

My *ex-husband* is a *pro-Communist* crackpot. Use hyphens after the prefix *ex-* and any prefix placed before a proper name, in this case *pro-* before *Communist*. In general, though, most words formed with prefixes are written as one word; for example, *antisocial* or *multicultural*.

The *post-mortem* revealed that her *brother in law* died of natural causes. This sentence contains two hyphenation errors. First, the compound word *post-mortem* should be written as a single word, *postmortem* (see comment on prefixes in the preceding example). Second, the compound noun *brother in law* should be hyphenated as *brother-in-law*.

Twentieth-century fiction is notable for its experimentation. **or** The fiction of the *twentieth century* is notable for its experimentation. In the first sentence *Twentieth-century* functions as a compound adjective modifying the noun *fiction* and so requires a hyphen. In the second sentence, *twentieth century* functions as a compound noun (specifically an object of the preposition *of*) and does not require a hyphen.

The *secretary treasurer* discouraged the group from making *highly-risky* investments. This sentence contains two hyphenation errors. First, the compound noun *secretary treasurer* requires a hyphen. Second, *-ly* adverbs such as *highly* are written as separate words when they precede adjectives such as *risky*.

Connecting Spelled-Out Numbers

Use hyphens to link compounds of spelled out numbers and to link numbers to nouns. For example:

twenty-fifth time

nine-page letter

132-page report

six-year-old

35-year-old

Whenever you have a question about dividing words and hyphenating compound words, use your dictionary. Dots usually mark syllables, and hyphens mark hyphenated compounds.

8F Numbers

Numbers can be spelled out or written as numerals. When to employ one style or the other depends on the writing context. In most academic writing in the humanities, and indeed in most writing geared for a general audience, numbers are usually spelled out as discussed next. In the sciences, however, numbers are usually written as numerals.

Unless you are asked to follow different conventions, use the following guidelines to handle numbers in writing:

1. Spell out numbers requiring two words or less and write numerals for numbers requiring three or more words. In practice, this means you will write out numbers *one* to *ninety-nine* and write numerals for *100* and above.

2. Spell out numbers that begin sentences. For long numbers this can lead to awkward sentences. In such instances, you should consider revising the sentence to move the number away from the beginning of the sentence so it can be written in numerals.

3. Make exceptions for numbers used in special figures. In these instances, numbers are usually written as numerals. Special figures of this type include days and years; pages, chapters, and volumes; acts, scenes, and lines; decimals, fractions, ratios, and percentages; temperatures; addresses; statistics; and amounts of money.

Consider the following examples:

The company mailed *twenty-one* parcels yesterday.

She bought *2,200* acres of ranch land with her lottery winnings.

One hundred and fifty-two cows drowned in the flood.

The Japanese attacked Pearl Harbor on December *7, 1941*.

You will find the answer on page *87* in chapter *5*.

The famous "To be, or not to be" soliloquy appears in act *3*, scene *1* of *Hamlet*.

The temperature reached *105*°F yesterday.

The suspect resided at *221* Dolores Street, apartment *3B*.

The winning margin was *2* to *1*.

With tax, the umbrella cost $*15.73*.

8G Spelling

One of the unfair facts of life is that the ability to spell is not equally distributed: Some people spell easily and some don't. If you're one of the latter, you'll need to put more time into getting your words right. A spellchecker is helpful, because it flags most misspelled words and suggests alternatives. If you are using one of these aids, however, be especially careful to look for misspelled homonyms. Rules of spelling sometimes help, though too many of them are probably a hindrance. Therefore only the most useful and dependable ones are included here.

Doubling a Final Consonant

When adding a suffix such as *-ing* or *-ed* to a word that ends in a consonant, double the final consonant to keep the internal vowel short; for example, *permit, permitted; stop, stopped*. Double the final consonant when all three of the following are true:

1. The word ends in a consonant preceded by a vowel.

2. The word is one syllable or the accent is on the final syllable.

3. The suffix begins with a vowel.

Here are some other examples:

hop	hopped	begin	beginning
sit	sitting	prefer	preferred
put	putting	occur	occurrence
win	winner	recap	recapped

Words Containing *ie* or *ei*

The familiar rhyme about using *ie* or *ei* is true most of the time—enough times that it is worth remembering: *i* before *e* except after *c* when the sound is long *e*. Thus words such as these follow the rule:

receive	believe	weight
ceiling	chief	beige
conceited	siege	eight

There are a few common exceptions: *caffeine, either, neither, seize,* and *weird*. Another common word that the rule does not address is *friend* (spelled *i* before *e*, but the sound is not long *e*).

Final *e*

To add an ending to a word that ends in a silent *e*, drop the *e* when the ending begins with a vowel:

believe + able = believable	believe + ed = believed
move + able = movable	move + ment = movement
hope + ing = hoping	hope + ful = hopeful

When the consonant preceding the final *e* is a soft *c* or *g*, the *e* is dropped only when the ending begins with *e* or *i*:

change + ing = changing	change + able = changeable
notice + ing = noticing	notice + able = noticeable
manage + er = manager	manage + ment = management
nice + er = nicer	nice + ly = nicely

Final *y*

To add an ending to a word with a final *y* preceded by a consonant, change the *y* to *i* except when your ending is *-ing*:

happy + ly = happily	study + ing = studying
apply + s = applies	apply + ing = applying
vary + ous = various	vary + ing = varying
try + ed = tried	try + ing = trying

When the final *y* is preceded by a vowel, keep the *y*:

play + ed = played	play + ful = playful
employ + ed = employed	employ + ment = employment

but

say + s = says	say + d = said
pay + ment = payment	pay + d = paid

Never change the *y* when adding an ending to a proper noun: *the Barrys*.

Plurals

Plural nouns ordinarily have an *s* ending:

boy + s = boys	car + s = cars

Words that end in *ch, s, sh, x,* or *z* require *-es*:

box + es = boxes	church + es = churches

Words ending in *o* are a little more troublesome. If the *o* is preceded by a vowel, add *s*:

radio + s = radios	video + s = videos

If the *o* is preceded by a consonant, ordinarily add *-es*:

hero + es = heroes	potato + es = potatoes

A few common words take either *s* or *-es*:

tornados, tornadoes	zeros, zeroes	volcanos, volcanoes

Some words form their plurals internally or do not have a plural form. Do not add an *s* to these words:

child, children	deer, deer
man, men	fish, fish
mouse, mice	moose, moose

Compound words ordinarily have an *s* at the end of the compound:

textbook, textbooks	snowshoe, snowshoes
text edition, text editions	snow goose, snow geese

But when the first word of the compound is the main word, add the *s* to it:

sisters-in-law   attorneys-general

Whenever you are in doubt about the correct plural ending, check your dictionary.

Homonyms

Some of the most troublesome words to spell are homonyms, words that sound alike but are spelled differently. Here is a partial list of the most common ones:

accept, except	maybe, may be
affect, effect	of, 've (have)
already, all ready	passed, past
cite, sight, site	than, then
forth, fourth	their, there, they're
it's, its	to, too, two
know, no	whose, who's
lead, led	your, you're

A few other words, not exactly homonyms, are sometimes confused:

breath, breathe	lightning, lightening
choose, chose	loose, lose
clothes, cloths	precede, proceed
dominant, dominate	quiet, quite

Check the meanings of any sound-alike words you are unsure of in your dictionary.

9 Review of Basic Grammar

Grammar is the set of rules used for communicating in a language. Words are the basic units of grammar, which classifies them by their function into the *parts of speech*. In English, grammar determines the form words take and the order in which they can be combined into *phrases, clauses,* and *sentences*. Sentences, unlike phrases and clauses, must represent complete thoughts and to do so each must contain at least one *subject* and one *predicate*. Sentences can also include *objects* and *complements*.

9A Parts of Speech

This section examines nine parts of speech: verbs, nouns, pronouns, adjectives, adverbs, prepositions, conjunctions, articles, and interjections. Some words can function as more than one part of speech. For example, the word "crow" can function as a noun (The *crow* stole food from our table) and a verb (The fans *crow* insults at the referee). For such words, determine the function the word plays within a sentence before you identify the part of speech it constitutes.

Verbs

Verbs express action (She *ran* for the senate) or a state of being (I *am* sick). Through changes in *form,* verbs can indicate *tense* (present, past, future, etc.);

person (first person, second person, or third person); *number* (singular or plural); *voice* (active or passive); and *mood* (indicative, imperative, and subjunctive). Other classifications of verbs include *linking verbs, transitive and intransitive verbs, helping verbs,* and *verbals.*

Form. Verbs have five primary forms:

Base	Present + s	Present Participle	Past	Past Participle
ask	asks	asking	asked	asked
climb	climbs	climbing	climbed	climbed
jump	jumps	jumping	jumped	jumped
move	moves	moving	moved	moved
reach	reaches	reaching	reached	reached
vanish	vanishes	vanishing	vanished	vanished
walk	walks	walking	walked	walked

The *base form* is used to indicate present tense action in the first-person singular (*I*) and plural (*we*), the second person (*you*), and the third-person plural (*they* or a plural noun).

We *hope* that you *drive* safely.

The hikers *vanish* into the fog.

The *present + s form* is made by adding an -*s* or -*es* to the base form and is used only to indicate present tense action in the third-person singular (*he, she, it,* or a singular noun).

She *walks* up the stairs.

The voter *reaches* for the ballot.

The *present participle form* is created by adding -*ing* to the base form. When used as a participle, this form functions as an adjective.

The *dripping* faucet kept him up all night.

When used as a *gerund,* the form functions as a noun.

Dancing was her favorite activity.

When joined with the verb *be* and helping verbs, the present participle form indicates the ongoing action of the progressive tense.

He *is studying* at the moment. Present progressive tense.

They *have been listening* to music. Past perfect progressive tense.

The *past form* is made by adding a -*d* or -*ed* to the base form. This form is used to indicate past action.

The committee *waited* for our answer.

He *moved* with the beat.

Verbs that express past action without adding a -*d* or -*ed* to the base form are known as *irregular verbs* (see the list below).

The *past participle form* is also made by adding a -*d* or -*ed* to the base form. In fact, for regular verbs, the past participle form and the past form are identical. When used as a participle, this form functions as an adjective.

The *wilted* flowers lay on the table.

When joined with the helping verbs *have* and *will* the past participle form indicates the perfect tenses.

We *have waited* for a long time. Present perfect tense.

She *will have finished* her paper by noon. Future perfect tense.

When joined with the verb *be,* the past participle form is used to indicate *passive voice.*

The guests *were escorted* to their table.

The plan *was approved* unanimously.

Just as they do in the past form, irregular verbs do not add -*d* or -*ed* to make the past participle form. Irregular verbs often change internally to indicate their past and past participle forms. Common irregular verbs and their past and past participle forms include the following:

Base	Past	Past Participle
be (is, am, are)	was, were	been
come	came	come
do	did	done
drink	drank	drunk
eat	ate	eaten
give	gave	given
go	went	gone
grow	grew	grown
see	saw	seen
take	took	taken
throw	threw	thrown
write	wrote	written

Tense. A verb's tense indicates when its action occurred. The *simple tenses* are used the most frequently. They depict action in a straightforward manner in the present, past, and future.

Present	The children *kiss* their grandmother.
Past	The children *kissed* their grandmother.
Future	The children *will kiss* their grandmother.

The *perfect tenses* express action that has been completed by a specific time or action that has already been completed before another action begins.

Present Perfect	The children *have kissed* their grandmother.
Past Perfect	The children *had kissed* their grandmother.
Future Perfect	The children *will have kissed* their grandmother.

The *progressive tenses* express ongoing actions.

Present Progressive	The children *are kissing* their grandmother.
Past Progressive	The children *were kissing* their grandmother.
Future Progressive	The children *will be kissing* their grandmother.
Present Perfect Progressive	The children *have been kissing* their grandmother.
Past Perfect Progressive	The children *had been kissing* their grandmother.
Future Perfect Progressive	The children *will have been kissing* their grandmother.

Person and Number. The relationship between person and number is intertwined so the two need to be discussed together. The subject's connection to the verb *as a speaker* is expressed through person. In the first person, the subject does the speaking (*I, we*); in the second person, the subject is spoken to (*you*); and in the third person, the subject is spoken about (*he, she, it, they*).

A verb's number can be either singular or plural and is determined by its subject. Singular verbs show the action of an individual subject (*I, you, he, she, it*) while plural verbs show the action of a collective subject (*we, you, they*). The verb form is the same for the singular and the plural in all of the tenses with the exception of present tense in the third-person singular, which adds an *-s* or *-es* to the base form (see *present + s* form on p. 467).

	Singular	Plural
First Person	*I forgive* the debt.	*We forgive* the debt.
Second Person	*You forgive* the debt.	(All of) *You forgive* the debt.
Third Person	*He (she, it) forgives* the debt.	*They forgive* the debt.

Voice. In a sentence written in the *active voice,* the subject is the doer of the verb's action. In a sentence written in the *passive voice,* the subject is not the doer of the verb's action. Instead, the doer of the verb's action is the object of a preposition or is not stated at all. Because the active voice is clearer, more direct, and less wordy than the passive voice, you should strive to write in the active voice whenever possible. Reserve use of the passive voice only for instances in which you do not know or want to name the doer of the verb's action.

Susan lost the car keys. Active voice: Here the subject, *Susan*, performs the action of the verb *lost*.

The car keys were lost by Susan. Passive voice: The information communicated in this example is the same as that expressed in the previous example, but now *car keys* have become the subject and the doer of the verb's action, *Susan*, is the object of the preposition *by*.

The car keys were lost. Passive voice: Here the subject remains *car keys* but the doer of the verb's action is not stated.

Mood. Mood expresses the writer's attitude toward the action of the verb. There are three forms of mood: indicative, imperative, and subjunctive. Verbs in the *indicative mood* make statements, ask questions, and declare opinions. For example:

He *said* that your argument *is* wrong. Makes a statement.

Did he really *say* that? Asks a question.

He *should rethink* his objection to my argument. Declares an opinion.

Verbs in the *imperative mood* issue commands, requests, or directions. When the subject of an imperative verb is not explicitly identified, it is understood to be *you*.

Don't touch the hot plate. Issues a command.

Class, please *read* the essays tonight. Issues a request.

Turn right at the next intersection. Issues directions.

Verbs in the *subjunctive mood* communicate wishes, make statements contrary to fact, list requirements and demands, and imply skepticism or doubt. They usually appear in clauses introduced by *if, that, as if*, and *as though*. Use the base form of the verb for the present tense subjunctive. For the past tense subjunctive of the verb *be*, use *were* for all subjects.

He wishes that he *were* a movie star. Communicates wish.

If I *were* to live for a thousand years, think of all that I would see. Makes statement contrary to fact.

The day care center requires that your sister *sign* a consent form and *provide* proof of immunization for her daughter. Lists requirements.

The lawyer acts as if his client *were* a saint. Implies skepticism.

Linking Verbs. Verbs that link the subject to a subject complement (see 9C Objects and Complements) are called linking verbs. These verbs commonly express states of being rather than action. Common linking verbs include *be, look, sound, taste, smell, feel, grow, appear, seem, become, remain*, and *get*.

I *am* tired.

You *look* thirsty.

Things *sound* grim over there.

She *felt* happy.

Your neighbors *seem* angry.

Helping Verbs. Some verbs require the addition of helping verbs (or auxiliary verbs) to communicate their meaning. The combination of a main verb and a helping verb forms a *verb phrase*. The most frequently used helping verbs are *be, do,* and *have*. These three helping verbs can also stand alone as main verbs: I *am* hungry; She *did* her chores; You *have* won. Other helping verbs, however, cannot stand alone as main verbs and can only be used in verb phrases. These helping verbs include *can, could, may, might, should, will,* and *would*. Helping verbs are often required to indicate tense, voice, and mood.

Mr. Nguyen *will* call you tomorrow. Future tense.

The students *have* completed the test. Present perfect tense.

Next month I *will have been* living here for three years. Future perfect progressive tense.

The report *was* delivered early. Passive voice.

We *can* help you. Indicative mood.

Did you leave the door open? Indicative mood.

Transitive and Intransitive Verbs. Transitive verbs express action at objects, which receive that action (see 9C Objects and Complements). Intransitive verbs do not express action at objects.

She *mailed* the letter to me. Transitive: the direct object *letter* receives the action of the transitive verb *mailed*.

The children *slept* peacefully. Intransitive: the verb *slept* does not express its action at an object—the adverb *peacefully* functions only to modify the verb.

Many verbs can function as both transitive and intransitive verbs.

The athlete *ate* the roast turkey. Transitive: the direct object *roast turkey* receives the action of the transitive verb *ate*.

The athlete *ate* like a pig. Intransitive: the verb *ate* does not express its action at an object—the adverbial phrase *like a pig* only modifies the verb.

Verbals. Verb forms that function as nouns, adjectives, or adverbs in sentences are known as *verbals*. There are three kinds of verbals: participles, gerunds, and infinitives. *Participles* function as adjectives. The present participle form adds *-ing* to the base form. The past participle form adds a *-d* or *-ed* to the base form of regular verbs (irregular verbs are often conjugated internally).

The *howling* wolf startled the hunters. The present participle *howling* modifies the subject *wolf*.

She threw the *chipped* vase into the trash. The past participle *chipped* modifies the direct object *vase*.

Gerunds function as nouns and use the present participle form, that is, *-ing* added to the base form of the verb.

Fishing takes patience.

The consequences of *drinking* and *driving* are often tragic.

Infinitives can function as nouns, adjectives, or adverbs. Infinitives begin with the word *to* followed by the base form of the verb.

Everyone wants *to fall in love*. The infinitive *to fall in love* acts as a direct object and so functions as a noun.

They had nothing *to eat* today. The infinitive *to eat* modifies the noun *nothing* and so acts as an adjective.

You must persevere *to succeed* in life. The infinitive *to succeed* modifies the verb phrase *must persevere* and so acts as an adverb.

Nouns

Nouns include people (ice skater, Malcolm X), places (playground, Grand Canyon), things (bicycle, Empire State Building), and concepts (happiness, liberty). *Common nouns* refer to people, places, things, or concepts that are representative of groups or classes (mechanic, colleges, keys, hardness). *Proper nouns* refer to specific people, places, things, or concepts (*President Chirac, Tokyo, the Titanic, Marxism*). Common nouns may be either concrete or abstract in character. *Concrete nouns* refer to things that have a tangible existence in the world (tears, lawyer, roast beef). *Abstract nouns,* on the other hand, refer to ideas and feelings that do not exist outside of our thoughts or emotions (sadness, justice, hunger). *Count nouns* can be counted and have singular (cat, cookie, bike) and plural forms (cats, cookies, bikes). *Noncount nouns* (or mass nouns) cannot be counted and do not possess plural forms (violence, copper, stability). *Collective nouns* refer to groups; although they are frequently used in the singular, they also possess plural forms (people, family, crowd, party, horde). Nouns may indicate possession by adding an apostrophe and *-s* to singular forms (Michael's car, cat's meow) and an apostrophe to the plural forms (dancers' clothes, birds' feathers). Nouns are often preceded by articles (*a, an, the*) or quantifiers (*one, many, some, a few, several*). They may also be modified by adjectives (*black* cat), adjective phrases (keys *on the table*), or adjective clauses (car *that was stolen last night*).

Pronouns

Pronouns act as substitutes for nouns. They perform the same functions as nouns, but whereas nouns actually name people, places, things, and concepts, pronouns only stand in for nouns. The noun to which a pronoun refers is known as the pronoun's *antecedent*.

Mrs. Ghatta had a nightmare while *she* slept on the couch. The subject *Mrs. Ghatta* is the antecedent of the pronoun *she*.

While *she* slept on the couch, *Mrs. Ghatta* had a nightmare. The subject *Mrs. Ghatta* remains the antecedent of the pronoun *she* even though the pronoun now precedes the subject in the sentence.

Pronouns are classified by function into the following groups: personal, relative, interrogative, reflexive/intensive, indefinite, and demonstrative. Personal, relative, and interrogative pronouns possess subjective, objective, and possessive case forms.

Personal Pronouns. These replace nouns that name people or things and possess subjective, objective, and possessive case forms.

Subjective	Objective	Possessive
I	me	my, mine
you	you	your, yours
he	him	his
she	her	hers
it	it	its
we	us	our, ours
they	them	their, theirs

The *subjective case form* stands in for nouns that function as subjects or subject complements.

They crossed the street. The pronoun *they* serves as the sentence's subject.

The fool is *he* who turns his back on wisdom. The pronoun *he* serves as the subject complement.

The *objective case form* stands in for nouns that function as objects of verbs or prepositions.

Ms. Lin paid *us* in cash. The pronoun *us* serves as an indirect object.

Their grievances seemed petty to *me*. The pronoun *me* serves as an object of the preposition *to*.

The *possessive case form* shows ownership. This form can function as a possessive adjective (*my, your, his, her, its, our, their*) or as both a possessive adjective and the noun or gerund it modifies (*mine, yours, his, hers, its, ours, theirs*).

Your cat ate *my* canary. The pronouns *Your* and *my* function as adjectives indicating ownership.

Theirs was an unhappy fate. The pronoun *Theirs* functions as both the possessive adjective *their* and the noun *fate*.

Relative Pronouns. These pronouns introduce adjective clauses. Relative pronouns that refer to people possess subjective, objective, and possessive case forms.

Subjective	Objective	Possessive
who	whom	whose
whoever	whomever	whosever

Relative pronouns that do not refer to people (*that, what, whatever, which, whichever, whose*) do not possess subjective, objective, and possessive case forms.

Ahmed, *who* lives next door, was promoted today. The pronoun *who* is the subject of *lives*.

She hung up on her boyfriend, *whom* she despised. The pronoun *whom* is the object of *despised*.

We greeted our friends, *whose* home we had watched for the last two weeks. The pronoun *whose* indicates ownership.

They bought a car *that* was within their price range. The pronoun *that* indicates ownership.

Interrogative Pronouns. These pronouns take the same forms as relative pronouns, including subjective, objective, and possessive case forms when they refer to people.

Interrogative pronouns, however, do not introduce adjective clauses. Instead, they introduce questions.

Who lost the argument?

To *whom* did the prize go?

Whose car is that?

What questions did he ask you?

Whatever happened to her?

Reflexive/Intensive Pronouns. Reflexive pronouns refer to subjects or objects introduced earlier in the same clause. Their function is to show action directed by the antecedent at itself. Reflexive pronouns include *myself, yourself, himself, herself, itself, oneself, ourselves, yourselves,* and *themselves.*

She asked me how I managed to keep cutting *myself* while shaving.

Please make *yourself* at home. The unstated subject of this sentence is understood to be *you.*

We tell *ourselves* the same stories over and over again.

The campers washed *themselves* in the river.

Intensive pronouns take the same forms as reflexive pronouns but are used only to emphasize the action of the antecedent, not to show action directed by the antecedent at itself.

She fixed the flat tire by *herself.*

It is surprising the resources one finds inside *oneself.*

Indefinite Pronouns. These pronouns refer to quantities or unspecified people and things. Indefinite pronouns include *a few, a lot, all, another, any, anybody, anyone, anything, anywhere, both, each, either, enough, everybody, everyone, everything, everywhere, few, many, more, most, much, neither, nobody, none, no one, nothing, one, several, some, somebody, someone, something,* and *somewhere.*

Anybody caught shoplifting will be prosecuted.

Few have sacrificed as much as we have.

One good deed deserves *another.*

I have called *everyone* together today to say *a few* words about *something* very important.

Demonstrative Pronouns. These pronouns (*this, that, these, those*) point to antecedents in such a way as to hold them up for special scrutiny or discussion.

That was a spectacular meal.

I will take *these* shoes, please.

Adjectives

Adjectives modify nouns and pronouns. They answer questions such as *How many? What kind? Which?* and *Whose?*

> She bought *five jumbo-sized* platters of appetizers for *tomorrow's* party at *Ken's* house. How many platters? *Five*. What kind of platters? *Jumbo-sized*. Which party? *Tomorrow's*. Whose house? *Ken's*.

Adjectives usually precede the words they modify but they can follow after words, or, as subject complements, even after the verb.

> The ocean, *cool* and *inviting,* lapped at our feet.

> The movie was *boring*.

Nouns and pronouns often function as adjectives, in both their subjective case forms and possessive forms. Indeed, a word may function as a noun in one part of a sentence and as an adjective elsewhere in the same sentence.

> *Some* children attend *summer* school; *some* do not. The word *some* functions as an adjective in its first instance and as a noun in its second instance. The word *summer*, frequently used as a noun, functions as an adjective modifying *school*.

Adjectives have positive, comparative, and superlative forms.

> Their house is *big*. Positive form.

> Their house is *bigger* than mine. Comparative form.

> Theirs is the *biggest* house on the block. Superlative form.

Adverbs

Adverbs modify verbs, adjectives, and other adverbs. They answer questions such as *How? How often? When?* and *Where?*

> *Yesterday,* we *narrowly* won the championship game. How did we win? *Narrowly*. When did we win? *Yesterday*. Both adverbs modify verbs.

> Our rivals play *nearby* and had beaten us *frequently*. Where do the rivals play? *Nearby*. How often had they beaten us? *Frequently*. Both adverbs modify verbs.

> It was a *desperately* needed victory. The adverb *desperately* modifies the adjective *needed*.

> The losing team left the field *very* quietly. The adverb *very* modifies the adverb *quietly*.

Adverbs can come before or after the words they modify. Sometimes, for the sake of rhythm or emphasis, adverbs can be placed at the beginning or end of the sentence.

> The detective *slowly* opened the door.

> *Slowly,* the detective opened the door.

> The detective opened the door *slowly*.

Adverbs, like adjectives, have positive, comparative, and superlative forms. For adverbs that end in *-ly,* the comparative adds the word *more* to the positive form while the superlative adds the word *most*.

She sings *beautifully*. Positive form.

She sings *more beautifully* than I do. Comparative form.

She sings *most beautifully* of us all. Superlative form.

Prepositions

Prepositions introduce *prepositional phrases* and show the relationship (place, destination, possession, time, cause, movement, purpose, etc.) between the *object of the preposition,* which is always a noun or pronoun, and another word or group of words. Common prepositions include *about, above, after, around, at, before, behind, below, beneath, between, beyond, by, down, for, from, in, inside, into, like, of, off, on, onto, out, over, past, since, through, to, toward, under, until, up, with,* and *without.*

The police car parked *in* our driveway. Place.

The protestors marched *toward* city hall. Destination.

This is the home *of* a World War II veteran. Possession.

We will arrive *at* 8:00 p.m. Time.

The water is dripping *from* the leak. Cause.

She walked *into* the theater. Movement.

The students studied *for* the final exam. Purpose.

Conjunctions

Conjunctions link one or more words, phrases, or clauses within a sentence. There are three types of conjunctions: coordinating, subordinating, and correlative.

Coordinating Conjunctions. These conjunctions join parallel words, phrases, and clauses (see 2A Parallelism). Coordinating conjunctions include *and, but, for, nor, or, so,* and *yet.*

The pitcher *and* the hitter confronted each other.

She wanted to go to the beach, *but* she had to stay home instead.

You can have orange juice *or* lemonade.

Subordinating Conjunctions. These conjunctions introduce subordinate (dependent) clauses. Subordinating conjunctions include *after, although, as, because, before, even if, even though, if, once, since, so, so that, than, that, unless, until, when, whenever, where, whereas, wherever, whether,* and *while.*

After she won the race, Robin celebrated with her family and friends.

We will not leave *until* Jim returns.

I was on the phone *when* the earthquake struck.

Correlative Conjunctions. Like coordinating conjunctions, correlative conjunctions join parallel words, phrases, and clauses. Correlative conjunctions, however, only occur in pairs. They include *both...and; either...or; just as...so; neither...nor; not only...but also;* and *whether...or.*

She wanted *both* to have a career *and* to start a family.

We will visit *either* the museum *or* the park this afternoon.

Articles

Articles introduce nouns. The word *the* is a *definite article* and it introduces nouns whose specific character is known (*The* cat walked down *the* path). The words *a* and *an* are *indefinite articles* and they introduce nouns whose specific character is not known (*A* cat walked down *a* path). *A* precedes words that begin with consonants; *an* precedes words that begin with vowels or a silent *h* (*an* hour).

Interjections

Interjections are words that express strong feelings, alarm, or surprise. They are common in speech and may be used in personal or informal writing, but are generally inappropriate for formal and academic writing. When they do appear in writing they typically stand alone as fragments. Common interjections include *boo, cool, oh, oh no, ouch, shhh, uh-oh, wow, yea,* and *yikes.* Profanity is often used as an interjection, particularly in speech, but it is considered offensive in most academic and professional settings.

9B Subjects and Predicates

The *subject* of a sentence is its main topic. The subject is always a noun, pronoun, noun phrase, or noun clause. The *predicate* makes a statement or asks a question about the subject. The predicate must always contain a verb but it can also contain adjectives, adverbs, nouns, pronouns, and other words.

Subjects

The simple subject is the noun or pronoun that represents the sentence's main topic. It is usually a single word, although proper nouns can run to two or more words (*General George Washington*). The complete subject contains the simple subject and any words or phrases that modify it.

Subject	Predicate
He	slept.
The man	had terrible nightmares that night.
The wearied, defeated prime minister	tossed fitfully in his bed.

Most of us at dinner that evening got sick the next day. The pronoun *Most* is the sentence's simple subject and *Most of us at dinner that evening* is the complete subject.

Compound subjects are two or more parallel nouns or pronouns linked by commas and coordinating conjunctions or correlative conjunctions.

Mishal, Zanab, and Amir swam out to the sailboat.

Playing to win and playing fair are not mutually exclusive concepts.

Neither you nor I will win the lottery.

Predicates

The simple predicate is the sentence's main verb. The complete predicate contains the simple predicate and any words or phrases that modify it.

> The strikers *picketed outside the factory's main gate despite the wind and rain.* The verb *picketed* is the sentence's simple predicate; the simple predicate and all of the words that follow after it represent the complete predicate.

Compound predicates represent two or more main verbs linked by commas and coordinating conjunctions or correlative conjunctions.

> We *laughed, ate, and drank* our way through the evening.

> He *tiptoed* to the door *and pressed* his ear up against its cold, hard wood.

> That afternoon she *not only aced* the exam *but* she *also submitted* her final paper to her instructor.

9C Objects and Complements

Objects are nouns or pronouns that appear within a sentence's predicate and complete its meaning. *Complements* are nouns or adjectives that rename or describe the sentence's subject or direct object.

Objects

There are three types of objects: direct objects, indirect objects, and objects of prepositions.

Direct Objects. These are nouns or pronouns that accept the action of *transitive verbs* (see 9A Parts of Speech). Direct objects answer questions such as *What?* or *Whom?* about their verbs.

> She kissed *her children* good night. Kissed whom? *Her children.*

> He wrote *the essay* on sustainable growth. Wrote what? *The essay.*

> The teacher gave *them* to us. Gave what? *Them.*

Indirect Objects. These are nouns or pronouns for which the action of the transitive verb is performed. Direct objects answer questions such as *For what? To what? For whom?* or *To whom?* about their verbs. Because indirect objects never appear without direct objects, one way to avoid confusing the two is to identify the direct object (DO) first and then the indirect object (IO).

> We mailed *them* the invitations. Mailed what? The invitations (DO). To whom? *Them* (IO).

> The county clerk issued *Michael and Caitlin* a marriage license. Issued what? A marriage license (DO). To whom? *Michael and Caitlin* (IO).

> Her father gave *their union* his blessing. Gave what? His blessing (DO). To what? *Their union* (IO).

Objects of Prepositions. These are nouns or pronouns that complete the meaning of *prepositional phrases* (see 9A Parts of Speech). When they appear in sentences with direct objects, objects of prepositions convey the same meaning as indirect objects. Objects of prepositions, however, can also appear in sentences that do not contain direct objects.

> We mailed the invitations to *them*.
>
> I left the keys in *the ignition*.
>
> For *the older couple,* the hike would be long and hard.

Complements

There are two types of complements: subject complements and object complements.

Subject Complements. These are nouns or adjectives that follow after a *linking verb* (see 9A Parts of Speech) and rename or describe the subject. Subject complements that are nouns rename their subjects and those that are adjectives describe their subjects.

> Margaret is *a lawyer*. The subject complement *a lawyer* is a noun.
>
> My grandfather is *ill*. The subject complement *ill* is an adjective.

Object Complements. These are nouns or adjectives that rename or describe the direct object. Object complements that are nouns rename their direct objects and those that are adjectives describe their direct objects.

> The panel voted Sagiko *the winner*. The object complement *the winner* is a noun.
>
> Many people consider travel *pleasurable*. The object complement *pleasurable* is an adjective.

9D Phrases

A *phrase* is a group of related words that lack a subject or a predicate or both. A phrase, then, can never express a complete thought as a sentence and independent clause can. Phrases modify words, groups of words, or the entire sentence. There are six types of phrases: prepositional phrases, participial phrases, gerund phrases, absolute phrases, infinitive phrases, and appositive phrases.

Prepositional Phrases

Prepositional phrases begin with a *preposition* (see 9A Parts of Speech) and contain a noun or pronoun and its modifiers, if any. Prepositional phrases act as adjectives and adverbs.

> The neighbors *across the street* own a speedboat. The prepositional phrase functions as an adjective modifying the noun *neighbors*.
>
> The satellite burned up *in the upper atmosphere*. The prepositional phrase functions as an adverb modifying the verb *burned up*.

Participial Phrases

Participial phrases contain *present* or *past participles* (see 9A Parts of Speech) and their modifiers or complements. Participial phrases act as adjectives.

The man *arrested yesterday* was an industrial spy. The participial phrase modifies the noun *man*.

The dancers *demonstrating the tango right now* are my friends. The participial phrase modifies the noun *dancers*.

Gerund Phrases

Gerund phrases contain *gerunds* (see 9A Parts of Speech) and their modifiers, objects, and complements. Gerund phrases function as nouns and therefore can serve as a subject, direct object, object of the preposition, object complement, and subject complement.

Dating over the Internet has become popular. The gerund phrase serves as the subject.

The children love *playing computer games*. The gerund phrase serves as the direct object.

He was exhausted from *running under the hot sun*. The gerund phrase serves as the object of the preposition.

We wished them luck *climbing the mountain*. The gerund phrase serves as an object complement.

Her favorite pastime is *knitting wool sweaters*. The gerund phrase serves as the subject complement.

Absolute Phrases

Absolute phrases contain a noun or pronoun, a present or past participle, and any modifiers. Absolute phrases modify an entire sentence, not just one word or group of words within the sentence. Whether they appear at the beginning, middle, or end of a sentence, absolute phrases are always set off with a comma.

Its whistle blowing, the ferry pulled away from the dock.

The patient, *his body convulsed with fever,* slipped into unconsciousness.

He stepped on the gas, *his heart racing with adrenaline*.

Infinitive Phrases

Infinitive phrases contain *infinitives* (see 9A Parts of Speech) and their modifiers, objects, or complements. Infinite phrases function as adjectives, adverbs, and nouns.

He wanted his son *to help him fix the leak*. The infinitive phrase modifies the noun *son* and so acts as an adjective.

She studied *to pass the exam*. The infinitive phrase modifies the verb *studied* and so acts as an adverb.

Before I made a decision, I needed *to think things over thoroughly*. The infinitive phrase acts as a direct object and so functions as a noun.

Appositive Phrases

Appositive phrases are nouns and their modifiers that rename the nouns or pronouns that immediately precede them. They are often set off with commas.

My neighbor, *a doctor,* is a very kind woman.

He has an engineering degree from Caltech, *one of the most prestigious universities in the country.*

9E Clauses

A clause is a group of words containing both a subject and a predicate. An *independent clause* can function on its own as a sentence.

Subject	Predicate
She	wept.
The woman who lives next door	personally delivered the letter to me today.

A *subordinate clause* (dependent clause) cannot function on its own as a sentence and must be linked to an independent clause by a subordinating conjunction or relative pronoun. There are three types of subordinate clauses: adjective clauses, adverb clauses, and noun clauses.

Adjective Clauses

Adjective clauses modify nouns or pronouns in an independent clause or in another subordinate clause. Adjective clauses begin with *relative pronouns* (see 9A Parts of Speech) such as *who, whom, whose, which,* and *that.*

The doctor *who delivered our baby* is from India.

She wrote a letter *that explained how she felt.*

Adverb Clauses

Adverb clauses usually modify verbs in an independent clause or in another subordinate clause, but on occasion they may also modify adjectives and adverbs. Adverb clauses begin with *subordinating conjunctions* (see 9A Parts of Speech) such as *after, although, as, because, before, if, since, so, than, that, unless, until, when, where,* and *while.*

After the movie was over, we strolled through the mall.

They planned to travel the world *until they ran out of money.*

She left the party *when her ex-boyfriend* arrived.

Noun Clauses

Noun clauses serve as a subject, object, or complement. They can begin with relative pronouns or subordinating conjunctions.

Where the ship sank no one knows. The noun clause serves as the subject.

She asked him *when he would be leaving.* The noun clause serves as the direct object.

I will not run from *what is coming.* The noun clause serves as the object of the preposition.

Their complaint was *that the contract had not been fulfilled.* The noun clause serves as the subject complement.

9F Basic Sentence Patterns

A sentence must contain a subject and a predicate. The complexity of predicates, however, means that sentences can follow one of five basic patterns:

Subject + Intransitive verb

Subject + Transitive verb + Direct object

Subject + Linking verb + Subject complement

Subject + Transitive verb + Indirect object + Direct object

Subject + Transitive verb + Direct object + Object complement

These five patterns form the foundation on which all sentences in the English language are written. The following examples show only the simplest uses of these patterns. Because all of the elements that make up these patterns can be modified by other words, phrases, and clauses, these sentence patterns can assume much more complicated forms in everyday writing.

Subject	Intransitive verb		
We	won.		

Subject	Transitive verb	Direct object	
Our team	defeated	our rivals.	

Subject	Linking verb	Subject complement	
My teammates	were	ecstatic.	

Subject	Transitive verb	Indirect object	Direct object
They	gave	us	the trophy.

Subject	Transitive verb	Direct object	Object complement
Our coach	declared	the game	a milestone.

9G Types of Sentences

Sentences are also classified by the way in which they use *clauses* (see 9E Clauses) into four categories: simple sentences, compound sentences, complex sentences, and compound-complex sentences.

Simple Sentences

A simple sentence is made up of one *independent clause*. The independent clause may contain compound *subjects*, compound *predicates*, and modifying *phrases*, but must not be linked with other clauses.

Some professional athletes are poor role models for children. Single subject and single predicate.

Some professional athletes and movie stars are poor role models for children. Compound subject and single predicate.

Some professional athletes lack social responsibility and are poor role models for children. Single subject and compound predicate.

Some professional athletes, *their interests focused exclusively on themselves,* lack social responsibility. Single subject, with modifying phrase (in italics) and single predicate.

Compound Sentences

A compound sentence is made up of two or more independent clauses (IC) linked by a semicolon or a comma and a *coordinating conjunction*. Each clause may contain compound subjects, compound predicates, and modifying phrases, but must not be linked with a subordinate clause.

——— IC ———   ——————— IC ———————

John was uneasy, but he didn't believe in werewolves. The two independent clauses are linked by a comma and the coordinating conjunction *but*.

——————— IC ———————   ——————— IC ———————

He *checked the lock and stood motionless;* there was someone or something growling on the other side of the door. The two independent clauses are linked with a semicolon.

Complex Sentences

A complex sentence is made up of one independent clause (IC) and one or more *subordinate clauses* (SC). Both the independent and subordinate clause(s) may contain compound subjects, compound predicates, and modifying phrases. Subordinate clauses always begin with *subordinating conjunctions* or *relative pronouns* (see 9A Parts of Speech).

——— IC ———   ——————— SC ———————

The lawyer laughed when my wife told the joke. The subordinate clause begins with the subordinating conjunction *when*.

——————— IC ———————   ——————— SC ———————

I reluctantly shook the hand of the lawyer who was representing my wife in the divorce. The subordinate clause begins with the relative pronoun *who*.

Compound-Complex Sentences

A compound-complex sentence contains two or more independent clauses (IC) and at least one subordinate clause (SC). The independent clauses must be linked by a semicolon or a comma and a coordinating conjunction. Each clause may contain compound subjects, compound predicates, and modifying phrases.

——— IC ———   ——— SC ———   ——————— IC ———————

They won't believe me until they see you, for you have completely changed. The first independent clause and its subordinate clause are linked to the second independent clause with a comma and the coordinating conjunction *for*.

10 Tips for ESL Writers

Many non-native writers of English find it challenging to master the language's complicated grammatical rules. This section offers advice in traditional problem areas for writers of English as a second language (ESL).

10A Articles

Articles introduce nouns, but the rules for determining how they do so are complex. *The* is the *definite article* that introduces nouns whose specific character is known (*The* cat), while *a* and *an* are *indefinite articles* that introduce nouns whose specific character is not known (*A* cat). To use definite and indefinite articles correctly, however, you also need to know whether the noun under consideration is a *count noun,* a *noncount noun,* or a *proper noun*.

Count Nouns

Count nouns can be counted and have singular forms (*cat, cookie, bike*) and plural forms (*cats, cookies, bikes*). Singular count nouns whose specific character is not known take the indefinite articles *a* and *an*; those whose specific character is known take the definite article *the*. Plural count nouns whose specific character is not known, that is, nouns that are referred to in general, do not take articles. Plural count nouns whose specific character is known take the definite article *the*.

> *An aardvark* turned up in my backyard. Singular count noun of unknown specific character—use the appropriate indefinite article, *a* or *an*.

> *The aardvark* befriended us. Singular count noun of known specific character—use the definite article *the*.

> *Aardvarks* are interesting animals. Plural count noun of unknown specific character—do not use an article.

> *The aardvarks* moved to our neighbor's backyard. Plural count noun of known specific character—use the definite article *the*.

Noncount Nouns

Noncount nouns (or mass nouns) cannot be counted and do not possess plural forms (*violence, copper, stability*). Noncount nouns whose specific character is not known, that is, nouns that are referred to in general, do not take articles. Noncount nouns whose specific character is known take the definite article *the*.

> *Peace* is universally valued around the world. Noncount noun of unknown specific character—do not use an article.

> *The peace* held while the negotiations dragged on. Noncount noun of known specific character—use the definite article *the*.

Proper Nouns

Proper nouns refer to specific people, places, things, or concepts (*President Chirac, Tokyo, the Titanic, Marxism*). Singular proper nouns generally do not take definite articles with the exception of the following: noun phrases (*the* Man in the Moon); geographic features (*the* Himalayas); architectural landmarks (*the* Brooklyn Bridge); titles of ships, aircraft, spacecraft, and vehicles (*the* Challenger); titles of political and religious institutions (*the* Senate, *the* Episcopalian Church); titles of political and religious leaders (*the* prime minister, *the* pope); titles of documents (*the* Emancipation Proclamation); and titles of periods and events (*the* Middle

Ages, *the* Great Depression). Plural proper nouns take definite articles with the exception of the titles of companies (General Mills).

President Bush spoke at the commencement. The singular proper noun *President Bush* does not take a definite article.

The president spoke at the commencement. The singular common noun *president* is the title of a political leader and so does take a definite article.

The De Beers are a very wealthy family. The plural proper noun *De Beers* takes a definite article.

De Beers is a very wealthy company. The plural proper noun *De Beers* is the title of a company and so does not take a definite article.

10B Verbs

The common verb errors and the basic functions and forms of verbs are discussed elsewhere in this handbook (see 4 Verbs and 9A Parts of Speech). Challenging areas for ESL writers can include the helping verbs *be, do,* and *have*; modal auxiliaries; phrasal verbs; and gerunds and infinitives.

Helping Verbs *be, do,* and *have*

Helping verbs (or auxiliary verbs) join with main verbs to create verb phrases. The most frequently used helping verbs are *be, do,* and *have,* which can also stand alone as main verbs. How to use these three helping verbs with main verbs can sometimes be confusing.

The Helping Verb *be*. Use the present forms of *be* (*am, is, are*) with the present participle (base form + *-ing*) to make the present progressive tense. Use the past forms of *be* (*was, were*) with the present participle to make the past progressive tense. The other progressive tenses require the addition of the helping verbs *have* and *will* (see the following examples) along with the forms of *be* and the present participle.

She *is working* at the moment. Present progressive.

I *was calling* overseas when the doorbell rang. Past progressive.

They *will be sailing* tomorrow. Future progressive.

Larry *has been sulking* since last night. Present perfect progressive.

We *had been skiing* for three hours when your brother showed up. Past perfect progressive.

You *will have been barbecuing* chicken all day long before the party is over. Future perfect progressive.

Use the present forms of *be* (*am, is, are*) with the past participle (base form + *-ed*) to create the present tense in the passive voice. Other tenses in the passive voice require the addition of the other helping verbs *will* and *have* along with the forms of *be* and the past participle.

The car *is stopped* at the light.

In some countries, the local elections *have been rigged* for many years.

The Helping Verb *do*. Use forms of *do* (*do, does, did*) with the base form of the verb to create a verb phrase. Use verb phrases of this sort to add emphasis or to re-state a claim that provokes doubt or disbelief. Add the modal auxiliary *not* to make negative claims.

We *do believe* in the judicial system.

She *does drive* carefully.

I *did mail* the letter to you.

He *does not know* the answer.

The Helping Verb *have*. Use the present forms of *have* (*have, has*) with the past participle (base form + *-ed*) to make the present prefect tense. Use the past forms of *have* (*had*) with the past participle to make the past perfect tense. The future perfect tense requires the addition of the helping verb *will* along with the present form of *have* and the past participle.

She *has purchased* a new car. Present perfect.

We *had vacationed* at the Grand Canyon before we went to Monument Valley. Past perfect.

They *will have painted* the house by this evening. Future prefect.

Modal Auxiliaries

Modal auxiliaries are helping verbs that cannot stand alone as main verbs. Joined with a main verb, modals express ability, intention, necessity, permission, possibility, or prohibition. Modals include *can, cannot, could, have to, may, might, must, must not, not, should,* and *would*. These modals do not change form, regardless of the main verb's tense or whether the main verb is singular or plural. They only have one form. When joining modals with main verbs, use the base form of the main verb immediately after the modal. Never use more than one modal with one main verb.

We *can* reach the stars if we try. Expresses ability.

We *cannot* get there tomorrow. Expresses prohibition.

I *have* to wash the dishes. Expresses necessity.

I *might* even clean out the refrigerator. Expresses possibility.

You *should* forget the past. Expresses advisability.

You *would* have a great time in Italy. Expresses probability.

Phrasal Verbs

A phrasal verb is an idiomatic verb phrase that contains a verb and one or two prepositions or adverbs. The meaning of the two- or three-word phrasal verb gener-ally cannot be understood by combining the literal meanings of its words. For example, the phrasal verb *turn down* does not mean "to turn downward" but rather "to reject or refuse." Common phrasal verbs include the following:

act up	run into
break down	stay up
call on	step in
catch on	take off
cut in	throw away
figure out	turn down
hang on	turn on
look into	walk out on
look out for	watch out for

Phrasal verbs are informal and often are inappropriate for academic and professional writing. If you do choose to use them in your writing, be sure you understand their correct meaning.

Gerunds and Infinitives

Gerunds function as nouns and use the present participle form (base form + *-ing*). Infinitives usually function as nouns but can also function as adjectives or adverbs. They begin with the word *to* followed by the base form of the verb. Gerunds and infinitives that follow after main verbs function as objects. Keep the following guidelines in mind when using gerunds and infinitives with main verbs.

1. **Verbs that do not change meaning whether followed by gerunds or infinitives:**

attempt	like
begin	love
can't stand	omit
continue	prefer
hate	start

In the following examples, below the meaning of the verb *hated* and the gerund *losing* is the same as the verb *hated* and the infinitive *to lose*.

We hated *losing* the game.

We hated *to lose* the game.

2. **Verbs that change meaning when followed by gerunds or infinitives:**

forget	stop
remember	try

In the following examples, notice how the meaning of the first sentence differs from the second.

I forgot *practicing* the piano yesterday. Forgot the subject of *practicing* yesterday.

I forgot *to practice* the piano yesterday. Forgot actually *to practice* yesterday.

3. **Verbs that can precede gerunds but not infinitives:**

admit	keep
appreciate	miss
avoid	postpone
cannot help	practice
consider	put off
delay	quit
deny	recall
discuss	resist
enjoy	risk
finish	suggest
imagine	tolerate

In the following examples, the gerund in the first sentence is correct and the infinitive in the second sentence represents an error.

She enjoys *painting* watercolors. Gerunds may be used after the verb *enjoy*.

She enjoys *to paint* watercolors. Infinitives may not be used after the verb *enjoy*.

4. **Verbs that can precede infinitives but not gerunds:**

agree	mean
ask	need
beg	offer
choose	plan
claim	pretend
decide	promise
expect	refuse
fail	venture
have	wait
hope	want
manage	wish

In the following examples, the infinitive in the first sentence is correct and the gerund in the second sentence represents an error.

They decided *to climb* the mountain. Infinitive may be used after the verb *decide*.

They decided *climbing* the mountain. Gerund may not be used after the verb *decide*.

10C Adjectives and Adverbs

The correct use of adjectives and adverbs can present challenges for all writers; however, for ESL writers in particular, the placement and word order of these modifiers can be troublesome.

Adjectives

Adjectives modify nouns and pronouns (see 9A Parts of Speech). Other words such as articles and pronouns can also act as adjectives and modify nouns and pronouns. When using multiple adjectives to modify one or more words in the sentence, use the word order listed here:

1. **Article, pronoun, and possessive noun:** *a, an, the, his, my, our, your, a lot, many, some, that, their, those, Steve's, the neighbor's,* etc.

2. **Adjectives indicating number or order:** *one, two, three, one hundred, one thousand, first, second, third, last, final,* etc.

3. **Adjectives indicating judgment, opinion, or evaluation:** *awful, astonishing, beautiful, excellent, evil, good, faithful, ugly, wicked,* etc.

4. **Adjectives indicating size:** *big, diminutive, giant, large, little, long, massive, minuscule, short,* etc.

5. **Adjectives indicating shape:** *boxy, circular, loose, rectangular, round, snug, square, tight, triangular, wide,* etc.

6. **Adjectives indicating condition:** *broken, damaged, fixed, functional, operating, repaired, reconditioned, running, undamaged, whole, working,* etc.

7. **Adjectives indicating age:** *aged, ancient, antique, fresh, immature, mature, new, old, young,* etc.

8. **Adjectives indicating color:** *black, blue, green, mauve, orange, purple, violet, white, yellow,* etc.

9. **Adjectives indicating nationality, ethnicity, and religion:** *African American, Anglo, Arabic, Armenian, Brazilian, Canadian, Chinese, Kenyan, Latin American, Mandarin, Buddhist, Catholic, Hindu, Presbyterian,* etc.

10. **Adjectives indicating material:** *aluminum, birch, copper, cotton, gold, iron, oak, metal, pine, plastic, platinum, polyester, silk, steel, wood,* etc.

11. **Nouns used as adjectives:** *bird* (brain), *dog* (house), *car* (park), *floor* (mat), *mosquito* (net), etc.

12. **The noun being modified.** Examples:

    His last undamaged birch-bark canoe sank yesterday.

    She found *some beautiful little green turquoise* beads at the flea market.

    My grandmother gave *that antique black Chinese silk* dress to my sister as a birthday gift.

Adverbs

Adverbs modify verbs, adjectives, and other adverbs (see 9A Parts of Speech). Adverbs can come before or after the words they modify. Sometimes, for the sake of rhythm or emphasis, adverbs can be placed at the beginning or end of the sentence. Although there is considerable flexibility in where you can place most adverbs, there are also some limitations. Use the following guidelines:

1. **Place adverbs indicating the author's or speaker's *perspective* at the front of the sentence:**

   Thankfully, I had recovered from the flu by then.

   Unfortunately, we won't be able to make your party tonight.

2. **Place adverbs indicating *order* at the front or end of the sentence:**

   First, we will consider the results of our fund-raising efforts.

   Proposals for overhauling the department will be discussed *last*.

3. **Place adverbs indicating *manner* immediately before the words they modify or at the end of the sentence:**

   They *softly* entered the room.

   She answered my questions *sheepishly*.

4. **Place adverbs indicating *time* immediately after any adverbs indicating *manner* or *place* or, if none exist, at the front or end of the sentence:**

   The earth shook *ferociously here yesterday*.

   Tomorrow, I am leaving for California.

   He writes reports *slowly*.

10D Prepositions

Prepositions introduce *prepositional phrases* and show the relationship (place, destination, possession, time, cause, movement, purpose, etc.) between the *object of the preposition,* which is always a noun or pronoun, and another word or group of words. The prepositions used to show place and time can be troublesome for non-native speakers of English.

Place

The prepositions showing place include *in, on,* and *at.* Use the preposition *in* to refer to an established physical, geographic, or political space (*in* the garage, *in* the Amazon, *in* Egypt). Use the preposition *on* as a synonym for *on top of* (*on* the coffee table, *on* the roof) and to indicate location on mass transportation, streets, book pages, building floors, and land (*on* the bus, *on* 114th Street, *on* page 177, *on* the eleventh floor, *on* the field). Use the preposition *at* to refer to specific locations, general locations, and addresses (*at* the Museum of Modern Art, *at* my mother's house, *at* the beach, *at* 23349 Westwood Boulevard).

The Band-Aids are *in* the medicine box.

Her apartment is *on* the fourth floor.

You are welcome to stay *at* my house.

Time

The prepositions showing time also include *in, on,* and *at.* Use the preposition *in* to refer to general time of day (except *night*), months, seasons, and years (*in* the afternoon, *in* December, *in* spring, *in* 1983). Use the preposition *on* to refer to days of the week and dates (*on* Friday, *on* the 28th, *on* July 4, 1776). Use the preposition *at* to refer to specific time of day and with *night* (*at* 1:15, *at* noon, *at* night).

I will see her *in* the evening.

We will see them *on* Friday.

He will see you *at* noon.

10E Participles

Present participles (base form of the verb + *-ing*) and *past participles* (base form of the verb + *-d* or *-ed*) can both function as adjectives in sentences. Their meanings are different, however, and they cannot be used interchangeably. In particular, participles that describe feelings and mental states can sometimes be troublesome for ESL writers. These participles include the following:

amazing / amazed	fascinating / fascinated
annoying / annoyed	frightening / frightened
boring / bored	interesting / interested
confusing / confused	pleasing / pleased
depressing / depressed	satisfying / satisfied
disappointing / disappointed	surprising / surprised
exciting / excited	terrifying / terrified
exhausting / exhausted	tiring / tired

To avoid errors with these participles and others, only use present participles to describe nouns and pronouns that *cause* a feeling or mental state. Similarly, only use past participles to describe nouns and pronouns that *experience* a feeling or mental state.

The lecture was *fascinating*. The noun being modified, *lecture*, causes the mental state, so the present participle *fascinating* is required.

We were *fascinated* by the lecture. The pronoun being modified, *We*, experiences the mental state, so the past participle *fascinated* is required.

The news is filled with *depressing* events. The noun being modified, *events*, causes the mental state, so the present participle *depressing* is required.

Julia was *depressed* by events in the news. The noun being modified, *Julia*, experiences the mental state, so the past participle *depressed* is required.

CREDITS

Text Credits

Page 33. From "Inventing the University" by David Bartholomae in *When a Writer Can't Write: Studies in Writer's Block and Other Composing-Process Problems*, ed. Mike Rose, The Guilford Press, 1985, pp. 134–65.

Page 46. Page From "The Epistemic Value of Curiosity" by Schmitt and Lahroodi in *Educational Theory*, 58.2 (2008): 125–48.

Page 53. From "Virtual Friendship and the New Narcissism" by Christine Rosen in *The New Atlantis*, Summer 2007, pp. 15–31.

Page 83. "Buckeye" copyright © 1995 by Scott Russell Sanders; first published in *Orion*; collected in the author's *Writing from the Center* (personal essays) (Indiana University Press, 1995); reprinted by permission of the author.

Page 89. "One More Lesson" is reprinted with permission from the publisher of *Silent Dancing: A Partial Remembrance of a Puerto Rican Childhood* by Judith Ortiz Cofer (© 1990 Arte Público Press–University of Houston).

Page 121. "Soup" by Anonymous, originally published in the *The New Yorker*. Copyright © 1989 Conde Nast Publications. All rights reserved.

Page 124. Excerpt from "A Darkening" from *The Worst Hard Time: The Untold Story of Those Who Survived the Great American Dust Bowl* by Timothy Egan. Copyright © 2005 by Timothy Egan. Reprinted by permission of Houghton Mifflin Harcourt Publishing Company. All rights reserved.

Page 127. "Learning About Work from Joe Cool" by Gib Akin from *Journal of Management Inquiry*, March 2000, 9: 57–61. Copyright © 2000 by Sage Publications. Reproduced by permission of Sage Publications.

Page 162. "Jack's Still Splashing About in the Shadows," a review of *Pirates of the Caribbean: Dead Man's Chest* by Mark Kermode, *The Observer*, July 6, 2006.

Page 166. "A Ton (Just Barely) of Fun," a review of a 2008 Lotus Exige car by Ezra Dyer from *The New York Times*, December 21, 2008. Copyright © 2008 The New York Times. All rights reserved. Used by permission and protected by the Copyright Laws of the United States. The printing, copying, redistribution, or retransmission of the Material without express written permission is prohibited.

Page 169. "Grand Theft Auto Takes on New York," a review of the *Grand Theft Auto IV* video game by Seth Schiesel from *The New York Times*, April 28, 2008. Copyright © 2008 The New York Times. All rights reserved. Used by permission and protected by the Copyright Laws of the United States. The printing, copying, redistribution, or retransmission of the Material without express written permission is prohibited.

Page 177. Screen capture of Epinions.com home page, April 20, 2009. These materials have been reproduced with the permission of eBay Inc. © 2009 EBAY INC. ALL RIGHTS RESERVED.

Page 199. "Housing and Our Military" by David S. Johnston, *USA Today,* January 7, 2009. Reproduced by permission of the author.

Page 202. "Green Dining" a 13 slide PowerPoint presentation including 6 photo from the Univ. of CA, Santa Cruz Dining Services. Reproduced by permission of the University of California Santa Cruz Dining Hall.

Page 205. "Why Bother?" by Michael Pollan from *The New York Times Magazine,* April 20, 2008. Reprinted by permission of International Creative Management, Inc. Copyright © 2008 by Michael Pollan for *The New York Times.*

Page 254. "A Teacher with Faith and Reason" by Jeff Jacoby, *The Boston Globe*, July 22, 2007. Reprinted by permission of The New York Times Company.

Page 257. "Is Humiliation an Ethically Appropriate Response to Plagiarism," Blog post by Loye Young on http://www.adjunctnation.com/archive/magazine/article/715/, Reprinted by permission of Adjunct Advocate Magazine.

Page 288. "The Myth of the Latin Woman: I Just Met A Girl Named Maria" by Judith Ortiz Cofer from *The Latin Deli*: *Prose and Poetry,* 1995. Reprinted by permission of The University of Georgia Press.

Page 294. "For the Muslim Prom Queen, There Are No Kings Allowed" by Patricia Leigh Brown. From *The New York Times,* June 9, © 2003, The New York Times. All rights reserved. Used by permission and protected by the Copyright Laws of the United States. The printing, copying, redistribution, or re-transmission of the Material without express written is prohibited.

Photo Credits

Page 2. Michael P. Cardacino/Creative Eye/MIRA.com

Page 13T. Kim Taylor © Dorling Kindersley

Page 13M. Chad Ehlers/Stock Connection

Page 13B. Andreas Von Einsiedel © Dorling Kindersley

Page 40. Getty Images–Stockbyte.

Page 45. © John M. Greim/Mira.com

Page 48. © Dorling Kindersley

Page 54. © Tate London/Art Resource

Page 62. Edward Weston, "Pepper #30," 1930. Photograph by Edward Weston. Collection Center for Creative Photography, The University of Arizona. © 1981 Arizona Board of Regents.

Page 74. Photofest NYC

Page 78. Bruce Ballenger

Page 93. © Roderick Chen/Alamy

Page 116. Jacques Jangoux/Photo Researchers, Inc.

Page 124. Research Division of the Oklahoma Historical Society

Page 133. Courtesy of the Library of Congress Prints and Photographs

Page 156. WALT DISNEY/THE KOBAL COLLECTION

Page 165. Lotus Cars USA, Inc. Photo by Rick Dole.

Page 173TL. © The Dorothea Lange Collection, Oakland Museum of California, City of Oakland.

THE
CURIOUS
RESEARCHER

Rethinking the Research Paper

Unlike most textbooks, this one begins with your writing, not mine. Find a fresh page in your notebook, grab a pen, and spend ten minutes doing the following exercise.

E X E R C I S E 1

Collecting Golf Balls on Driving Ranges and Other Reflections

Most of us were taught to think before we write, to have it all figured out in our heads before we pick up our pens. This exercise asks you to think *through* writing rather than *before,* letting the words on the page lead you to what you want to say. With practice, that's surprisingly easy using a technique called *fastwriting*. Basically, you just write down whatever comes into your head, not worrying about whether you're being eloquent, grammatical, or even very smart. It's remarkably like talking to a good friend, not trying to be brilliant and even blithering a bit, but along the way discovering what you think. If the writing stalls, write about that, or write about what you've already written until you find a new trail to follow. Just keep your pen moving.

STEP 1: Following is a series of sixteen statements about the research paper assignment. Check the five statements you think most students believe about the assignment. Then, in your notebook, write fast for five minutes about whether you think the statements you checked are true. Speculate about where these ideas about research papers come from and why they might make sense. If you disagree with any of the statements you checked, explore why wrongheaded ideas about the assignment have endured. Whenever you feel moved to do so, tell a story.

- It's okay to say things the instructor might disagree with.
- You need to follow a formal structure.
- You have to know your thesis before you start.
- You have to be objective.
- You can't use the pronoun *I*.
- You can use your own experiences and observations as evidence.
- The information should come mostly from books.
- You have to say something original.
- You're always supposed to make an argument.
- You can use your own writing voice.
- Summarizing what's known about the topic is most important.
- You're writing mostly for the instructor.
- You're supposed to use your own opinions.
- The paper won't be revised substantially.
- Form matters more than content.

STEP 2: Now, consider the truth of some other statements, listed below. These statements have less to do with research papers than with how you see facts, information, and knowledge and how they're created. Choose one of these statements* to launch a five-minute fastwrite. Don't worry if you end up thinking about more than one statement in your writing. Start by writing about whether you agree or disagree with the statement, and then explore why. Continually look for concrete connections between what you think about these statements and what you've seen or experienced in your own life.

There is a big difference between facts and opinions.

Pretty much everything you read in textbooks is true.

People are entitled to their own opinions, and no one opinion is better than another.

There's a big difference between a *fact* in the sciences and a *fact* in the humanities.

When two experts disagree, one of them has to be wrong.

No matter how difficult they are, most problems have one solution that is better than the others.

---

*Source for part of this list is Marlene Schommer, "Effects of Beliefs about the Nature of Knowledge," *Journal of Educational Psychology* 82 (1990): 498–504.

Very few of us recall the research papers we wrote in high school, and if we do, what we remember is not what we learned about our topics but what a bad experience writing them was. Joe was an exception. "I remember one assignment was to write a research paper on a problem in the world, such as acid rain, and then come up with your own solutions and discuss moral and ethical aspects of your solution, as well. It involved not just research but creativity and problem solving and other stuff."

For the life of me, I can't recall a single research paper I wrote in high school, but like Joe, I remember the one that I finally enjoyed doing a few years later in college. It was a paper on the whaling industry, and what I remember best was the introduction. I spent a lot of time on it, describing in great detail exactly what it was like to stand at the bow of a Japanese whaler, straddling an explosive harpoon gun, taking aim, and blowing a bloody hole in a humpback whale.

I obviously felt pretty strongly about the topic.

Unfortunately, many students feel most strongly about getting their research papers over with. So it's not surprising that when I tell my Freshman English students that one of their writing assignments will be an eight- to ten-page research paper, there is a collective sigh. They knew it was coming. For years, their high school teachers prepared them for the College Research Paper, and it loomed ahead of them as one of the torturous things you must do, a five-week sentence of hard labor in the library, or countless hours adrift in the Internet. Not surprisingly, students' eyes roll in disbelief when I add that many of them will end up liking their research papers better than anything they've written before.

I can understand why Joe was among the few in the class inclined to believe me. For many students, the library is an alien place, a wilderness to get lost in, a place to go only when forced. Others carry memories of research paper assignments that mostly involved taking copious notes on index cards, only to transfer pieces of information into the paper, sewn together like patches of a quilt. There seemed little purpose to it. "You weren't expected to learn anything about yourself with the high school research paper," wrote Jenn, now a college freshman. "The best ones seemed to be those with the most information. I always tried to find the most sources, as if somehow that would automatically make my paper better than the rest." For Jenn and others like her, research was a mechanical process and the researcher a lot like those machines that collect golf balls at driving ranges. You venture out to pick up information here and there, and then deposit it between the title page and the bibliography for your teacher to take a whack at.

Learning and Unlearning

I have been playing the guitar ever since the Beatles' 1964 American tour. In those days, *everyone* had a guitar and played in a group. Unfortunately, I never took guitar lessons and have learned in recent years that I have much "unlearning" to do. Not long ago, I finally unlearned how to do something as simple as tying my strings to the tuning keys. I'd been doing it wrong (thinking I was doing it right) for about forty years.

Recent theories suggest that people who have developed a great deal of prior knowledge about a subject learn more about it when they reexamine the truth of those beliefs, many of which may no longer be valid or may simply be misconceptions. The research paper, perhaps more than any other school assignment, is laden with largely unexamined assumptions and beliefs. Perhaps some of the statements in the first part of Exercise 1 got you thinking about any assumptions you might have about writing academic research papers. Maybe you had a discussion in class about it. You may be interested to know that I presented that same list of statements to 250 first-year writing students, and the statements are listed in the order they were most often checked by students. In that case, however, students checked the statements they *agreed* with. For example, 85 percent of the students surveyed agreed that "it's okay to say things the instructor might disagree with," something I find encouraging. However, 60 percent believed that they had to know their thesis before they began their papers, an attitude that implies discovery is not the point of research.

The second part of Exercise 1 might have you thinking about some beliefs and attitudes you haven't thought much about—what a "fact" is, the nature and value of "opinions," and how you view experts and authorities.

I hope that these beliefs about the assignment you are about to undertake and your perspectives on how knowledge is made and evaluated are views that you return to again and again as you work through this book. You may find that some of your existing beliefs are further reinforced, but I'd wager that you might find *you* have some unlearning to do, too.

Using This Book

The Exercises

Throughout *The Curious Researcher,* you'll be asked to do exercises that either help you prepare your research paper or actually help you write it. You'll need a research notebook in which you'll do the exercises and perhaps compile your notes for the paper. Any notebook will do, as long as there are sufficient pages and left margins. Your instructor may ask you to hand in the work you do in response to the exercises, so it might be useful to use a notebook with detachable pages.

Several of the exercises in this book ask that you use techniques such as fastwriting and brainstorming. This chapter began with one, so you've already had a little practice with the two methods. Both fastwriting and brainstorming ask that you suspend judgment until you see what you come up with. That's pretty hard for most of us because we are so quick to criticize ourselves, particularly about writing. But if you can learn to get comfortable with the sloppiness that comes with writing almost as fast as you think, not bothering about grammar or punctuation, then you will be rewarded with a new way to think, letting your own words lead you in sometimes surprising directions. Though these so-called creative techniques seem to have little to do with the serious business of research writing, they can actually be an enormous help throughout the process. Try to ignore that voice in your head that wants to convince you that you're wasting your time using fastwriting or brainstorming. When you do, they'll start to work for you.

The Five-Week Plan

But more about creative techniques later. You have a research paper assignment to do. If you're excited about writing a research paper, that's great. You probably already know that it can be interesting work. But if you're dreading the work ahead of you, then your instinct might be to procrastinate, to put it off until the week it's due. That would be a mistake, of course. If you try to rush through the research and the writing, you're absolutely guaranteed to hate the experience and add this assignment to the many research papers in the garbage dump of your memory. It's also much more likely that the paper won't be very good. Because procrastination is the enemy, this book was designed to help you budget your time and move through the research and writing process in five weeks. (See the box, "Steps to Writing Your Research Essay.") It may take you a little longer, or you may be able to finish your paper a little more quickly. But at least initially, use the book sequentially, unless your instructor gives you other advice.

This book can also be used as a reference to solve problems as they arise. For example, suppose you're having a hard time finding enough information on your topic or you want to know how to plan for an interview. Use the Table of Contents by Subject

Steps to Writing Your Research Essay

Week One

- Discover your subject.
- Develop "working knowledge" of your subject.
- Narrow your subject by finding your focusing question.

Week Two

- Plan a research strategy that balances library and Internet sources.
- Fine-tune search terms.
- Begin developing "focused knowledge" of your subject.
- Plan interviews or surveys.

Week Three

- Write about your findings.
- Try advanced searching techniques.
- Conduct interviews and surveys.

Week Four

- Write the first draft.

Week Five

- Clarify your purpose, and hone your thesis.
- Revise draft.
- Edit, proofread, and finalize citations.

as a key to typical problems and where in the book you can find some practical help with them.

Alternatives to the Five-Week Plan

Though *The Curious Researcher* is structured by weeks, you can easily ignore that plan and use the book to solve problems as they arise. The Contents by Subject in the front of the text is keyed to a range of typical problems that arise for researchers: how to find a topic, how to focus a paper, how to handle a thesis, how to search the Internet, how to organize the material, how to take useful notes, and so on. The overview of Modern Language Association (MLA) research paper conventions in Appendix B provides a complete guide to make it easier to find answers to your specific technical questions at any point in the process of writing your paper.

The Research Paper and the Research Report

In high school, I wrote a research "paper" on existentialism for my philosophy class. I understood the task as skimming a book or two on the topic, reading the entry on "existentialism" in the *Encyclopaedia Britannica,* making some note cards, and writing down everything I learned. That took about six pages. Was I expressing an opinion of some kind about existentialism? Not really. Did I organize the information with some idea about existentialism I wanted to relay to readers? Nope. Was I motivated by a question about that philosophy I hoped to explore? Certainly not. What I wrote was a research *report,* and that is a quite different assignment than most any research paper you'll be asked to write in college.

Discovering Your Purpose

For the paper you're about to write, the information you collect must be used much more *purposefully* than simply reporting what's known about a particular topic. Most likely, you will define what that purpose is. For example, you may end up writing a paper whose purpose is to argue a point—say, eating meat is morally suspect because of the way stock animals are treated at slaughterhouses. Or your paper's purpose may be to reveal some less-known or surprising aspect of a topic—say, how the common housefly's eating habits are not unlike our own. Or your paper may set out to explore a thesis, or idea, that you have about your topic—for example, your topic is the cultural differences between men and women, and you suspect the way girls and boys play as children reflects the social differences evident between the genders in adults.

Whatever the purpose of your paper turns out to be, the process usually begins with something you've wondered about, some itchy question about an aspect of the world you'd love to know the answer to. It's the writer's curiosity—not the teacher's—that is at the heart of the college research paper.

In some ways, frankly, *research reports* are easier. You just go out and collect as much stuff as you can, write it down, organize it, and write it down again in the paper. Your job is largely mechanical and often deadening. In the *research paper,* you take a much more active role in *shaping and being shaped by* the information you encounter. That's harder because you must evaluate, judge, interpret, and analyze. But it's also much more satisfying because what you end up with says something about who you are and how you see things.

Where Did the Research Paper Come From?

Do you want to know whom to blame or whom to thank? The undergraduate assignment first arose in the first decade of the 20th century, a development related to two things: the rapid growth of the size of university library collections and the transformation of American colleges into places that privileged research rather than cultivating character and eloquence.

It's hard to underestimate this revolution in the goal of American universities. Until after the Civil War, going to college meant preparing for a "gentlemanly" profession like religion or law, and the purpose of college was to make sure that graduates were well-spoken, well-read, and virtuous. In just a few decades, this goal was abandoned in favor of the idea that universities should advance human knowledge.

Documented research papers were the method for accomplishing this new mission. Professors wrote research papers, and then, naturally, they assigned them to their graduate students. As graduate students assumed undergraduate teaching roles, they started to assign research papers to their students.

The very first research papers were often called "source themes," expository essays that were casually written rather than formal. By the 1920s, however, the research paper hardened into a relatively rigid form—one that owed its existence less to genuine inquiry than to the worship of the qualities of scientific method: objectivity, impersonality, originality, and documentation. Most research paper assignments today are still captive to this history. They seem to focus more on formal requirements than to the larger purpose of the endeavor: discovery.

How Formal Should It Be?

When I got a research paper assignment, it often felt as if I were being asked to change out of blue jeans and a wrinkled Oxford shirt and get into a stiff tuxedo. Tuxedos have their place, such as at the junior prom or the Grammy Awards, but they're just not me. When I first started writing research papers, I used to think that I *had* to be formal, that I needed to use big words like *myriad* and *ameliorate* and to use the pronoun *one* instead of *I*. I thought the paper absolutely needed to have an introduction, body, and conclusion—say what I was going to say, say it, and say what I said. It's no wonder that the first college research paper I had to write—on Plato's *Republic* for another philosophy class—seemed to me as though it were written by someone else. I felt at arm's length from the topic I was writing about.

You may be relieved to know that not all research papers are necessarily rigidly formal or dispassionate. Some are. Research papers in the sciences, for example, often have very formal structures, and the writer seems more a reporter of results than someone who is passionately engaged in making sense of them. This *formal stance* puts the emphasis where it belongs: on the validity of the data in proving or disproving something, rather than on the writer's individual way of seeing something. Some papers in the social sciences, particularly scholarly papers, take a similarly formal stance, where the writer not only seems invisible but also seems to have little relation to the subject. There are many reasons for this approach. One is that *objectivity*—or as one philosopher put it, "the separation of the perceiver from the thing perceived"—is traditionally a highly valued principle among some scholars and researchers. For example, if I'm writing a paper on the effectiveness of Alcoholics Anonymous (AA), and I confess that my father—who attended AA—drank himself to death, can I be trusted to see things clearly?

Yes, *if* my investigation of the topic seems thorough, balanced, and informative. And I think it may be an even better paper because my passion for the topic will encourage me to look at it more closely. However, many scholars these days are openly skeptical about claims of objectivity. Is it really possible to separate the perceiver from the thing perceived? If nothing else, aren't our accounts of reality always mediated by the words we use to describe it? Can language ever be objective? Though the apparent impersonality of their papers may suggest otherwise, most scholars are not nearly as dispassionate about their topics as they seem. They are driven by the same thing that will send you to the library or the Web over the next few weeks—their own curiosity—and most recognize that good research often involves both objectivity and subjectivity. As the son of an alcoholic, I am motivated to explore my own perceptions of his experience in AA, yet I recognize the need to verify those against the perceptions of others with perhaps more knowledge.

When "Bad" Writing Is Good

You might find it tempting to simply dismiss formal academic writing as "bad" writing, particularly after writing the less formal research essay. But that would be a mistake. Some academic writing only *seems* bad to you because you're not familiar with its conventions—the typical moves writers in that discipline make—nor are you aware of the ongoing conversation in that field to which a particular academic article contributes. It's a little like stumbling into the electricians' convention at the Hyatt while they're discussing new regulations on properly grounding outlets. Unless you're an electrician, not a whole lot will make sense to you.

In a way, *The Curious Researcher* represents an apprenticeship in academic writing much like an apprenticeship to a master electrician. Among other things, you'll learn how to ground an outlet—learn some of the technical moves academic writers use, such as citation, incorporating source material, and using indexes—but even more important I hope you'll learn to *think* like an academic writer. Ironically, I think this is easier to practice by not necessarily writing formal academic research papers because they so often *conceal* the open-ended, even messy, process of inquiry. Less formal exploratory essays seem to make the process of inquiry more apparent.

Thinking Like an Academic Writer

What does it mean to *think* like an academic writer? Quite a few different things, of course, some of which vary from discipline to discipline. But there are a few habits of mind or perspectives that I think often shape academic inquiry no matter what the field.

1. Inquiry, especially initially, is driven by questions, not answers.
2. It is normal and often necessary to suspend judgment and to tolerate ambiguity.
3. New knowledge or perspectives are made through the back and forth of conversation in which the writer assumes at least two seemingly contrary roles: believer and doubter, generator and judge.

4. Writers take responsibility for their ideas, accepting both the credit for and the consequences of putting forth those ideas for dialogue and debate.

Your instructor may want you to write a formal research paper. You should determine if a formal paper is required when you get the assignment. (See the box, "Questions to Ask Your Instructor about the Research Assignment.") Also make sure that you understand what the word *formal* means. Your instructor may have a specific format you should follow or tone you should keep. But more likely, she is much more interested in your writing a paper that reflects some original thinking on your part and that is also lively and interesting to read. Though this book will help you write a formal research paper, it encourages what might be called a *research essay*, a paper that does not have a prescribed form though it is as carefully researched and documented as a more formal paper.

"Essaying" or Arguing?

Essay is a term that is used so widely to describe school writing that it often doesn't seem to carry much particular meaning. But I have something particular in mind.

The term *essai* was coined by Michel Montaigne, a sixteenth-century Frenchman; in French, it means "to attempt" or "to try." For Montaigne and the essayists who follow his tradition, the essay is less an opportunity *to prove* something than an attempt *to find out*. An essay is often exploratory rather than argumentative, testing the truth of an idea or attempting to discover what might be true. (Montaigne even once had coins minted that said *Que sais-je?*—"What do I know?") The essay is often openly subjective and frequently takes a conversational, even intimate, form.

Now, this probably sounds nothing like any research paper you've ever written. Certainly, the dominant mode of the academic research paper is impersonal and argumentative. But if you consider writing a *research essay* instead of the usual *research paper*, four things might happen:

1. *You'll discover your choice of possible topics suddenly expands.* If you're not limited to arguing a position on a topic, then you can explore any topic that you find puzzling in interesting ways and you can risk asking questions that might complicate your point of view.

Questions to Ask Your Instructor About the Research Assignment

It's easy to make assumptions about what your instructor expects for the research paper assignment. After all, you've probably written such a paper before and may have had the sense that the "rules" for doing so were handed down from above. Unfortunately, those assumptions may get in the way of writing a good paper, and sometimes they're dead wrong. If you got a handout describing the assignment, it may answer the questions below, but if not, make sure you raise them with your instructor when he gives the assignment.

- How would you describe the audience for this paper?
- Do you expect the paper to be in a particular form or organized in a special way? Or can I develop a form that suits the purpose of my paper?
- Do you have guidelines about format (margins, title page, outline, bibliography, citation method, etc.)?
- Can I use other visual devices (illustrations, subheadings, bulleted lists, etc.) to make my paper more readable?
- Can I use the pronoun *I* when appropriate?
- Can my own observations or experiences be included in the paper if relevant?
- Can I include people I interview as sources in my paper? Would you encourage me to use "live" sources as well as published ones?
- Should the paper *sound* a certain way (have a particular tone), or am I free to use a writing voice that suits my subject and purpose?

2. *You'll find that you'll approach your topics differently.* You'll be more open to conflicting points of view and perhaps more willing to change your mind about what you think. As one of my students once told me, this is a more honest kind of objectivity.

3. *You'll see a stronger connection between this assignment and the writing you've done all semester.* Research is something all writers do, not a separate activity or genre that exists only upon demand. You may discover that research can be a revision strategy for improving essays you wrote earlier in the semester.

4. *You'll find that you can't hide.* The research report often encourages the writer to play a passive role; the research essay doesn't easily tolerate passivity. You'll probably find this both liberating and frustrating. While you may likely welcome the chance to incorporate your opinions, you may find it difficult to add your voice to those of your sources.

You may very well choose to write a paper that argues a point for this assignment (and, by the way, even an essay has a point). After all, the argumentative paper is the most familiar form of the academic research paper. But I hope you might also consider essaying your topic, an approach that encourages a kind of inquiry that may transform your attitudes about what it means to write research.

The Research Essay and Academic Writing

"If I'm going to have to write formal research papers in my other classes, why should I waste my time writing an informal research essay?" That's a fair question. In fact, the research essay you're about to write *is* different in some ways from the more formal academic scholarship you may be reading as you research your topic (see Figure 1, "Research Essays vs. Research Papers"). And it's also a bit different from research papers you may write in other classes. But the *methods of thought*, what I call the "habits of mind" behind academic inquiry, are fundamentally the same when writing the research essay and the formal research paper.

Because the research essay makes visible what is often invisible in formal academic writing—the process of coming to know what you've discovered about your topic—it's a great introduction to what academic research is all about. And because it removes what is often an artifice of objectivity in research papers, the research essay is like a hound flushing a grouse from the brush—writers can't hide under the cover of invisible authorship, concealing themselves in the safety of "one wonders" or "this paper will argue." *Writers* wonder and argue. *Your* questions, analyses, or assertions take center stage in the research essay as they do just as fundamentally, though less explicitly, in formal academic research. The research essay is good practice for this essential element of all academic inquiry: what you think and how you came to think it.

Informal Research Essay

- Often explicitly subjective, using the first person
- Exploratory
- Written for an audience of nonexperts on the topic
- Few rules of evidence
- Thesis may be delayed rather than stated in introduction
- Writer may express tentativeness about conclusions
- Structure determined by purpose and subject
- *Process* of coming to know often included

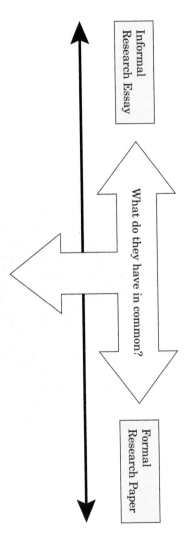

What do they have in common?

- Motive is to answer a question or solve a problem
- Establish context of what has already been said about the question or problem
- Doubt and ambiguity natural part of process
- Have a thesis or tentative claim
- Use evidence/information to explore or prove claim

Formal Research Paper

- Often avoids the first person
- Argumentative
- Written for other experts on the topic
- Established rules of evidence
- Thesis often stated in introduction
- Conclusions stated authoritatively
- Form usually prescribed
- Story of *how* conclusions were reached limited to methods

FIGURE 1 Research Essays vs. Research Papers

Becoming an Authority by Using Authorities

Whether formal or less so, all research papers attempt to be *authoritative.* That is, they rely heavily on a variety of credible sources beyond the writer who helped shape the writer's point of view. Those sources are mostly already published material, but they can also be other people, usually experts in relevant fields whom you interview for their perspectives. Don't underestimate the value of "live" and other nonlibrary sources. Authorities don't just live in books. One might live in the office next door to your class or be easily accessible through the Internet.

Though in research papers the emphasis is on using credible outside sources, that doesn't mean that your own experiences or observations should necessarily be excluded from your paper when they're relevant. In fact, in some papers, they are essential. For example, if you decide to write a paper on Alice Walker's novel *The Color Purple,* your own reading of the book—what strikes you as important—should be at the heart of your essay. Information from literary critics you discover in your research will help you develop and support the assertions you're making about the novel. That support from people who are considered experts—that is, scholars, researchers, critics, and practitioners in the field you're researching—will rub off on you, making your assertions more convincing, or authoritative.

Reading and talking to these people will also change your thinking, which is part of the fun of research. You will actually learn something, rather than remain locked into preconceived notions.

"It's Just My Opinion"

In the end, *you* will become an authority of sorts. I know that's hard to believe. One of the things my students often complain about is their struggle to put their opinions in their papers: "I've got all these facts, and sometimes I don't know what to say other than whether I disagree or agree with them." What these students often *seem* to say is that they don't really trust their own authority enough to do much more than state briefly what they feel: "Facts are facts. How can you argue with them?"

Step 2 of Exercise 1 that began this chapter may have started you thinking about these questions. I hope the research assignment you are about to start keeps you thinking about your beliefs about the nature of knowledge. Are facts unassailable? Or are they simply claims that can be evaluated like any others? Is the struggle to evaluate conflicting claims an obstacle to doing research, or the point of it? Are experts supposed to know all the answers? What makes one opinion more valid than another? What makes *your* opinion valid?

I hope you write a great essay in the next five or so weeks. But I also hope that the process you follow in doing so inspires you to reflect on how you—and perhaps all of us—come to know what seems to be true. I hope you find yourself doing something you may not have done much before: thinking about thinking.

Facts Don't Kill

You probably think the words *research paper* and *interesting* are mutually exclusive. A prevalent belief among my students is that the minute you start having to use facts in your writing, then the prose wilts and dies like an unwatered begonia. It's an understandable attitude. There are many examples of dry and wooden informational writing, and among them, unfortunately, may be some textbooks you are asked to read for other classes.

But factual writing doesn't have to be dull. You may not consider the article "The Bothersome Beauty of Pigeons" (see the following exercise) a research paper. It may be unlike any research paper you've imagined. While the piece includes citations and a bibliography—two features of most research papers—it reads more like a personal essay, with narrative strands, personal experiences and observations, and a personal voice. "The Bothersome Beauty of Pigeons" is an essay like those I encourage you to write—it grows from an experience I had while traveling in Italy that quickly became a research project on pigeons. I knew little about them except that a pair insisted on roosting under the eaves of my Boise, Idaho, home, clucking and cooing at all hours and splattering the bedroom window with droppings. I was not amused. When in Italy I felt a bit differently about pigeons as I watched them sweep in and out of the piazzas in great flocks, feeding at the feet of tourists.

The essay you are about to read explores my ambivalence about the birds, a question that naturally led me to research their habits and behaviors, methods of controlling them, and even a bit of philosophy that speculates about animal consciousness. While "The Bothersome Beauty of Pigeons" is not a formal academic research paper (I write those, too), it does reflect many of the features of academic writing and especially academic inquiry. For example, the essay is driven by questions, works toward a controlling idea or thesis, involves my willingness to suspend judgment, and attempts to build on the ideas of others to extend my own thinking. While the essay is personal—growing from my experience—it attempts to say something larger; it is an effort to comment on "our" experience, and uses research to help enrich those understandings.

The purpose of research writing is not simply to show readers what you know. It is an effort to *extend a conversation about a topic* that is ongoing, a conversation that includes voices of people who have already spoken, often in different contexts and perhaps never together. The research writer begins with his own questions, and then finds the voices that speak to them. He then writes about what others have helped him to understand. As you read "The Bothersome Beauty of Pigeons," look for the traces of this process of inquiry. It may also inspire you to have a similar adventure.

E X E R C I S E   2

Reflecting on "The Bothersome Beauty of Pigeons"

Read my research essay first for pleasure, and then reread it with a pen in your hand. Use two opposing pages of your notebook to explore your response to the piece. Begin on the left page by

- Jotting down, in quotes, your favorite line or passage from the essay.
- Copying a passage—a few lines or paragraph—that uses outside research. Choose one that you particularly liked or didn't like, or both.
- Composing, in your own words, what you think is the main idea or thesis of the essay. Begin by speculating about exactly what central question seemed to be behind the essay. What do you think I was trying to understand? What is it that I *came* to understand by the end of the essay?

Shift across to the opposing, or right, page of your notebook. Looking to the left at the notes you just took, begin a seven-minute fastwrite that explores your thinking in response to one or more of the following questions:

- When *you* write your research essay, what techniques or methods could you use to keep the essay interesting to readers even if it is fact-based?
- In what ways was "The Bothersome Beauty of Pigeons" *unlike* what you understood to be a research paper? Does it challenge those assumptions in ways that make you more interested in

research? What questions does the essay raise about what
you're supposed to do in your research assignment?

■ Explore your thoughts about the contents of the essay. Did you
find you could relate in some way to what the essay seemed to
say? Did you learn anything about yourself, or about pigeons, or
our relationships to nature that struck you in some way?

The Bothersome Beauty of Pigeons

by Bruce Ballenger

The cardboard display tables of the mostly African vendors in
Florence's largest piazzas are marvels of engineering. They are designed
to be light and portable, and to fold in an instant without disrupting the
orderly display of fashionable sunglasses, silver cigarette lighters, or art
posters. I watch these street entrepreneurs from the steps of the city's
great cathedral, Santa Maria della Fiore, as they work the roving bands
of Italian schoolchildren on school holiday. It is a hard sell. The vendors
line up side by side and though many sell exactly the same kinds of sunglasses or lighters or posters, they don't seem to aggressively compete
with each other; in fact, they borrow money from each other to make
change, and laugh together at quiet comments I can't hear.

For a few moments my attention to the scene strays, and when
I look back the vendors and their cardboard displays have simply
vanished. At first, I can't figure out a reason for the disappearing
act. Nor can I explain the street vendors' sudden return minutes
later, sweeping in like the flocks of pigeons that are everywhere in
these squares. Then I see the small Renault of the Florence polizia
driving slowly down an adjacent street, where two officers sit stiffly
in their crisp blue uniforms and white leather belts; the police seem
bored, indifferent, not even remotely interested in the sudden flight
their slow passage through the square inspires.

The vendors are apparently unlicensed and the police routinely
attempt to flush them out, but this is clearly a half-hearted campaign. Who can blame them? The vendors are everywhere, lingering
at the edge of crowds, a fraternity of friendly bandits clutching their
neatly folded cardboard tables, each equipped with a convenient handle of rope and duct tape. Within seconds of the officers' departure,
the vendors descend on the square again, once again unfolding their
tables to which the merchandise magically adhered.

I watch this flight and return again and again, and along with it
I notice the pigeons, who participate in a similar performance of their

own in these same squares. The birds are also everywhere, in bold flocks that peck at the heels of the sloppy eaters, each bird turning a greedy red eye up at the diner, the other eye fixed on the ground before it. It is impossible to ignore the pigeons, and tourists delight in tossing food and witnessing the free-for-all at their feet. I find myself looking for crumbs from the pannini I have just finished for lunch, wondering at my own impulse to feed a bird against which I had recently waged war.

Pigeons seem to inspire such paradoxical feelings. Pigeon racers in the Bronx tenderly kiss the beaks of their birds, finally home after flying 500 miles to their lofts after a remarkable feat of solar navigation (Blechman). Meanwhile, pigeon haters host Web sites like Pigeonsmakemesick.com and propose plans for ridding cities of the "vermin," including the tactical use of tennis rackets and loaves of bread (Thorne). Most of us, I think, can swing both ways in our feelings towards pigeons, an ambivalence that doesn't seem to apply to other "pests" because pigeons occupy an odd category of creatures that we can both love and hate, animals that are untidy and irritating yet, at times, utterly enchanting.

Florence does not feed a pigeon lover's longings nearly as well as Venice. In Florence's Piazza San Giovanni, where I sat, there were no seed sales, a business that thrives in Venice's St. Mark's square. For one euro, tourists there can buy a small bag of seeds to feed the pigeons, who respond to the encouragement by gathering in great flocks around the seed thrower. The birds lose their grace and shamelessly stumble over each other with eagerness, pecking wildly at the stone street and even eating out of the tourist's hand or perching on his head. This becomes a photographic occasion as tourists stand, arms outstretched before the great church, covered with pigeons.

One guidebook recommends that this feeding should be followed by throwing an article of clothing in the air, which like the police and the sunglass vendors, makes the pigeons take flight in a sudden pulse of wings, only to circle back in their greed and quickly land again at the tourists' feet (Steve 91). The same guidebook offers advice on dealing with pigeon droppings in one's hair—an obvious hazard for the pigeon lover and hater alike—suggesting that it's far better to wait until the stuff dries because it's easier to remove (85).

Such a thing goes completely against instinct. Among my most chilling childhood memories is politely heeding the patrol boy who commanded me to stop before I crossed the street in front of my home. He towered above me, no doubt growing some in memory, and I didn't see him gather the spit in his mouth to deposit on the top of my head. I ran home, heedless of traffic, my vision blurred by tears and my fingers wildly clawing at my fouled hair.

It is also, I think, instinctual for human beings to respond warmly to many other animals, particularly those that we find attractive. Pigeons would seem to qualify. They are, after all, close relatives to doves—the lovely white birds of peace—and despite the unsettling red eyes, brown in the youngsters, most *Columbia livia* have smoothly sculpted bodies of blue-gray, and a certain grace when they're not pecking at the stale remnants of someone's lunch. While people rant online about the pestilence of pigeons, it's easy to find organizations of pigeon lovers all over the Web, including the many pigeon fanciers who race them from the rooftops of New York City and other urban areas around the world. Apparently, the fighter George Foreman and actor Paul Newman are among them. Others admire the pigeons' intelligence, something that has been demonstrated by behaviorists like B. F. Skinner who selected pigeons as their primary study subjects. "Pound for pound," gushes Pigeons.com, citing a University of Montana study, "[the pigeon] is one of the smartest, most physically adept creatures in the animal kingdom" ("Resources"). One recent study even demonstrated that pigeons could learn to distinguish between a Van Gogh and a Chagall (Watanabe 147).

It takes special skills to thrive in the world's cities, and pigeons, also called rock doves, are endowed with several ecological advantages that allow them to indulge in "high risk" behavior and escape unscathed. The birds, introduced to North America from Europe in the 1600s, possibly find in urban canyons the high cliffs of their wild ancestors ("FAQs"), and from their high perches they can live and breed and look down on the rest of us.

But they have other evolutionary advantages as well, some of which save them from the well-placed kicks of pigeon-haters or the tires of speeding taxis. For one thing, they "suck" puddle water rather than take it in their beaks and throw their heads back to swallow it, something like the difference between drinking a juice box and slinging back a shot of tequila. Sucking is quicker, apparently, and in very short order they get the water they need, 10 to 15 percent of their body weight daily. In addition, because they can store food in a crop, a pouch in the throat, pigeons can quickly gorge on bread crumbs and seed as the birds weave between the shuffling feet of busy urbanites and then fly to a safe roost to digest what they gathered (Wells and Wells 324).

It's hard not to admire these traits that give the birds such biological success, and yet somehow these evolutionary gifts seem unfair and unearned. I'm disappointed that, say, bluebirds weren't given these advantages, birds that would use them more graciously, judiciously. Pigeons are punks. Looking them in the eye, I'm sure they know this but they just don't care. Yet looking at pigeons also reminds me of my own arrogance, and I both hate them and love them for it.

"The problem with pigeons," said Lia Bartolomei, an Italian who led me through the churches of Lucca one day, "is that they turn marble to dust" (Bartolomei). She then pointed to the small statues and marble carving on the church that were pocked and disfigured. The blame seemed clear. Apparently marble is particularly vulnerable to the acid in pigeon droppings, an unintended consequence of the birds' passion to roost on high places as their ancestors did on cliffs.

This is made worse by the pigeon's social nature. Unlike most other birds, they apparently are not particularly territorial, something that is obvious watching pigeons stumble over each other pursuing breadcrumbs. In great concentrations, the birds produce especially damaging piles of droppings, stuff that not only turns marble to dust but can be an ideal medium for fungus that can cause histoplasmosis and cryptococcossis, both lung infections in humans ("Health Hazards"). It costs the city of London $150,000 a year to clean up pigeon poop in Trafalgar Square alone ("Proposed").

It's the decay of marble monuments, the caked pigeon poop on city bridges, the messy nests on office buildings, and the health threats of dung fungus that long ago thrust the pigeon into the category of "pest." This is an undesirable label if you happen to be the plant or animal that earned it because life for such things can suddenly become complicated. The rock dove—cousin to the bird of peace, messenger for the Romans, brave racer for the homing pigeon enthusiast—also earned the unlovely name of "skyrat." Pigeon-haters find comrades on the Web and confer on the most effective poisons. Their anthem is folksinger Tom Lehrer's song "Poisoning Pigeons in the Park," a macabre tune noting that *When they see us coming, the birdies all try an' hide / But they still go for peanuts when coated with cyanide* (Lehrer). But despite the rants of pigeon-haters, (some of which are tongue-in-cheek) pigeons are not rats because among other things they aren't ugly. "Pests" like these make things complicated for us, too.

Like every urban area in the U.S., the pigeon thrives in Boise, Idaho, where I live, and recently I went to war with a pair determined to roost in the eaves of our turn-of-the century craftsman home. Let me be clear about one thing: I am a lover of wild birds, even hooligan crows who moodily gather in the neighborhood trees in late afternoon muttering curses. I never disliked pigeons, and even admired their success and intelligence. But the white and green streaks on my windows, and the pile of droppings at my back door turned me against them. The pigeons' indifference to my shouts and shirt waving whenever I found them on the eaves began to infuriate me.

It is human to rail against nature from time to time, and it may even be human nature. It's true that one of the ecological lessons of our time is that our determined efforts to dominate the natural world are not, generally, successful or wise. Ecologically speaking, then, the belief that we're apart from nature, that it can be easily "managed," doesn't help ensure our survival as a species; in fact, our grand engineering efforts often endanger our survival. But aren't these often matters of scale? Pigeon wars, like the battle against dandelions in a suburban lawn, may not matter as much in the ecological scheme of things, or at least this is what we tell ourselves. Still, these campaigns against the wild things that threaten our tidy world—bugs and weeds, rats and pigeons—can say a great deal about the ecology of emotion that shapes our response to nature.

Pigeons, unlike rats, aren't very good enemies. They *are* attractive, and the sweep of their flocks in and out of the squares and streets in Europe or America, expanding and contracting against the bright sky, can almost seem like breathing. Virginia Woolf compared the movement of the great flocks of starlings in the fall to the throwing of a net with "thousands of black knots" expanding and then contracting as the birds settle on the tops of trees (Woolf 5). From a distance, flocks of pigeons can seem like that, and unless you've imprinted images from Hitchcock's film *The Birds,* even the throbbing wings of dozens of the birds landing at your feet can be a little thrill.

Years ago, when I lived on the New England coast, I went on several whale watches to Stellwaggen Bank, an offshore area where there is an unusual concentration of the animals, including some of the rarest like the Right Whale. On every one of these trips, I noticed that there was a longing not only to see these great animals but to *get close* to them. I sensed this desire had as much to do with the longing to make contact—to look in the eye of a whale, to feel a mutual presence between watcher and animal—as it did the desire to simply get a good look at something that large. I wonder if it's that same longing that feeds the pigeon watchers in St. Mark's square as they feed the pigeons. This might explain why there could be such an outcry when, several years ago, London's mayor proposed to end the long history of pigeon feeding in London's Trafalgar Square.

"People come from abroad just to do it," said one critic of the proposal. "For many children the pigeons are the first contact they have with animals. If a pigeon lands on a child's shoulder, it will paint a good picture in their mind and who then know that animals are worth caring for" ("Proposed"). I'm not sure what is behind this longing to get close. But perhaps it appeals to the biological memory, buried deep, that we are indeed a part of nature, not apart from it. Eye contact is the closest thing we get to a language of intimacy with wild things, though we won't look a rat in the eye. We don't want to get close to just anybody.

Yet these two feelings, our separation and connection to the natural world, are always in conflict, even among those who have tutored themselves to believe in one rather than the other. This seems especially true when confronted with creatures like pigeons, who aren't easy to hate and aren't easy to love, who both foul the nest and yet possess the beauty of a gray river stone, smoothed by the timeless movement of current. All of this was on my mind as I pounded small nails into my pigeons' favorite perches under the eaves and cut the tops off of them to make them sharp, one of the many methods recommended by experts for "controlling" pigeons. Another popular method that uses something called Avitrol, corn bait laced with toxic chemicals, might even mean killing them. The language of "pest control," like the language of warfare, is not immune to euphemism.

Most of the tactics recommended against pigeons, however, are intended to simply make life uncomfortable for them, methods that are more likely, as one combatant put it, to create "a good public relations image" (Loven 3): a perception problem, by the way, that campaigns against rats don't have. These more benign methods of pigeon combat include "porcupine wire," electric wires on roosting places, or chemical pastes that the birds find distasteful. Several cities are experimenting with pigeon contraceptives. Shouting, water pistols, and twirling T-shirts provide momentary satisfaction but are not considered effective. It was a plastic long-eared owl with a head that moves in the wind that finally scared my pigeons away. I moved the owl every two days, and found a strange satisfaction in bullying the birds with what I imagine is their worst nightmare. A big owl with a twirling head would scare the devil out of me if I were a pigeon.

My pigeons moved next door where an elderly couple feed them bird seed and have the time and the willingness to clean up after their new charges; so it seems, in this case, things worked out for everyone. But the large flocks still haunt the piazzas in Florence and Venice, the squares in London, and similar places in nearly every city across the globe. Despite their ability to distinguish between a

Van Gogh and a Chagall, pigeons still deposit droppings that deface the great marble statues and facades—the works of art and architecture that are part of our human heritage—and yet people still buy bags of seed for about a dollar and pose for photographs, drenched in doves. Meanwhile, officials in these cities continue, sometimes quietly, to wage war against the birds.

Some historians believe that another war, this one in Viet Nam more than thirty years ago, was one that we could never win because politicians were unable to convince Americans to fully commit to it. That was a hard sell, too, because most Americans were smart enough to eventually realize that even with a full commitment the rewards of "winning" would not be worth the cost. We battle the birds with the same lack of conviction. Like Viet Nam, "pigeon control" is a war that we will never win because we also battle our own conflicting desires: the feeling that it is our obligation to protect and preserve humankind's great works and our hunger to coexist with at least the more appealing creatures with which we share space in our cities. We struggle, as we always have, with the sense that we are both a part of and apart from other species on the planet.

I've managed to scare the pigeons away from the eaves of my house. But it's not so easy to flush them from where they roost now in the back of my mind, cooing and clucking defiantly, daring me to hate them. I can't. This aggravates me because I know that part of the reason is, quite simply, that pigeons are not rats. It seems unlikely that pigeons know this, though certain philosophers believe that some animals know what it's like to *be* that animal (Nagel 435–50). If this is true, I imagine pigeons may be aware that they're fouling the head of a human being when they roost on the copy of Michelangelo's *David* in Florence's Piazza della Signoria. It is part of the pigeon "experience" to sit confidently on marble heads, knowing that the unthinking stone beneath their feet is neither a source of food nor threat, just a benign roost from which they can turn their red eyes to the humans on the ground below. We look back at them with amusement and disgust, curiosity and contempt—the conflicting feelings and desires that bothersome beauty in nature often arouses. Meanwhile, pigeons hasten the mortality of marble, turning a dream to dust.

Works Cited

Bartolomei, Lia. Personal Interview. 15 April 2002.
Blechman, Andrew. "Flights of Fancy." *Smithsonian Magazine* March 2002: 44–50.

"Frequently Asked Questions." Project Pigeon Watch. 5 May 2002 <http://birds.cornell.edu/ppw/faq.htm>.

"Health Hazards Associated with Bird and Bat Droppings." Illinois Department of Public Health-Health Beat. 2 May 2002 <http://www.idph.state.il.us/public/hb/hbb&bdrp.htm>.

Lehrer, Tom. "Poisoning Pigeons in the Park." 7 May 2002 <http://www.hyperborea.org/writing/pigeons.html>.

Loven, Judy. "Pigeons." Animal Damage Management: Purdue Cooperative Extension Service. April 2000. 4 pgs. 7 May 2002 <http://www.entm.purdue.edu/Entomology/ext/targets/ADM/index.htm>.

Nagel, Thomas. "What Is It Like to Be a Bat?" *Philosophical Review* 83 (1974): 435–50.

"Proposed Trafalgar Square Changes Ruffle Feathers." CNN.com. 15 November 2000. 2 May 2002 <www.cnn.com/2000/travel/news/11/15/Britain.trafalgar.ap/>.

"Resources: Interesting and Amazing Facts about Pigeons." Pigeons.com Resources. 2 May 2002 <http://www.pigeons.com/resources/facts.html>.

Steve, Rick. *Rick Steve's Italy, 2001.* Emeryville, CA: Avalon, 2001.

Thorne, Jacob. "Jacob Rants Semicoherently about Pigeons." 18 November 2002 <http://www.angelfire.com/art/glorious/pigeons.html>.

Watanabe, Shigeru. "Van Gogh, Chagall, and Pigeons: Picture Discrimination in Pigeons and Humans." *Animal Cognition* 4 (2001): 147–151.

Wells, Jeffrey V. and Allison Childs Wells. "Pigeons and Doves." *The Sibley Guide to Bird Life and Behavior.* Illust. David Allen Sibley. New York: Knopf, 2001, 319–325.

Woolf, Virginia. "Death of a Moth." *Eight Modern Essayists.* 6th ed. William Smart. New York: St. Martin's, 1995, 5–7.

The Question Habit

The most uninspired research writing lumbers along from fact to fact and quote to quote, saying "Look at what I know!" *Demonstrating* knowledge is not nearly as impressive as *using* it toward some end. And the best uses of research are to answer questions the writer is really interested in. In the next few days, your challenge is to find those questions.

The First Week

The Importance of Getting Curious

A few years back, I wrote a book about lobsters. At first, I didn't intend it to be a book. I didn't think there was that much to say about lobsters. But the more I researched the subject, the more questions I had and the more places I found to look for answers. Pretty soon, I had 300 pages of manuscript.

My curiosity about lobsters began one year when the local newspaper printed an article about what terrible shape the New England lobster fishery was in. The catch was down 30 percent, and the old-timers were saying it was the worst year they'd seen since the thirties. Even though I grew up in landlocked Chicago, I'd always loved eating lobsters after being introduced to them at age eight at my family's annual Christmas party. Many years later, when I read the article in my local newspaper about the vanishing lobsters, I was alarmed. I wondered, Will lobster go the way of caviar and become too expensive for people like me?

That was the question that triggered my research, and it soon led to more questions. What kept me going was my own curiosity. If your research assignment is going to be successful, you need to get curious, too. If you're bored by your research topic, your paper will almost certainly be boring as well, and you'll end up hating writing research papers as much as ever.

Learning to Wonder Again

Maybe you're naturally curious, a holdover from childhood when you were always asking, Why? Or maybe your curiosity paled as you got older, and you forgot that being curious is the best reason for wanting to learn things. Whatever condition it's in, your curiosity must be the driving force behind your research paper. It's the most essential ingredient. The important thing, then, is this: *Choose your research topic carefully. If you lose interest in it, change your topic to one that does interest you, or find a different angle.*

In most cases, instructors give students great latitude in choosing their research topics. (Some instructors narrow the field, asking students to find a focus within some broad, assigned subject. When the subject has been assigned, it may be harder for you to discover what you are curious about, but it won't be impossible, as you'll see.) Some of the best research topics grow out of your own experience (though they certainly don't have to), as mine did when writing about lobster overfishing or pigeons. Begin searching for a topic by asking yourself this question: *What have I seen or experienced that raises questions that research can help answer?*

Getting the Pot Boiling

A subject might bubble up immediately. For example, I had a student who was having a terrible time adjusting to her parents' divorce. Janabeth started out wanting to know about the impact of divorce on children and later focused her paper on how divorce affects father-daughter relationships.

Kim remembered spending a rainy week on Cape Cod with her father, wandering through old graveyards, looking for the family's ancestors. She noticed patterns on the stones and wondered what they meant. She found her ancestors as well as a great research topic.

Manuel was a divorced father of two, and both of his sons had recently been diagnosed with attention deficit disorder (ADD). The boys' teachers strongly urged Manuel and his wife to arrange drug therapy for their sons, but they wondered whether there might be any alternatives. Manuel wrote a moving and informative research essay about his gradual acceptance of drug treatment as the best solution for his sons.

For years, Wendy loved J. D. Salinger's work but never had the chance to read some of his short stories. She jumped at the opportunity to spend five weeks reading and thinking about her favorite author. She later decided to focus her research paper on Salinger's notion of the misfit hero.

Accidental topics, ideas that you seem to stumble on when you aren't looking, are often successful topics. For example, Amy spent some time in an America Online chat room one night, and the conversation took an interesting turn. Participants began to discuss the theory that suggests a correlation between depression and heavy computer use. Could that be true? She wondered. She decided to write a paper to find out.

Sometimes, one topic triggers another. Chris, ambling by Thompson Hall, one of the oldest buildings on his campus, wondered about its history. After a little initial digging, he found some 1970s newsclips from the student newspaper describing a student strike that paralyzed the school. The controversy fascinated him more than the building did, and he pursued the topic. He wrote a great paper.

If you're still drawing a blank, try the following exercise in your notebook.

EXERCISE 1.1

Building an Interest Inventory

STEP 1: From time to time I'll hear a student say, "I'm just not interested in *anything* enough to write a paper about it." I don't believe it. Not for a second. The real problem is that the student simply hasn't taken the time to think about everything he knows and everything he might want to know. Try coaxing those things out of your head and onto paper by creating an "interest inventory."

Start with a blank journal page, or if you're using a word processor, define columns—say, three per page. Title each column with one of the words below:

PLACES, TRENDS, THINGS, TECHNOLOGIES,
PEOPLE, CONTROVERSIES, HISTORY,
JOBS, HABITS, HOBBIES

Under each title, brainstorm a list of words (or phrases) that come to mind when you think about *what you know and what you might want to know* about the category. For example, under TRENDS you might be aware of the use of magnets for healing sore muscles, or you might know a lot about extreme sports. Put both down on the list. Don't censor yourself. Just write down whatever comes to mind, even if it makes sense only to you. This list is for your use only. You'll probably find that ideas come to you in waves—you'll jot down a few things and then draw a blank. Wait for the next wave to come and ride it. But if you're seriously becalmed, start a new column with a new word from the list above and brainstorm ideas in that category. Do this at least four times with different words. Feel free to return to any column to add new ideas as they come to you, and don't worry about repeated items. Some things simply straddle more than one category. For an idea of what this might look like, see what I did with this exercise (Figure 1.1).

CONTROVERSIES

Guantanamo bay
Iraq war
Palestine vs. Israel
Beijing Olympics
Steroids in baseball
Racism/sexism in politics
Gender identity
Homosexual marriage
Death penalty
When is a person created?
Right to euthanasia
Vegetative states
Drinking bottled water
Is organic stuff better?
Does the glass ceiling
    still exist?
Why are people poor?
Religion in the U.S.
    government
Sex lives of elected officials
What makes people fat?
Evolution in the school
    system
Gas vs. ethanol
Sales tax on groceries

JOBS

Prison guard
Garbage man
Sewer cleaners
Undertakers
TV anchor
Hotel housekeepers
Rap stars
Child stars
Interior decorators
Manicurists
Tailors
Cobblers
Tour guides

HABITS

Using a toothpick
Fingernail biting
Bouncing a leg
Verbal ticks, "so
    anyway . . ."
Wringing hands
Eating with mouth open
Chewing gum loudly
Laughing to oneself
Checking locks
Leaving cell phone on
Talking too loud
Nose picking
Hair twirling
Habits vs. superstitions
"God bless you"

TRENDS

Bluetooth headsets
Ipods
Drinking coffee
Crocs shoes
Giant purses
Designer everything
Organic products
Green/eco consciousness
"Some disease" awareness
Celebrity spokespeople
Internet television
Pets as children
Going to prison
Adult-oriented cartoons
Model/actress/singer
    combo
High-stakes kindergarten

HISTORY

The Holocaust
The Vietnam War
Ancient China
Who built the
    pyramids?
Why did the Aztecs
    die?
When did man leave
    Africa?
What was Pres.
    Washington like?
The Underground
    Railroad
Feudal Japan
Human sacrifices
Spanish Inquisition
Napoleonic wars

FIGURE 1.1   Amanda's Interest Inventory

TRENDS	HISTORY
Myspace	Stonecutter's guilds
Blogs	Nostradamus
Cohabitating	The Gold Rush
White teeth	Immigrants to the
Specialized TV channels	U.S. in the 1900s
Hardwood floors	The Triangle
Locavores	Shirtwaist fire
Wikipedia	The importance of the
Pink shirts for men	printing press
Heated car seats	Hygiene habits in
Splenda	ancient Greece
Energy drinks	Gender roles in
	ancient Egypt
	Torture chambers
	Footbinding
	Pre-Christian
	religions
	Canada's freedom
	from Europe.

Allot a total of twenty minutes to do this step: ten minutes to generate lists in four or more categories, a few minutes to walk away from it and think about something else, and the remaining time to return and add items to any column as they occur to you. (The exercise will also work well if you work on it over several days. You'll be amazed at how much information you can generate.)

STEP 2: Review your lists. Look for a single item in any column that seems promising. Ask yourself these questions: Is this something that raises questions that research can help answer? Are they potentially interesting questions? Does this item get at something you've always wondered about? Might it open doors to knowledge you think is important, fascinating, or relevant to your own life?

Circle the item.

Many interesting things surfaced on my lists. My TRENDS list seemed the richest. For example, when I finished Jon Krakauer's book *Into Thin Air,* a nonfiction account of a doomed Mt. Everest expedition, I was left wondering about the range of motivations that might account for the increasing popularity of that dangerous climb. On the same list I also wrote "decline of songbirds." I'm aware from personal experience and some limited reading that there has been a steady decline in songbird populations in North America during the last few decades. I spent many happy days watching warblers in the treetops behind my suburban Chicago home as a kid, and it makes me sad that those trees in some future month of May might be more silent. What's going on?

STEP 3: For the item you circled, generate a list of questions—as many as you can—that you'd love to explore about the subject. Here's what Amanda, one of my students, did with her topic on teeth whitening:

Are tooth whiteners safe?

What makes teeth turn browner over time?

How has society's definition of a perfect smile changed over time?

Are whiter teeth necessarily healthier than darker teeth?

Is it true that drinking coffee stains your teeth?

How much money is spent on advertising tooth whitening products each year?

What percentage of Americans feel bad about the shade of their teeth?

Do dentists ever recommend that people whiten their teeth?

Is there any way to keep your teeth from getting darker over time?

Can teeth get too white?

Why do I feel bad that my teeth aren't perfect?

Do other cultures have the same emphasis on perfectly white teeth as Americans do?

Are there the same standards for men's teeth and women's teeth?

What judgments do we make about people based simply on the color of their teeth?

How does America's dental hygiene compare with other countries? Is the "Austin Powers" myth really true?

The kinds of questions I came up with on my tentative topic seem encouraging. Several already seem "researchable," and several remind me that I *feel* something about those missing warblers. I may not have developed a hunger to know more yet, but it has piqued my interest. Do you have an appetite for anything yet?

Other Ways to Find a Topic

If you're still stumped about a tentative topic for your paper, consider the following:

■ *Surf the Net.* The Internet is like a crowded fair on the medieval village commons. It's filled with a range of characters— from the carnivalesque to the scholarly—all participating in a democratic exchange of ideas and information. There are promising research topics everywhere. Maybe begin with a site such as The Virtual Library (http://www.vlib.org), which tries to organize Internet resources by subject. Choose a subject that interests you, say autos or cognitive science, and follow any number of trails that lead from there into cyberspace.

■ *Search an index.* Visit your library's Web site and check an online index or database in a subject area that interests you. For example, suppose you're a psychology major and would like to find a topic in the field. Try searching PyschINFO, a popular database of psychology articles. Most databases can be searched by author, subject, keyword, and so on. Think of a general area you're interested in—say, bipolar disorder—and do a subject or keyword search. That will produce a long list of articles, some of which may have abstracts of summaries that will pique your interest. Notice the "related subjects" button? Click that and see a long list of other areas in which you might branch off and find a great topic.

■ *Browse Wikipedia.* While the online "free content" encyclopedia isn't a great source for an academic paper (see page 539), Wikipedia is a warehouse of potential research topic ideas. Start with the main page and take a look at the featured or newest articles. You can also browse articles by subject or category.

■ *Consider essays you've already written.* Could the topics of any of these essays be further developed as research topics? For example, Diane wrote a personal essay about how she found the funeral of a classmate alienating—especially the wake. Her essay asked what purpose such a ritual could serve, a question, she decided, that would best be answered by research. Other students wrote essays on the difficulty of living with a depressed brother or an alcoholic parent, topics that yielded wonderful research papers. A class assignment to read Ken Kesey's *One Flew Over the Cuckoo's Nest* inspired Li to research the author.

■ *Pay attention to what you've read recently.* What newspaper articles have sparked your curiosity and raised interesting questions?

Rob, a hunter, encountered an article that reported the number of hunters was steadily declining in the United States. He wondered why. Karen read an account of a particularly violent professional hockey game. She decided to research the Boston Bruins, a team with a history of violent play, and examine how violence has affected the sport. Don't limit yourself to the newspaper. What else have you read recently—perhaps magazines or books—or seen on TV that has made you wonder?

■ *Consider practical topics.* Perhaps some questions about your career choice might lead to a promising topic. Maybe you're thinking about teaching but wonder about current trends in teachers' salaries. One student, Anthony, was being recruited by a college to play basketball and researched the tactics coaches use to lure players. What he learned helped prepare him to make a good choice.

■ *Think about issues, ideas, or materials you've encountered in other classes.* Have you come across anything that intrigued you, that you'd like to learn more about?

■ *Look close to home.* An interesting research topic may be right under your nose. Does your hometown (or your campus community) suffer from a particular problem or have an intriguing history that would be worth exploring? Jackson, tired of dragging himself from his dorm room at 3:00 A.M. for fire alarms that always proved false, researched the readiness of the local fire department to respond to such calls. Ellen, whose grandfather worked in the aging woolen mills in her hometown, researched a crippling strike that took place there sixty years ago. Her grandfather was an obvious source for an interview.

■ *Collaborate.* Work together in groups to come up with interesting topics. Try this idea: Organize the class into small groups of five. Give each group ten minutes to come up with specific questions about one general subject—for example, American families, recreation, media, race or gender, health, food, history of the local area, environment of the local area, education, and so forth. Post these questions on newsprint as each group comes up with them. Then rotate the groups so that each has a shot at generating questions for every subject. At the end of forty minutes, the class will have generated perhaps a hundred questions, some uninspired and some really interesting. You can also try this exercise on the class website using the discussion board or group features.

What Is a Good Topic?

A few minutes browsing the Internet convinces most of my students that the universe of good research topics is pretty limited: global warming, abortion rights, legalization of pot, same sex marriage, and the like. These are usually the topics of the papers you can buy with your Visa card at sites like "freeessays.com" (yea, right). These are also often topics with the potential to bore both reader and writer to death because they inspire essays that are so predictable.

But beginning with a good question, rather than a convenient answer, changes everything. Suddenly, subjects are everywhere: What is with our cultural obsession about good teeth? Is it true that lawnmowers are among the most polluting engines around? What's the deal with the devastation of banana crops and how will that affect prices at Albertson's down the street? Even the old tired topics get new life when you find the right question to ask. For example, what impact will the availability of medical marijuana vending machines in California have on the legal debate in that state?

What's a good topic? Initially, it's all about finding the right question, and especially one that you are really interested in. (See the box on page 535.) Later, the challenge will be limiting the number of questions your paper tries to answer. For now, look for a topic that makes you at least a little hungry to learn more.

Checking Out Your Tentative Topic

Consider the potential of the tentative topic you've chosen by using this checklist:

- Does it raise questions I'd love to learn the answers to? Does it raise a lot of them?
- Do I feel strongly about it? Do I already have some ideas about the topic that I'd like to explore?
- Can I find authoritative information to answer my questions? Does the topic offer the possibility of interviews? An informal survey? Internet research?
- Will it be an intellectual challenge? Will it force me to reflect on what *I* think?
- Are a lot of people researching this topic or a similar one? Will I struggle to find sources in the library because other students have them?

Don't worry if you can't answer yes to all of these questions or if you can't answer any at all just yet. Being genuinely curious about your topic is the most important consideration.

Five Research Essays I'd Like to Read

- **The rise of reality shows.** I'm embarrassed to admit this but my daughter's got me watching what some critics call the penultimate TV reality show—Project Runway. The show annoys me. A lot. But if it's on, I'll sit down and watch with enjoyment and hate myself for doing it. What might explain both the appeal and the repugnance of this particular show, and perhaps reality shows generally?
- **Cell phones on airplanes.** Legislation was introduced in Congress recently to ban cell phones on American airlines while many European air carriers now allow them. Is this a good thing? Just because technology enables us to do something, should we do it?
- **The sociology of Mount Everest.** The first human successfully climbed the world's tallest mountain more than fifty years ago. On one day in 1993, forty people made it to the top. Climbing the mountain is now big business. What are people's motives for spending tens of thousands of dollars to be led to the summit? Have these motives changed? And what does it say about the changing definition of "adventure?"
- **The history of toothpaste.** People have brushed their teeth for ages, but Crest has only been around for a half-century or so. What did people use as toothpaste in medieval times? Was it effective? And what might the evolution of toothpaste say about human vanity or inventiveness or even ignorance?
- **The floating continent of plastic.** In a region of the North Pacific that few ever see, there is reportedly a huge island of litter, twice the size of Texas, composed mostly of plastic. The debris accumulates there because of a quirk in ocean currents. What danger does this pose to marine mammals or even to phytoplankton on which the ecosystem relies? What kinds of plastic is this island made of and what does this say about our appetite for convenience?

Making the Most of an Assigned Topic

If your instructor limits your choice of topics, then it might be a little harder to find one that piques your curiosity, but it will not be nearly as hard as it seems. It is possible to find an interesting angle on almost any subject, if you're open to the possibilities. If you're not convinced, try this exercise in class.

EXERCISE 1.2

The Myth of the Boring Topic

This exercise requires in-class collaboration. Your instructor will organize you into four or five small groups and give each group a commonplace object; it might be something as simple as a nail, an orange, a pencil, a can of dog food, or a piece of plywood. Whatever the object, it will not strike you as particularly interesting, at least not at first.

STEP 1: Each group's first task is to brainstorm a list of potentially interesting questions about its commonplace object. Choose a recorder who will post the questions as you think of them on a large piece of newsprint taped to the wall. Inevitably, some of these questions will be pretty goofy ("Is it true that no word rhymes with orange?"), but work toward questions that might address the *history* of the object, its *uses,* its possible *impact on people,* or *the processes* that led to its creation in the form in which you now see it.

STEP 2: After twenty minutes, each group will shift to the adjacent group's newsprint and study the object that inspired that group's questions. Spend five minutes thinking up more interesting questions about the object that didn't occur to the group before you. Add these to the list on the wall.

What Makes a Question "Researchable"?

- It's not too big or too small.
- It focuses on some aspect of a topic about which something has been said.
- It interests the researcher.
- Some people have a stake in the answer. It has something to do with how we live or might live, what we care about, or what might be important for people to know.
- It implies an approach, or various means of answering it.
- It raises more questions. The answer might not be simple.

STEP 3: Stay where you are or return to your group's original object and questions. Review the list of questions, and choose *one* you find both interesting and most "researchable" (see previous box). In other words, if you were an editorial team assigned to propose a researched article for a general interest magazine that focuses on this object, what might be the starting question for the investigation? The most interesting question and the most researchable question may or may not be the same.

In Idaho, where I live, there are stones called geodes. These are remarkably plain looking rocks on the outside, but with the rap of a hammer they easily break open to reveal glittering crystals in white and purple hues. The most commonplace subjects and objects are easy to ignore because we suspect there is nothing new to see or know about them. Sometimes it takes the sharp rap of a really good question to crack open even the most familiar subjects, and then suddenly we see that subject in a new light. What I'm saying is this: A good question is the tool that makes the world yield to wonder, and knowing this is the key to being a curious researcher. Any research topic—even if it's assigned by the instructor—can glitter for you if you discover the questions that make you wonder.

If all else fails, examine your assigned topic through the following "lenses." One might give you a view of your topic that seems interesting.

■ *People.* Who has been influential in shaping the ideas in your topic area? Do any have views that are particularly intriguing to you? Could you profile that person and her contributions?

■ *Trends.* What are the recent developments in this topic? Are any significant? Why?

■ *Controversies.* What do experts in the field argue about? What aspect of the topic seems to generate the most heat? Which is most interesting to you? Why?

■ *Impact.* What about your topic currently has the most effect on the most people? What may in the future? How? Why?

■ *Relationships.* Can you put one thing in relationship to another? If the required subject is Renaissance art, might you ask, "What is the relationship between Renaissance art and the plague?"

Admittedly, it is harder to make an assigned topic your own. But you can still get curious if you approach the topic openly, willing to see the possibilities by finding the questions that bring it to life for you.

Developing a Working Knowledge

If you have a tentative topic that makes you curious, then you're ready to do some preliminary research. At this stage in the process, it's fine to change your mind. As you begin to gently probe your subject, you may discover that there's another topic that interests you more—or perhaps a question that hadn't occurred to you. One of the advantages of developing a "working knowledge" of your topic at this stage is that these other possibilities may present themselves.

What's a working knowledge? William Badke, in his great book *Research Strategies*, calls a "working knowledge" of a topic the ability "to talk about it for one minute without repeating yourself." The advantage of developing a working knowledge of your tentative topic at this point is that it will help you find a focus, the problem that vexes more research writers than any other. Aside from giving you something new to talk about when conversation lags at Thanksgiving dinner, a working knowledge helps you to understand the following:

1. How your topic fits into the *context* of other subjects.
2. Some of the areas of controversy, debate, questions, or unresolved problems that ripple through expert conversation about your topic.

Knowing both of these things really helps when you want to stake out your own small piece of the larger landscape, and it helps you find the question that will mark your location and drive your investigation.

> ### Working Together
>
> In small groups, plan one-minute presentations of "working knowledge" you've developed on your topic doing Exercise 1.3. Following each presentation, ask group members to brainstorm a list of questions they have about your topic based on what you've said.

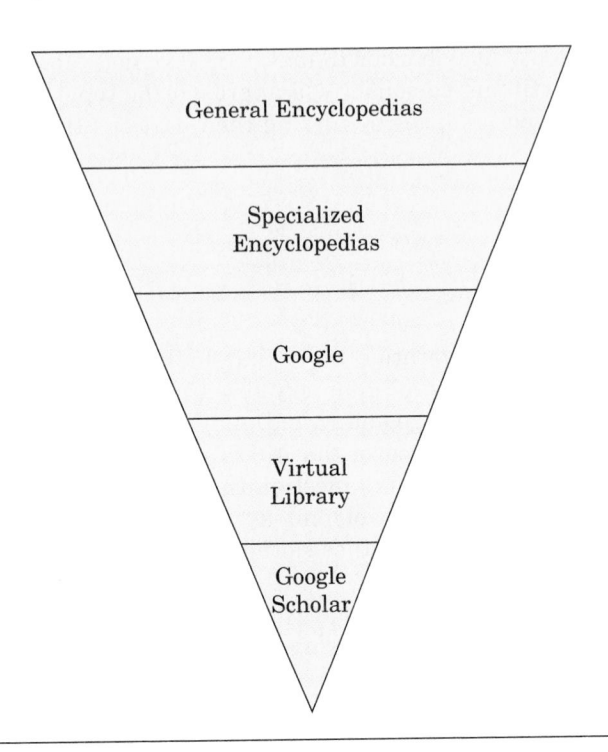

FIGURE 1.2   Working Knowledge Research Strategy

Research Strategies

There are many ways to develop a working knowledge of your topic, but generally the research strategy is like many others: Work from more general information to more specialized information (see Figure 1.2). That means, in this case, that you start with that old standby, the encyclopedia. That will not be your impulse, of course. You'll want to fire up Google and do a quick search, gather some online documents, and call it good. If at all possible, you'll want to avoid the library. But should you, even at this early stage in your investigation?

E X E R C I S E   1 . 3

Seeing the Broad View

Fortunately, one of the Web's strengths is subject coverage, and an online search will give you a good initial vantage point on your research topic. A logical starting point is an Internet version of the encyclopedia—the age-old reference for surveying a topic's landscape—and for most of us that means one thing: Wikipedia.

Wikipedia: Right or Wrong?

When you say "Wikipedia" to some academics, it's the equivalent of fingernails on a blackboard. Why do they cringe so? Because they see more and more students citing Wikipedia in their essays, and since articles on the site are authored by anyone, no matter his or her credentials on a topic, Wikipedia potentially violates one of the most important criteria for using any source in an academic paper: accuracy and reliability. There is some evidence, however, that the site compares fairly well with its more credible cousin, *Encyclopedia Britannica*. When they compared science articles in the two encyclopedias, researchers found that Wikipedia had an average of four inaccuracies while *Britannica* had three, and these were all relatively minor.* Still, in most cases, Wikipedia should not be a citation in your final paper, but it can be a useful starting point for your research when used cautiously.

WIKIPEDIA GOOD	WIKIPEDIA BAD
▪ On some topics, it has more current information on a subject than the conventional encyclopedia.	▪ Reliability is always suspect because authors may lack credentials.
▪ Because articles are authored by people around the world, some topics have a multicultural perspective.	▪ There is no attempt to be comprehensive, to give appropriate treatment to important subjects.
▪ Articles frequently include helpful hyperlinks.	▪ Many articles don't cite sources, so reliability and accuracy is difficult to check.
▪ Stable articles—those that have undergone substantial revision so that they represent consensus—approach the standard of a conventional encyclopedia.	▪ Some articles, particularly young ones on new topics, may reflect a strong bias because of their limited number of authors.

STEP ONE: Consult an online encyclopedia like Wikipedia, *Encyclopedia Britannica*, or one of the more scholarly wikis currently in development like Scholarpedia (www.scholarpedia.org) or Citizendium

*Jim Giles, "Special Report: Internet Encyclopedias Go Head to Head," *Nature* 438 (2005): 900–901.

(en.citizendium.org/wiki/Main_Page). You can also find a good list of the Web encyclopedias at the site www.refdesk.com. Try out several search terms on these sites until you find information relevant to your topic. Then, on the left page of your open notebook, jot at least three or four facts, interesting ideas, or quotations from the encyclopedias you consulted. Make sure you bookmark the pages so you can consult them later!

STEP TWO: Consult a specialized encyclopedia on your topic. These are more subject-focused works, obviously, that often have a wealth of information on a topic lacking in a more general work.

SPECIALIZED ENCYCLOPEDIAS

HUMANITIES	SOCIAL SCIENCES
Dictionary of Art	African-American Encyclopedia
International Dictionary	Dictionary of Psychology
of Films and Filmmakers	Encyclopedia of Marriage
Encyclopedia of World Art	and the Family
Encyclopedia of Religion	Encyclopedia of Psychology
Encyclopedia of Philosophy	The Blackwell Encyclopedia
Encyclopedia of African	of Social Psychology
American Culture and History	Encyclopedia of Educational
Encyclopedia of America	Research
Encyclopedia of Sociology	Encyclopedia of Social Work
Social History	Encyclopedia of World Cultures
	Encyclopedia of the Third World
	Encyclopedia of Democracy
	Guide to American Law:
	Everyone's Legal Encyclopedia

SCIENCE	OTHER
Dictionary of the History	Encyclopedia of the Modern
of Science	Islamic World
Dictionary of the History	The Baseball Encyclopedia
of Medicine	Encyclopedia of Women
Encyclopedia of the Environment	and Sports
Concise Encyclopedia of Biology	Encyclopedia of World Sport
Encyclopedia of Bioethics	The World Encyclopedia
Encyclopedia of Science	of Soccer
and Technology	Worldmark Encyclopedia
Macmillan Encyclopedias	of the Nations
of Chemistry and Physics	
Food and Nutrition Encyclopedia	

These specialized references abound. (My personal favorite is the *Encyclopedia of Hell*). The accompanying list provides a sampling of specialized encyclopedias. To find these and other focused references relevant to your topic, you'll probably have to go to your academic library. Few are online. To find specific titles, ask your reference librarian or search your campus library's online book index. Try searching using the subject area with the word "encyclopedia" or "dictionary" (e.g., Internet and encyclopedia).

STEP THREE: Go ahead and Google your topic (or use another general search engine). Typically, Google users do keyword rather than subject searches, trying out a few (usually two) search terms rather than working down through subject categories. Both strategies are useful, but for now choose some keywords that you think might produce good results. Try combining three or more words to narrow your search. Instead of *plastic pollution* (a half million hits) try *plastic pollution ocean seabirds* (seventy thousand hits). Don't forget the quotation convention on Google that allows you to search for a specific phrase. For instance, *"plastic continent" Pacific*. Bookmark useful documents.

STEP FOUR: As you probably know, information on the Web is horribly disorganized; it's a librarian's worst nightmare. But there are librarians and others who are knowledgeable about organizing information who have worked quietly for years trying to impose some order on the chaos. What they've done is created *subject directories* on the Web. Perhaps the most famous subject directory is Yahoo! (yahoo.com), but there are several other sites that feature directories that were specifically developed by library experts and educators, people who are concerned both with order and the value of information in cyberspace One of the best subject directories is The Virtual Library. It's not the largest, but it is managed by people—mostly volunteers—all over the world who are experts in the library's various subject areas, contributing and evaluating the best sites.

Visit The Virtual Library (vlib.org) and drill down into your subject, starting with the broadest category and then refining and narrowing as you go. (See Figure 1.3 and Figure 1.4). Again, bookmark particularly relevant documents.

STEP FIVE: One of the great innovations for academic researchers is specialized search engines that focus on scholarly sources. The best of these is Google Scholar, though there are others (see the

FIGURE 1.3 Managed by volunteers, The Virtual Library is one of the best subject directories on the Internet.

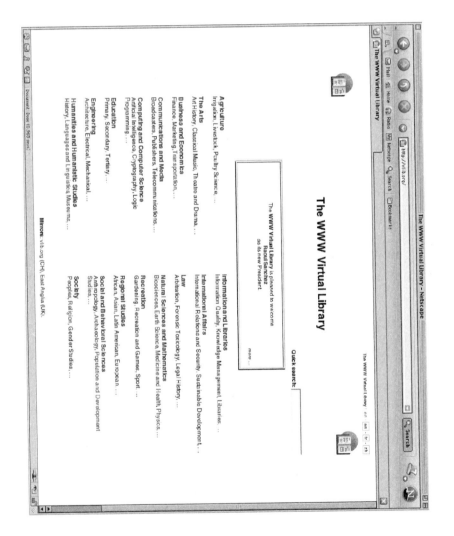

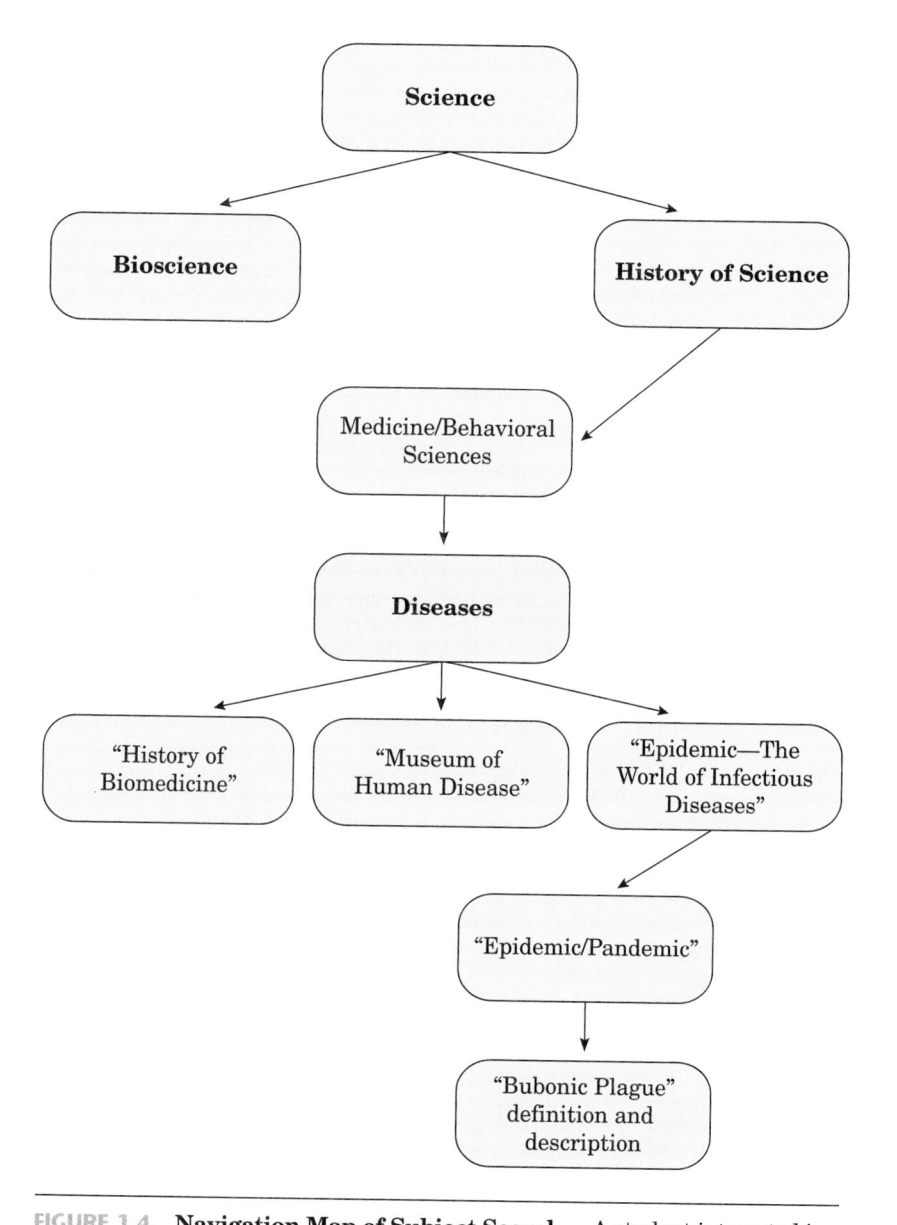

FIGURE 1.4   Navigation Map of Subject Search.   A student interested in the bubonic plague, a pandemic that wiped out nearly a third of Europe's population in the fourteenth century, began in the "Science" category at the Virtual Library. She followed the most promising trail down through the subject hierarchy (using the "back" button on her browser to get out of dead ends when necessary), and ended finally at a Museum of Natural History site with an interesting definition and description of the plague. On the way, she began to think about AIDs and the plague. Might she explore the connection between the two?

following list). Try one or more of these using the keywords that worked best for you in Step Three.

Academic Search Engines

Google Scholar http://scholar.google.com/
> Those folks from Google just won't rest on their laurels. This is a recent addition to their array of search tools. Its database includes articles and even some books.

Fields of Knowledge http://www.fieldsofknowledge.com/index.html
> A very useful site that asks experts (mostly college professors) to list the best sources they know on a subject.

Academic Index http://www.academicindex.net
> A "metasearch" engine that returns Web sites recommended by scholars and librarians on thousands of subjects.

Librarian's Index to the Internet http://lii.org/
> Indexes about 16,000 Web sites on the Internet, all of which, they pledge, is "information you can trust."

STEP SIX: Finally, conclude your working knowledge search by collecting the basic bibliographic information on the most useful sources you found. A convenient way to do this is to use a "citation machine," a Web-based program that automatically prompts you for the bibliographic information and then magically turns it into citations in whatever citation format you want. Don't trust one of these to generate references for your final essay—they can make mistakes—but they're great as a preliminary method for collecting a list of citations. Visit citationmachine.net (or another site) and enter in information about your best sources choosing APA or MLA format.

The Reference Librarian: A Living Source

Alas, there are still other reasons to visit the library, even at this early stage in your research. First and foremost is that the reference room is where reference librarians hang out, and these are people you should get to know. I recently told a reference librarian that I was having a hard time keeping up with the changes in library technology, and she said, "Things are changing so fast it even makes my head spin." Even blurred, the eyesight of reference librarians—people who know where to look and what to look for—is far better than ours. Reference specialists are invaluable to college researchers; without a doubt, they're the most important resource in the library.

Narrowing the Subject

It never occurred to me that photography and writing had anything in common until I found myself wandering around a lonely beach
one March afternoon with a camera around my neck. I had a fresh roll
of film and, full of ambition, I set out to take beautiful pictures. Three
hours later, I had taken only three shots, and I was definitely not having fun. Before quitting in disgust, I spent twenty minutes trying to
take a single picture of a lighthouse. I stood there, feet planted in the
sand, repeatedly bringing the camera to my face, but each time I looked
through the viewfinder, I saw a picture I was sure I'd seen before,
immortalized on a postcard in the gift shop down the road. Suddenly,
photography lost its appeal.

A few months later, a student sat in my office complaining that
he didn't have anything to write about. "I thought about writing an
essay on what it was like going home for the first time last weekend," he said. "But I thought that everyone probably writes about
that in freshman English." I looked at him and thought about lighthouse pictures.

Circling the Lighthouse

Almost every subject you will choose to write about for this
class and for this research paper has been written about before. The
challenge is not to find a unique topic (save that for your doctoral
dissertation) but to find an angle on a familiar topic that helps readers to see what they probably haven't noticed before. In "The Bothersome Beauty of Pigeons," I took the most common of subjects—the
urban pigeon—and took a close look at its habits and behaviors, finding in them an explanation for my conflicted feelings about "pests"
that are inconveniently attractive.

I now know that it was a mistake to give up on the lighthouse.
The problem with my lighthouse picture, as well as with my student's proposed essay on going home, was not the subject. It was that
neither of us had yet found our own angle. I needed to keep looking,
walking around the lighthouse, taking lots of shots until I found one
that surprised me, that helped me see the lighthouse in a new way,
in *my* way. Instead, I stayed put, stuck on the long shot and the
belief that I couldn't do better than a postcard photograph.

It is generally true that when we first look at something, we
mostly see its obvious features. That became apparent when I
asked my freshman English class one year to go out and take pictures of anything they wanted. Several students came back with

single photographs of Thompson Hall, a beautiful brick building on campus. Coincidentally, all were taken from the same angle and distance—straight on and across the street—which is the same shot that appears in the college recruiting catalog. For the next assignment, I asked my students to take multiple shots of a single subject, varying angle and distance. Several students went back to Thompson Hall and discovered a building they'd never seen before, though they walk by it every day. Students took abstract shots of the pattern of brickwork, unsettling shots of the clock tower looming above, and arresting shots of wrought iron fire escapes, clinging in a tangle to the wall.

The closer students got to their subjects, the more they began to see what they had never noticed before. The same is true in writing. As you move in for a closer look at some aspect of a larger subject, you will begin to uncover information that you—and ultimately your readers—are likely to find less familiar and more interesting. One writing term for this is *focusing*. (The photographic equivalent would be *distance from the subject.*)

From Landscape Shots to Close-Ups

The research reports many of us wrote in high school typically involved landscape photography. We tried to cram into one picture as much information as we could. A research report is a long shot. The college research essay is much more of a close-up, which means narrowing the boundaries of a topic as much as you can, always working for a more detailed look at some smaller part of the landscape.

You are probably not a photographer, and finding a narrow focus and fresh angle on your research topic is not nearly as simple as it might be if this were a photography exercise. But the idea is the same. You need to see your topic in as many ways as you can, hunting for the angle that most interests you; then go in for a closer look. One way to find your *focus* is to find your *questions*.

E X E R C I S E   1 . 4

Finding the Questions

Although you can do this exercise on your own, your instructor will likely ask that you do it in class this week. That way, students can help each other. (If you do try this on your own, only do Steps 3 and 4 in your research notebook.)

STEP 1: Take a piece of paper or a large piece of newsprint, and post it on the wall. At the very top of the paper, write the title of your tentative topic (e.g., *Plastics in the Ocean*).

STEP 2: Take a few minutes to briefly describe why you chose the topic.

STEP 3: Spend five minutes or so briefly listing what you know about your topic already (e.g., any surprising facts or statistics, the extent of the problem, important people or institutions involved, key schools of thought, common misconceptions, observations you've made, important trends, major controversies, etc.).

STEP 4: Now spend fifteen or twenty minutes brainstorming a list of questions *about your topic* that you'd like to answer through your research. Make this list as long as you can; try to see your topic in as many ways as possible. Push yourself on this; it's the most important step.

STEP 5: As you look around the room, you'll see a gallery of topics and questions on the walls. At this point in the research process, almost everyone will be struggling to find her focus. You can help each other. Move around the room, reviewing the topics and questions other students have generated. For each topic posted on the wall, do two things: Add a question *you* would like answered about that topic that's not on the list, and check the *one* question on the list you find most interesting. (It may or may not be the one you added.)

If you do this exercise in class, when you return to your newsprint, note the question about your topic that garnered the most interest. This may not be the one that interests you the most, and you may choose to ignore it altogether. But it is helpful to get some idea of what typical readers might want most to know about your topic.

You also might be surprised by the rich variety of topics other students have tentatively chosen for their research projects. The last time I did this exercise, I had students propose papers on controversial issues such as the use of dolphins in warfare, homelessness, the controversy over abolishment of fraternities, legalization of marijuana, and censorship of music. Other students proposed somewhat more personal issues, such as growing up with an alcoholic father, date rape, women in abusive relationships, and the effects of divorce on children. Still other students wanted to learn about more historical subjects, including the role of Emperor Hirohito in World War II, the student movement in the 1960s, and the Lizzie Borden murder case. A few students chose topics that were local. For example, one student recently researched the plight of 19th-century Chinese miners digging for gold in the mountains just outside of Boise. Another did an investigation of skateboard culture in town, a project that involved field observation, interviews, as well as library research.

EXERCISE 1.5

Finding the Focusing Question

Review the questions you or the rest of the class generated in Exercise 1.4, Steps 4 and 5, and ask yourself, Which questions on the list am I most interested in that could be the focus of my paper? Remember, you're not committing yourself yet.

STEP 1: Write the *one* question that you think would be the most interesting focus for your paper on the top of a fresh piece of newsprint or paper: This is your *focusing question.*

STEP 2: Now build a new list of questions under the first one. What else do you need to know to answer your focusing question? For example, suppose your focusing question is, *Why do some colleges use unethical means to recruit athletes?* To explore that focus, you might need to find out:

> Which colleges or universities have the worst records of unethical activities in recruiting?
>
> In which sports do these recruiting practices occur most often? Why?
>
> What are the NCAA rules about recruiting?
>
> What is considered an *unethical practice?*
>
> What efforts have been undertaken to curb bad practices?

Many of these questions may already appear on the lists you and the class generated, so keep them close at hand and mine them for ideas. Examine your tentative focusing question carefully for clues about what you might need to know. See also the box "Methods for Focusing Your Paper: An Example," which describes how one student completed this exercise.

EXERCISE 1.6

Finding the Relationship

One of the best ways to frame a research question is to use it to describe the relationship between your topic and something else. This is something researchers do all the time. For instance, suppose you're interested in anorexia, an eating disorder that afflicts a friend of yours. One way to get a handle on this big subject is to ask the following question: *What is the relationship between anorexia and* _____*?* How might you fill in the blank? Brainstorm some ideas that you think might show some interesting—and researchable—relationships. A "concept map" is one way to do this. Begin by writing your topic in capital letters in the middle of an unlined piece of paper, and then draw nodes with double-ended arrows that lead back to your topic. Write words and phrases in the nodes that suggest a possible relationship with your topic.

In this example, the map shows four possible relationships:

1. What is the relationship between anorexia and the anorexic's relationship with her father?
2. What is the relationship between anorexia and the anorexic's age? How young is she?
3. What is the relationship between anorexia and advertising?
4. What is the relationship between anorexia and the anorexic's history of sexual abuse?

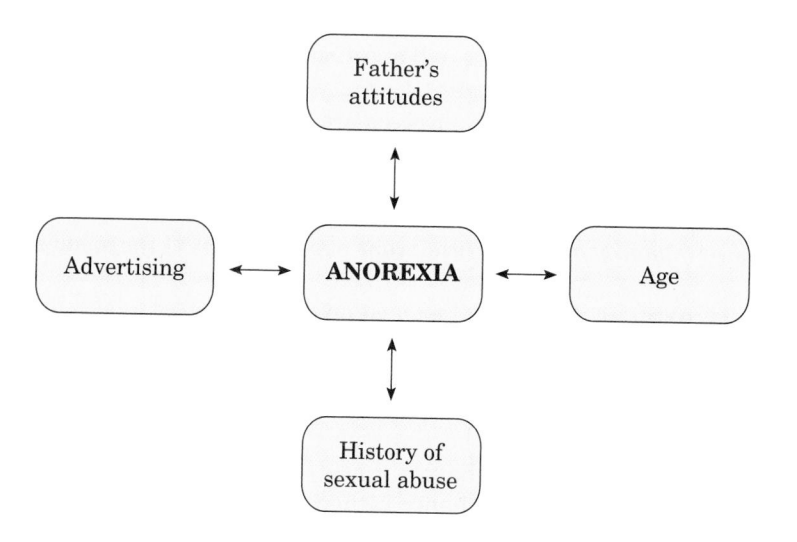

Other Ways to Narrow Your Subject

1. **Time.** Limit the time frame of your project. Instead of re-searching the entire Civil War, limit your search to the month or year when the most decisive battles occurred.
2. **Place.** Anchor a larger subject to a particular location. Instead of exploring "senioritis" at American high schools, research the phenomenon at the local high school.
3. **Person.** Use the particulars of a person to reveal generalities about the group. Instead of writing about the homeless problem, write about a homeless man.
4. **Story.** Ground a larger story in the specifics of a "smaller" one. Don't write about dream interpretation, write about a dream *you* had and use the theories to analyze it.

By marrying your topic to something else, and seeking to explore the relationship between them, you succeed in narrowing your focus. Now, instead of simply looking for information on anorexia—watch out for the avalanche!—you will be looking only for information that connects that topic with, say, anorexics' relationships with their fathers.

Possible Purposes for a Research Assignment

If you have a decent research question, you're off and running. But your first step should be to pause, look at your question, and think a bit about which of the following purposes are implied by the question you chose. Each of these purposes will profoundly influence the way you read your sources and how you approach writing the first draft. While any essay can use more than one of these purposes, which would you say is your *main* motive in writing your paper, at least at the moment?

1. **To explore.** You pose the question *because* you're unsure of the answer. This is what draws you to the topic. You're most interested in writing an essay, not a paper; that is, you want to write about what you found out in your research, and what you've come to believe is the best or truest answer to the question you pose. Your essay will have a thesis, but it will probably surface toward the end of the paper rather than at the beginning. This

is what I would call a *research essay* rather than a research paper, and it's the most open-ended form for academic inquiry.

2. **To argue.** You know you have a lot to learn about your topic, but you have a very strong hunch—or maybe even a strong conviction—about what the answer to your research question might be. Your initial purpose in writing the paper embraces your readers as well as yourself. You want to affect what they think, and even how they behave. Your thesis is a statement—*Muslim religious schools in Pakistan are not to blame for Islamic extremism*—that you can probably roughly articulate at the beginning of your project. It may very well change as you learn more, but when you write your paper, your purpose is to state a central claim and make it convincing. Frequently that claim is stated near the beginning of the paper.

3. **To analyze.** Some researchers collect data, examine it closely, and see how closely it conforms to what they initially thought to be true. They begin with a theory. Maybe you have a theory, too, and you want to test it by collecting information to see if you're right. For instance, you're doing field research on the culture of 15-year-old girls at a local school, focusing particularly on those on the social margins. Your theory is that a lot of these girls suffer from depression, and your interviews will provide information that you can analyze to discover if that's true. While you may not consider yourself much of a theorist, you are developing theories all the time about the way things are. This paper is a chance to test one of them using information you collect from your sources.

EXERCISE 1.7

Research Proposal

This is an important moment in the research process. How well you've crafted your research question will significantly influence the success of your project. You can change your mind later, but for now, jot down a brief proposal that outlines your research plan in your research notebook or to turn in to your instructor. It should include the following:

1. Focusing question
2. Primary purpose
   - *Explore:* What are additional questions that most interest you and might help you discover the answers to your research question?

Methods for Focusing Your Paper: An Example

A clear, narrow research question is the one thing that will give you the most traction when trying to get your research project moving. It's also one of the hardest steps in the process. Like gulping air after a dive into the deep end of a pool, our natural instinct at the beginning of a research project is to inhale too much of our subject. We go after the big question—why is poverty a problem?—and quickly wonder why we are submerged in information, struggling to find a direction. That's why I've spent so much time on a range of methods to craft a workable research question.

Here's an example of how one student used some of these approaches to satisfy both her general curiosity about the origins of terrorism and her need to write an essay about it that would be interesting, specific, and manageable over a five-week period. Helen used the *time, person, place,* and *story* methods as a means of refining her research question (see "Other Ways to Narrow Your Subject" on page 550). Any one of these questions would be a good starting place for her inquiry into terrorism.

Topic: Terrorism

Opening Question: What is the cause of terrorism by Islamic extremists?

1. Time as a Focusing Device—What might be the historical roots of Islamic extremism during the first jihad in the 7th century?

2. Person as a Focusing Device—Did President Jimmy Carter's policies in the Middle East contribute to the radicalization of some Islamic groups?

3. Place as a Focusing Device—Have Islamic religious schools in Pakistan contributed to the extremist thought and the radicalization of Muslim activists?

4. Story as a Focusing Device—What might the story of Shehzad Tanweer, one of the men who allegedly participated in the 2005 London bombings, reveal about how young men are radicalized?

- *Argue:* What is your tentative main claim or thesis?
- *Analyze:* What theory about your topic are you testing?
3. What, if any, prior beliefs, assumptions, preconceptions, ideas, or prejudices do you bring to this project? What personal experiences may have shaped the way you feel?

Reading for Research

EXERCISE 1.8

Ways of Reading to Write

1. Complete the following sentence in your journal or notebook:
   *The most important thing about **reading** for a research paper is*

   _____.

2. The following passage is from the opening chapter of John Yount's wonderful novel, *Trapper's Last Shot.* It's a pretty startling scene, powerfully narrated. Read the excerpt, and then in your journal compose an explanation of how you interpret the purpose of this scene as an opening to the novel. What themes and feelings does it seem to introduce that you predict might be central to the rest of the story? Don't forget to use specific passages from the excerpt to support your assertions.

   Chapter One

   The summer of 1960 was hot and dry in Cocke County, Georgia. No rain fell from the second week in June through the entire month of July. The loblolly pines turned yellow in the drought. The grass scorched and withered in the fields, and bare patches of red clay earth began to appear and to crack and cake in the sun like the bottoms of dried up lakes. The first day of August some clouds drifted in from the mountains in Tennessee and the Carolinas, and the air grew still and heavy, and for a while a thin rain fell as warm as sweat. But before the rain had quite stopped, the sun came out again, and steam began to rise from the fields and woods, from the dirt roads and concrete slab highways, and the countryside cooked like so many vegetables in a pot.

   The next day five boys started out to go swimming in the south fork of the Harpeth River. Except for a thin crust like a pastry shell over the pink dust, there was no evidence of the rain. As they walked toward the river, the heat droned and shimmered in the fields, and locusts sprang up before them to chitter away and drop down and then spring up again as they came on. When they got among the trees on the river bank, the oldest of them, who was fourteen, shucked quickly out of his britches and ran down the bank and out on a low sycamore limb and, without breaking stride, tucked up his legs and did a cannonball into the water. The surface all around, even to the farthest edge, roiled when he hit as if the pool were alive, but they didn't see the snakes at first. The boy's face was white as bleached bone when he came up. "God," he said to them, "don't come in!" And though it was no more than a whisper, they all heard. He seemed to struggle and wallow and make pitifully small headway though he was a strong swimmer. When he got in waist deep water, they could see the snakes hanging on him, dozens of them, biting and holding on. He was already staggering and crying in a thin, wheezy voice, and he brushed and slapped at the snakes trying to knock them off. He got almost to the bank before he fell, and though they wanted to help him, they couldn't keep from backing away. But he didn't need them then. He tried only a little while to get up before the movement of his arms and legs lost purpose, and he began to shudder and then to stiffen and settle out. One moccasin, pinned under his chest, struck his cheek again and again, but they could see he didn't know it, for there was only the unresponsive bounce of flesh.

From the novel *Trapper's Last Shot* by John Yount.

3. The following is an excerpt from an academic article on how college students think about their own masculinity. Obviously, this differs in many ways from the piece you just read. Your aim here is to carefully read the passage and write a summary of the author's main idea(s) based on your understanding of the text. A summary, you'll recall, is a brief capsulation of the important ideas in a much longer text. Write this summary in your journal and be prepared to share it with others in the class.

   Researchers' understanding of identity formation is commonly attributed to Erikson's (1968) developmental theory. According to Erikson, individuals gain a sense of who they are by confronting a universal sequence of challenges or crises (e.g., trust, intimacy, etc.) throughout their lives. Marcia (1966) operationalized Erikson's original theory and similarly suggested that identity formation is the most important goal of adolescence. Marcia viewed identity development as a process of experiencing a series of crises with one's ascribed childhood identity and subsequently emerging with new commitments. That is, as individuals consider new ideas that are in conflict with earlier conceptions, they weigh possibilities, potentially experiment with alternatives, and eventually choose commitments that become the core of a newly wrought identity. Individuals avoiding the process altogether, neither experiencing crises nor making commitments, are in a state of identity diffusion. Individuals may also be somewhere between these two possibilities by either simply maintaining a parentally derived ideology (foreclosed) or actively by experimenting with and resolving identity-related questions prior to commitment (moratorium).*

4. After you've completed the preceding three steps, spend some time fastwriting in your journal your responses to some of the following questions. These will also be discussed in class.
   - Did your approach to reading the two excerpts differ? How?
   - What are your "typical" reading strategies. Did you use them here?
   - What are your typical reading "behaviors," things such as underlining, highlighting, marginal notes, rereading, and so on? Would they vary with each excerpt?
   - To what extent did you take your own advice in your answer to Step 1 of this exercise;

The most important thing about reading for a research paper is

_____?

   - The two excerpts are clearly different kinds of writing—one is literary and the other academic. They're also different *forms* of writing. What are the key differences between them?
   - What problems did you encounter when you read these excerpts? How did you solve them?

Reading Rhetorically

We all learned to read in school, but we probably never really learned how to read *rhetorically*. Reading rhetorically means selecting particular reading strategies that are most effective in certain situations and for certain purposes and applying them. In high school, much of the writing about reading you may have done was in English class, writing critical essays about novels, poems, or short stories. In many ways, reading to write about a novel or a short story is quite different from reading to write research essays, something you may have discovered in

*T. L. Davis, "Voices of Gender Role Conflict: The Social Construction of College Men's Masculinity," *Journal of College Student Development* 43: 508–521.

Exercise 1.8. For one thing, there are very basic differences between a literary text and a research article. In a short story, the author's purpose may be *implicit*; you have to "read into" the evidence provided in a narrative to make some interpretation about its meaning. An academic article, on the other hand, is *explicit*. The author states his or her conclusions rather than inviting the reader to make a reasoned interpretation. In addition, academic writing, like the second excerpt in Exercise 1.8, uses specialized language and conventions—terms, references, evidence, and organizing principles that the people for whom the article was intended (usually other experts in the field) can understand. Stories have their own internal logic and language, but these are usually accessible to most readers even if the meaning is not.

Finally, we usually enjoy the *experience* of reading a story, or at least feel something in response to a good one, but we usually read articles with a much more practical purpose in mind: to acquire information.

Shouldn't the fundamental differences between these types of texts mean that the *way* we read them is also different? I think so. But we rarely think about our reading strategies, pretty much resorting to reading the way we always have in school. Maybe you never highlight, or maybe the pages you read are fields plowed with yellow rows. Maybe you make marginal notes when you read, or maybe you never write a thing. Maybe you always read everything just once, or maybe you read a text many times to make sure you understand it. Maybe you always read every word, or maybe you skim like a flat rock on smooth water. Whatever your reading practices, becoming aware of them is a first step to reading strategically.

Reading Like an Outsider

Why spend precious time thinking about your reading process? For the same reason this course focuses on the writing process: By becoming aware of *how* you do things that have become habits, you exercise more control over them. In many ways, this book is about challenging old habits and assumptions about research, and this includes approaches to reading when you have to write a research essay. For example, consider what's unique about this situation:

- In a general sense, you're just reading to collect information. But researchers use what they read in some particular ways: to provide support for their ideas, to create a context for the questions they're asking, and to complicate or extend their thinking.

- College research often requires students to read the specialized discourses of fields they're not familiar with. That means they must struggle with jargon and conventions that make reading particularly difficult.

■ Typically, the purpose of the research paper is not to report, but to explore, argue, or analyze. Information is in the service of the writer's own ideas about a topic.

■ In some classes (though probably not this one), the main audience for the research essay is an expert in the subject the writer is exploring.

In a way, the student researcher has to read like an outsider—or as essayist Scott Russell Sanders put it, "an amateur's raid in a world of specialists." What does this suggest about your reading strategy? First, it makes sense to develop a working knowledge of your topic *before* you tackle the more scholarly stuff. Research in reading suggests that knowledge of a subject makes a big difference in comprehension and retention of information. Second, your own purposes should firmly guide what you read and how you read it. Mentally juggle at least the three purposes I mentioned earlier—reading for example, for context, and for challenge. Third, anticipate your own resistance to the scholarly writing that seems "boring." It's boring because you're an outsider and haven't broken the code. The more you read in your subject area, the more you'll understand; the learning curve is steep. Fourth, in scholarly writing especially, quickly learn the organizing principles of the articles. For example, in the social sciences, articles often have *abstracts, introductions, methods,* and *discussion* sections. Each provides particular kinds of information that might be useful to you. It often isn't necessary to read an academic article from beginning to end. And finally, the most important thing: Read with a pen in your hand. In the next chapter, I'll introduce you to some notetaking strategies that encourage you to use writing to think about what you're reading *as* you're reading it. Write-to-learn activities such as fastwriting can help you take possession of information and help you write a stronger paper.

Reading Strategies for Research Writers

■ First develop a working knowledge.
■ Let your own purposes guide: example, context, challenge.
■ Anticipate your own resistance.
■ Learn the organizing principles of articles.
■ Read with a pen in your hand.

CHAPTER 2

The Second Week

Developing a Research Strategy

A few years ago, I wanted a pair of good birding binoculars for my birthday. I thought of the local store that seemed to carry the largest selection of binoculars, went down there, and within twenty minutes or so spent about $300 on some Swift binoculars, a brand that is highly regarded by wildlife watchers. Did you ever notice that is often *after* your purchase when you're most motivated to seek out information that reinforces your decision to buy something? Within days of buying the Swifts, I searched the Internet just to make certain that the model I bought was the one recommended by most birders. Sure enough, that seemed to be the case. Then I casually checked the prices on the binoculars, quite certain that I made a fairly good deal on them. To my horror I discovered that I had paid about $100 more than I had to.

Sometimes having no research strategy costs more than time.

A research essay is time consuming and, although you aren't risking money, the quality of your paper may make a big difference in your final grade. Your time and your grade are two reasons that it pays to be thoughtful about *how* you approach gathering and using information. A typical "strategy" is something like this: (1) get the assignment, (2) choose a topic, (3) wait until a few days before the paper is due, (4) madly search the Internet, (5) write the paper the night before you have to hand it in, (5) pray.

In fact, you've already approached this paper more strategically. In the last chapter, you spent time exploring possible topics, narrowing your focus, and developing research questions that will help guide your search for information. This will make a big difference in the efficiency of your research in the library and the Web. But what do experienced researchers know that will help you find what you're looking for fast, and use what you find effectively? Here's what you will learn this week:

1. A chronology for the search
2. How to control the language of your searches to get the best results
3. Advanced searching techniques for the library and the Web, and other sources of information including surveys and interviews
4. Evaluating what you find
5. Notetaking methods that will help you to begin writing your essay even before you begin the draft

Google vs. the Library

Despite all the fat, the carbs, and the empty calories, the convenience of a Big Mac is hard to ignore. Similarly, a few minutes feasting on the information served up by Google is far more convenient than searching an online database at the university library. Actually *going* there seems, well, out of the question. As one analyst put it recently, "Googling has become synonymous with research." Another called the relentless feast of online information "infobesity."

Should we be wringing our hands about this? The answer is yes, and no. The power and accessibility of Google and other Internet search tools has turned virtually everyone into a researcher. No question is too arcane, no quest completely hopeless when typing a few words into a search window allows you to lurch through millions of documents in a second. It's really hard to understate the wonder of this. Along with the junk, the results of Internet searches often turn up something useful, even for an academic paper. In fact, at least one study* suggests that when Google searches are matched with searches on library databases, the popular search engine doesn't do too badly. When researchers looked for relevant documents on four test topics, they found a total of 723 relevant sources. Google produced 237 of these, and the library databases turned up 163. Predictably, however, the documents from the library were generally a much higher quality—they were from more qualified sources, more up-to-date, more balanced,

---

*Jan Brophy and David Bawden. "Is Google Enough? Comparison of an Internet Search Engine with Academic Library Sources," *Aslib Proceedings: New Information Perspectives* 57 (2005): 498–512.

and more accurate. Still, while Google produced more stinkers, researchers concluded that 52 percent of its results were actually pretty good.

Undoubtedly, it's Google's accessibility that makes it so irresistible. In addition to avoiding a hike to the library or sorting through academic databases online, Google gives you results you can often find and use immediately. In the Google matchup with the library, 90 percent of the documents produced by the popular search engine were instantly accessible, full-text articles, while the library fared less well—only 65 percent of those results were full-text. In some cases, getting an article on a library database required interlibrary loan or a microfilm search.

Yet for all Google's appeal, in academic writing *quality matters.* A lot. You must always try to use accurate sources that are written by people who know what they're talking about. For those kinds of sources, your library is indispensable. The dilemma here is this: Do you value the accessibility of an Internet search above the quality of the library sources? At first, not many of my students struggle with this. Google wins, hands down. But savvy researchers know that's like juggling with one hand—you're making it much harder than it needs to be. In academic research, you need as much relevant, accurate information as you can get. The answer, obviously, is to learn how you can *complement* your Google searches with library searches.

A Complementary Research Strategy

Writers are always better off when they work from abundance. It is far better to have more information than you can use since this allows you to understand your subject more deeply and focus your investigation more narrowly. Attack your research question on multiple fronts—the Internet, the library, and interviews or surveys—and you're much more likely to succeed in finding out what you want to know (see Figure 2.1). This inclusive approach will help you accomplish the three things that make up a sound search strategy.

FIGURE 2.1   Maximize coverage of quality sources by investigating on three fronts.

1. Find *sufficient* information to fully explore a narrowly focused topic.
2. Find *varied* sources.
3. Find *quality* information.

Find Sufficient Information by Using the Best Search Terms

Around our house a few years back, the Harry Potter phenomenon had everyone muttering magic words. "Flipendo," said Julia, trying to turn the dog into a gerbil. "Wingardium leviosa," said Becca, who was determined to elevate her little sister six feet off the ground. Chopsticks substituted for magic wands. I knew this because we suddenly had too few when the take-out Chinese meal arrived; that was the only part of this magical revival that swept the household that I didn't much like.

Some writers foolishly think that there's magic involved in getting good words to the page when it's really much more simple and not at all mysterious: You have to have your seat in the chair and your fingers on the keyboard or curled around a pen. But there is a kind of magic you can perform as a researcher, and it also involves the right words uttered in the right order. *How* you phrase your search of a library database or the World Wide Web makes an enormous difference in the results. I've come to believe that this ability, almost more than any other, is the researcher's most important skill.

Controlled Language Searches Using Library of Congress Subject Headings

One of the things that is so good about libraries compared to the Web is that information there is organized. That's the good news. The bad news is that there is so much information to organize that librarians had to develop a special language for searching it. It's not alien language—the words are familiar—but it is a language that requires that certain words be used in the combinations that librarians use to organize information. These are *controlled language searches,* and they are much more common in the library than on the Web.

Skilled researchers who want to know what words to use in a library search turn to the *Library of Congress Subject Headings.* This five-volume book is in your library's reference room. The *LSCH,* also known as "the big red books," is a little-appreciated but incredibly useful catalog of the standard headings used by most librarians to index information (see Figure 2.2).

Subject heading in boldface. The notation "(May Subd Geog)" indicates that a subject may also be subdivided according to geographic location (e.g., Animal Rights—United States).

UF *stands for "used for." It lists less suitable terms for the same subject.*	**Animal rights** *(May Subd Geog) [HV4701-HV4959]* Here are entered works on the inherent rights attributed to animals. Works on the protection and treatment of animals are entered under Animal welfare.
	  UF Animal liberation
	    Animals' rights
	    Rights of animals
		When subjects correspond to Library of Congress (LC) class numbers (i.e., number classifications by subject areas), they are included here. These numbers can be very helpful if you just want to browse the shelves for books. Scope notes are sometimes added to explain headings.

BT *means "broader term," NT means "narrower term."*	BT Animal welfare—
	  Moral and ethical
	  aspects
	—Law and legislation
	  USE Animal welfare—
	  Law and legislation	

USE *is a code that lists the standard LC term under one that is not standard.*	—**Religious aspects**
	——**Baptists,**
	    [Catholic Church,
	    etc.]
	——**Buddhism,**
	    [Christianity, etc.]
	Animal running
	  USE Animal locomotion
	Animal sculptors
	  (May Subd Geog)
	  UF Animaliers
	  BT Sculptors
	    Zoological artists
		Subdivisions of the main subject heading, also in boldface.

FIGURE 2.2   There's no need to guess what subject headings to use when searching on your topic. The *Library of Congress Subject Headings* will get you off to the right start. Here a student looking for sources on animal liberation will discover that "Animal rights" is the heading to use.

Locate your topic in the book. You might begin by imagining a subject within which your topic probably falls, looking up that subject in the *LSCH,* and then finding a good match among the many subheadings listed. Look for the abbreviation BT, or "broader term," to see if you might be redirected to a more appropriate subject heading. Look especially at the NT, or "narrower term" listing. That may lead you to an appropriate description of the topic you've chosen.

As you're perusing the *Library of Congress Subject Headings*, get a sense of how your subject area is broken down. What are some other topics or subtopics within the area of knowledge you're considering? Do any sound more interesting? Are there other trails you might want to follow?

You want to save these *LSCH* terms for your topic for later. These will help you know the words to use when you search the library's online book index and many of the library's periodical databases. Essentially, you've just had a language lesson that allows you to speak "libraryese"—the words that will help you find information more directly and quickly.

Boolean Searching

Frequently, you'll be searching using a *combination* of keywords. For example, searching for books using the word "Wildfires" will produce an avalanche that will quickly bury you. Efficient research requires that you maximize the number of relevant results and minimize the number of irrelevant ones. That's where searches that use careful combinations of keywords are so important. Many libraries and some Internet search engines use something called "Boolean" connectors to help you do this when you search databases. George Boole, a British logician, invented the system more than a hundred years ago, and it still dominates library searching (it's somewhat less widespread on the Web).

The system essentially requires the use of the words AND, OR, and NOT between the search terms or keywords. The word AND, say, between the "Animal" and "Rights" will search a database for documents that include *both* of those terms.

The use of the connector OR between search terms, obviously, will produce a list of documents that contain either of the terms. That can be a lot of results. Sometimes by simply putting two words together, "Animal Rights," the OR is implied and you'll get the same results as if you used the word. This is often true when using a Web search engine.

The NOT connector is less frequently used but really can be quite helpful if you want to *exclude* certain documents. Suppose, for example, you were interested in researching the problem of homelessness in Washington State, where you live. To avoid getting information on Washington D.C., where it's also a problem, use the connector NOT.

Homeless AND Washington NOT D.C.

As you can see from the example above, it's possible to use the connectors between a number of terms, not just two. In fact, the art of creating keyword searches is using both the right words (those used by librarians) in the right combination (those that in combination sufficiently narrow your search and give you the best results).

One final search technique that can be very useful, especially in library searches, is something called "nesting." This involves the use of parentheses around two or more terms in a phrase. This prompts the computer to look for those terms first. For example, suppose you were searching for articles on the ethics of animal rights, but you were particularly interested in information in two states, Idaho and Montana. You might construct a search phrase like this one:

(Montana OR Idaho) AND animal AND rights AND ethics

Magic Words on the World Wide Web

In the last chapter, you did a subject search on the Web, using popular sites such as The Virtual Library that specialize in those kinds of searches. Far more common are searches that use so-called search engines such as Google. As you probably know, these are really quite remarkable software programs that in a split second "crawl" the Web, searching for documents that contain the keywords you type in. Lately, the magic of these search engines has been tarnished a bit by commercialism, allowing advertisers to purchase priority listings in search engine results and not always making that fact obvious to the searcher. But these search engines are still essential and getting better all the time.

Keyword searches are the most common methods of searching the Web. Unfortunately, there isn't consistency in search languages used by the many search engines available for scouring the Web. Some permit Boolean searching. Some use a variation on Boolean that involves symbols rather than words. But Google, the giant of search engines, has made all of this a bit simpler by providing a search form in which you simply enter the words or phrases that define your search (see Figure 2.3). You can find this when you click on the "Advanced Search" link, something that most student researchers rarely do.

FIGURE 2.3 Google's Advanced Search page makes it easy to take advantage of multiple search terms that will focus your query and produce better results.

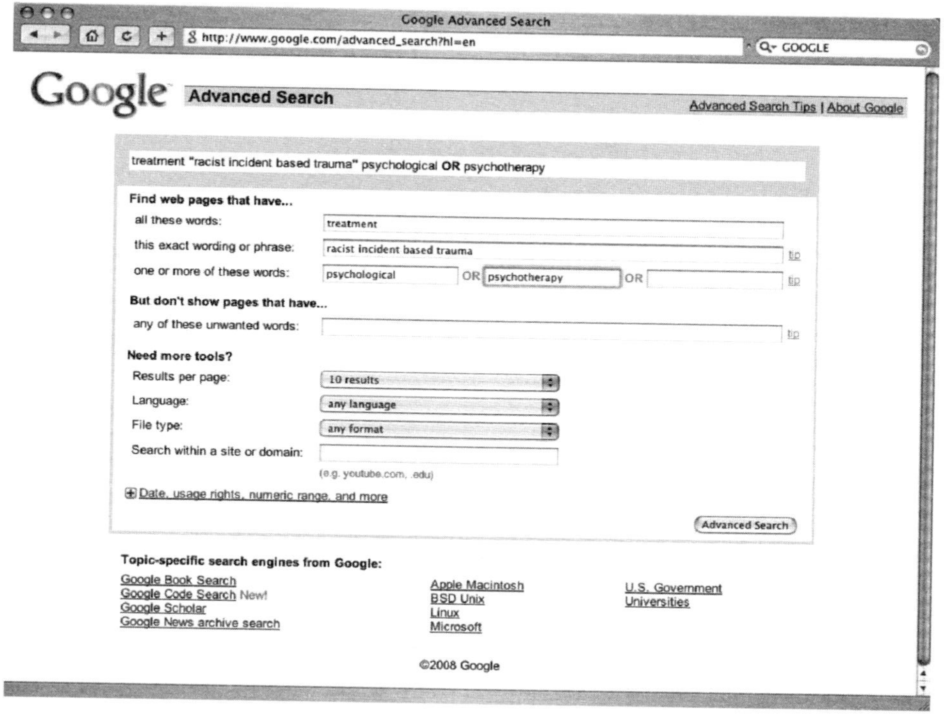

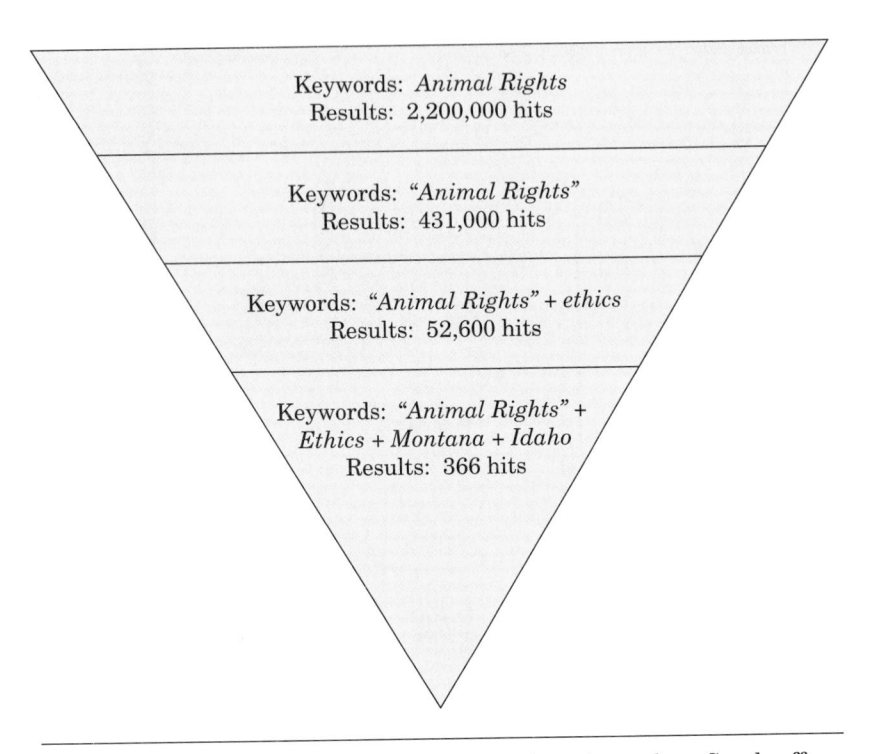

FIGURE 2.4   Effects of Keyword Elaboration. A search on Google offers dramatically different numbers of results as the keywords are refined and elaborated on. Whenever possible use three or more terms to narrow your results.

Because of the mind-boggling amount of information on the Web, careful keyword searches are critical. Researchers waste more online time either not finding what they wanted or sifting through layers and layers of irrelevant documents because of thoughtless keyword searches. For example, notice in Figure 2.4 how the search on the ethics of animal rights can be dramatically changed by adding terms. An initial search on Google simply using the broad keywords "animal rights" produced 2.2 million documents. Using quotations marks to search for only documents that include that phrase, along with three additional terms, winnowed those results to 366 hits, many of which will be relevant.

Find Varied Sources

One of the first things I notice when I'm reading research essay drafts is whether the writer leans too heavily on a single source. Does this author or article keep reappearing, again and again on page after page, like a pigeon at a favorite roost? This is not good. It

What Studies Say about How Students Research Online

- Most use a trial-and-error approach to searching.
- They rarely use anything more than basic searches, avoiding advanced searching features.
- Typically, they only use two search terms every session, and these search sessions last an average of 15–19 minutes.
- Only 8 percent use Boolean operators.
- 60 percent admit that they are overwhelmed by the amount of information available to them.
- Nearly three quarters use the Internet rather than the library.

typically means that the writer has too few sources and must keep turning to these few, or one source is especially relevant to the topic or the research question and the writer can't resist repeated invitations for the author to reappear.

Vary your sources. This not only means using a sufficient number so that your essay is informative but using different *kinds* of sources whenever you can.

In part, the kinds of sources you rely on in preparing your paper depend on your topic. Sandra has chosen as her tentative focusing question, *How has the Kosovo conflict influenced the way war crimes are prosecuted?* Because Sandra's topic addresses public policy and current events, she'll likely find a wealth of information in newspapers and magazines but not much in books. She certainly should check the academic indexes on this topic—a database called PAIS, or Public Affairs Information System, would be a good bet—because it's likely that political scientists have something to say on the subject. Pat's working on a piece about the debate over the use of "water-boarding" by U.S. officials when interrogating suspected terrorists. He may rely more heavily on opinion pieces by commentators on the political left and right than on more objective studies, and because it's a current topic he will probably find much of his information on the Internet.

There are several ways to think about how sources can be distinguished from each other.

- Are they primary or secondary sources?
- Are they objective or subjective?
- Are they stable or unstable?

Primary vs. Secondary Sources

One way of looking at information is to determine whether it's a *primary* or a *secondary* source. A primary source presents the original words of a writer—his speech, poem, eyewitness account, letter, interview, autobiography. A secondary source analyzes somebody else's work. Whenever possible, choose a primary source over a secondary one, since the primary source is likely to be more accurate and authoritative.

The subject you research will determine the kinds of primary sources you encounter. For example, if you're writing a paper on a novelist, then his novels, stories, letters, and interviews are primary sources. A topic on the engineering of the Chicago River in 1900, a partly historical subject, might lead to a government report on the project or a firsthand account of its construction in a Chicago newspaper. Primary sources for a paper in the sciences might be findings from an experiment or observations. For a paper in business, marketing information or technical studies might be primary sources. A videotape of a theatrical performance is a primary source, while the reviews in the local newspaper are secondary sources.

Objective vs. Subjective

For now, I'm going to sidestep the debate over whether *any* source can be fully objective and simply point out that, generally speaking, we can divide all sources into those that attempt to report facts that have been gathered systematically, minimizing author bias, and those that don't pretend to be anything more than the author's opinion, perhaps supported by evidence gleaned from objective sources. You can probably guess some examples of objective sources: experiments, survey results, carefully designed studies of many kinds. The best of these are "peer reviewed" (see page 574) to double-check their accuracy. As you know, many academics prize these objective sources as the best evidence. Subjective sources are all over the map. Imagine a continuum in which on one end are advertisements and on the other are research essays like the one you're working on, a project that reflects your own ideas about a topic based on what you discover others have said. Ads, of course, typically have little or no information and often make claims without supporting evidence. In the middle there are blogs, radio essays, newspaper op-ed pieces, popular nonfiction books, and so on.

You might assume that objective sources are always better. But there are many occasions when it makes perfect sense to draw on a subjective source. It depends, as always, on the topic. If your research question is related to a public controversy—say, the accuracy of claims that a certain product will make your teeth whiter— then you will undoubtedly cite these claims in your essay. When you do use subjective sources, however, you must try to make it clear in your work what the nature of the bias might be. Is the author a right-wing commentator, an environmentalist, a spokesperson for a special interest?

Stable or Unstable?

When information went digital, a new phenomenon emerged— sometimes the information would just simply disappear. That Web page that you cited in your draft with the great statistics on scooter fatalities is there one day and gone the next. Since one of the reasons why you cite sources in academic writing is that readers can consult a writer's sources, that missing Web page is a serious problem. Disappearing Web pages, of course, are hard to predict, but you can make some judgments about the stability of an online source. Has it been around for a long time? Is it routinely updated? Are print versions of an online document available? Is the site associated with a reputable institution?

Find Quality Sources

The aim of your research strategy is not only to find interesting information on your topic but also to find it in *authoritative* sources. What are these? The highest quality sources are those types found on the bottom of the pyramid (see Figure 2.5). These are works that are most likely to be written by and then reviewed by experts in their field. You find these "peer-reviewed" articles in scholarly journals, some of which are now available online as well as in the library. The downside of dealing with sources at the bottom of the authoritative pyramid is that they may be written in the *discourse* of the field; to you that will make it seem as if the writing is jargon-filled and hard to follow. Of course, as a nonspecialist you aren't the intended audience for the work. But if you can glean some useful information, facts, or ideas from journal articles—and you usually can—your essay will draw on the best sources available on the topic.

When Was It Published?

If you're researching the treatment of slaves in nineteenth-century New Orleans, then currency is obviously less of an issue

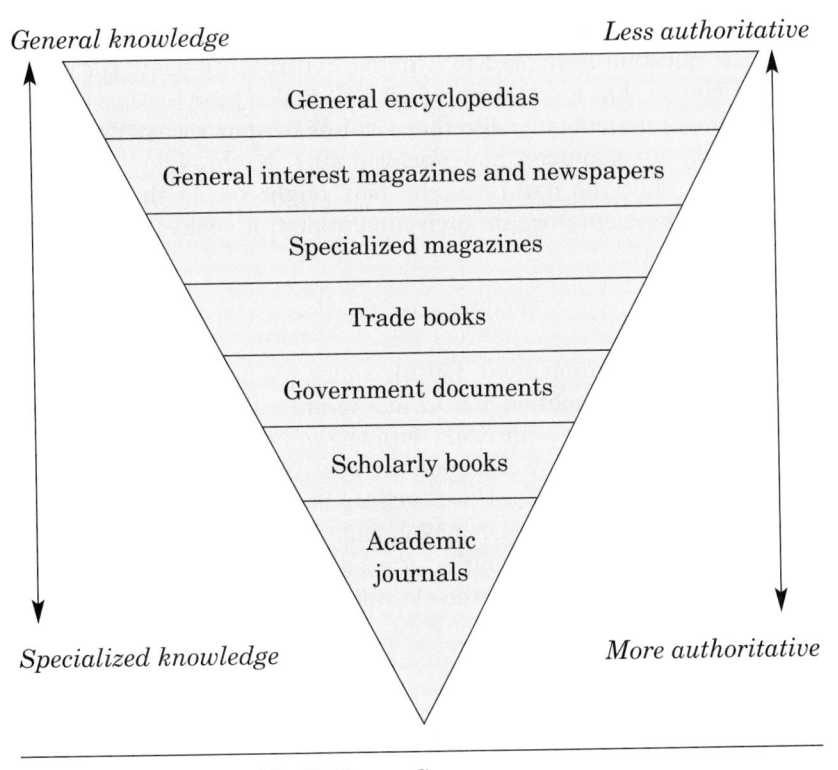

FIGURE 2.5   Pyramid of Library Sources

than it might be if your project were to explore the impact of the Toyota Prius on marketing practices for hybrid vehicles. Generally, in any project related to the social sciences, a recent publication date carries more weight, which is one reason that the APA citations emphasize date of publication. The currency of Web pages and online documents can also be important. A site that is regularly updated is obviously more likely to have the latest information on the topic.

Why Journal Articles Are Better Than Magazine Articles

If your topic has been covered by academic journal articles, rely heavily on these sources if you can. An article on, say, suicide among college students in a magazine like *Time* is less valuable than one in the *American Journal of Psychology*. Granted, the latter may be harder to read, but you're much more likely to learn something from a journal article because it's written by an expert and is usually narrowly focused. Also, because academic articles are carefully documented, you may be able to mine bibliographies for additional sources. And finally, scholarly work, such as that published in academic journals and books (usually published by university presses), is especially authoritative because it's subject to peer review. That means that every manuscript submitted for publication is reviewed by other authorities in the field, who scrutinize the author's evidence, methods, and arguments. Those articles that end up being published have truly passed muster.

Look for Often-Cited Authors

As you make your way through information on your topic, pay attention to names of authors whose works you often encounter or who are frequently mentioned in bibliographies. These individuals are often the best scholars in the field, and it will be useful to become familiar with their work and use it, if possible, in your paper. If an author's name keeps turning up, use it as another term for searching the card catalog library databases, or Google Scholar. Doing so might yield new sources you wouldn't necessarily encounter in other ways.

Not All Books Are Alike

When writing my high school research reports, I thought that a book was always the best source because, well, books are thick, and anyone who could write that much on any one subject probably knows what she's talking about. Naive, I know.

One of the things college teaches is *critical thinking*—the instinct to pause and consider before rushing to judgment. I've learned not to automatically believe in the validity of what an author is saying (as you shouldn't for this author), even if she did write a thick book about it.

If your topic lends itself to using primarily books as sources, then evaluate the authority of each before deciding to use it in your paper. This is especially important if your paper relies heavily on one particular book. Consider the following:

- Is the book written for a general audience or more knowledgeable readers?
- Is the author an acknowledged expert in the field?
- Is there a bibliography? Is the information carefully documented?
- How was the book received by critics? To find out quickly, search the Web with the author or title of the book using one of the academic search engines listed on page 544 in Chapter 1.

What Does "Peer Reviewed" Mean?

Broadly speaking, periodicals, books, Web sites, and magazines are one of two types: scholarly or popular. Popular publications include magazines like *Newsweek* or online sites like *Slate,* which are staff-written, usually by nonexperts for a more general audience. Scholarly publications are written and edited by experts for others in their fields, and the best of these are "peer reviewed." This means that before an article is published online or in print, a group of fellow experts read and comment on its validity, argument, factual accuracy, and so on. The article doesn't appear in print until this review is completed and the journal editor is satisfied that the other scholars think the work is respectable.

What does this mean to you? It means that you can count on the authoritative muscle of a peer-reviewed source to help you make a strong point in your paper.

Evaluating Online Sources

Librarians are gatekeepers protecting order, stability, and quality of information in the library. By comparison, the Internet is anarchy. Everyone knows that you have to be vigilant about trusting the accuracy, balance, and reliability of Web documents. Unfortunately, there's continuing evidence that student researchers still have a hard time assessing the quality of online sources. While many of the criteria for evaluating sources just mentioned apply equally to Web documents, they deserve special attention.

Here are some general guidelines to follow. Later I'll suggest a more vigorous approach for evaluating online sources:

■ *Always keep your purpose in mind.* For example, if you're exploring the lobbying methods of the National Rifle Association, then you will want to hear, and see, what this organization has to say on its Web site, knowing full well that this is not an unbiased source. The NRA Web pages are, however, both relevant and authoritative in this instance. After all, who knows more about the NRA than the NRA?

■ *Favor governmental and educational sources over commercial ones.* There are plenty of exceptions to this (like the one just mentioned), but in general you're wise to rely more heavily on material sponsored by groups without a commercial stake in your topic. How can you tell the institutional affiliation of sources? Sometimes it's obvious. They tell you. But when it's not obvious, the *domain name* provides a clue. The *.com* that follows a server name signifies a commercial site, while *.edu, .org,* or *.gov* usually signals an educational, nonprofit, or governmental entity. The absence of ads on a Web site also implies a site that is noncommercial.

■ *Favor authored documents over those without authors.* There's a simple reason for this: You can check the credentials of an author. You can do this by sending an e-mail message to him or her, a convenience often available as a link on a Web page, or you can do a quick search with the name on library indexes to see if that author has published other books or articles on your topic. If writers are willing to put their names on a document, they might be more careful about the accuracy and fairness of what they say.

■ *Favor documents that are also available in print over those only available online.* These might be articles that have appeared in magazines or newspapers or even journals. They might be conference reports or studies or even books. Sources that are published in more than one medium may be more credible because they undergo more scrutiny.

■ *Favor Web pages that have been recently updated over those that haven't been changed in a year or more.* Frequently at the bottom of a Web page there is a line indicating when the information was posted to the Internet and/or when it was last updated. Look for it.

■ *Favor Web sources that document their claims over those that don't.* Most Web documents won't feature a bibliography. That doesn't mean that they're useless to you, but be suspicious of a Web author who makes factual assertions without supporting evidence.

A Key to Evaluating Internet Sources.   As an undergraduate, I was a botany major. Among other things, I was drawn to plant taxonomy because the step-by-step taxonomic keys for discovering the names of unfamiliar plants gave the vegetative chaos of a Wisconsin meadow or upland forest a beautiful kind of logic and order. The key that follows is modeled after the ones I used in field taxonomy, but this one is a modest attempt to make some sense of the chaos on the Web for the academic researcher, particularly when the usual approaches for establishing the authority of traditional scholarship and publications fail. For one thing, many Internet documents are anonymous, and the date of publication isn't always clear. In some cases, even if there is an author of an online document, his or her affiliation or credentials may not be apparent.

If you're not sure whether a particular Web document will give your essay credibility, see Figure 2.6 and work through the following steps:

1. Does the document have an author or authors? If *yes,* go to Step 2. If *no,* go to Step 10.

Authored Documents

2. Does the document appear in an online journal or magazine that is "refereed"? In other words, is there any indication that every article submitted must be reviewed by other scholars in the field before it is accepted for publication? If *yes,* you've found a good source. If *no* (or you're unsure), go to Step 3.

3. Is the document from a government source? If *yes,* then it may be a good source. If *no,* go to Step 4.

4. Does the document appear in an online publication affiliated with a reputable educational institution or organization? If *yes,* its likely to be trustworthy. If *no,* go to Step 5.

5. Is *the author* affiliated with a reputable educational institution or organization? (For example, is he or she connected with a large university or a national nonprofit organization? Individuals associated with businesses or special interest groups may be reliable, though researchers should be vigilant about whether they have axes to grind and qualify the information to make that clear.) If *yes,* be encouraged. If *no,* move on to Step 6.

6. If the author isn't clearly affiliated with a reputable institution, does he or she offer any credentials that help establish his or her expertise to write on the topic? (For example, an advanced degree in the relevant discipline is encouraging.) If *no,* go to Step 7.

7. Did you find the document on a Web site that has earned high marks from scholarly reviewers and others interested in the reliability of Internet information? *Yes?* Great. *No?* Move on to Step 8.

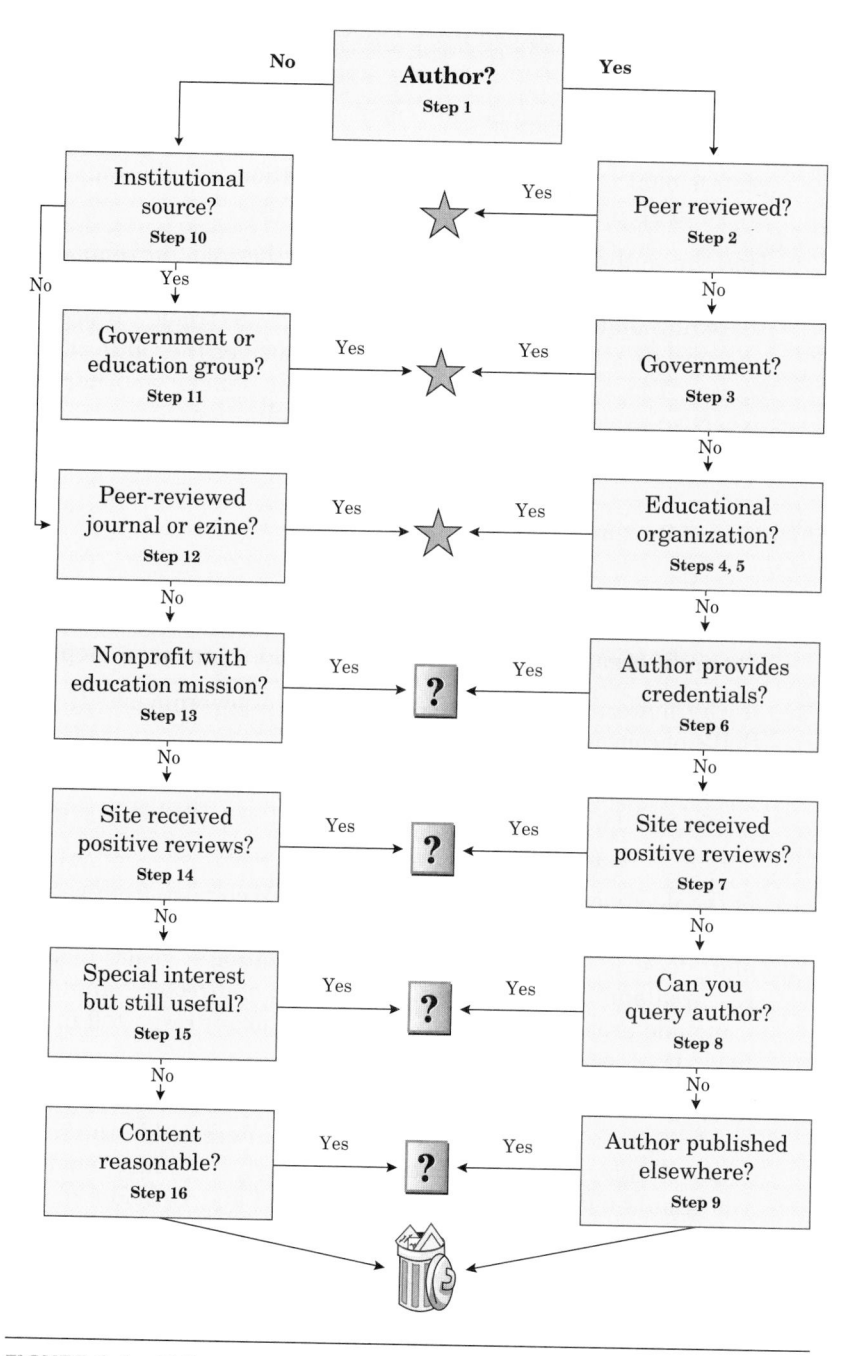

FIGURE 2.6 Follow the flowchart for a rigorous review of a Web document or page, beginning with whether the author is obvious or not. Sites that earn stars are generally more trustworthy. Those with question marks still may be useful, depending on the situation. Be particularly wary of information on commercial or special interest sites.

8. Does the author include an e-mail address link in the online document so that you can write to inquire about affiliations or professional credentials or other publications on the topic? If *no*, go to Step 9.

9. Has the author published elsewhere on the topic in reputable journals or other publications? Check this at the library by searching under the author's name in the electronic catalog or appropriate CD-ROM indexes. If *no*, reconsider the value of the source. You could be dealing with a lone ranger who has no expertise on your topic and no relevant affiliations.

Unauthored Documents

10. If the online document has no author, is it from an institutional source like a university, the state or federal government, or a nonprofit organization? If *yes*, go to Step 11. If *no*, go to Step 14.

11. Is the material from the federal or state government? If *yes*, that's encouraging. If *no*, go to Step 12.

12. Is the anonymous document published in an online journal or magazine? Is it refereed? (See Step 2.) If *yes*, it's likely a good source. If *no*, go to Step 13.

13. Is the document part of a publication or Web page from a non-government source whose mission is described in the document, and does it suggest that the organization's goals include research and education? Is there a board of directors, and does it include professionals and academics who are respected in the field? If *no*, go to Step 14.

14. Does the Web site in which the document is located get high marks from scholarly or other reviewers interested in the reliability of Internet information? If *no*, start to wonder whether you should use this source. Go to Steps 15 and 16 before giving up on it.

15. Even if the organization offering the information represents a special interest group or business with an axe to grind, the information may be useful as a means of presenting its point of view. Make sure, if you use it, that the information is qualified to make that obvious.

16. Do any of the usual criteria for evaluating a source apply to this anonymous document? Does it have a citations page, and do the

citations check out? Was it published on the Internet recently? Does the argument the writer is making seem sound? Do the facts check out? If the answer is *no* to all of the above, then don't trust the document. If you can answer *yes* to more than one of these questions, the material probably has marginal value in a college paper, though there might be exceptions.

A good researcher always takes a skeptical view of claims made in print; she should be even more wary of claims made in Internet documents. And while these approaches for evaluating online sources should help, it still can be pretty tricky deciding whom to take seriously in cyberspace. So to sort it all out, always ask yourself these questions: How important is this Internet document to my research? Do I really need it? Might there be a more reliable print version?

Developing Focused Knowledge

If working knowledge equips you to sustain a one-minute dinner conversation on your topic, then focused knowledge is enough for you to make a fifteen- or twenty-minute presentation to the rest of the class. You'll probably be able to answer all their questions, too. (See suggestions for class presentations on page 582 in the box, "Working Together: 'Could You Clarify, Mr. Ziegler?'"). You'll hardly be an expert, but you'll probably know a lot more about your topic than any of your peers.

Focused knowledge is the product of smart research this week and the next, refining your search terms, knowing where to look for the most useful information, and using your time efficiently. As you'll see later in this section, focused knowledge also depends on what you *do* with what you find. Are you able to not only collect information on your topic but think about its significance to your project? Remember that you'll be reading with at least three questions in mind:

1. Does this information help create a *context* for the question I'm posing?
   - Can it provide background on what has already been said about it, and who has said it?
   - Can it provide background on what is already known and when it was discovered?

- Can it provide background on why this is a question worth asking?
2. Does the information *support* or *develop* an idea or claim I'm making?
    - Is it evidence that what I'm saying might be true?
    - Does it help refine or qualify an idea I have about my topic?
3. Does this information *challenge* or *complicate* what I've been thinking about my topic?
    - Does it raise new questions I hadn't thought of?
    - Is it a point of view that is opposed to mine? If so, what do I think about it?
    - Does this change my thinking in some way?

What About a Thesis?

Ultimately, you must have something to say about your research question. But when should you know what that is?

Suspending Judgment?

Should you have a thesis or claim at this point? That depends on the purpose of your project. If it's exploratory, if your motive is to discover what you think, then it's too early to make any bold statements that answer the question you're researching. It might even be counterproductive. Inquiry-based investigations depend on your willingness to *suspend judgment* long enough to discover what you think.

What Do You Presume?

On the other hand, you might have a theory—some sense of the answer to your research question. We have theories all of the time, but we rarely test them against the evidence. I have a theory that every Labrador retriever I ever owned was a few cards short of a full hand in the intelligence department. Naturally, this prompts me to generalize about the breed. A research question arising from my experience is this: *What is the best way to evaluate canine intelligence?* Or put another way, who is really stupid—me or my dogs? Some theories, or presumptions, grow out of this. Here are a few of them.

1. My dogs' inability to follow simple commands, despite some training, is their fault.
2. Labs are usually pretty dumb.
3. Intelligence in dogs is fairly easy to evaluate.

Now would be an excellent time to make a list of your theories, assumptions, or beliefs about your topic. They will be invaluable guides for your research this week because you can examine these beliefs against the evidence and potentially break through to new understandings about your research question.

What Are You Arguing?

In some cases, you know what you think is the best answer to your research question even before you've done much investigation of the topic, and your motive is to build a convincing argument around that claim. For example, consider this claim: *Lawnmowers make a significant contribution to CO^2 emissions in the U.S.* Maybe this is something you heard or read somewhere from a reputable source, and it's something you strongly suspect is true. Maybe your instructor asked you to make that argument, or you're writing an opinion piece for an assignment. Conventional research papers are frequently organized from the beginning around a thesis or claim. If that's the kind of project you're working on, now would be a good time to craft a sentence that states your most important assertion or main idea. This may well be refined or even discarded later on as you learn more, but it will help with your research this week.

To generate a *tentative* thesis statement at this point, try finishing one of the following sentences:

1. While most people think _____ about _____, I think _____.

2. The most convincing answer to my research question is _____.

3. The main reason that _____ is a problem is _____, and the best solution is _____.

4. Among the causes of _____, the least understood is _____.

5. Though much has been said about _____, very little attention has been paid to _____.

6. All of the evidence so far about _____ points to _____ as a significant cause/solution/effect/problem/interpretation/factor.

With these three questions in mind—and a number of others that interest you—you'll be implementing your research strategy this week and next, looking at sources in the library and on the Web. The exercises that follow will help guide these searches, making sure that you don't overlook some key source or reference. Your instructor may ask you to hand in a photocopy of the exercise as a record of your journey.

Working Together: "Could You Clarify, Mr. Ziegler?"

By the end of this week, you should be ready to make a presentation to your class on your topic. Imagine that it's a press conference similar to the ones shown on television. You will give a fifteen-minute talk on your topic to your classmates, who will later, like veteran newspaper reporters, follow up with questions. Your presentation will be carefully timed. It shouldn't be any longer than the allotted time limit; any less than the allotted time suggests that you haven't yet developed a deeper knowledge of your topic.

Plan your presentation with the following things in mind:

- *Rather than simply report everything you've learned about your topic, try to give your talk some emphasis.* For example, focus on what you've learned so far that most surprised you and why. Or present the most common misconceptions about your topic and why they miss the mark. Or provide some background about why the question you're exploring is important and share some of the answers you've discovered so far. If your topic has a personal dimension, tell the story, and share how your research has helped you understand your experience differently.

- *Don't read a speech.* It's fine to have notes with you—in fact, it's a good idea—but try to avoid reading them. Make your presentation as interesting as you can. After all, this is a chance to discover what other people think about your topic—what interests them about it and what doesn't. This talk is a great chance to try out some approaches to your topic that you may later use to make your essay more compelling.

- *Consider visuals.* Itching to try out PowerPoint? Here's your chance. Also think about photographs, graphs, charts, and other visual ways to present your information.

- *Begin by stating your focusing question.* Every presentation should start by establishing what question is driving your investigation. You might even put this on the board when you begin.

While you listen to your peers' presentations, think about what questions they raise that interest you. These might be questions of clarification, questions about an assertion the presenters or one of their sources made, or areas that the speakers didn't cover but that you wonder about. Imagine that you're a hard-nosed reporter anxious to get the story right.

Library Research Techniques

Despite the appeal of the Web, the campus library remains your most important source of information for academic research. Sure, it can be aggravating. There's that missing book that was supposed to be there or that article that isn't available in full-text. You needed that article. Most of all, there's the sense of helplessness you might feel as a relative novice using a reference system that is bigger and more complicated than the library back home.

In the last chapter, you were introduced to basic library search strategies, knowledge that will help give you some mastery over the university library. In the exercise that follows, you'll expand on that knowledge, and at the same time you'll move from a working knowledge of your topic to a deeper understanding, one that will crystallize by reading and writing about what you find.

Finding Books

In the years since I wrote the first edition of *The Curious Researcher*, the old card catalog has completely disappeared. In its place is an electronic Web-based catalog that allows researchers to search for books even from home. This is a wonderful advance, one of the many ways technology has made researching easier, faster, and more efficient. But not everything has changed. Cataloging and indexing books is still done the old-fashioned way, and it helps to know how librarians organize books in the university library.

There are two systems for classifying books: the Dewey Decimal and the Library of Congress systems. Each is quite different. The Dewey system, reportedly conceived in 1873 by an Amherst College undergraduate while daydreaming in church, is numerical, dividing all knowledge into ten broad areas and further subdividing each of these into one hundred additional classifications. Adding decimal points allows librarians to subdivide things even further. Just knowing the *call number* of a book will tell you its subject.

The Library of Congress system, which uses both letters and numbers, is much more common in college libraries. This is the system with which you should become most familiar. Each call number begins with one or two letters, signifying a category of knowledge, which is followed by a whole number between 1 and 9,999. A decimal and one or more Cutter numbers sometimes follow. The Library of Congress system is pretty complex, but it's not hard to use. As you get deeper in your research, you'll begin to recognize call numbers that consistently yield useful books. It is sometimes helpful to simply browse those shelves for other possibilities.

Understanding Call Numbers*

The call number, that strange code on the spine of a library book, is something most of us want to understand just well enough to find that book on the shelf. How much do you need to know? First, you should know that there is more than the alphabet at work in arranging books by their call numbers and that call numbers tell you more than merely where books are shelved.

For example, the call number shown in Figure 2.7 tells you the subject area of the book, a little something about its author, and when the book was published. This is useful to know not only because

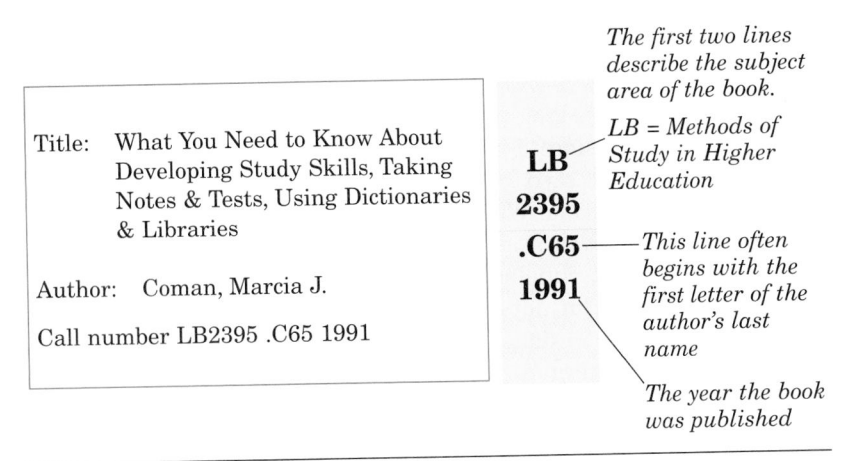

FIGURE 2.7   Deciphering the Call Number Code

*"Understanding Call Numbers" is adapted from the Web site of the Hawaii Community College library and used here with permission.

Read call numbers line by line:

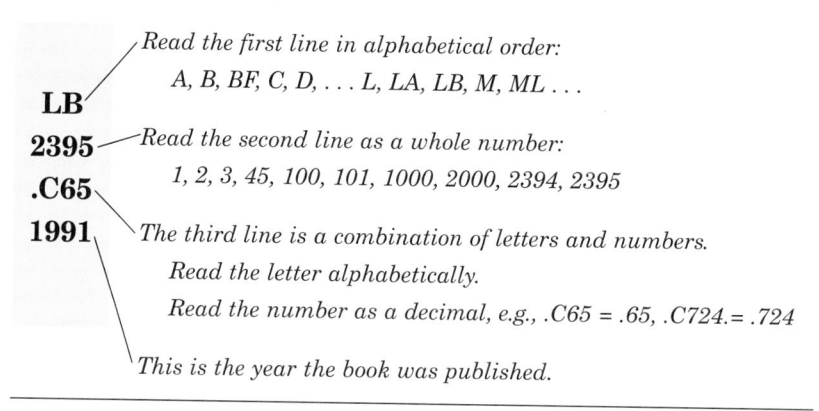

LB
2395 ——Read the second line as a whole number:
.C65
1991

Read the first line in alphabetical order:

   A, B, BF, C, D, . . . L, LA, LB, M, ML . . .

Read the second line as a whole number:

   1, 2, 3, 45, 100, 101, 1000, 2000, 2394, 2395

The third line is a combination of letters and numbers.
Read the letter alphabetically.
Read the number as a decimal, e.g., .C65 = .65, .C724.= .724

This is the year the book was published.

FIGURE 2.8   **Reading Call Numbers**

it will help you find the book, but it might prompt you to find other, possibly more recent books on the same subject on a nearby shelf.

Figure 2.8 shows you how to read call numbers. Read them from top to bottom (or left to right if displayed horizontally). While alphabetical and numerical order are key to understanding the sequencing of books in the library, the third line of a call number is a weird combination of letters and decimals. This always mystifies me.

In Figure 2.9, you can see how Library of Congress call numbers determine the arrangement of books on the shelf. The only tricky part is that odd letter and decimal combination in the third line of the call number. Note that the small decimal number (.B22) precedes a larger one (.B27). The year a book was published also determines its position on the shelf.

It's likely your college library, like mine, has retired its 3" × 5" cards and replaced them with an *online card catalog*. This online system uses a computer to do the same thing that you used to do, thumbing through the card catalog. And of course the computer is much faster.

E X E R C I S E   2 . 1

Library Investigations

STEP 1: It's the rare topic that isn't covered, in some way, in a book or part of one. Subject headings on your topic that you gleaned from *Library of Congress Subject Headings* really pay off when you use the electronic index to launch a search for relevant books. Begin with those, manipulating search terms on the search page of your online

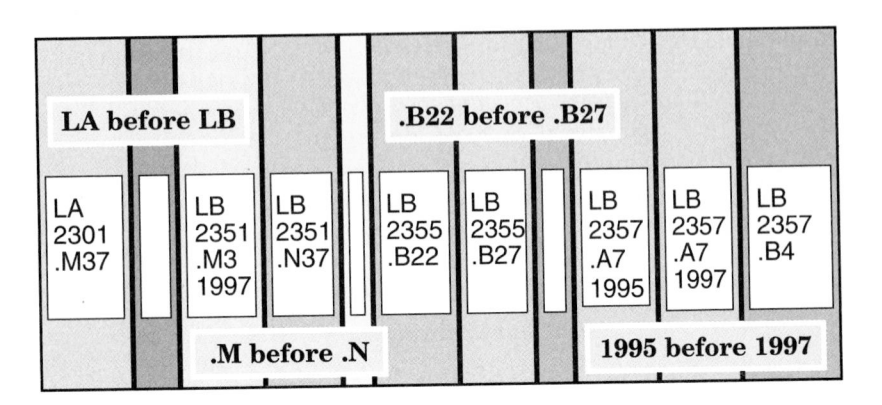

FIGURE 2.9   **How Books Are Arranged on the Library Shelf**

book index. Try several until you begin to see book titles that look promising. Figure 2.10 shows a sample search page.

Sort your results on a separate piece of paper from most promising to least promising. This is the beginning of your working bibliography and may be part of your progress report to your instructor this week. Use the following format for each entry. (It's based on

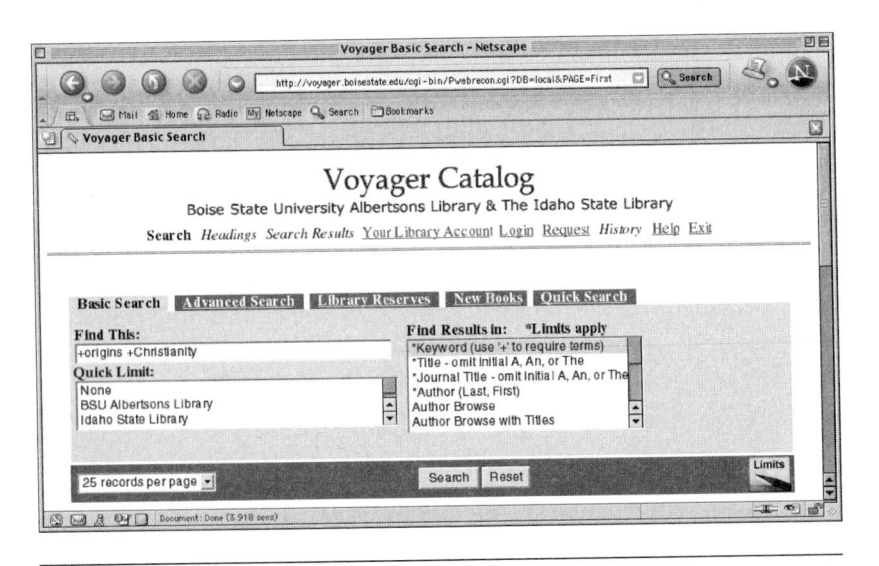

FIGURE 2.10   Online library indexes are now Web-based. The software varies, but nearly all of the search forms feature a range of search options, from basic to advanced, and ways to limit your search to certain databases, libraries, or terms. The terms you discover in the *Library of Congress Subject Headings* will help boost the relevance of the results.

the MLA method of listing citations, something you'll learn more about later.) You can also use an online "citation machine" like citationmachine.net to record the bibliographic information.

Call number: _____

Author(s): _____

Title: _____

Place of publication: _____

Date of publication: _____

Two- or three-sentence summary of what seems relevant about

each text to your project: _____

_____

_____

Coming Up Empty-Handed?

In the unlikely event that you can't find any books by searching directly using the online catalog, there's another reference you can check that will help locate relevant articles and essays that are *a part* of a book whose title may otherwise seem unpromising. Check to see if your library has a database called the Essay and General Literature Index. Search that database with your keywords or subject and see if it produces something useful. List the relevant results as instructed previously.

Checking Bibliographies

One tactic that might lead to a mother lode of sources for your essay is to look at the bibliographies at the back of (mostly) scholarly books (and articles). Don't ever set aside a promising book until you've checked the bibliography! Jot down complete bibliographic information from citations you want to check out later. Keep a running list of these in your research notebook.

Interlibrary Loan

If your library doesn't have the book (or article) you really want, don't despair. Most college libraries have a wonderful low- or no-cost service to students called interlibrary loan. The library will search the collections of other libraries to find what you're looking for and have it sent, sometimes within a week or less. Use the service by checking with the reference desk or your library's Web site.

Finding Magazine and Journal Articles Using Online Databases

It used to be that those green, well-thumbed volumes of the *Readers' Guide to Periodical Literature* were the only game in town if you were after an article published in a general-interest magazine. However, online databases have replaced indexes like the old *Readers' Guide.* Good riddance! While the *Guide* is still invaluable for finding articles published before 1990 (and as early as 1890) that may not be included in the new databases, the online indexes are much easier to use. See Figure 2.11. But perhaps the real weakness of the *Readers' Guide* and its online descendant, particularly for academic research, is that it's mostly an index of nonscholarly sources such as *Time, Redbook,* and *Sports Illustrated.* There's nothing wrong with these publications. In fact, you may end up using a few in your essay. But as you dig more

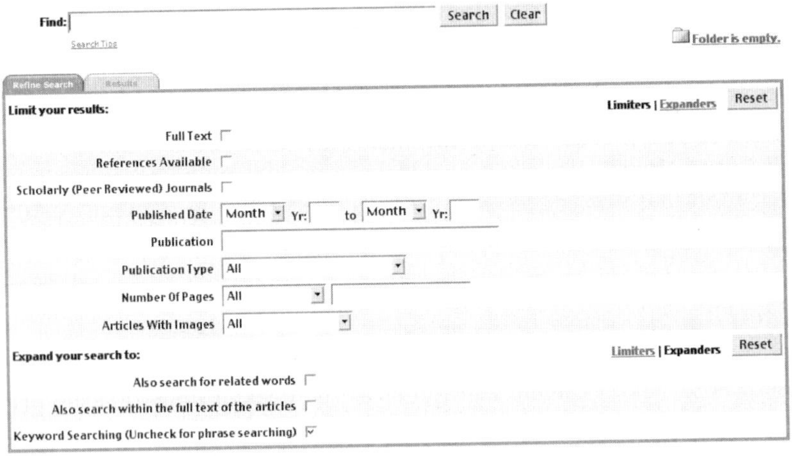

FIGURE 2.11   Since the periodical databases are huge, most search pages invite you to limit results not simply through careful use of search terms but by publication dates, full-text versions, peer-reviewed, and so on. A favorite choice is to ask only for articles that are available online in full text. The reason is obvious—it saves you a trip to the library to find the article in a bound volume. Remember, though, that full-text articles are not necessarily the best articles on your topic. The companies that sell the databases to libraries don't necessarily use quality as a criterion for which articles to offer in full-text.

deeply into your subject, you may find that the information in popular periodicals will often begin to tell you what you already know.

There are two kinds of article databases at your library: general subject databases that cover multiple disciplines and specialized databases that are discipline specific. Of course, I don't know which of these general databases you have at your library, but here are some of the most common:

GENERAL SUBJECT DATABASES

Academic OneFile

Academic Search Premier

ArticleFirst

IgentaConnect

General OneFile

Academic Search

JSTOR

Academic Universe on Lexis Nexis

EBSCO MasterFile

Many of these multidisciplinary databases include popular magazines, but they also index some scholarly journals as well. That's another reason they're so useful. For example, EBSCO MasterFile indexes nearly 3,000 journals and magazines and even provides full-text articles—rather than simply citations—from more than 1,800 periodicals. Increasingly, these databases include full-text articles, an extraordinary convenience for students working from home.

Specialized databases are subject specific. These are usually listed by discipline on your library's Web pages. The advantage of using these databases is that they will produce many more scholarly articles that might be relevant to your research question, though they may not all be full text. For a list of some of these, see the following table.

STEP 2: Visit your library's Web page that lists all of the available periodical databases. Begin your search by trying out one of the general subject databases. As before, if you find articles that seem relevant to your project, collect their bibliographic material or, if you're quite certain you might use the piece and it's available in full text, print out the articles. Most college libraries will allow you to mark citations you want to keep on the search form and later print them out as well. Now try an appropriate specialized database or two on your topic. As before, collect either bibliographic information on promising sources or print out full-text copies.

Your working bibliography for each promising source should include the following information:

Author: _____

Title: _____

Title of periodical: _____

Volume or issue number and date: _____

Pages covered by the article: _____

Two- or three-sentence comment about what information you hope to get from the article or what questions you hope it answers: _____

_____

_____

COMMON SPECIALIZED DATABASES

HUMANITIES	SCIENCE AND TECHNOLOGY	SOCIAL SCIENCES
America, History and Life	Applied Science & Technology Index	Anthropological Index
Arts and Humanities Search	CINAHL (Nursing)	ComAbstracts (Communication)
Art Index	Biological Abstracts	PsychINFO
MLA Bibliography (Literature and composition)	GeoRef (Geology) Abstracts	Social Work
Historical Abstracts	MathSciNet	Sociological Abstracts
Literary Index	Medline (Medicine)	Worldwide Political Science Abstracts
Music Index	Computer Literature Index	PAIS (Public Affairs)
Philosopher's Index	Health Reference Center	Criminal Justice Abstracts
Humanities Index	AGRICOLA (Agriculture)	Contemporary Women's Issues
Religion Index	General Science Index	Social Sciences Index

BUSINESS	EDUCATION
ABI/Inform	ERIC
FreeEDGAR	Education Index
Business Source Elite	Education Full Text

Finding Newspaper Articles with Online Databases

If your topic is local, current, or controversial, then it's likely that newspapers will be an important source of information for your essay. You'll rarely get much in-depth information or analysis from newspapers, but they can often provide good quotes, anecdotes, and case studies as well as the most current printed information on your topic. Newspapers are also sometimes considered primary sources because they provide firsthand accounts of things that have happened.

STEP 3: Guess what? There are databases of newspaper articles, too. See the accompanying list. They don't index the hometown paper, but they do provide citations to the so-called national newspapers such as *The New York Times, Washington Post, Los Angeles Times, The Wall Street Journal,* and *The Christian Science Monitor.* Bound indexes of several of these papers are in your university library, but nobody ever uses them anymore. What's good about the national newspapers is that they're among the most authoritative journalistic sources; in other words, because of their large and experienced staffs, the information they provide is more trustworthy.

NEWSPAPER DATABASES

National Newspaper Index

Proquest National Newspapers

Newspaper Source

Lexis-Nexis Academic Universe

Newspaper Abstracts

Custom Newspapers

Alternative Press Index

The larger papers also have their own Web sites where you may be able to search their archives and retrieve full-text articles. Sometimes they charge for this service. A convenient method for searching some of these sites is to use a news search engine that will consult thousands of papers in a few seconds. Here are several of the best of these search engines:

NEWSPAPER SEARCH ENGINES

Google News (http://news.google.com)

Yahoo News (http://news.yahoo.com)

AlltheWeb News (http://www.alltheweb.com/?cat=news)

You can also configure some of these sites to send you alerts when articles are published on a topic relevant to your project.

Occasionally, the local papers are also indexed online by the university library, and copies are available on microfilm. More and more frequently, however, local papers, like their larger counterparts in major cities, have their own Web sites where you use keyword searches to scour their archives.

Search for newspaper articles on your topic. Begin with one of the larger databases such as the National Newspaper Index, and then, depending on your topic, search the archives or online indexes of your local newspapers. If you find a promising full-text article on the Web, print it out. Also try to find a citation for a promising article on one of the databases and go to the microfilm room of your campus library, find the article, and copy it. If your topic just doesn't lend itself to a newspaper search, then use Google News or another of the newspaper search engines listed above and print an article that was posted today from a foreign newspaper. Choose the country from which your ancestors came.

Advanced Internet Research Techniques

I love the word "portal." It summons images of a little window on some vast space ship that frames the face of an open-mouthed observer looking in wonder at the vast reaches of the universe beyond. Researching on the Internet is a lot like peeping out of that window. There is just so much out there, billions of documents, gazillions of words, each a fragment of electronic data floating in cyberspace like dust motes in some vast sunbeam. Earlier in this chapter, you were reminded that this universe, while tantalizing, is also a librarian's nightmare. There's useful knowledge for academic writing out there, but it's hard to find and it's easy to get lost.

You're already better prepared for the search than most. Earlier you learned how to evaluate Web sources and design keyword searches. This is crucial knowledge. In Exercise 1.3 you also used some of the Web's key subject directories, several of which are maintained by librarians, actual human beings who sift and sort Internet materials and list those that are worthy. However, the more common method of searching the Web doesn't use a human being at all but a piece of software that electronically crawls the Web creating massive indexes of documents that respond to your keyword searches.

Types of Search Engines

The most popular search engine is Google, a search engine with an enormous database that is relatively simple to use. There are many other search engines like Google, including Ask, Yahoo!, AlltheWeb, Live Search, Alta Vista, and others. For current reviews and ratings of each of these, as well as research on what particular search engines do well and not so well, visit Search Engine Watch (http://searchenginewatch.com/) and click on the link for "Search 101." Google and the others are really quite amazing, but they do have limitations. For one thing, they only index pages on the Web that have hyperlinks pointing to them elsewhere, or whose creators have requested they be indexed by a particular search tool. In addition, these databases may not be current.

Search tools such as Yahoo! or Google aren't the only vehicles for scouring the Web. There are also specialized search engines that focus on particular subjects such as education, politics, and psychology, as well as search engines that specialize in going where conventional Web crawlers like Google do not go—the vast invisible Web, containing the types of documents that Google and other search engines cannot find or will not find. No one knows the size of the invisible Web, but it's probably much larger than the visible one.

Finally, there are so-called metasearch tools such as Dogpile (www.dogpile.com/) that are able to deploy multiple individual search engines in the service of a single search. These are very useful, particularly at the beginning of an Internet search on your topic. However, metasearch engines aren't quite as good as they sound because they skim off the top results from each individual search tool so you won't see the range of results you would get if you focus on one of the search engines with its own large database.

What's the key to maximizing the efficiency of your Internet research?

1. Maximize your coverage by using multiple search engines, not just your favorite one.
2. If possible, exploit subject directories put together by people, not software, concerned with quality content.
3. Be thoughtful about what and how many keywords you use to search. Generally, the more words—and especially phrases—you use, the more likely you are to generate relevant hits.

EXERCISE 2.2

Research on the Internet

STEP 1: Using some of the keyword combinations you developed for your topic, launch a search on one or more of the metasearch engines shown in the accompanying list. These tools are a good place to begin because of their breadth—you can quickly see the more popular sites on your topics and the various contexts in which information about it might be found.

METASEARCH ENGINES

Clusty (clusty.com)

Dogpile (www.dogpile.com)

Mamma (www.mamma.com)

Search.com (www.search.com)

Vivisimo (www.vivisimo.com)

SurfWax (www.surfwax.com)

Remember to play around with keywords, and don't forget the search language you learned earlier in this chapter. The "Help" button on whatever metasearch tool you use will give you the specifics on what connectors, Boolean or others, that search engine accepts.

Develop a "working bibliography" of Web pages (see Figure 2.12) that seem promising and print copies of them for note taking. For each page, include the following information, if available. A Web-based citation machine can help you with this.

Author (if any). _____

Title of page. _____

Publication name and date of print version (if any). _____

Name of online publication or database. _____

Online publication (volume or issue, date, page or paragraph

numbers). _____

Date you accessed the page. _____

Full Internet address. _____

A brief summary of what you found particularly promising or

interesting about the site. _____

Internet Research
Topic: The Intelligence of Crows
Focusing Question: Do crows exhibit unusual intelligence when compared with similar birds?

Working Bibliography

1. Hutchins, Lisa. "The Intelligence of Crows." Pica Productions. March 99. 2 July 2002 <http://www.users.qwest.net/~lhutchins/intelli_crows.htm>. Article reviews crow's problem-solving abilities and specific social behaviors like "mobbing."
2. "ASCAR's Frequently Asked Questions About Crows and Ravens." American Society of Crows and Ravens. ASCAR Online. 3 July 2002 <http://www.ascaronline.org/crowfaq.html>. FAQ page that includes some useful but limited information about crow behavior and common myths about the bird.
3. "Crow Family." Crow City. 3 July 2002 <http://website.lineone.net/~crowseed/crowcity/info/family.html>. British-based site discusses crow species in England with especially useful information on crows in Celtic mythology. Seems like a personal site.
4. Davies, Garweth Huw. "Bird Brains." PBS Online. 3 July 2002 <http://www.pbs.org/lifeofbirds/brain/index.html>. Page tells story of crows in Japan that use cars at intersections to open nuts. Also examines intelligence of other bird species. Linked to David Attenborough PBS program "The Life of Birds."

FIGURE 2.12   A sample working bibliography of Web sites related to topic on the intelligence of crows.

To make assembling this information easier, open a blank page in Word or some other word-processing program in another window while you search the Web. When you find a page you want to keep, highlight the address in your browser's address window, right-click to copy, go to your open page in Word, and right-click to paste. Because it's so important to get Internet addresses right, this copy-and-paste function can be very helpful.

STEP 2: Select *at least* two other single-search engines (see list) for a keyword search on your topic. Try two that you didn't use in Exercise 1.3 in the last chapter. Bookmark useful sites, and add what you find useful for your project to the working bibliography you started in Step 1. Though it's a bit of a pain, this working bibliography will be enormously useful later as you assemble the final draft of your essay.

In the searches you conduct for both steps of the exercise, you'll likely find links to pages that didn't appear in response to your original query. Follow these, too. The Web is aptly named since it presents knowledge through hyperlinks as multidisciplinary and interconnected.

POPULAR SINGLE SEARCH ENGINES

Google (www.google.com)

Yahoo! Search (search.yahoo.com)

Ask.com (www.ask.com)

Live search (www.live.com)

AltaVista (www.altavista.com)

Hotbot (www.hotbot.com)

Search.com (www.search.com)

AlltheWeb.com (www.alltheweb.com)

Looksmart (www.looksmart.com)

STEP 3: Specialized search engines that are subject-focused have proliferated on the Web in recent years, and these can be a boon to researchers because they often generate quite different results than general search portals, like Yahoo!. Google Scholar, the site you used briefly in the last chapter, is one of the best of these. Return there and do a more thorough investigation using some of the refined search terms you've developed in the last week. You can also find additional specialized search at the following sites.

SPECIALIZED SEARCH ENGINES SITES

Search Engine Guide (www.searchengineguide.com)

Pandia Powersearch (www.pandia.com/powersearch)

Virtual Search Engines (www.virtualfreesites.com)

Webquest (webquest.sdsu.edu/searching/specialized.html)

As before, bookmark all the documents or pages you discovered that seem useful, and add them to your working bibliography.

By now you're well on your way to developing focused knowledge of your topic. If you've successfully completed Exercises 2.1 and 2.2, you will have the following:

1. A working bibliography, annotated with your initial comments, of books, periodicals, and Web pages relevant to your topic. This will be invaluable later as you develop the bibliography for your essay.

2. Copies of promising articles or Web documents for note taking.

Living Sources: Interviews and Surveys

Arranging Interviews

A few years ago, I researched a local turn-of-the-century writer named Sarah Orne Jewett for a magazine article. I dutifully read much of her work, studied critical articles and books on her writing, and visited her childhood home, which is open to the public in South Berwick, Maine. My research was going fairly well, but when I sat down to begin writing the draft, the material seemed flat and lifeless. A few days later, the curator of the Jewett house mentioned that there was an eighty-eight-year-old local woman, Elizabeth Goodwin, who had known the writer when she was alive. "As far as I know, she's the last living person who knew Sarah Orne Jewett," the curator told me. "And she lives just down the street."

The next week, I spent three hours with Elizabeth Goodwin, who told me of coming for breakfast with the famous author and eating strawberry jam and muffins. Elizabeth told me that many years after Jewett's death, the house seemed haunted by her friendly presence. One time, when Elizabeth lived in the Jewett house as a curator, some unseen hands pulled her back as she teetered at the top of the steep stairs in the back of the house. She likes to believe it was the author's ghost.

This interview transformed the piece by bringing the subject to life—first, for me as the writer, and then later for my readers. Ultimately, what makes almost any topic compelling is discovering why it matters to *people*—how it affects their lives. Doing interviews with people close to the subject, both experts and nonexperts, is often the best way to find that out.

If you'd like to do some interviews, now is the time to begin arranging them.

Finding Experts

You may be hesitant to consider finding authorities on your topic to talk to because, after all, you're just a lowly student who knows next to nothing. How could you possibly impose on that sociology professor who published the book on anti-Semitism you found in the library? If that's how you feel, keep this in mind: *Most people, no matter who they are, love the attention of an interviewer, no matter who she is, particularly if what's being discussed fascinates them both.* Time and again, I've found my own shyness creep up on me when I pick up the telephone to arrange an interview. But almost invariably, when I get there and start talking with my interview subject, the experience is great for us both.

How do you find experts to interview?

■ *Check your sources.* As you begin to collect books, articles, and Internet documents, note their authors and affiliations. I get calls from time to time from writers who come across my book on lobsters in the course of their research and discover that I am at Boise State University. Sometimes the caller will arrange a phone interview or, if he lives within driving distance, a personal interview.

■ *Check the phone book.* The familiar Yellow Pages can be a gold mine. Carin, who was writing a paper on solar energy, merely looked under that heading and found a local dealer who sold solar systems to homeowners. Mark, who was investigating the effects of sexual abuse on children, found a counselor who specialized in treating abuse victims.

■ *Ask your friends and your instructors.* Your roommate's boyfriend's father may be a criminal attorney who has lots to say about the insanity defense for your paper on that topic. Your best friend may be taking a photography course with a professor who would be a great interview for your paper on the work of Edward Weston. One of your instructors may know other faculty working in your subject area who would do an interview.

■ *Check the faculty directory.* Many universities publish an annual directory of faculty and their research interests. On my campus, it's called the *Directory of Research and Scholarly Activities.* From it, I know, for example, that two professors at my university have expertise in eating disorders, a popular topic with student researchers.

■ *Check the* Encyclopedia of Associations. This is a wonderful reference book that lists organizations with interests ranging from promoting tofu to preventing acid rain. Each listing includes the name of the group, its address and phone number, a list of its publications, and a short description of its purpose. Sometimes, these organizations can direct you to experts in your area who are available for live interviews or to spokespeople who are happy to provide phone interviews.

■ *Check the Internet.* You can find the e-mail addresses and phone numbers of many scholars and researchers on the Internet, including those affiliated with your own university and ones nearby. Often, these experts are listed in online directories for their colleges or universities. Sometimes, you can find knowledgeable people by subscribing to a listserv or Internet discussion group on your topic. Occasionally, an expert will have her own Web page, and her e-mail address will provide a hypertext link. (For more details, see "Finding People on the Internet," on page 603.)

Finding Nonexperts Affected by Your Topic

The distinction between *expert* and *nonexpert* is tricky. For example, someone who lived through twelve months of combat in Vietnam certainly has direct knowledge of the subject, though probably he hasn't published an article about the war in *Foreign Affairs*. Similarly, a friend who experienced an abusive relationship with her boyfriend or overcame a drug addiction is, at least in a sense, an authority on abuse or addiction. Both individuals would likely be invaluable interviews for papers on those topics. The voices and the stories of people who are affected by the topic you're writing about can do more than anything else to make the information come to life, even if they don't have Ph.D.'s.

You may already know people you can interview about your topic. Last semester, Amanda researched how mother-daughter relationships change when a daughter goes to college. She had no problem finding other women anxious to talk about how they get along with their mothers. A few years ago, Dan researched steroid use by student athletes. He discreetly asked his friends if they knew anyone who had taken the drugs. It turned out that an acquaintance of Dan's had used the drugs regularly and was happy to talk about his experience.

If you don't know people to interview, try posting notices on campus kiosks or bulletin boards. For example, "I'm doing a research project and interested in talking to people who grew up in single-parent households. Please call 555–9000." Also poll other students in your class for ideas about people you might interview for your paper. Help each other out.

Making Contact

By the end of this week, you should have some people to contact for interviews. First, consider whether to ask for a personal, telephone, or e-mail interview or perhaps, as a last resort, to simply correspond by mail. The personal interview is almost always preferable; you not only can listen, but you can watch, observing your subject's gestures and the setting, both of which can be revealing. When I'm interviewing someone in her office or home, for example, one of the first things I may jot down are the titles of books on the bookshelf. Sometimes, details about gestures and settings can be worked into your paper. Most of all, the personal interview is preferable because it's more natural, more like a conversation.

Be prepared. You may have no choice in the type of interview. If your subject is off campus or out of state, your only options may be the telephone, e-mail, or regular mail.

When contacting a subject for an interview, first state your name and then briefly explain your research project. If you were referred to the subject by someone she may know, mention that. A comment like "I think you could be extremely helpful to me," or "I'm familiar with your work, and I'm anxious to talk to you about it," works well. That's called *flattery,* and as long as it isn't excessive or insincere, we're all vulnerable to it.

It is gracious to ask your prospective subject what time and place for an interview may be convenient for her. Nonetheless, be prepared to suggest some specific times and places to meet or talk. When thinking about when to propose the interview with an expert on your topic, consider arranging it *after* you've done some research. You will not only be more informed, but you will have a clearer sense of what you want to know and what questions to ask.

Conducting Interviews

You've already thought about whether interviews might contribute to your paper. Build a list of possible interview subjects and contact several of them. By the end of this week, you should begin interviewing.

I know. You wouldn't mind putting it off. But once you start, it will get easier and easier. I should know. I used to dread interviewing strangers, but after making the first phone call, I got some momentum going, and I began to enjoy it. It's decidedly easier to interview friends, family, and acquaintances, but that's the wrong reason to limit yourself to people you know.

Whom to Interview?   Interview people who can provide you with what you want to know. And that may change as your research develops. In your reading, you might have encountered the names of experts you'd like to contact, or you may have decided that what you really need is some anecdotal material from someone with experience in your topic. It's still not too late to contact interview subjects who didn't occur to you earlier. But do so immediately.

What Questions to Ask?   The first step in preparing for an interview is to ask yourself, What's the purpose of this interview? In your research notebook, make a list of *specific questions* for each person you're going to interview. Often, these questions are raised by your reading or other interviews. What theories or ideas encountered in your reading would you like to ask your subject about? What specific facts have you been unable to uncover that your interview subject may provide? What don't you understand that he could explain? Would you like to test one of your own impressions or ideas on your subject? What about the subject's work or experience would you like to learn? Interviews are wonderful tools for clearing up your own confusion and getting specific information that is unavailable anywhere else.

Now make a list of more *open-ended questions* you might ask each or all of the people you're going to talk to. Frankly, these questions are a lot more fun to ask because you're more likely to be surprised by the answers. For example:

- In all your experience with _____, what has most surprised you?
- What has been the most difficult aspect of your work?
- If you had the chance to change something about how you approached _____, what would it be?
- Can you remember a significant moment in your work on _____? Is there an experience with _____ that stands out in your mind?
- What do you think is the most common misconception about _____? Why?
- What are significant current trends in _____?
- Who or what has most influenced you? Who are your heroes?
- If you had to summarize the most important thing you've learned about _____, what would it be?
- What is the most important thing other people should know or understand?

As you develop both specific and open-ended questions, keep in mind what you know about each person—his work in the field and personal experience with your topic. You may end up asking a lot of the same questions of everybody you interview, but try to familiarize yourself with any special qualifications a subject may have or experiences he may have had. That knowledge might come from your reading, from what other people tell you about your subject, or from your initial telephone call to set up the interview.

Also keep in mind the *kinds* of information an interview can provide better than other sources: anecdotes, strong quotes, and sometimes descriptive material. If you ask the right questions, a live subject can paint a picture of his experience with your topic, and you can capture that picture in your paper.

During the Interview.   Once you've built a list of questions, be prepared to ignore it. Interviews are conversations, not surveys. They are about human interaction between two people who are both interested in the same thing.

I remember interviewing a lobsterman, Edward Heaphy, on his boat. I had a long list of questions in my notebook, which I dutifully asked, one after the other. My questions were mechanical, and so were his answers. I finally stopped, put my notebook down, and talked informally with Edward for a few minutes. Offhandedly, I asked, "Would you want your sons or daughter to get in the business?" It was a totally unplanned question. Edward was silent for a moment, staring at his hands. I knew he was about to say something important because, for the first time, I was attentive to him, not my notepad. "Too much work for what they get out of it," he said quietly. It was a surprising remark after hearing for the last hour how much Edward loved lobstering. What's more, I felt I had broken through. The rest of the interview went much better.

Much of how to conduct an interview is common sense. At the outset, clarify the nature of your project—what your paper is on and where you're at with it. Briefly explain again why you thought this individual would be the perfect person to talk to about it. I find it often helps to begin with a specific question that I'm pretty sure my subject can help with. But there's no formula. Simply be a good conversationalist: Listen attentively, ask questions that your subject seems to find provocative, and enjoy with your subject sharing an interest in the same thing. Also don't be afraid to ask what you fear are obvious questions. Demonstrate to the subject that you *really* want to understand.

Always end an interview by making sure you have accurate background information on your subject: name (spelled correctly), position, affiliation, age (if applicable), phone number. Ask if you can call him with follow-up questions, should you have any. And always ask your subject if he can recommend any additional reading or other people you should talk to. Of course, mention that you're appreciative of the time he has spent with you.

Notetaking.   There are basically three ways to take notes during an interview: Use a digital recorder, a notepad, or both. I adhere to the third method, but it's a very individual choice. I like digital recorders because I don't panic during an interview that I'm losing information or quoting inaccurately, but I don't want to spend hours transcribing the files. So I also take notes on the information I think I want to use, and if I miss anything, I consult the recording later. It's a backup. Sometimes, I find that there is no recording—the machine decided not to participate in the interview—and at least I have my notes. Again, a backup.

Get some practice developing your own note-taking technique by interviewing your roommate or taking notes on the television news. Devise ways to shorten often-used words (e.g., *t* for *the, imp* for *important,* and *w/o* for *without*).

The E-Mail Interview

The Internet opens up new possibilities for interviews; increasingly, experts (as well as nonexperts interested in certain subjects) are accessible through e-mail and newsgroups. While electronic communication doesn't quite approach the conversational quality of the conventional face-to-face interview, the spontaneous nature of e-mail exchanges can come pretty close. It's possible to send a message, get a response, respond to the response, and get a further response—all in a single day. And for shy interviewers and interviewees, an e-mail conversation is an attractive alternative.

Finding People on the Internet. Finding people on the Internet doesn't have to involve a needle and hay if you have some information on whom you're looking for. If you know an expert's name, his organizational affiliation, and his geographical location, several search tools may help you track down his e-mail address, if he has one. But perhaps the easiest way to use the Net to find someone to interview is through a Web document on your topic. For example, when researching this new edition of this book, I encountered an online version of the Alliance for Computers and Writing's proposals for MLA-style electronic citations, authored by Janice Walker. Walker's e-mail address was a hyperlink in that document, so had I wanted to ask her some questions, all I would have had to do was click on her name. Authors of Web pages frequently provide their addresses as links, inviting comments about their texts and the like. Thus, it seems safe to assume that they are probably willing to entertain questions from researchers, too.

Plucking an e-mail address from a Web page is the easiest way to find an interview subject. But what if you just have someone's name and organizational affiliation? Google them! This has become second nature for most of us when we're trying to track down that girlfriend or boyfriend from the eighth grade. It can be equally useful to hunt down experts on your research topic.

You can also find academics by visiting the Web sites of the universities or colleges where they teach and use the online faculty/staff directories to find their addresses. Obviously, this won't work if you don't know the name of the institutions with which a scholar is affiliated, but this is often listed in an academic's articles, books, or Web page. To find the home pages of hundreds of American universities and colleges, visit the following site: The Yahoo Education Directory (http://dir.yahoo.com/Education/Higher_Education/Colleges_and_Universities/). This is a very easy to use search page that allows you to find the home pages of universities in the United States. It includes links to a number of sites that also index colleges and universities as well as their various programs.

Making Contact by E-Mail.   Once you find the e-mail address of someone who seems a likely interview subject, proceed courteously and cautiously. One of the Internet's haunting issues is its potential to violate privacy. Be especially careful if you've gone to great lengths in hunting down the e-mail address of someone involved with your research topic; she may not be keen on receiving unsolicited e-mail messages from strangers. It would be courteous to approach any potential interview subject with a short message that asks permission for an online interview. To do so, briefly describe your project and why you thought this individual might be a good source for you. As always, you will be much more likely to get an enthusiastic response from someone if you can demonstrate your knowledge of her work on or experience with your topic.

Let's assume your initial contact has been successful and your subject has agreed to answer your questions. Your follow-up message should ask a *limited* number of questions—say, four or five—that are thoughtful and, if possible, specific. Keep in mind that while the e-mail interview is conducted in writing rather than through talking, many of the methods for handling conventional interviews still apply.

The Discussion Board Interview.   Discussion or message boards don't involve live conversations, like instant messaging, but they can be good places to find people—and sometimes experts—who are passionately interested in your research topic or question. How do you find one that might be relevant to your project? Try visiting one of the following directories that list these sites by subject.

- Google Directory (www.google.com/Top/Computers/Interent/On_the_Web/Message_Boards)
- BoardReader (boardreader.com)

■ BoardTracker (www.boardtracker.com)
■ MSN Groups (groups.msn.com)
■ Yahoo! Groups (groups.yahoo.com)

Deciding What to Ask. Another way to get some help with knowing what to ask—and what not to—is to spend some time following the discussion of list participants before you jump in yourself. You might find, for example, that it would be far better to interview one participant with interesting views rather than to post questions to the whole list.

But if you do want to query the discussion board, avoid posting a question that may have already received substantial attention from participants. You can find out what's been covered by consulting the list's FAQs (frequently asked questions). The issue you're interested in may be there, along with a range of responses from list participants, which will spare you the need to ask the question at all.

Planning Informal Surveys

Christine was interested in dream interpretation, especially exploring the significance of symbols or images that recur in many people's dreams. She could have simply examined her own dreams, but she thought it might be more interesting to survey a group of fellow students, asking how often they dream and what they remember. An informal survey, in which she would ask each person several standard questions, seemed worth trying.

You might consider it, too, if the responses of a group of people to some aspect of your topic would reveal a pattern of behavior, attitudes, or experiences worth analyzing. Informal surveys are decidedly unscientific. You probably won't get a large enough sample size, nor do you likely have the skills to design a poll that would produce statistically reliable results. But you probably won't actually base your paper on the survey results, anyway. Rather, you'll present specific, concrete information that *suggests* some patterns in your survey group, or, at the very least, some of your own findings will help support your assertions.

Defining Goals and Audience

Begin planning your informal survey by defining what you want to know and whom you want to know it from. Christine suspected that many students have dreams related to stress. She wondered if there were any similarities among students' dreams. She was also curious about how many people remember their dreams and how often, and if this might be related to gender. Finally, Christine wanted to find out whether people have recurring dreams and, if so, what those were about. There were other things she wanted to know, too. But she knew she had to keep the survey short, probably no more than seven questions.

If you're considering a survey, make a list in your research notebook of things you might want to find out and specify the group of people you plan to talk to. College students? Female college students? Attorneys? Guidance counselors? Be as specific as you can about your target group.

Types of Questions

Next, consider what approach you will take. Will you ask *open-ended questions,* which give respondents plenty of room to invent their own answers? For example, Christine might ask, *Describe any dreams that seemed related to stress?* The payoff for open-ended questions is that sometimes you get surprising answers. The danger, which seems real with Christine's question, is that you'll get no answer at all. A more *directed question* might be, *Have you ever dreamed that you showed up for class and didn't know that there was a major exam that day?* Christine will get an answer to this question—yes or no—but it doesn't promise much information. A third possibility is the *multiple-choice question.* It ensures an answer and is likely to produce useful information. For example:

Have you ever had any dreams similar to these?

a. You showed up for a class and didn't know there was a major exam.
b. You registered for a class but forgot to attend.
c. You're late for a class or an exam but can't seem to move fast enough to get there on time.
d. You were to give a presentation but forgot all about it.
e. None of the above.*

Ultimately, Christine decided to combine the open-ended question about stress and the multiple-choice approach, hoping that if one didn't produce interesting information, the other would (see Figure 2.13). She also wisely decided to avoid asking more than seven questions, allowing her subjects to respond to her survey in minutes.

*Reprinted with permission of Christine Bergquist.

The following survey contains questions about dreaming and dream content. The findings gathered from this survey will be incorporated into a research paper on the function of dreaming and what, if anything, we can learn from it. I'd appreciate your honest answers to the questions. Thank you for your time!

General Subject Information

Gender: ☐ Male ☐ Female

Age: _____

Major: _____

Survey Questions
(circle all letters that apply)

1. How often do you remember your dreams?
   A. Almost every night
   B. About once a week
   C. Every few weeks
   D. Practically never
2. Have you ever dreamt that you were:
   A. Falling?
   B. Flying?
3. Have you ever dreamt of:
   A. Your death?
   B. The death of someone close to you?
4. Have you ever had a recurring dream?
   A. Yes
   B. No
   If yes, How often? _____
            What period of your life? _____
            Do you still have it? _____
5. Have you ever had any dreams similar to these?
   A. You showed up for a class and didn't know there was a major exam.
   B. You're late for a class or an exam but can't seem to move fast enough to get there.
   C. You were to give a presentation but forgot all about it.
6. Do you feel your dreams:
   A. Hold some deep, hidden meanings about yourself or your life?
   B. Are meaningless?
7. Please briefly describe the dream you best remember or one that sticks out in your mind. (Use the back of this survey.)

FIGURE 2.13   Sample Informal Survey
Source: Reprinted with permission of Christine Bergquist.

Survey Design

A survey shouldn't be too long (probably no more than six or seven questions), it shouldn't be biased (asking questions that will skew the answers), it should be easy to score and tabulate results (especially if you hope to survey a relatively large number of people), it should ask clear questions, and it should give clear instructions for how to answer.

As a rule, informal surveys should begin as polls often do: by getting vital information about the respondent. Christine's survey began with questions about the gender, age, and major of each respondent (see Figure 2.13). Depending on the purpose of your survey, you might also want to know things such as whether respondents are registered to vote, whether they have political affiliations, what year of school they're in, or any number of other factors. Ask for information that provides different ways of breaking down your target group.

Avoid Loaded Questions.   Question design is tricky business. An obviously biased question—*Do you think it's morally wrong to kill unborn babies through abortion?*—is easy to alter by removing the charged and presumptuous language. (It is unlikely that all respondents believe that abortion is killing.) One revision might be, *Do you support or oppose providing women the option to abort a pregnancy during the first twenty weeks?* This is a direct and specific question, neutrally stated, that calls for a yes or no answer. The question would be better if it were even more specific.

Controversial topics, like abortion, are most vulnerable to biased survey questions. If your topic is controversial, take great care to eliminate bias by avoiding charged language, especially if you have strong feelings yourself.

Avoid Vague Questions.   Another trap is asking vague questions: *Do you support or oppose the university's alcohol policy?* In this case, don't assume that respondents know what the policy is unless you explain it. Since the campus alcohol policy has many elements, this question might be redesigned to ask about one of them: *The university recently established a policy that states that underage students caught drinking in campus dormitories are subject to eviction. Do you support or oppose this policy?* Other equally specific questions might ask about other parts of the policy.

Drawbacks of Open-Ended Questions.   Open-ended questions often produce fascinating answers, but they can be difficult to tabulate.

Christine's survey asked, *Please briefly describe the one dream you best remember or one that sticks out in your mind.* She got a wide range of answers—or sometimes no answer at all—but it was hard to quantify the results. Almost everyone had different dreams, which made it difficult to discern much of a pattern. She was still able to use some of the material as anecdotes in her paper, so it turned out to be a question worth asking.

Designing Your Multiple-Choice Questions. The multiple-choice question is an alternative to the open-ended question, leaving room for a number of *limited* responses, which are easier to quantify. Christine's survey had a number of multiple-choice questions.

The challenge in designing multiple-choice questions is to provide choices that will likely produce results. From her reading and talking to friends, Christine came up with what she thought were three stress-related dreams college students often experience (see question 5, Figure 2.13). The results were interesting (45 percent circled "B") but unreliable, since respondents did not have a "None of the above" option. How many respondents felt forced to choose one of the dreams listed because there was no other choice? Design choices you think your audience will respond to, but give them room to say your choices weren't theirs.

Continuum Questions. Question 6 (see Figure 2.13) has a similar choice problem in that it asks a direct either/or question: *Do you feel your dreams: (A) Hold some deep, hidden meanings about yourself or your life?* or *(B) Are meaningless?* Phrased this way, the question forces the respondent into one of two extreme positions. People are more likely to place themselves somewhere in between.

A variation on the multiple-choice question is the *continuum,* where respondents indicate how they feel by marking the appropriate place along a scale. Christine's question 6 could be presented as a continuum:

How do you evaluate the significance of your dreams? Place an "X" on the continuum in the place that most closely reflects your view.

My dreams always hold some meaning   *My dreams are meaningless*

Though it is a bit more difficult to tabulate results of a continuum, this method often produces reliable answers if the instructions are clear.

Planning for Distribution

Surveys can be administered in person, by phone, or online. Although there are some real advantages to administering the survey yourself (or lining up friends to help you do it), reflect on how much time you want to devote to gathering the information. How important will the survey be to your paper? Are the results crucial to your argument? If not, consider doing what Christine did: Print several hundred survey forms that are easy for respondents to fill out themselves, and distribute them with some help from your instructor or friends.

Conducting Surveys

Last week, you considered whether your topic lends itself to an informal survey. If it does, you generated three types of questions you might ask: *open-ended, multiple choice,* and *directed.* After all the reading you did this week, you likely have some fresh ideas of questions you might ask. Finalize the questions, and begin distributing the survey to the target group you defined earlier.

Distribution.   Surveys administered by telephone have some advantages. People are more likely to be direct and honest over the phone, since they are relatively anonymous. Surveys are also more likely to be completed correctly, since the answers are recorded by the survey giver. However, making multiple phone calls can be tedious and expensive, if your target group goes beyond the toll-free calling area. But you may have no choice, especially if the target group for your survey isn't exclusively on campus.

One alternative to conducting a telephone survey is to distribute the survey yourself. The university community, where large numbers of people are available in a confined area, lends itself to administering surveys this way, if there's a university audience you're interested in polling. A survey can be distributed in dormitories, dining halls, classes, or anywhere else the people you want to talk to gather. You can stand outside the student union and stop people as they come and go, or you can hand out your survey to groups of people and collect them when the participants have finished. Your instructor may be able to help distribute your survey to classes. I asked a number of my colleagues to distribute Christine's survey (see Figure 2.13) in their Freshman English classes, a required course representing a relatively random sample of freshmen. Since the survey only took five minutes to fill out, other instructors were glad to help, and in one day Christine was able to sample more than ninety students.

The campus and its activities often self-select the group you want to survey. Anna, writing a paper on date rape, surveyed exclusively women on campus, many of whom she found in women's dormitories. For his paper on the future of the fraternity system, David surveyed local "Greeks" at their annual awards banquet.

How large a sample should you shoot for? Since yours won't be a scientific survey, don't bother worrying about statistical reliability; just try to survey as many people as you can. Certainly, a large (say, more than one hundred) and representative sample will lend more credence to your claims about any patterns observed in the results.

The Internet Survey

You can create an online survey easily using a program like surveymonkey.com. These programs are remarkably easy to use, walking you through the process of designing questions, posting the survey, and even analyzing the results. For example, Survey-Monkey's free "basic" service will allow you to create a ten-question survey and collect up to a hundred responses. You can then post the survey on your blog, send it out to an email mailing list, or put a link on your web site. The challenge, as usual, is reaching the people you'd like to survey and getting them to respond.

Listservs, discussion boards, and even real-time communication tools such as chat rooms, all organize people with similar interests—and in some cases similar demographics. This makes cyberspace a potentially appealing place to conduct survey work. Consider, for example, posting three or four questions on your topic to a relevant discussion group or to a group that may reach an audience you'd like to survey. For example, Marty was working on an essay that explored the extent to which college students felt a generational identity. A search on Google Groups produced a Usenet group (alt.society.generation-x) that proved an ideal forum to respond to her questions.

CHAPTER 3

The Third Week

Writing in the Middle

I was never crazy about taking notes for a research paper. Notetaking seemed so tedious. Instead, I developed a love affair with the photocopier and walked around sounding like a slot machine, my pockets full of change, ready to bolt to the nearest copier whenever I encountered a promising article. I collected these articles to read later. I also checked out scores of books that seemed useful, rather than taking the time to skim them in the library and jot down notes on what seemed important. I was quite a sight at the end of the day, walking back to my dormitory or apartment, reeling under the weight of a mound of books and articles, all precariously balanced, defying natural laws.

When the time came to begin writing my paper, the work seemed agonizingly slow. I would consult my meager notes, thumb through two or three books from the stack, reread a dog-eared copy of an article, stop and think, write a line or two, stop and go back to a book, and then maybe write another line or two. I was always a slow writer, but I now realize that one major reason I got bogged down writing my research paper drafts was my inattention to note-taking. I paid the price for doing so little writing before I had to do the writing.

I now believe that the writing that takes place in the *middle* of the research process—the notetaking stage—may be as important, if not more so, than the writing that takes place at the end—composing the draft. Writing in the middle helps you take possession of your sources and establish your presence in the draft. It sharpens your thinking about your topic. And it is the best cure for unintentional plagiarism.

I realize I have a sales job to do on this. Writing in the middle, particularly if you've been weaned on notecards, feels like busywork. "It gets in the way of doing the research," one student told me. "I just want to collect as much stuff as I can, as quickly as I can. Notetaking slows me down." Though it may seem inefficient, writing as you read may actually make your research *more* efficient. Skeptical? Read on.

Becoming an Activist Notetaker

Notetaking can and probably should begin the process of writing your paper. Notetaking is not simply a mechanical process of vacuuming up as much information as you can and depositing it on notecards or in a notebook with little thought. Your notes from sources are your first chance to *make sense* of the information you encounter, to make it your own. You do need more time to take thoughtful notes, but doing so pays off in writing a draft more quickly and in producing a paper that reflects your point of view much more strongly.

I'll show you what I mean. Here's a passage from the essay "How the Web Destroys the Quality of Students' Research Papers" by David Rothenberg.

> But too much of what passes for information these days [on the Web] is simply *advertising* for information. Screen after screen shows you where you can find out more, how you can connect to this place or that. The acts of linking and networking and randomly jumping from here to there become as exciting or rewarding as actually finding anything of intellectual value.

As part of a conference presentation, I decided to write an essay that explores some of the issues raised in the article. I wondered, "Is David Rothenberg right when he argues that so far Web research has had a mostly negative impact on student writing?" The passage above struck me, and I wrote it down—word for word—on the left page of my journal. On the opposing page I began an open-ended fastwrite, exploring my reaction to Rothenberg's claim.

Here's what I found myself saying about four minutes into the fastwriting:

It strikes me that the real virtue of the Web might be its central weakness: Because so much of the Web is, as Rothenberg claims, insubstantial and unreliable, we have a wonderful opportunity to get students to consider that distinction between information and knowledge, between legitimate and specious claims to authority

... Where Rothenberg sees pitfalls, I see opportunities, I guess.

And here's what I ended up writing in my own essay, "A Net Full of Nothing?":

> I don't think most of my students think that the Internet makes research easier. It makes research more *convenient,* and that's why students' first instinct these days is to pull up a chair in front of a monitor rather than to journey into the stacks. For the foreseeable future, the campus library will remain the best place to cast a net for term papers, but I'm coming around to seeing that the Web may be an even better place for students to practice how to evaluate their catch. *Can the Internet's weakness as a source of knowledge tutor students in the opportunities for knowledge-making?* I'm not sure yet.

It's quite possible, of course, that I could have used some other way to come up with the idea that the Web's weaknesses as an information source might be one of its virtues. But time and again I've seen in my own writing—and in my students'—that this kind of open-ended, often messy writing *as I'm reading* a book or article or even a Web page produces surprises: new ways of seeing things, and sometimes even new ways of saying things. It is also a great way to talk to, with, and sometimes against the published author. Talking freely to yourself in writing about what you're reading, how you understand it, and how it relates to what you already think (or may have never thought of) is one of the best ways to make outside sources your own. Such writing to yourself also allows you to indulge in "the gift of perhaps," trying out ideas and posing questions you wouldn't dare to do in a draft because it would complicate things.

Writing in the middle is basically something you do everyday: Have a conversation. In this case you're doing it with a stranger who shares your interest in something and you're talking with texts. The exercise that follows is an opportunity to practice this new kind of dialogue.

Something like 85 percent of all American college students use the social networking site Facebook. Writer Christine Rosen speculates that sites like Facebook and MySpace have fundamentally changed the "taxonomy of friendship." Where we once developed good friendships with people by privately sharing the intimate details of our lives face-to-face, these social networking sites place a premium on divulging these details in public. In fact, the weirder you come across, the more you can distinguish yourself as unique and quirky, the more successful you can be at "acquiring" friends. Rosen argues that the kinds of things that earn you status on Facebook or MySpace are not the kinds of things that generally encourage meaningful relationships. Her essay, excerpted in Exercise 3.1, is titled "Virtual Friendship and the New Narcissism." You can find the full essay later in this chapter, on page 632.

EXERCISE 3 . 1

Getting a Word in Edgewise

Have a conversation with Christine Rosen about what you think about her argument. To get in the spirit of this, imagine that you are actually going to sit across from her at lunch as she explains some of her key claims. Rosen obviously knows more about the influence of social networking sites on our relationships with each other than you do; after all, you haven't thought about it as much as she has. But she is interested in what you think.

First, think to yourself about these issues by fastwriting for four minutes in your notebook in response to one or more of the following questions. Follow the writing wherever it goes.

1. If you're a Facebook or MySpace user, what kind of "portrait" do you think you've tried to paint of yourself on your site?
2. If you've never used a social networking site online, what do you think of the idea that Facebook or MySpace are "great places to connect with people and make friends?"
3. Tell a story of one of your experiences on one of these sites.

Now that you've prepared a little for your conversation with Rosen, imagine that you've met her at a restaurant and she says suddenly, "There are some things I've been thinking about and I'd really like to know your thoughts about them, particularly as a college student."

"Shoot," you say.

And then Rosen says this:

Today's online social networks are congeries of mostly weak ties—no one who lists thousands of "friends" on MySpace thinks of those people in the same way as he does his flesh-and-blood acquaintances, for example. It is surely no coincidence, then, that the activities social networking sites promote are precisely the ones weak ties foster, like rumor-mongering, gossip, finding people, and tracking the ever-shifting movements of popular culture and fad. If this is our small world, it is one that gives its greatest attention to small things.*

STEP 1: Begin a five-minute fastwrite in which you respond to Rosen's comment. Try to hold up your end of the conversation. Whenever the writing stalls, return to the passage above and find something else to respond to—ask questions, react, present your own ideas, try to restate what you think Rosen seems to be saying.

Lunch continues. Rosen seems genuinely interested in your response to her ideas. She sets her glass of water down after a sip, looks you in the eye, and says, "Okay, what do you think of this?":

> . . . [I]n the offline world, communities typically are responsible for enforcing norms of privacy and general etiquette. In the online world, which is unfettered by the boundaries of real-world communities, new etiquette challenges abound. For example, what do you do with a "friend" who posts inappropriate comments on your Wall? What recourse do you have if someone posts an embarrassing picture of you on his MySpace page? What happens when a friend breaks up with someone—do you defriend the ex? If someone "friends" you and you don't accept the overture, how serious a rejection is it? Some of these scenarios can be resolved with split-second snap judgments; others can provoke days of agonizing.

STEP 2: Begin another five-minute fastwrite in your notebook in which you respond to this latest proposition by your luncheon partner. Again, try to preserve the relatively informal, conversational quality of the situation.

Lunch is nearly over, and Rosen seems finished talking. You're wondering about who will pick up the check. Suddenly, Rosen says, "Sorry. There's just one more thing I'd like to say. Will you hear me out?"

Your pen is at the ready.

She says:

> The implications of the narcissistic and exhibitionistic tendencies of social networkers also cry out for further consideration. There are opportunity costs when we spend so much time

---

*Christine Rosen, "Virtual Friendship and the New Narcissism," *The New Atlantis: A Journal of Technology and Society* (Summer 2007): 15–31.

carefully grooming ourselves online. Given how much time we already devote to entertaining ourselves with technology, it is at least worth asking if the time we spend on social networking sites is well spent. In investing so much energy into improving how we *present* ourselves online, are we missing chances to genuinely *improve* ourselves?

STEP 3: You graciously respond to Rosen once more in a five-minute fastwrite.

Your instructor may have you read the full text of Rosen's article (Exercise 3.5) and ask you to compose an essay that grows out of this written conversation. What I most want you to notice at this point, however, is whether this dialogue with a published author has anything in common with conventional notetaking. If not, what are the differences? Later in this chapter, I suggest an approach to notetaking that combines conventional quotation, summary, and paraphrase with the kind of open-ended writing you accomplished here. It's a process that encourages the kind of *dialectical* thinking that is at the heart of inquiry, the movement back and forth between your observations and your ideas about them, between generating and judging, and collecting evidence and developing theories about what it might mean.

> **A Variation in Responding: Believing and Doubting**
>
> In each fastwrite response to Rosen, consider spending the first two minutes playing "the believing game" and the next two minutes "the doubting game." In other words, begin by thinking through writing about why Rosen might see things the way she does. What can you *understand* about her point of view? What might you agree with? Then shift your stance, and critically examine her claims. What is she ignoring? What fault do you find with her reasoning? How does your own experience offer contrary evidence?

Most *good* conversations make demands on both speakers. The most important of these is simply to listen carefully to what the other person is saying, even (and perhaps especially) if you don't agree. In couples therapy there's a method to help this along called "say back"—each partner has to listen first and then repeat what he or she heard the other say. Response or reaction comes later. Researchers entering into a conversation with their sources need to engage in the same practice: Listen or read carefully, first making an effort to understand a subject or author's arguments or ideas, and then exploring your response to them, as you did in the preceding exercise.

The academic equivalent of "say back" is paraphrasing or summarizing. Both are undervalued skills, I think, that require practice. Try your hand at it in the following exercise.

EXERCISE 3.2

"Say Back" to a Source

The following passage is from an article by linguist Deborah Tannen on the complexity of communication within families.

> Through talk, we create and shape our relationships. Through talk, we are comforted; through talk we are hurt. We look to family members for come-as-you-are acceptance, but instead of an intimate ally, we sometimes find an intimate critic. A small remark can spark a big conflict because with the family, no utterance stands alone. Every remark draws meaning from innumerable conversations that came before.*

In your notebook, rewrite the passage in your own words in roughly the same length—a *paraphrase*. You'll find it's easier to do if you first focus on understanding what Tannen is trying to say and then write without looking much at the passage, if possible. If this is an in-class exercise, exchange your rewrite with a partner. Then read the following section on plagiarism.

Recognizing Plagiarism

Simply put, *plagiarism* is using others' ideas *or* words as if they were your own. The most egregious case is handing in someone else's work with your name on it. Some schools also consider using one paper to meet the requirements of two classes to be a grave offense. But most plagiarism is unintentional. I remember being guilty of plagiarism when writing a philosophy paper my freshman year in college. I committed the offense largely because I didn't know what plagiarism was and I hadn't been adequately schooled in good scholarship (which is no excuse).

*Deborah Tannen, "I Heard What You Didn't Say," *The Washington Post,* May 13, 2001: B1.

I Read What You Said and Borrowed It, Okay?

Here's another passage from the same article by Deborah Tannen. In this excerpt she is talking about a situation with which we're all familiar. We're talking with a loved one and he or she makes a comment that seems innocuous—"I'll put the dishes in the dishwasher because I can pack more in"—but the comment is heard as a larger criticism: "You're not good at housework." There are what seem to be simple messages with equally simple motives, and then there are "metamessages" that we sometimes hear instead of the simple ones. What follows is Tannen's original passage, and what seems like a pretty good paraphrase.

Original passage: *Distinguishing the message from the metamessage (terms I have adopted from anthropologist Gregory Bateson) is necessary to ensure that family members work things out rather than working each other over. It's frustrating to have the same arguments again and again. But some arguments can be constructive—if family members use them to articulate and understand the metamessages they are intending and hearing.*

Paraphrase: Sometimes family members can have the same argument over and over and not realize that they're arguing about two different things. Linguist Deborah Tannen writes that it's important to distinguish between the message and the metamessages; a message may have a simple intention but it is heard as something quite different, something the speaker didn't intend at all. By articulating what was said and what was heard, arguments can be constructive rather than frustrating.

There are a couple of problems with this paraphrase but they might, at first, seem pretty subtle. Notice that the first line uses the phrase "have the same argument over and over" which, though worded slightly different, copies the pattern of Tannen's original "have the same arguments again and again." That won't do.

Worse, the paraphrase fails to include quotation marks around the borrowed phrase "the message and the metamessage." It also lifts "constructive" from the original without quotation marks and uses the word "articulating" in the paraphrase, without quotation marks, which also is uncomfortably close to Tannen's "articulate." But the bigger problem is not one I would expect you to notice yet. Even though the paraphrase uses an attribution tag—"Linguist Deborah Tannen writes . . ."—the paraphrase doesn't include a parenthetical

What Is Plagiarism?

Each college or university has a statement in the student handbook that offers a local definition. But that statement probably includes most or all of the following forms of plagiarism.

1. Handing in someone else's work—a downloaded paper from the Internet or one borrowed from a friend—and claiming that it's your own.
2. Using information or ideas that are not common knowledge from any source and failing to acknowledge that source.
3. Handing in the same paper for two different classes.
4. Using the exact language or expressions of a source and not indicating through quotation marks and citation that the language is borrowed.
5. Rewriting a passage from a source by minor substitutions of different words but retaining the same syntax and structure of the original.

citation, something like (Tannen 2) indicating the page number from which the passage was borrowed. We'll talk later about citation, but here's the key thing to remember: *Whenever you quote, paraphrase, or summarize a source, it must always be cited, even if you mention the author's name.*

Corrected paraphrase: Old family arguments may not really be about what family members have always thought they were about. Linguist Deborah Tannen writes that it's important to distinguish between **"the message and the metamessage"**; a message may have a simple intention but is heard as something quite different, something the speaker didn't intend at all. Even old family arguments can be **"constructive,"** says Tannen, if family members are careful to talk openly about this difference (**Tannen 2**).

Here are some simple tactics for avoiding plagiarism:

- It's fine to borrow distinctive terms or phrases from a source, but also signal that you've done so with quotation marks.
- Make a habit of using attribution tags, signaling to your reader who is the source of the idea, quotation, or fact. These tags include things such as, *Tannen argues, Tannen writes, According*

to Tannen, etc. For a lengthy list of these tags, see the box, "Active Verbs for Discussing Ideas," in Chapter 5.

■ *Always* cite borrowed material (more about how to do that later).

As a follow up to Exercise 3.2, return to the paraphrase you composed of the Tannen passage on talk within families. Do you need to edit or alter the paraphrase you wrote to avoid possible plagiarism problems? If you're in class, your instructor may ask you to work in pairs on this. What are the common plagiarism mistakes—almost always unintentional—that students in the class made when they paraphrased the passage in Exercise 3.2?

Why Plagiarism Matters

It may seem that all the fuss over plagiarism is just another example of English teachers' obsession with rules. In fact, the saddest days I've ever had as a writing teacher have always been when I've talked with a student about a paper she downloaded from the Internet or borrowed from her roommate. Most instructors hate dealing with plagiarism. It is, of course, a moral issue, but the motive to be careful about distinguishing what is yours and what you've borrowed isn't just a matter of "being good." It's really a gesture of gratitude. Research is always built on the work that came before it, and as you read and write about your topic, I hope that you come to appreciate the thoughtful writing and thinking of people before you who may have given you a new way of seeing or thinking.

Knowledge is a living thing (see Figure 3.1), growing like a great tree in multiple directions, adding and losing branches which keep reaching higher toward new understandings and truths.

The Common Knowledge Exception

While you always have to tell readers what information you have borrowed and where it came from, things that are "common knowledge" are excluded from this. Everyone knows, for example, that John Kennedy died in Dallas in November 1963. These and other widely known facts need not be cited. Neither do observations that anyone could make or common sayings, such as "home is where the heart is."

Why Cite?

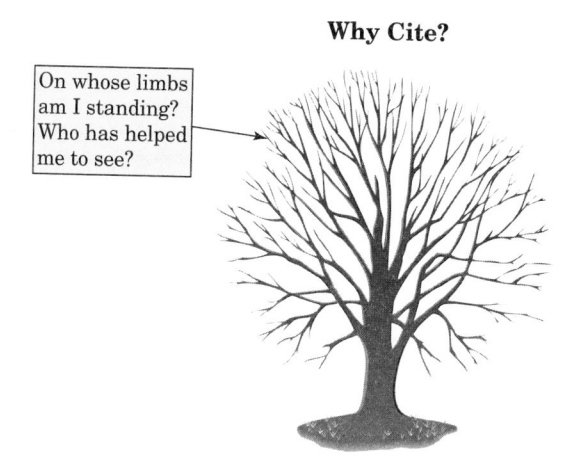

On whose limbs am I standing? Who has helped me to see?

FIGURE 3.1   Like a tree, knowledge in a discipline is a living thing, from time to time losing and adding branches, growing in new directions.

As researchers we are tree climbers, ascending the branches in an effort to see better. It's only natural that as we make this climb, we feel grateful for the strength of certain limbs under our feet. Citing and acknowledging sources is a way of expressing this gratitude.

Sources Are from Mars, Notetakers Are from Venus

I have to admit that I never read John Gray's bestseller about the complexity of communication between men and women, *Men Are from Mars, Women Are from Venus,* but I like the metaphor that sometimes it seems as if men and women are from different planets; I think the metaphor applies to notetaking, too. Consider how awkward it is to read someone else's words, make a concerted effort to understand what they mean, and then find your own words to restate the ideas. What's worse is that sometimes the authors are experts who use language you may not easily grasp or use reasoning in ways you can't easily follow. And then there are those authors who write so beautifully, you wonder how you could possibly say it better. Finally, there might be the fear that somehow you will goof and plagiarize the source's ideas or words.

For all of these reasons, the relationship between a source and a research writer is often complex. Both might as well be on different planets.

Paraphrasing

In Exercise 3.2, you practiced "say back," a technique that helps many married couples who are headed for divorce. As I mentioned, *paraphrase* is the academic equivalent of this therapeutic method for getting people to listen to each other. Try to say in your own words— and in about the same length as the author said it—what you understand that author to mean. This is hard, at first, because instead of just mindlessly quoting—a favorite alternative for many students— you have to *think*. Paraphrasing demands that you make your own sense of something. The time is well worth it. Why? Because not only are you lowering the risk of unintentional plagiarism and being fair to the source's ideas, *you are essentially writing a fragment of your draft*. Exercise 3.3 will help you develop these skills.

EXERCISE 3 . 3

Paraphrase Practice

At the heart of paraphrasing is this very simple idea: *Good writers find their own way of saying things*. That's your challenge here. Read each line or passage below until you think you thoroughly understand it, and then don't look at it again. Paraphrase the passage on a separate piece of paper finding your own way of saying what you understand the original passage to mean. Finally, review your paraphrase to make sure that any borrowed words or phrases from the original are within quotation marks in your paraphrase.

The lines and passages get progressively harder to paraphrase.

1. For most of the last 500 years, imitation was the sincerest form of architectural flattery.*

2. According to the National Institutes of Health,
   - Percentage of U.S.-born *Mexican* Americans who have suffered from some psychological disorder: 48
   - Percentage of Mexican immigrants who have: 29
   - Percentage of Mexico City residents who have: 23

*Witold Rybczynski, "When Architects Plagiarize It's Not Always Bad," *Slate*, Sept. 14, 2005; www.slate.com/id/2126270/?nav=tap3, Sept. 15, 2005.

3. Houseflies not only defecate constantly, but do so in liquid form, which means they are in constant danger of dehydration.*

4. An increasing number of Americans have come to view Islam as a religion that encourages violence while a declining number say Islam has a lot in common with their own religion. The public remains divided over whether churches should stay out of politics, even as large numbers say they are comfortable with expressions of faith by political leaders.†

Exercise 3.3 returns me to my original argument: Thoughtful notetaking pays off in the long run because you're essentially writing your essay in the middle of the process. Imagine what an advantage you'll have over those who wait until the night before the paper is due. Rather than pages of journal notes ripe for the picking, the night-before-it's-due clan is looking at bare branches. In a few pages, I'll suggest several notetaking methods that I think will give you the most to harvest; one of these, the double-entry journal, is a method that combines both the kind of listening that paraphrase demands and the open-ended exploratory thinking that you enjoyed in Exercise 3.1, the conversation with Rosen. But first, let's review another listening technique useful for academic writers: summary.

Summarizing

In order to sell a movie to Hollywood, a screenwriter should be able to summarize what it's about in a sentence. "*Juno* is a film about a smart, single, pregnant teenager who finds unexpected humor in her situation but finally finds that her wit is not enough to help her navigate the emotional tsunami her pregnancy triggers in the lives of those around her." That statement hardly does justice to the film—which is about so much more than that—but I think it basically captures the story and its central theme.

Obviously, that's what a *summary* is: a reduction of longer material into some brief statement that captures a basic idea, argument, or theme from the original. Like paraphrasing, summarizing often requires careful thought, since you're the one doing the distilling, especially if you're trying to capture the essence of a whole movie, article, or chapter that's fairly complex. But many times,

---

*Richard Conniff, "Why Did God Make Flies?" *Wonders* (New York: Owl, 1997).
†Pew Forum on Religion and Public Life, "Religion and Politics: Contention and Consensus," www.pewforum.org/docs/index.php?DocID=26, July 25, 2005.

summarizing involves simply boiling down a passage—not the entire work—to its basic idea.

EXERCISE 3.4

Summary Practice

Does Madonna make art? Does Jay-Z? Certainly Mozart did, right? Simon Frith, a scholar who writes about theories of popular music, thinks that we need an "aesthetic theory" to talk about pop music of all kinds but sees resistance to the idea. In the following passage, an excerpt from his book *Popular Music: Critical Concepts in Media and Cultural Studies*, Frith writes about this problem.

The excerpt is typical of the kinds of writing you'll encounter in scholarly books—it seems to use some unfamiliar jargon and follows a line of reasoning that may not be immediately obvious to you. That's why it will be a great opportunity for you to practice summary.

Carefully read the passage, and write a brief (two to four sentences) summary of his main point. Make sure to say it in your own words, and if you borrow any words from Frith, don't forget those quotation marks.

> Underlying all the other distinctions critics draw between "serious" and "popular" music is an assumption about the source of musical value. Serious music matters because it transcends social forces; popular music is aesthetically worthless because it is determined by them (because it is "useful" or "utilitarian"). This argument, common enough among academic musicologists, puts sociologists in an odd position. If we venture to suggest that the value of, say, Beethoven's music can be explained by the social conditions determining its production and subsequent consumption we are dismissed as philistines—aesthetic theories of classical music remain decidedly non-sociological. Popular music, by contrast, is taken to be good only for sociological theory. Our very success in explaining the rise of rock' n' roll or the appearance of disco proves their lack of aesthetic interest. To relate music and society becomes, then, a different task according to the music we are treating. In analyzing serious music, we have to uncover the social forces concealed in the talk of "transcendent" values; in analyzing pop, we have to take seriously the values scoffed at in the talk of social functions.*

*Simon Frith, *Popular Music: Critical Concepts in Media and Cultural Studies* (London: Routledge, 2004) 32.

A summary, where you distill only part of a larger source, is selective. You choose to emphasize some key part of a source because it fits your paper's purpose. But the same warning applies to selective summarizing as was given earlier about paraphrasing: Don't misrepresent the general thrust of the author's ideas. Ask yourself, Does my selective use of this source seem to give it a spin the author didn't intend? Most of the time, I think you will discover the answer is no.

Quoting

The quotation mark may be the student researcher's best friend, at least as demonstrated by how often papers are peppered by long quotes!

As a general rule, the college research paper should contain no more than 10 or 20 percent quoted material, but it's an easy rule to ignore. For one thing, quoting sources at the notetaking and drafting stages is quicker than restating material in your own words. When you quote, you don't have to think much about what you're reading; you just jot it down the way you see it and, if you have to, think about it later. That's the real problem with verbatim copying of source material: There isn't much thinking involved. As a result, the writer doesn't take possession of the information, shape it, and allow herself to be shaped by it.

That's not to say that you should completely avoid quoting sources directly as a method of notetaking. If you're writing on a literary topic, for example, you may quote fairly extensively from the novel or poem you're examining. Or if your paper relies heavily on interviews, you'll want to bring in the voices of your subjects, verbatim.

When to Quote. As a rule, jot down a quote when someone says or writes something that is distinctive in a certain way and when restating it in your own words wouldn't possibly do the thought justice. I'll never forget a scene from the documentary *Shoah,* an eleven-hour film about the Holocaust, which presented an interview with the Polish engineer of one of the trains that took thousands of Jews to their deaths. Now an old man and still operating the same train, he was asked how he felt now about his role in World War II. He said quietly, "If you could lick my heart, it would poison you."

It would be difficult to restate the Polish engineer's comment in your own words. But more important, it would be stupid even to try. Some of the pain and regret and horror of that time in history is embedded in that one man's words. You may not come across such a distinctive quote as you read your sources this week, but be alert to *how* authors (and those quoted by authors) say things. Is the prose unusual, surprising, or memorable? Does the writer make a point in an interesting way? If so, jot it down.

Heidi, in a paper on the children's television program *Sesame Street,* began by quoting a eulogy for Muppets creator Jim Henson. The quote is both memorable and touching. Heidi made an appropriate choice, establishing a tone that is consistent with her purpose: to respond to certain critics of the program. The fact that a quote sounds good isn't reason enough to use it. Like anything else, quotes should be used deliberately, with purpose.

There are several other reasons to quote a source as you're notetaking. Sometimes, it's desirable to quote an expert on your topic who is widely recognized in the field. Used to support or develop your own assertions, the voice of an authority can lend credit to your argument and demonstrate your effort to bring recognized voices into the discussion.

Another reason to quote a source is that his explanation of a process or idea is especially clear. Such quotes often feature metaphors. Robert Bly's *Iron John,* a book that looks at American men and their difficult journey into manhood, is filled with clear and compelling explanations of that process. As a son of an alcoholic father, I found Bly's discussion often hit home. Here, using a metaphor, he explains in a simple but compelling way how children in troubled homes become emotionally unprotected, something that often haunts them the rest of their lives:

> When a boy grows up in a "dysfunctional" family (perhaps there is no other kind of family), his interior warriors will be killed off early. Warriors, mythologically, lift their swords to defend the king. The King in a child stands for and stands up for the child's mood. But when we are children our mood gets easily overrun and swept over in the messed-up family by the more powerful, more dominant, more terrifying mood of the parent. We can say that when the warriors inside cannot protect our mood from being disintegrated, or defend our body from invasion, the warriors collapse, go into a trance, or die.*

I'm sure there's a more technical explanation for the ways parents in dysfunctional families can dominate the emotional lives of their children. But the warrior metaphor is so simple; that is, partly, its power. As you read or take notes during an interview, be alert to sources or subjects who say something that gets right to the heart of an important idea. Listen for it.

If your paper is on a literary topic—involving novels, stories, poems, and other works—then purposeful and selective quoting

---

*Robert Bly, *Iron John: A Book About Men* (Reading, MA: Addison-Wesley, 1990), 147.

is especially important and appropriate. The texts and the actual language the writers use in them are often central to the argument you're making. If you're writing about the misfit heroes in J. D. Salinger's novels, asserting that they embody the author's own character, then you'll have to dip freely into his books, quoting passages that illustrate that idea. (See Appendix C for an essay on literary topics that use quotes effectively.)

Quoting Fairly.   If you do choose to quote from a source, be careful to do three things: (1) Quote accurately, (2) make sure it's clear in your notes that what you're jotting down is quoted material, and (3) beware of distorting a quote by using it out of context. The first two guidelines protect you from plagiarism, and the last ensures that you're fair to your sources.

To guarantee the accuracy of a quote, you may want to photocopy the page or article with the borrowed material. A tape recorder can help in an interview, and so can asking your subject to repeat something that seems especially important. To alert yourself to which part of your notes is a quote of the source's words, try using oversized quotation marks around the passage so that it can't be missed.

Guarding against out-of-context quotations can be a little more difficult. After all, an isolated quote has already been removed from the context of the many other things a subject has said. That shouldn't be a problem if you have represented her ideas accurately. However, sometimes a quote can misrepresent a source by what is omitted. Simply be fair to the author by noting any important qualifications she may make to something said or written, and render her ideas as completely as possible in your paper.

EXERCISE 3.5

Dialogic Notetaking: Listening In, Speaking Up

There's the skills part of note taking—knowing how to cite, summarize, paraphrase, and quote correctly—and then there's the more interesting, harder part—making *use* of what you're reading to discover what you think. So far, we've talked about this latter process using the metaphor of conversation. In Exercise 3.1, you tried out this idea, responding in writing to Christine Rosen's ideas about the influence of social networking sites like Facebook on how we think about friendship. I asked you to imagine that this was literally a conversation between you and Rosen, except that the voices you heard were in writing rather than speech.

The Unending Conversation

Imagine that you enter a parlor. You come late. When you arrive, others have long preceded you, and they are engaged in a heated discussion, a discussion too heated for them to pause and tell you exactly what it is about. In fact, the discussion had already begun long before any of them got there, so that no one present is qualified to retrace for you all the steps that had gone before. You listen for a while, until you decide that you have caught the tenor of the argument; then you put in your oar. Someone answers; you answer him; another comes to your defense; another aligns himself against you, to either the embarrassment or gratification of your opponent, depending upon the quality of your ally's assistance. However, the discussion is interminable. The hour grows late, you must depart. And you do depart, with the discussion still vigorously in progress.

Kenneth Burke

This conversation metaphor doesn't originate with me. Lots of people use it to describe how all knowledge is made. One theorist, Kenneth Burke, famously explained that we might imagine that all scholarship on nearly any subject is much like a parlor conversation between people in the know (see box above). These are the experts who, over time, have contributed to the discussions about what might be true and who constantly ask questions to keep the conversation going.

As newcomers to this conversation, we don't really have much to contribute. It's important that we listen in so that we begin to understand what has already been said and who has said it. But at some point, even novices like us, are expected to speak up. We're not there to simply record what we hear. We're writers. We're supposed to discover something to say.

A lot of people have weighed in on the impact of technology on how we live, think, and feel. That conversation won't be contained by any parlor. Think convention hall, or maybe football stadium. But imagine that in one corner of that hall a smaller group is talking about the impact of social networking on our relationships with each other. Coincidentally, the moment you arrive Christine Rosen, who you met earlier, has the floor, and she's talking in more detail about the things she mentioned in the earlier exercise. You can hear what she's saying by reading a portion of her longer essay, "Virtual Friendship and the New Narcissism," starting on page 632.

STEP 1:

1. Begin by listening in. Read Christine Rosen's essay once straight through. Underline and mark passages that you think are:
   a. important to your understanding of the article,
   b. puzzling in some way,
   c. surprising, or
   d. connected with your own initial ideas and experiences.

2. Reread the opening paragraph, ending few paragraphs, and all of your marked passages, and then, without looking at the article, compose a two- or three-sentence summary of what you understand to be the most important thing the article is saying. Write this down on the left page of your notebook.

3. Find two passages in the article that you think are good examples of what you state in your summary. Copy these on the left page of your notebook, too.

STEP 2: Now speak up. Use the right side of your notebook to explore your thinking about what Rosen is saying. Look on the opposing left pages to remind yourself of some of her ideas and assertions. This is an open-ended fastwrite, but here are some prompts to get you writing and thinking:

- Tell the story of your thinking:
  - When I first started thinking about this topic, I thought _____, and then I thought _____, and then, and then . . . but now I think _____.

- Consider ways you've begun to think differently:
  - I used to think _____, but now I'm starting to think _____.

- Try both believing and doubting:
  - *The most convincing points Rosen makes in her essay are _____. or Though I don't necessarily agree with Rosen, I can understand why she would think that _____.*
  - And then: *The thing that Rosen ignores or fails to understand is _____. or The least convincing claim she makes is _____ because _____.*

- Use questions:
  - The most important question Rosen raises is _____.
  - The question that she fails to ask is _____.

Discuss in class how this notetaking exercise worked. What went well? What was difficult? How did your initial thoughts influence your reading of the article? Did your thinking change? Which of these techniques will you continue to use in your notetaking?

Virtual Friendship and the New Narcissism*

by Christine Rosen

Christine Rosen *is a senior editor of* The New Atlantis *and a fellow at the Ethics and Public Policy Center.*

For centuries, the rich and the powerful documented their existence and their status through painted portraits. A marker of wealth and a bid for immortality, portraits offer intriguing hints about the daily life of their subjects—professions, ambitions, attitudes, and, most importantly, social standing. Such portraits, as German art historian Hans Belting has argued, can be understood as "painted anthropology," with much to teach us, both intentionally and unintentionally, about the culture in which they were created.

Self-portraits can be especially instructive. By showing the artist both as he sees his true self and as he wishes to be seen, self-portraits can at once expose and obscure, clarify and distort. They offer opportunities for both self-expression and self-seeking. They can display egotism and modesty, self-aggrandizement and self-mockery.

Today, our self-portraits are democratic and digital; they are crafted from pixels rather than paints. On social networking websites like MySpace and Facebook, our modern self-portraits feature background music, carefully manipulated photographs, stream-of-consciousness musings, and lists of our hobbies and friends. They are interactive, inviting viewers not merely to look at, but also to respond to, the life portrayed online. We create them to find friendship, love, and that ambiguous modern thing called connection. Like painters constantly retouching their work, we alter, update, and tweak our online self-portraits; but as digital objects they are far more ephemeral than oil on canvas. Vital statistics, glimpses of bare flesh, lists of favorite bands and favorite poems all clamor for our attention—and it is the timeless human desire for attention that emerges as the dominant theme of these vast virtual galleries.

Although social networking sites are in their infancy, we are seeing their impact culturally: in language (where *to friend* is now a verb), in politics (where it is *de rigueur* for presidential aspirants to catalogue their virtues on MySpace), and on college campuses (where *not* using Facebook can be a social handicap). But we are only beginning to come to grips with the consequences of our use of these sites: for friendship, and for our notions of privacy, authenticity, community, and identity. As with any new technological advance, we must consider what type of behavior online social networking encourages. Does this technology, with its constant demands to collect (friends and status), and perform (by marketing ourselves), in some ways undermine our ability to attain what it promises—a surer sense of who we are and where we belong? The Delphic oracle's guidance was *know thyself*. Today, in the world of online social networks, the oracle's advice might be *show thyself*. . . .

Won't You Be My Digital Neighbor?

According to a survey recently conducted by the Pew Internet and American Life Project, more than half of all Americans between the ages of twelve and seventeen use some online social networking site. Indeed, media coverage of social networking sites usually describes them as vast teenage playgrounds—or wastelands, depending on one's perspective. Central to this narrative is a nearly unbridgeable generational divide, with tech-savvy youngsters redefining friendship while their doddering elders look on with bafflement and increasing anxiety. This seems anecdotally correct; I can't count how many times I have mentioned social networking websites to someone over the age of forty and received the reply, "Oh yes, I've heard about that MyFace! All the kids are doing that these days. Very interesting!"

Numerous articles have chronicled adults' attempts to navigate the world of social networking, such as the recent *New York Times* essay in which columnist Michelle Slatalla described the incredible embarrassment she caused her teenage daughter when she joined Facebook: "everyone in the whole world thinks its super creepy when adults have facebooks," her daughter instant-messaged her. "unfriend paige right now. im serious. . . . i will be soo mad if you dont unfriend paige right now. actually." In fact, social networking sites are not only for the young. More than half of the visitors to MySpace claim to be over the age of 35. And now that the first generation of college Facebook users have graduated, and the site is open to all, more than half of Facebook users are no longer students. What's more, the proliferation of niche social networking sites, including those aimed at adults, suggests that it is not only teenagers who will nurture relationships in virtual space for the foreseeable future.

What characterizes these online communities in which an increasing number of us are spending our time? Social networking sites have a peculiar psychogeography. As researchers at the Pew project have noted, the proto-social networking sites of a decade ago used metaphors of *place* to organize their members: people were linked through virtual cities, communities, and homepages. In 1997, GeoCities boasted thirty virtual "neighborhoods" in which "homesteaders" or "GeoCitizens" could gather—"Heartland" for family and parenting tips, "SouthBeach" for socializing, "Vienna" for classical music aficionados, "Broadway" for theater buffs, and so on. By contrast, today's social networking sites organize themselves around metaphors of the *person,* with individual profiles that list hobbies and interests. As a result, one's entrée into this world generally isn't through a virtual neighborhood or community but through the revelation of personal information. And unlike a neighborhood, where one usually has a general knowledge of others who live in the area, social networking sites are gatherings of deracinated individuals, none of whose personal boastings and musings are necessarily trustworthy. Here, the old arbiters of community—geographic location, family, role, or occupation—have little effect on relationships.

Also, in the offline world, communities typically are responsible for enforcing norms of privacy and general etiquette. In the online world, which is unfettered by the boundaries of real-world communities, new etiquette challenges abound. For example, what do you do with a "friend" who posts inappropriate comments on your Wall? What recourse do you have if someone posts an embarrassing picture of you on his MySpace page? What happens when a friend breaks up with someone—do you defriend the ex? If someone "friends" you and you don't accept the overture, how serious a rejection is it? Some of these scenarios can be resolved with split-second snap judgments; others can provoke days of agonizing.

Enthusiasts of social networking argue that these sites are not merely entertaining; they also edify by teaching users about the rules of social space. As Danah Boyd, a graduate student studying social networks at the University of California, Berkeley, told the authors of *MySpace Unraveled,* social networking promotes "informal learning.... It's where you learn social norms, rules, how to interact with others, narrative, personal and group history, and media literacy." This is more a hopeful assertion than a proven fact, however. The question that isn't asked is how the technology itself—the way it encourages us to present ourselves and interact—limits or imposes on that process of informal learning. All communities expect their members to internalize certain norms. Even individuals in the transient communities that form in public spaces obey these rules, for the most part; for example, patrons of libraries are expected to keep noise to a minimum. New technologies are challenging such norms—cell phones ring during church sermons; blaring televisions in doctors' waiting rooms make it difficult to talk quietly—and new norms must develop to replace the old. What cues are young, avid social networkers learning about social space? What unspoken rules and communal norms have the millions of participants in these online social networks internalized, and how have these new norms influenced their behavior in the offline world?

Social rules and norms are not merely the strait-laced conceits of a bygone era; they serve a protective function. I know a young woman—attractive, intelligent, and well-spoken—who, like many other people in their twenties, joined Facebook as a college student when it launched. When she and her boyfriend got engaged, they both updated their relationship status to "Engaged" on their profiles and friends posted congratulatory messages on her Wall.

But then they broke off the engagement. And a funny thing happened. Although she had already told a few friends and family members that the relationship was over, her ex decided to make it official in a very twenty-first century way: he changed his status on his profile from "Engaged" to "Single." Facebook immediately sent out a feed to every one of their mutual "friends" announcing the news, "Mr. X and Ms. Y are no longer in a relationship," complete with an icon of a broken heart. When I asked the young woman how she felt about this, she said that although she assumed her friends and acquaintances would eventually hear the news, there was something disconcerting about the fact that everyone found out about it instantaneously; and since the message came from Facebook, rather than in a face-to-face exchange initiated by her, it was devoid of context—save for a helpful notation of the time and that tacky little heart.

Indecent Exposure

Enthusiasts praise social networking for presenting chances for identity-play; they see opportunities for all of us to be little Van Goghs and Warhols, rendering quixotic and ever-changing versions of ourselves for others to enjoy. Instead of a palette of oils, we can employ services such as PimpMySpace.org, which offers "layouts, graphics, background, and more!" to gussy up an online presentation of self, albeit in a decidedly raunchy fashion: Among the most popular graphics used by PimpMySpace clients on a given day in June 2007 were short video clips of two women kissing and another of a man and an obese woman having sex; a picture of a gleaming pink handgun; and an image of the cartoon character SpongeBob SquarePants, looking alarmed and uttering a profanity.

This kind of coarseness and vulgarity is commonplace on social networking sites for a reason: it's an easy way to set oneself apart. Pharaohs and kings once celebrated themselves by erecting towering statues or, like the emperor Augustus, placing their own visages on coins. But now, as the insightful technology observer Jaron Lanier has written, "Since there are only a few archetypes, ideals, or icons to strive for in comparison to the vastness of instances of everything online, quirks and idiosyncrasies stand out better than grandeur in this new domain. I imagine Augustus' MySpace page would have pictured him picking his nose." And he wouldn't be alone. Indeed, this is one of the characteristics of MySpace most striking to anyone who spends a few hours trolling its millions of pages: it is an overwhelmingly dull sea of monotonous uniqueness, of conventional individuality, of distinctive sameness.

The world of online social networking is practically homogenous in one other sense, however diverse it might at first appear: its users are committed to self-exposure. The creation and conspicuous consumption of intimate details and images of one's own and others' lives is the main activity in the online social networking world. There is no room for reticence; there is only revelation. Quickly peruse a profile and you know more about a potential acquaintance in a moment than you might have learned about a flesh-and-blood friend in a month. As one college student recently described to the *New York Times Magazine:* "You might run into someone at a party, and then you Facebook them: what are their interests? Are they crazy-religious, is their favorite quote from the Bible? Everyone takes great pains over presenting themselves. It's like an embodiment of your personality."

It seems that in our headlong rush to join social networking sites, many of us give up one of the Internet's supposed charms: the promise of anonymity. As Michael Kinsley noted in *Slate,* in order to "stake their claims as unique individuals," users enumerate personal information: "Here is a list of my friends. Here are all the CDs in my collection. Here is a picture of my dog." Kinsley is not impressed; he judges these sites "vast celebrations of solipsism." . . .

The New Taxonomy of Friendship

There is a Spanish proverb that warns, "Life without a friend is death without a witness." In the world of online social networking, the warning might be simpler: "Life without hundreds of online 'friends' is virtual death." On these sites, friendship is the stated *raison d'être*. "A place for friends," is the slogan of MySpace. Facebook is a "social utility that connects people with friends." Orkut describes itself as "an online community that connects people through a network of trusted friends." Friendster's name speaks for itself.

But "friendship" in these virtual spaces is thoroughly different from real-world friendship. In its traditional sense, friendship is a relationship which, broadly speaking, involves the sharing of mutual interests, reciprocity, trust, and the revelation of intimate details over time and within specific social (and cultural) contexts. Because friendship depends on mutual revelations that are concealed from the rest of the world, it can only flourish within the boundaries of privacy; the idea of public friendship is an oxymoron.

The hypertext link called "friendship" on social networking sites is very different: public, fluid, and promiscuous, yet oddly bureaucratized. Friendship on these sites focuses a great deal on collecting, managing, and ranking the people you know. Everything about MySpace, for example, is designed to encourage users to gather as many friends as possible, as though friendship were philately. If you are so unfortunate as to have but one MySpace friend, for example, your page reads: "You have 1 friends," along with a stretch of sad empty space where dozens of thumbnail photos of your acquaintances should appear.

This promotes a form of frantic friend procurement. As one young Facebook user with 800 friends told John Cassidy in *The New Yorker,* "I always find the competitive spirit in me wanting to up the number." An associate dean at Purdue University recently boasted to the *Christian Science Monitor* that since establishing a Facebook profile, he had collected more than 700 friends. The phrase universally found on MySpace is, "Thanks for the add!"—an acknowledgment by one user that another has added you to his list of friends. There are even services like FriendFlood.com that act as social networking pimps: for a fee, they will post messages on your page from an attractive person posing as your "friend." As the founder of one such service told the *New York Times* in February 2007, he wanted to "turn cyber-losers into social-networking magnets."

The structure of social networking sites also encourages the bureaucratization of friendship. Each site has its own terminology, but among the words that users employ most often is "managing." The Pew survey mentioned earlier found that "teens say social networking sites help them manage their friendships." There is something Orwellian about the management-speak on social networking sites: "Change My Top Friends," "View All of My Friends" and, for those times when our inner Stalins sense the need for a virtual purge, "Edit

Friends." With a few mouse clicks one can elevate or downgrade (or entirely eliminate) a relationship.

To be sure, we all rank our friends, albeit in unspoken and intuitive ways. One friend might be a good companion for outings to movies or concerts; another might be someone with whom you socialize in professional settings; another might be the kind of person for whom you would drop everything if he needed help. But social networking sites allow us to rank our friends publicly. And not only can we publicize our own preferences in people, but we can also peruse the favorites among our other acquaintances. We can learn all about the friends of our friends—often without having ever met them in person.

Status-Seekers

Of course, it would be foolish to suggest that people are incapable of making distinctions between social networking "friends" and friends they see in the flesh. The use of the word "friend" on social networking sites is a dilution and a debasement, and surely no one with hundreds of MySpace or Facebook "friends" is so confused as to believe those are all real friendships. The impulse to collect as many "friends" as possible on a MySpace page is not an expression of the human need for companionship, but of a different need no less profound and pressing: the need for status. Unlike the painted portraits that members of the middle class in a bygone era would commission to signal their elite status once they rose in society, social networking websites allow us to *create* status—not merely to commemorate the achievement of it. There is a reason that most of the MySpace profiles of famous people are fakes, often created by fans: Celebrities don't need legions of MySpace friends to prove their importance. It's the rest of the population, seeking a form of parochial celebrity, that does.

But status-seeking has an ever-present partner: anxiety. Unlike a portrait, which, once finished and framed, hung tamely on the wall signaling one's status, maintaining status on MySpace or Facebook requires constant vigilance. As one 24-year-old wrote in a *New York Times* essay, "I am obsessed with testimonials and solicit them incessantly. They are the ultimate social currency, public declarations of the intimacy status of a relationship. . . . Every profile is a carefully planned media campaign."

The sites themselves were designed to encourage this. Describing the work of B.J. Fogg of Stanford University, who studies "persuasion strategies" used by social networking sites to increase participation, *The New Scientist* noted, "The secret is to tie the acquisition of friends, compliments and status—spoils that humans will work hard for—to activities that enhance the site." As Fogg told the magazine, "You offer someone a context for gaining status, and they are going to work for that status." Network theorist Albert-László Barabási notes that online connection follows the rule of "preferential attachment"—that is, "when choosing between two pages, one with twice as many links as the other, about twice as many people link to the more connected page." As a result, "while our individual choices are highly unpredictable, as a group we follow strict patterns." Our lemming-like pursuit of online status via the collection of hundreds of "friends" clearly follows this rule.

What, in the end, does this pursuit of virtual status mean for community and friendship? Writing in the 1980s in *Habits of the Heart*, sociologist Robert Bellah and his colleagues documented the movement away from close-knit, traditional communities, to "lifestyle enclaves" which were defined largely by "leisure and consumption." Perhaps today we have moved beyond lifestyle enclaves and into "personality enclaves" or "identity enclaves"—discrete virtual places in which we can be different (and sometimes contradictory) people, with different groups of like-minded, though ever-shifting, friends.

Beyond Networking

This past spring, Len Harmon, the director of the Fischer Policy and Cultural Institute at Nichols College in Dudley, Massachusetts, offered a new course about social networking. Nichols is a small school whose students come largely from Connecticut and Massachusetts; many of them are the first members of their families to attend college. "I noticed a lot of issues involved with social networking sites," Harmon told me when I asked him why he created the class. How have these sites been useful to Nichols students? "It has relieved some of the stress of transitions for them," he said. "When abrupt departures occur—their family moves or they have to leave friends behind—they can cope by keeping in touch more easily."

So perhaps we should praise social networking websites for streamlining friendship the way e-mail streamlined correspondence. In the nineteenth century, Emerson observed that "friendship requires more time than poor busy men can usually command." Now, technology has given us the freedom to tap into our network of friends when it is convenient for us. "It's a way of maintaining a friendship without having to make any effort whatsoever," as a recent graduate of Harvard explained to *The New Yorker*. And that ease admittedly makes it possible to stay in contact with a wider circle of offline acquaintances than might have been possible in the era before

Facebook. Friends you haven't heard from in years, old buddies from elementary school, people you might have (should have?) fallen out of touch with—it is now easier than ever to reconnect to those people.

But what kind of connections are these? In his excellent book *Friendship: An Exposé*, Joseph Epstein praises the telephone and e-mail as technologies that have greatly facilitated friendship. He writes, "Proust once said he didn't much care for the analogy of a book to a friend. He thought a book was better than a friend, because you could shut it—and be shut of it—when you wished, which one can't always do with a friend." With e-mail and caller ID, Epstein enthuses, you can. But social networking sites (which Epstein says "speak to the vast loneliness in the world") have a different effect: they discourage "being shut of" people. On the contrary, they encourage users to check in frequently, "poke" friends, and post comments on others' pages. They favor interaction of greater quantity but less quality.

This constant connectivity concerns Len Harmon. "There is a sense of, 'if I'm not online or constantly texting or posting, then I'm missing something,'" he said of his students. "This is where I find the generational impact the greatest—not the use of the technology, but the *overuse* of the technology." It is unclear how the regular use of these sites will affect behavior over the long run—especially the behavior of children and young adults who are growing up with these tools. Almost no research has explored how virtual socializing affects children's development. What does a child weaned on Club Penguin learn about social interaction? How is an adolescent who spends her evenings managing her MySpace page different from a teenager who spends her night gossiping on the telephone to friends? Given that "people want to live their lives online," as the founder of one social networking site recently told *Fast Company* magazine, and they are beginning to do so at ever-younger ages, these questions are worth exploring.

The few studies that have emerged do not inspire confidence. Researcher Rob Nyland at Brigham Young University recently surveyed 184 users of social networking sites and found that heavy users "feel less socially involved with the community around them." He also found that "as individuals use social networking more for entertainment, their level of social involvement decreases." Another recent study conducted by communications professor Qingwen Dong and colleagues at the University of the Pacific found that "those who engaged in romantic communication over MySpace tend to have low levels of both emotional intelligence and self-esteem."

The implications of the narcissistic and exhibitionistic tendencies of social networkers also cry out for further consideration. There are opportunity costs when we spend so much time carefully grooming ourselves online. Given how much time we already devote to entertaining ourselves with technology, it is at least worth asking if the time we spend on social networking sites is well spent. In investing so much energy into improving how we *present* ourselves online, are we missing chances to genuinely *improve* ourselves?

We should also take note of the trend toward giving up face-to-face for virtual contact—and, in some cases, a preference for the latter. Today, many of our cultural, social, and political interactions take place through eminently convenient technological surrogates— Why go to the bank if you can use the ATM? Why browse in a bookstore when you can simply peruse the personalized selections Amazon.com has made for you? In the same vein, social networking sites are often convenient surrogates for offline friendship and community. In this context it is worth considering an observation that Stanley Milgram made in 1974, regarding his experiments with obedience: "The social psychology of this century reveals a major lesson," he wrote. "Often it is not so much the kind of person a man is as the kind of situation in which he finds himself that determines how he will act." To an increasing degree, we find and form our friendships and communities in the virtual world as well as the real world. These virtual networks greatly expand our opportunities to meet others, but they might also result in our valuing less the capacity for genuine connection. As the young woman writing in the *Times* admitted, "I consistently trade actual human contact for the more reliable high of smiles on MySpace, winks on Match.com, and pokes on Facebook." That she finds these online relationships more *reliable* is telling: it shows a desire to avoid the vulnerability and uncertainty that true friendship entails. Real intimacy requires risk—the risk of disapproval, of heartache, of being thought a fool. Social networking websites may make relationships more reliable, but whether those relationships can be humanly satisfying remains to be seen.

Notetaking Techniques

In the first edition of *The Curious Researcher,* I confessed to a dislike of notecards. Apparently, I'm not the only one. Mention notecards, and students often tell horror stories. It's a little like talking about who has the most horrendous scar, a discussion that can prompt participants to expose knees and bare abdomens in public places. One student even mailed me her notecards—fifty bibliography cards and fifty-three notecards, all bound by a metal ring and color coded. She assured me that she didn't want them back—ever. Another student told me she was required to write twenty notecards a day: "If you spelled something wrong or if you put your name on the left side of the notecard rather than the right, your notecards were torn up and you had to do them over."

It is true, of course, that some students find recording information on notecards an enormously useful way of organizing information. And some teachers have realized that it's pretty silly to turn notetaking into a form that must be done "correctly" or not at all. For these reasons, I included suggestions about how to use notecards effectively in the first edition of this text. But in good conscience, I can't do it anymore. I no longer believe that 3" × 5" or 4" × 6" cards are large enough to accommodate the frequently messy and occasionally extended writing that often characterizes genuinely useful notes. Little cards get in the way of having a good conversation with your sources.

If conventional notecards encourage a monologue, then what method will encourage dialogue? Basically any notetaking strategy that encourages the two things that you've practiced so far in this chapter: listening and responding, collecting and evaluating. It's that movement back and forth between information and what you think of that information, between your observations of things and your ideas about them, between what you once understood and what you *now* understand, that will involve you in the process of *knowledge-making,* rather than simple information retrieval and reporting. Now this probably sounds pretty grandiose. Your research essay will probably not earn space in an academic journal. But as you begin to understand the difference between knowledge and information, you will earn yourself a place in an academic community that values people with their own ideas. Isn't that inviting?

I'm convinced that something as seemingly mundane as notetaking can be a key part of becoming a knower rather than a parrot. One method, in particular, seems especially effective at encouraging dialogue between the researcher and his sources: the double-entry journal.

The Double-Entry Journal

The double-entry approach (see Figure 3.2) is basically this: Use opposing pages of your research notebook (or opposing columns in a word document). On each left side, compile your notes from a source—paraphrases, summaries, quotes—and on each right side, comment on them. Imagine that line down the middle of the page—or that spiral binder that divides opposing pages—as the lunch table at

Four Motives for Using a Source

My daughter Julia wants a pug. This isn't good news because I don't think much of little dogs with sinus problems. I also heard a rumor that if a pug sneezes hard enough its eyes might pop and dangle by the optical nerve until the eyeball is greased and popped back into the eye socket. This posed a research question: *Are pugs typical of overbred dogs that tend to suffer from a range of physiological and psychological problems?*

Since this is a question that goes way beyond my personal experience, I naturally turn to outside sources to learn more. When most of us do research for an academic paper, we typically search for sources that exemplify or support a point we want to make. But inquiry-based projects often begin with questions, not a preconceived argument, so the search for sources becomes much more than an exercise in finding sources that support what you already want to say. For example:

1. **Sources Can Extend Your Thinking.** This is an essential motive for doing research, particularly early in the process. You want to learn more about your subject so that you can refine your research question and understand more fully what it is you're asking. For example, in an article in *Economist* magazine, I learn that kennel clubs, which began in England in the second half of the nineteenth century, have played a key role in "genetic painting" of dog breeds, a euphemism for genetic

(continued)

manipulation (1).* The article goes on to argue that it is the demands of these associations for a kind of "racial purity" that have contributed to overbreeding (2). Perhaps I should revise my research question: *What role has the Pug Dog Club of America (PDCA) played in promoting or confronting the problem of inbreeding in the dog?*

2. **Sources Can Provide Necessary Background.** In order to fully understand your topic there may be things you—and ultimately your readers—should know. For example, the *Encyclopedia of Animals*† tells me that pugs are one of the oldest breeds and live an average of eight years. The dog's genetic history is a long one, which may be a significant fact. The average life span of a pug also means that Julia will be a sophomore in college when the dog dies, which means her pug becomes my pug.

3. **Sources Can Support or Exemplify a Point You Want to Make.** This is the default approach to using a source. We have a point, claim, or assertion we want to support with the information we've found. For instance, here's a quotation that seems to confirm the claim that kennel clubs have indeed contributed to medical problems in dogs:

> The Kennel Club, the top canine body in Britain, working with breed-specific dog clubs has laid out the "right" looks—a narrow set of desirable characteristics that breeders try to match. "Judges judge against a standard, and it's rewarding and challenging for breeders to try to meet those standards," says Geoff Sampson, a geneticist who works for the Kennel Club. But that kind of judging has too often been unrewarding for the dog. In the quest to create the perfect pooch, close relatives will often be mated, sometimes even brother and sister or mother and son. The danger of this practice is that it increases the

---

**"It's a Dog's Life," *Economist*, December 12, 2002: 1–5; *Academic Search Premier*, EBSCOhost, Boise State University, www.epnet.com., August 8, 2005.
†"Pug," *Encyclopedia of Animals*, EBSCO Animals, Boise State University, www.epnet.com, August 8, 2005.

likelihood that puppies will inherit genetic diseases—
some 400 have now been identified in dogs.*

4. **Sources Can Present Opportunities for Analysis and
   Interpretation.** Sometimes you encounter information
   that raises new questions, and when it does, you have a
   chance to offer your own analysis or interpretation of how
   that information or assertion might be understood. For
   example, one article asserted that the whole movement to
   promote purebred dogs for show, which originated with
   the British Kennel Clubs in the nineteenth century, might
   be part of a larger, social push toward racial purity in people.
   That dog breeding may have "racist" origins is an explosive
   and fascinating assertion. While I concede this might
   have been true, is it a relevant claim today? Isn't it faulty
   reasoning to infer that the motives of some people 150 years
   ago remain the motives of people today?

   By the way, I could not find evidence that pugs blow
   out their eyeballs when they sneeze. Sadly, I can't use that
   as a reason for discouraging Julia about pug ownership
   unless I find some convincing evidence to support it. But
   I'll keep looking.

which you sat with Christine Rosen in the opening exercise of this
chapter. On the left sits the published author. You sit on the right.
Take care to listen to what the author said through paraphrase, summary, and quotation on the left, and then on the right respond with
your own commentary, questions, interpretations, clarifications, or
even feelings about what you heard. Your commentary can be pretty
open ended: What strikes you? What was confusing? What was surprising? How does the information stand up to your own experiences
and observations? Does it support or contradict your thesis (if you
have one at this point)?

How might you use the information in your paper? What purpose
might it serve? What do you think of the source? What further
questions does the information raise that might be worth investigating? How does the information connect to other sources you've read?

*Helen Gibson, "A Flawed Beauty," *Time Europe,* August 8, 2001: 2–3. MasterFile
Premier, EBSCOhost, Boise State University, www.epnet.com, August 8, 2005.

Notes from Source

- On the left page collect direct quotations, paraphrases, and summaries of key ideas that you cull from your source.

- Collect material that's relevant to your project, but also write down passages, facts, and claims from the source that you find surprising or puzzling or that generate some kind of emotional response in you.

- Make sure you write down this material carefully and accurately.

- Don't forget to include the page number from the source to the left of the borrowed material or idea.

Fastwrite Response

- On the right page, think through writing about some of the information you collected in the other column. This will likely be a messy fastwrite but a focused one.

- Try shifting between two stances: believing and doubting. Spend a few minutes writing about the possible merits of an author's ideas, assertions, or study. Then spend a few minutes writing about questions, doubts, or counterclaims you would raise.

- Whenever your writing dies, skip a space, look to the left, and find something else to respond to.

- Some questions to ponder as you're writing might include:
  1. What strikes me about this?
  2. What are my first thoughts when I consider this? And then what? And then? And then?
  3. What exactly does this make me think of or remember?
  4. How would I qualify or challenge this author's claim? In what ways do I agree with it?
  5. What else have I read that connects with this?
  6. How do I feel about this?

FIGURE 3.2 **Double-Entry Journal Method**

There are a variety of ways to approach the double-entry journal. If you're taking notes on a photocopied article or a book you own, try reading the material first and underlining passages that seem important. Then, when you're done, transfer some of that underlined material—quotes, summaries, or paraphrases—into the left column of your journal. Otherwise, take notes in the left column *as* you read.

While you take notes, or after you've finished, do some exploratory writing in the right column. This territory belongs to you. Here, through language, your mind and heart assert themselves over the source material. Use your notes in the left column as a trigger for writing in the right. Whenever your writing stalls, look to the left. The process is a little like watching tennis—look left, then right, then left, then right. Direct your attention to what the source says and then to what *you* have to say about the source. Keep up a dialogue.

Figures 3.3, 3.4, and 3.5 illustrate how the double-entry journal works in practice. Note these features:

- Bibliographic information is recorded at the top of the page. Do that first, and make sure it's complete.
- Page numbers are included in the far-left margin, right next to the information that was taken from that page. Make sure you keep up with this as you write.
- While the material from the source in the left column may be quite formal or technical—as it is in Figure 3.4—the response in the right column should be informal, conversational. Try to write in your own voice. Find your own way to say things. And don't hesitate to use the first person: *I*.
- As you read the writers' responses to their sources in Figures 3.3 and 3.4, notice how often the writers use their own writing to try to question a source's claim or understand better what that claim might be (e.g., "What the authors seem to be missing here . . ." and "I don't get this quote at all . . .").
- Seize a phrase from your source, and play out its implications; think about how it pushes your own thinking or relates to your thesis. For example, the student writing about the rise of home video (Figure 3.3) plays with the phrase "mode of consumption"—a particular way of using film that the author believes home video encourages—and she really takes off on it. It leads her to a meditation on what it's like to see movies in theaters and what might be lost in the transition to home viewing.
- Use questions to keep you writing and thinking. In both Figure 3.3 and 3.4, the writers frequently pause to ask themselves questions—not only about what the authors of the original sources might be saying but what the writers are saying to themselves as they write.

Ehrenstein, David. "Film in the Age of Video." Film Quarterly 49.3 (1996): 38–42. Print.

38 ". . . today the once distinct spheres of theatrical and home exhibition have been radically conflated."

Let's see. So the "spheres" of showing films in theaters and in home video have been "conflated." What I think he means is that movies are now produced with both means of showing them in mind, which would seem to have implications for how they're made these days. E. talks later in the article about this, I think, when he mentions how only the dimension of sound has been preserved from the old days of big screens in dark theaters. The "big image" is lost. I'm not sure what this means, exactly.

39 That's Entertainment 3, which started as video, is "less a spectacular to be enjoyed in a darkened theater than a work of historical and cultural research that invites detailed analysis—a mode of consumption that home video, by its very nature, encourages."

I like this phrase that home video represents a particular "mode of consumption" for film. You may see more than one film at a sitting, in a lighted room, and you can rewind and reexamine favorite scenes and images. There is something about sitting in the dark, too, watching a big screen with a few hundred other people. It's like you experience nothing but image because there's nothing else to see. And somehow the act of watching with strangers, instead of in your living room by yourself or with friends, creates a kind of community. But E. talks here about how even the theater experience is no longer "distinctive." But he doesn't really say why. What exactly was lost with the disappearance of the "movie palace?" Size, for one thing. Maybe that's one way that home video and movies in theater have been "conflated." Because, as E. says, films are now made for both video and theaters, and the "illusion

40 "There are any number of (video) sets devoted to films, old and new, that enable the average everyday consumer to examine cinema now as never before."

"The illusion of depth" is destroyed on home video.

41 "To remember the movie palaces, with enormous images floating in a velvety darkness, framed by curtains that never seemed to close on an ever-shifting

FIGURE 3.3   **Sample Double-Entry Journal.** This writer, taking notes on an article from a scholarly journal, collects and responds to summaries, quotes, and paraphrases from the source.

program (features, cartoons, shorts, news, coming attractions) is not to indulge in nostalgia but rather to note how radically cinematic object relations have changed. There's nothing in any way distinctive about the modern theatrical movie-going experience, save the sound.

42 "We have entered an era of lowered cinematic expectations."

Jacque Rivette: "The cinema is necessarily fascination and rape, that is how it acts on people; it is something pretty unclear, something one sees shrouded in darkness."

of depth" as well as size of the image is destroyed by home video, then there's really no need for the really big screen of the "movie palace." Instead, we now have theaters divided and subdivided into eight theaters. Screens have shrunk, rooms have shrunk, and the theater experience begins to approximate home video. That leads to this "era of lowered cinematic expectations."

I don't get this quote at all. How can Rivette compare the experience of watching a film as both "fascination and rape?" Does he mean that film does violence in the dark to viewers in the same way a rapist would?

Check Rivette cite.

FIGURE 3.3 (Continued)

What I like about the double-entry journal system (see Figure 3.5) is that it turns me into a really active reader as I'm taking notes for my essay. That blank column on the right, like the whirring of my computer right now, impatiently urges me to figure out what I think through writing. All along, I've said the key to writing a strong research paper is *making the information your own*. Developing your own thinking about the information you collect, as you go along, is one way to do that. Thoughtful notes are so easy to neglect in your mad rush to simply take down a lot of information. The double-entry journal won't let you neglect your own thinking, or at least, it will remind you when you do.

The double-entry system does have a drawback. Unlike index card systems, double-entry journals don't organize your information particularly well. A lot of page flipping is involved to find pieces of information as you draft your paper. But I find I often remember which sources have what information, partly because I thought about what might be important as I read and took notes on each source.

Prior, Molly. "Bright On: Americans' Insatiable Appetite for Whiter-Than-White Teeth Is Giving Retailers Something to Smile About." <u>Beauty Biz</u> 1 Sept. 2005: 36–43. Print.

Teeth are no longer just for eating with—their appearance is becoming more important as a factor in a person's image, and they need to be perfectly white. (36)

Cosmetics companies are now entering territory once reserved for dentists as more and more people care mostly about the aesthetics of their teeth and smile. (36)

"Sephora is so enthusiastic about the [tooth whitening] category, it named "smile" its fifth retail pillar, joining the four others (makeup, fragrance, skin care and hair care) earlier this year." (37)

"The trend has shed its clinical beginnings and assumed a new identity, smile care. Its new name has been quickly adopted by a growing troupe of retailers, who hope to lure consumers with a simple promise: A brighter smile will make you look younger and feel more confident." (37)

Instead of going to the dentist and taking care of their teeth so they function well, people are investing a cosmetic interest in their teeth. People selling tooth whitening products hope people associate whiter, more perfect teeth with higher self-esteem and social acceptance. (40)

"What says health, youth and vitality like a great smile?" (40)

I have noticed the increasing amount of importance that people put on the whiteness of their teeth, but this also seems to have increased with the amount of advertising for whitening products on TV and in magazines. I wonder if the whole thing is profit driven: hygiene companies wanted to make more money, so instead of just selling toothbrushes and toothpaste, they created a whitening product and then worked to produce a demand for it. I almost feel really manipulated, like everyone's teeth were fine the way they naturally existed, and then all the sudden a big company decided it needed to create a new product and sell it by making us feel bad about our smiles, and thus bad about ourselves.

The whole thing is sad, because once something becomes the societal "norm," we start to become obligated to doing it. If everyone's teeth are beige, it's no problem when yours are too. But when everyone has sparkling white teeth, then it looks funny if you let yours stay brown. It either says "I don't have the money to whiten my teeth," or "I don't care about my appearance."

Sometimes it feels people might also judge you as being dirty, because white teeth seem healthier and cleaner than brown teeth, or lazy, for not spending the time to whiten your teeth. All those things are negative, and create a negative cloud around our teeth where we once felt good, or at least ambivalent. I don't like the way I'm being told my smile isn't good enough the way it is. I feel like when I smile it should just be about showing happiness and conveying that to others, not a judgment about me as a person.

FIGURE 3.4 **Amanda's Double-Entry Journal.** Here, Amanda concentrates on collecting and responding to quoted material from the source.

Oppenhiemer, Todd. "The Computer Delusion." <u>TheAtlantic.com</u>. Atlantic Monthly Group, July 1997. Web. 15 Apr. 2009.

4 Alan Lesgood, director of Learning and Development Center at U of Pitt: The computer is an "amplifier," involves both sound "study practices and thoughtless ones." Which of the two will predominate?

5 Are computers "the filmstrips of the 90s"? Clifford Stoll, author of <u>Silicon Snake Oil</u>: "We loved them (filmstrips) because we didn't have to think for an hour, teachers loved them because they didn't have to teach and parents loved them because it showed their schools are high tech. But no learning happened."

8 Children with disabilities show most evidence of improvement with computer use.

10 A number of experts argue that visual learning produces much less than sensory learning. ". . . the senses have little status after kindergarten."

The article upended some of my thinking about the virtues of computer technology. What was most helpful for my project, though, were the comments about the need for learners to engage in sensory activity, and the idea that computers do not seem to encourage creativity. I'm not sure that the analysis holds for the activity of research, which unlike some of the examples—mostly high school and elementary—seem directed toward a whole range of teacher-guided instruction. The task of collecting research off the Web seems more directed and purposeful. But maybe not.

One quote that really stands out: "School is not about information, it's about <u>using</u> information." And here this seems relevant. The Web offers the student the illusion she's getting somewhere if she simply collects information, something that is easy to do surfing the Web. Like the photocopying machine, the Web will help the student research accumulated material but at what point will she think about it? How much does the student, for example, have to reflect before she decides to click the printer icon? At least with the photocopy machine, it costs money to print a copy, an incentive to think about whether the material is <u>worth</u> copying; this incentive is missing on the Web.

FIGURE 3.5 Here's one of my double-entry scribbles. I was researching how students use the Web for research and found a related article in the *Atlantic Monthly* titled "The Computer Delusion." In the right-hand column, I found myself taking off on a quotation: "Schooling is not about information, it's about using information."

Other Notetaking Techniques

The Research Log: A Jay Leno Approach

The research log is an alternative to the double-entry journal that promotes a similar "conversation" between writer and source, but with a few differences. One is that, like Jay Leno, the researcher starts with a monologue and always gets the last word. Another difference is that the research log may be more adaptable than the double-entry journal for researchers who prefer to write on computers. The standard format of the research log can serve as a template, which can be retrieved whenever you're ready to take notes on another source. Those notes can then be easily dropped into the draft as needed, using the "Cut and Paste" feature of your word-processing program. Obviously, the research log format works just as well in a paper notebook.

The basic approach is this:

1. Take down the full bibliographic information on the source (see Figure 3.6). Then read the article, book chapter, Web page, or whatever first, marking up your personal copy in the usual fashion by underlining, making marginal notes, and so on.

2. Your first entry will be a fastwrite that is an *open-ended response* to the reading under the heading "What Strikes Me Most." You could take the following stances or pose the following questions to guide this writing:

   ▪ Begin by playing the "believing game," exploring how the author's ideas, arguments, or findings are sensible. Then shift to the "doubting game," looking for gaps, questions, and doubts you have about what the source says.

   ▪ What strikes you as the most important thing the author is trying to say?

   ▪ What surprises you most?

   ▪ What do you remember best?

   ▪ What seems most convincing? Least convincing?

   ▪ How has it changed your thinking on the topic?

   ▪ How does it compare to other things you've read?

   ▪ What other research possibilities does it suggest?

3. Next, mine the source for nuggets. Take notes under the heading "Source Notes." These are quotations, summaries, paraphrases, or key facts you collect from the reading. They are probably some of the things you marked as you read the source initially.

4. Finally, follow up with one more fastwrite under the heading "The Source Reconsidered." This is a second, *more focused* look at the source in which you fastwrite about what stands out in the notes you took. Which facts, findings, claims, or arguments that you jotted down shape your thinking now? If the writing stalls, skip a line, take another look at your source notes, and seize on something else to write about.

Project: The Newest Commodity: The Smile

Citation: Tanner, Marty. "American Choppers." *New York Times*. New York Times, 20 Feb. 2005. Web. 4 Apr. 2009.

Date: 4/5/2009

What Strikes Me Most:
A prosthodontist is a dentist that specializes in making teeth look a certain way. While many people are born with smiles they are proud of, a prosthodontist can take any smile and modify it in any way. Unfortunately, more and more people are falling into a trap that there is only one "perfect" smile, and they are asking for their own mouths to be modified to create the perfect smile. This disgusts me because I think there should be as many smiles as there are people. It's becoming like a nose job or a face lift—some modification people make to their appearance to make it less like the countenance they were born with, and more like that "perfect" face. It makes me sad that another thing that is so distinctive to each person has actually become something we want to normalize. As a woman I feel like I'm told to be a size two, have straight, shiny hair, and have a little, cute nose, and have perfectly arched eyebrows, and have thick, pink lips. Now too I have to have the correct length and width teeth that are a sparkly B1 white. It makes me wonder why our culture goes from accepting one part of ourselves as standard and imperfect but acceptable, and makes it into something we need to modify.

I also think the prosthodontist to the stars, Dr. Levine, is really disingenuous in this article. While his job depends on people being unhappy with the way their teeth look, he tries to play the "good guy" card and say that people's smiles are looking too perfect, and that people need to have a great set of choppers, but not overly great. He

---

FIGURE 3.6 **Amanda's Research Log**

seems to want to make the polite statement that nobody has a perfect smile, but then through his profession his job is to make people believe they can get a perfect smile—and they don't already have one. I think that's kind of slimy.

Source Notes:
"Within certain strict boundaries, Levine likes to see some imperfection because it renders the hand of the dentist invisible. This is his art." Many famous people, like actors and actresses, think of their smile as a sort of symbol of their status that they can flash to attract attention. Many of these smiles are exactly the same, with the golden mean the proportion of the length of their top six front teeth, and with each individual tooth having a width that is 80% of the length. There is even a "perfect" amount of tooth that should show when a person's mouth is closed: around 3.7 mm. Patients can wear a fake set of teeth around their home before they have their smiles modified to see if what they imagine as being perfect actually looks bad. They can test drive their new set of teeth for friends and family so they don't end up with a mistake that looks like a pair of too-perfect dentures.

"Smiles are looking too much alike."
" . . . the man who credits himself with shaping Christie Brinkley's 'iconic American smile.'" Reality makeover programs like The Swan often use a prosthodontist as part of the makeover.

The Source Reconsidered:
When the article mentions Julia Roberts or the "iconic American smile" I know exactly what it means. In my mind, I truly have an image of that smile, and I realize now that's because every single starlet and commercial model seems to have that smile. Yet, when I look at my friends and all the people around me, there are so many different smiles. I have one friend with really short, stubby

FIGURE 3.6   (Continued)

teeth that are pretty brown around the edges, and I
admit that I notice it. But when she smiles, I tend
to look more at the rest of her face and the fact
that she's really happy than I do at her imperfect
teeth. It's like it's turning some natural human
emotion into some mass produced carbon copy. That's
why the whole smile care thing really bothers me.
Changing somebody's nose changes only their nose.
Changing someone's smile seems to control and modify the way they communicate a feeling, and that
is really bothersome. They are modifying something
far more personal than just their appearance,
they are changing the way they emote. That's
freaky.

FIGURE 3.6   (Continued)

Narrative Notetaking

Narrative notetaking (see Figure 3.7) is an episodic approach to
reading for research. It documents the writer's narrative of thought
about a source, developing several "layers" of response with each
reading and rereading; in that sense, it's a bit like the research log.
Narrative notetaking essentially turns the double-entry journal on

Focusing Question: How has cosmetic dentistry changed the way we
think of the smile, and what are the repercussions?

Source: Walker, Rob. "Consumed; Unstained Masses." New York Times.
New York Times, 2 May 2004. Web. 10 Apr. 2009.

First Layer: Story the Source

The prosthodontist Jonathan Levine works to change the way people's
teeth look. He created a product called GoSmile that works to whiten
people's teeth. At first he didn't think there was much use for it, but
then normal people started to want whiter teeth, and his business
has boomed.

FIGURE 3.7   **Amanda's Narrative Notets**

For a while many celebrities have cosmetically enhanced their teeth, but now normal people are as well. Saks and Sephora, two upscale retailers, started selling the product. Colgate and Crest, traditionally known for their toothpaste, also created products for over the counter whitening. These products seem to be booming in the early 2000s.

Many people are now feeling that white teeth are as much of a necessity as a washed face or brushed hair. It seems to be a sign of the times. Retailers are also making out hand over fist as more and more people buy whitening products.

One of the clever ways whitening products work is they tell consumers that they don't have to change their lifestyles to get whiter teeth. They can still drink dark beverages and eat colored foods, but just use a whitener to keep their teeth looking pristine. Americans seem to like products that make sure they can indulge in all the things they'd like, but avoid the negative repercussions of doing so.

People are now going to the dentist to make sure their teeth look good, rather than just for oral health. This can actually be seen as a benefit, because it means that people are at least going to the dentist.

It's not completely irrational that many people are hopping on the bandwagon of a more celebrity-like smile. People who are generally considered attractive make more money than average looking people, and it's another way to stand out positively in the crowd.

Second Layer: Rapid Summary

The American public is getting more and more vain, as evidenced by the fact that tooth whitening is growing in popularity. While only celebrities used to modify the appearance of their teeth, now average people are

FIGURE 3.7   (Continued)

doing it. Because of the value of appearance in our society, once we realize we can modify the way we look to our advantage, we seem to flock to it quickly. That's what's happening with the whole trend of smile care—we're using whiteners to change the way our teeth look so maybe we will be judged more profitably. And when a large percentage of society decides to buy something, there will always be corporations and retailers standing alongside to reap a profit.

Third Layer: Narrative of Thought

Before I started reading this article I thought that it was the capitalistic profit motive that had introduced whitening products and created a consumer demand for them. Now I understand that all of us as consumers have an equal responsibility with the companies that make and market such products, because we're the ones that buy them and change our standards of beauty. That makes me think that this is a complicated issue. While it's frustrating to feel like I can never be attractive enough, because the standard of attractiveness to which I'm held keeps getting harder and harder to meet, I'm the one that is interested in meeting it in the first place. While it would be easy to denigrate that as vanity, however, I can also see that being judged by others as attractive does have actual benefits, be it a higher salary or better treatment from strangers. In that case I'm put in a tough spot—I can work against the culture that tells me I don't look the right way, and feel negatively judged, or I can conform to it, and feel disappointed that I folded to social pressure. This isn't just an issue about people whitening their teeth for fun, it's about how society changes its standards and how quickly we assimilate to them—and why.

FIGURE 3.7   (Continued)

its side, creating layers of thought and information rather than columns, each layer building on the other; yet it also preserves the contrary thinking that makes the double-entry journal so valuable. The number of layers the writer makes depends on the value of the source to his or her project.

First Layer: Story the Source.   Read the source carefully from beginning to end, marking up your personal copy with underlining, marginal notes, highlighter, or whatever you use to signal important passages. Then in your notebook (or on your computer) quickly tell the story of the text and how it developed from beginning to end. This should be a rough chronological account or the source's chain of reasoning or development.

- How did the piece begin?
- And then where did it go from there?
- And then?
- How did it end?

When finished, draw a line under your entry.

Second Layer: Rapid Summary.   This step involves a rereading, but a selective one. Review the text, including your underlining and other marks to find ideas, concepts, or claims that seem to be *repeated* or that seem to be important assertions, claims, or findings. Circle or mark with Post-its® the lines or passages that seem most important to your understanding of the source's argument or findings, or that seem most relevant to your project. Now, *in your own words,* compose a few sentences that summarize your understanding of what the source is saying about your topic. Remember that a summary doesn't simply state the topic of the passage, but what the reading *says* about the topic.
Draw another line under this entry.

Third Layer: Narrative of Thought.   Now push the text aside for a moment and reflect on how it has contributed to your thinking about the topic. Begin a fastwrite that tells the story of your thinking since reading and writing about this source. Start with this "seed" sentence or ones like it:

Before I started reading this article/book/Web document/etc.,

I thought _____, but now I understand that _____. That

makes me think _____.

These three layers certainly don't have to be the end of the writing you do about a source, and you may find that one or more of the layers command most of your attention, perhaps generating much longer entries than those in the model, Figure 3.7. Customize this approach to make it most productive for you. For example, you might find that the third layer, "Narrative of Thought," might be more useful as an initial step, or you might find that the second layer of notes is a collection of quotes, summaries, or paraphrases from the source, rather than the rapid summary. Experiment and make narrative notetaking work for you. The most important thing with all of these notetaking techniques—the double-entry journal, the research log, or narrative notetaking—is that you're using writing to think *when you're in the middle,* engaging with the voices, views, and findings of the people you're reading.

Online Research Notebooks

Google Notebook offers some easy ways to organize yourself during the notetaking stage, especially if a lot of your research is taking place online. (See Figure 3.8.) To use it, create a Google account, and then follow the "more" link on the Google homepage to "even more." Scroll down to the "notebook" function.

Once you're in the notebook, start piecing together the research you have so far. A helpful thing to do is to cut and paste text from the Internet site you're using, and put that into the general body of the notebook. Make sure you keep track of all the citation information you'll need for the site here as well. Then, use the "comments" feature that shows up at the bottom of the text bubble to use some of the notetaking techniques you've learned in this chapter. Take your time—this isn't so much about copying information from the Internet but spending time mentally digesting it. Because you can take writing directly from the notebook and put it in your draft later on, making keen observations at this stage will lighten your writing workload later on.

Once you have both the information—which can include both text and images, whatever you find helpful—use the "add labels" function to help organize the information. That way when you go back through the data, it will be easy to piece together similar pieces of information into the same place. You can also divide your notes up into sections by following the "add section" link to break your notes up into different categories. It might be helpful to make each source a different section, so you can flip through and see what each independent author is saying.

If you want to find a specific phrase in your notebook, the search function at the top of the notebook lets you hunt down exactly the words you're looking for. If you can't remember who said what, the search is an easy way to minimize the fogginess that sometimes comes with an abundance of research.

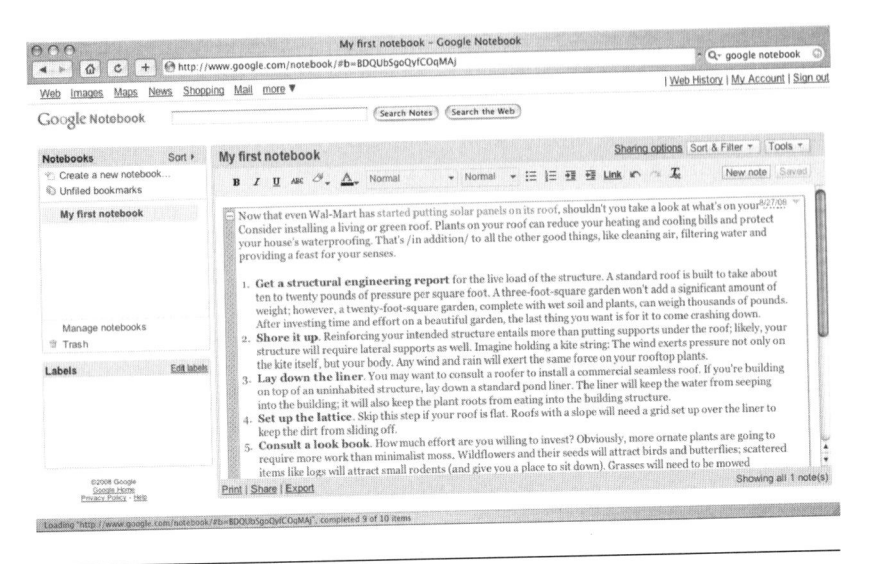

FIGURE 3.8   Sites like Google Notebook, seen here, or Zotero provide researchers with new methods of collecting and commenting on sources online. The key is to go beyond the cut-and-paste reflex and use the notetaking features as you would with a double-entry journal.

Whatever you choose to do, the notebook allows you to keep track of all the different perspectives you're getting, as well as all your own thoughts and ideas about the information. A little time put into keeping things straight will make your life easier when you start writing the body of your paper.

When You're Coming Up Short: More Advanced Searching Techniques

At the end of the third week of the research assignment last semester, Laura showed up at my office, looking pale.

"I spent all night at the library, and I couldn't find much on my topic," she said. "What I *could* find, the library didn't have—it was missing, or checked out, or wasn't even part of the collection. I may have to change my topic."

"I hate libraries!" she said, the color returning to her face.

Laura's complaint is one that I hear often at this point in the research process, especially from students who have dutifully tried to find a narrow focus for their papers, only to realize—they think—that there isn't enough information to make the topic work. They have tried the online catalog, periodical databases, and the Internet. The students found a few articles but not enough for a ten-page paper. Like Laura, they may decide to broaden their focus or bail out on their topic altogether, even though they're still interested in it.

I always give these frustrated students the same advice: Don't despair yet. And don't give up on your narrow focus or your topic until you've dug more deeply for information. There are still some more specialized indexes to try and some nonlibrary sources to consider. You are, in a sense, like the archaeologist who carefully removes the dirt from each layer of a dig site, looking to see what it might reveal. If little turns up, the next layer is systematically explored and then the next, until the archaeologist is convinced she's digging in the wrong place. Student researchers too often give up the dig before they've removed enough dirt, believing too quickly there's nothing there.

Advanced Library Searching Techniques

Here are some things you might not have considered to unearth more useful information on your research question. They are listed in the order you might try them.

1. *Vary search terms*. If you ignored the *Library of Congress Subject Headings* in Exercise 2.1, those huge red books in the library reference room, now is the time to crack them open. These will provide language for searches that is most likely to produce the best results in books and article databases. At the very least, try using some other search terms suggested by your research so far. You might, for instance, try searching using the names of people who have published on your topic.

2. *Search other databases*. Okay, so you've tried a general subject database like Academic OneFile, and even a specialized database like PsychINFO. But have you tried another general database like Academic Search Premier, or another specialized database like InfoTrac Psychology? Broaden your coverage.

3. *Check bibliographies*. Academic books and articles always include a list of references at the end. These can be gold mines. Look at all the sources like these that you've collected so far and scan the titles in the bibliographies that seem promising. Find these by searching the library databases.

4. *Use a bibliographic index.* These are databases that will provide you with a list of references on many topics. For example, the Bibliographic Index Plus not only will allow you to search for articles on your topic but may also return links to full-text versions.

5. *Consider using interlibrary loan services.* Your campus library will get you that article or book they don't have by borrowing the materials from another library. This is an incredibly useful service, often available online, but it's useless to procrastinators since delivery can take a week or two.

6. *Troll government documents.* The U.S. Government is the largest publisher in the world. If your research question is related to some issue of public policy, then there's a decent chance you'll find some government documents on the subject. Try the site FirstGov (see Figure 3.9), a useful index to the gazillions of government publications and reports.

Advanced Internet Search Techniques

It's more likely that you've tapped out relevant sources on the Internet than those in the library since many of us seem to always begin there. But make sure that you've tried some of the following search strategies on the Web.

1. *Vary search terms.* By now, you've gathered enough information on your topic to have some new ideas about terms or phrases that might yield good results. Say you're researching the origins of American blues music, and you discover that among its many traditions is something called the Piedmont style. Try searching using that phrase in quotation marks. Also consider doing Web searches on the names of experts who have contributed significantly to the conversation on your topic.

2. *Use advanced search features.* Few of us use the advanced search page on Google and other search engines. By habit, we just type in a few terms in the simple search window. But advanced searching will allow you to exploit methods that will give you better results—things like phrase searching in conjunction with Boolean operators like AND and OR.

3. *Use multiple search engines.* Don't call for retreat until you've gone beyond Google. Try Yahoo!, Ask.com, and similar search

FIGURE 3.9 FirstGov is a useful starting point for a search of government documents on your topic.

engines. Also try specialized search engines that are relevant to your subject (see Chapter 2).

4. *Search the invisible Web.* The vast majority of information on the Web is not accessible to everyday search engines. Much of this information exists in databases that web crawlers don't know how to categorize or is blocked from listing in search hits. That's unfortunate for academic researchers because educational institutions post many of these databases and documents. As usual, some savvy people have come up with methods of searching this frontier. Try some of the following:

- **Direct Search** http://www.freepint.com/gary/direct.htm
- **Infomine** http://infomine.ucr.edu/
- **Invisible Web Directory** http://www.invisible-web.net/

Thinking Outside the Box: Alternative Sources

Sometimes you need to be creative. Try finding sources on your research question in places you don't think to look.

1. *Search blogs.* It is easy to dismiss blogs as merely self-indulgent musings of people with nothing better to do, except that some blogs are written by people who really know what they're talking about. In addition, bloggers can be vigilant observers of new developments, breaking news stories, and cutting-edge opinion. There are a number of specialized search engines to scour the blogosphere. Perhaps the best is Google's.

2. *Search images.* Another source of material you may not have thought of is images available on the Internet. A photograph of a collapsed school building following the 2008 earthquake in central China will do much to dramatize your essay on the vulnerability of buildings to such a disaster. Or a historical essay on lynching in the South might be more powerful with a picture of a murder from the Library of Congress archives.

3. *Listen to archived radio or podcasts.* Suppose your research question focuses on Martin Luther King Jr. Why not listen to an interview of Taylor Branch, the man who wrote a three-volume biography of the civil rights leader? You can find it on NPR.org (see Figure 3.10). National Public Radio is a particularly good

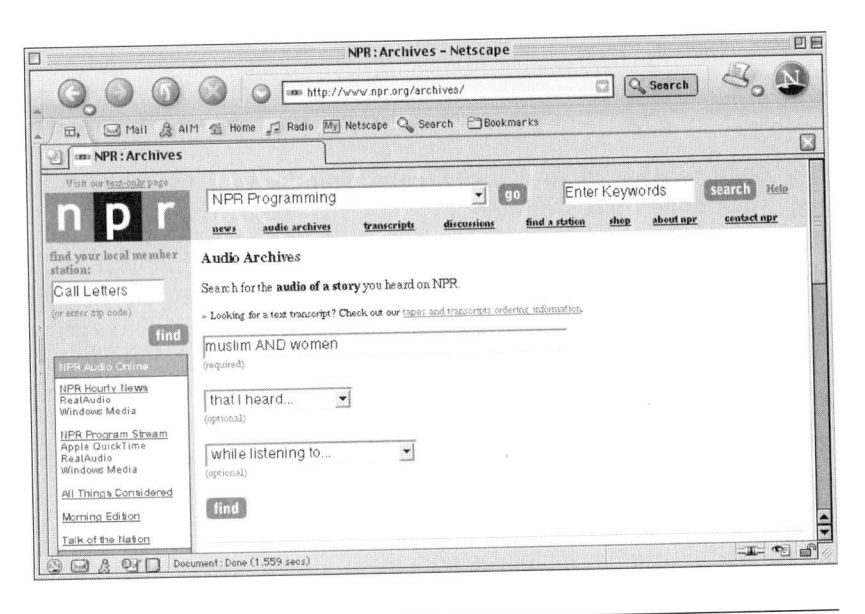

FIGURE 3.10   Searching the Archives at National Public Radio

source for material for academic projects. There are also a variety of search engines that will help you find podcasts on nearly any subject.

4. *Check out YouTube.* It isn't just about laughing babies anymore. YouTube is a rich archive of video that can provide material on many topics. For the project on Martin Luther King, Jr., for example, you might watch a video of his last speech. There are, of course, other sites that archive video, too. Truveo (http://www.truveo.com/) will help you search them all.

5. *Search iTunes U.* Across the U.S., colleges and universities are going online through Apple's iTunes U, putting up video and audio speeches, lectures, and other academic content. You can find iTunes U on iTunes, of course, and you can do a keyword search on multiple sites using "power search." The terms "global warming" produced 90 hits, including lectures, opinion, and reports from some of America's top universities. See Figure 3.11 for more advanced searching techniques.

Library	**Internet**	**Alternative Sources**
• Vary search terms	• Vary search terms	• Search blogs
• Search other databases	• Use advanced search features	• Search images
• Check bibliographies	• Use multiple search engines	• Listen to archived radio and podcasts
• Use a bibliographic index	• Search the invisible Web	• Watch videocasts
• Use interlibrary loan		• Search iTunes U
• Troll government documents		

FIGURE 3.11 **More Advanced Searching Techniques**

CHAPTER 4

The Fourth Week

Getting to the Draft

It is *not* 2 A.M. Your paper is *not* due in twelve hours but in one or two weeks. For some students, beginning to write a research paper this early—weeks before it's due—will be a totally new experience. An early start may also, for the first time, make the experience a positive one. I know that starting early will help ensure writing a better paper.

Still, there are those students who say they thrive on a looming deadline, who love working in its shadow, flirting with failure. "I work best that way," they say, and they wait until the last minute and race to the deadline in a burst of writing, often sustained by cigarettes and strong doses of caffeine. It works for some students. Panic is a pretty strong motivator. But I think most who defend this habit confuse their relief at successfully pulling off the assignment once again with a belief that the paper itself is successful.

Papers done under such pressure often aren't successful, and that is particularly true of the last-minute research paper, in which procrastination is especially deadly. Research writing is recursive. You often have to circle back to where you've already been, discovering holes in your research or looking at your subject from new angles. It's hard to fit in a trip back to the library the night before the paper is due, when you've just started the draft and need to check some information. This book is designed to defeat procrastination, and if, in the past few weeks, you've done the exercises, taken thoughtful notes, and attempted a thorough search for information, you probably have the urge to begin writing.

On the other hand, you may feel as if you don't know enough yet about your topic to have anything to say. Or you may be swamped with information, and your head may be spinning. What do you do with it all?

When Christy came to my office, she was three weeks into her research on a paper that asked, Why do diets fail? She really wanted to know, since she was having such a hard time with her own diet. Though she'd really done a good job collecting information, she was exasperated.

"I found a whole bunch of articles on how heredity affects obesity," she said, "and all this stuff on how people's upbringing determines how they eat. I also found some articles that said our bodies *want* to be certain weights."

It sounded pretty interesting to me.

"I've got all this information, but I'm worried that I'll lose my focus," she said. "*And so much of it seems contradictory.* I don't know what to think."

When the Experts Disagree

Christy was pretty sure she was in trouble because her sources sometimes didn't agree on the same things. I thought she was right where she should be: standing on the curb at a busy intersection, watching the experts on her topic collide and then go off in different directions. Knowledge in any field—nutrition, literature, or entomology—is not static. It is contested—pushed, pulled, probed, and even sometimes turned over completely to see what is underneath. Scholars and experts devote their lifetimes to disagreeing with each other, not because they enjoy being disagreeable but because when knowledge is contested, it is advanced.

When I researched lobsters, I discovered a fascinating scientific mystery: More than 90 percent of the lobsters that grow to the minimum legal size every year end up on someone's dinner table. At that size, most lobsters haven't even had a chance to breed. How is it possible, asked the scientists, that there are any lobsters left at that rate of exploitation? I discovered several explanations. Some people argued that the millions of lobster traps—each of which is designed to allow undersize lobsters to escape—serve as a kind of giant soup kitchen, providing extra food to lobsters. That, some experts said, accounts for lobsters' resilience. Other experts believed that laws protecting females carrying eggs have worked remarkably well. Still others believed that lobsters migrate into areas depleted by overfishing. Recently, another idea won favor with scientists. They suggested that large lobsters at the edge of the continental shelf are the "parental stock" for coastal lobsters, sending their larval offspring inshore on tides and currents.

Evaluating Conflicting Claims

As a writer—and in this case, a nonexpert—I had to sort through these conflicting opinions and decide which I thought were most convincing. I had to claim my point of view and later make it convincing to my own readers.

That was Christy's challenge, and it's your challenge, too. When you're thorough in your research, you're bound to find sources that square off against each other or come at your subject from different directions. What do you make of these competing claims and differing perspectives?

E X E R C I S E   4 . 1

Do Concealed Guns Reduce Crime?

Soon after the Virginia Tech and Northern Illinois University shooting rampages, a group called Students for Concealed Carry on Campus (SCCC) started organizing on American campuses. The group is determined to overturn gun bans at most schools and allow students who are otherwise legally qualified to carry concealed weapons on campus.

SCCC is part of a larger national debate about whether allowing people to carry concealed weapons will reduce crime. Currently, a number of states have either "shall issue" or more restrictive "may issue" laws regulating whether citizens can carry concealed weapons. The "shall issue" states are required to give their residents a permit to carry if they meet other legal qualifications to own a gun. The "may issue" states have more latitude to reject applicants. Considerably fewer states now have the "may issue" laws.

At the heart of the issue is the very sensible theory that if gun-toting criminals know that their potential victims might be carrying too, the criminals are much less likely to behave violently. But is this theory true? Certainly the NRA thinks so. On its Web site, the interest group notes that there is "not a single academic study that claims Right to Carry laws have increased state crime rates. The debate among academics has been over how large the benefits have been."

Actually, there is a lively academic debate about the impact of concealed gun laws on crime. What follows are the conclusions of two academic studies that come to two quite different conclusions about the issue. Read each claim carefully and then think about how you might decide which to believe.

Claim #1

In a landmark study that has profoundly influenced the debate over the potential benefits of right-to-carry laws, two researchers, John Lott and David Mustard, studied crime rates in U.S. counties, some of which have "shall issue" (SI) laws. This is what they found:

> Using cross-sectional time-series data for U.S. counties from 1977 to 1992, we find that allowing citizens to carry concealed weapons deters violent crimes, without increasing accidental deaths. If those states without right-to-carry concealed gun provisions had adopted them in 1992, county- and state-level data indicate that approximately 1,500 murders would have been avoided yearly. Similarly, we predict that rapes would have declined by over 4,000, robbery by over 11,000, and aggravated assaults by over 60,000. We also find criminals substituting into property crimes involving stealth, where the probability of contact between the criminal and the victim is minimal. Further, higher arrest and conviction rates consistently reduce

crime. The estimated annual gain from all
remaining states adopting these laws was at least
$5.74 billion in 1992. The annual social benefit
from an additional concealed handgun permit is as
high as $5,000.*

Claim #2

After Lott and Mustard published their study, researchers
engaged in a lively debate about its findings that "shall issue"
laws reduced crime. Among those that found different results was
a 2005 study excerpted below. Kovandzic, Marvel, and Vieratas
looked at U.S. cities with 100,000 or more residents to determine
the effect of "shall issue" laws on crime. This is what they found:

Our results provide little support for the findings
of Lott and Mustard (1997) and Lott (1998b, 2000),
that SI laws reduce violent crime. . . . Even if
criminals have timely information regarding the
passage of SI laws and the number of people
lawfully carrying guns in public, such information
is unlikely to have a significant impact on their
behavior and violent crime rates. According to
ethnographic research on active offenders, most
crime is opportunistic and does not involve
elaborate planning and potential costs are given
relative little consideration (Jacobs, 2000;
Jacobs, Topalli & Wright, 2003; Shover, 1996;
Wright & Decker, 1994, 1997). Even when offenders
do calculate the costs, they also factor in
their ability to manage or eliminate these

*John R. Lott and David B. Mustard, "Crime, Deterrence, and Right to Carry
Concealed Handguns," *Journal of Legal Studies* 26 (January 1997): 1–68.

potential costs (Hochstetler & Copes, 2003; Miller
& Jacobs, 1998). Research suggests that criminals
are extremely confident about their abilities to
control a situation and deal with whatever may
arise, including encountering an armed victim
(Jacobs, 2000; Wright & Decker, 1997).*

Who to Believe?

You have two competing claims from two respected sources.

1. How would you decide which of these claims is true? What else
   might you need to know to answer that question?
2. Now imagine two different situations. In one, you're writing a
   research essay that *explores* the question of whether SI laws
   reduce crime. In another, you're writing a paper that *argues*
   that these laws are effective at reducing crime. Would either
   situation affect how you might use these competing claims in
   your paper?
3. If you were going to come up with some general principles for
   evaluating the claims in sources what might they be?

Careful researchers are systematic in their evaluation of competing claims. After reading these two excerpts, can you imagine a
series of questions you might ask to help you determine whom to
believe when faced with this situation in the future? In groups, brainstorm such a list of questions on a piece of newsprint. Do these fall
into any categories?

Finally, on a fresh piece of newsprint, refine your list. Which
questions and in what order might you ask yourself when trying to
decide between conflicting claims? Discuss these lists in class.

E X E R C I S E   4 . 2

Reclaiming Your Topic

More than two weeks ago, you began researching a topic that
you may have known little about. But you were curious enough to

---

*Tomislav V. Kovandzic, Thomas B. Marvel, and Lynne M. Vieratas, "The Impact of
'Shall-Issue' Concealed Handgun Laws on Violent Crime Rates," *Homicide Studies*
9 (November 2005): 292–323.

dive in and immerse yourself in the research, listening to the voices of people who know more than you. You may feel, as Christy did, that your paper is beginning to slip away from you; there is just too much information, or the contradictions can't possibly be sorted out. It might seem presumptuous to think that your ideas matter. You may feel as if you're in over your head. After all, you're not an expert.

If you're not at all confused at this stage in the research process, that's great. Now is the time, through writing, to tighten your grasp on the material. But if you're feeling overwhelmed, writing now can help you get a grip. Try this exercise, which will take about forty minutes.

STEP 1: Spend ten or fifteen minutes reviewing all of the notes you've taken so far and skimming key articles or passages from books. Glance at your most important sources. Let your head swim with information.

STEP 2: Now clear your desk of everything but your research notebook. Remove all your notes and all your sources. You won't use them while doing the rest of this exercise. Trust that you'll remember what's important.

STEP 3: Now fastwrite about your topic for eight minutes. Tell the story of how your own thinking about your topic has evolved. When you began the project, what did you think? Then what happened, and what happened after that? What were your preconceptions about your topic? How have they changed? This is an open-ended fastwrite. Don't let the writing stall out. If you run out of things to say, talk to yourself through writing about your research, thinking about other trails you might follow. Time yourself.

STEP 4: Skip a few lines in your notebook. Write "Moments, Stories, People, and Scenes." Now fastwrite for another ten minutes, this time focusing on more specific case studies, situations, people, experiences, observations, and so on that stand out in your mind from the research done so far or perhaps from your own experience with the topic. Keep your pen moving for a full ten minutes. Time yourself.

STEP 5: Skip a few more lines. For ten minutes, quickly write a dialogue between you and someone else about your topic. You choose whom to converse with—a friend, your instructor. Don't plan the dialogue. Just begin with the question most commonly asked about your topic, and take the conversation from there, writing both parts of the dialogue.

STEP 6: Finally, skip a few more lines and write these two words in your notebook: "So What?" Now spend a few minutes trying to summarize the most important thing *you* think people should understand about your topic based on what you've learned so far. Distill these comments down to a sentence or two. This may be hard, but it's important. Remember, you can change your mind later.

An Application Example

What did doing Exercise 4.2 accomplish, besides giving you a cramp in your writing hand? If the exercise worked, you probably already know. By freeing yourself from the chorus of expert voices in your sources and thinking to yourself about what the ideas you've collected mean, you've taken possession of the information again. You may have reaffirmed your purpose in writing the paper.

In the preceding chapters, we've followed Amanda as she tackled her research questions about teeth whitening. (You can see her final research essay in Appendix B.) Here's how Exercise 4.2 helped her get a handle on where she wanted to go in the draft.* Notice how her project began with a relatively small question about whether the now widely available teeth whiteners worked to making a larger point about the fluidity of beauty standards, and how hard it is for people to keep up with them.

Amanda is thinking like a researcher. One question leads to another, and each allows her to see her topic in a fresh way. As she becomes more knowledgeable, Amanda begins to see what it is she might say. A thesis is emerging.

STEP 3

I first thought about this topic because I noticed how many whitening products were being advertised on TV and I looked for one in the store. I couldn't believe that it was $30 for an over-the-counter whitening system. Then I wondered if they actually worked. I know that looking at people in Hollywood, they do have really bright white teeth, and it seems like now more than ever makeover shows are focusing on the color of teeth. I started to wonder why we're whitening our teeth at all. Is it healthier? In a word, no. But when everyone else starts doing something, our standard of beauty begins to change, and then it's important for the rest of us to conform. This creates a challenge because standards of beauty keep

*The following excerpts are reprinted with permission of Amanda Stewart.

increasing more and more, and we keep increasing our expectations for ourselves. We add things to our beauty routines rather than subtract them. It also seems to make disadvantaged and lower class people more obvious—almost like a caste system. They can't afford laser hair removal, acne treatments, and cosmetic dentistry, so the rich people start to look more and more different from less wealthy people. We're creating dividing lines through appearance that segregate us even more.

Wow, does this all have to do with tooth whitening? A little bit, I guess. It has to do with appearance and the way we modify our appearance. I'm concerned I've strayed a little bit too far from my original topic, but that might be okay. Rather than looking at the health implications and the effectiveness of tooth whitening and all the "hows" I want to look more at the "whys."

I also am interested in the birth of mass cosmetic dentistry. As people have started to take better care of their teeth and hygiene has improved, dentists were making less money on all sorts of health procedures. They had to find a way to recoup that money, so they created a new niche of services—smile care. They found an endless source of revenue when they tapped into Americans' desire for improved appearance, and they can't ever underestimate our willingness to spend money to look better. It's funny how profit motive can piggyback on our vanity and create a sort of loop wherein we spend money to look better, and then companies know we're willing to spend money to look better, so they create a higher standard of beauty and a product that will help us meet that standard.

By focusing on specifics in Step 4, the second fastwrite, you should discover some ways to anchor your ideas about the topic to particular people, situations, and case studies you discovered in your reading or from your own experience. Making these connections will not only strengthen your own thinking; case studies and personal accounts often make compelling examples, important to your paper.

STEP 4

One intriguing character in tooth whitening is Dr. Levine, who talked about the perfect celebrity smile. He gave exact dimensions and proportions that create the same smile in all those Hollywood glamour gals that are known for their beautiful teeth. I can't believe that there's nearly a mathematical formula that tells us exactly what a perfect smile should look like. It's disturbing to me that we have standardized our smile as one thing.

One story that intrigued me was a female corporate worker that had her teeth worked on several times to change her image. She talked about big, powerful teeth and the way they made her look more assertive than small, dainty teeth. I never realized all the character judgments that are made based on teeth. Not only does the whiteness convey associations of youth, vitality, and health, but apparently a lot more than that. Also, we're not aware that we make these judgments the majority of the time. If a person walks around with a mouth full of brown snaggle-teeth, we assume they take poor care of themselves and are low-income.

I was shocked when I learned that tooth-brushing didn't become a common American phenomenon until after World War II, when soldiers picked up the habit of brushing their teeth while in the army, and then continued it when they got home and spread it to their families. The Europeans and Asians had popularized the habit much earlier, in the mid 19th century. I knew oral hygiene was a relatively new phenomenon, but I didn't realize it was that new. It makes me amazed by the number of advances we've made in five decades. We've gone from chewing on sticks to help freshen our breath, to brushing and flossing, to having veneers placed on and teeth realigned for better aesthetics. I couldn't believe the statistics on the number of Americans that felt dissatisfied with the appearance of their teeth, and couldn't shake the feeling that the numbers had probably doubled in the past ten years. I think something like 34 percent of people had tried a whitening product, while a much larger number had considered it. When I was young I never heard of anyone mentioning the whiteness of his or her teeth, and now it's nearly a universal concern.

Step 5, the dialogue writing activity, invites someone else to the discussion of your topic, challenging you to consider an audience. What might most people want to know about your topic? How might you explain the answers? These questions may later shape how you organize your paper.

Amanda's dialogue started with the question that began her research—Why do people whiten their teeth?—and then went from there, getting more and more specific. Can you visualize the inverted pyramid progression of her questions and answers?

It actually might be more productive to construct a more freewheeling dialogue than Amanda's. Have a real conversation with an imagined reader. Push yourself with questions that really get you thinking about your topic and that might help you see it in a fresh way.

Here's Amanda's dialogue:

STEP 5

Why do people whiten their teeth?

People seem to have started whitening their teeth because other people whiten their teeth, and they want to "keep up with the Joneses" so to speak. Once it's a societal beauty standard to have white teeth, you almost have to do it to stay in line with everyone else.

Why did the beauty standard change in the first place?

Dentists and big corporations like Colgate and Crest seem to have created the desire in consumers to have whiter teeth.

They wanted to make more money, so they created more products to be sold to Americans—like whiteners. Now there are gums, gel trays, toothpastes, mouthwashes, and even laser treatments that can get teeth white.

What if you don't whiten your teeth?

A lot of judgments are made about us based on our teeth—like our overall health, hygiene, and age. By keeping more natural-colored teeth, you are unconsciously sending a message to other people about yourself that may not be what you'd prefer they think of you. It's funny how for eons people accepted eggshell-colored teeth as being natural, but now they're unacceptable.

Doesn't this just make people feel bad?

To some degree, yes. Once advertisers are promoting an image and certain people are living up to it, the rest of us feel required to live up to it too. But the people creating whitening products don't really care whether or not we feel secure about ourselves in a natural state. They want money. But I'm not bashing them, because we also create the demand by buying products, and if nobody purchased them, there wouldn't be anymore placed on the market.

Finally, asking "So What?" in Step 6 should help you redefine your thesis, or the controlling idea of your paper. In fact, your thesis may change. But for now, you need some brief statement—a sentence or two—that summarizes the most important thing you want your readers to understand.

STEP 6

So what?

Rather than being just a simple conveyance of positive feeling, smiles have become status symbols—and models to be improved *through tooth-whiteners and cosmetic dentistry. Tooth-whitening products have changed the way people feel about their natural smiles, and are now used to create a prototype perfect smile.*

If you're not happy with your answer to "So What?" spend some more time thinking about it. Don't proceed too much further with writing until you have some kind of tentative thesis statement to keep in mind. Put your thesis on an index card or piece of paper, and post it over your desk as a reminder. Pull it down and revise it, if necessary, as you continue with research and writing. But keep that thesis up there on the wall, at least while you're writing the first draft.

If Exercise 4.2 didn't work for you, you may need to collect more information. Consider circling back to some of the advanced search strategy suggestions made in the third week (see Chapter 3). But if you feel ready to begin writing a draft, read on.

Deciding Whether to Say *I*

I'm a writer who seems unable to stop talking about myself. As a reader of this textbook, that should be apparent to you by now. I share anecdotes about my photography failures, my high school girlfriend, and my predilection for lobsters. I've chosen to do this, though I know that getting personal in a piece of writing is somewhat risky business. If it's excessive, self-disclosure can seem egotistical or narcissistic. Constant self-reference—"I believe that . . . " or "I always wondered about . . . " or "I feel that . . . "—is usually unnecessary. (After all, if you simply make the assertion without the attribution, it's pretty obvious that you believe it or feel it.) The overuse of *I* can also seem to get in the way of the real subject, which may not be you. The personal profile is one genre of nonfiction writing that often suffers from explicit authorial intrusion. And teachers of research papers, as you know, often seem downright hostile to the intruding *I*.

By now, you know I don't agree with the view that all research writing should be objective (as if such a thing were possible). And in the research *essay* that you are about to draft this week, I certainly invite you to consider using the first person, presenting your own observations and experiences as evidence (if they're relevant) and yes, even talking about yourself.

There are many reasons this might be a good idea. First, by signaling our personal experiences and prejudices about a topic, we make explicit not only our particular purposes in exploring it but also why we might have a reason for (or even a vested interest in) seeing it a certain way. Readers like to know a writer's motivation for writing about something and appreciate knowing how her experiences might influence her ways of seeing. But maybe even more important, when a writer stops pretending that the *text* talks instead of the *author* (e.g., "This paper will argue that . . .") and actually enters into her text, she is much more likely to initiate a genuine conversation with her readers *and* with her sources. This dialogue might very well lead to some new ways of seeing her topic—that is, after all, the purpose of inquiry.

Getting Personal Without Being Personal

Conversation takes place between people, and in writing that embodies conversation, readers sense what Gordon Harvey* called *presence*—an awareness that a writer is making sense of things in his own particular ways, that he has a personal stake in what is being said. This is most easily achieved when the writer *gets* personal by using the first person, sharing personal experiences and perspectives. I hope that you sense my presence in *The Curious Researcher* through my willingness to do such things.

But I also want you to see, as Harvey observes, that presence in writing can be registered in ways other than simply talking about yourself. That is, you can write a research essay this week that *doesn't* use the first person or isn't autobiographical and still provides your readers with a strong sense of your presence as an individual writer and thinker. This presence may be much more subtle when it's not carried on the first-person singular's sturdy back. But it still makes writing come to life.

Before you begin drafting your essay this week, you'll have to decide how you'd prefer to get personal—explicitly or implicitly. For some of you, the choices may be limited. For instance, if your essay is on the causes of World War I, then integrating your own personal experience with the subject is obviously not an option. Most topics, however, offer the possibility of self-disclosure, and unless your instructor advises otherwise, almost all can accommodate *I*. But when you choose not to get personal in direct ways, you can still establish a strong presence in your essay.

Beginning at the Beginning

John McPhee, a staff writer for *The New Yorker* magazine and one of the masters of writing the research-based essay, gave a talk some years back about beginnings, which vex many writers.

*Gordon Harvey, "Presence in the Essay," *College English* 56 (1994): 642–54.

Making Your Presence Felt

Here are some ways to establish your presence in your research essay without necessarily using the first person.

- *Control quotation.* Carefully consider how you use the voices of others—where in your essay and for what purpose—as well as what you choose to emphasize in what those voices said.
- *Find your own way of saying things.* Even when talking about what someone else has said, say it in a way that only you can.
- *Find your own way of seeing things.* How do others usually see your topic, and how do you see it differently?
- *Seize opportunities to comment.* More than anything else, what you **do** with information—evaluating it, relating it, defining it, interpreting it, establishing its significance—gives the essay your signature.

The first part—the lead, the beginning—is the hardest part of all to write. I've often heard writers say that if you have written your lead you have written 90 percent of the story. You have tens of thousands of words to choose from, after all, and only one can start the story, then one after that, and so forth. And your material, at this point, is all fresh and unused, so you don't have the advantage of being in the middle of things. You could start in any of many places. What will you choose?* Leads must be sound. They should never promise what does not follow. Leads, like titles, are flashlights that shine down into the story.

Flashlights or Floodlights?

I love this: *"Leads . . . are flashlights that shine down into the story."* An introduction, at least the kind I was taught to write in high school, is more like a sodium vapor lamp that lights up the whole neighborhood. I remember writing introductions to research papers that sounded like this:

```
There are many critical problems that face

society today. One of these critical problems is
```

*John McPhee, University of New Hampshire, 1977.

environmental protection, and especially the
conservation of marine resources. This paper
will explore one of these resources--the
whale--and the myriad ways in which the whale-
watching industry now poses a new threat to this
species' survival. It will look at what is happening today and what some people concerned with
the problem hope will happen tomorrow. It will
argue that new regulations need to be put
into effect to reduce boat traffic around our
remaining whales, a national treasure that
needs protection.

This introduction isn't that bad. It does offer a statement of
purpose, and it explains the thesis. But the window it opens on the
paper is so broad—listing everything the paper will try to do—that
readers see a bland, general landscape. What's to discover? The old
writing formula for structuring some papers—"Say what you're going
to say, say it, and then say what you said"—breeds this kind of introduction. It also gets the writer started on a paper that often turns
out as bland as the beginning.

Consider this alternative opening for the same paper:

Scott Mercer, owner of the whale-watching vessel
Cetecea, tells the story of a man and his son who
decide that watching the whales from inside their
small motorboat isn't close enough. They want to
swim with them. As Mercer and his passengers
watch, the man sends his son overboard with
snorkel and fins, and the boy promptly swims
towards a "bubble cloud," a mass of air exhaled
by a feeding humpback whale below the surface.
What the swimmer doesn't know is that, directly
below that bubble cloud, the creature is on

its way up, mouth gaping. They are both in for a
surprise. "I got on the P.A. system and told my
passengers, just loud enough for the guy in the
boat to hear me, that either that swimmer was
going to end up as whale food or he was going to
get slapped with a $10,000 fine. He got out of
the water pretty fast."

I think this lead accomplishes nearly as much as the bland version
but in a more compelling way. It suggests the purpose of the paper—to
explore conflicts between whale lovers and whales—and even implies
the thesis—that human activity around whales needs more regulation.
This lead is more like McPhee's "flashlight," pointing to the direction of
the paper without attempting to illuminate the entire subject in a paragraph. An interesting beginning will also help launch the writer into a
more interesting paper, for both reader and writer.

It's probably obvious that your opening is your first chance to
capture your reader's attention. But how you begin your research
paper will also have a subtle yet significant impact on the rest of
it. The lead starts the paper going in a particular direction; it also
establishes the *tone,* or writing voice, and the writer's relationships to the subject and the reader. Most writers at least intuitively know this, which is why beginnings are so hard to write.

Writing Multiple Leads

One thing that will make it easier to get started is to write three
leads to your paper, instead of agonizing over one that must be perfect.
Each different opening you write should point the "flashlight" in a
different direction, suggesting different trails the draft might follow.
After composing several leads, you can choose the one that you—and
ultimately, your readers—find most promising.

Writing multiple openings to your paper might sound hard, but
consider all the ways to begin:

■ *Anecdote.* Think of a little story that nicely frames what your
paper is about, as does the lead about the man and his son who
almost became whale food.

■ *Scene.* Begin by giving your readers a look at some revealing
aspect of your topic. A paper on the destruction of tropical rain

forests might begin with a description of what the land looks like after loggers have left it.

■ *Profile*. Try a lead that introduces someone who is important to your topic. Amanda's essay on the relationship between the popularity of tooth whitening and our changing notions of beauty might begin, for example, by describing Dr. Levine, the man who determined with mathematical precision the dimensions of the "perfect smile."

■ *Background*. Maybe you could begin by providing important and possibly surprising background information on your topic. A paper on steroid use might start by citing the explosive growth in use by high school athletes in the last ten years. A paper on a novel or an author might begin with a review of what critics have had to say.

■ *Quotation*. Sometimes, you encounter a great quote that beautifully captures the question your paper will explore or the direction it will take. Heidi's paper on whether *Sesame Street* provides children with a good education began by quoting a tribute from *U.S. News and World Report* to Jim Henson after his sudden death.

■ *Dialogue*. Open with dialogue between people involved in your topic. Dan's paper on the connection between spouse abuse and alcoholism began with a conversation between himself and a woman who had been abused by her husband.

■ *Question*. Pointedly ask your readers the questions you asked that launched your research or the questions your readers might raise about your topic. Here's how Kim began her paper on adoption: "Could you imagine going through life not knowing your true identity?"

■ *Contrast*. Try a lead that compares two apparently unlike things that highlight the problem or dilemma the paper will explore. Dusty's paper "Myth of the Superwoman" began with a comparison between her friend Susan, who grew up believing in Snow White and Cinderella and married at twenty-one, and herself, who never believed in princes or white horses and was advised by her mother that it was risky to depend on a man.

■ *Announcement*. Sometimes the most appropriate beginning *is* one like the first lead on whales and whale-watchers mentioned earlier, which announces what the paper is about. Though such openings are sometimes not particularly compelling, they are direct. A paper with a complex topic or focus may be well served by simply stating in the beginning the main idea you'll explore and what plan you'll follow.

E X E R C I S E   4 . 3

Three Ways In

STEP 1: Compose three different beginnings, or leads, to your research paper. Each should be one or two paragraphs (or perhaps more, depending on what type of lead you've chosen and on the length of your paper). Think about the many different ways to begin, as mentioned earlier, and experiment (see Figure 4.1). Your instructor may ask you to write the three leads in your research notebook or type them on a separate piece of paper and bring them to class.

STEP 2: Get some help deciding which opening is strongest. Circulate your leads in class, or show them to friends. Ask each person to check the one lead he likes best, that most makes him want to read on.

STEP 3: Choose the lead you like (even if no one else does). To determine how well it prepares your readers for what follows, ask a friend or classmate to answer these questions: Based on reading only the opening of the paper: (a) What do you predict this paper is about? What might be its focus? (b) Can you guess what central question I'm trying to answer? (c) Can you predict what my thesis might be? (d) How would you characterize the tone of the paper?

Amanda's Three Leads

Here are three openings that Amanda crafted for her draft on our cultural obsession with the "perfect smile." Which do you think is strongest?

1. I haven't felt much like smiling recently. It isn't that I've been particularly melancholy, or deprived of necessary joy. I've actually been hesitant to smile because lately I've felt insecure about my teeth. I brush and floss every day and see my dentist twice a year, just like any responsible hygiene patient does—but that doesn't seem to be enough anymore. My teeth need to be white. Now when I feel the corners of my mouth pucker upwards and I start to grin at someone, I can't stop thinking about my teeth. What once was a

David Hancock
Brock Dethier
English 201
12 March 1998

Leaping Dog Awakens Locals' Curiosity

LOGAN, UT—A dog with seemingly supernatural abilities astounded observers on the Quad at Utah State University Friday when it leaped nearly twenty feet high while trying to catch a frisbee.

The owner of the dog, Sam McDougle, aroused the suspicions of local residents when he suggested Logan water as a possible cause. "Don't feed him no special vitamins or nuthin', just dog food and tap water," McDougle said.

"I'm a little scared," commented Ruth Parkins about questionable elements in the water, "and I don't know that I'd want my kids turning into freaks." Authorities downplayed rumors of steroids and hormone stimulants contaminating the water source. "I wasn't there, but I'd say Mr. McDougle is quite a charlatan," said Doug Thompson, mayor of Logan.

According to witnesses, McDougle repeatedly tossed a frisbee high into the air, and the dog launched after it "like a Patriot Missile taking out some Scuds," said Air Force Lieutenant John Richards. "When I first saw him do it, I thought, 'well, ain't that neat,'" said McDougle. "But now I'm gonna need a lot bigger fence."

FIGURE 4.1   Here's the opening to a paper that doesn't fit neatly into any category. David's essay begins with a photograph of a dog jumping an unreasonable height and a mock newspaper article on the feat. His next page unravels the mystery—the photograph was doctored using a software program—and then the essay goes on to explore the dangers of digitally altered images. David asks, "Can we even trust photographs anymore?"

Source: Reprinted by permission of David Hancock.

simple visual expression of happiness has become a symptom of my overall doubts about my appearance.

2. Julie Beatty wants people to look at her as a more confident, strong person, so she's doing the only logical thing. She's shelling out over $12,500 for an overhaul on her teeth. While it sounds completely ridiculous to change a person's oral structure to create a different persona, Julie is a member of a booming group of people who are looking to change their smiles to change their lives. Whether or not Julie's straightening, whitening, and tooth reshaping will change her success as an executive is still unknown, but the popularity of cosmetic dentistry and smile care is an undeniable new phenomenon.

3. I can feel individual molecules of air battering at my teeth. It's the middle of the night, but I can't sleep because of the constant pain in my mouth. Even the weight of my lips pressing down on my teeth is agonizing, like I've spent the day being hit in the mouth with a hammer and have exposed nerves protruding throughout. I haven't been beaten up, though. The cause of all my agony is a 10 percent peroxide gel I've been smearing into trays and putting on my teeth for the past week to whiten them. All this pain is due to my vanity and desire for a bit more pearliness in my pearly whites. As I watch the numbers of the clock roll from 2:00 to 4:00, I wonder why I'm putting up with such dental distress just for a more gleaming smile.

It's easy to choose an opening that's catchy. But the beginning of your paper must also help establish your purpose in writing it, frame your focus, and perhaps even suggest your main point, or thesis. The lead will also establish the voice, or tone, the paper will adopt (see the following section). That's a big order for one or two paragraphs, and you may find that more than a couple of paragraphs are needed to do it. Tentatively select the one opening (or a combination of several) from this exercise that does those things best. I think you'll find that none of the leads you composed will be wasted; there will be a place for the ones you don't use somewhere else in the paper. Keep them handy.

Deciding on a Voice

How you begin has another subtle influence on your draft: It establishes the tone, or writing voice, you will adopt in your paper. Though you may think *writing voice* is not something you've considered much before, you probably paid a lot of attention to it when writing the essay that accompanied your college applications. Does this *sound* right? you wondered, considering whether what you wrote would impress the admissions officer. Did you sound like college material? You also know how to *change* your writing voice. You do it all the time. The voice you choose in an email to your professor with a question about an assignment will be different from the voice you use if you ask a friend about it. We develop this kind of rhetorical awareness through experience.

Of all the writing assignments you've done over the years, the research paper is probably the one in which you paid the most attention to writing voice. Research papers are supposed to sound a certain way, right? They're supposed to be peppered with words such as *myriad* and *thus* and *facilitate*. They're supposed to sound like, well, nobody you know—detached, mechanical, and ponderous.

These are understandable assumptions. So many of the sources you've read in the past weeks have sounded that way. It's also difficult to avoid sounding detached when you're writing about a topic that holds little interest for you. But the writing voice you choose for this or any other paper you write *is* a choice. Don't assume that all research papers are supposed to sound a certain way and that you must mindlessly conform to that voice.

Considering Purpose, Audience, Subject, and Who You Are

How do you choose a writing voice for a research paper? A lot of the decisions, including an appropriate voice or tone for your essay, depend on this: *for whom are you writing and how knowledgeable are they already about your topic*? This has a huge impact on many things—how you structure your essay, the kind of information you use, and even the genre you choose (see Figure 4.2). Generally, the more knowledgeable your audience is about your research topic, the more likely it is that you will need to minimize your personal presence in the work, organize the information using conventions that expert readers expect, and consider what kinds of information these people will find most persuasive, sometimes called "rules of evidence."

In some classes, you may write for your instructors about subjects in which they are experts, and you may need to adjust your approach. But most composition courses invite students to write for their peers. These are general readers, an audience that is not likely to know nearly as much as you already do about your research topic. Therefore you're probably not writing a technical paper for an audience of experts. And though your primary purpose is not to entertain readers, you *are* trying to make your essay as interesting to others as it is to you.

But no text, even the most formal, is completely voiceless. And in an essay, even a research essay, readers' sense that they are

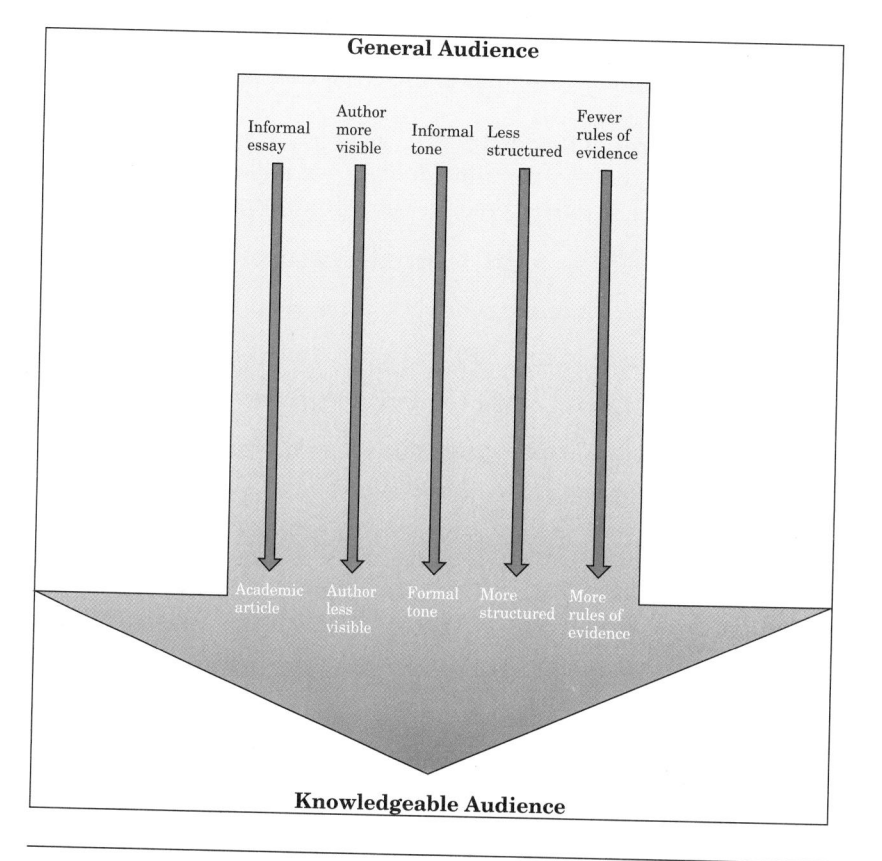

FIGURE 4.2   The Reader Effect. As your audience varies from those less informed about your research topic to those who are knowledgeable about it, your approach changes.

listening to the sound of a human being with a particular way of seeing things makes the writing come alive.

Fundamentally, your writing voice is a reflection of *who you are.* Your natural writing voice is different from mine, just as your spoken voice is. You can change your spoken voice, something you're probably pretty experienced at already. But you may need to learn to know and appreciate your writing voice—the voice that sounds like you. It might even be appropriate for this paper.

I faced a difficult decision about voice in writing this text. My purpose was to instruct students in research skills as well as to motivate them to find some enthusiasm for the assignment. In order to motivate my readers, I wanted to present the research paper in a new way. That purpose would not be served, I thought, by writing in the detached, impersonal voice most people associate with textbooks (and research papers). I chose to sound like *me,* hoping that when explained in my voice, the subject would seem more accessible and my own enthusiasm for research would come through.

The Differing Voices of Research.   The voice in a piece of writing often comes through in the very first line. In case you still think all research papers sound alike, listen to these first lines from student papers:

Ernst Pawel has said that *The Metamorphosis* by Franz Kafka "transcends the standard categories of literary criticism; it is a poisoned fairy tale about the magic of hate and the power of hypocrisy . . . charting the transmogrification of a lost soul in a dead bug" (279).

—From a paper on how Kafka writes the story to deal with his own childhood demons

As a waiter in a classy restaurant, I observe considerable variation in the way people dine, both in their treatment of other people and their skill at getting food and drink gracefully into their mouths.

— From an essay on the history of table manners

Even the sound of the word is vulgar.

—From a paper on ticks

Living during a period of war was something I had never experienced until the escalation of the recent Gulf crisis.

—From a paper on Igor Stravinsky's The Soldier's Tale

I have often worried in the past months if there was either something wrong with or missing from my brain.

—From a paper on dream interpretation

No more fat jokes.

—From a paper on a daughter coming to terms with her mother's cancer

These *are* different beginnings. But notice something all these beginnings share: They are concrete. None begins with a bland, broad stroke—some sweeping generalization or obvious statement (e.g., "War is an unhappy reality in today's society" or "Richard Wright's *Native Son* is about the African-American experience in America"). Rather, each gives the reader a specific handle on the topic. In some cases, the reader is given not only a concrete point of view but also, through a distinctive voice, is introduced to an individual writer, as well.

The voices in the previous examples could be considered along a continuum, beginning with the more formal and moving to the much less formal, ranging from the impersonal to the personal, from a less visible writer to one who steps forward immediately. Any one of these voices might be appropriate for your paper, depending on your subject, purpose, and audience, and on who you are.

As suggested earlier in this book, ask your instructor if you have some latitude in choosing a voice for your paper. (See "Things to Ask Your Instructor" in the Introduction.) If so, review the lead you tentatively chose in Exercise 4.3. Does it establish a voice that's appropriate, given your topic, purpose, and audience? Do you like the way it sounds? Should you change it? Would another lead sound better? If so, write a new lead or choose another from the several leads you wrote earlier.

Writing for Reader Interest

You've tentatively chosen a lead for your paper. You've selected it based on how well you think it frames your tentative purpose, establishes an appropriate tone or voice, and captures your readers' attention. Before you begin writing your draft, consider these four other strategies for writing a lively, interesting paper that will help keep readers turning pages.

1. How does your topic intersect with your readers' experiences?

2. Is there a way to put faces on your topic, to dramatize how it affects or is affected by particular people?

3. Can you find an ending that further clarifies, dramatizes, or emphasizes what you've come to understand about the answers to your research question?

4. Are there opportunities to surprise your readers, with interesting facts, arresting arguments, or highlighting a way of seeing something that is unexpected?

Working the Common Ground

Here's how David Quammen, a nature writer, begins an essay on the sexual strategy of Canada geese:

> Listen: *uh-whongk, uh-whongk, uh-whongk, uh-whongk,* and then you are wide awake, and you smile up at the ceiling as the calls fade off to the north and already they are gone. Silence again, 3 A.M., the hiss of March winds. A thought crosses your mind before you roll over and, contentedly, resume sleeping. The thought is: "Thank God I live here, right here exactly, in their path. Thank God for those birds." The honk of wild Canada geese passing overhead in the night is a sound to freshen the human soul. The question is why.*

If you live in Puerto Rico or anywhere beyond the late-night call of geese flying overhead, this lead paragraph may not draw you into Quammen's article on the birds' sexual habits. But for the many of us who know the muttering of geese overhead, suddenly the writer's question—why this is a sound "to freshen the human soul"—becomes our question, too. *We want to know what he knows because he starts with what we both know already:* the haunting sound of geese in flight.

David Quammen understands the importance of working the common ground between his topic and his readers. In "The Miracle of Geese," he begins with an experience that many of us know, and once he establishes that common ground, he takes us into the less familiar territory he encountered while researching Canada geese. And we willingly go. Quammen gives us a foothold on his topic that comes from our own experience with it.

One of my interests in writing an essay about pigeons was the conviction that I'm not alone in feeling ambivalent about the birds. Though "The Bothersome Beauty of Pigeons" doesn't begin, as David Quammen's essay does, by establishing this common ground, on several occasions I exploit moments I think readers will find familiar, including the anecdote about the war I waged on pigeons roosting under the eaves of my house. In smaller ways, I work common ground by using it in explanations, particularly when I'm trying to bring research information to life. For

*David Quammen, *The Flight of the Iguana* (New York: Delacorte, 1988), 233.

example, here's how I described the drinking habits of pigeons in the essay:

> [Pigeons] have other evolutionary advantages as well, some of which save them from the well-placed kicks of pigeon-haters or the tires of speeding taxis. For one thing, they "suck" puddle water rather than take it in their beaks and throw their heads back to swallow it, something like the difference between drinking a juice box and slinging back a shot of tequila. Sucking is quicker, apparently, . . .

In an earlier draft, I had merely described the water sucking habits of pigeons, but I sensed that the information would be far more interesting and understandable if I exploited a comparison that readers would find familiar: drinking juice boxes and taking shots of tequila.

As you draft your research paper, look for ways to work the common ground between your topic and your readers: What typically is their relationship to what you're writing about? What might they know about the topic but not have noticed? How does it touch their world? What would they want to know from their own experiences with your topic?

Steve, writing a paper about the town fire department that services the university, began by describing a frequent event in his dormitory: a false alarm. He then went on to explore why many alarms are not really so false after all. He hooked his readers by drawing on their common experience with his topic.

Some topics, like geese and divorce and alcoholism, may have very real connections to the lives of your readers. Many people have heard geese overhead, seen families broken apart, or watched parents or friends destroy themselves with booze. As you revise your paper, look for opportunities to encourage readers to take a closer look at something about your topic they may have seen before.

Topics for Which Common Ground Is Hard to Find.   Some topics don't yield common ground so directly. They may be outside the direct experiences of your readers. For example, Margaret was a history major, and, thankfully, she had never had the bubonic plague. Neither have the rest of us. But she was interested in writing a research essay on the impact of the fourteenth century epidemic on the lives of European women. This is an age and a disaster that in some ways is beyond the imagining of modern readers, though a skillful writer will look to highlight some of the similarities between our lives and those of the people she's writing about. One of these connections might be the modern AIDS epidemic in Africa, a disaster of truly epic proportions though it seems largely ignored by many Americans. Margaret might begin her essay with a brief glimpse at the devastation of families in South Africa today as a way of establishing the relevance of her 500-year-old topic.

Literary topics may also present a challenge in establishing common ground with readers, unless the author or work is familiar. But there are ways. When I was writing a paper on notions of manhood in Wallace Stegner's novels *The Big Rock Candy Mountain* and *Recapitulation,* I brought the idea of manhood home to my readers by describing my relationship with my own father and then comparing it to the relationship of two key characters in the books. Comparison to other more popular works that readers may know is often a way to establish some common ground.

Though it's unlikely that any of your classmates served on the ground in the recent Afghan war, images of that conflict—the debris-laden streets of Kabul, and the emergence of women in their burkas following the fall of the Taliban—are familiar to most of us through TV. This familiarity with such a distant place and culture might be a great way to establish the common ground with readers if, say, you were writing about the resurgence of female participation in the affairs of that nation.

In writing your paper, imagine the ways in which your topic intersects with the life of a typical reader, and in that way, bring the information to life.

Putting People on the Page

Essayist E. B. White once advised that when you want to write about humankind, you should write about a human. The advice to look at the *small* to understand the *large* applies to most writing, not just the research paper.

Ideas come alive when we see how they operate in the world we live in. Beware, then, of long paragraphs with sentences that begin with phrases such as *in today's society,* where you wax on with generalization after generalization about your topic. Unless your ideas are anchored to specific cases, observations, experiences, statistics, and, especially, people, they will be reduced to abstractions and lose their power for your reader.

Using Case Studies.   Strangely, research papers are often people-less landscapes, which is one of the things that can make them so lifeless to read. Lisa wrote about theories of child development, citing studies and schools of thought about the topic yet never applying that information to a real child, her own daughter, two-year-old Rebecca. In his paper decrying the deforestation of the Amazon rain forest, Marty never gave his readers the chance to hear the voices of the Indians whose way of life is threatened.

Ultimately, what makes almost any topic matter to the writer or the reader is what difference it makes to people.

Candy's paper on child abuse and its effect on language development, for example, opened with the tragic story of Genie, who, for nearly thirteen years, was bound in her room by her father and beaten whenever she made a sound. When Genie was finally rescued, she could not speak at all. This sad story about a real girl makes the idea that child abuse affects how one speaks (the paper's thesis) anything but abstract. Candy gave her readers reason to care about what she learned about the problem by personalizing it.

Sometimes, the best personal experience to share is your own. Have you been touched by the topic? Kim's paper about the special problems of women alcoholics included anecdotes about several women gleaned from her reading, but the paper was most compelling when she talked about her own experiences with her mother's alcoholism.

Using Interviews.   Interviews are another way to bring people to the page. In "Why God Created Flies," Richard Conniff brought in the voice of a bug expert, Vincent Dethier, who not only had interesting things to say about flies but who also spoke with humor and enthusiasm. Heidi's paper on *Sesame Street* featured the voice of a school principal, a woman who echoed the point the paper made about the value of the program. Such research essays are filled not just with information about the topic but with people who are touched by it in some way.

As you write your paper, look for opportunities to bring people to the page. Hunt for case studies, anecdotes, and good quotes that will help your readers see how your topic affects how people think and live their lives.

Writing a Strong Ending

Readers remember beginnings and endings. We already explored what makes a strong beginning: It engages the reader's interest, it's more often specific than general, and it frames the purpose of the paper, defining for the reader where it is headed. A beginning for a research paper should also state or imply its thesis, or controlling idea.

We haven't said anything about endings yet, or "conclusions," as they are traditionally described. What's a strong ending? That depends. If you're writing a formal research paper (in some disciplines), the purpose of the conclusion is straightforward: It should summarize major findings. But if you're writing a less formal research essay, the nature of the conclusion is less prescribed. It could summarize major findings, but it could also suggest new directions worth exploring, highlight an especially important aspect of the topic, offer a rethinking of the thesis, or end the story of the search. The conclusion could be general, or it could be specific.

Endings to Avoid.   The ending of your research paper could be a lot of things, and in a way, it's easier to say what it should *not* be:

■ Avoid conclusions that simply restate what you've already said. This is the "kick the dead horse" conclusion some of us were taught to write in school on the assumption that our readers probably aren't smart enough to get our point, so we'd better repeat it. This approach annoys most readers who *are* smart enough to know the horse is dead.

■ Avoid endings that begin with *in conclusion* or *thus*. Words such as these also signal to your reader what she already knows: that you're ending. Language such as this often begins a very general summary, which gets you into a conclusion such as the one mentioned above: dead.

■ Avoid endings that don't feel like endings—that trail off onto other topics, are abrupt, or don't seem connected to what came before them. Prompting your readers to think is one thing; leaving them hanging is quite another.

In some ways, the conclusion of your research paper is the last stop on your journey; the reader has traveled far with you to get there. The most important quality of a good ending is that it should add something to the paper. If it doesn't, cut it and write a new one.

What can the ending add? It can add a further elaboration of your thesis that grows from the evidence you've presented, a discussion of solutions to a problem that has arisen from the information you've uncovered, or perhaps a final illustration or piece of evidence that drives home your point.

Student Christina Kerby's research essay on method acting explores the controversy over whether this approach is selfish, subverting the playwright's intentions about a character's identity and replacing it with the actor's focus on her own feelings and identity. Christina's ending, however, first transcends the debate by putting method acting in context: It is one of several tools an actor can use to tap her emotions for a role. But then Christina humorously raises the nagging question about selfishness once more: Can we accept that Juliet is not thinking about the fallen Romeo as she weeps by his side but about her dead cat Fluffy? Here's Christina's ending:

Acting is no longer about poise, voice quality, and diction. It is also about feeling the part, about understanding the emotions that go into playing the part, and about possessing the skill necessary to bring those emotions to life within the character. . . . Whether an actor uses Stanislavski's method of physical actions to unlock the door to her subconscious or whether she attempts to stir up emotions from deep within herself using Strasberg's method, the actor's goal is to create a portrayal that is truthful. It is possible to pick out a bad actor from a mile away, one who does not understand the role because she does not understand the emotions necessary to create it. Or perhaps she simply lacks the means of tapping into them.

If genuine emotion is what the masses want, method acting may be just what every star-struck actress needs. Real tears? No problem. The

```
audience will never know that Juliet was not
lamenting the loss of her true love Romeo but
invoking the memory of her favorite cat Fluffy,
who died tragically in her arms.*
```

An ending, in many ways, can be approached similarly to a lead. You can conclude with an anecdote, a quotation, a description, a summary, or a profile. Go back to the discussion earlier in this chapter of types of leads for ideas about types of conclusions. The same basic guidelines apply.

One of the easiest ways to solve the problem of finding a strong ending is to have the snake bite its tail. In other words, find some way in the end of your essay to return to where the piece began. For example, if your research essay began with an anecdote that dramatized a problem—say, the destruction of old growth forests in Washington—you might return to that opening anecdote, suggesting how the solutions you explored in your essay might have changed the outcome. If you pose a question in the first few paragraphs, return to the question in the last few. If you begin with a profile of someone relevant to your topic, return to him or her in the end, perhaps amplifying on some part of your picture of the person. Although this approach is formulaic, it often works well because it gives a piece of writing a sense of unity.

Using Surprise

The research process—like the writing process—can be filled with discovery for the writer if he approaches the topic with curiosity and openness. When I began researching the *Lobster Almanac,* I was constantly surprised by things I didn't know: Lobsters are bugs; it takes eight years for a lobster in Maine to grow to the familiar one-pound size; the largest lobster ever caught weighed about forty pounds and lived in a tank at a restaurant for a year, developing a fondness for the owner's wife. I could go on and on. And I did in the book, sharing unusual information with my readers on the assumption that if it surprised me, it would surprise them, too.

As you write your draft, reflect on the surprising things you discovered about your topic during your research and look for ways to weave that information into the rewrite. Later, after you have written your draft, share it with a reader and ask for his ideas about what is particularly interesting and should be further developed. For now, think about unusual specifics you may have left out.

*Reprinted with permission of Christina B. Kerby.

However, don't include information, no matter how surprising or interesting, that doesn't serve your purpose. Christine's survey on the dreams of college freshmen had some fascinating findings, including some accounts of recurring dreams that really surprised her. She reluctantly decided not to say much about them, however, because they didn't really further the purpose of her paper, which was to discover what function dreams serve. On the other hand, Bob was surprised to find that some politically conservative politicians and judges actually supported decriminalization of marijuana. He decided to include more information about who they were and what they said in his revision, believing it would surprise his readers and strengthen his argument.

Organizing the Draft

Like a lot of school kids, I learned to write something called the "five-paragraph theme": introduction with thesis, three topic sentences, and three supporting details under each topic sentence. This was the container into which I poured all of my writing back then. Though it didn't produce particularly interesting writing, the five-paragraph structure was a reliable way to organize things. It was very well-suited to outlines. I vaguely remember this one from sixth grade:

I. China is a really big country
    A. The population of China is really big
    B. The geographic size of China is really big
    C. The economic dreams of China are really big.

What's useful about thinking of structure this way is the notion of hierarchy. There are some ideas that are subordinated to others, and some information that is subordinated to each idea. A problem with it, however, is the assumption that hierarchy is *always* the best way to organize information. For instance, essays can often make relevant digressions, or they might play with one way of seeing the topic and then another.

Perhaps a more basic problem with forms like the five-paragraph theme is the idea that structure is this kind of inert container that stands apart from the things you put into it and that it is immune to your particular motives in writing about something.

Yet structure is important. And it's even more important when writers begin a draft with an abundance of information. John McPhee has written popular nonfiction essays on people who study animal road kills, a guy who still makes birch bark canoes, and McPhee's own exploration of Atlantic City using the game Monopoly as a guide. He is a careful and meticulous researcher, accumulating material in multiple binders from his interviews, observations, and reading. By the time he sits down to write, he's looking at pages and pages of notes. McPhee's solution to this problem is to use note cards to organize his information on bulletin boards, moving them around until he gets a satisfying arrangement. "The piece of writing has a structure inside it," he says, and before he begins drafting he seeks to find it.

If you don't have much information to begin with, structure isn't such a problem. You simply end up using everything you have.

I'd like to encourage you, as you start drafting this week, to think about organizing your essay in a way that is more flexible and more responsive to your purposes in the piece, the audience for whom you're writing, your topic, and the assignment. For example, here are two ways to imagine how your research essay might come together.

- *Delayed thesis structure*—characteristic of the exploratory essay
- *Question-claim structure*—characteristic of the argumentative paper

While each method of organizing your research essay is distinct, they all share certain characteristics. For example, nearly any academic research paper includes the following items:

1. A point, a claim, a thesis, one main thing you are trying to say about the research question.
2. A review of what has already been said by others about it.
3. Specific information—evidence—that is the data from which your interpretations, conclusions, assertions, and speculations arise.
4. A method of reasoning through the question, some pattern of thought—narrative, argument, essaying—that writer and reader finds a convincing way to try to get at the truth of things.

Delayed Thesis Structure

If you chose your topic because you wanted to learn what you think—to find out rather than to prove—then you are essaying your research question. That's what I was doing in the beginning of this book when I was trying to figure out what to make of my conflicting feelings about pigeons. What is it about these creatures that makes them so easy to love and hate at the same time and what does that say about our responses to the natural world?

Quite naturally, then, I didn't begin my draft with a thesis—an answer to these questions—but sought to use my essay to try to sort this out. The "delayed thesis" structure uses the information from your research to think through your research question (see Figure 4.3).

In one version of this, you essentially tell the story of your thinking, a kind of "narrative of thought." The plot is something like, "This seems to be the problem and this is the question is raises for me. And here's what this person and that person have said about it, and this is what they said that makes me think." The story ends with some kind of statement that addresses this question: "What do I understand now about the question I initially asked that I didn't understand when I first asked it?"

However, exploratory research essays can take any number of forms. The structure that follows highlights five parts a research essay *might* include and lists some specific options for developing each. It might help you think about how to organize your draft this week.

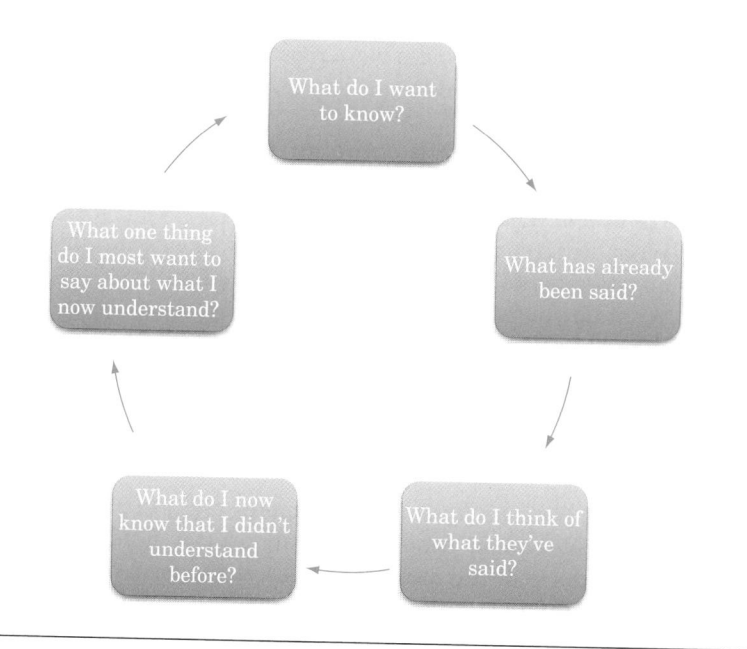

FIGURE 4.3   **The Delayed Thesis Structure.** This method of thinking through a research question might tell the story of your thinking and how what you've read and heard helps you to understand what you didn't understand before about your topic.

I. **Introduce the research problem or question and then your motive for exploring it.**
   a. Tell a story that dramatizes the problem.
   b. Describe your own experiences with it.
   c. What did you read, observe, or experience that made you curious about it?

II. **Establish the significance of the problem or question and why readers should care about it.**
   a. How many other people are affected?
   b. What difference will it make in people's lives?
   c. Why is this *particular* question significant?

III. **Describe and analyze what has already been written or said by others about the problem or question, and how this advances your understanding.**
   a. Who has made a significant contribution to the conversation about this?
   b. What have they said and how does that relate to your research question?
   c. What important questions do these other voices raise for you?

IV. **Explain what you find to be the most persuasive or significant answer to the research question (thesis)?**
   a. In the end, which voices were most convincing? Why?
   b. What might you add to the conversation?
   c. What do you want to say?

V. **Describe what you've come to understand about the topic that you didn't fully appreciate when you began the project. What is left to explore?**
   a. What difference will the discoveries you made about your question make in your life? In your readers' lives?
   b. What do you remain curious about?
   c. What questions are unresolved and what directions might more inquiry take if you were to continue?

Question–Claim Structure

While *The Curious Researcher* promotes essayed research as an excellent introduction to academic inquiry, most academic writing reports the products of the inquiry process in the form of argumentative papers. That may be the direction in which you want to take this draft after your research in recent weeks. Maybe you've developed strong feelings about your topic and you want to methodically build a case for a particular idea or assertion as a response to your research question.

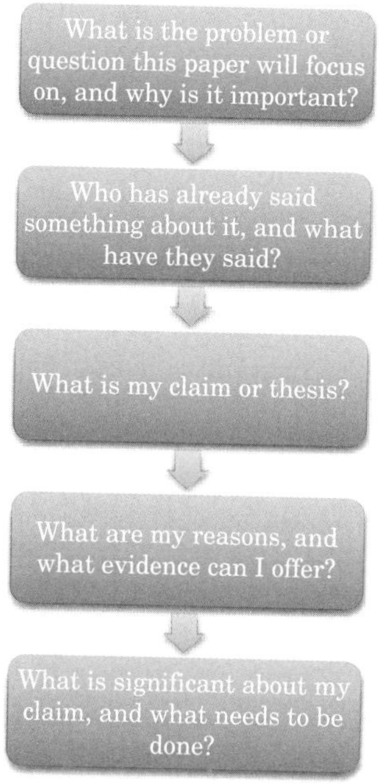

FIGURE 4.4 **The Question–Claim
Structure.** This structure, which is characteristic of the argumentative research paper,
signals the writer's purpose and point early
on and then sets out to prove it.

The question–claim structure is useful if your motive in the draft is to prove something. It has some similarities to the delayed thesis structure of the essay—for one thing it arises from a question—but this method for organizing your draft puts your answer to that question up front and then proceeds, using your research, to make the most convincing case (see Figure 4.4). It's a little like the automobile dealer who, after wandering the lot, decides to put the models he or she most wants to sell in the showroom window. You direct your readers' gaze away from the process of discovery to the product of that process: the point you want to make.

The question–claim structure may be the form of the research paper with which you're most familiar. Here's one way to think about organizing your draft using that approach.

I. **Introduce the problem or research question that is the
focus of the paper.**
   a. Provide factual background.
   b. Dramatize with an anecdote.
   c. Establish the significance of the problem by citing experts or other observers.
   d. Explain your purpose: To change audience attitudes? To call for some kind of action? To merely inform?

II. **Review the literature. What have others already said about the question?**
   a. Cite published studies, interviews, commentaries, experiments, and so on that are relevant to the question or problem.
   b. Which ideas or voices seem most important? Are there identifiable camps in the debate, or certain patterns of argument?
   c. Address popular assumptions. What do most people believe to be true?

III. **What will be *your* argument or thesis in the paper?**
   a. What does your understanding of the ongoing conversation about your research question lead you to believe is true?
   b. What is your position?
   c. What will you try to prove?

IV. **What are your reasons for believing what you believe and, for each one, what specific evidence did you find that you thought was convincing?**
   a. What kinds of evidence will your readers find most persuasive?
   b. Are there various kinds of evidence that can be brought to bear?
   c. How do your reasons square with those who might disagree with you?

V. **What is the significance of your claim? What's at stake for your audience? What might be other avenues for research?**
   a. What should we do? What might happen if we don't act?
   b. How does the thesis or claim that you propose resolve some part of the problem? What part remains unresolved?
   c. What questions remain?

Essaying or Arguing: An Example

Susan was writing an exploratory research essay on the relationship between attendance at preschool and academic success in elementary school. She decided to introduce her topic by describing her own dilemma with her son, Sam. She wanted to send him to preschool, but as a working college student she wasn't sure she could afford it. Her personal anecdote highlighted the problem many parents face and the question behind her research: Will children who don't attend preschool be at a disadvantage in primary school or not? In the middle section of her essay, Susan reported on several studies that looked at a range of skills that were affected by preschool experience and discussed which of these she found most significant, particularly in the context of her personal interviews with several local teachers. In the second to last section of her draft, Susan concluded that preschool does indeed make a difference, but particularly in the areas of reading and reasoning.

Imagine that Susan wants to revise her exploratory research essay into an argumentative research paper, a more conventional form for academic research. Would it be organized differently? While she still might begin with a personal anecdote as a way to dramatize the problem, Susan instead might choose a more factual approach. How many children in the United States attend preschool? How many don't? What are the trends? Are more parents struggling to find affordable preschools? Are fewer preschools available in disadvantaged areas? Is there a shortage of teachers? A significant difference would be where in the paper Susan puts her thesis. In the argumentative paper, the thesis usually appears toward the beginning (see Figure 4.4) and is stated explicitly: "I will argue in this essay that the preschool experience, which is being denied to a growing number of children in the United States, will put them at a serious disadvantage in reading and reasoning skills when they enter elementary school." Her essay would then go on to methodically establish the truth of this claim using her research. Susan might end her essay by suggesting how elementary teachers could address the learning deficits these children bring into their classrooms.

Writing with Sources

The need for *documentation*—that is, citing sources—distinguishes the research paper from most other kinds of writing. And let's face it: Worrying about sources can cramp your style. Many students have an understandable paranoia about plagiarism and tend, as mentioned earlier, to let the voices of their sources overwhelm their own. Students are also often distracted by technical details: Am I getting the right page number? Where exactly should this citation go? Do I need to cite this or not?

As you gain control of the material by choosing your own writing voice and clarifying your purpose in the paper, you should feel less constrained by the technical demands of documentation. The following suggestions may also help you weave reference sources into your own writing without the seams showing.

Blending Kinds of Writing and Sources

One of the wonderful things about the research essay is that it can draw on all four sources of information—reading, interviews, observation, and experience—as well as the four notetaking strategies discussed earlier—quotation, paraphrase, summary, and the writer's own analysis and commentary. Skillfully blended, these elements can make music.

Look at this paragraph from Heidi's paper on *Sesame Street*:

```
There is more to this show than meets the eye, cer-
tainly. It is definitely more than just a crowd of
furry animals all living together in the middle of
New York City. Originally intended as an effort to
educate poor, less privileged youth, Sesame Street
is set in the very middle of an urban development on
purpose (Hellman 52). As Jon Stone, one of the
show's founders and co-producers sees it, the pro-
gram couldn't be "just another escapist show set in
a tree house or a badger den" (52). Instead, the
recognizable environment gave something to the kids
they could relate to. " . . . It had a lot more real
quality to it than, say, Mister Rogers. . . . Kids say
the reason they don't like Mister Rogers is that
it's unbelievable," says Nancy Diamonti.*
```

The writing is lively here, not simply because the topic is interesting to those of us who know the program. Heidi has nicely blended her own commentary with summary, paraphrase, and quotation, all in a single paragraph. She has also been able to draw on multiple sources of information—an interview, some effective quotes from her reading, and her own observations of *Sesame Street*. We sense that the writer is *using* the information, not being used by it.

Handling Quotes. Avoid the temptation, as Heidi did, to load up your paragraphs with long or full quotes from your sources. I often see what I call "hanging quotes" in research papers. Embedded in a

*Used with permission of Heidi R. Dunham.

paragraph is a sentence or two within quotation marks. Though the passage is cited, there's no indication of who said it. Usually, the writer was uncertain about how to summarize or paraphrase or work *part* of the quotation into his own prose.

Use quotations selectively. And if you can, blend them into your own sentences, using a particularly striking or relevant part of the original source. For example, consider how quotes are used in this paragraph:

> Black Elk often spoke of the importance of the circle to American Indian culture. "You may have noticed that everything an Indian does is in a circle, and that is because the Power of the World always works in circles, and everything tries to be round. . . . The sky is round, and I have heard that the earth is round like a ball, and so are all the stars." He couldn't understand why white people lived in square houses. "It is a bad way to live, for there is not power in a square."

The quotes stand out, separate from the writer's own text. A better use of quotes is to work the same material smoothly into your own prose, doing something such as this:

> Black Elk believed the "Power of the World always works in circles," noting the roundness of the sun, the earth, and the stars. He couldn't understand why white people live in square houses: "It is a bad way to live, for there is not power in a square."

Occasionally, however, it may be useful to include a long quotation from one of your sources. A quotation that is longer than four lines should be *blocked,* or set off from the rest of the text by indenting it ten spaces from the left margin. Like the rest of the paper, a blocked quotation is also typed double-spaced. For example:

> According to Robert Karen, shame is a particu-
> larly modern phenomenon. He notes that in
> medieval times, people pretty much let loose, and
> by our modern tastes, it was not a pretty sight:
>
> > Their emotional life appears to have
> > been extraordinarily spontaneous and
> > unrestrained. From Joahn Huizinga's *The*
> > *Waning of the Middle Ages* we learn that the
> > average European town dweller was wildly
> > erratic and inconsistent, murderously
> > violent when enraged, easily plunged into
> > guilt, tears, and pleas for forgiveness,
> > and bursting with psychological eccentrici-
> > ties. He ate with his hands out of a common
> > bowl, blew his nose on his sleeve, defe-
> > cated openly by the side of the road, made
> > love, and mourned with great passion, and
> > was relatively unconcerned about such
> > notions as maladjustment or what others
> > might think. . . . In post-medieval centuries
> > what I've called situational shame spread
> > rapidly. . . . (61)

Note that the quotation marks are dropped around a blocked quotation. In this case, only part of a paragraph was borrowed, but if you quote one or more full paragraphs, indent the first line of each *three* spaces in addition to the ten the block is indented from the left margin.

We'll examine *parenthetical references* more fully in the next section, but notice how the citation in the blocked quotation above is placed *outside* the final period. That's a unique exception to the usual rule that a parenthetical citation is enclosed *within* the period of the borrowed material's final sentence.

Quick Tips for Controlling Quotations

Quotations from your sources can definitely be overused, especially when they seem dumped into the draft, untouched and unexamined, or used as a lazy substitute for paraphrase. But when it works, bringing the voices of others into your own writing can bring the work to life and make readers feel as if there is a genuine conversation going on.

Here are some quick tips for doing this effectively.

Grafting Quotes

Frequently, the best way to use quoted material is to graft it onto your own prose. Sometimes you just use a word or phrase:

> Some words for hangover, like ours, refer pro-saically to the cause: the Egyptians say they are "still drunk," the Japanese "two days drunk," the Chinese "drunk overnight."*

In other situations, especially when you want to provide a bit more emphasis to what a source has said, you might give over parts of several sentences to a source, like this:

> The makers of NoHang, on their Web page, say what your mother would: "It is recommended that you drink moderately and responsibly." At the same time, they tell you that with NoHang "you can drink the night away."

Sandwiching Quotes

A sandwich without the bread isn't a sandwich. Similarly, when you use a quotation, especially one that is a full sentence or more, it should be surrounded by your comments about it. Introduce the quotation: Who said it and why is he or she relevant? When did this person say it and in what context? How does the quote relate to the current discussion in your essay? Followup the quotation: What

---

*Joan Acocella, "A Few Too Many," *The New Yorker* 26 May 2008: 32–37.

do *you* think is important about what was just said? How does it address an important idea or question? What does the person quoted *fail* to say or fail to see?

Here's an example of what I mean:

> In fact, even back when leeches were held in contempt by the medical profession, Sawyer had a solid rationale for choosing them as his subject. Biology, as taught in the United States had left him frustrated: "For sex determination, we'd study *Drosophilia,* for physiology we'd study frogs, for genetics, bacteria. I thought there was more to be learned from studying one organism in detail than from parts of many." His American professors disdained this approach as a throw-back to nineteenth century biology.*

See how the writer here sets up the quotation? He provides background on the significance of what Sawyer, the leech biologist, was about to say. The guy was frustrated with how organisms were studied. The quotation is then sandwiched with a comment about how the quote reflects Sawyer's reputation as an antitraditionalist.

Billboarding Quotes

Another way you can control quotations is adding emphasis to billboard parts of a particular quote. Typically you do this by italicizing the phrase or sentence. It might look something like this:

> For the sake of Millennials—and, through them, the future of America—the most urgent adult task is to *elevate their expectations.* (Emphasis added)†

Note the parenthetical note that signals the original quote has been altered to give emphasis. In academic writing, this would also include a citation, but more about that later.

---

*Richard Conniff, *Spineless Wonders* (New York: Holt, 1996).
†Neil Howe and William Strauss, *Millennials Rising* (New York: Vintage, 2000).

Splicing Quotes

Sometimes you want to prune away unnecessary information from a quotation to place emphasis on that part that matters most to you or eliminates unnecessary information. Ellipsis points, those three dots (. . .) you sometimes see at the beginning, middle, or end of a sentence signal that some information has been omitted.

Take this passage for example:

> During the Gen-X child era, the American family endured countless new movements and trends—feminism, sexual freedom, a divorce epidemic, fewer G-rated movies, child-raising handbooks telling parents to "consider yourself" ahead of a child's needs, gay rights, Chappaquiddick, film nudity, a Zero Population Growth ethic, *Kramer vs. Kramer,* and *Roe v. Wade.* A prominent academic in 1969 proclaimed in the *Washington Post* that the family needed a "decent burial."

That's a pretty long list of movements and trends, and the reader could get a taste without serving up the whole thing. Ellipsis points can help:

> During the Gen-X child era, the American family endured countless new movements and trends—feminism, sexual freedom, a divorce epidemic . . . , [and a] prominent academic in 1969 proclaimed in the *Washington Post* that the family needed a "decent burial."

When you have to slightly reword the original text or alter the punctuation for a smoother splice, put the alteration in brackets. In the example, for instance, I turned what was a separate sentence in the original into a compound sentence using the conjunction *and.*

Handling Interview Material

The great quotes you glean from your interviews can be handled like quotations from texts. But there's a dimension to a quote from an interview that's lacking in a quote from a book: Namely, you participated in the quote's creation by asking a question, and in some cases, you were there to observe your subject saying it. This presents some new choices. When you're quoting an interview subject, should you enter your essay as a participant in the conversation, or should you stay out of the way? That is, should you describe yourself asking the question? Should you describe the scene of the interview, your subject's manner of responding, or your immediate reaction to what she said? Or should you merely report what was said and who said it?

Christina's essay, "Crying Real Tears: The History and Psychology of Method Acting," makes good use of interviews. Notice how Christina writes about one of them in the middle of her essay:

> During a phone interview, I asked my acting teacher,
> Ed Claudio, who studied under Stella Adler,
> whether or not he agreed with the ideas behind
> method acting. I could almost see him wrinkle his
> nose at the other end of the connection. He
> described method acting as "self-indulgent,"
> insisting that it encourages "island acting."
> Because of emotional recall, acting became a far
> more personal art, and the actor began to move
> away from the script, often hiding the author's
> purpose and intentions under his own.*

Contrast Christina's handling of the Claudio interview with her treatment of material from an interview with Dave Pierini later in her essay:

> Dave Pierini, a local Sacramento actor, pointed
> out, "You can be a good actor without using
> method, but you cannot be a good actor without
> at least understanding it." Actors are perhaps
> some of the greatest scholars of the human

*Reprinted with permission of Christina B. Kerby.

psyche because they devote their lives to the study and exploration of it. Aspiring artists are told to "get inside of the character's head." They are asked, "How would the character *feel*? How would the character *react*?"

Do you think Christina's entry into her report of the first interview (with Ed Claudio) is intrusive? Or do you think it adds useful information or even livens it up? What circumstances might make this a good move? On the other hand, what might be some advantages of the writer staying out of the way and simply letting her subject speak, as Christina chooses to do in her treatment of the interview with Dave Pierini?

Trusting Your Memory

One of the best ways to weave references seamlessly into your own writing is to avoid the compulsion to stop and study your sources as you're writing the draft. I remember that writing my research papers in college was typically done in stops and starts. I'd write a paragraph of the draft, then stop and reread a photocopy of an article, then write a few more sentences, and then stop again. Part of the problem was the meager notes I took as I collected information. I hadn't really taken possession of the material before I started writing the draft. But I also didn't trust that I'd remember what was important from my reading.

If, during the course of your research and writing so far, you've found a sense of purpose—for example, you're pretty sure your paper is going to argue for legalization of marijuana or analyze the symbolism on old gravestones on Cape Cod—then you've probably read purposefully, too. You *will* likely know what reference sources you need as you write the draft, without sputtering to a halt to remind yourself of what each says. Consult your notes and sources as you need them; otherwise, push them aside, and immerse yourself in your own writing.

Citing Sources

An Alternative to Colliding Footnotes

Like most people I knew back then, I took a typing class the summer between eighth grade and high school. Our instructional texts were long books with the bindings at the top, and we worked on standard Royal typewriters that were built like tanks. I got up to thirty words a minute, I think, which wasn't very good, but thanks to that class, I can still type without looking at the keyboard. The one thing I never learned, though, was how to turn the typewriter roller up a half space to type a footnote number that would neatly float above the line. In every term paper in high school, my footnotes collided with my sentences.

I'm certain that such technical difficulties were not the reason that most academic writers in the humanities and social sciences have largely abandoned the footnote method of citation for the parenthetical one, but I'm relieved, nonetheless. In the current system, borrowed material is parenthetically cited in the paper by indicating the author of the original work and the page it was taken from or the date it was published. These parenthetical citations are then explained more fully in the "Works Cited" page at the end of your paper where the sources themselves are listed.

By now, your instructor has probably told you which method of citing sources you should use: the Modern Language Association (MLA) style or the American Psychological Association (APA) style. Most English classes use MLA. A complete guide to MLA conventions is provided in Appendix B.

Before you begin writing your draft, go to Appendix A and read the section "Citing Sources in Your Essay." This will describe in some detail when and where you should put parenthetical references to borrowed material in the draft of your essay. Don't worry too much about the guidelines for preparing the final manuscript, including how to do the bibliography. You can deal with that next week.

I Hate These Theses to Pieces

Okay, here's a thesis:

    I hate thesis statements.

And you wonder, What is this guy talking about now? What do you mean you hate thesis statements? *All* thesis statements? Why?

You'd be right to wonder for two reasons. First, my thesis statement about thesis statements isn't very good: It is too sweeping, it is overstated (*hate?*), and it deliberately withholds information. Its virtues, if any, are its shock value and the fact that it *is*—as any thesis must be—an assertion, or claim. Second, you're wondering why a teacher of writing would make such a claim in the first place. Doesn't most writing have a thesis, either stated or implied? Isn't writing that lacks a thesis unfocused, unclear? Doesn't a research paper, in particular, need a strong thesis?

Let me try again. Here's a thesis:

```
The thesis statement often discourages inquiry
instead of promoting it.
```

Hmmm . . . This is less overstated, and the claim is qualified in a reasonable way (*often discourages*). This thesis is also a bit more informative because it ever so briefly explains *why* I dislike thesis statements: *They often discourage inquiry.* But how do they do that? For one thing, when you arrive at a thesis statement prematurely, you risk turning the process of exploring your topic into a ritual hunt for examples that simply support what you already think. With this purpose in mind, you may suppress or ignore ideas or evidence that conflicts with the thesis—that threatens to disrupt the orderly march toward proving it is true.

Well, then, you infer, you're not saying you dislike *all* thesis statements, just those that people make up too soon and cling to compulsively.

Yes, I think so. I prefer what I would call the *found thesis,* the idea that you discover or the claim you come to *after* some exploration of a topic. This type of thesis often strikes me as more surprising (or less obvious) and more honest. It suddenly occurs to me, however, that I just discovered the term *found thesis* at this very moment, and I discovered it by starting with a conventional claim: *I hate thesis statements.* Doesn't that undermine my current thesis about thesis statements, that beginning with one can close off inquiry?

Well, yes, come to think of it.

What might we conclude from all of this discussion about the thesis that you can apply to the draft you're writing this week?

1. If you're already committed to a thesis, write it down. Then challenge yourself to write it again, making it somewhat more specific and informative and perhaps even more qualified.

2. At this stage, the most useful thesis may not be one that dictates the structure and arrangement of your draft but one that provides a focus for your thinking. Using the information you've collected, play out the truth of your idea or claim, but also invite questions about it—as I did—that may qualify or even overturn what you initially thought was true. In other words, use your draft to *test* the truthfulness of your thesis about your topic.

3. If you're still struggling to find a tentative thesis, use your draft to discover it. Then use your found thesis as the focus for the revision.

4. Your final draft *does* need to have a strong thesis, or controlling idea, around which the essay is built. The essay may ultimately attempt to *prove* the validity of the thesis, or the final essay may *explore* its implications.

Driving Through the First Draft

You have an opening, a lot of material in your notes—much of it, written in your own words—and maybe an outline. You've considered some general methods of development, looked at ways to write with sources, and completed a quick course in how to cite them. Finish the week by writing through the first draft.

Writing the draft may be difficult. All writing, but especially research writing, is a recursive process. You may find sometimes that you must circle back to a step you took before, discovering a gap in your information, a new idea for a thesis statement, or a better lead or focus. Circling back may be frustrating at times, but it's natural and even a good sign: It means you're letting go of your preconceived ideas and allowing the discoveries you make *through writing* to change your mind.

A Draft Is Something the Wind Blows Through

Remember, too, that a *draft* is something the wind blows through. It's too early to worry about writing a research paper that's airtight, with no problems to solve. Too often, student writers think they have to write a perfect paper in the first draft. You can worry about plugging holes and tightening things up next week. For now, write a draft, and if you must, put a reminder on a piece of paper and post it on the wall next to your thesis statement or research question. Look at this reminder every time you find yourself agonizing over the imperfections of your paper. The reminder should say, "It Doesn't Count."

Keep a few other things in mind while writing your first draft:

1. *Focus on your tentative thesis or your research question.* In the draft consider your thesis a theory you're trying to prove but that you're willing to change. If your paper is more exploratory than argumentative, use your focusing question as a reminder of what you want to know. Remember your question can change, too, as you learn more about your subject.

2. *Vary your sources.* Offer a variety of different sources as evidence to support your assertions. Beware of writing a single page that cites only one source.

3. *Remember your audience.* What do your readers want to know about your topic? What do they need to know to understand what you're trying to say?

4. *Write with your notes.* If you took thoughtful notes during the third week—carefully transforming another author's words into your own, flagging good quotes, and developing your own analysis—then you've already written at least some of your paper. You may only need to finetune the language in your notes and then plug them into your draft.

5. *Be open to surprises.* The act of writing is often full of surprises. In fact, it should be, since *writing* is *thinking* and the more you think about something, the more you're likely to see. You might get halfway through your draft and discover the part of your topic that *really* fascinates you. Should that happen, you may have to change your thesis or throw away your outline. You may even have to reresearch your topic, at least somewhat. It's not necessarily too late to shift the purpose or focus of your paper (though you should consult your instructor before totally abandoning your topic at this point). Let your curiosity remain the engine that drives you forward.

CHAPTER 5

The Fifth Week

Revising for Purpose

My high school girlfriend, Jan, was bright, warm hearted, and fun, and I wasn't at all sure I liked her much, at least at first. Though we had a lot in common—we both loved sunrise over Lake Michigan, bird watching, and Simon and Garfunkel—I found Jan a little intimidating, a little too much in a hurry to anoint us a solid "couple." But we stuck together for three years, and as time passed, I persuaded myself—despite lingering doubts—that I couldn't live without her. There was no way I was going to break my white-knuckled hold on that relationship. After all, I'd invested all that time.

As a writer, I used to have similar relationships with my drafts. I'd work on something very hard, finally finishing the draft. I'd know there were problems, but I'd developed such a tight relationship with my draft that the problems were hard to see. And even when I recognized some problems, the thought of making major changes seemed too risky. Did I dare ruin the things I loved about the draft? These decisions were even harder if the draft took a long time to write.

Revision doesn't necessarily mean you have to sever your relationship with your draft. It's probably too late to make a complete break with the draft and abandon your topic. However, revision does demand finding some way to step back from the draft and change your relationship with it, seeing it from the reader's perspective rather than just the writer's. Revision requires that you loosen your grip. And when you do, you may decide to shift your focus or rearrange the information. At the very least, you may discover gaps in information or sections of the draft that need more development. You will certainly need to prune sentences.

The place to begin is *purpose*. You should determine whether the purpose of your paper is clear and examine how well the information is organized around that purpose.

Presumably, by now you know the purpose of your essay. If you hadn't quite figured it out before you wrote last week's draft, I hope writing the draft helped you clarify your purpose. It did? Great. Then complete the following sentence. Remember that here, you're trying to focus on the *main* purpose of your draft. There are probably quite a few things that you attempt to do in it, but what is the most central purpose?

The main purpose of my essay on _____ is to (use the appropriate word or words) *explain, argue, explore,*

*describe*_____.

Here's how Christina filled in the blanks for her essay on method acting:

The main purpose of my essay on ___*method acting*___ is to

(explain,) argue, explore, describe *the psychological aspects of method*

and its impact on American theater.

Another way of getting at purpose is to clarify your research question, something that you first considered about a month ago. It's likely that your research question has evolved since then. Sometimes, it becomes more narrowly focused and more specific. Say your question began with wondering how social networking sites change the way we think about friendship. Now the question is this: *What is MySpace doing about cyber-bullying, and is it necessary?* On the other hand, sometimes you see that you need to hitch your specific question to a larger idea, one that highlights the importance of your inquiry. For example, Amanda's piece on the trend of teeth whitening began with this research question: *How has cosmetic tooth whitening changed the way Americans feel about their teeth?* As she learned more she considered this question: *How does the tooth whitening trend reflect our culture's quickly changing definitions of beauty, and what does that mean for people who don't fit that definition?*

Go back to the beginning. What was your initial research question? What is it now?

EXERCISE 5.1

Wrestling with the Draft*

Writing with research is a wrestling match. You're the 120-pound weakling who may not have written many college research essays before trying to take on the heavyweight experts on your topic. You're fighting for your life, trying to use what these authorities say or think *for your own purposes,* without getting slammed to the floor for plagiarizing or meekly submitting a report rather than an essay. The challenge is to get control of the information, to muscle it to the ground using the strength of your own purposes. Establishing this control is one of the hardest parts of drafting research papers. Two extreme responses to this problem are giving up entirely and turning your paper over to your sources, letting them do all the talking, and pretending that you're not really wrestling with anyone and writing a paper that includes only your own opinions. Neither option is what you want.

Who won the wrestling match in your draft? To what extent did you succeed in using other people's ideas and information in the service of your own thoughts and purposes? One way to see who is getting the upper hand in the draft is to mark it up, noting where you've given control to your sources and where you've taken it back. This pattern can say an awful lot about how well you've done drafting a research essay where your own purposes rule.

1. For this exercise you'll use two highlighters, each a different color.

2. Choose a random page of your draft, somewhere in the middle.

3. First mark the parts in which you're a less active author. As you read the page, highlight every sentence, passage, or paragraph that reports facts, quotes sources, or otherwise presents information or ideas that belong to someone else.

4. Now, using the other highlighter, mark the parts in which you're an active author. Read the same page again, but this time highlight every sentence, passage, or paragraph that represents

---

*This exercise is adapted from one I borrowed from my colleague, Dr. Mike Mattison, who borrowed it from his former colleagues at University of Massachusetts–Amherst. Thanks to all.

your ideas, analysis, commentary, interpretation, definition, synthesis, or argument.

   5. Repeat the previous steps with two more pages of your draft.

   Which color dominates? Are you turning over too much of the text to your sources? Are you ignoring them and rattling on too much about what you think? And what do you notice about the pattern of color? Are you taking turns paragraph by paragraph with your sources, or is your own analysis and commentary nicely blended *within* paragraphs, so that the information is always anchored to your own thoughts? Do you surround quoted passages with your own voice and analysis? Who wins the wrestling match? See Figure 5.1 for an example of this exercise.

Our tooth whiteners are safer, and a study by James W. Curtis, DMD, discovered that bleaching through carbamide peroxide actually decreases the amount of plaque on teeth, but we're still doing it for beauty reasons rather than health ones (Nuss 28).

In her article "Bright On," Molly Prior notes that Procter & Gamble and Colgate-Palmolive revolutionized the whitening industry by bringing over-the-counter whiteners to drugstores everywhere at the turn of the twenty-first century (39). No longer did people have to pay high prices for professional whitening—they could do it themselves, at home, for a reasonable cost. In the past, a patient had to eat a bill of $1,000 for a laser whitening treatment, or $10,000 for a full set of veneers; now a package of Crest Whitestrips retails for only $29.99 (Gideonse). Suddenly, whiter teeth were available to everyone. While a shining smile once indicated wealth and the ability to splurge on cosmetic dentistry, it became affordable to the dentally discolored masses eager to emulate the lifestyles of the people they saw in magazines and on television.

Companies didn't create whitening products to fill a demand created by the public for whiter teeth. While Hollywood glitterati did pay high prices for iconic smiles, most people seemed happy with functional teeth. However, companies saw money to be made in creating a whiter norm for teeth, so they barraged the airwaves with advertisements featuring people complaining about the dullness and imperfection of their teeth. Natural teeth were denigrated as ugly. Crest and Colgate-Palmolive

---

FIGURE 5.1   Amanda Wins the Wrestling Match

The text highlighted in light gray is passages from Amanda's sources, and the darker highlights are passages in which she is commenting, clarifying, asserting, or interpreting. Notice the balance between light and dark gray. Clearly Amanda has a strong authorial presence. Also notice how quotations are surrounded by her commentary. By controlling quotations like this she is also using rather than being used by her sources.

wanted to make money, so appealed to the American obsession with beauty to secure a financial reason to smile. As Jonathan Levine, DDS, notes, "It's lately seeming much harder to go broke by overestimating the vanity of the American public" (Walker). The companies succeeded in making mouthfuls of money, netting $450 million dollars, and getting 45 percent of Americans to try some form of whitening (Prior 42). In effect, they appealed to our egos to get to our pocket books.

FIGURE 5.1 (Continued)

The Thesis as a Tool for Revision

Purpose and *thesis* have a tight relationship. When I write an essay, I'm essentially in pursuit of a point, and not infrequently, it playfully eludes me. Just when I think I've figured out exactly what I'm trying to say, I have the nagging feeling that it's not quite right—it's too simplistic or obvious, it doesn't quite account for the evidence I've collected, or it just doesn't capture the spirit of the discoveries I've made. If a thesis is often a slippery fish, then having a strong sense of purpose helps me finally get a grip on it.

Purpose (and its sister *focus*) is a statement of intention—this is what I want to do in this piece of writing. It not only describes how I've limited the territory but what I plan to do when I'm there. That's why the words *explain, argue, explore,* and *describe* are so important. They pinpoint an *action* I'll take in the writing, and they'll move me toward particular assertions about what I see. One of these assertions will seem more important than any other, and that will be my thesis.

Maybe my tendency to see thesis statements as slippery is because I dislike encountering main points in essays that act like schoolyard bullies—they overcompensate for their insecurity by loudly announcing, "Hey, listen to me, bub, *I'm* the main point around here, and whaddya going to do about it, huh?" Essays whose purpose is to argue something and take a broad and unqualified stand in favor of or against a whole category of people/positions/theories/ideas can be the worst offenders. Things are rarely that simple, and when they are, they usually aren't very interesting to write about.

Just as often, I encounter thesis statements that act more like the kids who get singled out by the bullies for harassment. They are meek or bland assertions that would be easy to pick apart if they weren't so uninteresting. Here's one: *Nuclear bombs are so powerful, so fast, and so deadly that they have become the weapon of today.* There *are* elements of an assertion here; the writer points out that modern nuclear weapons are *fast, powerful,* and *deadly.* But this is such an obvious claim that it probably isn't even worth stating. The phrase *weapon of today* would seem more promising if it was explained a bit. What is it about nations or warfare *today* that makes such weapons so appealing? Is the apparent passion for fast, deadly, and powerful nuclear weapons today analogous to anything—maybe the passion for designer labels, fax machines, and fast food?

EXERCISE 5.2

Dissecting the Fish

The main point in your research essay *may* be a straightforward argument—*Legalization of drugs will not, as some of its supporters claim, reduce violent crime*—or it may be an explanation or description of some aspect of your topic—*Method acting has revolutionized American theater.* But in either case, *use* the main point as a launching place for thinking about what you might do in the revision. Before you do anything else on your draft this week, consider doing the following:

■ In a sentence or two, write down the thesis or controlling idea that emerged in your draft last week. It may have been stated or implied, or perhaps after writing the draft, you have a clearer idea of what you're trying to say. In any case, write down your thesis.

■ Now generate a list of three or more questions that your thesis raises. These questions may directly challenge your assertion, or they may be questions—like those I raised earlier about the thesis about nuclear weapons—that help you further clarify or unpack what you're trying to say.

■ Next, rewrite your thesis statement at least three times. In each subsequent version, play with language or arrangement, add information, or get more specific about exactly what you're saying. For example:

1. Method acting has had a major impact on American theater.

2. The method—which turned Stanislavski's original focus on external actions inward, toward the actor's own feelings—has generated controversy since the beginning.

3. An actor using the method may be crying tears, but whether they're real or not depends on whom you ask: the actor, who is thinking about her dead cat in the midst of a scene about a dying lover, or the writer, who didn't have a dead cat in mind when she wrote it.

If this exercise works for you, several things will happen. Not only will you refine how you express your main point in the next draft, but you will also get guidance about how you might approach the revision—how you might reorganize it, what information you should add or cut, how you can further narrow your focus and even clarify your purpose. For example, the first version of the thesis on method acting provides the writer with little guidance about what information to *exclude* in the next draft. Aren't there lots of ways to show that method acting has had a major impact on American theater? The third version, on the other hand, is not only livelier and more interesting, it points the writer much more directly to what she should emphasize in the next draft: the conflict method acting creates over how theatrical roles are imagined, the license actors have with their material, and the ways that deception may be involved in a powerful performance using this technique.

What I'm suggesting here is this: Once you arrive at the controlling idea for your essay, it need not arrest your thinking about your topic, closing off any further discovery. A thesis is, in fact, a *tool* that will help you reopen the material you've gathered, rearrange it, and understand it in a fresh, new way.

Revision, as the word implies, means "re-seeing" or "reconceiving," trying to see what you failed to notice with the first look. That can be hard. Remember how stuck I was on that one picture of the lighthouse? I planted my feet in the sand, and the longer I stared through the camera lens, the harder it was to see the lighthouse from any other angle. It didn't matter that I didn't particularly like what I was seeing. I just wanted to take the picture.

You've spent more than four weeks researching your topic and the last few days composing your first draft. You may find that you've spent so much time staring through the lens—seeing your topic the way you chose to see it in your first draft—that doing a major revision is about as appealing as eating cold beets. How do you get the perspective to "re-see" the draft and rebuild it into a stronger paper?

Using a Reader

If you wanted to save a relationship, you might ask a friend to intervene. Then you'd get the benefit of a third-party opinion, a fresh view that could help you see what you may be too close to see.

A reader can do the same thing for your research paper draft. She will come to the draft without the entanglements that encumber the writer and provide a fresh pair of eyes through which you can see the work.

What You Need from a Reader

Your instructor may be that reader, or you might exchange drafts with someone else in class. You may already have someone whom you share your writing with—a roommate, a friend. Whomever you choose, try to find a reader who will respond honestly *and* make you want to write again.

What will be most helpful from a reader at this stage? Comments about your spelling and mechanics are not critical right now. You'll deal with those factors later. What the reader needs to point out is if the *purpose* of your paper is clear and if your thesis is convincing. Is it clear what your paper is about, what part of the topic you're focusing on? Does the information presented stay within that focus? Does the information clarify and support what you're trying to say? It would also be helpful for the reader to tell you what parts of the draft are interesting and what parts seem to drag.

EXERCISE 5.3

Directing the Reader's Response

Though you could ask your reader for a completely open-ended reaction to your paper, the following questions might help her focus on providing comments that will help you tackle a revision:

1. After reading the draft, what would you say is the main question the paper is trying to answer or focus on?
2. In your own words, what is the main point?
3. What do you remember from the draft that most convinces you that the ideas in the paper are true? What is least convincing?
4. Where is the paper most interesting? Where does the paper drag?

How your reader responds to the first two questions will tell you a lot about how well you've succeeded in making the purpose and thesis of your paper clear. The answer to the third question may reveal how well you've *used* the information gleaned from research. The reader's response to the fourth question will give you a preliminary reading on how well you engaged her. Did you lose her anywhere? Is the paper interesting?

A reader responding to Jeff's paper titled "The Alcoholic Family" helped him discover some problems that are typical of first drafts. His paper was inspired by his girlfriend's struggles to deal with her alcoholic father. Jeff wondered if he could do anything to help. Jeff's reader was touched by those parts of the paper where he discussed his own observations of the troubled family's behavior; however, the reader was confused about Jeff's purpose. "Your lead seems to say that your paper is going to focus on how family members deal with an alcoholic parent," the reader wrote to Jeff, "but I thought your main idea was that people outside an alcoholic family can help but must be careful about it. I wanted to know more about how you now think you can help your girlfriend. What exactly do you need to be careful about?"

This wasn't an observation Jeff could have made, given how close he is to the topic and the draft. But armed with objective and specific information about what changes were needed, Jeff was ready to attack the draft.

Attacking the Draft

The controlling idea of your paper—that thesis you posted on an index card above your desk a week or more ago—is the heart of your paper and should, in some way, be connected to everything else in the draft.

Though a good reader can suddenly help you see things you've missed, she will likely not give much feedback on what you should do to fix these problems. Physically attacking the draft might help. If you neatly printed your first draft, then doing this may feel sacrilegious—a little like writing in books. One of the difficulties with revision is that writers respect the printed page too much. When the draft is typed up, with all those words marching neatly down the page, it is hard to mess it up again. As pages emerge from the printer, you can almost hear the sound of hardening concrete. Breaking the draft into pieces can free you to clearly see them and how they fit together.

EXERCISE 5.4

Cut-and-Paste Revision

Try this cut-and-paste revision exercise (a useful technique inspired by Peter Elbow and his book *Writing with Power**):

1. Photocopy or print two copies of your first draft (one-sided pages only). Save the original; you may need it later.

2. Cut apart the copy of your research paper, paragraph by paragraph. (You may cut it into even smaller pieces later.) Once the draft has been completely disassembled, shuffle the paragraphs—get them wildly out of order so the original draft is just a memory.

3. Now go through the shuffled stack and find the *core paragraph,* the most important one in the whole paper. This is probably the paragraph that contains your thesis, or main point. This paragraph is the one that gets to the heart of what you're trying to say. Set it aside.

4. With your core paragraph directly in front of you, work your way through the remaining stack of paragraphs and make two new stacks: one of paragraphs that are relevant to your core and one of paragraphs that don't seem relevant, that don't seem to serve a clear purpose in developing your main idea. Be as tough as a drill sergeant as you scrutinize each scrap of paper. What you are trying to determine is whether each piece of information, each paragraph, is there for a reason. Ask yourself these questions as you examine each paragraph:

- Does it develop my thesis or further the purpose of my paper, or does it seem an unnecessary tangent that could be part of another paper with a different focus?
- Does it provide important *evidence* that supports my main point?
- Does it *explain* something that's key to understanding what I'm trying to say?
- Does it *illustrate* a key concept?
- Does it help establish the *importance* of what I'm trying to say?
- Does it raise (or answer) a *question* that I must explore, given what I'm trying to say?

You might find it helpful to write on the back of each relevant paragraph which of these purposes it serves. You may also discover

---

*Peter Elbow, *Writing with Power* (New York: Oxford University Press, 1981).

that *some* of the information in a paragraph seems to serve your purpose, while the rest strikes you as unnecessary. Use your scissors to cut away the irrelevant material, pruning back the paragraph to include only what's essential.

5. You now have two stacks of paper scraps: those that seem to serve your purpose and those that don't. For now, set aside your "reject" pile. Put your core paragraph back into the "save" pile, and begin to reassemble a very rough draft, using what you've saved. Play with order. Try new leads, new ends, new middles. As you spread out the pieces of information before you, see if a new structure suddenly emerges. *But especially, look for gaps—places where you should add information.* Jot down ideas for material you might add on a piece of paper; then cut up the paper and splice (with tape) each idea in the appropriate place when you reassemble the draft in the next step. You may rediscover uses for information in your "reject" pile, as well. Mine that pile, if you need to.

6. As a structure begins to emerge, begin taping together the fragments of paper and splicing ideas for new information. Don't worry about transitions; you'll deal with those later. When you're done with the reconstruction, the draft should look drafty—something the wind can blow through—and may be totally unlike the version you started with.

Examining the Wreckage

As you deal with the wreckage your scissors have wrought on your first draft, you might notice other problems with it. For example, you may discover that your draft has no real core paragraph, no part that is central to your point and purpose. Don't panic. Just make sure that you write one in the revision.

To your horror, you may find that your "reject" pile of paragraphs is bigger than your "save" pile. If that's the case, you won't have much left to work with. You may need to reresearch the topic (returning to the library this week to collect more information) or shift the focus of your paper. Perhaps both.

To your satisfaction, you may discover that your reconstructed draft looks familiar. You may have returned to the structure you started with in the first draft. If that's the case, it might mean your first draft worked pretty well; breaking it down and putting it back together simply confirmed that.

When Jeff cut up "The Alcoholic Family," he discovered immediately that his reader was right: Much of his paper did not seem clearly related to his point about the role outsiders can play in helping alcoholic families. His "reject" pile had paragraph after paragraph of information about the roles that alcoholic family members assume when there's a heavy drinker in the house. Jeff asked himself, What does that information have to do with the roles of outsiders? He considered changing his thesis, rewriting his core paragraph to say something about how each family member plays a role in dealing with the drinker. But Jeff's purpose in writing the paper was to discover what *he* could do to help.

As Jeff played with the pieces of his draft, he began to see two things. First of all, he realized that some of the ways members behave in an alcoholic family make them resistant to outside help; this insight allowed him to salvage some information from his "reject" pile by more clearly connecting the information to his main point. Second, Jeff knew he had to go back to the well: He needed to return to the library and recheck his sources to find more information on what family friends can do to help.

When you slice up your draft and play with the pieces, you are experimenting with the basic architecture of your essay. If it is going to hold up, certain fundamentals must be in place (see Figure 5.2). Before you move on to other revision strategies you need to be confident that your purpose—the inquiry question around which your investigation is organized—is stated clearly early in your essay.

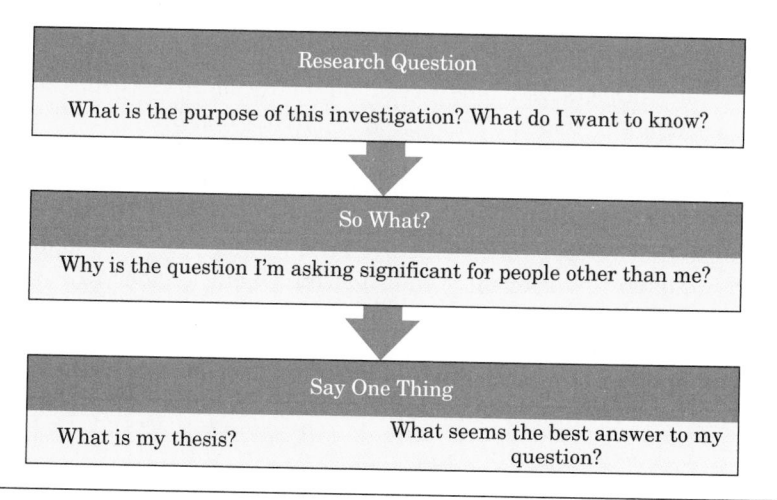

FIGURE 5.2   Three Things the Essay Must Do
As you revise your draft, you can measure your progress by asking whether you've answered these three basic questions: *Is the question I'm asking clear and sufficiently limited? Have I answered the "so what?" question? Is there one most important thing I'm trying to say?* If your draft explicitly answers each of these, then at least the boat will float and have a clear destination.

The significance of this question should be evident, too. Why should anyone care about the extinction of wild horses in the American West, for example? Why does it matter? The answer to this question often leads to the third essential element of your paper: What one thing are you trying to say? To lose wild horses is to diminish the cultural heritage of the West, one that goes beyond the mythical cowboy to include native people and early Spanish colonialists.

Revising for Information

I know. You thought you were done digging. But as I said last week, research is a recursive process. (Remember, the word is *research*, or "look again.") You will often find yourself circling back to the earlier steps as you get a clearer sense of where you want to go.

As you stand back from your draft, looking again at how well your research paper accomplishes your purpose, you'll likely see holes in the information. They may seem more like craters. Jeff discovered he had to reresearch his topic, returning to the library to hunt for new sources to help him develop his point. Since he had enough time, he repeated some of the research steps from the third week. This time, though, he knew exactly what he needed to find.

You may find that you basically have the information you need but that your draft requires more development. Candy's draft on how child abuse affects language included material from some useful studies from the *Journal of Speech and Hearing Disorders,* which showed pretty conclusively that abuse cripples children's abilities to converse. At her reader's suggestion, Candy decided it was important to write more in her revision about what was learned from the studies, since they offered convincing evidence for her thesis. Though she could mine her notes for more information, Candy decided to recheck the journal indexes to look for any similar studies she may have missed. As you begin to see exactly what information you need, don't rule out another trip to the library, even this late in the game.

Finding Quick Facts

The holes of information in your research paper draft may not be large at all. What's missing may be an important but discrete fact that would really help your readers understand the point you're making. For example, in Janabeth's draft on the impact of divorce on father-daughter relationships, she realized she was missing an important fact: the number of marriages that end in divorce in the United States. This single piece of information could help establish the significance of the problem she was writing about. Janabeth could search her sources for the answer, but there's a quicker way: fact books.

One of the Internet's greatest strengths is its usefulness in searching for specific facts. A few days ago, for example, my daughter Julia—who was studying China in the first grade—wanted to know the height of the Great Wall. The answer is thirty feet. We found it in minutes by consulting an online encyclopedia. As always, there are a range of statistical references on the Web. One place to start is the site that claims to be "the single best source for facts on the Net":

www.refdesk.com

I'm inclined to agree. The site has links to encyclopedias, biographical indexes, newspapers and magazines, dictionaries, and government information. Even better, refdesk.com has a convenient "Fast Facts" search engine that will return up-to-date information from a keyword search.

The standard print texts for researchers hunting down facts and statistics are still quite useful. They include the *Statistical Abstracts of the United States,* the *Information Please Almanac, Facts on File,* and the *World Almanac Book of Facts*—all published annually—but a number of these in abbreviated versions are now available on the Web. The U.S. Census Bureau site for example, is an incredibly rich source of demographic information on all kinds of subjects (see Figure 5.3).

Fact books and online sources can be valuable sources of information that will plug small holes in your draft. These references are especially useful during revision, when you often know exactly what fact you need. But even if you're not sure whether you can glean a useful statistic from one of these sources, they might be worth checking anyway. There's a good chance you'll find something useful.

Revising for Language

Most of my students have the impression that revision begins and ends with concerns about language—about *how* they said it rather than *what* they said. Revising for language is really a tertiary concern (though an important one), to be addressed after the writer has struggled with the purpose and design of a draft.

FIGURE 5.3   Home Page of U.S. Census Bureau

The U.S. Census Bureau offers a wealth of statistical information, including data from the 2000 census. The site, at www.census.gov, includes a search tool called "American Fact Finder" that will help you locate statistics about population, geography, business, housing, and industry. The results can be national statistics all the way down to data about a particular county.

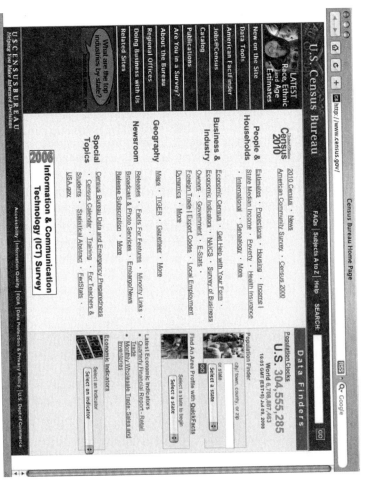

Once you're satisfied that your paper's purpose is clear, that it provides readers with the information they need to understand what you're trying to say, and that it is organized in a logical, interesting way, *then* focus your attention on the fine points of *how* it is written. Begin with voice.

Listening to the Voice

Listen to your paper by reading it aloud to yourself. You may find the experience a little unsettling. Most of us are not used to actively listening to our writing voices. But your readers will be listening.

As you read, ask yourself: Is this the voice you want readers to hear? Does it seem appropriate for this paper? Does it sound flat or wooden or ponderous in any places? Does it sound anything like you?

If revising your writing voice is necessary for any reason, begin at the beginning—the first line, the first paragraph—and rely on your ears. What sounds right?

You may discover that you begin with the right voice but lose it in places. That often happens when you move from anecdotal material to exposition, from telling a story to explaining research findings. To some extent, a shift in voice is inevitable when you move from one method of development to another, especially from personal material to factual material. But examine your word choices in those passages that seem to go flat. Do you sometimes shift to the dry language used by your sources? Can you rewrite that language in your own voice? When you do, you will find yourself cutting away unnecessary, vague, and pretentious language.

Rewriting in your own voice has another effect, too: It brings the writing to life. Readers respond to an individual writing voice. When I read David Quammen, an author whose work you've read in this text, it rises up from the page, like a hologram, and suddenly, I can see him as a distinct individual. I also become interested in how he sees the things he's writing about.

Avoid Sounding Glib

Beware, though, of a voice that calls more attention to itself than the substance of what you're saying. As you've no doubt learned from reading scholarly sources, much academic writing is voiceless, partly because what's important is not *who* the writer is but *what* he has to say.

Sometimes, in an attempt to sound natural, a writer will take on a folksy or overly colloquial voice, which is much worse than sounding lifeless. What impression does the following passage give you?

```
The thing that really blew my mind was that

marijuana use among college students had actually

declined in the past ten years! I was psyched to

learn that.
```

Ugh!

As you search for the right voice in doing your revision, look for a balance between flat, wooden prose, which sounds as if it were manufactured by a machine, and forced, flowery prose, which distracts the reader from what's most important: what you're trying to say.

How to Control Information

One of the basic challenges of writing with sources is integrating them seamlessly. In the past, you may have practiced the "data dump" strategy, or simply dropping factual information into your papers in little or big clumps. Of course, this won't do. Not only does it make the writing horribly dull, but it means that you're not *making use* of the information you worked so hard to find. Surrounding your sources with your own prose and purposes is an important skill you need to learn. Let's see how it might work. Here are three facts from the "Harper's Index," a monthly feature in *Harper's* magazine:

THREE FACTS

1. Percentage of Americans in 1983 who thought it was "possible to start out <u>poor</u> in this country . . . and become rich": 57 [New York Times–CBS News Poll]
2. Percentage who think this today: 80 [New York Times–CBS News Poll]
3. Percentage of U.S. <u>income</u> in 1983 and today, respectively, that went to the top 1 percent of earners: 9, 16 [National Bureau of Economic Research (Cambridge, Mass.)]*

Juxtaposed like this, these three facts tell a story which is merely implied if they stand alone. How might they be integrated smoothly into a paragraph that tells that story? Here's one possibility:

BLAND VERSION 1

```
According to polling data and the National Bureau

of Economic Research, the number of Americans who
```

*"Harper's Index," *Harper's*, September 2006, 13.

believe it is "possible to start out poor . . . and become rich" has increased by 23 percent since 1983. This growing faith in the rags-to-riches ideal comes despite the fact that, during the same period, the top 1 percent of wage earners nearly doubled their share of total income.

This isn't bad. Version 1 nicely uses the attribution tag, "According to . . . ," and includes information about the source of the information. The version is also careful to reword the original text. It obliquely states a possible implication of the facts, so the writer offers some analysis or interpretation of the information's significance. Still, it seems lifeless and dry.

LIVELIER VERSION 2

America's enduring belief in the promise of rising from rags to riches apparently blinds us to the facts. Surprisingly, while the richest 1 percent in the U.S. have nearly doubled their share of the nation's income since 1983, according to a New York Times-CBS poll, 23 percent more Americans since then have more faith in the proposition that it is "possible to start out poor . . . and become rich." It's possible that the success of the richest Americans in getting a larger slice of the pie inspires other Americans to believe they can get their piece, even if the leftovers continue to shrink.

This strikes me as far more lively and interesting, and a more seamless integration of the three facts. Do you think so? It's not hard to sense the difference between versions 1 and 2, but what accounts for them might at first seem pretty subtle. Note how the writer seems to surround the information with his own voice and purpose. In particular, consider the following points:

■ *Find your own way of saying things.* While the economic pie metaphor is hardly original, the writer uses it effectively to make the point that Americans can't seem to grasp the simple facts that contradict their beliefs.

■ *Surround factual information with your own analysis.* Version 1 leans on the facts and offers little comment on them. Version 2 begins with the suggestion that the facts imply how strongly. Americans want to believe in the American economic success mythology. The passage ends with an alternative explanation for the findings, which is just as quickly dismissed. The writer is working the material.

What else do you notice about the two versions?

Verbal Gestures

Remember Burke's metaphor for the knowledge-making process (see page 630)? He imagined a parlor full of people having an ongoing conversation about what might be true—arguing, agreeing, raising questions, suggesting new ideas, critiquing old ideas, everyone trying to push the conversation along. Any roomful of people in a conversation about things that cause disagreement is also a roomful of gestures. People wave off a point. They nod in assent. They raise a single finger to raise a new question or make a new point. They invite someone to step forward to speak, and ask another to step aside.

Similarly, an essay that is a writer's conversation with others about a question that matters to them also includes verbal gestures. These are words or phrases like the following ones. Some are gestures that invite some people in the room to provide *background* on the question so that everyone understands what has already been said. Other gestures signal *analysis,* or a closer examination and critique of something someone said. Sometimes these verbal gestures signify *speculation;* the writer just isn't quite sure what to think for sure but maybe. . . . Or they might indicate *alignment*—statements in which the writer is taking sides with a particular idea, position, or way of seeing.

Consider whether verbal gestures like these will help you manage the conversation about your topic.

BACKGROUND

Among the most important voices on _____, the most relevant to this inquiry are _____.

Most people _____.

The major sources of controversy are _____.

One idea emerges again and again, and it's _____.

Like most people, I believed that _____.

The unanswered questions are _____.

This much is clear, _____.

_____'s most important contribution is _____.

Most relevant is _____.

ANALYSIS

The most relevant point is _____.

In comparison, . . .

In contrast, . . .

What is most convincing is _____.

What is least convincing is _____.

What's most interesting is _____.

The surprising connection is _____.

Paradoxically, . . .

Actually, . . .

What isn't clear is _____.

SPECULATION

Perhaps . . .

Maybe . . .

It's possible that _____.

ALIGNMENT

Indeed . . .

Obviously . . .

Alternatively . . .

While others have argued that _____, I think _____.

On balance, the most convincing idea is _____.

What _____ has failed to consider is _____.

The more important question is _____.

Based on my research, _____.

A better explanation is _____.

It's hard to argue with _____.

What I understand now that I didn't understand before is _____.

Scrutinizing Paragraphs

How Well Do You Integrate Sources?

Go over your draft, paragraph by paragraph, and look for ways to *use* the information from your research more smoothly. Be especially alert to "hanging quotes" that appear unattached to any source. Attribution is important. To anchor quotes and ideas to people or publications in your paper, use words such as *argues, observes, says, contends, believes*, and *offers* and phrases such as *according to*. Also look for ways to use quotes selectively, lifting key words or phrases and weaving them into your own writing. What can you add that highlights what you believe is significant about the information? How does it relate to your thesis and the purpose of your paper?

Is Each Paragraph Unified?

Each paragraph should be about one idea and organized around it. You probably know that already. But applying this notion is a particular problem in a research paper, where information abounds and paragraphs sometimes approach marathon length.

If any of your paragraphs are similar to that—that is, they seem to run nearly a page or more—look for ways to break them up into shorter paragraphs. Is more than one idea embedded in the long version? Are you explaining or examining more than one thing?

Also take a look at your shorter paragraphs. Do any present minor or tangential ideas that belong somewhere else? Are any of these ideas irrelevant? Should the paragraph be cut? The cut-and-paste exercise (Exercise 5.4) may have helped you with this already.

Scrutinizing Sentences

Using Active Voice

Which of these two sentences seems more passive, more lifeless?

```
Steroids have been used by many high school
athletes.
```

or

```
Many high school athletes use steroids.
```

The first version, written in the passive voice, is clearly the more limp of the two. It's not grammatically incorrect. In fact, you may have found texts written in the passive voice to be pervasive in the reading you've done for your research paper. Research writing is plagued by passive voice, and that's one of the reasons it can be so mind numbing to read.

Passive voice construction is simple: The subject of the sentence—the thing *doing the action*—becomes the thing *acted upon* by the verb. For instance:

```
Clarence kicked the dog.
```

versus

```
The dog was kicked by Clarence.
```

Sometimes, the subject may be missing altogether, as in:

```
The study was released.
```

Who or *what* released it?

Active voice remedies the problem by pushing the subject up front in the sentence or adding the subject if he, she, or it is missing. For example:

```
High school athletes use steroids.
```

Knowing exactly who is using the drugs makes the sentence livelier.

Another telltale sign of passive voice is that it usually requires a *to be* verb: *is, was, are, were, am, be, being, been.* For example:

```
Alcoholism among women has been extensively
studied.
```

Search your draft for *be's,* and see if any sentences are written in the passive voice. (If you write on a computer, some word-processing programs will search for you.) To make a sentence active, replace the missing subject:

```
Researchers have extensively studied alcoholism
among women.
```

See the box, "Active Verbs for Discussing Ideas," which was compiled by a colleague of mine, Cinthia Gannett. If you're desperate for an alternative to *says* or *argues,* check out the 138 alternatives this list offers.

Using Strong Verbs

Though this may seem like nit-picking, you'd be amazed how much writing in the active voice can revitalize research writing. The use of strong verbs can have the same effect.

As you know, verbs make things happen. Some verbs can make the difference between a sentence that crackles and one that merely hums. Instead of this:

```
The study suggested that the widespread assump-
tion that oral sex is common among American
teenagers might be wrong.
```

write this:

```
The study shattered the common belief that
American teens increasingly indulge in oral sex.
```

Varying Sentence Length

Some writers can sustain breathlessly long sentences, with multiple subordinate clauses, and not lose their readers. Joan Didion is one of those writers. Actually, she also knows enough not to do it too often. She carefully varies the lengths of her sentences, going from a breathless one to one that can be quickly inhaled and exhaled. For example, here is how her essay "Dreamers of the Golden Dream" begins. Notice the mix of sentence lengths.

This is the story about love and death in the golden land, and begins with the country. The San Bernadino Valley lies only an hour east of Los Angeles by the San Bernadino Freeway but is in certain ways an alien place: not the coastal California of the subtropical twilights and the soft westerlies off the Pacific but a harsher California, haunted by the Mojave just beyond the mountains, devastated by the hot dry Santa Ana wind that comes down through the passes at 100 miles an hour and

Active Verbs for Discussing Ideas

accepts
acknowledges
adds
admires
affirms
allows
analyzes
announces
answers
argues
assaults
assembles
asserts
assists
believes
buttresses
categorizes
cautions
challenges
claims
clarifies
compares
complicates
concludes
condemns
confirms
conflates
confronts
confuses
considers
contradicts
contrasts
convinces
criticizes

critiques
declares
defends
defies
demands
denies
describes
determines
diminishes
disagrees
disconfirms
discusses
disputes
disregards
distinguishes
emphasizes
endorses
enumerates
exaggerates
experiences
experiments
explains
exposes
facilitates
formulates
grants
guides
handles
hesitates
highlights
hints
hypothesizes
identifies
illuminates

implies
infers
informs
initiates
insinuates
insists
interprets
intimates
judges
lists
maintains
marshalls
narrates
negates
observes
outlines
parses
perceives
persists
persuades
pleads
points out
postulates
praises
proposes
protects
provides
qualifies
quotes
ratifies
rationalizes
reads
reconciles
reconsiders

refutes
regards
rejects
relinquishes
reminds
repudiates
resolves
responds
retorts
reveals
reviews
seeks
sees
shares
shifts
shows
simplifies
states
stresses
substitutes
suggests
summarizes
supplements
supplies
supports
synthesizes
tests
toys with
treats
uncovers
urges
verifies
warns

Source: Reproduced with permission of Cinthia Gannett.

whines through the eucalyptus windbreaks and works on the nerves. October is a bad month for the wind, the month when breathing is difficult and the hills blaze up spontaneously. There has been no rain since April. Every voice seems a scream. It is the season of suicide and divorce and prickly dread, wherever the wind blows.*

The second sentence of Didion's lead is a whopper, but it works, especially since it's set among sentences that are more than half its length. Didion makes music here.

Examine your sentences. Are the long ones too long? You can usually tell if, when you read a sentence, there's no sense of emphasis or it seems to die out. Can you break an unnecessarily long sentence into several shorter ones? A more common problem is a string of short, choppy sentences. For example:

```
Babies are born extrasensitive to sounds. This
unique sensitivity to all sounds does not last.
By the end of the first year, they become deaf
to speech sounds not a part of their native
language.
```

This isn't horrible, but with some sentence combining, the passage will be more fluent:

```
Though babies are born extrasensitive to sounds,
this unique sensitivity lasts only through the
end of the first year, when they become deaf
to speech sounds not a part of their native
language.
```

Look for short sentences where you are repeating words or phrases and also for sentences that begin with pronouns. Experiment with sentence combining. The result will be not only more fluent prose but a sense of emphasis, a sense of the relationship between the information and your ideas about it.

*Joan Didion, *Slouching Toward Bethlehem* (New York: Pocket, 1968).

Editing for Simplicity

Thoreau saw simplicity as a virtue, something that's obvious not only by the time he spent beside Walden Pond but also by the prose he penned while living there. Thoreau writes clearly and plainly.

Somewhere, many of us got the idea that simplicity in writing is a vice—that the long word is better than the short word, that the complex phrase is superior to the simple one. The misconception is that to write simply is to be simple minded. Research papers, especially, suffer from this mistaken notion. They are often filled with what writer William Zinsser calls *clutter*.

E X E R C I S E 5 . 5

Cutting Clutter

The following passage is an example of cluttered writing at its best (worst?). It contains phrases and words that often appear in college research papers. Read the passage once. Then take a few minutes and rewrite it, cutting as many words as you can without sacrificing the meaning. Look for ways to substitute a shorter word for a longer one and to say in fewer words what is currently said in many. Try to cut the word count by half.

> The implementation of the revised alcohol policy
> in the university community is regrettable at the
> present time due to the fact that the administra-
> tion has not facilitated sufficient student
> input, in spite of the fact that there have been
> attempts by the people affected by this policy to
> make their objections known in many instances.
> (*55 words*)

Stock Phrases in Research Papers

Like many types of writing, the language of the college research paper is littered with words and phrases that find their way to the page the same way drinking root beer prompts my 12-year-old daughter and her friends to hold burping contests. One just seems to inspire the other. Following is a list of stock phrases that I often find in research papers. There is nothing grammatically wrong with these. It's simply that they are old, tired phrases and you can say the same thing more freshly with fewer words. Look for them in your draft and then edit them out.

TIRED PHRASES	FRESHER ALTERNATIVES
Due to the fact that . . .	*Because . . .*
At this point in time . . .	*Now . . .*
In my opinion, . . .	*(Unnecessary. We know it's your opinion)*
A number of . . .	*Many . . .*
A number of studies point to the fact that . . .	*Many researchers conclude (or argue) . . .*
In the event of . . .	*If . . .*
In today's society . . .	*Today we . . .*
In conclusion, . . .	*(Omit. If you're at the end of the paper you're probably concluding)*
Studies have found that . . .	*(Avoid. It's better to mention one or two)*
Until such time as . . .	*Until . . .*
Referred to as . . .	*Called . . .*
It should be pointed out that . . .	*(Omit. You are pointing it out.)*
Is in a position to . . .	*Can*
It is a fact that . . .	*(Omit. Just state the fact, ma'am)*
It may be said that . . .	*(Omit. Just say it)*
There can be little doubt that . . .	*It's likely . . .*
It is possible that . . .	*Perhaps . . .*

Preparing the Final Manuscript

I wanted to title this section "Preparing the Final Draft," but it occurred to me that *draft* doesn't suggest anything final. I always call my work a draft because until it's out of my hands, it never feels finished. You may feel that way, too. You've spent five weeks on this paper—and the last few days, disassembling it and putting it back together again. How do you know when you're finally done?

For many students, the deadline dictates that: The paper is due tomorrow. But you may find that your paper really seems to be coming together in a satisfying way. You may even like it, and you're ready to prepare the final manuscript.

Considering "Reader-Friendly" Design

Later in this section, we'll discuss the format of your final draft. Research papers in some disciplines have prescribed forms. Some papers in the social sciences, for example, require an abstract, an introduction, a discussion of method, a presentation of results, and a discussion of those results. These sections are clearly defined using subheadings, making it easier for readers to examine those parts of the paper they're most interested in. You probably discovered that in your own reading of formal research. You'll likely learn the formats research papers should conform to in various disciplines as you take upper-level courses in those fields.

While you should document this paper properly, you may have some freedom to develop a format that best serves your purpose. As you consider the format of your rewrite, keep readers in mind. How can you make your paper more readable? How can you signal your plan for developing the topic and what's important? Some visual devices might help, including:

- Subheadings
- Graphs, illustrations, tables
- Bulleted lists (like the one you're reading now)
- Block quotes
- Underlining and paragraphing for emphasis
- White space

Long, unbroken pages of text can appear to be a gray, uninviting mass to the reader. All of the devices listed help break up the text, making it more "reader friendly." Subheadings, if not over-used, can also cue your reader to significant sections of your paper and how they relate to the whole. Long quotes, those over four lines, should be blocked, or indented ten spaces (rather than the usual five spaces customary for indenting paragraphs), separating them from the rest of the text. (See Chapter 4, "Writing with Sources," for more on blocking quotes.) Bullets—dots or asterisks preceding brief items—can be used to highlight a quick list of important information. Graphs, tables, and illustrations also break up the text, but more importantly, they can help clarify and explain information. (See Section 2.15, "Placement of Tables, Charts, and Illustrations," in Appendix B.)

The format of the book you're reading is intended, in part, to make it accessible to readers. As you revise, consider how the look of your paper can make it more inviting and easily understood.

Following MLA Conventions

I've already mentioned that formal research papers in various disciplines may have prescribed formats. If your instructor expects a certain format, he has probably detailed exactly what that format should be. But in all likelihood, your essay for this class doesn't need to follow a rigid form. It will, however, probably adhere to the basic Modern Language Association (MLA) guidelines or the American Psychological Association (APA) guidelines.

Proofreading Your Paper

You've spent weeks researching, writing, and revising your paper. You want to stop now. That's understandable, no matter how much you were driven by your curiosity. Before you sign off on your research paper, placing it in someone else's hands, take the time to proofread it.

I was often so glad to be done with a piece of writing that I was careless about proofreading it. That changed about ten years ago, after I submitted a portfolio of writing to complete my master's degree. I was pretty proud of it, especially an essay about dealing with my father's alcoholism. Unfortunately, I misspelled that word—*alcoholism*—every time I used it. Bummer.

Proofreading on a Computer

Proofreading used to involve gobbing on correction fluid to cover up mistakes and then trying to line up the paper and type in the changes. Writing on a computer, you're spared from that ordeal. The text can be easily manipulated on the screen.

Software programs can also help with the job. Most word-processing programs, for example, come with spelling and grammar checkers.

These programs will count the number of words in your sentences, alerting you to particularly long ones, and will even point out uses of passive voice. I find some of these programs irritating because they evaluate writing ability based on factors such as sentence length, which may not be a measure of the quality of your work at all. But for a basic review, these programs can be extremely useful, particularly for flagging passive construction.

Many writers find they need to print out their paper and proofread the hard copy. They argue that they catch more mistakes if they proofread on paper than if they proofread onscreen. It makes sense, especially if you've been staring at the screen for days. A printed copy of your paper *looks* different, and I think you see it differently, maybe with fresher eyes and attitude. You might notice things you didn't notice before. You decide for yourself how and when to proofread.

Looking Closely

You've already edited the manuscript, pruning sentences and tightening things up. Now hunt for the little errors in grammar and mechanics that you missed. Aside from misspellings (usually typos), some pretty common mistakes appear in the papers I see. For practice, see if you can catch some of them in the following exercise.

EXERCISE 5.6

Picking Off the Lint

I have a colleague who compares proofreading to picking the lint off an outfit, which is often your final step before heading out the door. Examine the following excerpt from a student paper. Proofread it, catching as many mechanical errors as possible. Note punctuation mistakes, agreement problems, misspellings, and anything else that seems off.

```
In an important essay, Melody Graulich notes
how "rigid dichotomizing of sex roles" in most
frontier myths have "often handicapped and con-
fused male as well as female writers (187),"
```

```
she wonders if a "universel mythology" (198)
might emerge that is less confining for both of
them. In Bruce Mason, Wallace Stegner seems to
experiment with this idea; acknowledging the
power of Bo's male fantasies and Elsa's ability
to teach her son to feel. It is his strenth. On
the other hand, Bruces brother chet, who dies
young, lost and broken, seems doomed because he
lacked sufficient measure of both the feminine
and masculine. He observes that Chet had
"enough of the old man to spoil him, ebnough of
his mother to soften him, not enough of either
to save him (Big Rock, 521)."
```

If you did this exercise in class, compare your proofreading of this passage with that of a partner. What did each of you find?

Ten Common Mistakes

The following is a list of the ten most common errors (besides misspelled words) made in research papers that should be caught in careful proofreading. A number of these errors occurred in the previous exercise.

1. Beware of commonly confused words, such as *your* instead of *you're*. Here's a list of others:

their/there/they're	advice/advise
know/now	lay/lie
accept/except	its/it's
all ready/already	passed/past

2. Watch for possessives. Instead of *my fathers alcoholism*, the correct style is *my father's alcoholism*. Remember that if a noun ends in *s*, still add *'s: Tess's laughter*. If a noun is plural, just add the apostrophe: *the scientists' studies*.

3. Avoid vague pronoun references. The excerpt in Exercise 5.6 ends with the sentence, *He observes that Chet. . . .* Who's *he?* The

sentence should read, *Bruce observes that Chet.* . . . Whenever you use the pronouns *he, she, it, they,* and *their,* make sure each clearly refers to someone or something.

4. Subjects and verbs must agree. If the subject is singular, its verb must be, too:

```
The perils of climate change are many.
```

What confuses writers sometimes is the appearance of a noun that is not really the subject near the verb. Exercise 5.6 begins, for example, with this sentence:

```
In an important essay, Melody Graulich notes how
"rigid dichotomizing of sex roles" in most fron-
tier myths have "often handicapped and confused
male as well as female writers."
```

The subject here is not *frontier myths* but *rigid dichotomizing,* a singular subject. The sentence should read:

```
In an important essay, Melody Graulich notes how
"rigid dichotomizing of sex roles" in most fron-
tier myths has "often handicapped and confused
male as well as female writers."
```

The verb *has* may sound funny, but it's correct.

5. Punctuate quotes properly. Note that commas belong inside quotation marks, not outside. Periods belong inside, too. Colons and semicolons are exceptions—they belong *outside* quotation marks. Blocked quotes don't need quotation marks at all unless there is a quote within the quote.

6. Scrutinize use of commas. Could you substitute periods or semicolons instead? If so, you may be looking at *comma splices* or *run-on sentences.* Here's an example:

```
Since 1980, the use of marijuana by college
students has steadily declined, this was
something of a surprise to me and my friends.
```

The portion after the comma, *this was* . . . , is another sentence. The comma should be a period, and *this* should be capitalized.

7. Make sure each parenthetical citation *precedes* the period in the sentence you're citing but *follows* the quotation mark at the end of a sentence. In MLA style, there is no comma between the author's name and page number: (Marks 99).

8. Use dashes correctly. Though they can be overused, dashes are a great way to break the flow of a sentence with a related bit of information. You've probably noticed I like them. In a manuscript, type dashes as *two* hyphens (- -), not one.

9. After mentioning the full name of someone in your paper, normally use her *last name* in subsequent references. For example, this is incorrect:

```
Denise Grady argues that people are genetically

predisposed to obesity. Denise also believes

that some people are "programmed to convert

calories to fat."
```

Unless you know Denise or for some other reason want to conceal her last name, change the second sentence to this:

```
Grady also believes that some people are

"programmed to convert calories to fat."
```

One exception to this is when writing about literature. It is often appropriate to refer to characters by their first names, particularly if characters share last names (as in Exercise 5.6).

10. Scrutinize use of colons and semicolons. A colon is usually used to call attention to what follows it: a list, quotation, or appositive. A colon should follow an independent clause. For example, this won't do:

```
The most troubling things about child abuse

are: the effects on self-esteem and language

development.
```

In this case, eliminate the colon. A semicolon is often used as if it were a colon or a comma. In most cases, a semicolon should be used as a period, separating two independent clauses. The semicolon simply implies the clauses are closely related.

Using the "Find" or "Search" Function

If you're writing on a computer, use the "Find" or "Search" function—a feature in most word-processing programs—to help you track down consistent problems. You simply tell the computer what word or punctuation to look for, and it will locate all occurrences in the text. For example, if you want to check for comma splices, search for commas. The cursor will stop on every comma, and you can verify if it is correct. You can also search for pronouns to locate vague references or for words (like those listed in item 1) you commonly misuse.

Avoiding Sexist Language

One last proofreading task is to do a *man* and *he* check. Until recently, sexism wasn't an issue in language. Use of words such as *mankind* and *chairman* was acceptable; the implication was that the terms applied to both genders. At least, that's how use of the terms was defended when challenged. Critics argued that words such as *mailman* and *businessman* reinforced ideas that only men could fill these roles. Bias in language is subtle but powerful. And it's often unintentional. To avoid sending the wrong message, it's worth making the effort to avoid sexist language.

If you need to use a word with a *man* suffix, check to see if there is an alternative. *Congressperson* sounds pretty clunky, but *representative* works fine. Instead of *mankind,* why not *humanity?* Substitute *camera operator* for *cameraman.*

Also check use of pronouns. Do you use *he* or *his* in places where you mean both genders? For example:

```
The writer who cares about his topic will bring
it to life for his readers.
```

Since a lot of writers are women, this doesn't seem right. How do you solve this problem?

1. Use *his or her, he or she,* or that mutation *s/he.* For example:

```
The writer who cares about his or her topic will
bring it to life for his or her readers.
```

This is an acceptable solution, but using *his or her* repeatedly can be awkward.

2. Change the singular subject to plural. For example:

```
Writers who care about their topics will bring
them to life for their readers.
```

This version is much better and avoids discriminatory language altogether.

3. Alternate *he* and *she, his* and *hers* whenever you encounter an indefinite person. If you have referred to a writer as *he* on one page, make the writer *she* on the next page, as long as you are not talking about the same person. Alternate throughout.

Looking Back and Moving On

This book began with your writing, and it also will end with it. Before you close your research notebook on this project, open it one last time and fastwrite your response to the following questions. Keep your pen moving for seven minutes.

> How was your experience writing this research paper different from writing others? How was it the same?

When students share their fastwrites, this comment is typical: "It was easier to sit down and write this research paper than others I've written." One student last semester added, "I think it was easier because before writing the paper, I got to research something I wanted to know about and learn the answers to questions that mattered to me." If this research project was successful, you took charge of your own learning, as that student did.

Your research paper wasn't necessarily fun. Research takes time, and writing is work. Every week, you had new problems to solve. But if the questions you asked about your topic mattered, then you undoubtedly had moments, perhaps late at night in the library, when you encountered something that suddenly cracked your topic open and let the light come pouring out. The experience can be dazzling. It's even great when it's merely interesting.

What might you take away from this research paper that will prepare you for doing the next one? At the very least, I hope you've cultivated basic research skills: how to find information efficiently, how to document, how to avoid plagiarism, and how to take notes. But I also hope that you've learned more. Perhaps you've recovered a part of you that may have been left behind when you turned eleven or twelve—the curiosity that drove you to put bugs in mayonnaise jars, read about China, disassemble a transistor radio, and wonder about Mars. Curiosity is a handy thing in college. It gets you thinking. And that's the idea.

UNO Sample Essays and a Sample Assignment

School Lunches: What's Really Served?

Erianua Dickerson

Salisbury steak, mashed potatoes, corn, and a fruit cup sound like an appetizing lunch served in a school cafeteria. Though it may seem appealing to taste, this meal is quite unhealthy. The steak and potatoes, which are processed, and the corn and fruit, coming from a can, make up a typical meal that's prepared in school cafeterias. Choices are very limited, resulting in the students bringing their own lunch, indulging in junk foods from concessions, or ultimately giving in to eat the lunch that's provided by the cafeteria.

The average school in the U.S. has a contract with a Food Service Provider (FSP) that supplies food to be served for breakfast and lunch. Each school system selects an FSP through a bidding process and enters into an exclusive contract with that company (Cook 21). This contract can be updated annually to improve lunches that are being served or to use the same food products that had been distributed previously. The FSPs not only have control over what foods are served, but also over the preparation of the meals and the utensils the students use.

Generally, FSPs distribute food that is processed, pre-packaged, or pre-plated. Processed foods are foods that have been altered from their natural state, sometimes for safety or occasionally for convenience. Foods that are processed have become a growing topic of debate because they can be very unhealthy and fattening. Processed meats are the worst of these foods, and the most common include hot dogs, bologna, sausage, ham, and other packaged meats. Many processed foods are made with trans fat, saturated fats, and large amounts of sodium and sugar (Jegtvig par. 4).

Food processing isn't uncommon; in fact, it can be dated back to the prehistoric ages when salt-preservation was often used to preserve meat. Later, canning methods were introduced and salt-preservation wasn't used as much. Modern food processing technology in the 19th and 20th century was largely developed to serve military needs ("Food Processing"). When food is processed, it undergoes many steps that include drying, evaporation, distillation, extraction, filtration, and mixing. After this process is completed, the food lacks many essential nutrients, which have been depleted during the process.

School lunches are loaded with calories and fat that contribute to the unhealthy eating habits of kids. Students are commonly served mozzarella sticks, fries, and hamburgers that are packed with preservatives and additives. Pizza is regularly served in schools throughout the country and, in some cases, every day. One pizza option has more than twenty-five different ingredients, including azodicarbonamide, which is used as a bleach for foods or a defoaming agent in plastics, and datem and sodium stearoyl lactyale, two food additives for blending the ingredients together (Rotondaro par. 9). Ketchup, syrup, chocolate milk, and canned fruits are saturated with high-fructose corn syrup, which has been linked to the rise in obesity.

Obesity has become a rising epidemic, and focus is turning to the schools. Schools are now attempting to help students make healthier choices by cutting calories and serving more fruit; in some cases, though, the school has created an illusion for students and parents because the food choices still aren't healthy. Pre-packaged fruit, such as apple slices, are often misunderstood to be "fresh fruit," but in actuality, they are far from fresh. The simple-sounding toasted cheese sandwich on oat bread is a case in point: the list of ingredients shows that the frozen sandwich contains more than thirty ingredients—including high-fructose corn syrup (Rotondaro par. 5). Salad bars have been added, but they often contain salad dressing that may have more calories than a hamburger.

The percentage of children who are overweight has doubled since 1980, and among adolescents, the rates have tripled ("Fighting Obesity"). Along with obesity, the processed foods served at schools can contribute to the risk of colorectal, kidney, and stomach cancer. Unhealthy school lunches may also increase the incidence of diabetes type II, heart disease, and hypertension. Most adolescents who are obese become obese adults and have a chance of producing obese children.

Some positive changes are in place to alter lunches served in schools. In the last few years, the issue has grown from a small grassroots effort to a national cause célèbre, championed by the likes of Tom Collichio (*Top Chef*), Jamie Oliver (*Naked Chef*), and first lady Michelle Obama (Cook 21). The Senate passed the Healthy, Hunger-Free Kids Act that makes vital changes to the USDA's Free and Reduced Meal Program. This program was under the scope of critics for maintaining outdated nutritional guidelines and being underfunded; now the program reimburses schools $2.68 per meal, a cost that is not only supposed to cover food but cafeteria facilities and staff as well (Cook 21). By deciding to participate in the FSP decision-making process, schools can choose exactly what they want to serve, making a choice between fresh or processed foods.

Another rising approach to tackle unhealthy foods in schools is the schoolyard garden. This program basically allows students to grow a garden that they tend to on a weekly basis and use what's grown in the garden to prepare fresh school lunches. Many positive reviews have come from this program, which has increased its popularity nationwide. Students find the work in the schoolyard garden to be pleasurable and also educational while the work subtly creates a sense of personal responsibility and pride in students' school and environment.

Researchers are continuously looking for strategies and ways to influence students to eat healthier meals at school. Cornell researchers developed successful tricks that entice students to make healthier decisions, such as keeping ice cream in freezers without glass tops so that the ice cream isn't visible. Along with this strategy, researchers tried moving salad bars closer to the register to tempt students to choose a salad as a part of their lunch. The plan is to get kids to make better choices, not to deny them anything. Bans on soda and junk food have backfired in some places; some students have abandoned school meal programs that have tried to force-feed healthy choices (Marchione par. 5). Researchers are taking a psychological approach to increase healthy eating in schools, and tricks, such as hiding chocolate milk behind the plain milk and placing fruits into pretty baskets, are becoming successful.

Healthy school lunches have become increasingly important because what's served in school cafeterias can determine children's health and ultimately their future. All school officials should consider opening a contract with a FSP that will provide healthy foods. Students should look further into school yard gardens, and parents can get more involved. Many children and teens settle for food that's full of fats and sugars because there aren't many choices in the schools to choose from. Simple steps to influence children to make healthier eating decisions can change a life, a school, or maybe even a generation.

Works Cited

Cook, Andy. "Leading The Lunch Line." *Edible New Orleans* Autumn 2010: 20–24. Print.

"Fighting Obesity: What Schools Can Do." *District Administration*. N.p., Aug. 2006. Web. 1 Nov. 2010.

"Food Processing." History. *Wikipedia*. N.p., 26 Oct. 2010. Web. 2 Nov. 2010.

Jegtiv, Shereen. "What Are Processed Foods?" *About.com*. N.p., 1 Sept. 2009. Web. 1 Nov. 2010.

Marchione, Marilyn. "School Cafeterias Set to Serve Up Psychology." *The Times-Picayune* [New Orleans] 13 Oct. 2010: 1+. Print.

Rotondaro, Sgobbo, Summers Hays, Vinnie Rob, and Mariah Elizabeth. "Survey: School Lunches, Full of Processed Foods, Still Get Failing Health." *NY Daily News*. N.p., 31 Jan. 2010. Web. 1 Nov. 2010.

Scratch Cooking

Madison Margaret Wright

Scratch is a noun, a verb, and even an adjective. It's bad to do if you have the Chicken Pox. It's great if you're a golfer. It could mean disqualification if you're set to race a horse or a car, but in the kitchen, it means food cooked from its natural state, with no prior preparation or alteration of the ingredients. Food cooked "the way Mom used to make it." To me, it signifies food cooked the way it was meant to be. However, is this type of cooking even feasible for the majority of us today?

For as long as man has brought food back to his tribe or family, and into his dwelling or home, people have been coming up with new cooking techniques. Last week for a birthday celebration, I made a coconut cream pie. I rolled out the dough, whipped the cream by hand, toasted the coconut shavings until they were a beautiful shade of golden brown, and baked the hand-formed crust to perfection. Does it sound as if it was made from scratch? Most people today would say so, but technically, I didn't get my coconut from a tree. I didn't crack it open and shave it myself. I didn't get the milk from Ol' Bessy mooing in my backyard, either, even though my ingredients were fresh from the market. By my own literal definition, this is not cooking from scratch. So I ask myself, is it simply the thought that mattered?

To create a dish from actual scratch is a very involved process. We must only eat protein that has been taken from the wild or raised by animal husbandry. We must only enjoy fresh fruits and vegetables harvested at the height of their season. We can only drink milk if we squeeze it from an animal ourselves. It doesn't get any fresher than this, and delectable meals can be fashioned in this manner. Unfortunately, this doesn't fit the lifestyle of most Americans today. We don't all have farms, and we don't all raise livestock. More importantly, we don't all have the time or the inclination to devote so much of ourselves to sustenance. In fact, the society we live in dictates that most of us specialize. Farmers farm, teachers teach, and cooks cook. As a result, we have stores with everything we need. These run the gamut from the independent farmer's market to the enormous, corporate Sam's Clubs and Costco's, and many more in between.

The farmer's markets can provide beautiful, local, seasonal veggies and fruits for the shopper with enough time and money to negotiate the different stalls and buy the incredible, albeit pricey, products. Cooking beautiful food starts with beautiful ingredients, and the farmer's market shopper is closer than anyone, other than the farmer, to actually cooking from scratch. In my opinion, one of the best byproducts of indulging in this type of mentality is embracing seasonality.

Soft shell crabs might be my favorite food in the world to eat. I spend over half the year pining after the briny burst of flavor supplied by a bite into a properly fried softy. When the season finally arrives, few things make me happier. I know soft shells are available year round from either freezers or foreign seas, but none compare to a fresh blue crab pulled from the Gulf of Mexico and brought to my kitchen still kicking and pinching. My love for these crustaceans is so intense that I gladly go without them for months at a time to avoid the counterfeit flavor of frozen or Chinese crab supplies. While many fellow Louisianans would also apply this logic to local crawfish and shrimp, we forget that it likewise holds true for the bright red tomatoes or crispy heads of lettuce that magically occupy our supermarket shelves year-round. What, then, does the supermarket culture signify about our current world?

The superstore is a twentieth century phenomenon that for good or bad has changed the way we shop forever. From toilet paper to candy bars, Italian reds to English cucumbers, at the enormous warehouses we call grocery stores, we can buy just about anything. As a result of their bulk buying power, these stores have the ability to pass their savings on to the customer. These lower price points, in addition to the allure of one-stop shopping for today's busy professional, means infinitely more refrigerators are filled with these items than the fresh, seasonal produce bought off the back of a pick-up truck at a bi-weekly farmer's market. Although not always the freshest or perhaps not even in season, these fruits and vegetables still can provide the home cook with a myriad of delicious options. Unfortunately, the disconnect between the farmer and shopper results in lazy, uninformed cooking. This is the world where Stouffer's and Lean Cuisine thrive. Seemingly the antithesis of scratch cooking, the lazy shopper can still get further away from the natural progression of food from farm to table. With the 1950's invention of the drive-thru or fast food, we can order something different for each family member off a menu, drive up to the window, and "presto," dinner is served! In "Is It Really Stupid to Cook?" *The New York Times* writer Mark Bittman states, "[F]ast food isn't 'bad' because it's fast—it's bad because of crummy ingredients." It all comes back to what you are eating and where it comes from. Our Happy Meals and groceries can both come in a brown bag. But behold, delivery! Just like heat-and-serve frozen meals, food brought to your door requiring nothing more than a tip completely takes the beauty of cooking out of the kitchen.

According to an article by Ta-Nehisi Coates, the senior editor of *The Atlantic,* "Understanding the Blueberry Muffin," "[C]ooking from scratch creates a consciousness about food. It creates a respect, an understanding of what, exactly, you're putting in your body." This is so true, but you can cook a healthy meal from "scratch" and not spend hours in the kitchen. For example, one of my favorite dishes to make calls for chopped roasted chicken, but instead of roasting a chicken for an hour (not even including preparation time) I can buy a rotisserie chicken from the local grocery store, and I'm half way done cooking. Is that cheating? Yes. Am I still cooking from scratch if I take a short cut? Technically, no, but the definition of cooking is simply the art or practice of preparing food. Nowhere in this definition is a caveat requiring the preparation to be completed one hundred percent by me. With our busy schedules and unpredictable eating habits, eating at home is important now more than ever. We can bring the family to table without breaking our backs over the stove. With the technology we have, cooking can mean something different.

It is unrealistic to imagine that we all have gardens or raise livestock to put food on our tables. Michael Pollan's *New York Times* Bestseller, *In Defense of Food, An Eater's Manifesto,* says, "Food is also about . . . our relationship to the natural world, and about expressing our identity." What better way to get back to basics than to be in the kitchen, cooking? So just because it was bought at the store instead of picked or butchered by you, we seem to think it was not homemade. It might not be made from scratch grandma's way, but it was made with love all the same.

Works Cited

Bittman, Mark. "Is It Really Stupid to Cook?" *The New York Times* 12 Oct. 2009. *NYTimes.com*. Web. 8 Sept. 2010. <http://dinersjournal.blogs.nytimes.com/2009/10/12/is-it-really-stupid-to-cook/?scp=22&sq=bittman%20cooking%20from%20scratch&st=cse>.

Coates, Ta-Nehisi. "Understanding the Blueberry Muffin." *The Atlantic* 12 Oct. 2009. *TheAtlantic.com*. Web. 7 Sept. 2010. <http://www.theatlantic.com/culture/archive/2009/10/understanding-the-blueberry-muffin/28242/>.

Pollan, Michael. "An Eater's Manifesto." Introduction. *In Defense of Food: An Eater's Manifesto*. New York: Penguin, 2008. 8.

That Old Sound

Teppei Tada

I love my ax. It is a very old, probably about a hundred-year-old clarinet. This vintage instrument was previously owned by a great Japanese jazz clarinetist Shin Sudo, who was known for his New Orleans-style playing. He played actively and appeared at several jazz festivals in different countries, including the New Orleans Jazz and Heritage Festival. At the height of his career, right after making a record with the legendary New Orleans drummer Ernie Elly, he was diagnosed with cancer. I have never met him because he had already stopped playing clarinet when I started playing clarinet. When he passed away in 2002, his friend asked me to play his clarinet. Actually, nobody wanted to play his horn because it is an Albert system clarinet, which is an older type of clarinet seldom played these days. I did not play the Albert clarinet at the time, but I had always wanted to try. I have played it ever since.

When somebody says clarinet, it usually means the Boehm system clarinet. Both the Albert and the Boehm system of clarinets developed from the same ancestor called the Muller system clarinet in the same period during the middle of the nineteenth century. The Albert system clarinet was very popular in the early twentieth century because somehow the Boehm clarinet did not spread in the U.S. until about the 1940s. By the end of World War II, the majority of clarinet players switched to the Boehm clarinet and most companies stopped making the Albert clarinet. The main difference between the Albert and the Boehm clarinets is the fingerings. The Boehm clarinet has more keys and holes than the Albert clarinet. Having more keys offers many alternate fingering options and enables a musician to play more complicated passages and faster phrasings. Nowadays, the

Boehm system clarinet is generally considered as a more advanced instrument and no one likes to play the Albert clarinet except a few New Orleans jazz players. Those New Orleans jazz players believe that the Albert system clarinet is better than the Boehm system to play New Orleans jazz because it helps them feel closer to the tradition of New Orleans jazz.

What Albert clarinet players mostly talk about are its tone and high volume. They say the Albert clarinet has a better tone, and the tone of the Boehm clarinet is too thin. George Lewis, one of the most influential New Orleans jazz clarinet players and the very first member of the Preservation Hall Jazz Band, says, "I didn't like the tone of Boehm system—it was too keen . . . [the tone of the Boehm clarinet] was not as deep as the Albert" (Bethell 289). Lewis was famous for his thick tone and became an icon of the Albert system by touring around the world. People thought he had that thick tone because he played the Albert clarinet, and quite a few clarinetists switched to the Albert clarinet after listening to his performance.

Another well-known Albert clarinetist, Edmond Hall, a member of the Louis Armstrong All Stars in the 1950s, claims that the Albert clarinet has a bigger tone than the Boehm clarinet: "You get a bigger tone out of the Albert than you do on a Boehm . . . [for] a six piece Dixieland band, I don't think a Boehm clarinet fits . . ." (Russell 209). He had a huge tone and a very powerful playing style. He played many clarinets, which have slightly different fingering systems, in his career, but he had never played the Boehm clarinet.

Many Albert clarinetists think that the better and bigger tone comes from the large size of the bore, the inside diameter of an instrument. Omer Simeon, an Albert clarinetist who is most known for the recordings with Jelly Roll Morton in the late 1920s, says, "The bore [of the Albert clarinet] seems a little larger [than the Boehm clarinet] . . . that's what makes the tone [of the Albert clarinet] a little broader" (Russell 199). This is a very common opinion among Albert clarinetists. But Boehm clarinet players do not agree. They say that a player himself and a mouthpiece, a small piece of equipment which is attached on the top of an instrument and goes directly into a player's mouth, affects the sound more significantly. Jazz saxophone and clarinet player/composer Roger Aldridge argues, "[O]ne can get a bigger sound . . . by simply using a mouthpiece that's a better match to yourself (as a player) and your playing style rather than making a big deal about bore size." He himself used to play an old Boehm clarinet, which had a slightly larger bore than the current Boehm clarinet, but switched to a current one after finding his ideal mouthpiece.

Other Albert clarinetists think that the tone is related to the number of the holes on the body of the instrument. They say that the Albert system clarinet has fewer holes than the Boehm clarinet, and, therefore, it makes a richer tone. Some Albert clarinet players even take unnecessary metal keys, which are only for alternate fingerings, off the instruments and seal the tone holes to improve the tone. New Orleans local Albert clarinet player, Raymond Burke, insists that "Albert has a much better tone. . . . I think the less keys and holes you have on a clarinet the better" (Russell 213). He was so particular about the tone that he actually took off a metal key and sealed the tone hole. Some players also mention that the wood of the Albert clarinet is usually very old and it produces an aged, richer tone. But on the other hand, some classical players insist that it is necessary to change instruments every few years because the wood itself gets old and the tone is gone. There are so many different opinions. The problem is that all the opinions are not based on any acoustic evidence but just their own impressions.

To find a more theoretical answer about the relation between the bore size, the tone holes, the age of the wood, and the sound of the clarinet, I stopped asking musicians and went to a physics professor's office at the University of New Orleans. The Physics Department of UNO has been offering an interesting class called Physics of Music, taught by Professor Juliette Ioup. The class is about the acoustics of different musical instruments, as well as the basic physics of the sound, such as vibration, wavelength, sound speed, and harmonics. According to Professor Ioup, a bigger bore makes a bigger sound because the volume is related to the amount of the air: "The amplitude of a sound wave is a measure of how much the air molecules are vibrating . . . ; [therefore,] a large amount of air volume moving means a louder sound." It is simple. But her comment about the tone holes and the deterioration of the wood was a little different from what I had expected. She did not say that having fewer holes was better or worse and that newer wood was better or worse: "The tone or timbre or quality or color of the sound is very subjective and difficult to measure quantitatively." It means that those things, which both Albert and Boehm players believe to have an effect on the tone, are insignificant when examined scientifically.

It became clear that, acoustically, the Albert clarinet was not any better for New Orleans jazz than the Boehm clarinet—except for its volume. If so, why has the Albert clarinet continued to enjoy popularity in New Orleans jazz since the 1940s? Why do some players even switch from the Boehm to the Albert clarinet in the middle of their careers? Jazz clarinetist Evan Christopher, known for his New Orleans-style playing, explains that switching to the Albert system clarinet is "a commitment [to New Orleans jazz]." During the interview, he told me that he had already established his musical style before switching to the Albert system clarinet, but playing the Albert clarinet gave him confidence. Oscar Font, a jazz musician, photographer, and a writer in Barcelona who runs the web site "Albert System—The Jazz Clarinet," says that the reason why he plays this "uncomfortable Albert System clarinet" is that he is "respectuous [sic] to the old jazz clarinet tradition." They do not say anything about particular tone or style. They play the Albert system not for acoustic reasons but for mental, emotional, or nostalgic reasons. Their remarks reminded me of the fact that music is an art, and there is no way to measure beauty. The beautiful tone comes from inside a player.

Ironically, the guy who is considered as the best New Orleans-style clarinetist alive is not an Albert clarinet player. Boehm clarinet player Michael White has been chosen as the best New Orleans jazz clarinetist by New Orleans local magazine *Off Beat* for several years. He appears on many musical occasions as a representative of New Orleans jazz. When I interviewed him, he had just finished a recording session for a rock/blues superstar Eric Clapton. White has a different concept of New Orleans jazz from other musicians: "New Orleans jazz is a reflection of people's life. How they [people in New Orleans] speak, how they walk, how they dance . . ." His explanation is very convincing to me. Through doing the research, I got the feeling that the New Orleans clarinet sound cannot be defined as certain musical characteristics—the key is having some kind of image, which is personally related to the tradition of New Orleans jazz. Someone might think of a certain clarinetist in the past, and others might think of certain tunes. The Albert system clarinet can help a musician to think that way because it is the instrument that has been played by many great New Orleans jazz clarinetists such as George Lewis, Edmond Hall, Omer Simeon, and Raymond Burke. It is a traditional instrument, which symbolizes the old New Orleans sound.

I remember when Michael White heard me playing the Albert system clarinet for the first time. He smiled at me saying, "You've got that sound!" Although he plays the Boehm clarinet, we shared the same "that old New Orleans sound" at that moment. White would have thought of the people on the street. I am not sure what I thought of, but it might have been that Japanese clarinet player Shin Sudo talking to me through his horn. I love my ax. It is the link to that old sound.

Works Cited

Aldridge, Roger, "Difference Between Selmer Large Bores." *Sax On The Web Forum*. N.p. 11 Dec. 2006. Web. 28 Oct. 2010.

Bethell, Tom. *George Lewis: A Jazzman From New Orleans*. London: University of California Press, 1977. 289. Print.

Christopher, Evan. Personal interview. 22 Oct. 2010.

Font, Oscar. "Welcome." *Albert System—The Jazz Clarinet.* N.p. n.d. Web. 28. Oct. 2010.

Ioup, Juliette. Personal interview. 22. Oct. 2010.

Russell, Bill. *New Orleans Style.* New Orleans: Jassology Press, 1994. 199–214. Print.

White, Michael. Personal interview. 21 Oct. 2010.

Land of Opportunities vs. Dreams to Create Opportunities

Krishna Pokharel

Twelve years ago, a child who just migrated to the national capital from a rural Nepalese village, Jaisithok, was absolutely astounded by the wonders of technology. A light bulb clearing out the darkness of the night became the most wonderful thing he had ever seen. That little child, on his first night in the city, compared his miserable past life that would end by each sunset to his luxurious present where nights and days were the same. That young boy, then, thought of his villagers, who suffered a fateful life due to the unavailability of electricity. Then he said to himself, "I will light a bulb in my village," and decided to become an engineer.

That child, who still aspires to see the light bulbs in his village, is still alive in me, and I am studying Mechanical Engineering here at University of New Orleans (UNO) to make those dreams come true. While I am on my path toward fulfilling my childhood goals, I am always asked where I would use my engineering expertise. Will I remain here in the United States like so many of my countrymen have, or will I go back? However, my answer has always been the same: "I will go back." The best place to utilize my engineering skills would be in rural Nepalese villages because those places have been awaiting development for decades, and it is my personal goal to raise the living standard of my countrymen.

A lack of electricity has not only resulted in a miserable life for the people in my village, but it has also hindered their economic development. They carry out all their chores before the sun crosses the horizon because the onset of dusk halts the life of the village. For instance, housewives are supposed to cook before sunset, and students are required to complete their homework by then. Otherwise, those tasks should be done in the dim light of kerosene lamps, which is very inconvenient. How unfortunate are those people who, despite being the richest in water resources in the world, are lost in the abyss of darkness every night? The Institute of Engineers (India), in a survey, states that "Nepal, which has multi-stage hydro power potential, can convert itself into [a] 'hydro-power dollar' country just like Gulf nations that are affluent 'petro dollar' countries." Despite such economic potential of the numerous rampantly-flowing perennial rivers, a lack of skilled manpower has caused an insufficient production leading to the lack of such a basic necessity as electricity. A simple mini-scale hydropower, wind-energy project, or even a solar-power system, can significantly change the lives of these people. The only prerequisites are trained and qualified engineers, like me, who have a vision for the future.

My personal choice of where I would work depends entirely on the beneficiaries of my engineering skills. Are they United States citizens, who have been enjoying the wonders of technology for decades, or are they those living in rural Nepal, who have been struggling against darkness for centuries? The answer is very obvious to me. Those rural Nepalese, who are facing the lack of electricity, are the people who need me more. Hence, without any hesitation, I would be more than happy to serve my own people.

Though it is very difficult to set up a power plant initially, it is not impossible. Dristy Shrestha, a Middlebury College student, describes her success in a mini-hydro project in Nepal: "I wanted to apply and do something in my country." This past May, she, with the help of the local workforce, built a small dam and a power house and re-directed a portion of the river so that the flowing water would pass through the turbines in the power house (Vara). The successful completion of her project is providing a direct benefit to more than forty houses in the village. Her achievement not only proves that mini-hydro power projects are beneficial to the locals, but it also inspires me in my dreams to light my village with electricity.

Mechanical Engineering, my academic discipline, is a branch of engineering that deals with the design and use of machines and tools, like turbines, to generate power ("Mechanical Engineering"). Hence, my field of study allows me to equip myself with knowledge and various skills to build and operate the hydroelectric turbines to generate electricity. With the talent acquired here, I can set up some mini-hydro power projects that could significantly alter the lifestyle of more than fifty households in my village and nearby. Not only could the locals light their houses, but they could also run some small-scale industries or businesses and add an additional income source to their traditional agrarian lives.

The benefit of having power seems very significant in the kitchen. Villagers can run electrical equipment, such as rice-cookers, instead of burning wood logs to cook, which would ease their lifestyle drastically because they would not have to spend hours to collect wood from the local forest. In addition, they can store food for longer using a refrigerator, which will reduce the food that gets wasted and also lessens their daily expenses. Students can prevent hurting their eyes trying to read and write in the faint light. In short, the availability of electricity will help them to live better lives. Hence, my effort in those villages can significantly raise the living standard of the locals.

Despite all these benefits I plan on providing to my people, some critics will still suggest that I avoid going back into the same life of misery from where I originally came. Even my parents, who now are in Kathmandu, the capital city of Nepal, want me to work in the United States and earn more money. Some of my friends argue that there is no career prospect back home, especially because of the lack of companies that can possibly hire me. Even if one of the few companies hires me, I would get a much lower salary, around six hundred dollars per month (at most) compared to thousands of dollars that I can possibly get here. Yes, I acknowledge that the above-mentioned things are true, but I will be happier to serve my poor people rather than to live for my wealthy boss. Five to six hundred dollars per month is more than enough to live a quality life in Nepal. At least, I will gain satisfaction when I try to empower others with electrical power. Earning more satisfaction with less money is far better than earning more money with no satisfaction. Furthermore, I believe that my education will be fruitful only if I apply it in the best interest of those who are not as privileged as I am. As an engineer, it would be my ethical responsibility to help people in solving their real-life problems.

In addition, I may also have to face the reluctance of the villagers toward having hydropower in the village. They might say that they are happy the way they are now by highlighting some of side effects of having a dam. First, they may believe that construction of dams and operations of power-plants would be too costly, leading to a high per unit price of electricity which they may not be able to afford. Second, there may be no one in the village skilled at operating the machines. Third, the water reservoir may lead to flooding in the village, taking away acres of fertile land, their primary source of income. However, these problems can be conquered once the villagers show some enthusiasm. Though convincing the locals that the construction of the mini-power plant will be as difficult as climbing Mt. Everest, it is not impossible. They can be encouraged toward the construction of the power plant by my explaining to them the economical benefits of having electricity in the village. Construction of the dam with the local materials like wood and stones and with the voluntary help of the locals will minimize the cost. Furthermore, once the plant is set up, only a few people are needed to operate the machines and run the plant. The local people can do it by themselves once they are trained. That way, not only will the locals benefit from the employment opportunities, but they will also be able to afford to have electricity in their houses because the production cost will be low. One researcher, Shankar Karki, a student of University of Technology, Sydney, states that "[t]he cost-effectiveness of small sized plants in the generation expansion also leads to decrease in electricity prices as well" (Karki). Thus, his research also proves that mini-power plants are cost-effective. In addition, the flow of the water can be controlled with the use of shutters in the dam to prevent the possibility of flooding.

A popular adage says, "Home is where the heart is," and my heart has always remained where my villagers are. The objective of my life will be fulfilled only if I go there to serve my people, who need me and my experience of the U.S., and show them a glimpse of the development that they have been deprived of for centuries. Giving the underprivileged an equal share of "right" in our society, and teaching people about their role in creating a prosperous society for themselves, is the goal of my education. And I am enthused to fulfill it by launching myself into those untouched parts of my country where people not just await tangible changes but also a pioneer to lead them with hope and motivation. Whenever I fall in a dilemma of choosing between right and wrong, or perhaps better and the best, I let my heart decide. And thus, I have decided to go back after completing my studies here in the U.S. and perform my share of duties to my motherland.

Works Cited

"Institution of Engineers Favours Tie-Up with Nepal for Hydro Power." *Business Line*. THE HINDU group of publications. 12 Dec. 2009. Web. 28 Feb. 2010.

Karki, Shankar. "Implications of Small Hydropower Plants in Power Sector Development: A Case of Nepal." Pg 5. *Energy Planning and Policy Program*, University of Technology, Sydney. Web. 21 March. 2010

"Mechanical Engineering." The American Heritage® Dictionary of the English Language, Fourth Edition. Houghton Mifflin Company, 2004. Web. 09 Mar. 2010 http://dictionary.reference.com/browse/mechanical engineering>.

Vara, Roz. "Nepali Student Returns Home, Illuminates Rural Village." *The Middlebury Campus. The Student Weekly of Middlebury College*. 3 Dec. 2009. Web. 28 Feb. 2010.

Getting to School a Little Faster

Timothy Brathwaite

Pedal stroke after pedal stroke, we rocketed up the hill. Our brows were furrowed and solemn as we focused all efforts on the task. It had been four miles of cycling at a nauseating pace, and although our bodies cried out for mercy, we showed them no attention. As we crested the cruel and destructive hill, our minds awoke from their vegetative state—after all, the hard part was done, and our success was secure. All that remained was a one-and-a-half mile downhill stretch of land to school in downtown Brooklyn, where we would fly through the terrain on two wheels to immortalize the ride and become greater than we were in the past. However, before we could celebrate and bask in the light of victory, a dark cloud of exhaust fumes blotted out our view of the sun and mocked all our efforts. Traffic was congested all the way down the hill for as far as our eyes could see. Dipping and weaving through vehicle after vehicle, we fought valiantly to save that which we had just worked so hard to create, but it was to no avail because the traffic was just too thick. In a dejected manner, we watched as the seconds went by and then minutes; our hope of getting to school faster than ever before was beginning to fade. With each passage of time, our success was diluted until it finally became a failure, and our epic ride was ruined in a maze of stalled vehicles.

Traffic congestion is a huge problem that does more than just raze the yearly tradition of three students in New York City: it erodes the fabric of our economy and lowers the quality of life for many commuters. One partial solution, which has been proposed, and which has been successful in other cities around the world, is a program called congestion pricing. New York City (NYC) officials should support the practice and use of congestion pricing because it has the ability to simultaneously alleviate traffic problems in two complementary ways, making it one of the most effective tools available to the city.

The first and most obvious way that congestion pricing reduces traffic problems is by providing drivers with an economic incentive not to drive. By applying a fee to motorists who add to the congestion of a particular area, some drivers will choose not to drive into the zone because they feel that the benefits of auto commuting do not outweigh the costs of the fee they must pay. This theory is not just a mere conjecture; it has been field tested in cities around the world and has proven to be very effective at lowering the amount of traffic that a locale faces. For example, David Lewis, the chief economist at the HDR corporation and formerly the principal economist of the U.S. Congressional Budget Office, states, "Since [the] introduction of this fee, automobile traffic in central London has declined by a reported 20 percent, average traffic speeds have increased 37 percent, and peak period congestion delays are down 30 percent for autos and 50 percent for buses" (12, 36). Other places that have adopted congestion pricing with positive results include Stockholm, Sweden and Singapore (Traffic Congestion Mitigation Commission 37; Khan 84). It has often been said that history repeats itself, and if this is the case, then NYC should extend full support to the theory of congestion pricing. According to the Partnership for New York City, a group of 200 CEO's from NYC who fund economic impact studies, congestion causes ". . . more than $13 billion in annual costs to businesses and consumers, billions in lost economic output, and tens of thousands of lost jobs . . ." ("Growth or Gridlock" 2). Charging a fee to enter crowded sections of the city will decrease clogging of the streets and thereby diminish the various costs that the city is forced to endure.

In addition to decreasing congestion and the negative effects it places on the city's economy, congestion pricing generates substantial revenues that will be used to improve NYC's transportation system. According to the New York State Traffic Congestion Mitigation Commission (TCMC), a 17 member commission created to review plans that aim to reduce overcrowding of state roadways, the pricing schemes, which are being reviewed, have the ability to generate between $420 million and $520 million per year in net revenue (35). These funds will help bring mass transit to parts of the city, which are currently underserved, make needed repairs to the system, and increase the carrying capacity citywide to accommodate those who will switch to mass transit in lieu of driving. By securing funds to invest in public transportation, the city can make this mode of travel more appealing to drivers, which will induce greater transit usage and further lower congestion. As a consequence of less traffic, the speed and reliability of bus systems will improve (Santos and Fraser 273). This cycle of decreased road demands causes improved service of the city's mass transit, which should reduce road demand even more, utilizing the city's streets in the most effective and least costly manner (Leape 168). Furthermore, congestion pricing is a self-sufficient mechanism that covers its own operating costs and still generates a profit, which is used to support other projects. Alternative methods of reducing traffic, such as increased enforcement of traffic laws, investments in new information technology, and roadway improvements, all require money but fail to pay for themselves or contribute to other efforts.

While congestion pricing will raise significant amounts of money for the city, some people are concerned about where this money will come from. Opponents of congestion pricing frequently state that the fee should not be implemented because it is an unfair and regressive tax, which harms the working class (Brodsky 10). Admittedly, the plan put forth by Mayor Bloomberg, which would charge a flat rate of eight dollars on any cars entering the pricing zone and four dollars for trips within the zone, is a regressive tax; affluent individuals pay a lower proportion of their income to cover the fee while less prosperous people pay more of their income to cover the fee. However, the charge is not compulsory for the majority of New York City residents, and it can be alleviated through exemptions and tax credits to poor/middle class residents who have no reasonable alternatives to driving into the pricing zone. As reported by the TCMC, less than one percent of New York City residents who travel to work by car are poor or middle class and "lack a viable alternative to paying a . . . toll" (44). The majority of New York City commuters have options, and if they do not want to pay the fee, they can simply take mass transit. As for the fairness of congestion pricing, the personal costs of driving are only "about $0.52 per vehicle mile" while the external costs of driving are between "$0.13 per vehicle mile to $0.29 per vehicle mile." At the moment, these external costs are distributed amongst all of the inhabitants of the region, including the vast majority who do not travel through the central business district by automobile (Lewis 8). This is not fair. Congestion pricing will reduce the burden on society by charging those who create the costs in the first place. It does not make sense to bypass an opportunity to improve the city's transit system and shrink congestion because of unwarranted fears; congestion pricing actually benefits the working class far more than it harms them because the majority of non-affluent workers take mass transit to work and will see the revenues from the excise be used to improve public transportation.

Another belief that congestion pricing skeptics have is that the fee will actually hurt the economy. Groups such as Keep NYC Congestion Tax Free, a coalition of groups that opposes the pricing plan, believe that people will reduce their spending and avoid coming to NYC because of the fee to enter the area; this decreased patronage would cause businesses to lose millions of dollars and cut back on the amount of jobs they provide (18). While these concerns make sense intuitively, the results of road pricing have not shown this to be the case. Reviews of the implementation of congestion pricing in Singapore state that "Singapore has benefited economically from all its demand management programs" (Khan 85), and evaluations of London's pricing scheme reveal that there has been ". . . no significant effect for total central London retail sales" (Leape 169). In either scenario, the claims that a congestion fee would negatively impact businesses and the economy have been invalidated.

Part of the reasons why road pricing may not damage the economy as the opposition fears is that the economy is already harmed by congestion; therefore, relieving congestion should actually help the economy. While it is possible to find some industries and businesses that will be hurt by a reduction in the crowding of the area's streets, the city overall benefits from an improved flow of traffic. For instance, data from the Partnership for New York City shows that, in the arts and entertainment industry, the boroughs of Brooklyn, Queens, Staten Island, and the Bronx actually see a total increase of $59.6 million in revenue per year and 458 jobs due to congestion; however, this is less than half of the $182.2 million and 1,406 jobs that Manhattan loses every year to the overcrowding of the city's roadways ("Growth or Gridlock" 38). The groups that are against congestion pricing are typically from the outer boroughs such as Queens and Brooklyn, the very boroughs that may see a decline in their profits and employment levels if the amount of traffic decreases. Although it is completely natural for parties from these outer boroughs to try to protect the livelihood of the businesses in their areas, it is not in the best interest of the entire city. By utilizing congestion pricing, officials can facilitate the creation of more jobs and profit for city residents and employers while helping far more people than they hurt.

As New York City looks ahead to the future, it can expect a growth in its population, and unless large steps are taken, a growth in its levels of congestion as well. There is most likely no single remedy for the transportation issues that the city faces, but congestion pricing should definitely play a large role in whatever action is taken. Specifically, introducing road pricing in Manhattan's Central Business District can help reduce traffic citywide. It was found that in parts of the outer boroughs, such as Downtown Brooklyn and Long Island City Queens, most of the congestion is "caused primarily by through traffic to Manhattan, which is also overlapped with the intensive local traffic" ("Growth or Gridlock" 15). I revel in such discoveries because they give me hope that travel experiences in my own borough of Brooklyn can become more efficient and pleasant. Maybe one day in the future, with the advent of congestion pricing and more open road space, my friends and I will not have to sit in traffic jams, and we might find ourselves getting to school a little faster.

Works Cited

Brodsky, Richard L. *Interim Report: An Inquiry into Congestion Pricing as Proposed in PlaNYC 2030 and S.6068.* New York State Assembly. Committee on Corporations, Authorities and Commissions. 9 July 2007. 11 Nov. 2008 <http://assembly.state.ny.us/member_files/092/20070710/>.

"Congestion Pricing in the Manhattan Central Business District: Let's Look Hard Before We Leap." *Keep NYC Free.* May 2007. Keep NYC Congestion Tax Free. 11 Nov. 2008 <http://www.keepnycfree.com/reports/index.php>.

"Growth or Gridlock: The Economic Case for Traffic Relief and Transit Improvement for a Greater New York." *Partnership for New York City.* 04 Dec 2006. Partnership for New York City. 11 Nov. 2008 <http://www.pfnyc.org/pressReleases/2006/pr_120406_congestion.htm>.

Khan, Ata M. "Reducing Traffic Density: The Experience of Hong Kong and Singapore." *Journal of Urban Technology* 8 (2001): 69–87. SocIndex. Ebscohost. University of New Orleans Library. 11 Nov. 2008 <http://www.ebscohost.com>.

Leape, Jonathan. "The London Congestion Charge." *Journal of Economic Perspectives* 20 (2006): 157–76. Business Source Complete. Ebscohost. University of New Orleans Library. 11 Nov. 2008 <http://www.ebscohost.com>.

Lewis, David. "Americas Traffic Congestion Problem: Toward a Framework for Nationwide Reform." *Hamilton Project: Discussion Papers* (2008): 2–36. Academic Search Complete. Ebscohost. University of New Orleans Library. 11 Nov. 2008 <http://www.ebscohost.com>.

New York State Department of Transportation Traffic Congestion Mitigation Commission. *Report to the Traffic Congestion Mitigation Commission & Recommended Implementation Plan.* Jan. 2008 11 Nov. 2008. <https://www.nysdot.gov/programs/congestion_mitigation_commission/final-recommendation>

Santos, Georgina, and Gordon Fraser. "Road Pricing: Lessons from London." *Economic Policy* 21 (2006): 263–310. Business Source Complete. Ebscohost. University of New Orleans Library. 11 Nov. 2008 <http://www.ebscohost.com>.

A Topic Proposal and a Classical Argument Essay Related to Students' Majors or Future Professions

by Laura Kappel, Instructor of English
at the University of New Orleans

Choosing a Topic

The general topic for this assignment is a **question or issue in your major field of study or something related to your future profession.** This question should be something that you are genuinely curious about. You should begin by asking yourself several questions to help you come up with a focus:

Why did I choose this major?

What about my past—experiences, skills, knowledge, interest— draws me to this field?

What do I hope to do with this major?

What kinds of topics in this major appeal to me the most?

What are the current issues in this field; that is, what are scholars and professionals in this field writing about or discussing at conferences?

Who can I talk to in this field to help me get more information about this? Who are the people I know who are currently working in this field?

How can I begin to do some preliminary research to help me find a focused topic?

Who would my audience be for this paper? Who would have some vested interest in learning more about my research? (Think about individuals and/or groups or organizations.)

As you begin to focus your topic, you will need to find an angle on your topic, which should be a debatable issue since the research paper will be taking the form of a classical argument that has at least two sides to it. However, in the early stage of research, you should keep your topic options open and not eliminate anything immediately just because you do not see it as debatable. There may be more sides to this issue once you start researching it. **Also, it is very important that you do not choose a question to write about which you already have an answer to.** Researching and writing should lead to your exploration and discovery of that answer.

Writing the Proposal

The topic proposal should be one long paragraph or two paragraphs, between one and two pages long, which present between one and three questions related to your major, which you are hoping to explore in your research. The proposal should explain why you think this question/these questions would be worth pursuing and should tell how you came up with this focus. The proposal should also answer as many of the above-mentioned questions as possible, painting a clear picture about your personal connection to this topic and the relationship between this topic and your major.

The proposal should also briefly explain your next steps in researching this topic.

Sample Topic Questions from Former Students

- An Education major asked, "Should teachers be held accountable for failing students?"
- An Education major asked, "Should cursive writing be taught in elementary schools?"
- An Engineering student asked, "Should the bridges in the New Orleans area be reevaluated?"
- A Spanish major asked, "Is the classroom experience necessary for successful language learning?"
- A Psychology major asked, "Can talk therapy be a substitute for drug therapy?"
- A Psychology major asked, "Is Dance and Music Therapy an effective alternative therapy?"
- A Film Studies major asked, "Does a distorted timeline in thriller movies enhance or detract from the plot?"
- A future medical student asked, "Is becoming a nurse practitioner as advantageous as becoming a doctor?"
- A Predentistry major asked, "Are dentists adequately addressing dental fears in patients?"
- An accounting major asked, "Was the Sarbanes Oxley Act effective?"
- A Pre-pharmacy major asked, "Are generic drugs are as effective as name-brand drugs?"
- A Finance major asked, "Can microfinancing help the poor people in Bangladesh?"
- A Music major asked, "Which kind of clarinet more effectively creates a New Orleans jazz sound?"
- A Nursing major asked, "What are the problems with hospital food?"

Writing the Essay

The essay will be in the form of a classical argument, which will present a stance taken on an issue related to your central question and which will look at two or more sides of that issue. Thus, once you have researched your topic question, you will need to find a debatable issue related to it so that you can present at least two different sides of this argument. The essay should be about five–six pages long (approximately 1250–1500 words) and should include at least six sources, one of which must be from a library database such as Academic Search Complete or LexisNexis. At least one source should be from a nonprint genre (such as an interview, survey, radio or television segment [using the transcript is fine], sound clip, photograph, map, chart, etc.). The other sources should be reliable, recent, and professional. Try to include at least one direct quotation per paragraph, and be sure it is well-integrated with contextual information preceding the quote and commentary/analysis following it. These quotations must be documented using the Modern Language Association (MLA) format, and a Works Cited page must be included. *The quoted material should take up no more than roughly 15–20% of the content of your paper.*

Basic Classical Argument Structure

- ❏ Introduction: Presentation of the issue and of the thesis statement which takes a side.
- ❏ Paragraphs giving reasons to support the thesis.
- ❏ Paragraphs summarizing the opposition view.
- ❏ Paragraphs refuting the opposition view.
  NOTE: Sometimes the summary and refutation of the opposition points can occur in the same paragraph.
- ❏ Conclusion

Audience

As you work on this paper, keep a dual audience in mind. One is other people in your major, field, or chosen profession who have a vested interest in learning more about this issue. The other group is your classmates and instructor. Thus, you must explain your topic in a way that individuals who are not in that field will be able to understand it easily.

Other Guidelines

1. You need to define the audience in a section below the title and just before the text of the first paragraph. Write the word "Audience:" and then briefly explain the specific people or types of people this essay seeks to convince and say something about their values and beliefs related to your chosen issue. The audience should be people who are opposed to your argument or who are not informed yet about the issue. The audience also includes your classmates and the instructor, so base your content accordingly. This section should be three-four lines long, double-spaced.

2. Somewhere in the essay, explain your personal connection to the topic. (For example, you can explain why you have chosen this major or field of study.)

3. In addition to making logical appeals (**logos**) through giving evidence and citing testimony, try to make appeals to **pathos** by evoking certain emotions in the readers or by referring to common values between you and your readers in relation to the topic. Establish your own **ethos** (credibility) by showing that you have researched the topic fully, by presenting opposing views fairly and with respect, by following the correct style and formatting guidelines, and by adhering to editorial correctness (few errors in grammar, spelling, and punctuation). When citing the work of others, refer to their credentials to enhance their ethos, and be sure to explain your own expertise on this topic.

4. Touch all the bases:
   - Sensing—Include descriptive detail with references to the five senses. Use narrative sections (where appropriate) to tell a story to illustrate a point.
   - Thinking—Give logical reasons and evidence for your points. Be sure to have a clear main point stated in the thesis. Establish a clear structure/organization through well-formed topic sentences. Say something original about your topic by showing that you have thought about it in an innovative way.
   - Intuiting—Include a good variety of sentence styles. Use figurative and symbolic language, and try to include at least one original metaphor.
   - Valuing/Feeling—State the significance of your ideas by referring to larger values you hold as important.

5. Use a variety of rhetorical strategies. Some of the more common ones include the following:
   ✓ Description
   ✓ Narration
   ✓ Cause/effect
   ✓ Example and illustration
   ✓ Process analysis
   ✓ Classification and division
   ✓ Analogy
   ✓ Comparison and contrast
   ✓ Definition

Outcomes of this Assignment

This assignment allows students to explore a topic of their interest, to learn what people are saying about that topic, and to become a part of that dialogue by adding their own perspective on the issue. Students learn to see writing as a process that involves many stages, starting with curiosity and a desire to know and ending with a finished product that reflects their process of inquiry, exploration, discovery, and expression of ideas. While going through these stages, students learn the value of researching and revising as they become the expert in the classroom, the one person who most likely knows more about that chosen topic than anyone else in the class.

APPENDIX B

Guide to MLA Style

This section contains guidelines for preparing your essay in the format recommended by the Modern Language Association, or MLA. Part One, "Citing Sources in Your Essay," will be particularly useful as you write your draft; it provides guidance on how to parenthetically cite the sources you use in the text of your essay. Part Two, "How the Essay Should Look," will help you with formatting the manuscript after you've revised it, including guidelines for margins, tables, and pagination. Part Three, "Preparing the 'Works Cited' Page," offers detailed instructions on how to prepare your bibliography at the end of your essay; this is usually one of the last steps in preparing the final manuscript. Finally, Part Four presents a sample research essay in MLA style, which will show you how it all comes together.

Checklist before Handing in a Paper in MLA Style

- My name, instructor's name, course, and date are in the upper left-hand corner of the first page (see pages 792–793).
- All my pages are numbered using my last name next to the appropriate page number (see pages 793–794).
- My "Works Cited" page begins on a new page, not at the bottom of the last page of text.
- Everything, including my "Works Cited" page(s), is double-spaced.
- Because my printer cartridge has enough ink, every page of the paper's text is readable.
- There are no commas in my parenthetical citations between the author's name and the page number (see page 782).
- All my parenthetical citations are *inside* the periods at the ends of sentences, unless the citation appears at the end of a "blocked" quote (see pages 782 and 796–797).
- Parenthetical citations of Web sources *don't* include the URLs (see pages 819–828).
- My paper has a title but no separate title page (unless my instructor says otherwise).
- The entries in my "Works Cited" page(s) are listed alphabetically, and every line after the first one in an entry is indented five spaces.

Directory of MLA Style

Part One: Citing Sources in Your Essay

1.1 When to Cite

Before examining the details of how to use parenthetical citations, remember when you must cite sources in your paper:

1. Whenever you quote from an original source
2. Whenever you borrow ideas from an original source, even when you express them in your own words by paraphrasing or summarizing
3. Whenever you borrow factual information from a source that is *not common knowledge*

The Common Knowledge Exception. The business about *common knowledge* causes much confusion. Just what does this term mean? Basically, *common knowledge* means facts that are widely known and about which there is no controversy.

Sometimes, it's really obvious whether something is common knowledge. The fact that the Super Bowl occurs in late January or early February and pits the winning teams from the American and National Football Conferences is common knowledge. The fact that former president Ronald Reagan was once an actor and starred in a movie with a chimpanzee is common knowledge, too. And the fact that most Americans get most of their news from television is also common knowledge, though this information is getting close to leaving the domain of common knowledge.

But what about Carolyn's assertion that most dreaming occurs during rapid eye movement (REM) sleep? This is an idea about which all of her sources seem to agree. Does that make it common knowledge?

It's useful to ask next, How common to whom? Experts in the topic at hand or the rest of us? As a rule, consider the knowledge of your readers. What information will not be familiar to most of your readers or may even surprise them? Which ideas might even raise skepticism? In this case, the fact about REM sleep and dreaming goes slightly beyond the knowledge of most readers, so to be safe, it should be cited. Use common sense, but when in doubt, cite.

1.2 The MLA Author/Page System

Starting in 1984, the Modern Language Association (MLA), a body that, among other things, decides documentation conventions for papers in the humanities, switched from footnotes to the author/page parenthetical citation system. The American Psychological Association (APA), a similar body for the social sciences, promotes use of the author/date system.

You will find it fairly easy to switch from one system to the other once you've learned both. Since MLA conventions are appropriate for English classes, we will focus on the author/page system in the following sections. (For a comparison of the basic features of APA and MLA see Table 1.)

The Basics of Using Parenthetical Citation.   The MLA method of in-text citation is fairly simple: As close as possible to the borrowed material, you indicate in parentheses the original source (usually, the author's name) and the page number in the work that material came from. For example, here's how you'd cite a book or article with a single author using the author/page system:

> From the very beginning of *Sesame Street* in
> 1969, kindergarten teachers discovered that
> incoming students who had watched the program
> already knew their ABCs (Chira 13).*

The parenthetical citation here tells readers two things: (1) This information about the success of *Sesame Street* does not originate with the writer but with someone named *Chira,* and (2) readers can consult the original source for further information by looking on page 13

---

*This and the following "Works Cited" example are used with permission of Heidi R. Dunham.

Table 1   Key Differences between MLA and APA Formats

MLA	APA
Capitalizes most words in book and article titles on works cited page	Only capitalizes the first letter of titles and proper nouns on reference page
Uses author's full first and last name on works cited page	Uses author's last name along with first and middle initials on reference page
Uses the word "and" to combine authors' names in in-text citations and on works cited page if there is more than one author for a source	Uses an ampersand (&) to combine authors' names in in-text citations and on reference page if a source has more than one author
In-text citations use author's last name and pages cited	In-text citations use author's last name and date; page numbers aren't required
In-text citations use no punctuation between author's name and page number	In-text citations use a comma between author's last name and date
Page numbers are listed simply as a number in in-text citations	Page numbers are denoted with a "p." or "pp." in in-text citations
No cover sheet	Cover sheet, with running head
Uses page number on first page	Uses page number on first page— usually the cover sheet
Running head contains author's last name and the page number	Running head contains the first words of the paper's title and the page number
No subheadings within the paper	Uses subheadings within the paper; often begins with an abstract
Tables and figures integrated into the body of the paper	Tables and figures kept separate from the main text

of Chira's book or article, which is cited fully at the back of the paper in the "Works Cited." Here is what readers would find there:

```
               Works Cited
 Chira, Susan. "Sesame Street at 20: Taking
      Stock." New York Times 15 Nov. 1989: 13.
      Print.
```

Here's another example of parenthetical author/page citation from another research paper. Note the differences from the previous example:

> "One thing is clear," writes Thomas Mallon,
> "plagiarism didn't become a truly sore point
> with writers until they thought of writing as
> their trade. . . . Suddenly his capital and
> identity were at stake" (3-4).

The first thing you may have noticed is that the author's last name—Mallon—was omitted from the parenthetical citation. It didn't need to be included, since it had already been mentioned in the text. *If you mention the author's name in the text of your paper, then you only need to parenthetically cite the relevant page number(s).* This citation also tells us that the quoted passage comes from two pages rather than one.

1.2.1 PLACEMENT OF CITATIONS

Place the citation as close as you can to the borrowed material, trying to avoid breaking the flow of the sentences, if possible. To avoid confusion about what's borrowed and what's not—particularly in passages longer than a sentence—mention the name of the original author *in your paper*. Note that in the next example the writer simply cites the source at the end of the paragraph, not naming the source in the text. Doing so makes it hard for the reader to figure out whether Blager is the source of the information in the entire paragraph or just part of it:

> Though children who have been sexually abused
> seem to be disadvantaged in many areas,
> including the inability to forge lasting
> relationships, low self-esteem, and crippling
> shame, they seem advantaged in other areas.
> Sexually abused children seem to be more
> socially mature than other children of their
> same age group. It's a distinctly mixed
> blessing (Blager 994).

In the following example, notice how the ambiguity about what's borrowed and what's not is resolved by careful placement of the author's name and parenthetical citation in the text:

```
Though children who have been sexually abused
seem to be disadvantaged in many areas, including
the inability to forge lasting relationships, low
self-esteem, and crippling shame, they seem
advantaged in other areas. According to Blager,
sexually abused children seem to be more socially
mature than other children of their same age
group (994). It's a distinctly mixed blessing.
```

Citations That Go with the Flow

There's no getting around it—parenthetical citations can be like stones on the sidewalk. Readers stride through a sentence in your essay and then have to step around the citation at the end before they resume their walk. Yet citations are important in academic writing because they help readers know who you read or heard that shaped your thinking.

However, you can minimize citations that trip up readers and make your essay more readable.

- Avoid lengthy parenthetical citations by mentioning the name of the author in your essay. That way, you usually only have to include a page number in the citation.
- Try to place citations where readers are likely to pause anyway—for example, the end of the sentence, or right before a comma.
- Remember you *don't* need a citation when you're citing common knowledge or referring to an entire work by an author.
- If you're borrowing from only one source in a paragraph of your essay, and all of the borrowed material comes from a single page of that source, don't bother repeating the citation over and over again with each new bit of information. Just put the citation at the end of the paragraph.

In this latter version, it's clear that Blager is the source for one sentence in the paragraph, and the writer is responsible for the rest. Generally, use an authority's last name, rather than a formal title or first name, when mentioning her in your text. Also note that the citation is placed *inside* the period of the sentence (or last sentence) that it documents. That's almost always the case, except at the end of a blocked quotation, where the parenthetical reference is placed after the period of the last sentence. The citation can also be placed near the author's name, rather than at the end of the sentence, if it doesn't unnecessarily break the flow of the sentence. For example:

```
Blager (994) observes that sexually abused
children tend to be more socially mature than
other children of their same age group.
```

1.2.2 WHEN YOU MENTION THE AUTHOR'S NAME

It's generally good practice in research writing to identify who said what. The familiar convention of using attribution tags such as "According to Fletcher . . . " or "Fletcher argues . . . " and so on helps readers attach a name with a voice, or an individual with certain claims or findings. When you do mention the author of a source, then you can drop his or her name for the parenthetical citation and just list the page number. For example,

```
Robert Harris believes that there is "widespread
uncertainty" among students about what consti-
tutes plagiarism (2).
```

You may also list the page number directly after the author's name.

```
Robert Harris (2) believes that there is
"widespread uncertainty" among students about
what constitutes plagiarism.
```

1.2.3 WHEN THERE IS NO AUTHOR

Occasionally, you may encounter a source in which the author is anonymous—the article doesn't have a byline, or for some reason the author hasn't been identified. This isn't unusual with pamphlets, editorials, government documents, some newspaper articles, online sources, and short filler articles in magazines. If you can't parenthetically name the author, what do you cite?

Most often, cite the title (or an abbreviated version, if the title is long) and the page number. If you choose to abbreviate the title, begin with the word under which it is alphabetized in the "Works Cited" list. For example:

```
Simply put, public relations is "doing good and
getting credit" for it (Getting Yours 3).
```

Here is how the publication cited above would be listed at the back of the paper:

```
Works Cited

Getting Yours: A Publicity and Funding Primer
      for Nonprofit and Voluntary Organizations.
Lincoln: Contact Center, 2008. Print.
```

For clarity, it's helpful to mention the original source of the borrowed material in the text of your paper. When there is no author's name, refer to the publication (or institution) you're citing or make a more general reference to the source. For example:

```
An article in Cuisine magazine argues that the
best way to kill a lobster is to plunge a knife
between its eyes ("How to Kill" 56).
```

   or

```
According to one government report, with the
current minimum size limit, most lobsters
end up on dinner plates before they've had
a chance to reproduce ("Size" 3-4).
```

1.2.4 WORKS BY THE SAME AUTHOR

Suppose you end up using several books or articles by the same author. Obviously, a parenthetical citation that merely lists the author's name and page number won't do, since it won't be clear *which* of several works the citation refers to. In this case, include the author's name, an abbreviated title (if the original is too long), and the page number. For example:

> The thing that distinguishes the amateur from
> the experienced writer is focus; one "rides off
> in all directions at once," and the other finds
> one meaning around which everything revolves
> (Murray, *Write to Learn* 92).

The "Works Cited" list would show multiple works by one author as follows:

> Works Cited
>
> Murray, Donald M. *Write to Learn*. 8th ed.
>
>   Boston: Heinle, 2004. Print.
>
> ---. *A Writer Teaches Writing*. Boston:
>
>   Heinle, 2004. Print.

It's obvious from the parenthetical citation which of the two Murray books is the source of the information. Note that in the parenthetical reference, no punctuation separates the title and the page number, but a comma follows the author's name. If Murray had been mentioned in the text of the paper, his name could have been dropped from the citation.

How to handle the "Works Cited" list is explained more fully later in this appendix, but for now, notice that the three hyphens used in the second entry are meant to signal that the author's name in this source is the same as in the preceding entry.

1.2.5 INDIRECT SOURCES

Whenever you can, cite the original source for material you use. For example, if an article on television violence quotes the author of a book and you want to use the quote, try to hunt down the book. That way, you'll be certain of the accuracy of the quote and you may find some more usable information.

Sometimes, however, finding the original source is not possible. In those cases, use the term *qtd. in* to signal that you've quoted or paraphrased a quotation from a book or article that initially appeared elsewhere. In the following example, the citation signals that Bacon's quote was culled from an article by Guibroy, not Bacon's original work:

> Francis Bacon also weighed in on the dangers of imitation, observing that "it is hardly possible at once to admire an author and to go beyond him" (qtd. in Guibroy 113).

1.2.6 PERSONAL INTERVIEWS

If you mention the name of your interview subject in your text, no parenthetical citation is necessary. On the other hand, if you don't mention the subject's name, cite it in parentheses after the quote:

> Instead, the recognizable environment gave something to kids they could relate to. "And it had a lot more real quality to it than, say, *Mister Rogers* . . . ," says one educator. "Kids say the reason they don't like *Mister Rogers* is that it's unbelievable" (Diamonti).

Regardless of whether you mention your subject's name, you should include a reference to the interview in the "Works Cited." In this case, the reference would look like this:

> Works Cited
>
> Diamonti, Nancy. Personal Interview. 5 Nov. 1999.

1.2.7 SEVERAL SOURCES IN A SINGLE CITATION

Suppose two sources both contributed the same information in a paragraph of your essay? Or perhaps even more common is when you're summarizing the findings of several authors on a certain topic—a fairly common move when you're trying to establish a context for your own research question. How do you cite multiple authors in a single citation? In the usual fashion, using author name and page number, but separating each with a semicolon. For example,

> A whole range of studies have looked closely at the intellectual development of college

```
students, finding that they generally

assume "stages" or "perspectives" that

differ from subject to subject (Perry 122;

Belenky et al. 12).
```

If you can, however, avoid long citations because they can be cumbersome for readers.

Sample Parenthetical References for Other Sources. MLA format is pretty simple, and we've already covered some of the basic variations. You should also know five additional variations, as follow:

1.2.8 AN ENTIRE WORK

If you mention the author's name in the text, no citation is necessary. The work should, however, be listed in the "Works Cited."

```
Leon Edel's Henry James is considered by many to

be a model biography.
```

1.2.9 A VOLUME OF A MULTIVOLUME WORK

If you're working with one volume of a multivolume work, it's a good idea to mention which volume in the parenthetical reference. The citation below attributes the passage to the second volume, page 3, of a work by Baym and three or more other authors. The volume number always precedes the colon, which is followed by the page number:

```
By the turn of the century, three authors

dominated American literature: Mark Twain,

Henry James, and William Dean Howells (Baym

et al. 2: 3).
```

1.2.10 SEVERAL SOURCES FOR A SINGLE PASSAGE

Occasionally, a number of sources may contribute to a single passage. List them all in one parenthetical reference, separated by semicolons:

```
American soccer may never achieve the popu-

larity it enjoys in the rest of the world, an

unfortunate fact that is integrally related to
```

the nature of the game itself (Gardner 12;
"Selling Soccer" 30).*

1.2.11 A LITERARY WORK

Because so many literary works, particularly classics, have
been reprinted in so many editions, it's useful to give readers more
information about where a passage can be found in one of these editions. List the page number and then the chapter number (and any
other relevant information, such as the section or volume), separated
by a semicolon. Use arabic rather than roman numerals, unless your
teacher instructs you otherwise:

> Izaak Walton warns that "no direction can be
> given to make a man of a dull capacity able to
> make a Flie well" (130; ch. 5).

When citing classic poems or plays, instead of page numbers,
cite line numbers and other appropriate divisions (book, section, act,
scene, part, etc.). Separate the information with periods. For
example, (*Othello* 2.3.286) indicates act 2, scene 3, line 286 of
Shakespeare's work.

1.2.12 AN ONLINE SOURCE

In most cases, online documents don't have page numbers,
though you may find that when you print out the material, the
printer assigns page numbers, usually beginning with "1." The key
question to ask yourself is this: Are these numbers *permanent?* This
is usually not the case. Different printers might give electronic documents different page numbers.

When a document or Web page lacks permanent page numbers
you don't need to include them in your parenthetical citation. For
example, here's a passage from an authorless article from the Web
that lacks page numbers. The citation would therefore just include
the title of the page in quotation marks.

> Many women who wait to begin a family may
> wonder if prior birth control choices nega-
> tively affect their fertility. It's not
> uncommon, for instance, for a woman to take

---

*Jason Pulsifer, University of New Hampshire, 1991. Used with permission.

```
oral  contraceptives  for  10  years  or  longer.  The
birth  control  pill  itself  doesn't  affect  long-
term  fertility  ("Infertility:  Key  Q  and  A").
```

On the other hand, PDF files frequently have permanent pagination, particularly if the document is a copy of the original article. In that case, the page numbers should be used in your citation.

Part Two: Format

2.1 The Layout

There is, well, a certain fussiness associated with the look of academic papers. The reason for it is quite simple—academic disciplines generally aim for consistency in format so that readers of scholarship know exactly where to look to find what they want to know. It's a matter of efficiency. How closely you must follow the MLA's requirements for the layout of your essay is up to your instructor, but it's really not that complicated. A lot of what you need to know is featured in Figure B1.

2.1.1 PRINTING

Print your paper on white, $8\frac{1}{2}$" × 11" paper. Make sure the printer has sufficient ink or toner.

2.1.2 MARGINS AND SPACING

The old high school trick is to have big margins. That way, you can get the length without the information. Don't try that trick with this paper. Leave one-inch margins at the top, bottom, and sides of your pages. Indent the first line of each paragraph five spaces and blocked quotes ten spaces. Double-space all of the text, including blocked quotes and "Works Cited."

2.1.3 TITLE PAGE

Your paper doesn't need a separate title page. Begin with the first page of text. One inch below the top of the page, type your name,

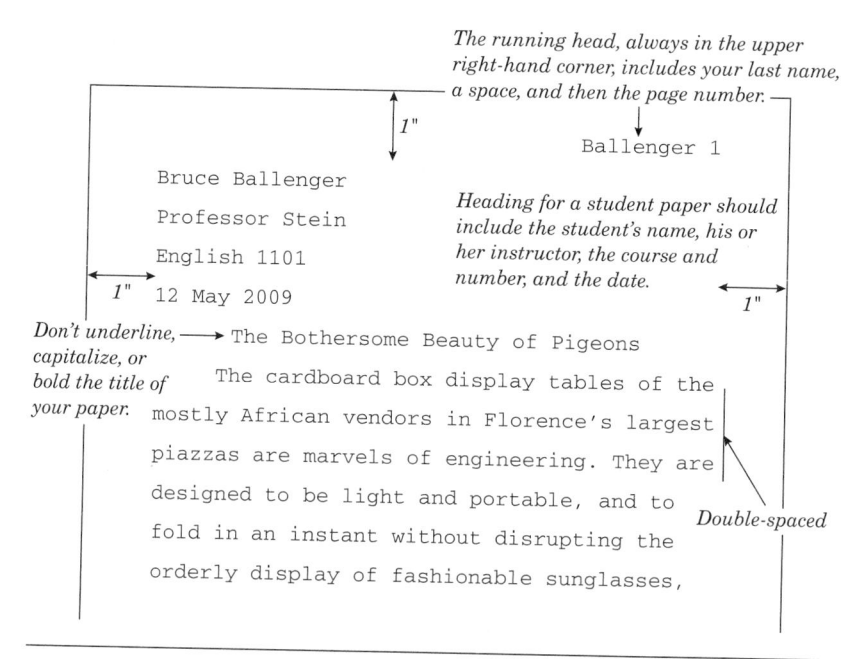

The running head, always in the upper right-hand corner, includes your last name, a space, and then the page number.

1"

Ballenger 1

Bruce Ballenger

Professor Stein

English 1101

1" 12 May 2009

Heading for a student paper should include the student's name, his or her instructor, the course and number, and the date.

1"

Don't underline, → The Bothersome Beauty of Pigeons
capitalize, or
bold the title of   The cardboard box display tables of the
your paper.   mostly African vendors in Florence's largest

piazzas are marvels of engineering. They are

designed to be light and portable, and to   *Double-spaced*

fold in an instant without disrupting the

orderly display of fashionable sunglasses,

FIGURE B1   **The Basic Look of an MLA-Style Paper**

your instructor's name, the course number, and the date (see following). Below that, type the title, centered on the page. Begin the text of the paper below the title.

    Karoline Ann Fox

    Professor Dethier

    English 401

    15 December 2008

        Metamorphosis, the Exorcist,

           and Oedipus

    Ernst Pawel has said that Franz Kafka's *The*

Metamorphosis . . . *

---

*Reprinted with permission of Karoline A. Fox.

Note that every line is double-spaced. The title is not italicized (unless it includes the name of a book or some other work that should be italicized) or boldfaced.

2.1.4 PAGINATION

Make sure that every page after the first one is numbered. That's especially important with long papers. Type your last name and the page number in the upper-righthand corner, flush with the right margin: Ballenger 3. Don't use the abbreviation *p.* or a hyphen between your name and the number.

2.1.5 PLACEMENT OF TABLES, CHARTS, AND ILLUSTRATIONS

With MLA format, papers do not have appendixes. Tables, charts, and illustrations are placed in the body of the paper, close to the text that refers to them. Number illustrations consecutively (Table 1 or Figure 3), and indicate sources below them (see Figure B2). If you use a chart or illustration from another text, give the full citation. Place any table caption above the table, flush left. Captions for illustrations or diagrams are usually placed below them.

2.1.6 HANDLING TITLES

The MLA guidelines about handling titles are, as the most recent *Handbook* observes, "strict." The general rule is that the writer should capitalize the first letters of all principal words in a title, including any that follow hyphens. The exceptions include

Table 1   Percentage of Students Who Self-Report Acts of Plagiarism

Acts of Plagiarism	Never/ Rarely	Some- times	Often/ Very Freq.
Copy text without citation	71	19	10
Copy paper without citation	91	5	3
Request paper to hand in	90	5	2
Purchase paper to hand in	91	6	3

Source: Scanlon, Patrick M., and David R. Neumann; "Internet Plagiarism among College Students," *Journal of College Student Development* 43.3 (2002): 379; print.

FIGURE B2   **Example of Format for a Table**

articles (*a, an,* and *the*), prepositions (*for, of, in, to*), coordinating conjunctions (*and, or, but, for*), and the use of *to* in infinitives. These exceptions apply *only if the words appear in the middle of a title;* capitalize them if they appear at the beginning or end.

In May 2008, the MLA updated its citation style, and among the changes is a no-brainer in this era of word processing: a shift to *italicizing* titles of works rather than <u>underlining</u> them. The APA figured this out about a decade ago.

The new rules for deciding whether to italicize a title or place it in quotation marks (the usual alternative) makes this distinction:

1. If the work is "published independently," italicize it. These works are typically books, Web sites, online databases, TV broadcasts, plays, periodicals, and so on.
2. If the title is part of a larger work—say, an article in a periodical or an episode of a TV program—then place it in quotation marks.

Here are some examples:

The Curious Researcher (book)

A Streetcar Named Desire (play)

"Once More to the Lake" (essay in a collection)

New York Times (newspaper)

"Psychotherapy" (encyclopedia article)

2.1.7 LANGUAGE AND STYLE

Names.   Though it may seem as if you're on familiar terms with some of the authors you cite by the end of your research project, it's not a good idea to call them by their first names. Typically, initially give the full names of people you cite, and then only their last names if you mention them again in your essay.

Ellipsis Points.   Those are the three (always three) dots that indicate you've left out a word, phrase, or even whole section of a quoted passage. It's often wise to do this since you want to emphasize only certain parts of a quotation rather than burden your reader with unnecessary information, but be careful to preserve the basic intention and idea of the author's original statement. Ellipsis points can come at the beginning of a quotation, in the middle, or at the end, depending where it is you've omitted material. For example,

> "After the publication of a controversial picture that shows, for example, either dead or grieving victims . . . , readers in telephone calls and in letters to the editor, often attack the photographer for being tasteless . . . "

Quotations.   Quotations that run more than four lines long should be blocked, or indented ten spaces from the left margin. The quotation should be double-spaced and quotation marks should be omitted. In an exception from the usual convention, the parenthetical citation is placed *outside* the period at the end of the quotation. A colon is a customary way to introduce a blocked quotation. For example,

> Chris Sherman and Gary Price, in *The Invisible Web*, contend that much of the Internet, possibly most, is beyond the reach of researchers who use conventional search engines:
>
> > The problem is that vast expanses of the Web are completely invisible to general-purpose search engines like AltaVista, HotBot, and Google. Even worse, this "Invisible Web" is in all likelihood growing significantly faster than the visible Web that you're familiar with. It's not that search engines and Web directories are "stupid" or even badly engineered. Rather, they simply can't "see" millions of high quality resources that are available exclusively on the Invisible Web. So what is this Invisible Web and

```
why aren't search engines doing anything
about it to make it visible? (xxi)
```

Part Three:
Preparing the "Works Cited" Page

The "Works Cited" page ends the paper. (This may also be called the "References Cited" or "Sources Cited" page, depending on the nature of your sources or the preferences of your instructor.) In the old footnote system (which, by the way, is still used in some humanities disciplines), this section used to be called "Endnotes" or "Bibliography." There are also several other lists of sources that may appear at the end of a research paper. An "Annotated List of Works Cited" not only lists the sources used in the paper but also includes a brief description of each. A "Works Consulted" list includes sources that may or may not have been cited in the paper but shaped your thinking. A "Content Notes" page, keyed to superscript numbers in the text of the paper, lists short commentaries or asides that are significant but not central enough to the discussion to be included in the text of the paper.

The "Works Cited" page is the workhorse of most college papers. The other source lists are used less often. "Works Cited" is essentially an alphabetical listing of all the sources you quoted, paraphrased, or summarized in your paper. If you have used MLA format for citing sources, your paper has numerous parenthetical references to authors and page numbers. The "Works Cited" page provides complete information on each source cited in the text for the reader who wants to know. (In APA format, this page is called "References" and is only slightly different in how items are listed.)

In March 2009, the Modern Language Association (MLA) changed the citation rules for "Works Cited" pages. A groan issued from classrooms across America. But it's not so bad. Really. The changes actually make sense. Here are the highlights:

1. **Italics good, underlining bad.** From now on the titles of independent works (i.e., books, periodicals, Web sites, and so on) in citations are to be italicized rather than underlined. Welcome to the 21st century.

2. **Adios to long and ugly Web addresses.** Unless your online source can't be found any other way, you no longer have to include the URL for the source in your citation.

3. **Provide a medium.** Every source citation now indicates the "medium of publication." The most common are the following: Print, Web, Film, CD, Performance, Interview, Video, and Audio.

3.1 Format

Alphabetizing the List. "Works Cited" follows the text of your paper on a separate page. After you've assembled complete information about each source you've cited, put the sources in alphabetical order by the last name of the author. If the work has multiple authors, use the last name of the first listed. If the source has no author, then alphabetize it by the first key word of the title. If you're citing more than one source by a single author, you don't need to repeat the name for each source; simply place three dashes followed by a period (---.) for the author's name in subsequent listings.

Indenting and Spacing. Type the first line of each entry flush left, and indent subsequent lines of that entry (if any) five spaces. Double-space between each line and each entry. For example:

```
                                          Hall 10

                    Works Cited
Biernacki, Patrick. Pathways from Heroin
     Addiction. Philadelphia: Temple UP, 1986.
     Print.
Brill, Leon. The De-Addiction Process. Springfield:
     Thomas, 1972. Print.
Epstein, Joan F., and Joseph C. Gfroerer. "Heroin
     Abuse in the United States." National Clear-
     inghouse for Alcohol and Drug Information. US
     Dept. of Health and Human Services, Aug.
     1997. Web. 24 Nov. 2008.
Hall, Lonny. Personal interview. 1 Mar. 2009.
Kaplan, John. The Hardest Drug: Heroin and Public
     Policy. Chicago: U of Chicago P, 1983. Print.
"Methadone." Encyclopaedia Britannica. 1999 ed.
     1999. CD-ROM.
```

Shaffner, Nicholas. *Saucerful of Secrets: The Pink Floyd Odyssey*. New York: Dell, 1992. Print.

Strang, John, and Michael Gossop. *Heroin Addiction and Drug Policy: The British System*. New York: Oxford UP, 1994. Print.

Swift, Wendy, et al. "Transitions between Routes of Heroin Administration: A Study of Caucasian and Indochinese Users in South-Western Sydney, Australia." *Addiction* (1999): 71-82. Print.

3.2 Citing Nonperiodical Publications (Books)

You usually need three pieces of information to cite a book: the name of the author or authors, the title, and the publication information. Occasionally, other information is required. The *MLA Handbook** lists this additional information in the order it would appear in the citation. Remember, any single entry will include a few of these things, not all of them. Use whichever are relevant to the source you're citing.

1. Name of the author
2. Title of the book (or part of it)
3. Number of edition used
4. Number of volume used
5. Where published, by whom, and the date
6. Page numbers used
7. Medium of publication (*Print*)
8. Name of the series
9. Any annotation you'd like to add.

Each piece of information in a citation is followed by a period and one space (not two).

Title. As a rule, the titles of books are italicized, with the first letters of all principal words capitalized, including those in any subtitles. Titles that are not italicized are usually those of pieces found

---

*Modern Language Association, *MLA Handbook for Writers of Research Papers*, 7th ed. (New York: MLA, 2009). Print.

within larger works, such as poems and short stories in anthologies. These titles are set off by quotation marks. Titles of religious works (the Bible, the Koran) are neither italicized nor enclosed within quotation marks. (See the guidelines in "Handling Titles," in Part Two.)

Edition.   If a book doesn't indicate any edition number, then it's probably a first edition, a fact you don't need to cite. Look on the title page. Signal an edition like this: *2nd ed., 3rd ed.,* and so on.

Publication Place, Publisher, and Date.   Look on the title page to find out who published the book. Publishers' names are usually shortened in the "Works Cited" list: for example, *St. Martin's Press, Inc.,* is shortened to *St. Martin's.*

It's sometimes confusing to know what to cite about the publication place, since several cities are often listed on the title page. Cite the first. For books published outside the United States, add the country name along with the city to avoid confusion.

The date a book is published is usually indicated on the copyright page. If several dates or several printings by the same publisher are listed, cite the original publication date. However, if the book is a revised edition, give the date of that edition. One final variation: If you're citing a book that's a reprint of an original edition, give both dates. For example:

```
Stegner, Wallace. Recapitulation. 1979. Lincoln:

    U of Nebraska P, 1986. Print.
```

This book was first published in 1979 and then republished in 1986 by the University of Nebraska Press.

Page Numbers.   Normally, you don't list page numbers of a book. The parenthetical reference in your paper specifies that. But if you use only part of a book—an introduction or an essay—list the appropriate page numbers following the publication date. Use periods to set off the page numbers. If the author or editor of the entire work is also the author of the introduction or essay you're citing, list her by last name only in subsequent citations. For example:

```
Lee, L. L., and Merrill Lewis. Preface. Women,

    Women Writers, and the West. Ed. Lee and

    Lewis. Troy: Whitston, 1980. v-ix. Print.
```

Sample Book Citations

3.2.1 A BOOK BY ONE AUTHOR

Armstrong, Karen. *The Spiral Staircase*. New
York: Knopf, 2004. Print.

In-Text Citation: (Armstrong 22)

3.2.2 A BOOK BY TWO AUTHORS

Ballenger, Bruce, and Michelle Payne. *The Curious
Reader*. New York: Longman, 2006. Print.

In-Text Citation: (Ballenger and Payne 14)

3.2.3 A BOOK WITH MORE THAN THREE AUTHORS
If a book has more than three authors, list the first and substitute the term *et al.* for the others.

Jones, Hillary, et al. *The Unmasking of Adam*.
Highland Park: Pegasus, 1992. Print.

In-Text Citation: (Jones et al. 21-30)

3.2.4 SEVERAL BOOKS BY THE SAME AUTHOR

Baldwin, James. *Tell Me How Long the Train's Been
Gone*. New York: Dell-Doubleday, 1968. Print.

---. *Going to Meet the Man*. New York: Dell-
Doubleday, 1948. Print.

In-Text Citation: (Baldwin, *Going* 34)

3.2.5 AN ENTIRE COLLECTION OR ANTHOLOGY

Crane, R. S., ed. *Critics and Criticism:
Ancient and Modern*. Chicago: U of
Chicago P, 1952. Print.

In-Text Citation: (Crane xx)

3.2.6 A WORK IN A COLLECTION OR ANTHOLOGY

The title of a work that is part of a collection but was originally published as a book should be underlined. Otherwise, the title of a work in a collection should be enclosed in quotation marks.

Bahktin, Mikhail. *Marxism and the Philosophy of Language*. *The Rhetorical Tradition*. Ed. Patricia Bizzell and Bruce Herzberg. New York: St. Martin's, 1990. 928-44. Print.

In-Text Citation: (Bahktin 929-31)

Jones, Robert F. "Welcome to Muskie Country." *The Ultimate Fishing Book*. Ed. Lee Eisenberg and DeCourcy Taylor. Boston: Houghton, 1981. 122-34. Print.

In-Text Citation: (Jones 131)

3.2.7 AN INTRODUCTION, PREFACE, FOREWORD, OR PROLOGUE

Scott, Jerie Cobb. Foreword. *Writing Groups: History, Theory, and Implications*. By Ann Ruggles Gere. Carbondale: Southern Illinois UP, 1987. ix-xi. Print.

In-Text Citation: (Scott x-xi)

Rich, Adrienne. Introduction. *On Lies, Secrets, and Silence*. By Rich. New York: Norton, 1979. 9-18. Print.

In-Text Citation: (Rich 12)

3.2.8 A BOOK WITH NO AUTHOR

American Heritage Dictionary. 4th ed. Boston: Houghton, 2000. Print.

In-Text Citation: (*American Heritage Dictionary* 444)

3.2.9 AN ENCYLOPEDIA

"City of Chicago." *Encyclopaedia Britannica.*
1999 ed. Print.

In-Text Citation: ("City of Chicago" 397)

Citing online encyclopedias is a bit different from citing paper ones. Online versions should include the name of the publisher or sponsor of the Web site and the date you accessed the site. It's also common that online encyclopedias lack page numbers.

"Diarrhea." *Columbia Encyclopedia Online.*
Columbia UP, 2008. Web. 10 June 2008.

In-Text Citation: ("Diarrhea")

Wikipedia raises eyebrows among many academics who don't consider it a particularly authoritative source, but should you need to cite it, include the date and time of the latest revision of the page you're citing.

"Social Networking Services." *Wikipedia.*
Wikimedia Foundation, 7 June 2008. Web.
11 June 2008.

In-Text Ciation: ("Social Networking")

3.2.10 A BOOK WITH AN INSTITUTIONAL AUTHOR

Hospital Corporation of America. *Employee Benefits Handbook.* Nashville: HCA, 2004.
Print.

In-Text Citation: (Hospital Corporation of America 5-7)

3.2.11 A BOOK WITH MULTIPLE VOLUMES

Include the number of volumes in the work between the title and publication information.

```
Baym, Nina, ed. The Norton Anthology of American
    Literature. 6th ed. 2 vols. New York:
    Norton, 2002. Print.
```

In-Text Citation: (Baym 2: 3)

If you use one volume of a multivolume work, indicate which one along with the page numbers, adding the total number of volumes in the work as supplementary information.

```
Anderson, Sherwood. "Mother." The Norton Anthol-
    ogy of American Literature. Ed. Nina Baym
    6th ed. Vol 2. New York: Norton, 2002.
    1115-31. Print. 2 vols.
```

In-Text Citation: (Anderson 1115)

3.2.12 A BOOK THAT IS NOT A FIRST EDITION

Check the title page to determine whether the book is *not* a first edition (2nd, 3rd, 4th, etc.); if no edition number is mentioned, assume it's the first. Put the edition number right after the title.

```
Ballenger, Bruce. The Curious Researcher.
    5th ed. Boston: Longman, 2007. Print.
```

In-Text Citation: (Ballenger 194)

Citing the edition is necessary only for books that are *not* first editions. This includes revised editions (*Rev. ed.*) and abridged editions (*Abr. ed.*).

3.2.13 A BOOK PUBLISHED BEFORE 1900

For a book this old, it's usually unnecessary to list the publisher.

```
Hitchcock, Edward. Religion of Geology.
    Glasgow, 1851. Print.
```

In-Text Citation: (Hitchcock 48)

3.2.14 A TRANSLATION

Montaigne, Michel de. *Essays*. Trans. J. M. Cohen.

Middlesex: Penguin, 1958. Print.

In-Text Citation: (Montaigne 638)

3.2.15 GOVERNMENT DOCUMENTS

Because of the enormous variety of government documents, citing them properly can be a challenge. Since most government documents do not name authors, begin an entry for such a source with the level of government (U.S. Government, State of Illinois, etc., unless it is obvious from the title), followed by the sponsoring agency, the title of the work, and the publication information. Look on the title page to determine the publisher. If it's a federal document, then the *Government Printing Office* (abbreviated *GPO*) is usually the publisher.

United States. Bureau of the Census. *Statistical*

Abstract of the United States. Washington:

GPO, 1990. Print.

In-Text Citation: (United States, Bureau of the

Census 79-83)

3.2.16 A BOOK THAT WAS REPUBLISHED

A fairly common occurrence, particularly in literary study, is to find a book that was republished, sometimes many years after the original publication date. In addition, some books first appear in hard cover and then are republished in paperback. To cite, put the original date of publication immediately after the book's title, and then include the more current publication date, as usual, at the end of the citation. Do it like so:

Ballenger, Bruce, and Barry Lane. *Discovering*

the Writer Within: 40 Days to More

Imaginative Writing. 1989. Shoreham:

Discover Writing P, 2008. Print.

In-Text Citation: (Ballenger and Lane 31)

3.2.17 AN ONLINE BOOK

Citing a book you found online requires more information than the usual citation for a book you can hold in your hands. As usual, include the author's name (if listed), an italicized title, and publication information. What you include in publication information depends on whether the text was published exclusively online or is also based on a print version. If only a digital book, include the date of electronic publication and the group or organization that sponsored it. If the book also appeared on paper, add the usual information (if provided) about the print version (city of publication, publisher, and date). The citation ends, finally, with the medium of publication (*Web*) and the date you accessed the title. For example,

> Badke, William. *Research Strategies: Finding Your*
> *Way through the Information Fog.* Lincoln:
> Writers Club P, 2000. *iUniverse.* Web.
> 12 July 2008.

In-Text Citation: (Badke)

3.3 Citing Periodical Print Publications

Periodicals—magazines, newspapers, journals, and similar publications that appear regularly—are cited similarly to books but sometimes involve different information, such as date, volume, and page numbers. Online articles have their own special requirement (see Section 3.5). The *MLA Handbook* lists the information to include in a periodical citation in the order in which it should appear:

1. Name of the author
2. Article title
3. Periodical title
4. Series number or name
5. Volume number
6. Issue number
7. Date
8. Page numbers
9. Medium of publication (*Print*)

Author's Name.   List the author(s) as you would for a book citation.

Article Title.   Unlike book titles, article titles are usually enclosed in quotation marks.

Periodical Title.   Italicize periodical titles, dropping introductory articles (*Aegis,* not *The Aegis*). If you're citing a newspaper your readers may not be familiar with, include in the title—enclosed in brackets but not underlined—the city in which it was published. For example:

```
MacDonald, Mary. "Local Hiker Freezes to
     Death." Foster's Daily Democrat [Dover, NH]
     28 Jan. 1992: 1. Print.
```

Volume Number.   Most academic journals are numbered as volumes (or occasionally feature series numbers); the volume number should be included in the citation. Popular periodicals sometimes have volume numbers, too, but these are not included in the citations. Indicate the volume number immediately after the journal's name. Omit the tag *vol.* before the number.

Issue Number. Most scholarly journals have issue numbers as well as volume numbers. Include the issue number in your citation if one is given. Cite the volume number, then a period, followed by the issue number, with no space between the period and the issue number. Volume 12, issue 1, would appear in your citation as "12.1."

Date.   When citing popular periodicals, include the day, month, and year of the issue you're citing—in that order—following the periodical name. Academic journals are a little different. Since the issue number indicates when the journal was published within a given year, just indicate that year. Put it in parentheses following the volume number and before the page numbers (see examples following).

Page Numbers.   Include the page numbers of the article at the end of the citation, followed by a period. Just list the pages of the entire article, omitting abbreviations such as *p.* or *pp.* It's common for articles in newspapers and popular magazines *not* to run on consecutive pages. In that case, indicate the page on which the article begins, followed by a "+" *(12+)*.

Newspaper pagination can be peculiar. Some papers wed the section (usually a letter) with the page number *(A4)*; other papers simply begin numbering anew in each section. Most, however, paginate continuously. See the following sample citations for newspapers for how to deal with these peculiarities.

Online sources, which often have no pagination at all, present special problems. For guidance on how to handle them, see the section "Citing Web Publications" later in this part of the appendix.

Sample Periodical Citations

3.3.1 A MAGAZINE ARTICLE

```
Oppenheimer, Todd. "The Computer Delusion."
     Atlantic Monthly July 1997: 47-60.
     Print.
```

In-Text Citation: (Oppenheimer 48)

```
Zimmer, Marc. "How to Find Students' Inner
     Geek." Chronicle of Higher Education
     12 Aug. 2005: B5. Print.
```

In-Text Citation: (Zimmer B5)

3.3.2 A JOURNAL ARTICLE

For articles in scholarly journals, include both the volume and issue numbers (unless there is no issue number).

```
Allen, Rebecca E., and J. M. Oliver.
     "The Effects of Child Maltreatment
     on Language Development." Child Abuse
     and Neglect 6.2 (1982): 299-305.
     Print.
```

In-Text Citation: (Allen and Oliver 299-300)

```
Goody, Michelle M., and Andrew S. Levine.
     "Health-Care Workers and Occupational
     Exposure to AIDS." Nursing Management
     23.1 (1992): 59-60. Print.
```

In-Text Citation: (Goody and Levine 59)

Increasingly, researchers turn to online library databases to search for journal articles. A fuller discussion of how to cite articles from academic databases follows in Section 3.5, but here is the basic format: Cite the article as you would a print periodical, then add the title of the database in italics, the medium of publication (*Web*), and the date you accessed the article.

> Boettger, Suzaan. "Global Warnings." *Art in*
> *America* June-July 2008: 154-60. *Academic*
> *OneFile*. Web. 10 June 2008.

In-Text Citation: (Boettger 154)

3.3.3 A NEWSPAPER ARTICLE

Some newspapers have several editions (morning edition, late edition, national edition), and each may contain different articles. If an edition is listed on the masthead, include it in the citation.

> Mendels, Pamela. "Internet Access
> Spreads to More Classrooms." *New York*
> *Times* 1 Dec. 1999, late ed.: C1+.
> Print.

In-Text Citation: (Mendels C1)

Some papers begin numbering pages anew in each section. In that case, include the section number if it's not part of pagination.

> Brooks, James. "Lobsters on the Brink."
> *Portland Press* 29 Nov. 1999, sec. 2: 4.
> Print.

In-Text Citation: (Brooks 4)

Increasingly, full-text newspaper articles are available online using library databases such as Newspaper Source or through the newspapers themselves. Citing newspaper articles from library databases involves adding information about the name of the database in italics (e.g., *Newspaper Source*), the medium of publication (*Web*), and the date you accessed the article.

Here's what the citation would look like:

```
"Lobsterman Hunts for Perfect Bait."
     AP Online 7 July 2002. Newspaper
     Source. Web. 13 July 2008.
```

In-Text Citation: ("Lobsterman")

Here's an example of a citation for an article I found on the newspaper's own Web site:

```
Sterngold, James. "Lessons from '92 Keep
     Angry City Calm." New York Times.
     New York Times, 10 July 2002. Web.
     12 July 2008.
```

In-Text Citation: (Sterngold)

3.3.4 AN ARTICLE WITH NO AUTHOR

```
"The Understanding." New Yorker 2 Dec.
     1991: 34-35. Print.
```

In-Text Citation: ("Understanding" 35)

3.3.5 AN EDITORIAL

```
"Paid Leave for Parents." Editorial.
     New York Times 1 Dec. 1999: 31.
     Print.
```

In-Text Citation: ("Paid Leave" 31)

Opinion articles harvested from online newspapers include date of publication, the name of the site's publisher, medium of publication (*Web*), and the date of access.

```
McGurn, William. "Obama, Religion, and
     the Public Square." Wall Street
```

Journal. Dow Jones, 8 June 2008. Web. 10 June 2008.

In-Text Citation: (McGurn)

3.3.6 A LETTER TO THE EDITOR

Ault, Gary Owen. "A Suspicious Stench." Letter. *Idaho Statesman* 18 Aug. 2005: 14. Print.

In-Text Citation: (Avlt 14)

3.3.7 A REVIEW

Page, Barbara. Rev. of *Allegories of Cinema: American Film in the Sixties*, by David E. James. *College English* 54 (1992): 945-54. Print.

In-Text Citation: (Page 945-46)

3.3.8 AN ABSTRACT

It's usually better to have the full text of an article for research purposes, but sometimes all you can come up with is an abstract, or short summary of the article that highlights its findings or summarizes its argument. Online databases frequently offer abstracts when they don't feature full-text versions of an article.

To cite an abstract, begin with information about the full version, and then include the information about the source from which you got the abstract. If the title of the source fails to make it obvious that what you are citing is an abstract (i.e., it's not called something such as *Psychological Abstracts*), include the word "abstract" after the original publication information, but don't underline it or put it in quotation marks. In this example, the source of the abstract is a periodical database called MasterFILE Premier. In addition, I include the medium of publication (*Web*) and the date I accessed the abstract online.

Edwards, Rob. "Air-raid Warning." *New Scientist* 14 Aug. 1999: 48-49.

```
Abstract. MasterFILE Premier. Web.

1 May 2009.
```

In-Text Citation: (Edwards)

The following citation is from another useful source of abstracts, the *Dissertation Abstracts International*. In this case, the citation is from the print version of the index.

```
McDonald, James C. "Imitation of Models in the
      History of Rhetoric: Classical, Belletris-
      tic, and Current-Traditional." U of Texas,
      Austin. DAI 48 (1988): 2613A. Print.
```

In-Text Citation: (McDonald 2613A)

3.4 Citing Other Sources

3.4.1 AN INTERVIEW

If you conducted the interview yourself, list your subject's name first, indicate what kind of interview it was (telephone interview, e-mail interview, or personal interview), and provide the date.

```
Hall, Lonny. Personal interview. 1 Mar. 2005.
```

In-Text Citation: (Hall)

Or avoid parenthethical reference altogether by mentioning the subject's name in the text: According to Lonny Hall, . . .

If you're citing an interview done by someone else (perhaps from a book or article) and the title does not indicate that it was an interview, you should, after the subject's name. Always begin the citation with the subject's name.

```
Stegner, Wallace. Interview. Conversations
      with Wallace Stegner. By Richard Eutlain
      and Wallace Stegner. Salt Lake: U of
      Utah P, 1990. Print.
```

In-Text Citation: (Stegner 22)

Or if there are other works by Stegner on the "Works Cited" page:

(Stegner, *Conversations* 22)

As radio and TV interview programs are increasingly archived on the Web, these can be a great source of material for a research essay. In the example below, the interview was on a transcript I ordered from the *Fresh Air* Web site. Note that the national network, National Public Radio, *and* the local affiliate that produced the program, WHYY, are included in the citation along with the air date.

Mairs, Nancy. Interview. *Fresh Air*. Natl. Public
    Radio. WHYY, Philadelphia, 7 June 1993.
    Web. 15 Apr. 2009.

In-Text Citation: (Mairs)

The following citation is for an interview published on the Web. The second date listed is the date of access.

Messner, Tammy Faye Bakker. Interview. *The Well*
    Rounded Interview. Well Rounded Entertain-
    ment, Aug. 2000. Web. 14 July 2008.

In-Text Citation: (Messner)

3.4.2 SURVEYS, QUESTIONNAIRES, AND CASE STUDIES

If you conducted the survey or case study, list it under your name and give it an appropriate title.

Ball, Helen. "Internet Survey." Boise State U,
    1999. Print.

In-Text Citation: (Ball)

3.4.3 RECORDINGS

Generally, list a recording by the name of the performer and italicize the title. Also include the recording company, catalog number, and year. (If you don't know the year, use the abbreviation *n.d.*) Include the medium (*CD, Audiocassette, LP*, etc.).

```
Orff, Carl. Carmina Burana. Cond. Seiji Ozawa.

     Boston Symphony. RCA, 6533-2-RG, n.d. CD.
```

In-Text Citation: (Orff)

When citing a single song from a recording, put it in quotation marks:

```
Larkin, Tom. "Emergence." Oceans. Enso, 1997.

     CD.
```

In-Text Citation: (Larkin)

3.4.4 TELEVISION AND RADIO PROGRAMS

List the title of the program (italicized), the station, and the date. If the episode has a title, list that first in quotation marks. You may also want to include the name of the narrator or producer after the title.

```
All Things Considered. Interview with Andre

     Dubus. Natl. Public Radio. WBUR, Boston,

     12 Dec. 1990. Radio.
```

In-Text Citation: (All Things Considered)

```
"U.S. to Limit Sales Related to Amphetamine

     Scourge." All Things Considered. Natl.

     Public Radio. WBUR, Boston, 18 Aug. 2005.

     Radio.
```

In-Text Citation: ("U.S. to Limit")

3.4.5 FILMS, VIDEOTAPES, AND DVDS

Begin with the title (italicized), followed by the director, the distributor, and the year. You may also include names of writers, performers, or producers. End with the date and any other specifics about the characteristics of the film or videotape that may be relevant (length and size).

```
Saving Private Ryan. Dir. Steven Spielberg.

     Perf. Tom Hanks, Tom Sizemore, and Matt

     Damon. Paramount, 1998. Videocassette.
```

In-Text Citation: (Saving)

You can also list a video or film by the name of a contributor you'd like to emphasize.

```
Capra, Frank, dir. It's a Wonderful Life.
     Perf. Jimmy Stewart and Donna Reed. RKO
     Pictures, 1946. Film.
```

In-Text Citation: (Capra)

3.4.6 ARTWORK

List each work by artist. Then cite the title of the work (italicized), the year of its creation, and where it's located (institution and city). If you've reproduced the work from a published source, include that information as well.

```
Homer, Winslow. Casting for a Rise. 1889.
     Hirschl and Adler Galleries, New York.
     Ultimate Fishing Book. Ed. Lee Eisenberg
     and DeCourcy Taylor. Boston: Houghton,
     1981. Print.
```

In-Text Citation: (Homer 113)

3.4.7 AN ADVERTISEMENT

Citing an advertisement in a periodical is straightforward. First list the company behind the ad, then include the word *Advertisement,* followed by publication information.

```
Volkswagen. Advertisement. Men's Health
     August 2005: 115. Print.
```

In-Text Citation: (Volkswagen)

3.4.8 LECTURES AND SPEECHES

List each by the name of the speaker, followed by the title of the address (if any) in quotation marks, the name of the sponsoring organization, the location, and the date. Also indicate what kind of address it was (lecture, speech, etc.).

```
Naynaha, Siskanna. "Emily Dickinson's Last
     Poems." Sigma Tau Delta, Boise, 15 Nov.
     1999. Lecture.
```

Avoid the need for parenthetical citation by mentioning the speaker's name in your text.

3.4.9 PAMPHLETS

Cite a pamphlet as you would a book.

`New Challenges for Wilderness Conservationists.`

   `Washington: Wilderness Society, 1973.`

   `Print.`

In-Text Citation: `(New Challenges)`

3.5 Citing Publications on CD-ROM or DVD-ROM

While the encyclopedia is the most familiar *portable* database on CD-ROM, there are many others, including full-text versions of literary classics, journal article abstracts, indexes, and periodicals. These databases on disk are less common because much of the same information has migrated online, but you will still encounter them. Citation of these materials requires much of the usual information and in the usual order. But it will also include the name of the *vendor,* or company that distributed it (for example, SilverPlatter or UMI-Proquest), and the *date of electronic publication* (or the release date of the disk or tape).

There are two categories of portable databases: (1) those that are issued periodically, like magazines and journals, and (2) those that are not routinely updated, like books. Citing a source in each category requires some slightly different information.

3.5.1 A NONPERIODICAL PUBLICATION ON CD-ROM OR DVD-ROM

This is cited much like a book, with the medium of publication added.

- Author. If no author is given, list the editor or translator, followed by the appropriate abbreviation (*ed., trans.*).
- Publication title (italicized) or title of the portion of the work you're using (if relevant)
- Name of editor, compiler, or translator (if relevant)
- Edition or release or version (if relevant)
- Place of publication
- Name of publisher and date of publication
- Medium of publication (*CD-ROM, DVD-ROM,* etc.)

For example:

> Shakespeare, William. *Romeo and Juliet*. Vers.
>   1.5. New York: CMI, 1995. Diskette.

In-Text Citation: (Shakespeare)

> "Psychotherapy." *Microsoft Encarta*. 2005 ed.
>   Everett: Microsoft, 2006. CD-ROM.

In-Text Citation: ("Psychotherapy")

3.5.2 MATERIAL FROM A PERIODICALLY PUBLISHED DATABASE ON CD-ROM OR DVD-ROM

Frequently a periodical database is a computer version—or an analogue—of a printed publication. For example, *The New York Times* has a disk version, as does *Dissertation Abstracts*. Both databases refer to articles also published in print; therefore, the citation often includes two dates: the original publication date and the electronic publication date. Note the location of each in the citations below.

> Haden, Catherine Ann. "Talking about the Past
>   with Preschool Siblings." *DAI* 56 (1996).
>   Emory U, 1995. CD-ROM. *Dissertation
>   Abstracts Ondisc*. UMI-ProQuest. Mar. 1996.
>
> Kolata, Gina. "Research Links Writing Style to
>   the Risk of Alzheimer's." *New York Times*
>   21 Feb. 1996: A1. CD-ROM. *Newspaper
>   Abstracts*. UMI-ProQuest. 1996.*

In-Text Citation: (Kolata)

Frequently, a periodically issued electronic source doesn't have a printed analogue. In that case, obviously, you can't include publication information about the printed version.

---

*Sometimes information about an electronic source is unavailable. In that case, include what information you have. For example, in this example, I was unable to find the month of publication for the *Newspaper Abstracts* and had to omit that piece of information from the citation.

3.6 Citing Web Publications

So much has changed since I wrote the first edition of *The Curious Researcher* in the early nineties, and I'm not a bit nostalgic. Internet access to academic databases and full-text articles that you can print out at home have made research dramatically more convenient. In addition, Google Scholar has opened up a universe of online information. Academic organizations like the Modern Language Association (MLA), folks who decide the intricacies of citing these online sources, have struggled to keep up with the changes. This edition of *The Curious Researcher* includes the latest citation information as of this writing, but to stay current, always check the latest edition of the *MLA Handbook for Writers of Research Papers* or the *MLA Style Manual*. Multiple copies are usually stashed somewhere in your library's reference room, though you may have to talk to an actual human being to find out where they are.

Electronic-source citations usually include at least two dates: the *date of electronic publication* and the *date of access* (when you visited the site and retrieved the document). There is a good reason for listing both dates: Online documents are changed and updated frequently—when you retrieve the material matters. If the online document you are using originally appeared in print, it might be necessary to include three dates: the print publication date, the online publication date, and your access date.

The most recent MLA style guidelines have streamlined the way sources found on the Web and through online databases are cited. In most cases, you do not need to include a URL or Internet address for your source unless that's the only way a reader would be able to find it.

It's important to remember that you cannot simply copy and paste a URL or bookmark into your list of works cited. Web publications are cited much like print sources are, but you sometimes need to include additional information to tell your readers where and when you accessed an online source.

For a work cited only on the Web, your citation needs to include these elements:

1. The author's name

2. The title of the work

3. The title of the Web site (in italics)

4. The version or edition used (if necessary)

5. The publisher or sponsor of the Web site

6. The date of publication (day, month, year; use *n.d.* if no date is listed)

7. The medium of publication (*Web*)

8. The date you accessed the site (day, month, year)

For example:

Coates, Ta-Nehisi. "Sensitive Thugs, Y'all All
     Need Hugs." *The Atlantic.com.* Atlantic
     Monthly Group, 5 Feb. 2009. Web. 6 Feb.
     2009.

Note: If you cannot find a publisher or sponsor listed for the Web site, use *N.p.*

To cite articles you find through an online database, begin by giving the information for the article as you would for a print source (see Section 3.3 above) and then add the following:

1. The title of the database (in italics)

2. The medium of publication (*Web*)

3. The date you accessed the article (day, month, year)

For example:

Liu, Eric Zhi Feng, and Chun Hung Liu.
     "Developing Evaluative Indicators for
     Educational Computer Games." *British
     Journal of Educational Technology* 40.1

```
(2009): 174-78. Academic Search Complete.
Web. 5 Feb. 2009.
```

Note: If no page numbers are listed, use *n. pag.*

Is It Also in Print?   Databases from computer services or networks feature information available in printed form (like a newspaper or magazine) and online, or information available exclusively online. This distinction is important. If the online source has a printed version, include information about it in the citation. For example:

```
Worth, Robert W. "Sunnis Protest Charter
    as Leaders Struggle to Finalize It."
    New York Times 26 Aug. 2005: A1.
    NYTimes.com. Web. 27 Aug. 2005.
```

In-Text Citation: (Worth)

Note that the first date lists when the print version appeared, the second date when the researcher accessed the document.

Material that appeared online only is somewhat simpler to cite since you'll only need to include information about the electronic version.

```
Beyea, Suzanne C. "Best Practices of
    Safe Medicine Administration."
    Aorn Journal. Apr. 2005. Web. 26
    Aug. 2005.
```

In-Text Citation: No page or paragraph numbers were used in this document, so simply list the author's last name: (Beyea). Or avoid parenthetical citation altogether by mentioning the name of the source in your essay (for example: "According to Suzanne Beyea, medications are . . . ").

You may be missing citation information on some Internet material—like page numbers and publication dates—that are easy to find in printed texts. Use the information that you have. Keep in mind that the relevant information for a citation varies with the type of electronic source.

Sample Online Citations

3.6.1 AN ARTICLE

Ketcham, Christopher. "They Shoot Buffalo,
     Don't They?" *Harper's Magazine*. Harper's
     Magazine Foundation, June 2008. Web.
     10 June 2008.

In-Text Citation: (Ketcham 72)

"Freeman Trial Delayed over Illness."
     USA Today. Gannett, 26 May 2008. Web.
     26 May 2008.

In-Text Citation: ("Freeman")

Dvorak, John C. "Worst Case Scenarios."
     PC Magazine Online. Ziff Davis Media,
     26 May 2008. Web. 1 June 2008.

In-Text Citation: (Dvorak 2)

3.6.2 AN ARTICLE OR ABSTRACT IN A LIBRARY DATABASE

One of the great boons to researchers in recent years is the publication of full-text versions of articles as part of the online databases available on your campus library's Web pages. Quite a few databases, such as MasterFILE or Newspaper Source, offer this service, and more are adding it every year. Some that don't offer full-text versions of articles offer abstracts, and even these can be useful. Citing articles or abstracts from library databases requires some information beyond what is usually required for citing other online articles. Specifically, you need

- The name of the database (e.g., Newspaper Source)
- The date you accessed the database to get the article

All of this information is pretty easy to come up with. Figure B3 lists the Web addresses of some of the most popular of these providers, along with some of the databases each features. Note in the following example that information on the print version of the article is provided first, and then information about the database and its provider is shown.

Database Provider	Databases	Web Address
Britannica Online	Encyclopaedia Britannica	http://www.britannica.com
EBSCOhost	Academic Search Elite, Academic Search Premier, Business Source Elite, Computer Source, Health Source, MasterFile Elite, MasterFile Premier, Newspaper Source, Nursing and Allied Health Collection, World Magazine Bank	http://www.epnet.com
Gale Group Databases	Contemporary Authors, Biography Index, Expanded Academic ASAP, General Business File ASAP, General Reference Center, Health Reference Center, Info Trac, Literary Index	http://www.infotrac.galegroup.com

FIGURE B3   URLs of Popular Databases

The table lists the Web addresses for most of the major companies that provide databases for libraries. Usually a database has a specific name, such as *Expanded Academic ASAP*, as shown in the second column, and then a service that provides it, a name that you can usually find somewhere on the search page of the database. For Expanded Academic ASAP, for example, it's a provider called *Gale Group*, shown in the first column.

FIGURE B3   (Continued)

LexisNexis	Academic Universe, Government Periodicals Universe, History Universe, Statistical Universe	http://www.lexisnexis.com/
OCLC First Search	Art Index, Book Review, Contemporary Women's Issues, EconLit, Essay and General Literature Index, Reader's Guide Abstracts, Social Science Index, WorldCat	http://newfirstsearch. oclc.org
ProQuest	ABI/INFORM, Academic Research Library, Magazine Index, National Newspapers, Wall Street Journal	http://www.bellhowell. infolearning.om/proquest
SilverPlatter/ Web SPIRS	Agricola, Biological Abstracts, CINHAL, EconLit, Essay and General Literature Index, Philosopher's Index, PsychINFO	http://webspirs. silverplatter.com
Wilson Web	Applied Science and Technology Abstracts, Art Index, Bibliographic Index, Biography Index, Book Review Digest, Education Index, General Science Index, Reader's Guide, Humanities Index, Social Science Index, World Authors	http://hwwilsonweb.com/

Winbush, Raymond A. "Back to the Future: Campus Racism in the 21st Century." *Black Collegian* Oct. 2001: 102-03. *Expanded Academic ASAP*. Web. 12 Apr. 2002.

In-Text Citation: (Winbush)

When citing an abstract from a library database, include the word "abstract" in the citation. For example,

```
Erskine, Ruth. "Exposing Racism, Exploring
     Race." Journal of Family Therapy
     24 (2002): 282-97. Abstract. EBSCO
     Online Citations. Web. 3 Dec. 2002.
```

In-Text Citation: (Erskine)

3.6.3 AN ONLINE BOOK

I can't imagine why anyone would read the *Adventures of Huckleberry Finn* online, but it's available, along with thousands of other books and historical documents in electronic form. If you use an online book, remember to include publication information (if available) about the printed version in the citation.

```
Twain, Mark. Adventures of Huckleberry Finn.
     New York: Harper, 1912. Google Book Search.
     Web. 10 Feb. 2008.
```

In-Text Citation: (Twain) Or better yet, since there are no page numbers, mention the author in the text rather than citing him parenthetically: In the *Adventures of Huckleberry Finn*, Twain recreates southern dialect . . .

When citing part of a larger work, include the title of that smaller part in quotation marks before the title of the work. Also notice that the text cited below is part of an online scholarly project. Include the name of the project, the editor and compiler of the work if listed, and its location.

```
Service, Robert. "The Mourners." Rhymes
     of a Red Cross Man. 1916. Ed. A. Light.
     Aug. 1995. Project Gutenberg. Web.
     1 July 2008.
```

In-Text Citation: (Service)

3.6.4 A WEB SITE OR PAGE FROM A WEB SITE

If you're citing a Web site, you're referring to either the entire site or a particular page on it. This distinction is important. A citation for an entire Web site includes its name, when it was posted or revised, the sponsoring organization, date of access, and medium of publication. For example,

Son of Citation Machine. Landmark Project, 2009.

   Web. 12 Feb. 2009.

In-Text Citation: (*Son of Citation Machine*)

More commonly, though, you'll be citing a page on a larger Web site, and this must include not just the title of the Web site but the title of the Web *page* from which you're getting information.

Rogers, Scott. "The Stupid Vote." *The*

   Conservative Voice. Salem Web Network,

   7 June 2008. Web. 10 June 2008

   <http://www.theconservativevoice.com/

   article/32556.html>.

In-Text Citation: (Rogers)

3.6.5 AN ONLINE POSTING

An online post can be a contribution to an e-mail discussion group like a listserv, a post to a bulletin board or usenet group, or a WWW forum. The description *Online posting* is included after the title of the message (usually drawn from the subject line). List the date the material was posted, the access date, and the online address as you would for any other online citation.

Alvoeiro, Jorge. "Neurological Effects of

   Music." Online posting. *sci.psychology.misc*

   Newsgroup. 20 June 1996. Web. 10 Aug. 1996.

In-Text Citation: (Alvoeiro)

The following example is from an e-mail discussion group. The address at the end of the citation is from the group's archives, available on the Web. If you don't have an Internet address for the post you want to cite, include the e-mail address of the group's moderator or supervisor.

Ledgerberg, Joshua. "Re: You Shall Know
    Them." Online posting. 2 May 1997. Dar-
    win Discussion Group. Web. 27 May 2008.

In-Text Citation: (Ledgerberg)

3.6.6 AN E-MAIL MESSAGE

Kriebel, David. "Environmental Address."
    E-mail to the author. 8 June 2008.

In-Text Citation: (Kriebel)

3.6.7 A SOUND CLIP OR PODCAST

Gonzales, Richard. "Asian American Political
    Strength." Natl. Public Radio. 27 May 2008.
    Web. 12 July 2008.

In-Text Citation: (Gonzales)

Mondello, Bob. "Charlton Heston, Old-School
    Gentleman, Dies at 84." 8 May 2008.
    Podcast. "NPR Movies." Natl. Public Radio.
    10 April 2008.

In-Text Citation: (Mondello)

3.6.8 AN ONLINE VIDEO

"Daughter Turns Dad In." Online video clip.
    CNN.com. Cable News Network, 4 Apr. 2008.
    Web. 10 Apr. 2008.

In-Text Citation: ("Daughter Turns")

Shimabukuro, Jake. "Ukelele Weeps by

    Jake Shimabukuro." Online video clip.

    YouTube. You Tube, 4 Apr. 2008. Web.

    6 Apr. 2008.

In-Text Citation: (Shimabukuro)

3.6.9 AN INTERVIEW

Boukreev, Anatoli. Interview. *Outside.*

    Mariah Media, 14 Nov. 2007. Web.

    27 May 2008.

In-Text Citation: (Boukreev)

3.6.10 A BLOG ENTRY OR BLOG COMMENT

For a blog entry, include the author's name, title of the entry, the phrase "Weblog entry," name of the blog, sponsoring organization (if any), date of update, your date of access, and the entry's URL.

Dent, Shirley. "Written on the Body: Literary

    Tattoos." Weblog entry. *The Blog: Books.*

    Guardian News and Media, 9 June 2008.

    Web. 10 June 2008.

In-Text Citation: (Dent)

If you want to cite a comment on a blog—and sometimes they're pretty interesting—then include the author's name (or screen name), a title, if there is one, and, if not, the first few words of the post, "[Weblog comment]," and the date it was posted. Then include the information on the blog, which is the subject of the comment.

MargotBlackSheep. "Tattoos Exist in Every

    Culture." Weblog comment. 10 June 2008.

Dent, Shirley. "Written on the Body:

Literary Tattoos." *The Blog: Books*.

Guardian News and Media, 9 June 2008.

Web. 10 June 2008.

In-Text Citation: (MargotBlackSheep)

3.6.11 AN ONLINE IMAGE

Online images often don't give you much to go on. If there is a name of the artist and title of the image, include them. If not, at least describe the image, and include the name of the sponsoring organization or site, and when you downloaded it.

"China Town Engulfed." Online image. 12 May

2008. *BBC News*. BBC, 8 June 2008. Web.

10 June 2008.

Part Four:
Student Essay in MLA Style

Throughout *The Curious Researcher* you've followed Amanda Stewart's progress on her research essay, reading excerpts from her research notebook as she tried many of the exercises in the book. Her investigation of the cultural phenomenon of teeth whitening proves, once again, that there are no boring topics, only bad questions. Teeth whitening, at first blush, hardly seems a subject worthy of academic study. But as you will see in the essay that follows, "In Search of the Great White," Amanda manages to take something as ordinary as the American obsession with white teeth and draws out its larger implications. Are standards of beauty moving targets that we all must chase? And at what cost?

Amanda Stewart

Prof. Ballenger

English 101

20 April 2008

In Search of the Great White

Lately I haven't felt much like smiling. It's not that I broke up with my boyfriend or failed a class—it's that my teeth are dingy brown. As part of the "great un-whitened masses," I feel self-conscious every time I go to grin. While my teeth have been the same color my entire life, I've never felt bad about showing them in public before. Until the 1990s, most people's teeth pretty much looked like mine, but since then they've steadily been getting whiter. White teeth are now as important as plucked eyebrows or brushed hair. In fact, in 2002 Americans increased the amount they had spent on whitening from the previous year by 90 percent, apparently it isn't just my imagination— smiles have gone from just white to fluorescent. Now that it's standard to have a blazing smile, I feel like a mottled eggshell in a sea of pearly whites. The tooth-whitening phenomenon gives insight into broader social phenomena: why do standards for physical appearance keep changing, and why do we rush to stay in style? How does this change the way we feel about our natural appearances? The microcosm of tooth whitening shows the greater sphere of beauty is about meeting the expectations around us rather than feeling secure in our natural appearances.

Despite the recent boom in tooth whitening, people have been concerned about the appearance of their teeth for a while. In the Middle Ages, barbers began trimming out excess teeth along with hair, and started cleaning them as well. They also applied nitric acid to whiten teeth, though it ate through the enamel and ushered in rapid tooth decay. Despite the pain and destruction of nitric acid, people continued to use it until Italians discovered the value of fluoride in the 1800s. Even by then, white teeth were a status symbol for the upper class to flaunt. Thankfully, our tooth whiteners *are* safer. A study by James W. Curtis, DMD, discovered that bleaching through carbamide peroxide actually decreases the amount of plaque on teeth; but we're still doing it for beauty reasons rather than health ones (Nuss 28).

This well-crafted lead starts with the personal—what it is at stake for the writer in exploring the topic—and then moves to the more universal—how the phenomenon raises larger questions that matter to all of us. We want to follow this lead because the writer has given us a reason to.

In her article "Bright On," Molly
Prior notes that Procter & Gamble and
Colgate-Palmolive revolutionized the
whitening industry by bringing over-the-
counter whiteners to drugstores everywhere
at the turn of the twenty-first century
(39). No longer did people have to pay
high prices for professional whitening—
they could do it themselves, at home, for
a reasonable cost. In the past, a patient
had to eat a bill of $1,000 for a laser
whitening treatment, or $10,000 for a
full set of veneers; now a package of
Crest Whitestrips retails for only
$29.99 (Gideonse). Suddenly, whiter
teeth were available to everyone. While
a shining smile once indicated wealth
and the ability to splurge on cosmetic
dentistry, it became affordable to the
dentally discolored masses eager to emulate the lifestyles of the people they
saw in magazines and on television.

Companies didn't create whitening
products to fill a demand created by the
public for whiter teeth. While Hollywood
glitterati did pay high prices for iconic
smiles, most people seemed happy with
functional teeth. However, companies saw
money to be made in creating a whiter norm

Amanda has spent the last few paragraphs providing background on her research question, and in a key move, offers a comment on the significance of what she has covered so far. This sentence tacks down the information, attaching it to the writer's purpose.

Stewart 4

for teeth, so they barraged the airwaves with advertisements featuring people complaining about the dullness and imperfection of their teeth. Natural teeth were denigrated as ugly. Crest and Colgate-Palmolive wanted to make money, so they appealed to the American obsession with beauty to secure a financial reason to smile. As Jonathan Levine, DDS, notes, "It's lately seeming much harder to go broke by overestimating the vanity of the American public" (Walker). The companies succeeded in making mouthfuls of money, netting $450 million dollars, and getting 45 percent of Americans to try some form of whitening (Prior 42). In effect, they appealed to our egos to get to our pocket books.

When selling whiter smiles, retailers typically appeal to our need for approval. Our mouths are no longer simply havens for gingivitis and halitosis, but self-esteem as well. Procter & Gamble's marketing director, David Dintenfass, says, "Today, beauty and confidence have a lot to do with having a white smile. And isn't confidence what beauty is all about?" (Prior 42). Obviously Dintenfass has a desire for all of us to want whiter teeth; that's his

Stewart 5

paycheck. But notice how he's no longer
selling whiter teeth to us. He is selling
confidence. The mouth has changed from
first being a masticatory portal, to an
important aspect of physical appearance,
to a status symbol. We are now being
judged as people based on the appearance
of our teeth. The trend towards making
the perfect smile a commodity is more
disturbing than other movements to
change beauty standards, however, because
changing our smiles changes the way we
express a basic emotion. We are now modifying the way a feeling is expressed,
which can change the way we actually feel.
Smiles are now as much about making a
statement as displaying a feeling.

Last winter I went out for coffee on
a date, and over the course of the evening
I started to loosen up and laugh. Halfway
through the flirting, I realized I had
been flashing my dingy teeth at my date,
and I clammed up out of self-conscious-
ness. I was afraid he wouldn't want to
be around a girl with such nasty teeth: I
felt ugly. After I stopped smiling,
though, I felt awkward and uncomfortable.
With my lips sealed to my teeth, pantomim-
ing my enjoyment, I felt inhibited and

This paragraph is a great example of how a writer can surround fact with commentary. Note how Amanda provides a layer of commentary to begin the paragraph, provides a quote, and then adds another layer of commentary teasing out its significance to her project.

confined. In squelching my smile I squashed my joy, and made the evening much less fun than it could have been. In retrospect I shouldn't have cared what a near stranger thought about my teeth, but it's hard to ignore others' perceptions and feel secure that my beauty can be as unique to me as my fingerprints.

Julie Beatty, a mining executive in San Francisco, is much like me in her discomfort with her natural teeth. She epitomizes the type of consumer Procter & Gamble's Dintenfass is marketing directly to—an upper-class woman (Ives). She has spent $12,500 to make-over her smile by straightening, enlarging, and whitening her teeth. She hopes to appear aggressive and masculine with her new smile, because her naturally small and rounded teeth conveyed her to be "easygoing, kind of a pushover," according to Dr. Joe Carrick, president of the American Academy of Cosmetic Dentistry (Gideonse). The fact that changing Julie's teeth changes the way other people treat her—and she feels about herself—is disturbing. Society's increasing shift towards encapsulating a person into certain specific aspects of

Here Amanda uses a case study to anchor her information to a particular person affected by it. By giving the issue a "face" it becomes less abstract.

appearance like their teeth shows both
an over-reliance on looks and an under-
reliance on character.

Propelling people to whiten and
change their teeth is dentist to the
stars Jonathan Levine. He created GoS-
mile, a portable whitening system, after
his wife convinced him people believed
it was a "real lifestyle opportunity"
(Walker). Levine started marketing his
product to the general public not to
just create whiter teeth, but to convey
an image of a whole, healthy lifestyle.
Levine believes that using his product,
and improving one's image helps to
"ameliorate deficiencies in pulchri-
tude," or, more simply, to move a
person higher up the social ladder
(Walker). That explains why 72 percent
of consumers want whiter teeth (Ives).
Collier Strong, an LA makeup artist,
believes "now public awareness has risen
to the point where if you don't have
nice teeth, people look at you and ask
themselves, why not? . . . How primitive!"
(Walker). We are no longer just a
normal-looking people with healthy,
natural teeth—we are backwards Ludites
hanging far behind the times.

People whitening their teeth aren't having an easy time, either. Sona Balanian, a publicist in LA, spent $500 on getting her teeth whitened at the dentist-run clinic BriteSmile. "I'm embarrassed to admit I spent that much," she says, "but I live in Hollywood and everyone has perfect teeth" (Prior 41). Unfortunately, she will probably run into the same problem that Laurie Hardjowirogo has. Laurie has been using bleaching trays from her dentist once a month for the past five years. "Now my much whiter teeth seem like they're the way they're supposed to be. But I don't know if I have a fair assessment anymore because so many people are doing it. I don't know where the bar is anymore" (Naversen Geraghty 158). She obviously believes cosmetic dentist Clifford Williams, who preaches, "White is not white enough. Everyone wants 'TV teeth'"(Prior 42). There is no way to gauge what is a little too white or too perfect anymore; it's hard to hit the moving target of beauty standards.

It would be hard to make up a quote that drives the writer's point about the standards of beauty being a "moving target" better than this one.

I still don't want to whiten my teeth to follow the trend and step into the trap created by conglomerates and dentists looking only to line their pocketbooks, but I'm having a hard time feeling judged as dirty and poor simply because my teeth don't sparkle. I wish the standards of beauty relied more on what was natural and less on what was being promoted by groups with vested interests. It's hard to fight back against social standards, because it's a battle one must undergo alone. I can't stop people from judging me by my teeth, and I can't make others stop using whitening products. I can, however, become confident enough in myself and my value as a person to eschew whatever beauty trends come down the pipeline, and steel myself in the fact that my value doesn't change when standards do. I'm going to look away from the whitening strips and toothpastes, and into myself to find my smile.

Stewart 10

Works Cited

Gideonse, Ted. "Move Over, Mona Lisa." *Newsweek*.

Newsweek, 14 Dec. 1998. Web. 20 May 2008.

Ives, Nat. "The Giants of Tooth Whitening See

Spinoff Products Expanding a Fast-growing

Market." *New York Times*. New York Times,

10 May 2008. Web. 23 Apr. 2003.

Naversen Geraghty, Laurel. "Great White Hope."

Prevention 58.6 (2006): 152-60. Print.

Nuss, Ellen. "How Safe Is Tooth Bleaching?"

Dental Assistant 73.3 (2004): 26-29. Print.

Prior, Molly. "Bright on: Americans' Insatiable

Appetite for Whiter-Than-White Teeth Is

Giving Retailers Something to Smile About."

Beauty Biz 1 Sept. 2005: 36-43. Print.

Walker, Rob. "Consumed; Unstained Masses." *New

York Times*. New York Times, 2 May 2004.

Web. 19 Apr. 2008.

"Works Cited" always begins a new page.

Understanding Research Assignments

About fifteen years ago, in a dark, dimly lit basement floor of the University of New Hampshire library, I discovered the textbook that may have had the very first research paper assignment for undergraduates. Charles Baldwin's 1906 *A College Manual of Rhetoric* encouraged students to write essays based on reading that emphasized "originally" compiling facts so that the writer gives "already known" information his or her "own grouping and interpretation." In an article that year, Baldwin noted that "from the beginning a student should learn that his use of the library will be a very practical measure of his culture."

In the century since then, the college research paper is probably the most common genre of student writing in the university. It is a fixture in composition classes and many other courses that require a "term paper." Naturally, this is why there are books like *The Curious Researcher*—to help students understand these assignments and give them guidance in the process of writing them. As you know, a major thrust of this book is the research *essay* rather than the formal research paper. My argument is that this more exploratory, possibly less formal, researched piece is the best way to introduce you to the spirit of inquiry that drives most academic research. The habits of mind that come from essaying, along with the research and writing skills that accompany them, should help you whenever you're asked to write a paper that involves research.

There's another skill that's invaluable when you encounter a research paper assignment in another class: Knowing how to interpret what exactly you're being asked to do. This involves reading your writing assignment rhetorically. In other words, analyze the *situation* for each assignment: How does it fit into other writing projects in the course? What particular purpose does this assignment have? What do you know about the instructor's particular attitudes about research and about writing? How do you figure out the best approaches to the research project? Apparently, students' struggle to do this well is a huge problem. In one study, for example, 92 percent of students said that the most frustrating part of doing research was figuring out what their professor wanted.*

Instructors aren't trying to be obtuse. They want you to understand the assignment, and most have made an effort to be clear. While there's not much you can do about *how* the assignment is conceived or described, you can be savvier at analyzing the assignment's purpose and guidelines.

I've recently conducted a review of research paper assignments from courses across the disciplines, and actually there are striking similarities between them. I tried to read them as a student would, actively looking for guidance about how to approach the assignment and also alert to subtleties that students might miss.

Analyzing the Purpose of the Assignment

One of the things I hear most often from my students who have research assignments in other classes is that the instructor "doesn't want my opinion in the paper." Frankly, I'm often skeptical of this. College writing assignments typically are about what or how you think. But because research papers involve considerable time collecting and considering the ideas of others, it's easy to assume that you're supposed to be a bystander.

Actually, even some instructors seem to equate the term "research paper" with merely reporting information. "This is not a research paper," said one assignment. "The idea here is not to pack in as much information as you can, but instead to present a thoughtful and clearly written analysis." Another noted that "although this is a research paper, the focus is fundamentally on your own analysis and interpretation. . . ."

What these instructors are at pains to point out is that, contrary to what you might think, they are actively interested in what you think. They want students to *do* something with the information they collect. But merely having an opinion isn't enough. As one assignment put it, "You are not being graded on your opinion, but your ability to communicate and support a point of view (your thesis)."

*Alison Head, "Beyond Google: How Do Students Conduct Academic Research?" *First Monday* 12.8 (2007). 30 March 2008 <http://www.firstmonday.org/issues/issue12_8/head/>.

However, the ability to write a convincing paper still begs the question of the larger purposes of the assignment. The assignments I reviewed sometimes talk about encouraging "critical thinking" or helping students enter "a scholarly conversation." A few talk about "advancing your knowledge" about a topic or learning the conventions of research writing in a particular discipline. But many, unfortunately, don't talk about a purpose for the assignment at all. Instead, these frequently focus on the method of inquiry, and most often it is the requirement that your paper make an argument.

Argumentative Research: Open or Closed?

The language that research assignments use to emphasize argument is quite often very explicit: "You are to write a research paper on a subject related to Southeast Asia. *Make an argument* about the overall significance of your topic to some aspect of life in Southeast Asia." Not much ambiguity there. Similarly, some assignments ask that you "take a position" on a topic. Argumentative research papers are most often organized around a thesis, and some assignment descriptions go to great lengths to explain what makes a strong one (usually sufficiently narrow, addressing a significant question, and explicitly stated).

What may not be obvious, however, is how much latitude you have in letting your research revise your thesis or even dramatically change your initial point of view. Most often, instructors *expect* the research to change your thinking, and they often use the term "working thesis" to describe your initial position. These are the more open-ended assignments that might specify that the crafting of a final thesis can occur late rather than early in the research process. These are also assignments that emphasize a focus on a *research question* much like we've discussed in this book.

More rarely, an assignment will imply a closed approach: First identify a thesis and then seek evidence from your research that will support it. This is the conventional thesis-support model in which the expectation is that you will use your thesis, and not your research question, to dictate not just the structure of your paper but the goal of your research. These kinds of assignments tend to not mention that a thesis might be revised and are silent on how it arises from a research question or problem.

Always ask your instructor about whether your reading of the assignment as more closed-ended is accurate. The key questions are these:

- Where should the thesis in this assignment come from?
- What process do you suggest for arriving at it?
- Finally, might it be revised—even substantially—later in the process?

In a more open-ended research paper, the inquiry-based methods of *The Curious Researcher* directly apply. For example, crafting a researchable question is an important route to coming up with a strong working thesis, and the dialogue or double-entry journal can help you think through how your research might develop or revise that thesis. The strict thesis-example paper seems to have little opportunity for inquiry. Indeed, the emphasis in these assignments is frequently on the formal qualities of the paper—how well it's organized around a thesis, the proper use of citations, and mechanical correctness. Developing an outline at the front end of the project is usually helpful. However, there's no reason that after developing working knowledge of your topic you can't use exercises like "Reclaiming Your Topic" (Exercise 4.2) in Chapter 4, or "Dissecting the Fish" (Exercise 5.2) in Chapter 5 to help you come up with a strong thesis, especially since that's such an important part of a thesis-example paper.

Audience

For whom are you writing? So much hinges on the answer to this question: the tone of the paper, how specialized its language might be, the emphasis you give on providing background on the research question, and the degree to which you stress reader interest. Despite the importance of audience, research paper assignments frequently fail to mention it at all. This omission can often mean one thing: You are writing for your instructor. It actually might surprise you how often this isn't the case. If your assignment includes peer review of drafts or class presentations, then you may be writing for a more generalized audience. Sometimes this is explicit: "Your paper should be understood by a broader audience than scholars in your field. You will have to explain concepts and not expect your audience to understand in-housing jargon." If the audience for your paper isn't clear, ask your instructor this simple question:

- Who is the audience for this assignment—readers like the instructor who are knowledgeable about the topic or readers who are not?

Emphasis on Formal Qualities

An informal essay is casual in tone, has a strong individual voice, and is structured to explore a question—*to find out* rather than *to prove*. It certainly has a thesis, but it is a delayed thesis, appearing not in the introduction but toward the end of the essay. The writer's questions are the organizing principles of the essay rather than the exercise of making a point and logically providing evidence to support it. It does, however, have some formal qualities, including careful citation and attribution, the marshalling of appropriate evidence to explore the topic, and a sensible organization that moves from question to answers.

Research paper assignments in other classes are likely to put considerably more emphasis on a structure based on logic and reasoning. Put another way, these papers, unlike an informal essay, report the *products* of the process of researching the question rather than follow the thinking that led to them. The chief product, of course, is your thesis—the thing you are trying to say—and typically you're expected to place this in the introduction of your paper. Fairly often research paper assignments instruct you to state your thesis or position explicitly in a sentence. In keeping with the approach of this book, assignments often ask that you develop a research question from which the thesis emerges. As one put it, "[The] introduction should make three points: It should briefly introduce your question and its significance, state your answer, and orient the reader regarding your way of proceeding. This is the place to say, 'I'm going to argue. . . .'"

Also pay close attention to what context the assignment asks you to establish for your research question—course discussion, literature review, or both. Some instructors are keen on having you write a paper that somehow extends the course's readings or discussion points. Others want you to become familiar with the scholarly conversation that might extend beyond the class. Here's a question to ask about this:

- What is the more important context for establishing the significance of my research question or thesis—what we talked about in class or what I discover when I review the relevant literature?

The logical structure of an argumentative research paper doesn't vary much (see the discussion about this in Chapter 4), although in some disciplines you will be instructed to use the organizational conventions of the field; for example, scientific papers might require an abstract, introduction, methods, results, discussion, and conclusion, in that order. Generally, the body of your paper must draw on evidence from your research to support your thesis, though frequently your assignment requires that you also consider opposing points of view. How are they misguided? In what ways do they fail to address your research question? Also pay attention to whether your assignment asks you to tightly tether each paragraph to the thesis using topic sentences that address how that paragraph supports it.* Outlining the topic sentences before you draft your essay can help you with this.

Since one of the aims of teaching research writing is to help you understand its conventions, assignments almost always discuss the need for proper citation, correct format, a required number of scholarly sources, attention to grammar and mechanics, and so on. You need to determine the relative importance of this. Some research paper assignments, for example, devote much more ink to describing the required format—location of page numbers, font, margins—and the need for "perfect" grammar than they do a discussion of the research process, formulating a thesis, or the larger goals of the assignment. In this case, you might give these conventions more attention. If you're not sure about this, ask this question:

- When you evaluate the paper, what is the relative importance of getting the format right? Do you give that concern as much weight as the quality of your thesis or the soundness of your thinking?

As you know, *The Curious Researcher* encourages essays in which writers have a strong presence. The easiest way to do this is to enter the text directly by using the first person, though in an

---

*Some teachers heavily stress the use of topic sentences in paragraph writing, though there is considerable evidence that much writing, including academic prose, doesn't consistently feature topic sentences.

earlier chapter we explored other ways to do this. Research paper assignments rarely mention whether you can use "I." Silence on this question usually means that you should not. One of the conventions of much academic writing is a more formal register, the sense that the paper speaks rather than the writer. Yet a considerable number of the assignments I reviewed encouraged students to write with "voice" and lively, vigorous prose. The most effective way to inject voice into your research writing is to find your own way of saying things, something that "writing in the middle"—the note taking strategies encouraged in this book—should help you with. Assignments that say nothing about voice or style probably expect what one assignment described as writing that is "formal in tone, working to establish an authoritative, critical and analytical voice." If you're unsure about this, consider asking your instructor the following question:

- Should the voice in my paper mimic the scholarly sources I'm reading, or can it be somewhat less formal, perhaps sounding a bit more like me?

Types of Evidence: Primary or Secondary

You might remember a figure earlier in *The Curious Researcher* that illustrates how some of the key elements of a paper—tone, structure, and writerly presence—shift as the audience becomes more scholarly. One of the most important of these elements is the type of evidence. In popular writing—say, articles in *Wired* or *Discover* or op-ed pieces in the newspaper—the types of evidence that writers use to convince readers are quite varied. Personal experience and observation, for instance, are often excellent ways to support a point. But as you begin writing research papers in academic disciplines, you need to pay attention to what your instructor considers *appropriate* evidence in that field and for that particular assignment. Scientific papers, for example, often rely on experimental data. Literature papers lean most heavily on evidence culled from the literary text you're writing about. Papers in anthropology might rely on field observations.

Sometimes assignments explicitly talk about appropriate evidence for your paper. More often they do not. Generally speaking, research papers that are assigned in lower-division courses won't require you to conduct experiments or generate field notes. They will likely ask you to draw evidence from already published, or secondary sources, on your topic. But this isn't always the case. A history paper, for example, might require that you study a primary text, perhaps letters by historical figures, political documents, or archived newspapers. This is something you need to know. If the types of evidence you should use in your paper aren't clear, ask this question:

- What types of evidence should I rely on for this paper? Primary or secondary sources? And is personal experience and observation, if relevant, appropriate to use?

In the spirit of writing a conventional conclusion, let me restate what might be apparent by now: The most important thing you must do when you get a research assignment is read the handout carefully, considering what you've already learned in the class about writing in that discipline. I read a lot of research paper assignments, and they usually provide very good guidance. But if they don't, that's never an excuse for floundering. Ask, ask, ask. Your instructor wants you to.